The Economics of the Environment

Edited by

Wallace E. Oates

Professor of Economics
University of Maryland
and University Fellow
Resources for the Future, US

An Elgar Critical Writings Reader

Published by
Edward Elgar Publishing Limited
Gower House
Croft Road
Aldershot
Hants GU11 3HR
England

Edward Elgar Publishing Company
Old Post Road
Brookfield
Vermont 05036
USA

Paperback edition 1994

British Library Cataloguing in Publication Data
Economics of the Environment. – New ed. –
(Elgar Critical Writings Reader Series)
  I. Oates, Wallace E. II. Series
  333.7

ISBN 1 85898 002 X

Printed in Great Britain at the University Press, Cambridge

Contents

Acknowledgements

The editor and publishers wish to thank the following who have kindly given permission for the use of copyright material.

Academic Press, Inc. for articles: W. David Montgomery (1972), 'Markets in Licenses and Efficient Pollution Control Programs', *Journal of Economic Theory*, **5**, 395–418; Alan Randall, Berry Ives and Clyde Eastman (1974), 'Bidding Games for Valuation of Aesthetic Environmental Improvements', *Journal of Environmental Economics and Management*, **1**, 132–49; Paul B. Downing and William D. Watson, Jr. (1974), 'The Economics of Enforcing Air Pollution Controls', *Journal of Environmental Economics and Management*, **1** (3), 219–36; Zvi Adar and James M. Griffin (1976), 'Uncertainty and the Choice of Pollution Control Instruments', *Journal of Environmental Economics and Management*, **3** (3), 178–88; Jon D. Harford (1978), 'Firm Behavior Under Imperfectly Enforceable Pollution Standards and Taxes', *Journal of Environmental Economics and Management*, **5** (1), 26–43; William O'Neil, Martin David, Christina Moore and Erhard Joeres (1983), 'Transferable Discharge Permits and Economic Efficiency: The Fox River', *Journal of Environmental Economics and Management*, **10** (4), 346–55; Eugene P. Seskin, Robert J. Anderson, Jr. and Robert O. Reid (1983), 'An Empirical Analysis of Economic Strategies for Controlling Air Pollution', *Journal of Environmental Economics and Management*, **10** (2), 112–24; Daniel F. Spulber (1985), 'Effluent Regulation and Long-Run Optimality', *Journal of Environmental Economics and Management*, **12** (2), 103–16; Winston Harrington, Alan J. Krupnick and Walter O. Spofford, Jr. (1989), 'The Economic Losses of a Waterborne Disease Outbreak', *Journal of Urban Economics*, **25**, 116–37.

American Economic Association for articles: John V. Krutilla (1967), 'Conservation Reconsidered', *American Economic Review*, **LVII** (4), 777–86; Robert U. Ayres and Allen V. Kneese (1969), 'Production, Consumption, and Externalities', *American Economic Review*, **LIX**, 282–97; William J. Baumol (1972), 'On Taxation and the Control of Externalities', *American Economic Review*, **LXII** (3), 307–22; Anthony C. Fisher, John V. Krutilla and Charles J. Cicchetti (1972), 'The Economics of Environmental Preservation: A Theoretical and Empirical Analysis', *American Economic Review*, **LXII**, 605–19; David S. Brookshire, Mark A. Thayer, William D. Schulze and Ralph C. D'Arge (1982), 'Valuing Public Goods: A Comparison of Survey and Hedonic Approaches', *American Economic Review*, **LXXII**, 165–77; Nancy E. Bockstael and Kenneth E. McConnell (1983), 'Welfare Measurement in the Household Production Framework', *American Economic Review*, **LXXIII**, 806–14; W. Michael Hanemann (1991), 'Willingness To Pay and Willingness To Accept: How Much Can They Differ?', *American Economic Review*, **81** (3), 635–47; Robert W. Hahn (1989), 'Economic Prescriptions for Environmental Problems: How the Patient Followed the Doctor's Orders', *Journal of Economic Perspectives*, **3** (2), 95–114.

Canadian Journal of Economics for article: J.H. Dales (1968), 'Land, Water, and Ownership', *Canadian Journal of Economics*, **I** (4), 791–804.

Basil Blackwell Ltd. for articles: Ralph Turvey (1963), 'On Divergences between Social Cost and Private Cost', *Economica*, New Series, **XXX**, 309–13; W.J. Baumol and David F. Bradford (1972), 'Detrimental Externalities and Non-Convexity of the Production Set', *Economica*, New Series, **XXXIX**, 160–76; William J. Baumol and Wallace E. Oates (1971), 'The Use of Standards and Prices for Protection of the Environment', *Swedish Journal of Economics*, **73**, 42–54; Karl-Göran Mäler (1971), 'A Method of Estimating Social Benefits from Pollution Control', *Swedish Journal of Economics*, **73**, 121–33.

R.H. Coase for his own article: (1960), 'The Problem of Social Cost', *Journal of Law and Economics*, **III**, 1–44.

Elsevier Science Publishers B.V. for articles: Marc J. Roberts and Michael Spence (1976), 'Effluent Charges and Licenses Under Uncertainty', *Journal of Public Economics*, **5**, 193–208; Wallace E. Oates and Diana L. Strassmann (1984), 'Effluent Fees and Market Structure', *Journal of Public Economics*, **24**, 29–46; Winston Harrington (1988), 'Enforcement Leverage When Penalties Are Restricted', *Journal of Public Economics*, **37**, 29–53; Ronald G. Ridker and John A. Henning (1967), 'The Determinants of Residential Property Values with Special Reference to Air Pollution', *Review of Economics and Statistics*, **XLIX**, 246–57.

John Wiley & Sons, Inc. for articles: Burton A. Weisbrod (1964), 'Collective-Consumption Services of Individual-Consumption Goods', *Quarterly Journal of Economics*, **LXXVIII**, 471–7; Kenneth J. Arrow and Anthony C. Fisher (1974), 'Environmental Preservation, Uncertainty, and Irreversibility', *Quarterly Journal of Economics*, **LXXXVIII**, 312–19.

Resources for the Future for excerpts: Marion Clawson (1959), *Methods of Measuring the Demand for and Value of Outdoor Recreation*, RFF Reprint 10, 1–36; Jack L. Knetsch and Robert K. Davis (1966), 'Comparisons of Methods for Recreation Evaluation' in Allen V. Kneese and Stephen C. Smith (eds), *Water Research*, Baltimore: Johns Hopkins Press, 125–42.

Review of Economic Studies Ltd. for article: Martin L. Weitzman (1974), 'Prices *vs.* Quantities', *Review of Economic Studies*, **XLI**, 477–91.

University of Chicago Press for articles: Sherwin Rosen (1974), 'Hedonic Prices and Implicit Markets: Product Differentiation in Pure Competition', *Journal of Political Economy*, **82**, 34–55; Michael Hazilla and Raymond J. Kopp (1990), 'Social Cost of Environmental Quality Regulations: A General Equilibrium Analysis', *Journal of Political Economy*, **98** (1), 853–73.

University of Wisconsin Press for article: Thomas H. Tietenberg (1980), 'Transferable Discharge Permits and the Control of Stationary Source Air Pollution: A Survey and Synthesis', *Land Economics*, **56** (4), 391–416.

Every effort has been made to trace all the copyright holders but if any have been inadvertently overlooked the publishers will be pleased to make the necessary arrangement at the first opportunity.

In addition the publishers wish to thank the library of the London School of Economics and Political Science and The Alfred Marshall Library, Cambridge University, for their assistance in obtaining these articles.

Introduction

In the early days of the 'Environmental Revolution' in the late 1960s and early 1970s, the role of economic analysis in the design and implementation of policies for protection of the environment was viewed with suspicion, and in some instances with outright hostility, by many environmentalists. Economic forces were seen by many as the basic source of environmental degradation, and effective policy had to combat these forces, not cooperate with them. Much of the early legislation embodied this perspective. In the United States, for example, the Clean Air Act of 1970 forbad the use of benefit-cost analysis in the determination of standards for environmental quality; such standards were to be set to protect the public health without regard to costs of attainment. Following on its heels, the Clean Water Act in 1972 set as the national objective the elimination of *all* discharges of pollutants into navigable waters.

There has taken place an interesting and important evolution of attitudes over the last two decades, one in which environmentalists and legislators have come to accept a more constructive role for the economic analysis of environmental problems. This shift in perspective has, I believe, several sources: the failure to make as much progress on the environmental front as had been hoped, with the realization that part of this failure has been the result of relatively ineffective policies, a gradual increase in the level of understanding and sophistication in many parts of the environmental policy-making community, and simply a generally more sympathetic stance towards decentralized, market-oriented approaches to policy. The current age is one in which market forces are getting a good press, with serious interest in, and receptivity to, the use of market forces for the solution of social problems. The notion of harnessing profit incentives on behalf of environmental protection has (as it should) a good deal of appeal. And this has manifested itself explicitly in the policy arena. In the United States, the 1990 Amendments to the Clean Air Act introduce a nationwide system of tradeable discharge permits for the regulation of sulphur emissions to address the problem of acid rain. In Europe, there are new forms of 'Green Taxes' being discussed and introduced as mechanisms for environmental management. Economic analysis and economic incentives for pollution control are coming to play an important role in the design and implementation of environmental policy.

The objective of this volume is to assemble a collection of key papers in the field of environmental economics to provide a 'working collection' for scholars, graduate students and policy analysts in the field. This, incidentally, represents something of a shift from the initial vision of the book. At the outset, Edward Elgar and I thought in terms of reprinting the seminal papers in environmental and natural resource economics – a collection of the 'classics'. Such a volume would have provided a useful reference consisting of the original sources in the field. However, in the course of the evolution of this volume, a change in its orientation took place, a change that has involved a narrowing of its scope in one way and a broadening in another.

First, we decided to narrow the coverage in terms of subject matter. This volume is now limited to the field of environmental economics; the major papers in natural resource economics (dealing with the economics of renewable and non-renewable resources) will appear in another volume edited by Geoffrey Heal of Columbia University.

Second, the scope of the collection has been broadened to include not just the 'classics', but a number of more recent papers that are on the current frontiers of research in environmental economics. Indeed, one such paper was published only last year. The volume thus incorporates both the early seminal papers in environmental economics and a selection of recent pieces making important contributions, both theoretical and empirical, to the economic analysis of environmental problems. This will expose the reader both to the original sources of environmental economics and to the flavour and direction of ongoing research. Finally, I have included several papers that I think are extremely useful pedagogical vehicles for some of the basic ideas in the field.

For purposes of this volume, then, I have chosen to distinguish environmental economics from its close cousin, natural resource economics. The division between the two fields is admittedly a little fuzzy in places. But I take natural resource economics to address as its central concern the intertemporal allocation of renewable and non-renewable resources. With its origins in the seminal paper by Harold Hotelling in 1931, the theory of natural resource economics typically applies dynamic control methods of analysis to problems of intertemporal resource usage. This has led to a vast literature on such topics as the management of fisheries, forests, minerals and energy resources. In contrast, I take the province of environmental economics to encompass two major issues: the regulation of polluting activities and the valuation of environmental amenities.

The collection is organized in the following way. After an overview in Part I provided by the famous Ayres-Kneese paper on the relationship between the environment and the economy, the volume turns to the 'pure theory' of environmental policy. Part II thus consists of papers addressing the economic theory of externalities and its formal policy implications. These studies develop the basic economic logic of environmental regulation and extend it to a setting of uncertainty.

Part III brings us closer to the actual design and implementation of policy measures, for it is a big step from theorems on the blackboard to the determination of real policy. These papers start us down this road by exploring the range of available policy instruments in a setting where environmental targets are given (perhaps by existing legislation). In this context, the problem is that of designing policy measures to achieve predetermined environmental objectives. The papers in this section explore alternative policy instruments, offer some empirical findings on their likely effectiveness, and describe and assess our experience with incentive-based policies for environmental management.

Part IV turns to the important issue of measuring the benefits and costs of environmental amenities. Environmental programmes have become expensive: many countries are now expending on the order of 2 per cent of their GDP on environmental protection, and these expenditure shares are likely to grow. This places a high premium on 'getting things right'. We need to know both what benefits we obtain from pollution control and what it costs. Such information does not come easily. Many of the benefits from environmental protection take the form of health amenities: reduced illness and lowered mortality. It is a delicate as well as conceptually difficult matter to produce estimates of such benefits in monetary terms. Moreover, other benefits may take an aesthetic form; these likewise present formidable measurement problems. Finally, there is a whole category of so-called 'non-use benefits' that individuals derive from simply knowing that certain environmental amenities exist, even though they may never make use of them.

Environmental economists have devised a number of techniques for the estimation of such benefits. In some instances, market behaviour can provide either direct or indirect clues as to what people are willing to pay for improved environmental quality. The premium, for example, that a house in an area with relatively clean air commands over a similar residence in a location with dirtier air can provide an indication of the monetary value that people place on reduced air pollution. In other instances, for non-use values for example, researchers have turned to 'contingent valuation' methods by which they ask respondents for their willingness-to-pay for specified improvements to the environment. There has been much progress in the development of reliable procedures for eliciting sensible and usable responses on valuation directly from individuals. Part IV, in sum, presents a collection of papers that explore different approaches to determining individuals' willingness-to-pay for environmental amenities. In addition, the article by Hazilla and Kopp offers a rigorous treatment of the measurement of the costs of environmental programmes.

Part V turns to the issue of enforcement. Using the literature on tax evasion and enforcement as a point of departure, several environmental economists have provided some important insights into the way polluters are likely to respond to imperfectly enforceable policies and how the environmental authority might best frame such policies to obtain widespread compliance. The enforcement literature offers some promising ideas for the design of an effective structure of penalties to induce sources to comply with environmental regulations.

In the last section, I have slipped into the fuzzy intersection between environmental and natural resource economics to include three major papers on the issue of conservation. In the course of selecting items for inclusion in this volume, I asked a group of environmental and resource economists to list what they saw as the most important, seminal articles in the field. Interestingly, the Arrow-Fisher paper on environmental preservation was the most frequently cited piece. It appears here along with two earlier papers that explicitly address the issue of preservation in the light of the irreversibility of certain forms of environmental degradation.

I hope that this collection of essays will be helpful both to individuals working in the field and also to those coming into environmental economics by providing access to the major papers in a systematic way; the collection will take the reader through the seminal articles in the field and provide a taste of some of the recent and ongoing research. In this regard, I might call attention to a comprehensive survey paper ('Environmental Economics: A Survey') that my colleague, Maureen Cropper, and I have written and that is scheduled to appear in the June 1992 issue of the *Journal of Economic Literature*. This survey provides a useful companion piece to the contributions in this volume by placing individual papers in the context of the broader field of environmental economics.

Finally, I want to thank Edward and Sandy Elgar for their encouragement and support in this enterprise and for their more general interest in the economics of the environment. This interest manifests itself in a series, *New Horizons in Environmental Economics*, that I am editing for the Elgars and that will make available new and significant contributions to the economic analysis of the environment.

Part I
Environmental Economics:
An Overview

[1]

Production, Consumption, and Externalities

By ROBERT U. AYRES AND ALLEN V. KNEESE[*]

"For all that, welfare economics can no more reach conclusions applicable to the real world without some knowledge of the real world than can positive economics" [21].

Despite tremendous public and governmental concern with problems such as environmental pollution, there has been a tendency in the economics literature to view externalities as exceptional cases. They may distort the allocation of resources but can be dealt with adequately through simple *ad hoc* arrangements. To quote Pigou:

> When it was urged above, that in certain industries a wrong amount of resources is being invested because the value of the marginal social net product there differs from the value of the marginal private net product, it was tacitly assumed that in the main body of industries these two values are equal [22][1].

And Scitovsky, after having described his cases two and four which deal with technological externalities affecting consumers and producers respectively, says:

> The second case seems exceptional, because most instances of it can be and usually are eliminated by zoning ord-

nances and industrial regulations concerned with public health and safety. The fourth case seems unimportant, simply because examples of it seem to be few and exceptional [25].

We believe that at least one class of externalities—those associated with the disposal of residuals resulting from the consumption and production process—must be viewed quite differently.[2] They are a normal, indeed, inevitable part of these processes. Their economic significance tends to increase as economic development proceeds, and the ability of the ambient environment to receive and assimilate them is an important natural resource of increasing value.[3] We will argue below that

[*] The authors are respectively visiting scholar and director, Quality of the Environment Program, Resources for the Future, Inc. We are indebted to our colleagues Blair Bower, Orris Herfindahl, Charles Howe, John Krutilla, and Robert Steinberg for comments on an earlier draft. We have also benefited from comments by James Buchanan, Paul Davidson, Robert Dorfman, Otto Eckstein, Myrick Freeman, Mason Gaffney, Lester Lave, Herbert Mohring, and Gordon Tullock.

[1] Even Baumol who saw externalities as a rather pervasive feature of the economy tends to discuss external diseconomies like "smoke nuisance" entirely in terms of particular examples [3]. A perspective more like that of the present paper is found in Kapp [16].

[2] We by no means wish to imply that this is the only important class of externalities associated with production and consumption. Also, we do not wish to imply that there has been a lack of theoretical attention to the externalities problem. In fact, the past few years have seen the publication of several excellent articles which have gone far toward systematizing definitions and illuminating certain policy issues. Of special note are Coase [9], Davis and Whinston [12], Buchanan and Stubblebine [6], and Turvey [27]. However, all these contributions deal with externality as a comparatively minor aberration from Pareto optimality in competitive markets and focus upon externalities between two parties. Mishan, after a careful review of the literature, has commented on this as follows: "The form in which external effects have been presented in the literature is that of partial equilibrium analysis; a situation in which a single industry produces an equilibrium output, usually under conditions of perfect competition, some form of intervention being required in order to induce the industry to produce an "ideal" or "optimal" output. If the point is not made explicitly, it is tacitly understood that unless the rest of the economy remains organized in conformity with optimum conditions, one runs smack into Second Best problems" [21].

[3] That external diseconomies are integrally related to economic development and increasing congestion has been noted in passing in the literature. Mishan has commented: "The attention given to external effects in

AYRES AND KNEESE: EXTERNALITIES   283

the common failure to recognize these facts may result from viewing the production and consumption processes in a manner that is somewhat at variance with the fundamental law of conservation of mass.

Modern welfare economics concludes that if (1) preference orderings of consumers and production functions of producers are independent and their shapes appropriately constrained, (2) consumers maximize utility subject to given income and price parameters, and (3) producers maximize profits subject to the price parameters; a set of prices exists such that no individual can be made better off without making some other individual worse off. For a given distribution of income this is an efficient state. Given certain further assumptions concerning the structure of markets, this "Pareto optimum" can be achieved via a pricing mechanism and voluntary decentralized exchange.

If waste assimilative capacity of the environment is scarce, the decentralized voluntary exchange process cannot be free of uncompensated technological external diseconomies unless (1) all inputs are fully converted into outputs, with no unwanted material residuals along the way,[4] and all final outputs are utterly destroyed in the process of consumption, or (2) property rights are so arranged that all relevant environmental attributes are in private ownership and these rights are exchanged in competitive markets. Neither of these conditions can be expected to hold in an actual economy and they do not.

Nature does not permit the destruction of matter except by annihilation with anti-matter, and the means of disposal of unwanted residuals which maximizes the internal return of decentralized decision units is by discharge to the environment, principally, watercourses and the atmosphere. Water and air are traditionally examples of free goods in economics. But in reality, in developed economies they are common property resources of great and increasing value presenting society with important and difficult allocation problems which exchange in private markets cannot resolve. These problems loom larger as increased population and industrial production put more pressure on the environment's ability to dilute and chemically degrade waste products. Only the crudest estimates of present external costs associated with residuals discharge exist but it would not be surprising if these costs were in the tens of billions of dollars annually.[5] Moreover, as we shall emphasize again, technological means for processing or purifying one or another type of waste discharge do not destroy the residuals but only alter their form. Thus, given the level, patterns, and technology of production and consumption, recycle of materials into productive uses or discharge into an alternative medium are the only general options for protecting a particular environmental medium such as water. Residual problems must be seen in a broad regional or economy-wide context rather

---

the recent literature is, I think, fully justified by the unfortunate, albeit inescapable, fact that as societies grow in material wealth, the incidence of these effects grows rapidly . . . " [21]; and Buchanan and Tullock have stated that as economic development proceeds, "congestion" tends to replace "co-operation" as the underlying motive force behind collective action, i.e., controlling external diseconomies tends to become more important than cooperation to realize external economies [7].

[4] Or any residuals which occur must be stored on the producer's premises.

[5] It is interesting to compare this with estimates of the cost of another well known misallocation of resources that has occupied a central place in economic theory and research. In 1954, Harberger published an estimate of the welfare cost of monopoly which indicated that it amounted to about .07 percent of GNP [15]. In a later study, Schwartzman calculated the allocative cost at only .01 percent of GNP [24]. Leibenstein generalized studies such as these to the statement that " . . . in a great many instances the amount to be gained by increasing allocative efficiency is trivial . . . " [19]. But Leibenstein did not consider the allocative costs associated with environmental pollution.

than as separate and isolated problems of disposal of gas, liquid, and solid wastes.

Frank Knight perhaps provides a key to why these elementary facts have played so small a role in economic theorizing and empirical research.

> The next heading to be mentioned ties up with the question of dimensions from another angle, and relates to the second main error mentioned earlier as connected with taking food and eating as the type of economic activity. The basic economic magnitude (value or utility) is service, not good. It is inherently a stream or flow in time . . . [18].[6]

Almost all of standard economic theory is in reality concerned with services. Material objects are merely the vehicles which carry some of these services, and they are exchanged because of consumer preferences for the services associated with their use or because they can help to add value in the manufacturing process. Yet we persist in referring to the "final consumption" of goods as though material objects such as fuels, materials, and finished goods somehow disappeared into the void—a practice which was comparatively harmless so long as air and water were almost literally free goods.[7] Of course, residuals from both the production and consumption processes remain and they usually render disservices (like killing fish, increasing the difficulty of water treatment, reducing public health, soiling and deteriorating buildings, etc.) rather than services. Control efforts are aimed at eliminating or reducing those disservices which flow to consumers and producers whether they want them or not and which, except in unusual cases, they cannot control by engaging in individual exchanges.[8]

I. *The Flow of Materials*

To elaborate on these points, we find it useful initially to view environmental pollution and its control as a materials balance problem for the entire economy.[9] The inputs to the system are fuels, foods, and raw materials which are partly converted into final goods and partly become waste residuals. Except for increases in inventory, final goods also ultimately enter the waste stream. Thus goods which are "consumed" really only render certain services. Their material substance remains in existence and must either be reused or discharged to the ambient environment.

In an economy which is closed (no imports or exports) and where there is no net accumulation of stocks (plant, equipment, inventories, consumer durables, or residential buildings), the amount of residuals inserted into the natural environment must be approximately equal to the weight of basic fuels, food, and raw materials entering the processing and production system, plus oxygen taken from the atmosphere.[10] This result, while obvious

---

[6] The point was also clearly made by Fisher: "The only true method, in our view, is to regard uniformly as income the *service* of a dwelling to its owner (shelter or money rental), the *service* of a piano (music), and the *service* of food (nourishment) . . . " (emphasis in original) [14].

[7] We are tempted to suggest that the word consumption be dropped entirely from the economist's vocabulary as being basically deceptive. It is difficult to think of a suitable substitute, however. At least, the word consumption should not be used in connection with goods, but only with regard to services or flows of "utility."

[8] There is a substantial literature dealing with the question of under what conditions individual exchanges can optimally control technological external diseconomies. A discussion of this literature, as it relates to waterborne residuals, is found in Kneese and Bower [17].

[9] As far as we know, the idea of applying materials balance concepts to waste disposal problems was first expressed by Smith [26]. We also benefitted from an unpublished paper by Joseph Headley in which a pollution "matrix" is suggested. We have also found references by Boulding to a "spaceship economy" suggestive [4]. One of the authors has previously used a similar approach in ecological studies of nutrient interchange among plants and animals; see [1].

[10] To simplify our language, we will not repeat this essential qualification at each opportunity, but assume it applies throughout the following discussion. In addition, we must include residuals such as NO and NO_2 arising from reactions between components of the air itself but occurring as combustion by-products.

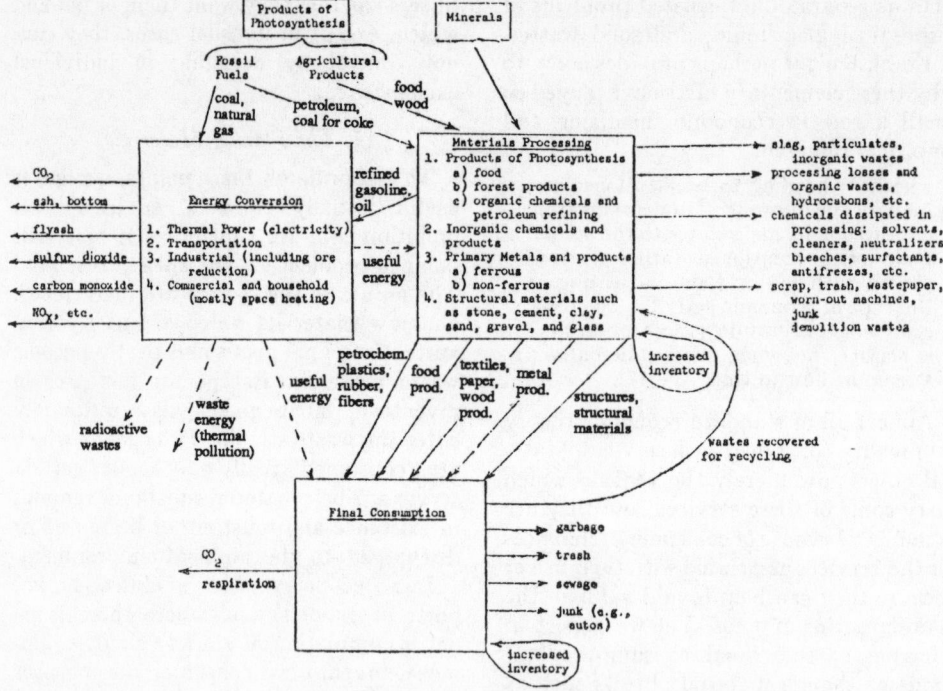

FIGURE 1.—MATERIALS FLOW

upon reflection, leads to the, at first rather surprising, corollary that residuals disposal involves a greater tonnage of materials than basic materials processing, although many of the residuals, being gaseous, require no physical "handling."

Figure 1 shows a materials flow of the type we have in mind in greater detail and relates it to a broad classification of economic sectors for convenience in our later discussion, and for general consistency with the Standard Industrial Classification. In an open (regional or national) economy, it would be necessary to add flows representing imports and exports. In an economy undergoing stock or capital accumulation, the production of residuals in any given year would be less by that amount than the basic inputs. In the entire U.S. economy, accumulation accounts for about 10–15 percent of basic annual inputs, mostly in the form of construction materials, and there is some net importation of raw and partially processed materials amounting to 4 or 5 percent of domestic production. Table 1 shows estimates of the weight of raw materials produced in the United States in several recent years, plus net imports of raw and partially processed materials.

Of the active inputs,[11] perhaps three-quarters of the overall weight is eventually discharged to the atmosphere as carbon (combined with atmospheric oxygen in the form of CO or CO_2) and hydrogen (combined with atmospheric oxygen as H_2O) under current conditions. This results from combustion of fossil fuels and from animal respiration. Discharge of carbon dioxide can be considered harmless in the short run. There are large "sinks" (in the form of vegetation and large water bodies,

[11] See footnote to Table 1.

TABLE 1—WEIGHT OF BASIC MATERIALS PRODUCTION
IN THE UNITED STATES PLUS NET IMPORTS,
1963 (10⁶ tons)

	1963	1964	1965
Agricultural (incl. fishery and wildlife and forest) products			
Food {Crops (excl. livestock feed)	125	128	130
Food {Livestock	100	103	102
Other products	5	6	6
Fishery	3	3	3
Forestry products (85 per cent dry wt. basis)			
Sawlogs	53	55	56
Pulpwood	107	116	120
Other	41	41	42
Total	434	452	459
Mineral fuels	1,337	1,399	1,448
Other minerals			
Iron ore	204	237	245
Other metal ores	161	171	191
Other nonmetals	125	133	149
Total	490	541	585
Grand total[a]	2,261	2,392	2,492

[a] Excluding construction materials, stone, sand, gravel, and other minerals used for structural purposes, ballast, fillers, insulation, etc. Gangue and mine tailings are also excluded from this total. These materials account for enormous tonnages but undergo essentially no chemical change. Hence, their use is more or less tantamount to physically moving them from one location to another. If this were to be included, there is no logical reason to exclude material shifted in highway cut and fill operations, harbor dredging, land-fill, plowing, and even silt moved by rivers. Since a line must be drawn somewhere, we chose to draw it as indicated above.

Source: R. U. Ayres and A. V. Kneese [2, p. 630].

mainly the oceans) which reabsorb this gas, although there is evidence of net accumulation of CO_2 in the atmosphere. Some experts believe that the latter is likely to show a large relative increase, as much as 50 per cent by the end of the century, possibly giving rise to significant —and probably, on balance, adverse— weather changes.[12] Thus continued com-

[11] See [30]. There is strong evidence that discharge of residuals has already affected the climate of individual cities; see Lowry [20].

bustion of fossil fuels at a high rate could produce externalities affecting the entire world. The effects associated with most residuals will normally be more confined, however, usually limited to regional air and water sheds.

The remaining residuals are either gases (like carbon monoxide, nitrogen dioxide, and sulfur dioxide—all potentially harmful even in the short run), dry solids (like rubbish and scrap), or wet solids (like garbage, sewage, and industrial wastes suspended or dissolved in water). In a sense, the dry solids are an irreducible, limiting form of waste. By the application of appropriate equipment and energy, most undesirable substances can, in principle, be removed from water and air streams[13]— but what is left must be disposed of in solid form, transformed, or reused. Looking at the matter in this way clearly reveals a primary interdependence between the various waste streams which casts into doubt the traditional classification of air, water, and land pollution as individual categories for purposes of planning and control policy.

Residuals do not necessarily have to be discharged to the environment. In many instances, it is possible to recycle them back into the productive system. The materials balance view underlines the fact that the throughput of new materials necessary to maintain a given level of production and consumption decreases as the technical efficiency of energy conversion and materials utilization increases. Similarly, other things being equal, the longer that cars, buildings, machinery, and other durables remain in service, the fewer new materials are required to compensate for loss, wear, and obsolescence— although the use of old or worn machinery (e.g., automobiles) tends to increase other residuals problems. Technically efficient combustion of (desulfurized) fossil fuels

[12] Except CO_2, which may be harmful in the long run, as noted.

would leave only water, ash, and carbon dioxide as residuals, while nuclear energy conversion need leave only negligible quantities of material residuals (although thermal pollution and radiation hazards cannot be dismissed by any means).

Given the population, industrial production, and transport service in an economy (a regional rather than a national economy would normally be the relevant unit), it is possible to visualize combinations of social policy which could lead to quite different relative burdens placed on the various residuals-receiving environmental media; or, given the possibilities for recycle and less residual-generating production processes, the overall burden to be placed upon the environment as a whole. To take one extreme, a region which went in heavily for electric space heating and wet scrubbing of stack gases (from steam plants and industries), which ground up its garbage and delivered it to the sewers and then discharged the raw sewage to watercourses, would protect its air resources to an exceptional degree. But this would come at the sacrifice of placing a heavy residuals load upon water resources. On the other hand, a region which treated municipal and industrial waste water streams to a high level and relied heavily on the incineration of sludges and solid wastes would protect its water and land resources at the expense of discharging waste residuals predominantly to the air. Finally, a region which practiced high level recovery and recycle of waste materials and fostered low residual production processes to a far reaching extent in each of the economic sectors might discharge very little residual waste to any of the environmental media.

Further complexities are added by the fact that sometimes it is possible to modify an environmental medium through investment in control facilities so as to improve its assimilative capacity. The clearest, but far from only, example is with respect to

watercourses where reservoir storage can be used to augment low river flows that ordinarily are associated with critical pollution (high external cost situations).[14] Thus internalization of external costs associated with particular discharges, by means of taxes or other restrictions, even if done perfectly, cannot guarantee Pareto optimality. Investments involving public good aspects must enter into an optimal solution.[15]

To recapitulate our main points briefly: (1) Technological external diseconomies are not freakish anomalies in the processes of production and consumption but an inherent and normal part of them. (2) These external diseconomies are quantitatively negligible in a low-population or economically undeveloped setting, but they become progressively (nonlinearly) more important as the population rises and the level of output increases (i.e., as the natural reservoirs of dilution and assimilative capacity become exhausted).[16] (3) They cannot be properly dealt with by considering environmental media such as air and water in isolation. (4) Isolated and *ad hoc* taxes and other restrictions are not sufficient for their optimum control, although they are essential elements in a more systematic and coherent program of environmental quality management. (5) Public investment programs, particularly including transportation systems, sewage disposal, and river flow regulation, are intimately related to the amounts and

[14] Careful empirical work has shown that this technique can fit efficiently into water quality management systems. See Davis [11].

[15] A discussion of the theory of such public investments with respect to water quality management is found in Boyd [5].

[16] Externalities associated with residuals discharge may appear only at certain threshold values which are relevant only at some stage of economic development and industrial and population concentrations. This may account for their general treatment as "exceptional" cases in the economics literature. These threshold values truly were exceptional cases for less developed economies.

effects of residuals and must be planned in light of them.

It is important to develop not only improved measures of the external costs resulting from differing concentrations and duration of residuals in the environment but more systematic methods for forecasting emissions of external-cost-producing residuals, technical and economic trade-offs between them, and the effects of recycle on environmental quality.

In the hope of contributing to this effort and of revealing more clearly the types of information which would be needed to implement such a program, we set forth a more formal model of the materials balance approach in the following sections and relate it to some conventional economic models of production and consumption. The main objective is to make some progress toward defining a system in which flows of services and materials are simultaneously accounted for and related to welfare.

II. *Basic Model*

The take off point for our discussion is the Walras-Cassel general equilibrium model,[17] extended to include intermediate consumption, which involve the following quantities:

resources and services

$r_1, \cdots \cdots \cdots \cdots, r_M$

products or commodities

$X_1, \cdots \cdots \cdots \cdots, X_N$

resource prices

$v_1, \cdots \cdots \cdots \cdots, v_M$

product or commodity prices

$p_1, \cdots \cdots \cdots \cdots, p_N$

final demands

$Y_1, \cdots \cdots \cdots \cdots, Y_N$

[17] The original references are Walras [28] and Cassel [8]. Our own treatment is largely based on Dorfman *et al.* [13].

The M basic resources are allocated among the N sectors as follows:

$$r_1 = a_{11}X_1 + a_{12}X_2 + \cdots + a_{1N}X_N$$
$$r_2 = a_{21}X_1 + a_{22}X_2 + \cdots + a_{2N}X_N$$
$$\vdots$$
$$r_M = a_{M1}X_1 + a_{M2}X_2 + \cdots + a_{MN}X_N$$

(1a) or

$$r_j = \sum_{k=1}^{N} a_{jk}X_k \qquad j = 1, \cdots, M$$

In (1a) we have implicitly assumed that there is no possibility of factor or process substitution and no joint production. These conditions will be discussed later. In matrix notation we can write:

(1b) $[r_{j1}]_{M,1} = [a_{jk}]_{M,N} \cdot [X_{k1}]_{N,1}$

where $[a]$ is an $M \times N$ matrix.

A similar set of equations describes the relations between commodity production and final demand:

(2a) $X_k = \sum_{l=1}^{N} A_{kl}Y_l \qquad k = 1, \cdots, N$

(2b) $[X_{k1}]_{N,1} = [A_{kl}]_{N,N} \cdot [Y_{l1}]_{N,1}$

and the matrix $[A]$ is given by

(3) $[A] = [I - C]^{-1}$

where $[I]$ is the unit diagonal matrix and the elements C_{ij} of the matrix $[C]$ are essentially the well known Leontief input coefficients. In principle these are functions of the existing technology and, therefore, are fixed for any given situation.

By combining (1) and (2), we obtain a set of equations relating resource inputs directly to final demand, viz.,

(4a)
$$r_j = \sum_{k=1}^{N} a_{jk} \sum_{l=1}^{N} A_{kl}Y_l = \sum_{k,l=1}^{N} a_{jk}A_{kl}Y_l$$
$$= \sum_{l=1}^{N} b_{jl}Y_l \qquad j = 1, \cdots, M$$

or, of course, in matrix notation (4b).

(4b)
$$[r_{j1}]_{M,1} = [a_{jk}]_{M,N} \cdot [A_{kl}]_{N,N} \cdot [Y_{l1}]_{N,1}$$
$$= [b_{jl}]_{M,N} \cdot [Y_{l1}]_{N,1}$$

We can also impute the prices of N intermediate goods and commodities to the prices of the M basic resources, as follows:

(5a) $\quad p_k = \sum_{j=1}^{M} v_j b_{jk} \quad k = 1, \cdots, N$

(5b) $\quad [p_{1k}]_{1,N} = [v_{1j}]_{1,M} \cdot [b_{jk}]_{M,N}$

To complete the system, it may be supposed that demand and supply relationships are given, a priori, by Pareto-type preference functions:

(6) Demand: $\quad Y_k = F_k(p_1, \cdots, p_N)$
$$k = 1, \cdots, N$$

(7) Supply: $\quad r_k = G_k(v_1, \cdots, v_M)$
$$k = 1, \cdots, M$$

where, of course, the p_j are functions of the v_j as in (5b).

In order to interpret the X's as physical production, it is necessary for the sake of consistency to arrange that outputs and inputs always balance, which implies that the C_{ij} must comprise *all* materials exchanges including residuals. To complete the system so that there is no net gain or loss of physical substances, it is also convenient to introduce two additional sectors, viz., an "environmental" sector whose (physical) output is X_0 and a "final consumption" sector whose output is denoted X_f. The system is then easily balanced by explicitly including flows both to and from these sectors.

To implement this further modification of the Walras-Cassel model, it is convenient to subdivide and relabel the resource category into tangible raw materials $\{r^m\}$ and services $\{r^s\}$:

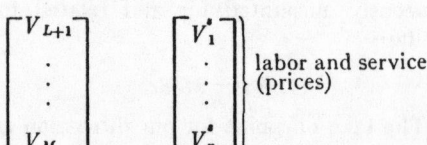

becomes

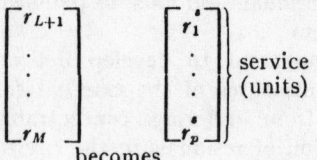

service (units)

where, of course,

(8) $\quad\quad L + P = M$

It is understood that services, while not counted in tons, can be measured in meaningful units, such as man-days, with well defined prices. Thus, we similarly relabel the price variables as follows:

$$\begin{bmatrix} V_1 \\ \cdot \\ \cdot \\ \cdot \\ V_L \end{bmatrix} \quad \begin{bmatrix} V_1^m \\ \cdot \\ \cdot \\ V_L^m \end{bmatrix} \text{raw material (prices)}$$

becomes

$$\begin{bmatrix} V_{L+1} \\ \cdot \\ \cdot \\ \cdot \\ V_M \end{bmatrix} \quad \begin{bmatrix} V_1^s \\ \cdot \\ \cdot \\ V_p^s \end{bmatrix} \text{labor and service (prices)}$$

The coefficients $\{a_{ij}\}$, $\{b_{ij}\}$ are similarly partitioned into two groups,

e.g., b_{1j} $\quad\quad b_{1j}^m$

b_{Lj} $\quad b_{Lj}^m$
$b_{L+1,j}$ becomes b_{1j}^s

b_{Mj} $\quad b_{pj}^s$

These notational changes have no effect whatever on the substance of the model, although the equations become somewhat more cumbersome. The partitioned matrix notation simplifies the restatement of the basic equations. Thus (1b) becomes (9), while (5b) becomes (10).

$$
(9) \qquad M\left\{\begin{bmatrix} \vdots \\ r \\ \vdots \end{bmatrix} = \begin{bmatrix} r^m \\ \cdots \\ r^s \end{bmatrix}\begin{matrix} \}L \\ \\ \}P \end{matrix} = M\left\{\begin{bmatrix} L & b^m \\ & \cdots & \\ P & b^s \end{bmatrix}\overbrace{}^{N} Y \right\}N\right.
$$

$$
(10) \qquad \underset{N}{[p_1, \cdots, p_N]} = [v^m \vdots v^s]\underset{\underbrace{L \;\; P}_{M}}{\begin{bmatrix} b^m \\ \cdots \\ b^s \end{bmatrix}}\underbrace{}_{N} M
$$

$$
= [\cdots v^m \cdots]\begin{bmatrix} \vdots & b^m & \vdots \\ \vdots & \cdots & \vdots \end{bmatrix} + [\cdots v^s \cdots]\begin{bmatrix} \vdots & b^s & \vdots \\ \vdots & \cdots & \vdots \end{bmatrix}
$$

The equivalent of (5a) is:

$$
(11) \qquad p_k = \underbrace{\sum_{j=1}^{L} b_{jk}^m v_j^m}_{\substack{\text{prices imputed} \\ \text{to cost of raw} \\ \text{materials}}} + \underbrace{\sum_{j=1}^{P} b_{jk}^s v_j^s}_{\substack{\text{prices imputed} \\ \text{to cost of} \\ \text{services}}}
$$

where $k = 1, \cdots, N$

We wish to focus attention explicitly on the flow of materials through the economy. By definition of the Leontief input coefficients (now related to materials flow), we have:

$C_{kj}X_j$ (physical) quantity transferred from k to j

$C_{jk}X_k$ quantity transferred from j to k

Hence, material flows *from* the environment to all other sectors are given by:

$$
(12) \qquad \begin{aligned} \sum_{k=1}^{N} C_{0k}X_k &= \sum_{j=1}^{L} r_j^m = \sum_{j=1}^{L}\sum_{k=1}^{N} a_{jk}^m X_k \\ &= \sum_{j=1}^{L}\sum_{k=1}^{N} b_{jk}^m Y_k \end{aligned}
$$

using equation (1), as modified.[18] Obvi-

ously, comparing the first and third terms,

$$
(13) \qquad \underbrace{C_{0k}}_{\substack{\text{total material} \\ \text{flow (0 to } k)}} = \underbrace{\sum_{j=1}^{L} a_{jk}^m}_{\substack{\text{all raw materials} \\ (0 \text{ to } k)}}
$$

Flows into and out of the environmental sector must be in balance:

$$
(14) \qquad \underbrace{\sum_{k=1}^{N} C_{0k}X_k}_{\substack{\text{sum of all raw} \\ \text{material flows}}} = \underbrace{\sum_{k=1}^{N} C_{k0}X_0 + C_{f0}X_0}_{\substack{\text{sum of all return} \\ \text{(waste) flows}}}
$$

Material flows to and from the final sector must also balance:

$$
(15) \qquad \begin{aligned} &\underbrace{\sum_{k=1}^{N} C_{kf}X_f}_{\substack{\text{sum of all} \\ \text{final goods}}} \\ &= \underbrace{\sum_{k=1}^{N} C_{fk}X_k}_{\substack{\text{sum of all} \\ \text{materials} \\ \text{recycled}}} + \underbrace{C_{f0}X_0}_{\substack{\text{waste residuals} \\ \text{(plus accumulation}^{19})}} \end{aligned}
$$

[19] For convenience, we can treat accumulation in the final sector as a return flow to the environment. In truth, structures actually *become* part of our environment, although certain disposal costs may be deferred.

[18] Ignoring, for convenience, any materials flow from the environment *directly* to the final consumption sector.

Of course, by definition, X_f is the sum of the final demands:

$$(16) \qquad X_f = \sum_{j=1}^{N} Y_j$$

Substituting (16) into the left side of (15) and (2a) into the right side of (15), we obtain an expression for the waste flow in terms of final demands:

$$(17) \quad C_{f0}X_0 = \sum_{j=1}^{N} \sum_{k=1}^{N} (C_{if} - C_{fj}A_{jk})Y_k$$

The treatment could be simplified slightly if we assumed that there is no recycling per se. Thus, in the context of the model, we could suppose that all residuals return to the environmental sector,[20] where some of them (e.g., waste paper) become "raw materials." They would then be indistinguishable from new raw materials, however, and price differentials between the two would be washed out. In principle, this is an important distinction to retain.

III. *Inclusion of Externalities*

The physical flow of materials between various intermediate (production) sectors and the final (consumption) sector tends to be accompanied by, and correlated with, a (reverse) flow of dollars.[21] However, the physical flow of materials from and back to the environment is only partly reflected by actual dollar flows, namely, land rents and payments for raw materials. There are three classes of physical exchange for which there exist no counterpart economic transactions. These are: (1) private use for production inputs of "common property" resources, notably air, streams, lakes, and the ocean; (2) private use of the assimila-

tive capacity of the environment to "dispose of" or dilute wastes and residuals; (3) inadvertent or unwanted material inputs to productive processes—diluents and pollutants.

All these goods (or "bads") are physically transferred at zero price, not because they are not scarce relative to demand—they often are in developed economies—or because they confer no service or disservice on the user—since they demonstrably do so—but because there exist no social institutions that permit the resources in question to be "owned," and exchanged in the market.

The allocation of resources corresponding to a Pareto optimum cannot be attained without subjecting the above-mentioned nonmarket and involuntary exchanges to the moderation of a market or a surrogate thereof. In principle, the influence of a market might be simulated, to a first approximation, by introducing a set of shadow (or virtual) prices.[22] These may well be zero, where supply truly exceeds demand, or negative (i.e., costs) in some instances; they will be positive in others. The exchanges are, of course, real.

The Walras-Cassel model can be generalized to handle these effects in the following way:

1. One can introduce a set of R common-property resources or services of raw materials $\{r_1^{cp}, \cdots, r_R^{cp}\}$ as a subset of the set $\{r_i\}$; these will have corresponding virtual prices $\{v_j^{cp}\}$, which would constitute an "income" from the environment. Such resources include the atmosphere; streams, lakes, and oceans; landscape; wildlife and biological diversity; and the indispensable assimilative capacity of the environment (its ability to accept and neutralize or recycle residuals).[23]

[20] In calculating actual quantities, we would (by convention) ignore the weight of oxygen taken free from the atmosphere in combustion and return as CO_2. However, such inputs will be treated explicitly later.

[21] To be precise, the dollar flow governs and is governed by a combined flow of materials and services (value added).

[22] A similar concept exists in mechanics where the forces producing "reaction" (to balance action and reaction) are commonly described as "virtual forces."

[23] Economists have previously suggested generalization of the Walras-Cassel model to take account of public goods. One of the earliest appears to be Schles-

2. One can introduce a set of S environmental *disservices* imposed on consumers of material resources, by forcing them to accept unwanted inputs $\{r_1^u, \cdots, r_s^u\}$ (pollutants, contaminants, etc.); these disservices would have negative value, giving rise to *negative* virtual prices $\{u_j\}$.[24]

The matrix coefficients $\{a_{ij}\}$ and $\{b_{ij}\}$ can be further partitioned to take account of this additional refinement, and equations analogous to (9), (10), and (11) can be generalized in the obvious way. Equation (6) carries over unchanged, but (7) must be appropriately generalized to take account of the altered situation. Actually, (7) breaks up into several groups of equations:

(18)
$$r_k^m = G_k^m(p_1, \cdots, p_N)$$
$$k = 1, \cdots, L$$

(19)
$$r_k^s = G_k^s(p_1, \cdots, p_N)$$
$$k = 1, \cdots, P$$

However, as we have noted at the outset, the supplies of common-property resources and environmental services or disservices are *not* regulated directly by market prices of other goods and services. In the case of common-property resources, the supplies are simply constants fixed by nature or otherwise determined by accident or noneconomic factors.

The total value of these services performed by the environment cannot be

calculated but it is suggestive to consider the situation if the natural reservoir of air, water, minerals, etc., were very much smaller, as if the earth were a submarine or "spaceship" (i.e., a vehicle with no assimilative and/or regenerative capacity). In such a case, all material resources would have to be recycled,[25] and the cost of all goods would necessarily reflect the cost of reprocessing residuals and wastes for reuse. In this case, incidentally, the ambient level of unrecovered wastes continuously circulating through the resource inventory of the system (i.e., the spaceship) would in general be nonzero because of the difficulty of 100 percent efficient waste-removal of air and water. However, although the quantity of waste products in constant circulation may fluctuate within limits, it cannot be allowed to increase monotonically with time, which means that as much material must be recycled, on the average, as is discarded. The value of common resources plus the assimilation services performed by the environment, then, is only indirectly a function of the ambient level of untreated residuals per se, or the disutility caused thereby, which depend on the cost efficiency of the available treatment technology. Be this as it may, of course, the bill of goods produced in a spaceship economy would certainly be radically different from that we are familiar with. For this reason, no standard economic comparison between the two situations is meaningful. The measure of worth we are seeking is actually the difference between the total welfare "produced" by a spaceship economy, where 100 percent of all residuals are promptly recycled, vis-à-vis the existing welfare output on earth, where resource inventories are substantial and

---

inger [23]. We are indebted to Otto Eckstein for calling our attention to this key reference.

[24] The notion of introducing the possibility of negative prices in general equilibrium theory has apparently been discussed before, although we are not aware of any systematic development of the idea in the published literature. In this connection, it is worth pointing out the underlying similarity of negative prices and effluent taxes—which have been, and still are being considered as an attractive alternative to subsidies and federal standard-setting as a means of controlling air and water pollution. Such taxes would, of course, be an explicit attempt to rectify an imbalance caused by a market failure.

[25] Any consistent deviation from this 100 per cent rule implies an accumulation of waste products, on the average, which, by definition, is inconsistent with maintaining an equilibrium.

complete recycling need not be contemplated for a very long time to come.

This welfare difference might well be very large, although we possess no methodological tools for quantifying it. In any case, the resource inventory and assimilative capacity of the environment probably contribute very considerably to our standard of living.

If these environmental contributions were paid for, the overall effect on prices would presumably to be push them generally upward. However, the major *differential* effect of undervaluing the environmental contribution is that goods produced by high residual-producing processes, such as papermaking, are substantially underpriced vis-à-vis goods which involve more economical uses of basic resources. This is, however, not socially disadvantageous per se: that is, it causes no misallocation of resources unless, or until, the large resource inventory and/or the assimilative capacity of the environment are used up. When this happens, however, as it now has in most highly industrialized regions, either a market must be allowed to operate or some other form of decision rule must be introduced to permit a rational choice to be made, e.g., between curtailing or controlling the production of residuals or tolerating the effects (disservice) thereof.

It appears that the natural inventory of most common resources used as inputs (e.g., air as an input to combustion and respiratory processes) is still ample,[26] but the assimilative capacity of the environment has already been exceeded in many areas, with important external costs resulting. This suggests a compromise treat-

ment. If an appropriate price could be charged to the producers of the residuals and used to compensate the inadvertent recipients—with the price determined by appropriate Pareto preference criteria—there would be no particular analytic purpose in keeping books on the exchange of the other environmental benefits mentioned, although they are quantitatively massive. We will, therefore, in the remainder of the discussion omit the common-property variables $\{r_j^{cp}\}$ and the corresponding virtual-price variables $\{v_j^{cp}\}$ defined previously, retaining only the terms $\{r_j^u\}$ and $\{u_{jk}\}$. The variable $\{r_j^u\}$ represents a physical quantity of the jth unwanted input. There are S such terms, by assumption, whose magnitudes are proportional to the levels of consumption of basic raw materials, subject to the existing technology. However, residuals production is not immutable: it can be increased or decreased by investment, changes in materials processing technology, raw material substitutions, and so forth.

At first glance it might seem entirely reasonable to assert that the *supplies* of unwanted residuals received will be functions of the (negative) prices (i.e., compensation) paid for them, in analogy with (7). Unfortunately, this assertion immediately introduces a theoretical difficulty, since the assumption of unique coefficients $\{a_{ij}\}$ and $\{C_{ij}\}$[27] is not consistent with the possibility of factor or process substitution or joint-production, as stated earlier. To permit such substitutions, one would have to envision a very large collection of alternative sets of coefficients: one complete set of a's and C's for each specific combination of factors and processes. Maximization of any objective function (such as GNP) would involve solving the entire system of equations as many times as there are combinations of factors and pro-

---

[26] Water is an exception in arid regions; in humid regions, however, water "shortages" are misnomers: they are really consequences of excessive use of watercourses as cheap means of waste disposal. But some ecologists have claimed that oxygen depletion may be a very serious long-run problem; see Cole [10].

[27] Or $\{b_{ij}\}$ and $\{A_{ij}\}$.

$$(21) \qquad [r] = \begin{bmatrix} r^m \\ r^e \\ r^u \end{bmatrix} = M \left\{ \underbrace{\begin{bmatrix} \begin{bmatrix} a^m \\ \cdots \\ a^e \\ \cdots \\ a^u \end{bmatrix} \end{bmatrix} X }_{N} \right\} \quad N = \begin{bmatrix} \begin{bmatrix} b^m \\ \cdots \\ b^e \\ \cdots \\ b^u \end{bmatrix} Y \end{bmatrix}$$

cesses, and picking out that set of solutions which yields the largest value. Alternatively, if the a's and C's are assumed to be continuously variable functions (of each other), the objective function could also, presumably, be parameterized. However, as long as the a's and C's are uniquely given, the supply of the kth unwanted residual is only marginally under the control of the producer, since it will be produced in strict relationship to the composition of the bill of final goods $\{Y_j\}$.

Hence, for the present model it is only correct to assume

$$(20) \qquad r_k^u = G_k^u(Y_1, \cdots, Y_N)$$

This limitation does not affect the existence of an equilibrium solution for the system of equations; it merely means that the shadow prices $\{u_{jk}\}$ which would emerge from such a solution for given coefficients $\{a_{ij}\}$, $\{b_{ij}\}$, and $\{C_{ij}\}$ might be considerably higher than the real economic optimum, since the latter could only be achieved by introducing factor and process changes.

Of course, the physical inputs are also related to the physical outputs of goods, as in (21).

Written out in full detail (21) is equivalent to:

$$(22) \quad \text{raw materials} \quad r_k^m = \sum_{j=1}^{N} a_{kj}^m X_j = \sum_{j=1}^{N} b_{kj}^m Y_j$$

$$k = 1, \cdots, L$$

$$(23) \quad \text{labor and technical services} \quad r_k^e = \sum_{j=1}^{N} a_{kj}^e X_j = \sum_{j=1}^{N} b_{kj}^e Y_j$$

$$k = 1, \cdots, P$$

$$(24) \quad \text{unwanted inputs} \quad r_k^u = \sum_{j=1}^{N} a_{kj}^u X_j = \sum_{j=1}^{N} b_{kj}^u Y_j$$

$$k = 1, \cdots, S$$

where, of course,

$$(25) \qquad L + P + S = M$$

The corresponding matrix equation for the prices of goods, in terms of production costs, is

$$(26) \qquad [p_1, \cdots, p_N] = [v^m \vdots v^e \vdots u] \begin{bmatrix} b^m \\ \cdots \\ b^e \\ \cdots \\ b^u \end{bmatrix}$$

Written out in the standard form, we obtain

$$(27) \qquad p_k = \underbrace{\sum_{j=1}^{L} b_{jk}^m v_j^m}_{\substack{\text{cost of raw} \\ \text{materials}}} + \underbrace{\sum_{j=1}^{P} b_{jk}^e v_j^e}_{\substack{\text{cost of labor} \\ \text{and technical} \\ \text{services}}}$$

$$+ \underbrace{\sum_{j=1}^{S} b_{jk}^u v_j^u}_{\substack{\text{cost (compensa-} \\ \text{tion) for pro-} \\ \text{viding environ-} \\ \text{mental disser-} \\ \text{vices}}}$$

$$k = 1, \cdots, N$$

Evidently, the coefficients b_{jk}^u are empirically determined by the structure of the regional economy and its geography. It is assumed that a single overall (negative) price for each residual has meaning, even though each productive sector—and even each consumer—has his own individual utility function. Much the same assumption is conventionally made, and accepted, in the case of positive real prices.

All of the additional variables now fit into the general framework of the original Walras-Cassel analysis. Indeed, we have $2N+2M-1$ variables (r_i, Y_i, p_i, v_i) (allowing an arbitrary normalization factor for the price level) and $2N+2M-1$ independent equations.[28] If solutions exist for the Walras-Cassel system of equations, the arguments presumably continue to hold true for the generalized model. In any case, a discussion of such mathematical questions would carry us too far from our main theme.

IV. *Concluding Comments*

The limited economics literature currently available which is devoted to environmental pollution problems has generally taken a partial equilibrium view of the matter, as well as treated the pollution of particular environmental media, such as air and water, as separate problems.[29] This no doubt reflects the propensity of the theoretical literature to view externalities as exceptional and minor. Clearly, the partial equilibrium approach in particular is very convenient theoretically and empirically for it permits external damage and control cost functions to be defined for each particular case without reference to broader interrelationships and adjustments in the economy.

[28] There is one redundant equation in the system, which expresses the identity between gross product and gross income for the system as a whole (sometimes called "Walras law").

[29] See, for example, the essays in Wolozin [29].

We have argued in this paper that the production of residuals is an inherent and general part of the production and consumption process and, moreover, that there are important trade-offs between the gaseous, liquid, or solid forms that these residuals may take. Further, we have argued that under conditions of intensive economic and population development the environmental media which can receive and assimilate residual wastes are not free goods but natural resources of great value with respect to which voluntary exchange cannot operate because of their common property characteristics. We have also noted, in passing, that the assimilative capacity of environmental media can sometimes be altered and that therefore the problem of achieving Pareto optimality reaches beyond devising appropriate shadow prices and involves the planning and execution of investments with public goods aspects.

We have exhibited a formal mathematical framework for tracing residuals flows in the economy and related it to the general equilibrium model of resources allocation, altered to accommodate recycle and containing unpriced sectors to represent the environment. This formulation, in contrast to the usual partial equilibrium treatments, implies knowledge of all preference and production functions including relations between residuals discharge and external cost and all possible factor and process substitutions. While we feel that it represents reality with greater fidelity than the usual view, it also implies a central planning problem of impossible difficulty, both from the standpoint of data collection and computation.

What, if any, help can the general interdependency approach we have outlined offer in dealing with pollution problems effectively and reasonably efficiently? A minimal contribution is its warning that partial equilibrium approaches, while more tractable, may lead to serious errors. Second, in projecting waste residuals for an economy—a regional economy would usually be the most relevant for planning and control—the inter-industry materials flow model can provide a much more conceptually satisfying and accurate tool for projecting future residuals production than the normal aggregative extrapolations.[30] The latter not only treat gaseous, liquid, and solid wastes separately, but do not take account of input-output relations and the fact that the materials account for the region must balance.

We think that in the next few years it will be possible to make improved regional projections of residuals along the lines sketched above. Undoubtedly, there will also be further progress in empirically estimating external costs associated with residuals discharge and in estimating control costs via various alternative measures. On the basis of this kind of information, a control policy can be devised. However, this approach will still be partial. Interrelations between the regional and national economy must be treated simplistically and to be manageable, the analysis must confine itself to a specific projected bill of goods.

The basic practical question which remains to be answered is whether an iterated series of partial equilibrium treatments—e.g., focusing on one industry or region at a time, *ceteris paribus*—would converge toward the general equilibrium

[30] Some efforts to implement these concepts are already underway. Walter Isard and his associates have prepared an input-output table for Philadelphia which includes coefficients representing waterborne wastes (unpublished). The recent study of waste management in the New York Metropolitan region by the Regional Plan Association took a relatively broad view of the waste residuals problem [31]. Relevant data on several industries are being gathered. Richard Frankel's not yet published study of thermal power in which the range of technical options for controlling residuals, and their costs, is being explored is notable in this regard. His and other salient studies are described in Ayres and Kneese [2].

solution, or not. We know of no theoretical test of convergence which would be applicable in this case but, in the absence of such a criterion, would be willing to admit the possible relevance of an empirical sensitivity test more or less along the following lines: take a major residuals-producing industry (such as electric power) and parametrize its cost structure in terms of emission control levels, allowing all technically feasible permutations of factor (fuel) inputs and processes. It would be a straightforward, but complicated, operations research problem to determine the minimum cost solution as a function of the assumed (negative) price of the residuals produced. If possible industry patterns—factor and process combinations—exist which would permit a high level of emission control at only a small increase in power production cost, then it might be possible to conclude that for a significant range of (negative) residuals prices the effect on power prices —and therefore on the rest of the economy —would not be great. Such a conclusion would support the convergence hypothesis. If, on the other hand, electric power prices are very sensitive to residuals prices, then one would at least have to undertake a deeper study of consumer preference functions to try to determine what residuals prices would actually be if a market mechanism existed. If people prove to have a strong antipathy to soot and sulfur dioxide, for instance, resulting in a high (negative) price for these unwanted inputs, then one would be forced to suspect that the partial equilibrium approach is probably not convergent to the general equilibrium solution and that much more elaborate forms of analysis will be required.

REFERENCES

1. R. U. AYRES, "Stability of Biosystems in Sea Water," Tech. Rept. No. 142, Hudson Laboratories, Columbia University, New York 1967.

AYRES AND KNEESE: EXTERNALITIES   297

2. —— AND A. V. KNEESE, "Environ-
mental Pollution," in U.S. Congress,
Joint Economic Committee, *Federal
Programs for the Development of Human
Resources*, Vol. 2, Washington 1968.

3. W. J. BAUMOL, *Welfare Economics and
the Theory of the State*. Cambridge 1967.

4. K. E. BOULDING, "The Economics of the
Coming Spaceship Earth," in H. Jarrett,
ed., *Environmental Quality in a Growing
Economy*, Baltimore 1966, pp. 3–14.

5. J. H. BOYD, "Collective Facilities in
Water Quality Management," Appendix
to Kneese and Bower [17].

6. J. W. BUCHANAN AND WM. C. STUBBLE-
BINE, "Externality," *Economica*, Nov.
1962, *29*, 371–84.

7. —— AND G. TULLOCK, "Public and
Private Interaction under Reciprocal
Externality," in J. Margolis, ed., *The
Public Economy of Urban Communities*,
Baltimore 1965, pp. 52–73.

8. G. CASSEL, *The Theory of Social Economy*. New York 1932.

9. R. H. COASE, "The Problem of Social
Cost," *Jour. Law and Econ.*, Oct. 1960,
3, 1–44.

10. L. COLE, "Can the World be Saved?"
Paper presented at the 134th Meeting of
the American Association for the Advancement of Science, December 27,
1967.

11. R. K. DAVIS, *The Range of Choice in
Water Management*. Baltimore 1968.

12. O. A. DAVIS AND A. WHINSTON, "Externalities, Welfare, and the Theory of
Games," *Jour. Pol. Econ.*, June 1962,
70, 241–62.

13. R. DORFMAN, P. SAMUELSON AND R. M.
SOLOW, *Linear Programming and Economic Analysis*. New York 1958.

14. I. FISHER, *Nature of Capital and Income*.
New York 1906.

15. A. C. HARBERGER, "Monopoly and Resources Allocation," *Am. Econ. Rev.*,
Proc., May 1954, *44*, 77–87.

16. K. W. KAPP, *The Social Costs of Private
Enterprise*. Cambridge 1950.

17. A. V. KNEESE AND B. T. BOWER,
*Managing Water Quality: Economics,
Technology, Institutions*. Baltimore 1968.

18. F. H. KNIGHT, *Risk, Uncertainty, and
Profit*. Boston and New York 1921.

19. H. LEIBENSTEIN, "Allocative Efficiency
vs. 'X-Efficiency,'" *Am. Econ. Rev.*,
June 1966, *56*, 392–415.

20. W. P. LOWRY, "The Climate of Cities,"
Sci. Am., Aug. 1967, *217*, 15–23.

21. E. J. MISHAN, "Reflections on Recent
Developments in the Concept of Exter-
nal Effects," *Canadian Jour. Econ. Pol.
Sci.*, Feb. 1965, *31*, 1–34.

22. A. C. PIGOU, *Economics of Welfare*. London 1952.

23. K. SCHLESINGER, "Über die Produk-
tionsgleichungen der ökonomischen
Wertlehre," *Ergebnisse eines mathemati-
schen Kolloquiums*, No. 6. Vienna, F.
Denticke, 1933.

24. D. SCHWARTZMAN, "The Burden of
Monopoly," *Jour. Pol. Econ.*, Dec. 1960,
68, 627–30.

25. T. SCITOVSKY, "Two Concepts of External Economies," *Jour. Pol. Econ.*,
Apr. 1954, *62*, 143–51.

26. F. SMITH, *The Economic Theory of Industrial Waste Production and Disposal*,
draft of a doctoral dissertation, North-
western Univ. 1967.

27. R. TURVEY, "On Divergencies between
Social Cost and Private Cost," *Economica*,
Nov. 1962, *30*, 309–13.

28. L. WALRAS, *Elements d'economie politi-
que pure*, Jaffé translation. London 1954.

29. H. WOLOZIN, ed., *The Economics of Air
Pollution*. New York 1966.

30. CONSERVATION FOUNDATION, *Implications of Rising Carbon Dioxide Content
of the Atmosphere*. New York 1963.

31. REGIONAL PLAN ASSOCIATION, *Waste
Management*, a Report of the Second
Regional Plan. New York 1968.

Part II
The Theory of Environmental Regulation

[2]

On Taxation and the Control of Externalities

By William J. Baumol*

It is ironic that just at the moment when the Pigouvian tradition has some hope of acceptance in application it should find itself under a cloud in the theoretical literature. James Buchanan has argued that its recommended taxes and subsidies may even increase resource misallocation in the presence of monopoly. Otto Davis and Andrew Whinston (1962) have, in effect, raised doubts about its applicability in the presence of oligopoly. And Ronald Coase has asserted that the tradition has not selected the correct taxation principle for the elimination of externalities, and may not even have chosen the right individuals to tax or to subsidize. In this paper I will suggest that these authors have led the discussion in our profession to focus on the wrong difficulties. In doing so they have, albeit inadvertently, drawn attention away from some of the most important limitations of the Pigouvian prescription as an instrument of policy and from consideration of the means that might prove effective in practice.

The main purpose of the paper is to show that, taken on its own grounds, the conclusions of the Pigouvian tradition are, in fact, impeccable. Despite the various criticisms that have been raised against it in the large numbers case, which is of primary importance in reality and to which Pigou's analysis directs itself, his tax-subsidy programs are generally those required for an optimal allocation of resources. Moreover, I will attempt to show that where an externality is (like the usual pollution problem) of the public goods variety, neither compensation to nor taxation of those who are affected by it is compatible with optimal resource allocation. Pigouvian taxes (subsidies) upon the generator of the externality are all that is required.

However, as is well known, the Pigouvian proposals suffer from a number of serious shortcomings as operational criteria when one seeks to implement them precisely as they emerge from the theory. I therefore discuss a modified approach that recommends itself more for its promise of effectiveness, than its theoretical nicety. It consists of two basic steps: the setting of standards, more or less arbitrarily, of levels of pollution, congestion and the like, that are considered to be tolerable, and the design of taxes and effluent charges whose rates are shown by experience to be sufficient to achieve the selected standards of acceptability. Such a system of charges will, at least in principle, effect any preselected reduction in,

* Professor of economics, Princeton University and New York University. I would like to express my gratitude to the National Science Foundation whose assistance helped materially in the completion of the paper and to my colleagues James Litvack, Wallace Oates, and David Bradford, to my students Mark Gaudry and Bryan Boulier, and to Peter Bohm, James Buchanan, Ronald Coase, Karl-Göran Mäler, Herbert Mohring, and Ralph Turvey who have given me many very helpful suggestions, and saved me from a number of serious errors. Mohring and J. Hayden Boyd have written an extremely illuminating paper dealing, among other relevant matters, with the portions of the Coase-Buchanan-Turvey arguments in the case where the polluters and their victims "can and do negotiate." Since the present paper concerns itself only with the "relevant" large numbers case where there is no negotiation, it deliberately makes no attempt to consider the interesting negotiation case examined so helpfully by Mohring and Boyd.

say, the pollution content of our rivers, at minimum cost to society. It automatically achieves an efficient allocation of the required reduction in emissions among the offending firms *even if they are neither pure competitors nor profit maximizers*. Thus, a persuasive case can be made for the use of taxes and subsidies to control externalities, even if they will not produce an optimal allocation of resources in the complex world of reality.

I. The Coase Argument in the Case Without Negotiation

Recommendations designed for the competitive case can clearly run into difficulties in the presence of monopolistic elements. Buchanan reminds us that, if a polluting monopolistic industry already restricts the outputs of its products below their competitive levels, the imposition of an effluent charge to restrict output still further is hardly likely to be appropriate. And Davis and Whinston (1962) show for the case of externalities under oligopoly that it is rather difficult to come up with an ideal set of taxes since in the small numbers case just about anything is possible by way of pricing and output levels. However, these arguments have little direct bearing on the Pigouvian analysis because it is couched entirely in terms of pure competition (on this see Stanislaw Wellicz' illuminating discussion), which, in view of the large numbers involved in virtually all of the externalities problems that worry us today, is entirely apropos.

Coase's arguments, buttressed by impressive legal erudition, are less easily dealt with. He offers us a number of illuminating observations, among them the interesting point (see his Section IV) that (in the relatively unimportant cases) where only a small number of decision makers is involved, a process of voluntary bargaining and side payments among those con-

cerned by an externality may produce an optimal allocation of resources, even in the absence of liability for damage. This implies that where small numbers are involved, the imposition of a "corrective" Pigouvian tax may be too much of a good thing it can produce a misallocation rather than eliminating it.

Coase suggests, however, that even in cases where there is no negotiation among the parties affected by an externality the Pigouvian taxes and subsidies may be the wrong remedy—that they may only modify the character of the misallocation of resources. Coase's central argument appears to be the following: Every social cost is inherently reciprocal in nature. The nearby residents who breathe smoke spewn by a factory must share with the management of the factory the responsibility for the resulting social cost. True, if the factory were closed up the social cost would disappear. But the same holds for its neighbors—were they to move away no one would suffer smoke nuisance. Put another way, just as the smoke emitted by the factory imposes at least a psychic cost on its neighbors, the latter's insistence on the installation of purification devices or a reduction in the pollution-producing activity imposes a cost on the factory.

This position, though at first glance very odd (the murder victim too, is then always an accessory to the crime), grows more persuasive as one considers it further. Coase does not raise the issue as a matter of distributive justice. Rather, he suggests, because of the reciprocal structure of the externality, the traditional taxes and subsidies are likely to lead to a misallocation of resources.[1] If it is socially less costly to

[1] Thus Coase starts out with

... the case of a confectioner, the noise and vibrations from whose machinery disturbed a doctor in his work. To avoid harming the doctor would inflict harm on [be costly to] the confectioner. The problem posed by this case was essentially whether it was worthwhile, as a

remove the neighbors from the vicinity of the factory than to reduce the quantity of pollutants emitted by the plant (taking into account the location preferences of the current residents), surely the former is the course of action which is more desirable socially.

In that case, should not a tax sometimes be levied, at least in part on those who choose to live near the factory rather than upon the factory owners?[2] Otherwise might not too many persons be induced to move near the factory thus, incidentally, increasing the magnitude of the Pigouvian tax since the social damage caused by the smoke must then rise correspondingly?

A simple model shows readily that, properly stated, the prescription of the Pigouvian tradition is (at least formally) correct. An appropriately chosen tax, levied only on the factory (without payment of

---

result of restricting the methods of production which could be used by the confectioner, to secure more doctoring at the cost of a reduced supply of confectionery products. [Section II, p. 2]

[2] If the factory owner is to be made to pay a tax equal to the damage caused, it would clearly be desirable to institute a double tax system and to make residents of the district pay an amount equal to the additional cost incurred by the factory owner (or the consumers of his products) in order to avoid the damage. [Coase, Section IX, p. 41] An even stronger statement on this subject occurs in Buchanan and Stubblebine (Section III):

... full Pareto equilibrium can *never* be attained via the imposition of unilaterally imposed taxes and subsidies until all marginal externalities are eliminated. If a tax subsidy method, rather than 'trade,' is to be introduced, it should involve bi-lateral taxes (subsidies). Not only must *B*'s behavior be modified so as to insure that he will take the costs externally imposed on *A* into account, but *A*'s behavior must be modified so as to insure that he will take the costs 'internally' imposed on *B* into account. [italics added]

However, in a recent letter Buchanan commented:

In my own thinking . . . I did not ever think of this sort of [double] tax at all, and it would have surely seemed bizarre to me to suggest that taxes be levied on both the factory and the laundries. What we were proposing was the Wicksellian public-goods approach. Suppose that existing property rights allow the factory to put out the smoke . . . There is a public goods problem here; the residents get together, impose a tax on *themselves* to subsidize the factory to install the smoke prevention device.

---

compensation to local residents) is precisely what is needed for optimal resource allocation under pure competition. No tax on nearby residents is required or, taken in real terms, is even compatible with optimal resource allocation. Thus the obvious and apparently common interpretation of the Coase position is simply invalid. We will see, however, that the issue Coase himself intended to raise was rather more subtle and his conclusions are not necessarily at variance with the Pigouvian prescription as I interpret it.

II. Analysis: Should the Victims of Externalities be Taxed or Compensated?

To formalize the argument we construct an elementary general equilibrium model designed to represent in most explicit form the conditions envisioned in the Coase argument, departing from it only by an assumption of universal perfect competition, including thereby the critical stipulation that costs of negotiated and voluntary control of externalities are prohibitive. In addition, we adopt the simplifying premises that there is only one scarce resource, labor, and that the externality (smoke) only affects the cost of production of neighboring laundries, rather than causing disutility for consumers. It is easy to show (see for example, fn. 5) that neither of these simplifications, nor the assumption that there are only four activities, affects the substance of the discussion. We utilize the following notation: Let

x_1, x_2, x_3, and x_4 be the outputs of the economy's four activities, I, II, III, and IV

R be the total supply of the labor resource available

x_5 be the unused quantity of labor (which is assumed to be utilized as leisure)

x_{ij} be the quantity of x_i consumed by individual j $(i = 1, \ldots, 5)$ $(j = 1, \ldots, m)$

p_1, p_2, p_3, p_4, and p_5 be the prices of the four outputs and leisure

$u_j(x_{1j}, \ldots, x_{5j})$ be the utility function of individual j, and

$c_1(x_1)$, $c_2(x_1, x_2)$, $c_3(x_3)$ and $c_4(x_4)$ be the respective total labor cost functions for our four outputs

Here x_1 is an output whose production imposes external costs on the manufacture of x_2 (say, industry II is the oft-cited laundry industry whose costs are increased by I's smoke). To permit the full range of Coase's alternatives (moving of the factory's neighbors and elimination of smoke by the factory), each of these two products is taken to have a perfect substitute. The substitute for x_1 is x_3 whose production yields no externalities, but whose cost is different (presumably higher) than that of x_1. We may think of commodity III as identical with I, but produced in a factory equipped with smoke elimination equipment. Similarly, industry IV is taken to offer the same output as II but its operations have been relocated (at a cost) in order to avoid the effects of the externalities.[3] Thus, by changing the ratio between x_2 and x_4 the model can relocate as much of the laundry output as is desired.

All prices are expressed in terms of hours of labor so that, identically,

$$(1) \qquad p_5 = 1$$

[3] Since product III is a perfect substitute for product I and product IV is a perfect substitute for product II, the utility function for individual j can be written as $u_j(x_{1j}+x_{3j}, x_{2j}+x_{4j}, x_{5j})$. This is, of course, a special case of the more general utility function utilized in the text, and as the reader can verify, the conclusions are totally unaffected by the use of the particular form of the utility function just described.

Pareto optimality then requires maximization of the utility of any arbitrarily chosen individual, say m, subject to the requirement that there be no loss in utility to any of the $m-1$ other persons, i.e.; given any feasible level for these other persons' utility. Thus the problem is[4] to maximize

$$u_m(x_{1m}, \ldots, x_{5m})$$

subject to

$$u_j(x_{1j}, \ldots, x_{5j}) = k_j \text{ (constant)}$$
$$(j = 1, 2, \ldots, m-1)$$

$$\sum_{j=1}^{m} x_{ij} = x_i \qquad (i = 1, \ldots, 5)$$

and the labor requirement (production function) constraint

$$c_1(x_1) + c_2(x_1, x_2) + c_3(x_3) + c_4(x_4) + x_5 = R$$

We immediately obtain our Lagrangian

$$L = \sum_{j=1}^{m} \lambda_j [u_j(x_{1j}, \ldots, x_{5j}) - k_j]$$
$$+ \sum_i \nu_i (x_i - \sum_j x_{ij})$$
$$(2) \qquad + \mu[R - c_1(x_1) - c_2(x_1, x_2)$$
$$- c_3(x_3) - c_4(x_4) - x_5]$$

where we may take $\lambda_m = 1$, $k_m = 0$.

We use the notation u_{ji} to represent $\partial u_j / \partial x_{ij}$ and c_{ik} to represent $\partial c_i / \partial x_k$ (or dc_i / dx_k, where appropriate).

Then, differentiating in turn with respect to the x_{ij} and the x_i we obtain the first-order conditions

$$\partial L / \partial x_{ij} = \lambda_j u_{ji} - \nu_i = 0 \quad (i = 1, \ldots, 5)$$
$$(j = 1, \ldots, m)$$

$$\partial L / \partial x_1 = -\mu(c_{11} + c_{21}) + \nu_1 = 0$$
$$\partial L / \partial x_i = -\mu c_{ii} + \nu_i = 0 \quad (i = 2, 3, 4)$$
$$\partial L / \partial x_5 = -\mu + \nu_5 = 0$$

[4] For a more sophisticated variant of this model, using the techniques of non-linear programming, see Robert Meyer.

Now, from consumer equilibrium analysis, we know that for any two commodities, a and b, and any two prices, p_a and p_b, we have $p_a/p_b = u_{ja}/u_{jb}$ $(j = 1, \cdots, m)$ or $\omega_j p'_i = u_{ji}$ for all i and some ω_j.

Hence, $\lambda_j u_{ji} = \lambda_j \omega_j p_i$, so that writing $s_j = \lambda_j \omega_j$ the first of our first-order conditions becomes $\nu_i = s_j p_i$ for all individuals, j. Consequently the value of s_j must equal the same number, $s = \nu_i/p_i$ for every individual, and that first equation of the first-order conditions now becomes simply $\nu_i = s p_i$ for all i. Substituting this expression for ν_i into the other first-order conditions, we obtain

$$sp_1 = \mu(c_{11} + c_{21})$$
$$sp_i = \mu c_{ii} \qquad (i = 2, 3, 4)$$
(3) $\quad sp_5 = s = \mu \quad$ since $p_5 = 1$ [by (1)]

By (3) we may then divide through the preceding conditions by $s = \mu$, and they therefore reduce just to[5]

$$p_1 = c_{11} + c_{21}$$
$$p_2 = c_{22}$$
(4) $\qquad p_3 = c_{33}$
$$p_4 = c_{44}$$
$$p_5 = 1$$

In other words, the optimal price for the externality-generating product is equal to the (Pareto optimal) level of its entire

[5] The analysis can also take account of constraints on the availability of land at the relevant locations, which give rise to rents that equalize costs at all locations actually utilized. If S_a and S_b represent the availability of land near and away from the factory, respectively, presumably we would add to the labor constraint in the model the two additional land-use constraints $g_a(x_1, x_2, x_3) + s_a = S_a$ and $g_b(x_4) + s_b = S_b$, with the quantities of unused land, s_a and s_b perhaps entering the utility functions. It then follows, just as before, that the equilibrium conditions are now $p_1 = c_{11} + c_{21} + p_a g_{a1}$; $p_2 = c_{22} + p_a g_{a2}$; $p_3 = c_{33} + p_a g_{a3}$; $p_4 = c_{44} + p_b g_{b4}$; $p_5 = 1$; $p_a = \rho_a/\mu$; $p_b = \rho_b/\mu$; where ρ_a and ρ_b are the Lagrange multipliers for the new constraints and p_a and p_b are the (labor) prices of land at the two locations. Our previous conclusions are, thus, totally unaffected. Only the smoke producer's product sells for more than its marginal private cost of labor plus land.

social[6] marginal cost, $c_{11} + c_{21}$, while the optimal price for any item, i, which generates no externalities is simply its marginal private cost, c_{ii}. To obtain these prices in our world of pure competition, one need merely levy an excise tax on item I equal to c_{21} (labor hours) dollars per unit, just as the Pigouvian tradition requires. Assuming the appropriate concavity-convexity conditions hold, this will automatically satisfy the necessary and sufficient conditions for the Pareto optimal output levels.[7] In the competitive case, where negotiation is impractical, that is all there is to the matter. The generalization to the case of n outputs, each of them imposing externalities on a number of the others, is immediate.

It is important to observe that, *the solution calls for neither taxes upon x_2, the neighboring laundry output, nor compensation to that industry for the damage it suffers.*

One way to look at the reason is that our model (and the pollution model in general) refers to the important case of *public* externalities. The laundry whose output is

[6] The social cost is not c_{21} alone but is the sum of the private and the external costs together (see the illuminating terminological discussion by D. W. Pearce and Stanley Sturmey). Note that the tax, implicitly, is a tax on *smoke* not a tax on x_1, the output of the smoke producing industry. For if s is the quantity of smoke and t the unit tax we may write $t = c_{21} = (\partial c_2/\partial s)(ds/dx_1)$ and obviously the firm can reduce its tax rate by decreasing the second of these terms, the smokiness of its product. This point has been emphasized by Charles Plott, who showed that a fixed tax per unit of x_1 might even conceivably increase s, if s were an inferior input.

[7] Moreover, measured in real terms this is the only tax arrangement that satisfies the optimality requirements, neglecting the possibility of a lump sum tax or subsidy which does not affect the marginal conditions. F. Trenery Dolbear has shown that it is generally not possible to find an optimal tax rate that compensates fully those who suffer the effects of the externality. Since no compensation is paid to industry II, the solution that is derived here does not run into Dolbear's problem. We also do not run into the problem of a multiplicity of solutions corresponding to the various points on Dolbear's contract curve because we are dealing with a world of pure competition with a given initial distribution.

damaged by smoky air does not, by an increase in its own output, make the air cleaner or dirtier for others. As with all public goods, an increase in one user's consumption does not reduce the available supply to others.[8] Hence, the appropriate price (compensation) to a user of a public good (victim of a public externality) is *zero* except, of course, for lump sum payments. Thus, perhaps, rather than saying there is no price that will yield an optimal quantity of a public good (externality), it may be more illuminating to say that a double price is required: a nonzero price (tax) to the supplier of the good, and a zero price to the consumer. Of course, no ordinary price can do this job, but a Pigouvian tax, without compensation to those affected by an externality, can indeed do the trick.

III. What Prevents an Excessive Influx of Neighbors?

When only smoke emission is taxed, with the tax level based on the magnitude of x_2, nearby laundry output, what will prevent too many laundries from moving

[8] In his discussion of these matters Coase seems at one point to skate awfully close to an error analogous to the confusion between pecuniary and technological externalities. He writes (section IX):

The tax that would be imposed would . . . increase with an increase in the number of those in the vicinity . . . But people deciding to establish themselves in the vicinity of the factory will not take into account [the resulting] fall in the value of production which results from their presence. This failure to take into account costs imposed on others is comparable to the action of a factory-owner in not taking account the harm resulting from his emission of smoke.   [p. 42]

This is analogous to the argument that where the supply curve of labor is rising an increase in output by firm *A* must produce externalities, by raising *B*'s labor costs. But, of course, this merely represents a transfer from *B* to his workers and is not a real net cost to society. For that reason, as is well known, pecuniary externalities do *not* lead to resource misallocation. Like a price change, the variation in taxes constitutes a pecuniary externality. Both have real consequences but they are merely "movements along" the production and utility functions, i.e., any given vector of inputs will be able to produce the same outputs as before the change in tax rates, and any vector of output levels will still be able to yield the same utility levels.

near the smoky factory? The answer is that, when the tax on the externality producer is set properly, the externalities themselves keep down the size of the nearby population. Moreover, the level of the tax will control both the magnitude of smoke emission and thereby (indirectly), the size of the nearby population. A high tax rate will discourage smoke and hence encourage migration into the neighborhood. A low tax rate will encourage smoke and, hence, drive residents away. A tax on smoke alone is all that is needed to control the magnitudes of *both* variables. That is why, as shown by the mathematics of the preceding section, just a tax on the smoke producer is sufficient to produce an optimal allocation of resources among all the activities in our model.[9]

A diagram may help to make the point clearer. Figure 1 shows the response of our two industries' outputs to a change in the tax rate on the polluting industry, I. We see that as the tax rate varies, industry I's output response follows the curve RR'. Thus, if the tax level is t, the output of industry I will be x_{1t}. But, because of the externalities, the output of industry II, in turn, reacts to the output of I. This relationship is described by reaction curve PP'. With $x_1=x_{1t}$ we see that $x_2=x_{2t}$.

The tax rate on II can vary all the way from $t=0$, yielding output combination (x_{10}, x_{20}), to a prohibitive tax rate, t_p, that drives I out of business altogether, so that $x_1=0$ and $x_2=x_{2p}$. Obviously, the ratio x_1/x_2 then decreases monotonically as the tax rate increases and, assuming continuity, there will be some intermediate tax rate at which the two activities will be in balance. The tax will keep x_1 in check while the external cost imposed by x_1 on industry II will keep x_2 to the right relative level. There is no need for a separate tax on II to achieve this goal.

[9] See the Appendix for a discussion of an argument by Buchanan and Stubblebine which is related to Coase's.

BAUMOL: CONTROL OF EXTERNALITIES   313

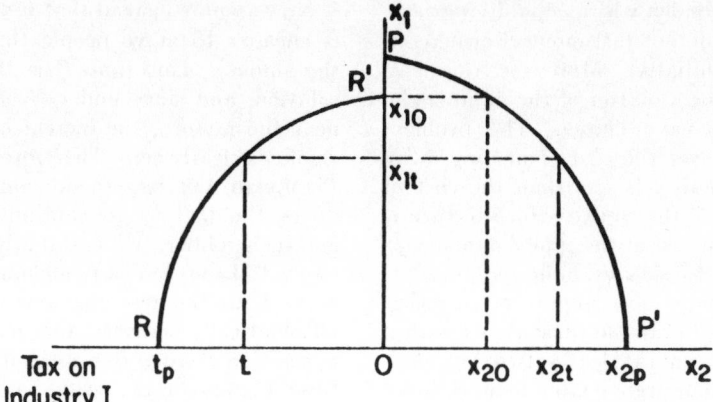

FIGURE 1

In order for this arrangement to work it is clearly necessary that the laundries *not* be compensated (at the margin) for the smoke damage they suffer. If they received in compensation an amount which varied with the magnitude of the smoke damage, that externality would not restrict the level of laundry activity near the factory. If the laundry operators' smoke costs were offset by damage compensation payments, obviously they would lose the economic incentive to eschew the vicinity of the smoky factory[10] and then Coase's tax on laundries would indeed be required to keep them away. But then the tax would be needed only to sop up the compensation payments which should never have been given in the first place.

IV. Multiple Local Maxima in the Coase Model

Coase's discussion is, however, right in pointing out the possibility that the econ-

[10] Of course, as smoke cost increases in the neighborhood of the factory, rents will fall to some extent and serve as partial compensation to the laundries. However, this does not change the analysis fundamentally. It is analogous to the case of rise in the price of an input which, as is well known, will tend to reduce the output of competitive firms, even though prices of other complementary inputs fall as a result. As the discussion of footnote 5 shows, explicit consideration of the price of land does not change the character of the solution.

omy may make the wrong choice between smoke elimination and laundry relocation: however the source of the problem, a multiplicity of local maxima, does not emerge clearly. Coase writes:

> Assume that a factory which emits smoke is set up in a district previously free from smoke pollution, causing damage valued at $100 per annum. Assume that the taxation solution is adopted and that the factory owner is taxed $100 per annum as long as the factory emits the smoke. Assume further that a smoke-preventing device costing $90 per annum to run is available. In these circumstances, the smoke-preventing device would be installed.
>
> . . . Yet the position achieved may not be optimal. Suppose that those who suffer the damage could avoid it by moving to other locations or by taking various precautions which would cost them, or be equivalent to a loss in income of, $40 per annum. Then there would be a gain in the value of production of $50 if the factory continued to emit its smoke and those now in the district moved elsewhere or made other adjustments to avoid the damage.   [Section IX]

One curious feature of this example is its assumption that while smoke damage is $100, the cost of moving to other locations is only $40. Under these circumstances one may well wonder why people living near the factory do not just move elsewhere on their own initiative. Moreover, this may not simply be a matter of the numbers he happens to have chosen. The problem arises whenever the cost of moving away from the factory is less than the cost of elimination of the smoke, which in turn is less than the cost of the smoke damage, as the logic of Coase's example requires.

It is perhaps more important to recognize that the example presents us with a choice between (at least) two local optima. As will be argued later, a multiplicity of maxima is generally rendered more likely by the presence of externalities so that this issue is not a pecularity of Coase's illustrations. The first of the two local optima in Coase's example (call it solution A) involves zero smoke emission and a full complement of residents near the factory. In the second optimum (solution B) no one remains in residence next to the factory and there is no restriction in smoke emission by the plant. Assuming that the (undesirable) initial position is the only other possibility, as Coase seems to suggest, which of these two will in fact be the global optimum depends on the cost of moving everyone away (m dollars) and the cost of elimination of the smoke (s dollars).

Assume with Coase that the initial cost of smoke damage is $100, that $s < 100$, but that $s < m$ so that it is cheaper to eliminate the smoke than to move the factory's neighbors. In this case, A is obviously the optimal solution. Since inhabitants surround the plant, and smoke emission, by assumption, cannot be changed by small amounts, the incremental social damage of an increase in smoke emission is $100. Thus the correct Pigouvian tax is $100 and, since $s < 100$, with such a tax it will pay the factory to do the right thing by society—to install the smoke eliminator.

Now assume instead that $m < s < 100$ (it is cheaper to move people than to stop the smoke). This time B is the optimal solution, and since under B no one lives near the factory, the incremental cost of smoke is clearly zero. Therefore the proper Pigouvian tax is zero, a value that induces the factory to continue smoking, and its neighbors will find it advantageous (since $100 > m$) to exit (coughing) from the area. Thus the zero Pigouvian tax value automatically satisfies the requirements of solution B when B is optimal just as the $100 Pigouvian tax leads to solution A when A is optimal.

Of course, if B happens to be the true global optimum and society mistakenly imposes the $100 Pigouvian tax appropriate for (local) optimum A, the economy may well end up with the inferior equilibrium A. This is the usual difficulty one encounters whenever there is a multiplicity of maxima, a problem that Pigou so clearly recognized (pp. 140, 224).

V. Departures from the Optimum and Adjustments in the Tax

If there is a departure from the optimal solution, for whatever reason, the value of the Pigouvian tax need not change. If, for example, B is the global optimum so that the optimal tax is zero, that tax need not be increased if a few (misguided) individuals choose to move back near the factory so that additional smoke now incurs (say) $50 in damage. *At the optimal solution* the marginal cost of smoke is zero, and the equilibrium Pigouvian tax remains zero—it does not increase to $50.

Here we have arrived at the issue which, I now understand, was really Coase's main point in the portion of his article we are considering. He writes in a letter:

  . . . Let us assume your optimum tax is imposed. Now suppose that A establishes himself near the plant which produces the damaging emissions and thus increases the amount of damage. Would your tax increase? My guess is that it would not (certainly if your tax system is right it should not). The tax system I was attacking was one which would in these circumstances, automatically lead to an increase in the tax as the damage increased.

This point is, surely, quite different from the issue he is usually interpreted to have raised (see the quotations in fn. 1, above, which suggest how the "usual interpretation" arose). It is, however, not inconsistent with the optimal solution derived in the previous section nor is it inconsistent with what I take to be the Pigouvian tradition.

But even on this issue Coase's strictures are not necessarily valid. Suppose that a regulator, having no way of calculating the *optimal* values of the Pigouvian tax is, however, able to determine the value of any marginal social damage at any point in time. *Faut de mieux* he therefore sets a tax rate equal to *current* marginal social damage on the smoke producer. This causes him to reduce his smoke, and so brings more laundries into the neighborhood. The tax is then readjusted to equal the new (higher) value of damage per puff of smoke, more laundries move in, and so on. Will this process of trial and error adjustments of the tax level, always setting it equal to current marginal smoke damage, converge to the optimum of Section II? That is, will the sequence of tax values converge to the optimal Pigouvian tax level, and will resource allocation approach optimality? That now seems to be Coase's main question.

Obviously, such a learning process always involves wastes and irreversabilities, just like the process of convergence of competitive prices to their equilibrium values in the absence of externalities. But if we follow the usual practice of assuming away these costs, one can show that the

process may be expected to converge to the optimum, provided the equilibrium is unique and stable. That is, there is then nothing inherently different about gradually moving taxes and prices towards their equilibrium here, and the process of adjustment toward competitive equilibrium when there are no externalities.

Specifically, letting s_t represent the tax per unit on commodity 1 at time t, and G_i be the ith adjustment function we may set

$$dx_{1t}/dt = G_1\left[p_{1t} - s_t - c_{11}(x_{1t})\right]$$
$$(5) \quad dx_{2t}/dt = G_2\left[p_{2t} - c_{22}(x_{1t}, x_{2t})\right]$$
$$dx_{it}/dt = G_i\left[p_{it} - c_{ii}(x_{it})\right] \quad (i = 3, 4)$$

$$(6)\, s_t = c_{21}(x_{1t}, x_{2t}) \quad p_{it} = f_i(x_{1t}, \ldots, x_{5t})$$

and where, as usual, we take

$$(7) \qquad\qquad G_i(0) = 0$$
$$(8) \qquad\qquad G_i' > 0$$

Going back to Section II, when optimality conditions (4) hold, we see by substituting them into (5) that all $dx_{it}/dt = 0$, i.e., (4) is indeed an equilibrium position for the dynamic system (5)–(8). Furthermore, any solution that does not satisfy (4) must involve at least one nonzero argument in the adjustment functions (5), and so no solution that fails to satisfy (4) can be an equilibrium.

It follows that if the dynamic system (5)–(8) is stable, and the solution to (4) is unique, the process with taxes set equal to *current* marginal damage and imposed *only on the polluter* will converge toward the optimum. One does not need to have calculated the optimal tax values from the beginning and stick to them.

The reason this process of simultaneous learning and adjustment does not work in Coase's example is that it involves (at least) two local maxima, as we have already noted. And in such a case, obviously, the adjustment mechanism may

well take us to the wrong maximum. Unfortunately, as we will see presently, in the
presence of externalities, a multiplicity of
maxima is all too likely to be with us.

VI. Implementation Problems

Despite the validity in principle of the
tax-subsidy approach of the Pigouvian
tradition, in practice it suffers from serious
difficulties. For we do not know how to
estimate the magnitudes of the social costs,
the data needed to implement the Pigouvian tax-subsidy proposals. For example,
a very substantial portion of the cost of
pollution is psychic; and even if we knew
how to evaluate the psychic cost to some
one individual we seem to have little hope
of dealing with effects so widely diffused
through the population.[11]

This would not necessarily be very
serious if one could hope to learn by experience. One might try any plausible set
of taxes and subsidies and then attempt,
by a set of trial and error steps, to approach the desired magnitudes. Unfortunately, convergence toward the desired
solution by an iterative procedure of this
sort requires some sort of measure of the
improvement (if any) that has been
achieved at each step so that the next trial
step can be adjusted accordingly. But we
do not know the socially optimal composition of outputs, so we simply have no
way of judging whether a given change in
the trial tax values will even have moved
matters in the right direction.

[11] For an excellent discussion of some of the work done
in trying to implement Pigouvian taxes in practice, see
Allen Kneese and Blair Bower, esp. ch. 6 and 8. The
difficulty of determining the magnitude of the Pigouvian
tax-subsidy level is one of Coase's major points, one
that seems often to be overlooked in discussions of his
paper. Thus Coase writes in a letter, "The view I expressed in my article was not that such an optimum tax
system (levied solely on the damage producing firm)
was inconceivable but that I could not see how the data
on which it would have to be based could be assembled."
An interesting approach to application for the small
numbers case that is based on the decomposition principle of mathematical programming is presented by
Davis and Whinston (1966).

These difficulties are compounded by
another characteristic of externalities
which has already been mentioned—the
likelihood that in the presence of externalities there will be a multiplicity of local
maxima (see Richard Portes, D. A.
Starrett, and Baumol). Consequently, even
if an iterative process were possible it
might only drive us toward a local maximum, and may thus fail to take advantage
of the really significant opportunities to
improve economic welfare.

A simple model in the spirit of that of
Section II can be used to show that the
presence of "strong" externalities can be
expected to produce a violation of the
convexity conditions in whose absence one
normally finds a multiplicity of local optima.

Let us assume (to permit the use of a
two-dimensional diagram) that there exist
only the first two of our four activities
(the smoky output, x_1, and nearby
laundry, x_2), and that their respective cost
functions are, as before, $c_1(x_1)$ and
$c_2(x_1, x_2)$. As a result, the equation of the
production possibility locus is

$$c_1(x_1) + c_2(x_1, x_2) = R$$

For convenience let us use k as a parameter measuring the strength of the
(marginal) externality.[12] Assume first that
there are diminishing returns (increasing
costs) in the production of the two outputs,
and that there are no marginal external
effects so that $k=0$. (At the margin industry I's output produces no smoke or
smoke is harmless to industry II.) In that
case it is easy to show that the production
possibility locus must satisfy dx_2^2/dx_1^2
<0, i.e., that the locus must assume the
general shape AC_0B in Figure 2 with the
concavity property required by the second-
order conditions.

Now, suppose that the activity of in-

[12] E.g., k may be interpreted as $\partial^2 c_2/\partial x_1 \partial x_2$, i.e., the
additional marginal resources cost of output 2 resulting
from a unit increase in output 1.

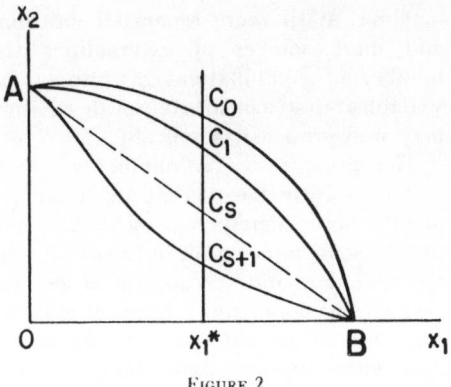

FIGURE 2

dustry I does produce some external damage ($k > 0$). What happens to the production possibility locus? First I will argue that neither of its end points, A or B, will normally be affected. At point B, laundry output, x_2, is zero. Hence, no matter how much smoke is produced, there is no laundry output to be damaged. Point B is therefore invariant with the magnitude of k. Similarly, at A, the smoke creating output is zero. Consequently, no matter how smoky the process of producing output II may be (no matter how large the value of k) the total smoke emitted will be (output x_1) · (smoke per unit of output) $= 0$, since the first of these factors is zero. Thus the position of point A remains invariant with the magnitude of k.

The effect on intermediate points such as C_0 on the locus is quite different. As k increases it takes increasing quantities of resources to produce a given volume of laundry. Thus, with any fixed value of x_1, say x_1^*, as k increases, the quantity of laundry that can be turned out with a given quantity of resources, R, must decline. Point C_0 will be pushed down to some lower point, C_1. With a still greater value of k it will be lowered still further. As smoke damage increases without limit it will take larger and larger quantities of resources to turn out a given quantity of laundry and eventually we approach a

limit point γ on the horizontal axis, at which it is no longer possible to produce clean clothes with any finite quantity of resources.

Now draw in straight line segment AB whose position does not vary with k since neither A nor B does. It is clear that as k increases we will eventually come to some point C_s beyond which all remaining points in the sequence $C_{s+1}, C_{s+2}, \ldots$ lie below AB. Beyond this point, obviously, the second-order conditions must be violated, as the production possibility curve approaches the axes, AOB.

Thus we see that the presence of sufficiently strong detrimental externalities will generally produce a violation of the second-order conditions. Only in the presence of insignificant externalities can one have any degree of confidence that the convexity conditions will hold.[13]

It is easy to offer an intuitive reason indicating how the presence of externalities increases the likelihood of a multiplicity of maxima, a reason that suggests that the problem is very real and potentially very serious in practice. Where a particular activity reduces the efficiency of another it becomes plausible that the optimal level of that activity, at least at some particular locations, is zero. If there are one hundred possible locations for the plants of a smoke-producing industry the worst possible solution might be to place some plants in each candidate location. *Any* solution leaving at least some combination of smoke-free areas may be preferable, and may well constitute a local maximum.

To make the point more concretely, suppose we are dealing with an island separated by a ridge of mountains that pre-

---

[13] The analysis can be extended to the case of n activities and externalities that enter utility as well as production functions. The analysis here confines itself to externalities producing inefficiencies on the production side following a suggestion of Jacob Marschak that the argument is more persuasive if framed in these terms.

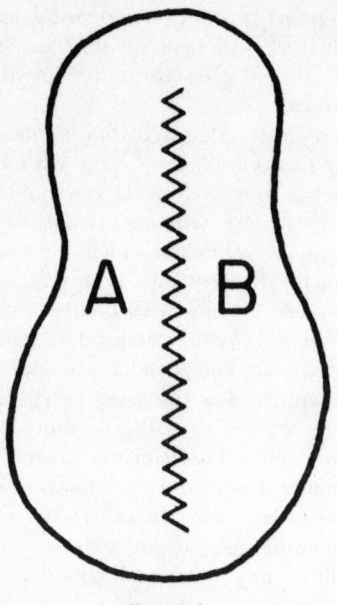

FIGURE 3

vent smoke from going from one side to the other (Figure 3). Let S_a and S_b be the volume of smoke-producing activity located on the two respective sides of the island, and let P_a and P_b be the corresponding number of residents living there. Let $S_a + S_b = S$ and $P_a + P_b = P$. Then, if the social cost of the smoke is great enough, there will obviously be at least two local optima: $(P_a = P, P_b = 0, S_a = 0, S_b = S)$ and $(P_a = 0, P_b = P, S_a = S, S_b = 0)$. For either of these arrangements keeps the smoke and the people apart. This does not mean, of course, that the two solutions are equally desirable. If A offers great scenic attractions while B is closer to raw materials we may expect the former of the two local maxima to be preferable. We cannot preclude the possibility of a third (interior) maximum, for once there is some industrial activity on each of the two sides of the island there may be some least cost distribution of people and industrial activity. But we see that we may well expect to encounter *at least* two local

maxima. With more separated locations and more sources of externalities the number of combinations of zero-valued variables that constitute local maxima may well grow astronomically.

The presence of a number of local maxima clearly means that an "improvement" may merely represent a move toward some minor peak in the social welfare function and it can, therefore, impose serious opportunity losses on society. All in all, we are left with little reason for confidence in the applicability of the Pigouvian approach, literally interpreted. We do not know how to calculate the required taxes and subsidies and we do not know how to approximate them by trial and error.

VII. An Alternative Approach—Adjustment of Taxes to Achieve Acceptable Externality Levels

There is an alternative approach to the matter that seems perfectly natural. On issues as important as those we are discussing, given the limited information at our disposal, it is perfectly reasonable to act on the basis of a set of minimum standards of acceptability. If, say, we treat the sulphur content of the atmosphere as one of the outputs of the economic system, it is not unreasonable to select some maximal level of this pollutant that is considered satisfactory and to seek to determine a tax on the offending inputs or outputs capable of achieving the chosen standard. This is precisely the approach employed in the formulation of stabilization policy, where it is decided that an employment rate exceeding w percent and a rate of inflation exceeding v percent per year are simply unacceptable, and fiscal and monetary measures are then designed accordingly.[14]

[14] As this discussion indicates, I join Wellicz in refusing to abandon externalities policy entirely to Little's "administrative decisions" (p. 184) or to Ralph Turvey's "applied economist" (p. 313). For further discus-

The advantages (as well as the limitations) of this approach are clear—unlike the Pigouvian procedure, it promises to be operational because it requires far less information for its implementation. Moreover, it utilizes global measures and avoids direct controls with all of their heavy administrative costs and their distortions of consumer choice and inefficiencies. It does not use the police and the courts as the prime instrument to achieve the desired modification of the outputs of the economy. Its effects are long lasting, not depending on the vigor of an enforcement agency, which all too often proves to be highly transitory. Unlike most other measures that have been proposed in the area it need not add to the mounting financial burdens of the state and local governments. Finally, it can be shown that, unlike any system of direct controls, it promises, at least in principle, to achieve decreases in pollution or other types of damage to the environment at minimum cost to society.[16]

One can expect an acceptability criterion procedure to be operational because policy makers think quite naturally in terms of minimum acceptability standards, and while it is no doubt an exaggeration to say that they can arrive at them easily, there are all sorts of precedents indicating that such standards can be decided upon in practice.

Though we are unlikely to be able to determine in advance precisely a set of tax values that will achieve the desired output standards, the output level achieved by a given tax arrangement is readily observed and, at least in principle, it is possible to learn by trial and error, continuing the direction of change of any tax modifications that turn out to bring outputs closer to their target levels. Since the procedure is a satisficing rather than a maximizing approach the possibility of a multiplicity of maxima is not relevant.

That is to say, one generally expects a considerable number of solutions to satisfy a particular set of acceptability conditions (various resource allocation patterns may be able to achieve a given set of reductions in pollution levels) *whether or not the second-order conditions are satisfied.* If several of these do so, then the essence of the satisficing approach is that one simply utilizes the first of the acceptable solutions that is discovered. One gives up any attempt to achieve any standard of optimality (other than minimization of cost[16] for a given degree of protection of the environment) and rests content with *any* solution that happens to satisfy the standards that have been selected.

---

sion see Baumol and Wallace Oates. For an earlier proposal that is very similar in spirit, see John H. Dales, ch. 6.

[16] This proposition has been suggested elsewhere (see, for example, Kneese and Bower, chs. 5 and 7; Larry Ruff, p. 79), and will be fairly obvious to anyone familiar with the analysis of the allocative effects of price changes and their efficiency properties. Specifically, suppose it is desired to reduce the pollution content of a river by k percent. Obviously a k percent reduction in the number of gallons emitted by each of the plants discharging wastes into the river will generally not be the desired solution. The theorem in question then asserts the following:

Given the production of any desired vector of final outputs by the plants along the river, a tax per gallon of effluent sufficient to reduce the overall pollution content of the river to the desired level will automatically achieve this decrease at minimum total cost to all plants combined.

The proof of the theorem is a straightforward exercise in constrained maximization (see Baumol and Oates). It works, of course, because the lower the marginal cost of reduction in pollution outflows of a particular plant, the larger the reductions it will pay it to undertake to avoid the corresponding tax payment.

What is surprising about the proposition, if anything, is that, unlike many results in welfare analysis, it does not require the firms along the river, or any other firms,

to be perfect competitors, nor does it have to assume that they maximize profits rather than share of market or growth or some other target variable. All it requires is that the firms wish to produce whatever output they select at minimum cost to themselves.

[16] Of course it is conceivable that there may be more than one local *cost* minimum. In that case an effluent charge that yields an acceptable pollution level may not yield the global cost minimum. This may be something that practical policy simply has no way of avoiding.

Thus, the acceptability criterion approach does not dispose of the difficulties involved in finding a true optimum—rather it sweeps those difficulties under the rug. Even with pollution reduced to acceptable levels, there will remain the possibility that the (undiscovered) global optimum offers us a world far better than what we have managed to achieve—if only we knew how to attain it. But if we permit ourselves to be paralyzed by councils of perfection we may have still greater cause for regret.

It may be that with time we can learn to improve the workings of a set of standards of acceptability. If, say, it turns out to be unexpectedly cheap to attain the initial pollution standards, it may be reasonable to tighten the standards on the presumption that marginal costs will not yet have equalled the marginal social benefits. Successive modifications in the criteria based on experience and revaluation may produce results that on the whole are not too bad.

If firms are put on notice that the acceptability standards may well be modified in the future this may lead them to construct what George Stigler describes as more flexible plants,—plants which are designed to keep down the cost of response to changes in standards. Of course, flexibility itself is not costless. However, it may be precisely what is appropriate for a society which is only beginning to learn how to grapple with its environmental problems.

APPENDIX

Buchanan, Stubblebine and Taxation of Both Parties to an Externality

Buchanan and Stubblebine have raised objections to the Pigouvian solution similar to those offered by Coase (see fn. 2, above). Much of their discussion deals with the case where voluntary negotiation in the presence of externalities will lead automatically to a

Pareto optimum. As already admitted, in this case a Pigouvian tax will only cause trouble. However, the authors also appear to offer an argument against the Pigouvian tax for the case in which negotiation is absent.

Their argument, if I understand it correctly, is that after industry I adjusts to a Pigouvian tax on its output, for that industry the marginal yield of an increase in x_1 is zero. However, for industry II, at the point γ the marginal yield of x_1 is $c_{21} < 0$. There must, consequently, be potential gains from trade between the two industries. They state:

> So long as $[(\partial c_2/\partial x_1)/(\partial c_2/\partial x_2)]$ remains nonzero, a Pareto-relevant marginal externality remains, despite the fact that the full 'Pigouvian solution' is attained. The apparent paradox here is not difficult to explain. Since, as postulated, [II] is not incurring any cost in securing the change in [I's] behavior, and since there remains, by hypothesis, a marginal diseconomy, further 'trade' can be worked out between the two parties. . . . The important implication to be drawn is that full Pareto equilibrium can never be attained via the imposition of unilaterally imposed taxes and subsidies . . .
> [Section III, pp. 382–83]

No doubt this is true—in a competitive situation two interrelated industries can generally increase their joint profits ("gain from trade") by collusion at the expense of the general public. In the case under discussion, if the output of x_1 is reduced it is true that industry I will lose nothing and industry II will gain c_{21}. However, society as a whole will experience no net gain.

Since the analysis deals exclusively with resource *allocation* we must assume that the labor released by the reduced value of x_1 will be employed elsewhere to produce more of some other output or more leisure. Consequently, the goods or services represented by the t units in taxes must be redistributed to the general public either by remission of another tax, increased provision of government services or some other means.

We may now evaluate the consequences of a unit increase in the output of x_1 on the entire society by summing up the direct effects on each of the three groups immediately

BAUMOL: CONTROL OF EXTERNALITIES 321

	Industry I	Industry II	Consumers	General Public
Incremental gain or revenue	p		$u_1 = c_{11} + t$	$t = c_{21}$
Incremental cost	$(c_{11}+t) = (c_{11}+c_{21})$	c_{21}	p	

concerned: industry I, industry II, consumers, and the consequences of the tax receipts for the general public (which encompasses all consumers and producers, including those already mentioned). These are shown in the table above Adding up the incremental gains and revenues we see that the net social gain is zero, precisely as optimality requires. There is only a redistribution from industry II to the general public.

In a recent letter Buchanan comments:

As for the nonoptimality of a unilaterally imposed tax, the problem here is that income effects enter to make the benefit-receiving side change behavior so that still further adjustments would be necessary . . . Our point was that this new position would not be one of full equilibrium if income effects enter. The laundries would now find that they secure the benefits of cleaner air without cost to themselves. Presumably this would make them do more laundry. This change in behavior would in turn change the apparent optimal solution. Admittedly, the imposed solution qualifies as Pareto-optimal if further trading is prohibited. And here Pareto-equilibrium does take on a different meaning from Pareto-optimal. Gains-from-trade exist, as you agree and, once these take place, we are not in an optimal solution.

In this paper I deal with the case where trading fails to take place not because it is prohibited, but because (as seems characteristic of our most important externalities problems in reality) large numbers make trading virtually impossible to arrange (where have we seen automobile drivers pay one another to cut down their exhaust?). Moreover, one must distinguish between the role of Buchanan's income effect and that of "further trading." Of course, further trading can destroy the optimality of the results achieved by a Pigouvian tax. For, as just

argued, in that case the two affected groups gain by exploiting the community. On the other hand, the "income effect"—the influx of laundries near the factory as clean air becomes cheaper is precisely the reason a tax on the smoke producer alone can lead *everyone* to behave Pareto optimally (see Section III).

REFERENCES

W. J. Baumol, "External Economies and Second-order Optimality Conditions," *Amer. Econ. Rev.*, June 1964, *54*, 358–72.

——— and W. E. Oates, "The Use of Standards and Pricing for Protection of the Environment," *Swedish J. Econ.*, Mar. 1971, *73*, 42–54.

J. M. Buchanan, "External Diseconomies, Corrective Taxes and Market Structure," *Amer. Econ. Rev.*, Mar. 1969, *59*, 174–7.

——— and W. C. Stubblebine, "Externality," *Economica*, Nov. 1962, *29*, 371–84.

R. H. Coase, "The Problem of Social Cost," *J. Law Econ.*, Oct. 1960, *3*, 1–44.

J. H. Dales, *Pollution, Property, and Prices*, Toronto 1968.

O. A. Davis and A. Whinston, "Externalities, Welfare and the Theory of Games," *J. Polit. Econ.*, June 1962, *70*, 241–62.

——— and ———, "On Externalities, Information, and the Government-Assisted Invisible Hand," *Economica*, Aug. 1966, *33*, 303–18.

F. T. Dolbear, Jr. "On the Theory of Optimum Externality," *Amer. Econ. Rev.*, Mar. 1967, *57*, 90–103.

A. V. Kneese and B. T. Bower, *Managing Water Quality: Economics, Technology, Institutions*, Baltimore 1968.

I. M. D. Little, *A Critique of Welfare Economics*, 2d ed., New York 1957.

H. Mohring and J. H. Boyd, "Analyzing 'Externalities': 'Direct Interaction' vs. 'Asset

Utilization' Frameworks," *Economica*, forthcoming.

R. A. Meyer, Jr., "Externalities as Commodities," *Amer. Econ. Rev.*, Sept. 1971, *61*, 736-40.

D. W. Pearce and G. S. Sturmey, "Private and Social Costs and Benefits: A New Terminology," *Econ. J.*, Mar. 1966, *76*, 152-57.

A. C. Pigou, *The Economics of Welfare*, 4th ed., London, 1932.

C. R. Plott, "Externalities and Corrective Taxes," *Economica*, Feb. 1966, *33*, 84-7.

R. D. Portes, "The Search for Efficiency in the Presence of Externalities," forthcoming.

L. E. Ruff, "The Economic Common Sense of Pollution," *Publ. Interest*, spring 1970, *19*, 69-85.

D. A. Starrett, "Fundamental Non-Convexities in the Theory of Externalities," Harvard 1971, unpublished.

G. J. Stigler, "Production and Distribution in the Short Run," *J. Polit. Econ.*, June 1939, *47*, 305-27.

R. Turvey, "On Divergences Between Social Cost and Private Cost," *Economica*, Aug. 1963, *30*, 309-13.

S. Wellicz, "On External Economies and the Government-Assisted Invisible Hand," *Economica*, Nov. 1964, *31*, 345-62.

[3]

JOURNAL OF ENVIRONMENTAL ECONOMICS AND MANAGEMENT 12, 103–116 (1985)

Effluent Regulation and Long-Run Optimality

DANIEL F. SPULBER[1]

Department of Economics, University of Southern California, University Park, Los Angeles, California 90089

Received January 14, 1983; revised September 9, 1983

The long-run efficiency properties of regulatory instruments are examined in a multiple-input framework. The effluent tax and tradeable permit are shown to be efficient with free entry and exit of small firms. The across-the-board effluent standard results in excessive entry and excessive industry pollution. © 1985 Academic Press, Inc.

1. INTRODUCTION

A regulator faced with free entry of firms is concerned not only with the implications of public policy for the discharges from a representative firm but also with the total pollution observed at the long-run market equilibrium. The regulator must take into account not only the effects of regulations upon the net marginal returns of the firm but must also consider the total profit of the firm and incentives for entry and exit. This paper shows that effluent charges and tradeable effluent permits lead to long-run optimality with entry of small firms. The difference between firm payments and environmental damages is interpreted as the rent accruing to the environmental resource. This result applies only to the competitive case with small polluters. The analysis presented here allows a comparison and clarification of the literature on small and large polluters.

In a multi-input framework, with social damages dependent upon total effluents, effluent charges are shown here to result in socially optimal entry, confirming an assertion of Baumol and Oates [2, p. 179, fn. 16], and the important result of Schulze and D'Arge [15]. By taking *average* as well as marginal damages into account, the effluent charge results in optimal firm scale levels and the correct input mix. At the free entry market equilibrium, the firm subject to an effluent tax will operate above or below the private minimum efficient scale depending upon whether average external costs exceed or are less than marginal external costs.

Since public policy to reduce effluents is often directed at reducing the effluent-generating activity, some policy recommendations include a tax on the final output of the polluting firm. In some theoretical analyses, a relation between the output of the firm and the effluent level is identified and a Pigouvian output tax is applied. This approach should not be followed by policymakers since an output tax does not provide firms with the correct incentives for either input substitution or market entry. It is shown that while a lump-sum transfer is needed to provide correct entry incentives when a Pigouvian output tax is applied, no such transfer is needed if the tax is correctly applied to effluents, contrary to [5]. Even if optimal firm scale and

---

[1] I thank the referees for helpful suggestions. The support of the National Science Foundation under Grant SES 82-19121 is gratefully acknowledged. Any errors are my responsibility.

103

104   DANIEL F. SPULBER

industry size may be attained with an output tax—lump-sum transfer scheme, firms
will not have proper incentives for input substitution. This is significant since output
taxes will not lead firms to undertake optimal pollution abatement and effluent
treatment.

Effluent standards are reexamined in a free entry framework and are shown to
create long-run distortions even if firms are identical. If the optimal per firm
standard is employed, excessive entry will occur driving total pollution above the
social optimum and driving the production level of each firm below the socially
minimum efficient scale. If the policymaker must meet an overall standard of
environmental quality using quotas, this will require the share of each firm to be set
below the optimal per firm level.

2. THE SOCIAL OPTIMUM

The regulation of an industry which generates pollution is now examined. Firms
are assumed to be identical and to behave competitively. Firms purchase inputs x_j at
given input prices r_j, $j = 1, \ldots, m$. A newly established firm incurs positive fixed
costs F. The firm's inputs are used to produce output q, with production function
$q = f(x_1, \ldots, x_m)$, where f is twice differentiable, increasing and concave. For each
vector of inputs firms generate an externality e as an unwanted by-product of
production, $e = h(x_1, \ldots, x_m)$, where h is convex and differentiable. The pollution
generating function h captures the effects of the *scale* of the firm as well as the
effects of different *input combinations* on total effluent production. The function h
may be *decreasing* in some inputs to represent the employment of inputs for
pollution abatement.

External costs of effluent generation are given by the social damage function
$D(E)$ where $E = ne$ represents *total effluent*, the effluent produced by each firm, e,
times the number of firms n. The damage function, D, is assumed to be differentiable $dD(E)/dE \equiv D'(E) > 0$ with increasing marginal damage and $D(0) = 0$. Total
damages can only depend upon the *total effluent* levels. If the spatial distribution of
effluent is important, this can easily be handled by redefining effluent levels at
different locations as different pollutants.[2] For both air and water pollution, it is the
concentration of pollutants within an air shed or water body that is of greatest
importance.

The policymaker's problem is to choose industry output, inputs, and the number
of firms in a partial equilibrium setting so as to maximize social welfare subject to
technological constraints. Let $P(\cdot)$ represent the market inverse demand. Social
welfare is defined as total consumer surplus net of private production costs and
external environmental damages. The Lagrangian for the policy maker is

$$L = \int_0^{nq} P(s)\, ds - n \sum_{j=1}^{m} r_j x_j - nF - D(ne) + n\xi(f(x) - q) + n\delta(e - h(x)).$$

$$(1)$$

where ξ and δ are the shadow prices for the production and effluent constraints,

---

[2] Although a single effluent model is considered here, the results generalize easily to multiple effluent
types.

respectively. The first-order necessary conditions include

$$\frac{\partial L}{\partial q} : P(nq) - \xi = 0 \tag{2}$$

$$\frac{\partial L}{\partial e} : - D'(ne) + \delta = 0 \tag{3}$$

$$\frac{\partial L}{\partial x_j} : - r_j + \xi \frac{\partial f(x)}{\partial x_j} - \delta \frac{\partial h(x)}{\partial x_j} = 0 \qquad j = 1, \ldots, m \tag{4}$$

$$\frac{\partial L}{\partial n} : P(nq)q - \sum_{j=1}^{m} r_j x_j - F - D'(ne)e = 0. \tag{5}$$

The optimal allocation and shadow prices $(q^*, x^*, e^*, n^*, \xi^*, \delta^*)$ solve (2)–(5) and $q = f(x)$, $e = h(x)$. Substituting (2) and (3) into (4) yields

$$P(n^*q^*)\frac{\partial f(x^*)}{\partial x_j} = r_j + D'(n^*e^*)\frac{\partial h(x^*)}{\partial x_j}, \qquad j = 1, \ldots, m. \tag{6}$$

Thus, *the marginal revenue product of each input should equal the marginal factor cost to society.* This implies that the firm's *input mix* is as important as its effluent level. This requires the firm to devote the proper amount of resources to inputs which reduce pollution and to choose the correct level of inputs for abatement and pretreatment of effluents. This result indicates why policies aimed at regulating specific pollution-generating inputs or requiring abatement inputs must fail in comparison with direct regulation of effluents.

The first-order condition (5) requires the number of firms to be such that private profit per unit of effluent for each firm equals marginal social damages. This may be interpreted as a zero economic profit condition. The principal optimality conditions are thus (5) and (6).

3. THE EFFLUENT TAX

3a. *Long-Run Optimality*

Consider the long-run impact of an effluent tax $t > 0$. Given the market price P, each firm chooses its output, inputs, and effluent level subject to its production constraints. The Lagrangian for the firm's problem is therefore

$$L = Pq - \sum_{j=1}^{m} r_j x_j - F - te + \lambda(f(x) - q) + \sigma(e - h(x)). \tag{7}$$

106   DANIEL F. SPULBER

The first-order necessary conditions include

$$\frac{\partial L}{\partial q} : P - \lambda = 0 \tag{8}$$

$$\frac{\partial L}{\partial e} : - t + \sigma = 0 \tag{9}$$

$$\frac{\partial L}{\partial x_j} : - r_j + \lambda \frac{\partial f(x)}{\partial x_j} - \sigma \frac{\partial h(x)}{\partial x_j} = 0, \qquad j = 1, \ldots, m. \tag{10}$$

The firm sets the shadow price on the effluent constraint equal to the effluent tax, and the shadow price on the production constraint equal to the market price. Thus, (10) implies

$$P \frac{\partial f(x)}{\partial x_j} = r_j + t \frac{\partial h(x)}{\partial x_j}, \qquad j = 1, \ldots, m. \tag{11}$$

Note that the effluent tax t affects the firm's marginal rate of technical substitution by adding the marginal cost of an input in effluent production to the input's factor price.

Besides solving the problem of choosing inputs and outputs, firms make entry and exit decisions. Entry occurs until profits are zero given the effluent tax.[3] Thus, at the long-run market equilibrium, $Pq - \sum_{j=1}^{m} r_j x_j - F - te = 0$, where $P = P(nq), q = f(x), e = h(x)$, and the input levels solve (11) for all firms.

Now, let the tax t^* equal the shadow price on the effluent constraint in (1), $t^* = \delta^* = D'(n^*e^*)$. Thus, t^* equals *marginal social damages* at the social optimum.

PROPOSITION 1.   *Given the effluent tax $t^* = D'(n^*e^*)$, the long-run market equilibrium is socially optimal.*

Correct incentives for entry are obtained from the *total* tax payment $D'(n^*e^*)e^*$. With free entry, factor payments exhaust revenue at the long-run equilibrium, the market price equals $P(n^*q^*)$, and thus condition (5) is satisfied. Also, the effluent tax, t^*, in Eq. (11) causes the firm to *correctly value the productive inputs* by adding their marginal social cost $D'(n^*e^*)\partial h(x^*)/\partial x_j^*$ to the factor price, so that condition (6) is satisfied.

The economic intuition for the result is as follows. All economic inputs that are priced *competitively* at marginal factor cost are paid more than their variable costs when marginal costs exceed average variable costs. This difference is referred to as quasirent, the return to the input producer's fixed inputs. How does this apply to the environment? The society bearing the burden of pollution damage may be seen as both the *owner* of the environment (air, water, etc.) and the *supplier* of environmental services. Environmental services are, in this case, the storage of pollutants provided at the cost of damages to producers and consumers. The difference between the total tax payment and the total social damages may be interpreted as

---

[3]Starrett and Zeckhauser [17] note that, in a fixed price model with concave production functions, the charges paid by the polluting firm will not affect its decision as to whether or not to produce. This will not hold if nonconvexities are present, see [17]. The reason that entry is affected by effluent charges in our model is that firms face fixed setup costs and the output price is given by a downward sloping demand function so that price is lowered by entry.

the rent accruing to ownership of the scarce factor, the environment. The environmental rent should not be treated differently from rents to other natural resources such as land or mineral resources. The costs of providing the resource services are social costs and are borne directly by consumers and firms. The total of firm payments equals the *sum of social damage costs* and *environmental rent* and provides incentives for optimal entry. Since firms are small, entry of a firm does not significantly alter the equilibrium rent.

The result in Proposition 1 relies on the assumption that all firms are *small*, with negligible effects on marginal social damages resulting from entry of an additional firm. The papers [6, 9, 14, 10, 3] examine *large scale* entry of firms and show that the total tax bill paid by individual firms may be too great.[4] The argument is that since the firm's tax bill (output times marginal damages) exceeds the damages caused *by that firm's entry*, then entry is excessively discouraged in the long run. These results are correct because when there is a change in the marginal social opportunity cost of a factor over the range of usage of that factor by a firm, the marginal increase in rent paid by an entering firm will exceed the social costs of supplying the factor. Thus, with large-scale entry, there is a need for an adjusted emission tax or permits scheme where the total cost to firms equals the area under the marginal social damage curve. This may be achieved, for example, using a Pigouvian tax–lump-sum transfer scheme or using the rental emission permits plan in Collinge and Oates [6], which satisfies both the short-run optimality condition and long-run entry–exit condition when entry of large polluters occurs.

3b. The Scale of the Firm

The *long-run* optimality of the effluent tax with small firms is best illustrated in terms of the social cost of producing the output of an individual firm.

$$C(q) = \min_{(x_j)} \left[\sum_{j=1}^{m} r_j x_j + F + t^* h(x) \right] \tag{12}$$

subject to $f(x) = q$, where $t^* = D'(n^* e^*)$. The problem may be solved for inputs as a function of output for a given tax and given input prices, $x_j = \gamma_j(q; t^*, r) = \gamma_j(q), j = 1, \ldots, m$. The effluent tax leads the firm to equate marginal social cost to output price,

$$\frac{dC(q)}{dq} = \sum_{j=1}^{m} \left(r_j + t^* \frac{\partial h(x)}{\partial x_j} \right) \frac{\partial x_j}{\partial q}$$

$$= \sum_{j=1}^{m} P \frac{\partial f(x)}{\partial x_j} \frac{\partial x_j}{\partial q}$$

$$= P. \tag{13}$$

Furthermore, from the zero profit entry condition, we see that price also equals

[4]See Collinge and Oates [6, p. 348], Rose-Ackerman [14, p. 514], Gould [10, p. 560], and Dolbear [9, p. 99]. Schulze and D'Arge [15, p. 766, fn. 8] disagree with Dolbear [9] regarding the excess of tax payments over damage costs. The two cases depend upon whether firms are large or small relative to the marginal damages caused by entry of an additional firm.

average social costs for each firm

$$P = \frac{1}{q^*}\left[\sum_{j=1}^{m} r_j x_j^* + F + t^* e^*\right] = \frac{C(q^*)}{q^*}. \tag{14}$$

Thus $dC(q^*)/dq^* = C(q^*)/q^*$ and *average social costs are minimized.*

Combining (13) and (14) and substituting for $t^* = D'(n^*e^*)$ we obtain

$$\left(\frac{\sum_{j=1}^{m} r_j x_j^* + F}{q^*} - \sum_{j=1}^{m} r_j \frac{\partial x_j^*}{\partial q^*}\right) = \left(D'(n^*e^*) \sum_{j=1}^{m} \frac{\partial h(x^*)}{\partial x_j^*} \frac{\partial x_j^*}{\partial q^*} - \frac{D'(n^*e^*)h(x^*)}{q^*}\right).$$

$$\tag{15}$$

Thus the difference between the firm's average private costs and marginal private costs equals the negative of the difference between the firm's average external costs and marginal external costs. This implies the following result.

PROPOSITION 2. *Given the optimal effluent tax, if the firm's average damages exceed (are less than) marginal damages, the firm will operate above (below) the private minimum efficient scale.*

This result emphasizes the importance of the effluent tax when average and marginal damages are not equal. One must be very careful in interpreting average damages. These refer to the external costs imposed by a firm per unit of final output q. It is because of returns to scale in the firm's generation of pollutants that the firm may have a decreasing, increasing, or u-shaped average damage curve. This should not be confused with the form of the social damage function $D(ne)$ which is a function of effluents *not outputs.* The firm takes marginal social damages t^* as given. The result explains why the separate entry regulations suggested by Carlton and Loury [5] are not needed when effluents rather than outputs are taxed, see Section 5 below. Since small firms have a negligible impact on marginal social damages, the firm takes marginal social damages t^* as constant. Thus the shape of the firm's external cost function $t^*e(q)$ is strictly dependent upon its own pollution-generating technology.

It should be added that the effluent tax achieves the socially optimal input and output levels without a specification of the effluent-output relation for the firm. In addition, the tax gives incentives for complex input substitution by the firm. There is a tendency on the part of regulators to focus on output controls, input restrictions (e.g., low-sulfur fuel oil) or technological requirements (e.g., the best practicable BPT or available BAT technology requirements in water quality regulation). The effluent tax avoids these thorny regulatory requirements.

4. TRADEABLE EFFLUENT PERMITS

The literature on effluent permits has focused attention upon industries with a fixed number of firms.[5] The optimality properties of permits carry over to the free

[5]See the important work of Dales [7, 8] and the survey in Tietenberg [18]. The proper functioning of the permit market requires a sufficient number of firms, see Starrett and Zeckhauser [17] on "thinness" of markets. Hahn [11] presents a simple model of firm demand for effluent permits where the firm selects its effluent level based upon the cost of abatement opportunities. The demand for permits is examined here under more general assumptions on firm technology.

entry case. Suppose that E permits are issued where l indicates the number of permits purchased by a firm. The market price of a permit is v. The firm's supply function as well as its demand for inputs will depend upon the price of permits. We can also obtain the firm's demand for permits. The firm solves a Lagrangian problem analogous to (7) where $l = e$, $v = t$, and $\beta = \sigma$ is the shadow price on the pollution constraint,

$$L = Pq - \sum_{j=1}^{m} r_j x_j - F - vl + \lambda(f(x) - q) + \beta(l - h(x)). \qquad (16)$$

The constraint that permits exceed effluents, $l \geqslant h(x)$ is always binding since the firm will never purchase excess permits. The firm sets the shadow price on the permit constraint $l \geqslant h(x)$ equal to the market price of a permit, $\beta = v$. The firm's problem (16) may be solved for the firm's supply function, input demand, and permit demand functions, $q^s = q(P, r, v)$, $x_j^D = x_j(P, r, v)$, $j = 1, \ldots, m$, and $l^D = l(P, r, v)$.[6]

Since entry depends on the price of permits, the aggregate market demand for permits is $L^d(v) = n(v)l^D(v)$. This is downward sloping in v.[7] The demand for permits has an interesting economic interpretation. It is the marginal valuation of environmental services to the polluting industry. Given the total number of permits issued $\bar{E}$, the market price v^* allocates the permits across firms in the industry (see Fig. 1a). If the total number of permits issued equals the socially optimal pollution level E^*, then the optimum level is attained by the market in permits (see Fig. 1b). At v^*, the marginal value of environmental services equals the marginal social cost of providing those services represented by the marginal damage function. If the area under the marginal damage curve equals total damage costs then the shaded area in Fig. 1b is the rent accruing to the owners of the environmental resource.

Given the total number of effluent permits equal to the social optimum E^*, compare the solution to the firm's problem (16) with the social optimum, (2) to (5).

PROPOSITION 3. *Given the total number of permits E^*, then, at the equilibrium in the market for effluent permits, the optimal assignment of effluent levels is achieved and the long-run industry equilibrium is optimal.*

To see this, let $t = v^*$ in (8) to (10). Suppressing P and r, the firm's inputs $x^D = x(v^*)$ and output $q^s = q(v^*)$ solve (11) and since $l = h(x)$ is a binding constraint, $n(v^*)l^D(v^*) = E^*$. Since the zero profit entry condition holds at the market equilibrium $v^* = D'(E^*)$, and the optimality conditions (5) and (6) are satisfied.

---

[6] Sufficient conditions for the permit demand to be downward sloping are given in Spulber [16].

[7] To see this, write the zero profit entry condition with permits, $\pi(r, v, n) = 0$, where $\pi(r, v, n) = P(nq)q - \sum_{j=1}^{m} r_j x_j - F - vl$. Differentiate π with respect to v holding n constant, $\partial \pi / \partial v = -l^D(v)$. Differentiate π with respect to n,

$$\frac{\partial \pi}{\partial n} = \frac{-P'(nq)C''(q)q}{P'(nq)n - C''(q)} < 0$$

where $C(q; R, v)$ is the firm's cost function. Thus, the equilibrium number of firms is decreasing in the permit price, $\partial n / \partial v = -(\partial \pi / \partial v)/(\partial \pi / \partial n) < 0$. Therefore the aggregate demand is downward sloping since $\partial L^D(v)/\partial v = n(v)\partial l^D(v)/\partial v + l^D(v)\partial n(v)/\partial v$.

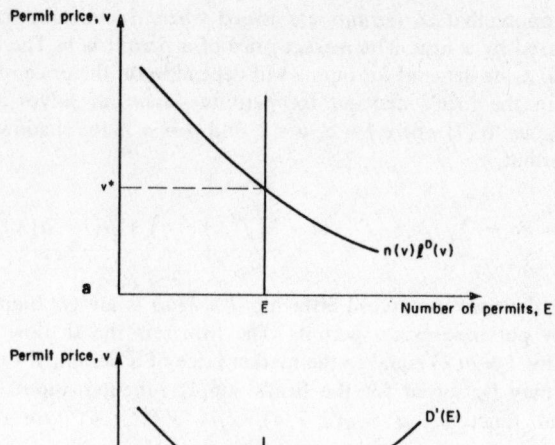

FIGURE 1

An additional interpretation of the permit market equilibrium is obtained by rewriting (11),

$$\frac{P\big(n(v^*)q^s(v^*)\big)\,\partial f\big(x^D(v^*)\big)/\partial x_j - r_j}{\partial h\big(x^D(v^*)\big)/\partial x_j} = v^*, \qquad j = 1,\ldots,m. \qquad (17)$$

Thus, the net marginal revenue from the environmental services associated with each factor equals the price of the environmental service, that is, the permit price. The net returns to use of the environmental service may be interpreted as an inverse demand or willingness to pay schedule.

5. THE OUTPUT TAX

A Pigouvian tax is generally taken to mean a tax (or subsidy) per unit of emissions generated by a firm.[8] Frequently, for convenience or as a teaching device, the Pigouvian tax is described as a tax on the final output of the firm and the output is

---

[8] Baumol and Oates [2, p. 45] state that "[i]nputs and outputs that generate smoke are, of course, subject to tax but only in proportion to the smoke they produce." In practice, there may not be a proportional relationship between a firm's final output and its emissions. As Plott [13] finds, a tax per unit of output may increase a firm's emissions if they are an inferior input, see also Baumol [1, p. 311, fn. 6]. Burrows [3, fn. 2] notes that the original Pigou analysis refers to "'taxes' on external-cost-generating activities such as petrol duty and motor vehicle license tax." Burrows [3, p. 495] interprets the Pigouvian tax as being a charge per unit of effluent emission.

in some way associated with the firm's effluent emissions. In this context, the tax creates incentives for the firm to reduce its output and in so doing reduce its emissions. This approach sometimes causes confusion since it seems to imply that public policy to reduce emissions can be achieved with output taxes. Further confusion exists in the theoretical regulation literature where conclusions about Pigouvian taxes are obtained from models with output taxes. This section shows why an output tax cannot work when input substitution affects the effluents generated by the firm. Even if output can be directly associated with effluents, the output tax cannot work since it will result in nonoptimal entry of firms into the regulated industry. Insight is gained into how the effluent tax provides correct entry incentives by examining the transfer needed to correct the output tax.

Consider first the short run with a fixed number of firms n. Assume that only a single input is used in production, $x \in R_+$. Then, $e = h(x) = h(f^{-1}(q))$. Thus, the marginal damages per firm may be calculated as a function of output

$$\frac{1}{n}\frac{\partial D\big(nh\big(f^{-1}(q)\big)\big)}{\partial q} = D'(ne)\frac{h'(x)}{f'(x)}. \tag{18}$$

The Pigouvian output tax, τ, equals marginal damages per firm, with e^*, x^* as the optimal effluent and input levels, $\tau \equiv D'(ne^*)h'(x^*)/f'(x^*)$. *Given the Pigouvian output tax τ and given one input, the optimal allocation is achieved.* The firm chooses its input x to maximize profit, $\pi = Pf(x) - \tau f(x) - rx$. The first-order condition for the firm is then $(P - \tau)f'(x^*) = r$. Substituting for τ and rearranging terms, the optimal effluent equation for a fixed number of firms (6) is obtained,

$$Pf'(x^*) = r + D'(ne^*)h'(x^*) \tag{19}$$

for $e^* = h(x^*)$. The result that the output tax is optimal holds because only the *scale* of each firm is important. The result will not hold if the firm may substitute inputs in production, each of which may have different marginal products in output and pollution production.

For $x \in R_+^m$, $m \geqslant 2$, and a constant number of firms, the output tax does not affect the firm's private cost minimization. Thus, for an output tax τ

$$(P - \tau)\frac{\partial f(x)}{\partial x_j} = r_j, \qquad j = 1, \dots, m, \tag{20}$$

so that the firm's input choices are not directly affected,

$$\frac{\partial f(x)/\partial x_j}{\partial f(x)/\partial x_i} = \frac{r_j}{r_i}, \qquad i \neq j; \qquad i, j = 1, \dots, m. \tag{21}$$

This differs from the social cost minimization condition, from (11),

$$\frac{\partial f(x)/\partial x_j}{\partial f(x)/\partial x_i} = \frac{r_j + D'(nh(x))\partial h(x)/\partial x_j}{r_i + D'(nh(x))\partial h(x)/\partial x_i}. \tag{22}$$

Therefore, under an output tax the firm will have an incorrect input mix and the firm may not engage in the right amount of effluent pretreatment activities.

PROPOSITION 4. *For $m \geq 2$ and a constant number of firms, the output tax does not achieve an optimal allocation.*

The Pigouvian output tax does not yield an optimal outcome in the long run even for the single input case. Given output tax τ equal to $D'(ne)h'/f'$ the entry equation is

$$P(nq)f(x) - D'(ne)\frac{h'(x)}{f'(x)}f(x) - rx - F = 0. \tag{23}$$

For the effluent tax equal to $D'(n^*e^*)$, the entry equation is

$$P(n^*q^*)f(x^*) - D'(n^*e^*)e^* - rx^* - F = 0. \tag{24}$$

Clearly, a lump-sum tax (or subsidy) per firm equal to

$$T^* = f(x^*)\left[D'(n^*e^*)\frac{e^*}{f(x^*)} - D'(n^*e^*)\frac{h'(x^*)}{f'(x^*)} \right] \tag{25}$$

will result in the correct number of firms entering the industry. This follows from the optimality of the Pigouvian output tax when the proper entry incentives are provided. This implies the following result.

PROPOSITION 5. *For a single input and with free entry of firms, the optimal effluent tax equates the difference between the firms' marginal private costs and average private costs to the transfer needed to correct the Pigouwian tax per unit of output.*

To see this, note that from Proposition 2, the difference between marginal private costs (MPC) and average private costs (APC) equals

$$\text{MPC} - \text{APC} = \left[D'(n^*e^*)\frac{e^*}{q^*} - D'(n^*e^*)\frac{h'(x^*)}{f'(x^*)} \right] \tag{26}$$

when the optimal effluent tax is applied. But this difference exactly equals T^*/q^* as given by Eq. (25).

Consider now the regulation literature in which output taxes are used. Schulze and D'Arge [15] show that an output tax leads to optimal resource allocation with small firms given the damage function $D(nq)$. In our framework, this is true if for a single input $T^* = 0$ in (25), or $h(x)/f(x) = h'(x)/f'(x)$ which holds, for example, when effluents are linear in output, $e = h(x) = b \cdot f(x)$. In this case, the result in [15] supports our model.

---

[9]Clearly an effluent tax may fail to be optimal if the damage function has the form $D(n, e)$. However, this form is meaningless in general since only total effluents can cause damage, not the number of firms.

Carlton and Loury [5] assert that the Pigouvian effluent tax does not lead to long-run optimality without a corrective lump-sum transfer. Carlton and Loury [5] employ a social damage function dependent upon the scale and number of firms $\overline{D}(n,q)$ and study the Pigouvian output tax.[9] It is shown in [5] that the lump-sum transfer equals

$$T = q\left[\frac{1}{q}\frac{\partial \overline{D}(n,q)}{\partial n} - \frac{1}{n}\frac{\partial \overline{D}(n,q)}{\partial q}\right]. \tag{26}$$

and that (p. 564): "The optimal lump sum tax... will be positive (negative) when average pollution damage is falling (rising) at the optimal firm output."

In [5], the failure of the Pigouvian tax is attributed to the difficulty of trying to control the number of firms and the scale of firms with just one policy instrument. Proposition 5 above suggests that the problem lies not in the *number* of instruments. Rather, the problem lies in the *choice* of instruments. When a tax is placed on the firm's effluent, the firm's average and marginal private costs will differ by exactly the amount of the transfer per unit of output that is needed to correct the Pigouvian output tax. The output tax–transfer scheme in [5] generally will not work in a multi-input model. First, to verify the one input case within our framework, the damage function $\overline{D}(n,q)$ is obtained by substituting for $e = h(x)$, $x = f^{-1}(q)$, $\overline{D}(n,q) \equiv D(nh(f^{-1}(q))) = D(ne)$. Thus, we have

$$\frac{\partial \overline{D}(n,q)}{\partial n} = D'(ne)e \tag{27}$$

$$\frac{\overline{D}(n,q)}{\partial q} = D'(ne)\frac{nh'(x)}{f'(x)} \tag{28}$$

where $x = f^{-1}(q)$. Substituting for $\partial \overline{D}(n,q)/\partial n$ and $\partial \overline{D}(n,q)/\partial q$ in (26) clearly $T = T^*$ as obtained in our optimality condition (25). The optimality of a Pigouvian output tax and lump-sum transfer system in a one-input framework should not be used as a guide to policy in a multi-input framework. The Carlton and Loury [5] result depends heavily on the assumption that pollution damages are a function of the *scale* and *number* of firms. As we have shown above, the firm's input mix is of importance. It is generally not possible to associate firm scale with effluent and thus with social damages. Thus, the Pigouvian output tax–lump-sum transfer scheme in [5] may be adjusted to obtain any desired scale and number of firms but the firm's input mix and the resulting effluent levels will be far from optimal. Equation (20) may be solved for $x_j = x_j(q)$, $j = 1, \ldots, n$. Then the social damage function may be written as a function of n and q, $\overline{D}(n,q) \equiv D(ne) = D(nh(x_1(q), \ldots, x_n(q)))$. The Pigouvian output tax and lump-sum transfer may be adjusted to set q and n. However, the social costs of achieving this allocation will be far greater than necessary due to the misallocation of inputs represented by (20). The misallocation will not occur if h is a positive linear transformation of f. Given the different effects of various inputs such as labor, capital, resources, and energy on pollution generation and abatement, this seems highly unlikely in practice.

The negative result of Burrows [3] assumes that damages are *additive* across firms, i.e., total damages equal $nD(q)$, see [3, fn. 5]. Thus external damages caused by firms are *local* and *independent*. An alternative specification of different pollution impacts at N locations might allow entry of firms at each location. Let the regulator choose industry size n_i and output q_i at each location $i = 1, \ldots, N$ to maximize

$$\int_0^Q P(s)\, ds - \sum_{i=1}^N n_i C(q_i) - \sum_{i=1}^N n_i F - \sum_{i=1}^N D_i(n_i q_i),$$

where $Q = \sum_{i=1}^N n_i q_i$ is total output and $D_i(n_i q_i)$ is damage at each location. An output tax at each location $t_i = D_i'(n_i q_i)$ will lead to correct output *and* entry incentives, as in [15].

6. THE EFFLUENT STANDARD

It is well known that for a fixed number of firms, effluent standards may not yield an optimal allocation when firm technologies differ.[10] When firms are identical, standards are generally viewed as the quantity dual of the optimal effluent tax. However, effluent standards fail in the long run even when firms are identical. The economic intuition is that effluent standards give firms a valuable property right to a particular use of the environment thus encouraging excessive entry.

Suppose that a regulator wishes to select per-firm emissions levels using an effluent standard. For simplicity assume that there are two productive inputs used in production, $q = f(x_1, x_2)$ and that pollution is generated by use of one of the inputs $e = h(x_2)$. The optimal per-firm pollution level e^* solves (7). Let $\bar{x}_1, \bar{x}_2, \bar{q}, \bar{n}$ denote the market equilibrium in the long run given the effluent standard e^*. Note that since the constraint is still binding, $\bar{e} = e^*$ and $\bar{x}_2 = x_2^*$. The market equilibrium is defined by the marginal revenue product condition, $P(\bar{n}\bar{q})f_1(\bar{x}_1, \bar{x}_2) = r_1$, and the zero profit entry condition, $P(\bar{n}\bar{q})f(\bar{x}_1, \bar{x}_2) - r_1\bar{x}_1 - r_2\bar{x}_2 - F = 0$. These conditions imply the following.

PROPOSITION 6. *Given an across-the-board effluent standard equal to the socially optimal per-firm pollution level, each firm operates below the social minimum efficient scale, excessive entry occurs, and total pollution exceeds the social optimum.*

The argument is as follows. The entry condition implies

$$P(n^*q^*)f(x_1^*, x_2^*) - r_1 x_1^* - D'(n^* e^*)e^* = P(\bar{n}\bar{q})f(\bar{x}_1, \bar{x}_2) - r_1\bar{x}_1. \quad (29)$$

Thus,

$$P(n^*q^*)f(x_1^*, x_2^*) - r_1 x_1^* > P(\bar{n}\bar{q})f(\bar{x}_1, \bar{x}_2) - r_1\bar{x}_1. \quad (30)$$

From the marginal revenue product condition, (30) implies

$$f^*(x_1^*, x_2^*)/f_1^*(x_1^*, x_2^*) - x_1^* > f(\bar{x}_1, \bar{x}_2)/f_1(\bar{x}_1, \bar{x}_2) - \bar{x}_1. \quad (31)$$

Thus, $x_1^* > \bar{x}_1$ since $\bar{x}_2 = x_2^*$ and $(f/f_1) - x_1$ is increasing in x_1. Given $x_1^* > \bar{x}_1$, output is therefore greater at the social optimum $q^* > \bar{q}$ and $f_1(x_1^*, x_2^*) < f_1(\bar{x}_1, \bar{x}_2)$. Thus, from the marginal revenue product condition $P(n^*q^*) > P(\bar{n}\bar{q})$ which implies $n^* < \bar{n}$ because demand is downward sloping.

The effluent standard does not affect total profits which therefore allows *excessive entry*. This raises total output, thus lowering the market price for any output level and leading to lower output for each firm. The increased entry leads to greater total pollution. This last result confirms a conjecture of Burrows [4, fn. p. 362], that "a larger industry under regulation could, however lead to higher *industry* use of the environment." With free entry, lower prices cause firms to reduce the unregulated inputs leading to lower output per firm. This may create a confusing situation for a regulator who will face complaints from firms in the industry who must cut back their production at the same time that more firms are entering the industry. The firms may call for entry restrictions as a means of controlling pollution. Thus, regulators may be forced to a scheme that combines per-firm emissions requirements with limited entry regulation.

Suppose that the regulator is attempting to meet an *overall legal environmental standard E* by assigning per-firm shares *e* such that $ne \leqslant E$. The Lagrangian for the policymaker's problem is then

$$L = \int_0^{nq} P(s)\, ds - n \sum_{j=1}^{m} r_j x_j - nF + n\xi(f(x) - q) + \alpha(E - nh(x)) \quad (32)$$

where the regulator chooses x, q, and n, where $\alpha \geqslant 0$ is a Kuhn–Tucker multiplier. The problem (32) yields an identical solution to the social optimum problem (1) if $E = n^*e^*$. Let $(\bar{q}, \bar{x}, \bar{e}, \bar{n}, \bar{\xi}, \bar{\alpha})$ solve (32). An effluent tax equal to the shadow price on the overall effluent constraint $\bar{\alpha}$ will yield an optimal allocation in the long run. Thus, the effluent tax is the social welfare maximizing policy instrument for meeting an overall environment standard. For a binding environmental constraint, the shadow price $\bar{\alpha}$ is positive so that an across-the-board standard assigning equal shares of the environmental constraint to each firm equal to $E/\bar{n}$ will result in excessive entry thus raising the social costs of achieving the environmental standard.

PROPOSITION 7. *Given a binding overall environmental standard and free entry, the across-the-board share per firm must be set below the optimal level $\bar{e}$.*

Proposition 7 follows from Eq. (4) which implies that firm profits are positive at the social optimum when $\bar{\alpha} > 0$,

$$P(\bar{n}\bar{q})\bar{q} - \sum_{j=1}^{m} r_j \bar{x}_j - F = \bar{\alpha}h(\bar{x}) > 0. \quad (33)$$

Thus, meeting a legal standard by an across-the-board quota will place excessive burdens upon firms. If fixed costs are relatively small relative to net revenues, excessive entry will require tight pollution restrictions on individual firms. Regulators will face requests from firms to limit entry or to approach the lower standard $\bar{e}$ gradually perhaps by placing stricter requirements upon newly entering firms.

7. CONCLUSION

The results obtained in this paper reaffirm the importance of directing public policy toward pricing the use of the environment. The policy instruments which achieve long-run optimality in a competitive market with small firms are the effluent

116   DANIEL F. SPULBER

tax and the tradeable effluent permit. Direct intervention through output taxes or output controls, entry tariffs, or restrictions, or effluent constraints will create further distortions in the allocation of resources. Given an effluent charge or permit price equal to marginal social damages, the total of firm payments equals the sum of environmental rent and external damages. These two components provide optimal incentives for entry in the long run.

REFERENCES

1. W. J. Baumol, On taxation and the control of externalities, *Amer. Econ. Rev.* **62**, 307–332 (1972).
2. W. J. Baumol and W. E. Oates, "The Theory of Environmental Policy," Prentice–Hall, Englewood Cliffs, N.J. (1975).
3. P. B. Burrows, Pigouvian taxes, polluter subsides, regulation, and the size of a polluting industry, *Canad. J. Econ.* **12**, 495–501 (1979).
4. P. B. Burrows, Pollution control with variable production processes, *J. Pub. Econ.* **8**, 357–367 (1977).
5. D. W. Carlton and G. C. Loury, The limitations of Pigouvian taxes as a long-run remedy for externalities, *Quart. J. Econ.*, 559–566 (1980).
6. R. A. Collinge and W. E. Oates, Efficiency in pollution control in the short and long runs: A system of rental emission permits, *Canad. J. Econ.* **15** (2) 346–354 (1982).
7. J. H. Dales, "Pollution, Property and Prices," Toronto Univ. Press, Toronto (1968).
8. J. H. Dales, Land, water and ownership, *Canad. J. Econ.* (1968).
9. F. T. Dolbear Jr., On the theory of optimum externality, *Amer. Econ. Rev.* **57**, 90–103 (1967).
10. J. R. Gould, Total conditions in the analysis of external effects, *Econ. J.* **87**, 558–564 (1977).
11. R. W. Hahn, "A Theoretical Analysis of the Demand for Emission Licenses," California Institute of Technology, Social Science Working Paper No. 392 (1981).
12. A. V. Kneese and B. T. Bower, "Managing Water Quality: Economics, Technology, Institutions," Johns Hopkins Press, Baltimore, Md. (1968).
13. C. R. Plott, Externalities and corrective taxes, *Economica* **33**, 84–87 (1966).
14. S. Rose-Ackerman, Effluent charges: A critique, *Canad. J. Econ.* **6**, 512–528 (1973).
15. W. Schulze and R. C. D'Arge, The Coase proposition, informational constraints and long-run equilibrium, *Amer. Econ. Rev.* **64**, 763–772 (1974).
16. D. F. Spulber, "Effluent Regulation and Long Run Optimality," Institute for Marine and Coastal Studies, Working Paper, University of Southern California (1983).
17. D. Starrett and R. J. Zeckhauser, Treating external diseconomies—Markets or taxes?, *in* "Statistical and Mathematical Aspects of Pollution Problems," (J. W. Pratt, Ed.), pp. 65–84, Dekker, New York (1974).
18. T. H. Tietenberg, Transferable discharge permits and the control of stationary source air pollution: A survey and synthesis, *Land Econ.* **56**, 391–416 (1980).

[4]

Detrimental Externalities and Non-Convexity of the Production Set

By W. J. BAUMOL and DAVID F. BRADFORD[1]

This paper undertakes to show that detrimental externalities tend to induce non-convexity of the social production possibility set. In particular we show that if externalities are sufficiently strong, convexity conditions must break down.

It is not our objective here to review in any detail the difficulties caused by non-convexity. Some of these consequences have long been recognized and are widely known.[2] However, until the recent appearance of papers by Starett [8], Portes [5], Kolm [3] and Baumol [2], it was apparently not recognized that externalities themselves are a source of non-convexity. These more recent writings suggest more than one connection between the two phenomena. However, one particularly straightforward relationship seems to have received little or no attention. With sufficiently strong interactive effects non-convexity follows from the simple fact that if *either* of two mutually interfering activities is operated at zero level the other suffers no hindrance. The goal of this paper is to explore this phenomenon and show very clearly how it is that sufficiently severe detrimental externalities of the form described and non-convexity necessarily go together.

In the first three sections we show both with the aid of illustrative examples and more general analysis that detrimental externalities of sufficient magnitude must always produce non-convexity in the production possibility set for two activities: one generating the externality and one affected by it. In Section IV we show that the problem is reduced but not generally eliminated by the possibility of spatial separation of offender and offended. Achievement of the "right" spatial separation turns out not always to be a simple matter, however. Section V contains some speculations about the way in which the number of local peaks in

[1] We would like to express our deep gratitude to Mrs. E. E. Bailey for her thorough review of an earlier version of this paper and her very helpful comments, and to the National Science Foundation for its generous support of our research.
[2] Pigou, for example, commented that "... if several arrangements are possible, all of which make the values of the marginal social net products equal, each of these arrangements does, indeed, imply what may be called a *relative maximum* for the [national] dividend but only one of these maxima is the unequivocal, or absolute, maximum. ... It is not necessary that all positions of relative maximum should represent larger dividends than all positions which are not maxima. On the contrary, a scheme of distribution approximating that which yields the absolute maximum, but not itself fulfilling the condition of equal marginal yields, would probably imply a larger dividend than most of the schemes which do fulfil this condition and so constitute relative maxima of a minor character." Pigou [4], p. 140. References in square brackets are listed on p. 176, below.

the production function grows with the number of interacting activities. In Section VI we discuss the possibility of using Pigovian taxes to sustain desirable behaviour, and in a concluding section we review briefly the problems for social policy inherent in the sort of non-convexity we have been analysing.

An appendix contains a formal demonstration of the workability of Pigovian taxes in this context. It is shown that as long as individual production sets are convex, all socially efficient output vectors *can* be

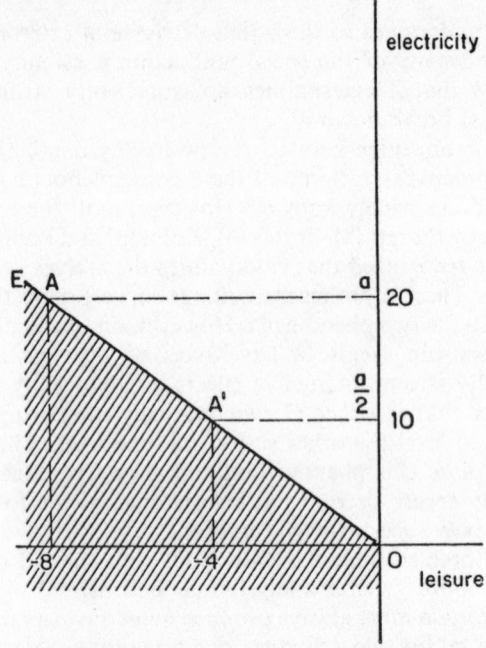

= production set of electricity industry

FIGURE 1a

sustained as a sum of profit-maximizing output choices under taxes designed to equate marginal social and private costs.

I. A SIMPLE MODEL

Consider a two-output, one-input economy in which each output is produced by a single industry. To avoid compounding problems we shall assume that each industry has a convex technology in terms of its own inputs and outputs.[1] However, the presence of detrimental externalities

[1] Thus, if v_i is the quantity of input to industry i and x_i is its output, and if (v_i^*, x_i^*) and (v_i^{**}, x_i^{**}) are two feasible input–output combinations (holding

means that increases in the output of one of the industries raises the other's costs of production, which is to say the amount of input required to produce any given output. What we wish to show is that if this detrimental externality is strong enough, then the social production set must be non-convex.[1]

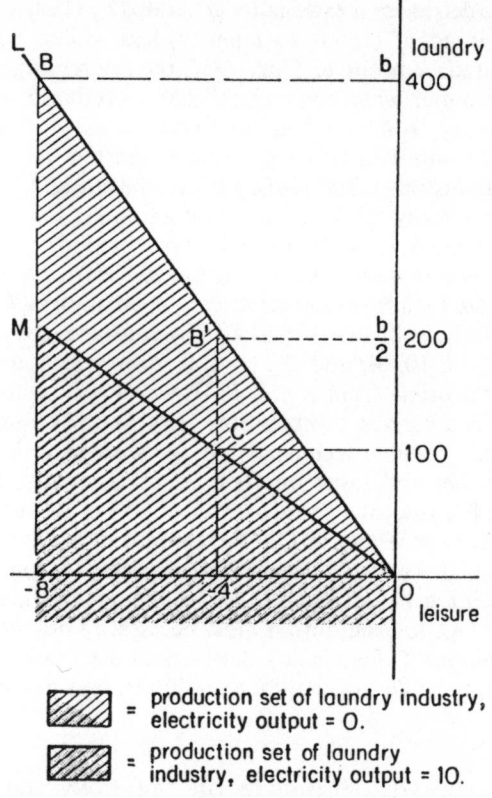

FIGURE 1b

For consistency with the general analysis in the Appendix let us carry through this example following the practice of measuring inputs as

---

constant inputs and outputs in other sectors), then $0 < \alpha < 1$ implies that $(\alpha v_i^* + (1-\alpha)v_i^{**}, \alpha x_i^* + (1-\alpha)x_i^{**})$ is also a feasible input–output combination. Convexity of a production set is sometimes referred to as "generalized non-increasing returns", by which is meant that a·convex technology cannot exhibit increasing returns to scale and that it obeys the law of diminishing marginal rates of substitution among factors and among outputs, and diminishing marginal productivity of outputs by factors.

[1] In the notation of the preceding footnote, the social production set is the set of all vectors $(v_1 + v_2, x_1, x_2)$ such that (v_1, x_1) and (v_2, x_2) are *simultaneously* feasible for their respective industries.

negative outputs. Hence, our economy can be described as having three outputs: for concreteness—leisure, electricity and laundry. The shaded region of Figure 1a shows the production set (the set of attainable net output vectors) for the electricity industry, bounded by the ray *OE*. Figure 1b displays the production set for the laundry industry under two alternative assumptions about output in the electricity industry. The detrimental externality generated by electricity means that, for a given input of labour to laundry, less will be produced when electricity output is positive. Thus, *OM*, the ray serving as the laundry production frontier when some electricity is produced, must lie below *OL*, the laundry frontier when no electricity is produced. To make things easy for ourselves we have assumed constant returns to scale for each of the industries taken alone—hence the straight-line boundaries.

The non-convexity of the social production set for this economy is easily demonstrated. Consider two social production vectors on frontiers *OE* and *OL*: vector *A* on *OE* (−8 leisure, 20 electricity, 0 laundry), and vector *B* on *OL* (−8 leisure, 0 electricity, 400 laundry). Obviously both of these are technically feasible, as are (by constant returns to scale) the vectors *A*′: (−4, 10, 0), and *B*′: (−4, 0, 200), which are, respectively, half way to the origin from *A* and *B*. However, the vector $V = (-8, 10, 200)$, which is a convex combination of *A* and *B* since $V = A' + B' = \frac{1}{2}A + \frac{1}{2}B$, is *not* feasible technically. If we wish to give up 8 units of leisure altogether and insist on 10 units of electricity, requiring 4 of these units of leisure, the most we can obtain is 100 units of laundry (point *C*). More generally, if *L* is the amount of leisure devoted to the two outputs and *a* and *b* represent the respective outputs of electricity and laundry if *L* is devoted exclusively to the one or the other, then the assignment of $\frac{1}{2}L$ to each output must necessarily provide less than $b/2$ of laundry output if there is any detrimental externality present. Point *B*′ is never attainable under these conditions, and non-convexity *must* follow.

II. An Alternative Version of the Non-Convexity Argument

In Figure 2 let X_1 and X_2 represent, respectively, quantities of electricity and laundry. Dropping our earlier assumption of constant marginal rate of transformation between outputs, let *ORAR*′ represent the convex set of output combinations attainable from a fixed amount of labour in the absence of externalities. For expository convenience, introduce a parameter *k* measuring the strength of the externality. In terms of our example, *k* can be taken to measure the mean addition to the resources cost of cleaning a given batch of laundry which occurs when an added unit of electricity output causes smoke to increase. By definition, then, along *RAR*′, which corresponds to the absence of external effects, the value of *k* (call it k_a) is zero.

Consider what happens to the production possibility locus as the value of *k* is increased. We will show that the position of the end-points

R and R' will be totally unaffected, while all other points on the locus will be shifted downward. Point R will be unaffected by a rise in the value of k since, whatever the social cost of smoke, at that point there will be no increase in damage because, by assumption, there is no smoke produced in the absence of any electricity output. Similarly, the location of R' is invariant with k since at that point no resources are devoted to laundry production, and hence there can be no increase in the resources cost of laundry output. There simply is no laundry to be damaged, so that electricity can smoke away without causing any harm to others. However, consider some intermediate level of electricity output, say x_1^*. Here an increase in k means that with a given amount of electricity and a given quantity of resources, a smaller quantity of clean

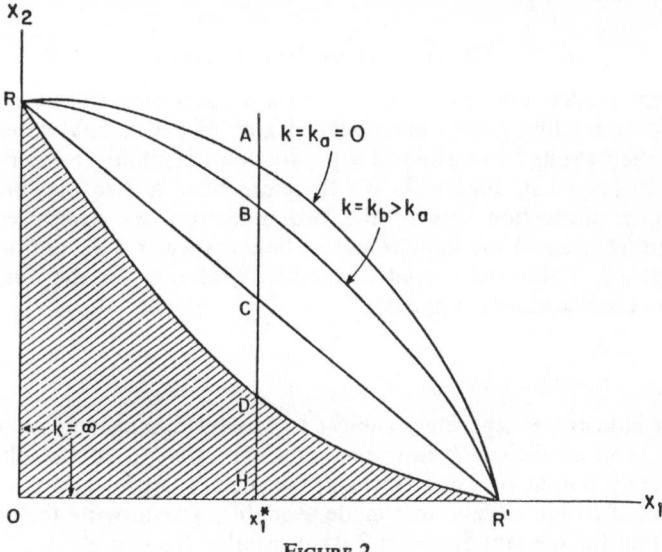

FIGURE 2

laundry can be produced than before. Consequently point A must shift downward to some lower point, B, and the entire possibility locus becomes something like RBR'. With further increases in the value of k, point A will be shifted lower still. If at some value of k it is pulled below line segment RCR', the possibility set becomes a non-convex region[1] such as shaded region $ORDR'$. But we know that if the external damage is sufficiently serious (i.e. for sufficiently high values of k), A must cut below C, for if the marginal smoke output is so great and so noxious that no quantity of resources can get laundry as clean as it would be ·

[1] Figure 2 can be connected directly to the inter-related individual production sets of Figures 1a and 1b. Points R and R' respectively represent the social output vectors $(-8, 0, 400)$, i.e. point B in Figure 1a, and $(-8, 20, 0)$, i.e. point A in Figure 1a. With constant returns to scale and a single input the production frontier in the absence of externalities must be the line segment RCR'. However, with electricity output at $x_1^* = 10$ in Figure 2, the most laundry we can obtain in the presence of the externality is $HD = 100$, not $HC = 200$.

in the absence of smoke, then A must fall all the way to the horizontal axis (point H). That is, in the limit, the possibility locus then must consist simply of the axis segments ROR'.

The simplicity of the preceding argument may belie its generality and rigour. The point is that with any pair of commodities one of which interferes with the production of the other there will be no such interference if one or the other is not produced. On the other hand if the interference is sufficiently great, the maximal output of the activity suffering the external damage will approach zero for *any* non-zero level of output of the other, and a non-convexity in the feasible set is unavoidable. Note finally that if there is a non-convexity in the production set for *any* pair of commodities, the full *n*-dimensional production set is also non-convex.

III. A Further Illustration

Some readers may prefer to deal with a concrete algebraic example explicitly relating a measure of the degree of detrimental externality with the "wrong" curvature of a production possibility frontier of the type displayed in Figure 2. We therefore offer a case in which the separate production sets of the two industries are strictly convex. Again let v_i stand for the amount of labour (negative leisure) used in industry i, x_1 for the output of electricity, and x_2 for the output of laundry services, and suppose

$$(1) \qquad v_1 = x_1^2/2$$
$$v_2 = x_2^2/2 + kx_1x_2.$$

Each industry is separately subject to strictly diminishing returns to scale. The coefficient k now measures the strength of the effect of electricity output on laundry costs; the effect is detrimental if $k > 0$. If a total of v units of labour is made available, we can write the implicit equation for the laundry–electricity possibility frontier as

$$(2) \qquad v = x_1^2/2 + kx_1x_2 + x_2^2/2,$$
$$x_1 \geqq 0, \ x_2 \geqq 0.$$

We can deal with any such differentiable possibility locus in an obvious manner, calculating its second derivative and showing generally that when the externality parameter k becomes sufficiently large that derivative must take positive values. The present illustration, however, permits us to show this result more directly. If $k=0$ (no externality), (2) describes a quarter circle in an (x_1, x_2) co-ordinate system. This boundary obviously has the "right" curvature. For small positive k, the boundary continues to be concave to the origin. However, when $k=1$, (9) becomes the equation of a straight line $[(x_1 + x_2)^2 = 2v]$; and for larger values of k, non-convexity of the production set occurs.

In the preceding example non-convexity only happens to appear with a fixed large value of k, i.e. for $k=1$. However, generally the appearance of the non-convexity will depend both on the magnitude of the externality parameters and on the values of x_1 and x_2. For example, suppose in the preceding example we leave the electricity cost function unchanged but make the laundry resource requirement function

$$v_2 = x_2 + kx_1x_2.$$

Then the production possibility locus is given by

$$v = v_1 + v_2 = x_1^2/2 + kx_1x_2 + x_2.$$

A straightforward calculation of the second derivative shows that convexity will now be violated if and only if

$$2k^2x_2 + kx_1 > 1.$$

Clearly, for k or x_1 or x_2 sufficiently large, this requirement will not be satisfied. In this illustrative example, the maximum feasible values of x_2 occur in the vicinity of $x_1 = 0$. Here we have $x_2 \simeq v$, and it is not difficult to imagine values of k and v that will violate the preceding convexity requirement. If v is very large, say of the order of thousands or millions of units, even a very small value of k will violate the second-order conditions. For example, if $v = 10,000$, then any $k > 0.01$ will have this effect.

IV. Spatial Separation as a Palliative

A lower bound to the degree of non-convexity in the social production set arising from detrimental externalities is provided by the possibility

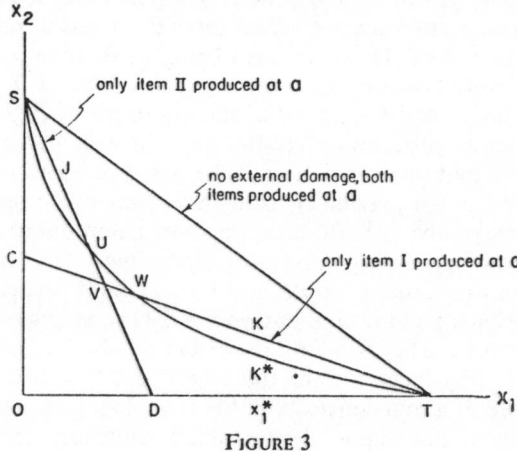

FIGURE 3

of separating the generators and their victims geographically, moving the laundries from the vicinity of the electricity producers, or *vice versa*. This is illustrated by the following example.

Assume once more that we have two outputs, 1 and 2 (electricity and laundry), and that these can be produced at either of two locations, a and b, with respective output levels, x_{1a}, x_{2a}, x_{1b} and x_{2b}. To begin with, we take all substitution relationships in the absence of externalities to be perfectly linear. Let us assume also that, were there no externalities, it would pay to produce both items at the same location, say a. In Figure 3 line segment ST represents the production possibility locus for our two items when external damage is zero and both are manufactured at the more economical location, a. SD represents the more restricted set of output levels[1] that remains possible if x_2 were still produced at a but the production of x_1 were moved to b. Since b is assumed to be a less suitable site, all of SD must lie below ST, with the exception of end-point S which corresponds to production of x_2 alone, and which, since all of that activity takes place at a, must provide the same output level as can be achieved when there is no restriction on the use of site a. Similarly, line segment CT represents the production possibilities when manufacture of x_2 is moved to b while that of x_1 takes place at a.

Now suppose that externalities generated by the production of x_1 at a grow serious, so that the locus corresponding to manufacture of both items at a shifts from the line segment ST to the convex locus $SUWT$, by the process described in the discussion of Figure 1. Then, if society wishes to produce, say, quantity x_1^* of item 1, it can only obtain $x_1^* K^*$ of x_2 if both goods continue to be produced at a. However, by separating the two production processes—shifting the manufacture of item 2 to site b—the community can increase its output of commodity 2 to $x_1^* K$.

Obviously, then, if we take into account the possibility of spatial separation of output processes, the production possibility locus becomes $SJUWKT$. In no event can externalities force this locus to retreat closer to the origin than SVT. However, even here, the feasible region $OSVT$ cannot be convex, because the boundary point V must lie below the line ST. Figures 4a and 4b generalize the argument of Figure 3 to the case of non-linear substitution relationships in which it is no longer necessarily true that one location, a, is the best place for both outputs. Once again, ST is the possibility locus in the absence of externalities. However, some of one or both items may now be produced at b as well as at a. The two possibility curves corresponding to the two ways of separating the two outputs are PR and CD. These two curves need no longer have even a point in common with ST. Nor, as Figure 4b shows, need they intersect. They will limit the extent to which externalities can pull the possibility locus toward the origin, but they cannot prevent the appearance of a non-convexity in the feasible region, as Figures 4a and 4b indicate. For suppose externalities transform the locus ST, along which the activities are not separated, into the curve SJT. The true possibility locus will now be $SWVUT$, yielding a feasible region $OSWVUT$ (shaded areas) that is non-convex.

[1] This shrinking of the possibility set takes into account any resources which must be devoted to transport as a result of the separation of activities.

168   ECONOMICA   [MAY

These diagrams illustrate the proposition that sufficiently severe externalities make locational specialization economical. An example of the application of this point is seen in the Ruhr region in Germany, where the Emscher River valley has been completely devoted to waste disposal, while two other river basins have been preserved free from pollution.

The diagrams also bring out the disconcerting possibility that *which locational specialization is optimal may well depend upon the desired output proportions*. Thus, in Figure 4a, with fairly strong externalities the production possibility function is *SWVUT*. For output combinations

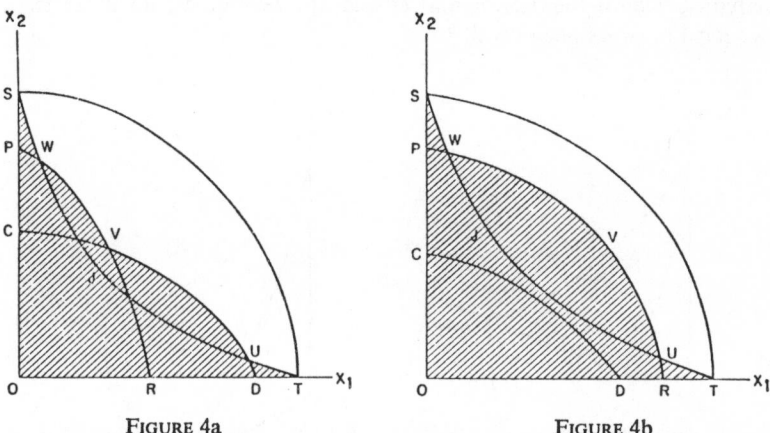

FIGURE 4a   FIGURE 4b

along segment *WV* all of x_2 is produced at *a*, all x_1 at *b*. Along segment *VU* the specialization is reversed. The danger of an incorrect choice by planners in this context appears clear. If it should turn out that, unpolluted, the Emscher River valley is uniquely well suited to growing marijuana it may turn out to have been a mistake to pick that one rather than one of the others for the area's sewer.

V. Generalization to *n* Activities

The arguments of the preceding sections have dealt with a world in which there are only two activities. Generalization of the argument to deal with more than two activities is immediate.[1] In a world of *n* outputs convexity can be guaranteed only if *each* of the partial possibility loci representing substitution between a pair of commodities is concave. Any single exception like that in Figure 2 means that at least two local

[1] Our discussion has also confined itself only to *detrimental* externalities. In principle, the presence of external benefits can also produce a multiplicity of local maxima, but here it is not so clear that the problem is likely to be serious. On this see Baumol [2], pp. 366–7.

1972]   EXTERNALITIES AND NON-CONVEXITY OF PRODUCTION SET   169

maxima become possible. Thus the analysis holds whether the economy encompasses two outputs or n.

There is, however, one aspect of the matter that does require explicit analysis in terms of n activities. One may well ask how the number of local maxima is likely to grow with the number of activities. Here we can offer a few observations about polar cases which suggest that in at least some cases the number of local maxima may grow very rapidly with the number of activities involved. First, however, we deal with a case in which a proliferation of activities does not necessarily increase the number of local maxima.

Polar case (*a*): If one activity imposes external costs on m other activities, even if the detrimental effects are very great, no more than two local maxima need result.[1]

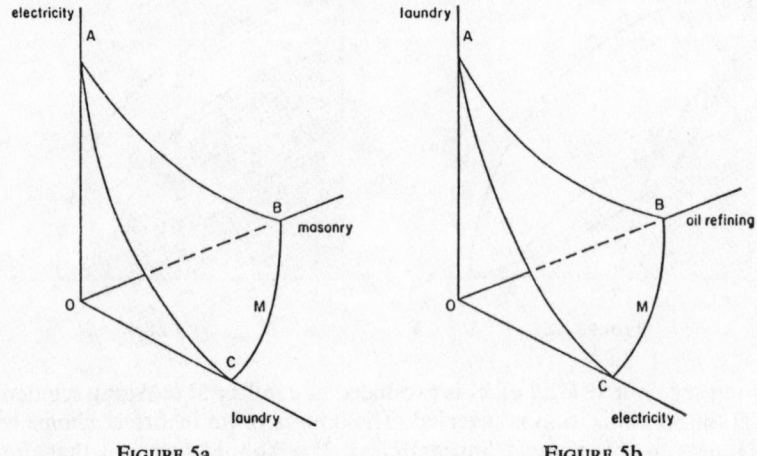

FIGURE 5a   FIGURE 5b

Polar case (*b*): A similar result holds when n activities impose external costs on one other activity.

In Figure 5a, the smoke from electricity production increases laundry cost and makes it more expensive to produce deterioration-resistant masonry. The production locus will then tend toward the form indicated (surface ABC). Since laundry and masonry activity impose no adverse external effects upon one another, their production possibility

---

[1] This does not preclude the possibility that there will be more than two maxima if the relevant functions violate the appropriate concavity–convexity conditions in the absence of externalities. Even where the maximum would otherwise be unique, externalities which are of intermediate strength may lead to three (or more) local maxima—characteristically two corner maxima produced by the externalities, and one interior maximum, a vestige of the unique maximum that would occur in the absence of externalities. Complications such as these and the possibility of irregularities in the relevant hypersurfaces probably limit the profitability of a more rigorous discussion of the subject of this section.

locus will have the normal shape (concave to the origin) illustrated by curve CB. However, for the reasons indicated in the discussion of Figure 2, if smoke damage grows sufficiently serious the other two partial loci will have shapes like those of AC and AB. We may then expect two local maxima, one at A and perhaps another at a point such as M. The interpretation of Figure 5b is exactly the same, and we merely pause to draw the reader's attention to the remarkable similarity between the diagram for the two-victim-one-polluter case and that for one victim and two polluters.

Next we come to cases involving more complex patterns of inter-dependence and show that here the number of local maxima may indeed increase with the number of activities involved. We have the following case.

Polar case (c): If each of n activities produces and suffers from very strong detrimental externalities and spatial separation is not possible, n local optima can be expected.

Here, in the limit as external damage becomes sufficiently great, it will be optimal (indeed it will only be possible) to carry on just one of the n activities. The choice of the activity to continue in operation clearly gives us our n local maxima (i.e. there are exactly n such choices available). If matters are not quite so serious, so that only a smaller number, k, of activities need be discontinued, it may be con-jectured that the number of local maxima will increase (to the number of combinations of n activities chosen k at a time).

Finally, we deal with the possibility of spatial separation, which, unlike its role in our earlier discussion, seems to aggravate the growth in number of maxima with the number of activities involved. We have the following case.

Polar case (d): If there are n activities each of which produces and suffers from externalities and there are just n discrete locations into which they can be separated, then, if the externalities are sufficiently severe, we can expect at least $n!$ local maxima. For we have n candidates for the first location and, for each such choice, there remain $n-1$ candidates for the second location, then $n-2$ candidates for the third, etc., i.e. there are altogether $n!$ different ways of achieving the desired isolation.

In practice, in some respects, this probably exaggerates the number of possibilities; in other ways it understates them. There really is no fixed finite number of discrete locations, and so one will normally have more than n geographic areas in which to locate n activities. If that is the right way of looking at the matter, it is clear that the number of local maxima (i.e. the number of ways of isolating each activity) will exceed $n!$. On the other hand, airborne pollution is known to travel over enormous distances. In that sense we may have no hiding-place from one another's emissions. We may then find ourselves back at the one-location case with its smaller number of local maxima but its more difficult problems of social damage.

VI. Convexity in Social and Individual Possibility Sets

In one respect the externality-induced non-convexity poses a less serious problem for social control than one might expect. For, as all of our examples indicate (see, notably, Figure 1), non-convexity in the social production possibility set is compatible with convexity in the sets over which individual producers make their choices. This has the consequence that it is possible through the use of prices and taxes alone to induce any individual firm to choose any designated point on its production possibility frontier, and hence to use these devices to sustain any designated point on the social possibility frontier, despite its "wrong" curvature. This may be contrasted, for example, with the case of non-convexity due to increasing returns to the scale of individual producers' production. Here, if every producer's average costs decline continually with scale over some substantial range, a producer confronted by a fixed price will either turn out zero output or some large quantity of output. Output combinations calling for intermediate levels of production of the good in question cannot be attained with the aid of the price mechanism alone.

The general principle may be illustrated with the example of Section III, involving two producers with input cost functions, (1). As it happens, if the input is inelastically supplied, in this case *any* pair of output choices by the two producers will be on the production possibility frontier. It need, then, only be demonstrated that any attainable (x_1, x_2) combination will be chosen in some price situation. Let the prices p_1 for electricity (x_1) and p_2 for laundry (x_2) be chosen, and let labour be given a price of unity. The profit functions of the two firms are given by

$$(3) \quad \begin{aligned} \pi_1 &= p_1 x_1 - x_1^2/2 \\ \pi_2 &= p_2 x_2 - x_2^2/2 - k x_1 x_2. \end{aligned}$$

The individual production sets being strictly convex in "own" variables, the profit functions are strictly concave in own variables. Hence (as may be checked by calculating second partials) first-order conditions (4) are sufficient as well as necessary:

$$(4) \quad \begin{aligned} x_1 &= p_1 \\ k x_1 + x_2 &= p_2. \end{aligned}$$

Eqs. (4) are invertible, which means that any desired pair (x_1, x_2) can be obtained as a solution to them for some combination of prices.

More generally, it is not true that all sets of profit-maximizing choices by producers will produce a socially efficient output combination, for we must usually worry about equating marginal rates of substitution and transformation by all producers, where any given pair of producers is likely to have many input–input, input–output and output–output pairs in common (e.g. all firms use some labour *and* some capital). The required adjustments to the prices facing an individual producer are, of course, Pigovian taxes, adding to the cost of inputs and subtracting from amounts received for outputs sums designed to bring into equality marginal private and marginal social cost. We reserve for an Appendix a formal demonstration of this fact.

VII. CONCLUDING COMMENTS: WHAT'S WRONG WITH NON-CONVEXITY?

There is only limited comfort to be derived from the knowledge that a sufficiently ingenious use of Pigovian taxes can keep a competitive economy at any desired point that is technologically efficient so long as detrimental externalities are the only source of non-convexity. Pigovian taxes cannot change the shapes of the technological relationships in the economy, and hence cannot remove the problems of evaluation of efficiency which non-convexity introduces. It seems appropriate therefore to conclude by reviewing this problem briefly.

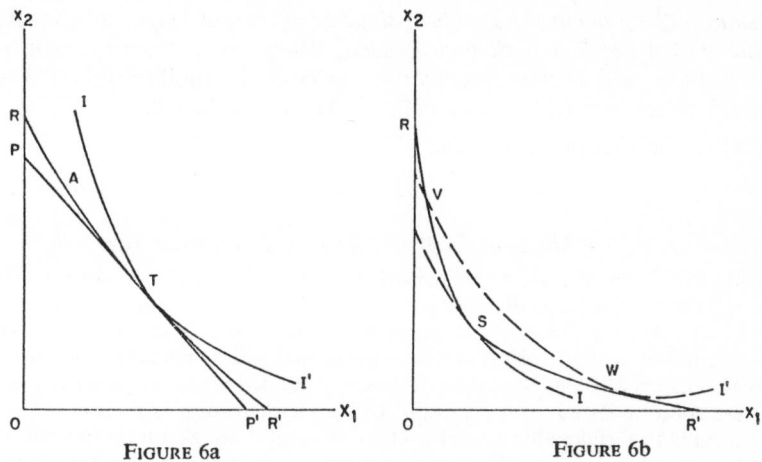

FIGURE 6a   FIGURE 6b

Let us, then, bring consumers into the picture. In Figure 6a let II' be a social indifference curve, so constructed that along it social welfare is constant and that its slope at any point equals the common slope of all consumers' indifference curves at the corresponding distribution of the two goods (see Samuelson [7] or Baumol [1] ch. 3, sec. IX, and Appendix). A social-welfare-maximizing state involving positive outputs of the two goods must be characterized by tangency of a social indifference curve with the production possibility frontier, as at point T in Figure 6a. As we have just suggested, so long as the only source of non-convexity is the presence of detrimental externalities, such a point can be sustained as a tax-adjusted competition equilibrium, in which producers are maximizing profits and individuals utility in the small and in the large.

However, note that, while convexity of preferences suffices to assure us that an equilibrium which maximizes the value of output at consumer prices over all feasible output vectors is Pareto-optimal (i.e. social-welfare-maximizing for some individualistic welfare function), the converse does not hold. It js no longer true that the availability of outputs that are more valuable (at current equilibrium consumer prices) implies that current output is not Pareto-optimal. In Figure 6a, for example, feasible outputs to the north-east of *PP'* are more valuable than output *T*, yet are socially inferior. A Pigovian-tax-compensated competitive equilibrium may thus be globally Pareto-optimal, as is *T* of Figure 6a; or a global minimum of social welfare among outputs which are technically efficient, as is *S* in Figure 6b; or a local, but not a global, social welfare maximum, as is *W* in Figure 6b.

In a world in which detrimental externalities are sufficiently severe to cause non-convexity of the social production possibility set, prices can no longer be depended upon to give us the right signals. *Even if we know the entire set of feasible output vectors, equilibrium prices usually tell us nothing about the Pareto-optimality of current output or even the direction in which to seek improvement.* While tax instruments will be effective in guiding the economy, the choice of the equilibrium point at which to settle must be made collectively by cost–benefit techniques.

Princeton University, Princeton, N.J.

APPENDIX

A Formal Model of External Effects and Corrective Taxes

In this Appendix we put forward a general definition of detrimental externalities of the sort discussed above. There is, of course, no single clear favourite among the possible generalizations of the effect whereby one single producer's expansion of his single output affects adversely the input requirements of other producers. However, the definition we propose does seem appropriate and does contain the simple definition as a special case Armed with this definition we show that social efficiency requires individual efficiency when external effects are all detrimental. A producer's net output vector (including negative entries for inputs) is "individually efficient" if no dominating net output vector is available to him without changing some other producer's net output choice. Finally, we show that when each individual producer's choice set is convex *any* socially efficient net output vector can be sustained by profit-maximizing production with externality-offsetting taxes.

Let $x^i = x_1^i, \ldots, x_n^i$ be the net output vector of the *i*th producer, where negative entries represent net inputs. We assume that x^i is chosen from a *feasible set* S^i. For the usual reasons (see, e.g. Quirk and Saposnik [6]) we assume that S^i always includes the origin and the negative orthant of Euclidian *n*-space (free disposal), and that S^i has no elements in the strictly positive orthant (no outputs without inputs).

The size and shape of S^i depend in general on the net output choices of *other producers.* Let X stand for the matrix of net output choices of the m producers in the economy, whose k, jth element, x_j^k, is the net output of commodity j by producer k. We shall represent the dependence of S^i on the choices of other producers as a functional relationship, mapping X into subsets of n-space, and denote this relationship by $S^i = S^i(X)$. Thus $S^i(X)$ is defined as the set $\{x^i | x^1, \ldots, x^{i-1}, x^{i+1}, \ldots, x^m\}$. We shall say that *these relationships embody detrimental external effects if for any two different producers k and i*

$$\lambda > 1 \Rightarrow S^i(\ldots \lambda x_j^k \ldots) \subset S^i(X),$$

where $(\ldots \lambda x_j^k \ldots)$ *denotes the matrix obtained from X by replacing x_j^k with λx_j^k.* This definition implies that a producer tends to hurt other producers by increasing the intensity of any net output *or* net input. Obviously a definition of beneficial external effects would be obtained by reversing the set inclusion sign in this definition. The definition could also be made specific to a particular element x_j^k so that some variables could exhibit detrimental, some beneficial, external effects. We confine our attention to relationships involving only detrimental externalities, which by the definition, include the case of zero externality.

Under this definition it follows trivially that socially efficient production (total net output of some one item maximized for any set of given totals of the other net outputs) requires efficiency on the part of each individual producer. For if a producer has chosen an individually inefficient net output vector he can alter his choice in a way which preserves his net output but reduces his net input usage. Since the external effect of the latter action must in our case *enhance* the productive opportunities of the other producers, such a choice is clearly required by social efficiency.

Since, by assumption, the feasible set of each producer, considering only variations in the vector under his control, is convex, any point in that set which is efficient from the producer's point of view will be a profit-maximizing choice for some vector of prices. And since, as we have just shown, any socially efficient point will be composed of a sum of points efficient for each producer, it follows that any socially efficient net output vector can be sustained as a profit-maximizing point for all producers if the prices are appropriately adjusted for each producer by a set of taxes. It remains only to show that the "appropriate" taxes are precisely equal to the marginal external damages arising from changes in output and input choices.

For this demonstration it will be convenient to assume that the feasible set of the ith producer is defined by the inequality $f^i(X) \leq 0$, where f^i is a differentiable function. Recall that X is a *matrix* of which the typical element, x_j^i, specifies the net output (negative for inputs) of the jth commodity by the ith producer. Fixing net output vectors x^j for $j \neq i$, $f^i(X) = 0$ defines the "private production possibility frontier" constraining x^i, the net output vector choice of the ith producer. By assumption, the set of vectors x^i satisfying $f^i(X) \leq 0$ in this case is convex.

If the rows of the matrix $\bar{X}$ sum to a point on the social production possibility frontier, then it is a solution to the non-linear programming problem

$$\underset{X}{\text{maximize}} \sum_{i=1}^{m} x_1^i,$$

subject to

$$\sum_{i=1}^{m} \bar{x}_k^i - \sum_{i=1}^{m} x_k^i \leq 0 \quad (k=2, \ldots, n)$$

$$f^j(X) \leq 0 \quad (j=1, \ldots, m).$$

By a simple extension of the Kuhn–Tucker theorem on optimization with inequality constraints, necessary conditions for a solution to this problem are that there exist non-negative multipliers $\lambda_2, \ldots, \lambda_n$, corresponding to the constraints requiring minimum amounts of commodities other than commodity 1, and $\gamma_1, \ldots, \gamma_m$, corresponding to the individual production constraints, such that

$$1 - \sum_{j=1}^{m} \gamma_j f_{i1}^j = 0 \qquad (i=1, \ldots, m)$$

$$\lambda_h - \sum_{j=1}^{m} \gamma_j f_{kh}^j = 0 \qquad (k=1, \ldots, m)$$
$$(h=2, \ldots, n).$$

(The notation f_{kh}^j stands for the partial derivative of f^j with respect to x_h^k.) By the usual interpretation, λ_j equals the amount of commodity 1 (in effect here the *numeraire* commodity) obtained by a unit reduction in the amount of commodity j produced. The multiplier γ_k is the value (in commodity 1 terms) of the extra output which could be obtained if firm k's production constraint were relaxed by requiring $f^k(X) \leq 1$ instead of $f^k(X) \leq 0$.

Consider next the profit-maximizing problem faced by producer i faced with a vector p of prices *and* a vector t^i of taxes:

$$\underset{x^i}{\text{maximize}} \sum_{j=1}^{m} (p_j - t_j^i) x_j^i,$$

subject to

$$f^i(X) \leq 0,$$

where all variables other than the "own", vector, x^i, are treated as exogenously fixed in the constraint. By the Kuhn–Tucker theorem, if x^i is a solution there necessarily exists a non-negative multiplier, δ^i, such that

$$p_j - t_j^i - \delta^i f_{ij}^i(X) = 0 \qquad (j=1, \ldots, m).$$

Furthermore, since the constraint set is convex, these conditions, together with the constraint, are sufficient as well as necessary for a constrained maximum. The multiplier δ^i indicates the profit which would be *lost* to the ith producer if his production constraint were "tightened" by one unit.

Now we need only put the two problems together. If $\bar{X}$ is a set of individual producer vectors summing to a point on the social production possibility function, use the Lagrange multipliers from the associated non-linear programming problem and set

$$p_1 = 1, \quad p_2 = \lambda_2, \quad \ldots, \quad p_n = \lambda_n \qquad (i=1, \ldots, m)$$

$$t_{ik} = \sum_{\substack{j=1 \\ j \neq 1}}^{m} \gamma_j f_{ik}^j, \qquad (k=1, \ldots, n).$$

We see that $\bar{x}^i$ satisfies the necessary and sufficient conditions for a profit maximum for producer i, with the multiplier δ^i of his problem equal to γ_i in the economy-wide problem.

To interpret this result note that, for $j \neq i$, f_{ik}^j is, in effect, the constriction in the jth production constraint per unit increase in the ith producer's net output of the kth good. Hence $\gamma_j f_{ik}^j$ is the external cost, in *numeraire* units, of such an increase, imposed by the ith producer on the jth per unit increase in x_k^i, and $\sum\limits_{j \neq i}^{m} \gamma_j f_{ik}^j$ is the total external social cost per unit increase in x_k^i. Furthermore, since $\delta^i = \gamma_i$, the external social cost will also exactly equal the marginal external profit loss per unit increase in output of X_k by firm i observed when the proper corrective taxes are applied.

REFERENCES

[1] Baumol, W. J., *Welfare Economics and The Theory of the State*, 2nd ed., Cambridge, Mass., 1965.
[2] ——, "External Economies and Second-Order Optimality Conditions", *American Economic Review*, vol. 54 (1964), pp. 358–72.
[3] Kolm, S. C., "Les Non-Convexités d'Externalité", CEPREMAP Rapport No. 11, mimeograph, 1971.
[4] Pigou, A. C., *The Economics of Welfare*, 4th ed., 1932.
[5] Portes, R. D., "The Search for Efficiency in the Presence of Externalities", in Paul Streeten (ed.), *Unfashionable Economics: Essays in Honour of Lord Balogh*, 1970, pp. 348–61.
[6] Quirk, J. and R. Saposnik, *Introduction to General Equilibrium Theory and Welfare Economics*, New York, 1968.
[7] Samuelson, P. A., "Social Indifference Curves", *Quarterly Journal of Economics*, vol. 70 (1956), pp. 1–22.
[8] Starett, D., "On a Fundamental Non-Convexity in the Theory of Externalities", Harvard Institute of Economic Research, Discussion Paper 115, 1970.

[5]

The Journal of

LAW &

ECONOMICS

VOLUME III   OCTOBER 1960

THE PROBLEM OF SOCIAL COST

R. H. COASE
University of Virginia

I. The Problem To Be Examined[1]

THIS paper is concerned with those actions of business firms which have harmful effects on others. The standard example is that of a factory the smoke from which has harmful effects on those occupying neighbouring properties. The economic analysis of such a situation has usually proceeded in terms of a divergence between the private and social product of the factory, in which economists have largely followed the treatment of Pigou in *The Economics of Welfare*. The conclusions to which this kind of analysis seems to have led most economists is that it would be desirable to make the owner of the factory liable for the damage caused to those injured by the smoke, or alternatively, to place a tax on the factory owner varying with the amount of smoke produced and equivalent in money terms to the damage it would cause, or finally, to exclude the factory from residential districts (and presumably from other

---

[1] This article, although concerned with a technical problem of economic analysis, arose out of the study of the Political Economy of Broadcasting which I am now conducting. The argument of the present article was implicit in a previous article dealing with the problem of allocating radio and television frequencies (The Federal Communications Commission, 2 J. Law & Econ. [1959]) but comments which I have received seemed to suggest that it would be desirable to deal with the question in a more explicit way and without reference to the original problem for the solution of which the analysis was developed.

1

areas in which the emission of smoke would have harmful effects on others). It is my contention that the suggested courses of action are inappropriate, in that they lead to results which are not necessarily, or even usually, desirable.

II. The Reciprocal Nature of the Problem

The traditional approach has tended to obscure the nature of the choice that has to be made. The question is commonly thought of as one in which A inflicts harm on B and what has to be decided is: how should we restrain A? But this is wrong. We are dealing with a problem of a reciprocal nature. To avoid the harm to B would inflict harm on A. The real question that has to be decided is: should A be allowed to harm B or should B be allowed to harm A? The problem is to avoid the more serious harm. I instanced in my previous article[2] the case of a confectioner the noise and vibrations from whose machinery disturbed a doctor in his work. To avoid harming the doctor would inflict harm on the confectioner. The problem posed by this case was essentially whether it was worth while, as a result of restricting the methods of production which could be used by the confectioner, to secure more doctoring at the cost of a reduced supply of confectionery products. Another example is afforded by the problem of straying cattle which destroy crops on neighbouring land. If it is inevitable that some cattle will stray, an increase in the supply of meat can only be obtained at the expense of a decrease in the supply of crops. The nature of the choice is clear: meat or crops. What answer should be given is, of course, not clear unless we know the value of what is obtained as well as the value of what is sacrificed to obtain it. To give another example, Professor George J. Stigler instances the contamination of a stream.[3] If we assume that the harmful effect of the pollution is that it kills the fish, the question to be decided is: is the value of the fish lost greater or less than the value of the product which the contamination of the stream makes possible. It goes almost without saying that this problem has to be looked at in total *and* at the margin.

III. The Pricing System with Liability for Damage

I propose to start my analysis by examining a case in which most economists would presumably agree that the problem would be solved in a completely satisfactory manner: when the damaging business has to pay for all damage caused *and* the pricing system works smoothly (strictly this means that the operation of a pricing system is without cost).

A good example of the problem under discussion is afforded by the case of straying cattle which destroy crops growing on neighbouring land. Let us suppose that a farmer and a cattle-raiser are operating on neighbouring proper-

[2] Coase, The Federal Communications Commission, 2 J. Law & Econ. 26–27 (1959).

[3] G. J. Stigler, The Theory of Price 105 (1952).

ties. Let us further suppose that, without any fencing between the properties, an increase in the size of the cattle-raiser's herd increases the total damage to the farmer's crops. What happens to the marginal damage as the size of the herd increases is another matter. This depends on whether the cattle tend to follow one another or to roam side by side, on whether they tend to be more or less restless as the size of the herd increases and on other similar factors. For my immediate purpose, it is immaterial what assumption is made about marginal damage as the size of the herd increases.

To simplify the argument, I propose to use an arithmetical example. I shall assume that the annual cost of fencing the farmer's property is $9 and that the price of the crop is $1 per ton. Also, I assume that the relation between the number of cattle in the herd and the annual crop loss is as follows:

Number in Herd (Steers)	Annual Crop Loss (Tons)	Crop Loss per Additional Steer (Tons)
1	1	1
2	3	2
3	6	3
4	10	4

Given that the cattle-raiser is liable for the damage caused, the additional annual cost imposed on the cattle-raiser if he increased his herd from, say, 2 to 3 steers is $3 and in deciding on the size of the herd, he will take this into account along with his other costs. That is, he will not increase the size of the herd unless the value of the additional meat produced (assuming that the cattle-raiser slaughters the cattle), is greater than the additional costs that this will entail, including the value of the additional crops destroyed. Of course, if, by the employment of dogs, herdsmen, aeroplanes, mobile radio and other means, the amount of damage can be reduced, these means will be adopted when their cost is less than the value of the crop which they prevent being lost. Given that the annual cost of fencing is $9, the cattle-raiser who wished to have a herd with 4 steers or more would pay for fencing to be erected and maintained, assuming that other means of attaining the same end would not do so more cheaply. When the fence is erected, the marginal cost due to the liability for damage becomes zero, except to the extent that an increase in the size of the herd necessitates a stronger and therefore more expensive fence because more steers are liable to lean against it at the same time. But, of course, it may be cheaper for the cattle-raiser not to fence and to pay for the damaged crops, as in my arithmetical example, with 3 or fewer steers.

It might be thought that the fact that the cattle-raiser would pay for all crops damaged would lead the farmer to increase his planting if a cattle-raiser came to occupy the neighbouring property. But this is not so. If the crop was previously sold in conditions of perfect competition, marginal cost was equal to price for the amount of planting undertaken and any expansion would have reduced the profits of the farmer. In the new situation, the existence of crop damage would mean that the farmer would sell less on the open market but his receipts for a given production would remain the same, since the cattle-raiser would pay the market price for any crop damaged. Of course, if cattle-raising commonly involved the destruction of crops, the coming into existence of a cattle-raising industry might raise the price of the crops involved and farmers would then extend their planting. But I wish to confine my attention to the individual farmer.

I have said that the occupation of a neighbouring property by a cattle-raiser would not cause the amount of production, or perhaps more exactly the amount of planting, by the farmer to increase. In fact, if the cattle-raising has any effect, it will be to decrease the amount of planting. The reason for this is that, for any given tract of land, if the value of the crop damaged is so great that the receipts from the sale of the undamaged crop are less than the total costs of cultivating that tract of land, it will be profitable for the farmer and the cattle-raiser to make a bargain whereby that tract of land is left un-cultivated. This can be made clear by means of an arithmetical example. Assume initially that the value of the crop obtained from cultivating a given tract of land is \$12 and that the cost incurred in cultivating this tract of land is \$10, the net gain from cultivating the land being \$2. I assume for purposes of simplicity that the farmer owns the land. Now assume that the cattle-raiser starts operations on the neighbouring property and that the value of the crops damaged is \$1. In this case \$11 is obtained by the farmer from sale on the market and \$1 is obtained from the cattle-raiser for damage suffered and the net gain remains \$2. Now suppose that the cattle-raiser finds it profitable to increase the size of his herd, even though the amount of damage rises to \$3; which means that the value of the additional meat production is greater than the additional costs, including the additional \$2 payment for damage. But the total payment for damage is now \$3. The net gain to the farmer from cultivat-ing the land is still \$2. The cattle-raiser would be better off if the farmer would agree not to cultivate his land for any payment less than \$3. The farmer would be agreeable to not cultivating the land for any payment greater than \$2. There is clearly room for a mutually satisfactory bargain which would lead to the abandonment of cultivation.[4] But the same argument applies not only to the whole tract cultivated by the farmer but also to any

---

[4] The argument in the text has proceeded on the assumption that the alternative to cultivation of the crop is abandonment of cultivation altogether. But this need not be so. There may be crops which are less liable to damage by cattle but which would not be as profitable as the crop grown in the absence of damage. Thus, if the cultivation of a new crop would yield a return to the farmer of \$1 instead of \$2, and the size of the herd which would cause \$3 damage with the old crop would cause \$1 damage with the new crop, it would be profitable to the cattle-raiser to pay any sum less than \$2 to induce the farmer

THE PROBLEM OF SOCIAL COST   5

subdivision of it. Suppose, for example, that the cattle have a well-defined route, say, to a brook or to a shady area. In these circumstances, the amount of damage to the crop along the route may well be great and if so, it could be that the farmer and the cattle-raiser would find it profitable to make a bargain whereby the farmer would agree not to cultivate this strip of land.

But this raises a further possibility. Suppose that there is such a well-defined route. Suppose further that the value of the crop that would be obtained by cultivating this strip of land is $10 but that the cost of cultivation is $11. In the absence of the cattle-raiser, the land would not be cultivated. However, given the presence of the cattle-raiser, it could well be that if the strip was cultivated, the whole crop would be destroyed by the cattle. In which case, the cattle-raiser would be forced to pay $10 to the farmer. It is true that the farmer would lose $1. But the cattle-raiser would lose $10. Clearly this is a situation which is not likely to last indefinitely since neither party would want this to happen. The aim of the farmer would be to induce the cattle-raiser to make a payment in return for an agreement to leave this land uncultivated. The farmer would not be able to obtain a payment greater than the cost of fencing off this piece of land nor so high as to lead the cattle-raiser to abandon the use of the neighbouring property. What payment would in fact be made would depend on the shrewdness of the farmer and the cattle-raiser as bargainers. But as the payment would not be so high as to cause the cattle-raiser to abandon this location and as it would not vary with the size of the herd, such an agreement would not affect the allocation of resources but would merely alter the distribution of income and wealth as between the cattle-raiser and the farmer.

I think it is clear that if the cattle-raiser is liable for damage caused and the pricing system works smoothly, the reduction in the value of production elsewhere will be taken into account in computing the additional cost involved in increasing the size of the herd. This cost will be weighed against the value of the additional meat production and, given perfect competition in the cattle industry, the allocation of resources in cattle-raising will be optimal. What needs to be emphasized is that the fall in the value of production elsewhere which would be taken into account in the costs of the cattle-raiser may well be less than the damage which the cattle would cause to the crops in the ordinary course of events. This is because it is possible, as a result of market transactions, to discontinue cultivation of the land. This is desirable in all

---

to change his crop (since this would reduce damage liability from $3 to $1) and it would be profitable for the farmer to do so if the amount received was more than $1 (the reduction in his return caused by switching crops). In fact, there would be room for a mutually satisfactory bargain in all cases in which a change of crop would reduce the amount of damage by more than it reduces the value of the crop (excluding damage)—in all cases, that is, in which a change in the crop cultivated would lead to an increase in the value of production.

cases in which the damage that the cattle would cause, and for which the cattle-raiser would be willing to pay, exceeds the amount which the farmer would pay for use of the land. In conditions of perfect competition, the amount which the farmer would pay for the use of the land is equal to the difference between the value of the total production when the factors are employed on this land and the value of the additional product yielded in their next best use (which would be what the farmer would have to pay for the factors). If damage exceeds the amount the farmer would pay for the use of the land, the value of the additional product of the factors employed elsewhere would exceed the value of the total product in this use after damage is taken into account. It follows that it would be desirable to abandon cultivation of the land and to release the factors employed for production elsewhere. A procedure which merely provided for payment for damage to the crop caused by the cattle but which did not allow for the possibility of cultivation being discontinued would result in too small an employment of factors of production in cattle-raising and too large an employment of factors in cultivation of the crop. But given the possibility of market transactions, a situation in which damage to crops exceeded the rent of the land would not endure. Whether the cattle-raiser pays the farmer to leave the land uncultivated or himself rents the land by paying the land-owner an amount slightly greater than the farmer would pay (if the farmer was himself renting the land), the final result would be the same and would maximise the value of production. Even when the farmer is induced to plant crops which it would not be profitable to cultivate for sale on the market, this will be a purely short-term phenomenon and may be expected to lead to an agreement under which the planting will cease. The cattle-raiser will remain in that location and the marginal cost of meat production will be the same as before, thus having no long-run effect on the allocation of resources.

IV. The Pricing System with No Liability for Damage

I now turn to the case in which, although the pricing system is assumed to work smoothly (that is, costlessly), the damaging business is not liable for any of the damage which it causes. This business does not have to make a payment to those damaged by its actions. I propose to show that the allocation of resources will be the same in this case as it was when the damaging business was liable for damage caused. As I showed in the previous case that the allocation of resources was optimal, it will not be necessary to repeat this part of the argument.

I return to the case of the farmer and the cattle-raiser. The farmer would suffer increased damage to his crop as the size of the herd increased. Suppose that the size of the cattle-raiser's herd is 3 steers (and that this is the size of the herd that would be maintained if crop damage was not taken into account). Then the farmer would be willing to pay up to $3 if the cattle-raiser would reduce his herd to 2 steers, up to $5 if the herd were reduced to 1 steer and would pay up to $6 if cattle-raising was abandoned. The cattle-raiser would therefore receive $3 from the farmer if he kept 2 steers instead of 3. This $3 foregone is therefore part of the cost incurred in keeping the third steer. Whether the $3 is a payment which the cattle-raiser has to make if he adds the third steer to his herd (which it would be if the cattle-raiser was liable to the farmer for damage caused to the crop) or whether it is a sum of money which he would have received if he did not keep a third steer (which it would be if the cattle-raiser was not liable to the farmer for damage caused to the crop) does not affect the final result. In both cases $3 is part of the cost of adding a third steer, to be included along with the other costs. If the increase in the value of production in cattle-raising through increasing the size of the herd from 2 to 3 is greater than the additional costs that have to be incurred (including the $3 damage to crops), the size of the herd will be increased. Otherwise, it will not. The size of the herd will be the same whether the cattle-raiser is liable for damage caused to the crop or not.

It may be argued that the assumed starting point—a herd of 3 steers—was arbitrary. And this is true. But the farmer would not wish to pay to avoid crop damage which the cattle-raiser would not be able to cause. For example, the maximum annual payment which the farmer could be induced to pay could not exceed $9, the annual cost of fencing. And the farmer would only be willing to pay this sum if it did not reduce his earnings to a level that would cause him to abandon cultivation of this particular tract of land. Furthermore, the farmer would only be willing to pay this amount if he believed that, in the absence of any payment by him, the size of the herd maintained by the cattle raiser would be 4 or more steers. Let us assume that this is the case. Then the farmer would be willing to pay up to $3 if the cattle raiser would reduce his herd to 3 steers, up to $6 if the herd were reduced to 2 steers, up to $8 if one steer only were kept and up to $9 if cattle-raising were abandoned. It will be noticed that the change in the starting point has not altered the amount which would accrue to the cattle-raiser if he reduced the size of his herd by any given amount. It is still true that the cattle-raiser could receive an additional $3 from the farmer if he agreed to reduce his herd from 3 steers to 2 and that the $3 represents the value of the crop that would be destroyed by adding the third steer to the herd. Although a different belief on the part of the farmer (whether justified or not) about the size of the herd that the cattle-raiser would maintain in the absence of payments from him may affect the total payment he can be induced to pay, it is not true that this different belief would have any effect on the size of the herd that the cattle-raiser will actually keep. This will be the same as it would be if the cattle-raiser had to pay for damage caused by his cattle, since a receipt foregone of a given amount is the equivalent of a payment of the same amount.

It might be thought that it would pay the cattle-raiser to increase his herd above the size that he would wish to maintain once a bargain had been made, in order to induce the farmer to make a larger total payment. And this may be true. It is similar in nature to the action of the farmer (when the cattle-raiser was liable for damage) in cultivating land on which, as a result of an agreement with the cattle-raiser, planting would subsequently be abandoned (including land which would not be cultivated at all in the absence of cattle-raising). But such manoeuvres are preliminaries to an agreement and do not affect the long-run equilibrium position, which is the same whether or not the cattle-raiser is held responsible for the crop damage brought about by his cattle.

It is necessary to know whether the damaging business is liable or not for damage caused since without the establishment of this initial delimitation of rights there can be no market transactions to transfer and recombine them. But the ultimate result (which maximises the value of production) is independent of the legal position if the pricing system is assumed to work without cost.

V. The Problem Illustrated Anew

The harmful effects of the activities of a business can assume a wide variety of forms. An early English case concerned a building which, by obstructing currents of air, hindered the operation of a windmill.[5] A recent case in Florida concerned a building which cast a shadow on the cabana, swimming pool and sunbathing areas of a neighbouring hotel.[6] The problem of straying cattle and the damaging of crops which was the subject of detailed examination in the two preceding sections, although it may have appeared to be rather a special case, is in fact but one example of a problem which arises in many different guises. To clarify the nature of my argument and to demonstrate its general applicability, I propose to illustrate it anew by reference to four actual cases.

Let us first reconsider the case of *Sturges v. Bridgman*[7] which I used as an illustration of the general problem in my article on "The Federal Communications Commission." In this case, a confectioner (in Wigmore Street) used two mortars and pestles in connection with his business (one had been in operation in the same position for more than 60 years and the other for more than 26 years). A doctor then came to occupy neighbouring premises (in Wimpole Street). The confectioner's machinery caused the doctor no harm until, eight years after he had first occupied the premises, he built a consulting room at the end of his garden right against the confectioner's kitchen. It was then found that the noise and vibration caused by the confectioner's machin-

[5] See Gale on Easements 237–39 (13th ed. M. Bowles 1959).

[6] See Fontainebleu Hotel Corp. v. Forty-Five Twenty-Five, Inc., 114 So. 2d 357 (1959).

[7] 11 Ch. D. 852 (1879).

THE PROBLEM OF SOCIAL COST   9

ery made it difficult for the doctor to use his new consulting room. "In particular . . . the noise prevented him from examining his patients by auscultation[8]
for diseases of the chest. He also found it impossible to engage with effect in
any occupation which required thought and attention." The doctor therefore
brought a legal action to force the confectioner to stop using his machinery.
The courts had little difficulty in granting the doctor the injunction he
sought. "Individual cases of hardship may occur in the strict carrying out of
the principle upon which we found our judgment, but the negation of the
principle would lead even more to individual hardship, and would at the same
time produce a prejudicial effect upon the development of land for residential
purposes."

The court's decision established that the doctor had the right to prevent
the confectioner from using his machinery. But, of course, it would have been
possible to modify the arrangements envisaged in the legal ruling by means of
a bargain between the parties. The doctor would have been willing to waive
his right and allow the machinery to continue in operation if the confectioner
would have paid him a sum of money which was greater than the loss of income which he would suffer from having to move to a more costly or less convenient location or from having to curtail his activities at this location or, as
was suggested as a possibility, from having to build a separate wall which
would deaden the noise and vibration. The confectioner would have been willing to do this if the amount he would have to pay the doctor was less than the
fall in income he would suffer if he had to change his mode of operation at
this location, abandon his operation or move his confectionery business to
some other location. The solution of the problem depends essentially on
whether the continued use of the machinery adds more to the confectioner's
income than it subtracts from the doctor's.[9] But now consider the situation if
the confectioner had won the case. The confectioner would then have had the
right to continue operating his noise and vibration-generating machinery
without having to pay anything to the doctor. The boot would have been on
the other foot: the doctor would have had to pay the confectioner to induce
him to stop using the machinery. If the doctor's income would have fallen
more through continuance of the use of this machinery than it added to the
income of the confectioner, there would clearly be room for a bargain whereby
the doctor paid the confectioner to stop using the machinery. That is to say,
the circumstances in which it would not pay the confectioner to continue to
use the machinery and to compensate the doctor for the losses that this would
bring (if the doctor had the right to prevent the confectioner's using his

[8] Auscultation is the act of listening by ear or stethoscope in order to judge by sound
the condition of the body.

[9] Note that what is taken into account is the change in income after allowing for alterations in methods of production, location, character of product, etc.

machinery) would be those in which it would be in the interest of the doctor to make a payment to the confectioner which would induce him to discontinue the use of the machinery (if the confectioner had the right to operate the machinery). The basic conditions are exactly the same in this case as they were in the example of the cattle which destroyed crops. With costless market transactions, the decision of the courts concerning liability for damage would be without effect on the allocation of resources. It was of course the view of the judges that they were affecting the working of the economic system—and in a desirable direction. Any other decision would have had "a prejudicial effect upon the development of land for residential purposes," an argument which was elaborated by examining the example of a forge operating on a barren moor, which was later developed for residual purposes. The judges' view that they were settling how the land was to be used would be true only in the case in which the costs of carrying out the necessary market transactions exceeded the gain which might be achieved by any rearrangement of rights. And it would be desirable to preserve the areas (Wimpole Street or the moor) for residential or professional use (by giving non-industrial users the right to stop the noise, vibration, smoke, etc., by injunction) only if the value of the additional residential facilities obtained was greater than the value of cakes or iron lost. But of this the judges seem to have been unaware.

Another example of the same problem is furnished by the case of *Cooke v. Forbes*.[10] One process in the weaving of cocoa-nut fibre matting was to immerse it in bleaching liquids after which it was hung out to dry. Fumes from a manufacturer of sulphate of ammonia had the effect of turning the matting from a bright to a dull and blackish colour. The reason for this was that the bleaching liquid contained chloride of tin, which, when affected by sulphuretted hydrogen, is turned to a darker colour. An injunction was sought to stop the manufacturer from emitting the fumes. The lawyers for the defendant argued that if the plaintiff "were not to use . . . a particular bleaching liquid, their fibre would not be affected; that their process is unusual, not according to the custom of the trade, and even damaging to their own fabrics." The judge commented: ". . . it appears to me quite plain that a person has a right to carry on upon his own property a manufacturing process in which he uses chloride of tin, or any sort of metallic dye, and that his neighbour is not at liberty to pour in gas which will interfere with his manufacture. If it can be traced to the neighbour, then, I apprehend, clearly he will have a right to come here and ask for relief." But in view of the fact that the damage was accidental and occasional, that careful precautions were taken and that there was no exceptional risk, an injunction was refused, leaving the plaintiff to bring an action for damages if he wished. What the subsequent developments

[10] L. R. 5 Eq. 166 (1867–1868).

were I do not know. But it is clear that the situation is essentially the same as that found in *Sturges v. Bridgman,* except that the cocoa-nut fibre matting manufacturer could not secure an injunction but would have to seek damages from the sulphate of ammonia manufacturer. The economic analysis of the situation is exactly the same as with the cattle which destroyed crops. To avoid the damage, the sulphate of ammonia manufacturer could increase his precautions or move to another location. Either course would presumably increase his costs. Alternatively he could pay for the damage. This he would do if the payments for damage were less than the additional costs that would have to be incurred to avoid the damage. The payments for damage would then become part of the cost of production of sulphate of ammonia. Of course, if, as was suggested in the legal proceedings, the amount of damage could be eliminated by changing the bleaching agent (which would presumably increase the costs of the matting manufacturer) and if the additional cost was less than the damage that would otherwise occur, it should be possible for the two manufacturers to make a mutually satisfactory bargain whereby the new bleaching agent was used. Had the court decided against the matting manufacturer, as a consequence of which he would have had to suffer the damage without compensation, the allocation of resources would not have been affected. It would pay the matting manufacturer to change his bleaching agent if the additional cost involved was less than the reduction in damage. And since the matting manufacturer would be willing to pay the sulphate of ammonia manufacturer an amount up to his loss of income (the increase in costs or the damage suffered) if he would cease his activities, this loss of income would remain a cost of production for the manufacturer of sulphate of ammonia. This case is indeed analytically exactly the same as the cattle example.

Bryant v. Lefever[11] raised the problem of the smoke nuisance in a novel form. The plaintiff and the defendants were occupiers of adjoining houses, which were of about the same height.

Before 1876 the plaintiff was able to light a fire in any room of his house without the chimneys smoking; the two houses had remained in the same condition some thirty or forty years. In 1876 the defendants took down their house, and began to rebuild it. They carried up a wall by the side of the plaintiff's chimneys much beyond its original height, and stacked timber on the roof of their house, and thereby caused the plaintiff's chimneys to smoke whenever he lighted fires.

The reason, of course, why the chimneys smoked was that the erection of the wall and the stacking of the timber prevented the free circulation of air. In a trial before a jury, the plaintiff was awarded damages of £40. The case then went to the Court of Appeals where the judgment was reversed. Bramwell, L.J., argued:

[11] 4 C.P.D. 172 (1878–1879).

. . . it is said, and the jury have found, that the defendants have done that which caused a nuisance to the plaintiff's house. We think there is no evidence of this. No doubt there is a nuisance, but it is not of the defendant's causing. They have done nothing in causing the nuisance. Their house and their timber are harmless enough. It is the plaintiff who causes the nuisance by lighting a coal fire in a place the chimney of which is placed so near the defendants' wall, that the smoke does not escape, but comes into the house. Let the plaintiff cease to light his fire, let him move his chimney, let him carry it higher, and there would be no nuisance. Who then, causes it? It would be very clear that the plaintiff did, if he had built his house or chimney after the defendants had put up the timber on theirs, and it is really the same though he did so before the timber was there. But (what is in truth the same answer), if the defendants cause the nuisance, they have a right to do so. If the plaintiff has not the right to the passage of air, except subject to the defendants' right to build or put timber on their house, then his right is subject to their right, and though a nuisance follows from the exercise of their right, they are not liable.

And Cotton, L.J., said:

Here it is found that the erection of the defendants' wall has sensibly and materially interfered with the comfort of human existence in the plaintiff's house, and it is said this is a nuisance for which the defendants are liable. Ordinarily this is so, but the defendants have done so, not by sending on to the plaintiff's property any smoke or noxious vapour, but by interrupting the egress of smoke from the plaintiff's house in a way to which . . . the plaintiff has no legal right. The plaintiff creates the smoke, which interferes with his comfort. Unless he has . . . a right to get rid of this in a particular way which has been interfered with by the defendants, he cannot sue the defendants, because the smoke made by himself, for which he has not provided any effectual means of escape, causes him annoyance. It is as if a man tried to get rid of liquid filth arising on his own land by a drain into his neighbour's land. Until a right had been acquired by user, the neighbour might stop the drain without incurring liability by so doing. No doubt great inconvenience would be caused to the owner of the property on which the liquid filth arises. But the act of his neighbour would be a lawful act, and he would not be liable for the consequences attributable to the fact that the man had accumulated filth without providing any effectual means of getting rid of it.

I do not propose to show that any subsequent modification of the situation, as a result of bargains between the parties (conditioned by the cost of stacking the timber elsewhere, the cost of extending the chimney higher, etc.), would have exactly the same result whatever decision the courts had come to since this point has already been adequately dealt with in the discussion of the cattle example and the two previous cases. What I shall discuss is the argument of the judges in the Court of Appeals that the smoke nuisance was not caused by the man who erected the wall but by the man who lit the fires. The novelty of the situation is that the smoke nuisance was suffered by the man who lit the fires and not by some third person. The question is not a trivial

THE PROBLEM OF SOCIAL COST   13

one since it lies at the heart of the problem under discussion. Who caused the smoke nuisance? The answer seems fairly clear. The smoke nuisance was caused both by the man who built the wall *and* by the man who lit the fires. Given the fires, there would have been no smoke nuisance without the wall; given the wall, there would have been no smoke nuisance without the fires. Eliminate the wall *or* the fires and the smoke nuisance would disappear. On the marginal principle it is clear that *both* were responsible and *both* should be forced to include the loss of amenity due to the smoke as a cost in deciding whether to continue the activity which gives rise to the smoke. And given the possibility of market transactions, this is what would in fact happen. Although the wall-builder was not liable legally for the nuisance, as the man with the smoking chimneys would presumably be willing to pay a sum equal to the monetary worth to him of eliminating the smoke, this sum would therefore become for the wall-builder, a cost of continuing to have the high wall with the timber stacked on the roof.

The judges' contention that it was the man who lit the fires who alone caused the smoke nuisance is true only if we assume that the wall is the given factor. This is what the judges did by deciding that the man who erected the higher wall had a legal right to do so. The case would have been even more interesting if the smoke from the chimneys had injured the timber. Then it would have been the wall-builder who suffered the damage. The case would then have closely paralleled *Sturges v. Bridgman* and there can be little doubt that the man who lit the fires would have been liable for the ensuing damage to the timber, in spite of the fact that no damage had occurred until the high wall was built by the man who owned the timber.

Judges have to decide on legal liability but this should not confuse economists about the nature of the economic problem involved. In the case of the cattle and the crops, it is true that there would be no crop damage without the cattle. It is equally true that there would be no crop damage without the crops. The doctor's work would not have been disturbed if the confectioner had not worked his machinery; but the machinery would have disturbed no one if the doctor had not set up his consulting room in that particular place. The matting was blackened by the fumes from the sulphate of ammonia manufacturer; but no damage would have occurred if the matting manufacturer had not chosen to hang out his matting in a particular place and to use a particular bleaching agent. If we are to discuss the problem in terms of causation, both parties cause the damage. If we are to attain an optimum allocation of resources, it is therefore desirable that both parties should take the harmful effect (the nuisance) into account in deciding on their course of action. It is one of the beauties of a smoothly operating pricing system that, as has already been explained, the fall in the value of production due to the harmful effect would be a cost for both parties.

Bass v. Gregory[12] will serve as an excellent final illustration of the problem. The plaintiffs were the owners and tenant of a public house called the Jolly Anglers. The defendant was the owner of some cottages and a yard adjoining the Jolly Anglers. Under the public house was a cellar excavated in the rock. From the cellar, a hole or shaft had been cut into an old well situated in the defendant's yard. The well therefore became the ventilating shaft for the cellar. The cellar "had been used for a particular purpose in the process of brewing, which, without ventilation, could not be carried on." The cause of the action was that the defendant removed a grating from the mouth of the well, "so as to stop or prevent the free passage of air from [the] cellar upwards through the well. . . ." What caused the defendant to take this step is not clear from the report of the case. Perhaps "the air . . . impregnated by the brewing operations" which "passed up the well and out into the open air" was offensive to him. At any rate, he preferred to have the well in his yard stopped up. The court had first to determine whether the owners of the public house could have a legal right to a current of air. If they were to have such a right, this case would have to be distinguished from *Bryant v. Lefever* (already considered). This, however, presented no difficulty. In this case, the current of air was confined to "a strictly defined channel." In the case of *Bryant v. Lefever*, what was involved was "the general current of air common to all mankind." The judge therefore held that the owners of the public house could have the right to a current of air whereas the owner of the private house in *Bryant v. Lefever* could not. An economist might be tempted to add "but the air moved all the same." However, all that had been decided at this stage of the argument was that there could be a legal right, not that the owners of the public house possessed it. But evidence showed that the shaft from the cellar to the well had existed for over forty years and that the use of the well as a ventilating shaft must have been known to the owners of the yard since the air, when it emerged, smelt of the brewing operations. The judge therefore held that the public house had such a right by the "doctrine of lost grant." This doctrine states "that if a legal right is proved to have existed and been exercised for a number of years the law ought to presume that it had a legal origin."[13] So the owner of the cottages and yard had to unstop the well and endure the smell.

---

[12] 25 Q.B.D. 481 (1890).

[13] It may be asked why a lost grant could not also be presumed in the case of the confectioner who had operated one mortar for more than 60 years. The answer is that until the doctor built the consulting room at the end of his garden there was no nuisance. So the nuisance had not continued for many years. It is true that the confectioner in his affidavit referred to "an invalid lady who occupied the house upon one occasion, about thirty years before" who "requested him if possible to discontinue the use of the mortars before eight o'clock in the morning" and that there was some evidence that the garden wall had been subjected to vibration. But the court had little difficulty in disposing of this line of argument: ". . . this vibration, even if it existed at all, was so slight, and the com-

THE PROBLEM OF SOCIAL COST   15

The reasoning employed by the courts in determining legal rights will often seem strange to an economist because many of the factors on which the decision turns are, to an economist, irrelevant. Because of this, situations which are, from an economic point of view, identical will be treated quite differently by the courts. The economic problem in all cases of harmful effects is how to maximise the value of production. In the case of *Bass v. Gregory* fresh air was drawn in through the well which facilitated the production of beer but foul air was expelled through the well which made life in the adjoining houses less pleasant. The economic problem was to decide which to choose: a lower cost of beer and worsened amenities in adjoining houses or a higher cost of beer and improved amenities. In deciding this question, the "doctrine of lost grant" is about as relevant as the colour of the judge's eyes. But it has to be remembered that the immediate question faced by the courts is *not* what shall be done by whom *but* who has the legal right to do what. It is always possible to modify by transactions on the market the initial legal delimitation of rights. And, of course, if such market transactions are costless, such a rearrangement of rights will always take place if it would lead to an increase in the value of production.

VI. The Cost of Market Transactions Taken into Account

The argument has proceeded up to this point on the assumption (explicit in Sections III and IV and tacit in Section V) that there were no costs involved in carrying out market transactions. This is, of course, a very unrealistic assumption. In order to carry out a market transaction it is necessary to discover who it is that one wishes to deal with, to inform people that one wishes to deal and on what terms, to conduct negotiations leading up to a bargain, to draw up the contract, to undertake the inspection needed to make sure that the terms of the contract are being observed, and so on. These operations are often extremely costly, sufficiently costly at any rate to prevent many transactions that would be carried out in a world in which the pricing system worked without cost.

In earlier sections, when dealing with the problem of the rearrangement of legal rights through the market, it was argued that such a rearrangement would be made through the market whenever this would lead to an increase in the value of production. But this assumed costless market transactions. Once the costs of carrying out market transactions are taken into account it is clear that such a rearrangement of rights will only be undertaken when the increase in the value of production consequent upon the rearrangement

---

plaint, if it can be called a complaint, of the invalid lady . . . was of so trifling a character, that . . . the Defendant's acts would not have given rise to any proceeding either at law or in equity" (11 Ch.D. 863). That is, the confectioner had not committed a nuisance until the doctor built his consulting room.

is greater than the costs which would be involved in bringing it about. When it is less, the granting of an injunction (or the knowledge that it would be granted) or the liability to pay damages may result in an activity being discontinued (or may prevent its being started) which would be undertaken if market transactions were costless. In these conditions the initial delimitation of legal rights does have an effect on the efficiency with which the economic system operates. One arrangement of rights may bring about a greater value of production than any other. But unless this is the arrangement of rights established by the legal system, the costs of reaching the same result by altering and combining rights through the market may be so great that this optimal arrangement of rights, and the greater value of production which it would bring, may never be achieved. The part played by economic considerations in the process of delimiting legal rights will be discussed in the next section. In this section, I will take the initial delimitation of rights and the costs of carrying out market transactions as given.

It is clear that an alternative form of economic organisation which could achieve the same result at less cost than would be incurred by using the market would enable the value of production to be raised. As I explained many years ago, the firm represents such an alternative to organising production through market transactions.[14] Within the firm individual bargains between the various cooperating factors of production are eliminated and for a market transaction is substituted an administrative decision. The rearrangement of production then takes place without the need for bargains between the owners of the factors of production. A landowner who has control of a large tract of land may devote his land to various uses taking into account the effect that the interrelations of the various activities will have on the net return of the land, thus rendering unnecessary bargains between those undertaking the various activities. Owners of a large building or of several adjoining properties in a given area may act in much the same way. In effect, using our earlier terminology, the firm would acquire the legal rights of all the parties and the rearrangement of activities would not follow on a rearrangement of rights by contract, but as a result of an administrative decision as to how the rights should be used.

It does not, of course, follow that the administrative costs of organising a transaction through a firm are inevitably less than the costs of the market transactions which are superseded. But where contracts are peculiarly difficult to draw up and an attempt to describe what the parties have agreed to do or not to do (e.g. the amount and kind of a smell or noise that they may make or will not make) would necessitate a lengthy and highly involved document, and, where, as is probable, a long-term contract would be desir-

---

[14] See Coase, The Nature of the Firm, 4 Economica, New Series, 386 (1937). Reprinted in Readings in Price Theory, 331 (1952).

THE PROBLEM OF SOCIAL COST   17

able;[15] it would be hardly surprising if the emergence of a firm or the extension of the activities of an existing firm was not the solution adopted on many occasions to deal with the problem of harmful effects. This solution would be adopted whenever the administrative costs of the firm were less than the costs of the market transactions that it supersedes and the gains which would result from the rearrangement of activities greater than the firm's costs of organising them. I do not need to examine in great detail the character of this solution since I have explained what is involved in my earlier article.

But the firm is not the only possible answer to this problem. The administrative costs of organising transactions within the firm may also be high, and particularly so when many diverse activities are brought within the control of a single organisation. In the standard case of a smoke nuisance, which may affect a vast number of people engaged in a wide variety of activities, the administrative costs might well be so high as to make any attempt to deal with the problem within the confines of a single firm impossible. An alternative solution is direct Government regulation. Instead of instituting a legal system of rights which can be modified by transactions on the market, the government may impose regulations which state what people must or must not do and which have to be obeyed. Thus, the government (by statute or perhaps more likely through an administrative agency) may, to deal with the problem of smoke nuisance, decree that certain methods of production should or should not be used (e.g. that smoke preventing devices should be installed or that coal or oil should not be burned) or may confine certain types of business to certain districts (zoning regulations).

The government is, in a sense, a super-firm (but of a very special kind) since it is able to influence the use of factors of production by administrative decision. But the ordinary firm is subject to checks in its operations because of the competition of other firms, which might administer the same activities at lower cost and also because there is always the alternative of market transactions as against organisation within the firm if the administrative costs become too great. The government is able, if it wishes, to avoid the market altogether, which a firm can never do. The firm has to make market agreements with the owners of the factors of production that it uses. Just as the government can conscript or seize property, so it can decree that factors of production should only be used in such-and-such a way. Such authoritarian methods save a lot of trouble (for those doing the organising). Furthermore, the government has at its disposal the police and the other law enforcement agencies to make sure that its regulations are carried out.

It is clear that the government has powers which might enable it to get some things done at a lower cost than could a private organisation (or at any

[15] For reasons explained in my earlier article, see Readings in Price Theory, n. 14 at 337.

rate one without special governmental powers). But the governmental administrative machine is not itself costless. It can, in fact, on occasion be
extremely costly. Furthermore, there is no reason to suppose that the restrictive and zoning regulations, made by a fallible administration subject to
political pressures and operating without any competitive check, will necessarily always be those which increase the efficiency with which the economic system operates. Furthermore, such general regulations which must
apply to a wide variety of cases will be enforced in some cases in which they
are clearly inappropriate. From these considerations it follows that direct
governmental regulation will not necessarily give better results than leaving
the problem to be solved by the market or the firm. But equally there is no
reason why, on occasion, such governmental administrative regulation should
not lead to an improvement in economic efficiency. This would seem particularly likely when, as is normally the case with the smoke nuisance, a large
number of people are involved and in which therefore the costs of handling
the problem through the market or the firm may be high.

There is, of course, a further alternative, which is to do nothing about
the problem at all. And given that the costs involved in solving the problem
by regulations issued by the governmental administrative machine will often
be heavy (particularly if the costs are interpreted to include all the consequences which follow from the Government engaging in this kind of activity),
it will no doubt be commonly the case that the gain which would come from
regulating the actions which give rise to the harmful effects will be less than
the costs involved in Government regulation.

The discussion of the problem of harmful effects in this section (when the
costs of market transactions are taken into account) is extremely inadequate.
But at least it has made clear that the problem is one of choosing the appropriate social arrangement for dealing with the harmful effects. All solutions
have costs and there is no reason to suppose that government regulation is
called for simply because the problem is not well handled by the market or
the firm. Satisfactory views on policy can only come from a patient study
of how, in practice, the market, firms and governments handle the problem
of harmful effects. Economists need to study the work of the broker in
bringing parties together, the effectiveness of restrictive covenants, the problems of the large-scale real-estate development company, the operation of Government zoning and other regulating activities. It is my belief that economists,
and policy-makers generally, have tended to over-estimate the advantages
which come from governmental regulation. But this belief, even if justified,
does not do more than suggest that government regulation should be curtailed. It does not tell us where the boundary line should be drawn. This, it
seems to me, has to come from a detailed investigation of the actual results

THE PROBLEM OF SOCIAL COST   19

of handling the problem in different ways. But it would be unfortunate if this investigation were undertaken with the aid of a faulty economic analysis. The aim of this article is to indicate what the economic approach to the problem should be.

VII. THE LEGAL DELIMITATION OF RIGHTS AND THE ECONOMIC PROBLEM

The discussion in Section V not only served to illustrate the argument but also afforded a glimpse at the legal approach to the problem of harmful effects. The cases considered were all English but a similar selection of American cases could easily be made and the character of the reasoning would have been the same. Of course, if market transactions were costless, all that matters (questions of equity apart) is that the rights of the various parties should be well-defined and the results of legal actions easy to forecast. But as we have seen, the situation is quite different when market transactions are so costly as to make it difficult to change the arrangement of rights established by the law. In such cases, the courts directly influence economic activity. It would therefore seem desirable that the courts should understand the economic consequences of their decisions and should, insofar as this is possible without creating too much uncertainty about the legal position itself, take these consequences into account when making their decisions. Even when it is possible to change the legal delimitation of rights through market transactions, it is obviously desirable to reduce the need for such transactions and thus reduce the employment of resources in carrying them out.

A thorough examination of the presuppositions of the courts in trying such cases would be of great interest but I have not been able to attempt it. Nevertheless it is clear from a cursory study that the courts have often recognized the economic implications of their decisions and are aware (as many economists are not) of the reciprocal nature of the problem. Furthermore, from time to time, they take these economic implications into account, along with other factors, in arriving at their decisions. The American writers on this subject refer to the question in a more explicit fashion than do the British. Thus, to quote Prosser on Torts, a person may

make use of his own property or . . . conduct his own affairs at the expense of some harm to his neighbors. He may operate a factory whose noise and smoke cause some discomfort to others, so long as he keeps within reasonable bounds. It is only when his conduct is unreasonable, *in the light of its utility and the harm which results* [italics added], that it becomes a nuisance. . . . . As it was said in an ancient case in regard to candle-making in a town, "Le utility del chose excusera le noisomeness del stink."

The world must have factories, smelters, oil refineries, noisy machinery and blasting, even at the expense of some inconvenience to those in the vicinity and the plaintiff may be required to accept some not unreasonable discomfort for the general good.[16]

The standard British writers do not state as explicitly as this that a comparison between the utility and harm produced is an element in deciding whether a harmful effect should be considered a nuisance. But similar views, if less strongly expressed, are to be found.[17] The doctrine that the harmful effect must be substantial before the court will act is, no doubt, in part a reflection of the fact that there will almost always be some gain to offset the harm. And in the reports of individual cases, it is clear that the judges have had in mind what would be lost as well as what would be gained in deciding whether to grant an injunction or award damages. Thus, in refusing to prevent the destruction of a prospect by a new building, the judge stated:

I know no general rule of common law, which . . . says, that building so as to stop another's prospect is a nuisance. Was that the case, there could be no great towns; and I must grant injunctions to all the new buildings in this town. . . .[18]

In *Webb v. Bird*[19] it was decided that it was not a nuisance to build a schoolhouse so near a windmill as to obstruct currents of air and hinder the working of the mill. An early case seems to have been decided in an opposite direction. Gale commented:

In old maps of London a row of windmills appears on the heights to the north of London. Probably in the time of King James it was thought an alarming circumstance, as affecting the supply of food to the city, that anyone should build so near them as to take the wind out from their sails.[20]

In one of the cases discussed in section V, *Sturges v. Bridgman,* it seems clear that the judges were thinking of the economic consequences of alternative decisions. To the argument that if the principle that they seemed to be following

[16] See W. L. Prosser, The Law of Torts 398–99, 412 (2d ed. 1955). The quotation about the ancient case concerning candle-making is taken from Sir James Fitzjames Stephen, A General View of the Criminal Law of England 106 (1890). Sir James Stephen gives no reference. He perhaps had in mind *Rex. v. Ronkett,* included in Seavey, Keeton and Thurston, Cases on Torts 604 (1950). A similar view to that expressed by Prosser is to be found in F. V. Harper and F. James, The Law of Torts 67–74 (1956); Restatement, Torts §§826, 827 and 828.

[17] See Winfield on Torts 541–48 (6th ed. T. E. Lewis 1954); Salmond on the Law of Torts 181–90 (12th ed. R.F.V. Heuston 1957); H. Street, The Law of Torts 221–29 (1959).

[18] Attorney General v. Doughty, 2 Ves. Sen. 453, 28 Eng. Rep. 290 (Ch. 1752). Compare in this connection the statement of an American judge, quoted in Prosser, op. cit. supra n. 16 at 413 n. 54: "Without smoke, Pittsburgh would have remained a very pretty village," Musmanno, J., in Versailles Borough v. McKeesport Coal & Coke Co., 1935, 83 Pitts. Leg. J. 379, 385.

[19] 10 C.B. (N.S.) 268, 142 Eng. Rep. 445 (1861); 13 C.B. (N.S.) 841, 143 Eng. Rep. 332 (1863).

[20] See Gale on Easements 238, n. 6 (13th ed. M. Bowles 1959).

THE PROBLEM OF SOCIAL COST   21

were carried out to its logical consequences, it would result in the most serious practical inconveniences, for a man might go—say into the midst of the tanneries of
Bermondsey, or into any other locality devoted to any particular trade or manufacture of a noisy or unsavoury character, and by building a private residence upon
a vacant piece of land put a stop to such trade or manufacture altogether,

the judges answered that

whether anything is a nuisance or not is a question to be determined, not merely by
an abstract consideration of the thing itself, but in reference to its circumstances;
What would be a nuisance in *Belgrave Square* would not necessarily be so in *Bermondsey;* and where a locality is devoted to a particular trade or manufacture carried
on by the traders or manufacturers in a particular and established manner not constituting a public nuisance, Judges and juries would be justified in finding, and may be
trusted to find, that the trade or manufacture so carried on in that locality is not a
private or actionable wrong.[21]

That the character of the neighborhood is relevant in deciding whether something is, or is not, a nuisance, is definitely established.

He who dislikes the noise of traffic must not set up his abode in the heart of a
great city. He who loves peace and quiet must not live in a locality devoted to
the business of making boilers or steamships.[22]

What has emerged has been described as "planning and zoning by the judici-
ary."[23] Of course there are sometimes considerable difficulties in applying
the criteria.[24]

An interesting example of the problem is found in *Adams v. Ursell*[25] in
which a fried fish shop in a predominantly working-class district was set up
near houses of "a much better character." England without fish-and-chips is
a contradiction in terms and the case was clearly one of high importance.
The judge commented:

It was urged that an injunction would cause great hardship to the defendant
and to the poor people who get food at his shop. The answer to that is that it does
not follow that the defendant cannot carry on his business in another more suitable
place somewhere in the neighbourhood. It by no means follows that because a
fried fish shop is a nuisance in one place it is a nuisance in another.

In fact, the injunction which restrained Mr. Ursell from running his shop
did not even extend to the whole street. So he was presumably able to move
to other premises near houses of "a much worse character," the inhabitants

[21] 11 Ch.D. 865 (1879).

[22] Salmond on the Law of Torts 182 (12th ed. R.F.V. Heuston 1957).

[23] C. M. Haar, Land-Use Planning, A Casebook on the Use, Misuse, and Re-use of Urban
Land 95 (1959).

[24] See, for example, Rushmer v. Polsue and Alfieri, Ltd. [1906] 1 Ch. 234, which deals with
the case of a house in a quiet situation in a noisy district.

[25] [1913] 1 Ch. 269.

of which would no doubt consider the availability of fish-and-chips to out-weigh the pervading odour and "fog or mist" so graphically described by the plaintiff. Had there been no other "more suitable place in the neighbour-hood," the case would have been more difficult and the decision might have been different. What would "the poor people" have had for food? No English judge would have said: "Let them eat cake."

The courts do not always refer very clearly to the economic problem posed by the cases brought before them but it seems probable that in the interpre-tation of words and phrases like "reasonable" or "common or ordinary use" there is some recognition, perhaps largely unconscious and certainly not very explicit, of the economic aspects of the questions at issue. A good example of this would seem to be the judgment in the Court of Appeals in *Andreae v. Selfridge and Company Ltd.*[26] In this case, a hotel (in Wigmore Street) was situated on part of an island site. The remainder of the site was acquired by Selfridges which demolished the existing buildings in order to erect another in their place. The hotel suffered a loss of custom in consequence of the noise and dust caused by the demolition. The owner of the hotel brought an action against Selfridges for damages. In the lower court, the hotel was awarded £4,500 damages. The case was then taken on appeal.

The judge who had found for the hotel proprietor in the lower court said:

I cannot regard what the defendants did on the site of the first operation as having been commonly done in the ordinary use and occupation of land or houses. It is neither usual nor common, in this country, for people to excavate a site to a depth of 60 feet and then to erect upon that site a steel framework and fasten the steel frames together with rivets. . . . Nor is it, I think, a common or ordinary use of land, in this country, to act as the defendants did when they were dealing with the site of their second operation—namely, to demolish all the houses that they had to demolish, five or six of them I think, if not more, and to use for the purpose of demolishing them pneumatic hammers.

Sir Wilfred Greene, M.R., speaking for the Court of Appeals, first noted

that when one is dealing with temporary operations, such as demolition and re-build-ing, everybody has to put up with a certain amount of discomfort, because operations of that kind cannot be carried on at all without a certain amount of noise and a certain amount of dust. Therefore, the rule with regard to interference must be read subject to this qualification. . . .

He then referred to the previous judgment:

With great respect to the learned judge, I take the view that he has not approached this matter from the correct angle. It seems to me that it is not possible to say . . . that the type of demolition, excavation and construction in which the defendant company was engaged in the course of these operations was of such an abnormal and unusual nature as to prevent the qualification to which I have referred coming

[26] [1938] 1 Ch. 1.

THE PROBLEM OF SOCIAL COST   23

into operation. It seems to me that, when the rule speaks of the common or ordinary use of land, it does not mean that the methods of using land and building on it are in some way to be stabilised for ever. As time goes on new inventions or new methods enable land to be more profitably used, either by digging down into the earth or by mounting up into the skies. Whether, from other points of view, that is a matter which is desirable for humanity is neither here nor there; but it is part of the normal use of land, to make use upon your land, in the matter of construction, of what particular type and what particular depth of foundations and particular height of building may be reasonable, in the circumstances, and in view of the developments of the day. . . . Guests at hotels are very easily upset. People coming to this hotel, who were accustomed to a quiet outlook at the back, coming back and finding demolition and building going on, may very well have taken the view that the particular merit of this hotel no longer existed. That would be a misfortune for the plaintiff; but assuming that there was nothing wrong in the defendant company's works, assuming the defendant company was carrying on the demolition and its building, productive of noise though it might be, with all reasonable skill, and taking all reasonable precautions not to cause annoyance to its neighbors, then the plaintiff might lose all her clients in the hotel because they have lost the amenities of an open and quiet place behind, but she would have no cause of complaint. . . . [But those] who say that their interference with the comfort of their neighbors is justified because their operations are normal and usual and conducted with proper care and skill are under a specific duty . . . to use that reasonable and proper care and skill. It is not a correct attitude to take to say: 'We will go on and do what we like until somebody complains!' . . . Their duty is to take proper precautions and to see that the nuisance is reduced to a minimum. It is no answer for them to say: 'But this would mean that we should have to do the work more slowly than we would like to do it, or it would involve putting us to some extra expense.' All these questions are matters of common sense and degree, and quite clearly it would be unreasonable to expect people to conduct their work so slowly or so expensively, for the purpose of preventing a transient inconvenience, that the cost and trouble would be prohibitive. . . . In this case, the defendant company's attitude seems to have been to go on until somebody complained, and, further, that its desire to hurry its work and conduct it according to its own ideas and its own convenience was to prevail if there was a real conflict between it and the comfort of its neighbors. That . . . is not carrying out the obligation of using reasonable care and skill. . . . The effect comes to this . . . the plaintiff suffered an actionable nuisance; . . . she is entitled, not to a nominal sum, but to a substantial sum, based upon those principles . . . but in arriving at the sum . . . I have discounted any loss of custom . . . which might be due to the general loss of amenities owing to what was going on at the back. . . .

The upshot was that the damages awarded were reduced from £4,500 to £1,000.

The discussion in this section has, up to this point, been concerned with court decisions arising out of the common law relating to nuisance. Delimitation of rights in this area also comes about because of statutory enactments. Most economists would appear to assume that the aim of governmental action in this field is to extend the scope of the law of nuisance by designating as nuisances activities which would not be recognized as such by the common law. And there can be no doubt that some statutes, for example, the Public Health Acts, have had this effect. But not all Government enactments are of this kind. The effect of much of the legislation in this area is to protect businesses from the claims of those they have harmed by their actions. There is a long list of legalized nuisances.

The position has been summarized in *Halsbury's Laws of England* as follows:

Where the legislature directs that a thing shall in all events be done or authorises certain works at a particular place for a specific purposes or grants powers with the intention that they shall be exercised, although leaving some discretion as to the mode of exercise, no action will lie at common law for nuisance or damage which is the inevitable result of carrying out the statutory powers so conferred. This is so whether the act causing the damage is authorised for public purposes or private profit. Acts done under powers granted by persons to whom Parliament has delegated authority to grant such powers, for example, under provisional orders of the Board of Trade, are regarded as having been done under statutory authority. In the absence of negligence it seems that a body exercising statutory powers will not be liable to an action merely because it might, by acting in a different way, have minimised an injury.

Instances are next given of freedom from liability for acts authorized:

An action has been held not to be against a body exercising its statutory powers without negligence in respect of the flooding of land by water escaping from watercourses, from water pipes, from drains, or from a canal; the escape of fumes from sewers; the escape of sewage: the subsidence of a road over a sewer; vibration or noise caused by a railway; fires caused by authorised acts; the pollution of a stream where statutory requirements to use the best known method of purifying before discharging the effluent have been satisfied; interference with a telephone or telegraph system by an electric tramway; the insertion of poles for tramways in the subsoil; annoyance caused by things reasonably necessary for the excavation of authorised works; accidental damage caused by the placing of a grating in a roadway; the escape of tar acid; or interference with the access of a frontager by a street shelter or safety railings on the edge of a pavement.[27]

The legal position in the United States would seem to be essentially the same as in England, except that the power of the legislatures to authorize what would otherwise be nuisances under the common law, at least without giving compensation to the person harmed, is somewhat more limited, as it is subject to constitutional restrictions.[28] Nonetheless, the power is there and cases more or less identical with the English cases can be found. The

[27] See 30 Halsbury, Law of England 690–91 (3d ed. 1960), Article on Public Authorities and Public Officers.

[28] See Prosser, op. cit. supra n. 16 at 421; Harper and James, op. cit. supra n. 16 at 86–87.

THE PROBLEM OF SOCIAL COST   25

question has arisen in an acute form in connection with airports and the operation of aeroplanes. The case of *Delta Air Corporation v. Kersey, Kersey v. City of Atlanta*[29] is a good example. Mr. Kersey bought land and built a house on it. Some years later the City of Atlanta constructed an airport on land immediately adjoining that of Mr. Kersey. It was explained that his property was "a quiet, peaceful and proper location for a home before the airport was built, but dust, noises and low flying of airplanes caused by the operation of the airport have rendered his property unsuitable as a home," a state of affairs which was described in the report of the case with a wealth of distressing detail. The judge first referred to an earlier case, *Thrasher v. City of Atlanta*[30] in which it was noted that the City of Atlanta had been expressly authorized to operate an airport.

By this franchise aviation was recognised as a lawful business and also as an enterprise affected with a public interest . . . all persons using [the airport] in the manner contemplated by law are within the protection and immunity of the franchise granted by the municipality. An airport is not a nuisance per se, although it might become such from the manner of its construction or operation.

Since aviation was a lawful business affected with a public interest and the construction of the airport was autorized by statute, the judge next referred to *Georgia Railroad and Banking Co. v. Maddox*[31] in which it was said:

Where a railroad terminal yard is located and its construction authorized, under statutory powers, if it be constructed and operated in a proper manner, it cannot be adjudged a nuisance. Accordingly, injuries and inconveniences to persons residing near such a yard, from noises of locomotives, rumbling of cars, vibrations produced thereby, and smoke, cinders, soot and the like, which result from the ordinary and necessary, therefore proper, use and operation of such a yard, are not nuisances, but are the necessary concomitants of the franchise granted.

In view of this, the judge decided that the noise and dust complained of by Mr. Kersey "may be deemed to be incidental to the proper operation of an airport, and as such they cannot be said to constitute a nuisance." But the complaint against low flying was different:

. . . can it be said that flights . . . at such a low height [25 to 50 feet above Mr. Kersey's house] as to be imminently dangerous to . . . life and health . . . are a necessary concomitant of an airport? We do not think this question can be answered in the affirmative. No reason appears why the city could not obtain lands of an area [sufficiently large] . . . as not to require such low flights. . . . For the sake of public convenience adjoining-property owners must suffer such inconvenience from noise and dust as result from the usual and proper operation of an airport, but their private rights are entitled to preference in the eyes of the law where the inconvenience is not one demanded by a properly constructed and operated airport.

[29] Supreme Court of Georgia. 193 Ga. 862, 20 S.E. 2d 245 (1942).

[30] 178 Ga. 514, 173 S.E. 817 (1934).   [31] 116 Ga. 64, 42 S.E. 315 (1902).

Of course this assumed that the City of Atlanta could prevent the low flying and continue to operate the airport. The judge therefore added:

From all that appears, the conditions causing the low flying may be remedied; but if on the trial it should appear that it is indispensable to the public interest that the airport should continue to be operated in its present condition, it may be said that the petitioner should be denied injunctive relief.

In the course of another aviation case, *Smith v. New England Aircraft Co.*,[32] the court surveyed the law in the United States regarding the legalizing of nuisances and it is apparent that, in the broad, it is very similar to that found in England:

It is the proper function of the legislative department of government in the exercise of the police power to consider the problems and risks that arise from the use of new inventions and endeavor to adjust private rights and harmonize conflicting interests by comprehensive statutes for the public welfare. . . . There are . . . analogies where the invasion of the airspace over underlying land by noise, smoke, vibration, dust and disagreeable odors, having been authorized by the legislative department of government and not being in effect a condemnation of the property although in some measure depreciating its market value, must be borne by the landowner without compensation or remedy. Legislative sanction makes that lawful which otherwise might be a nuisance. Examples of this are damages to adjacent land arising from smoke, vibration and noise in the operation of a railroad . . . ; the noise of ringing factory bells . . . ; the abatement of nuisances . . . ; the erection of steam engines and furnaces . . . ; unpleasant odors connected with sewers, oil refining and storage of naphtha. . . .

Most economists seem to be unaware of all this. When they are prevented from sleeping at night by the roar of jet planes overhead (publicly authorized and perhaps publicly operated), are unable to think (or rest) in the day because of the noise and vibration from passing trains (publicly authorized and perhaps publicly operated), find it difficult to breathe because of the odour from a local sewage farm (publicly authorized and perhaps publicly operated) and are unable to escape because their driveways are blocked by a road obstruction (without any doubt, publicly devised), their nerves frayed and mental balance disturbed, they proceed to declaim about the disadvantages of private enterprise and the need for Government regulation.

While most economists seem to be under a misapprehension concerning the character of the situation with which they are dealing, it is also the case that the activities which they would like to see stopped or curtailed may well be socially justified. It is all a question of weighing up the gains that would accrue from eliminating these harmful effects against the gains that accrue from allowing them to continue. Of course, it is likely that an extension of Government economic activity will often lead to this protection against

[32] 270 Mass. 511, 523, 170 N.E. 385, 390 (1930).

action for nuisance being pushed further than is desirable. For one thing, the Government is likely to look with a benevolent eye on enterprises which it is itself promoting. For another, it is possible to describe the committing of a nuisance by public enterprise in a much more pleasant way than when the same thing is done by private enterprise. In the words of Lord Justice Sir Alfred Denning:

... the significance of the social revolution of today is that, whereas in the past the balance was much too heavily in favor of the rights of property and freedom of contract, Parliament has repeatedly intervened so as to give the public good its proper place.[33]

There can be little doubt that the Welfare State is likely to bring an extension of that immunity from liability for damage, which economists have been in the habit of condemning (although they have tended to assume that this immunity was a sign of too little Government intervention in the economic system). For example, in Britain, the powers of local authorities are regarded as being either absolute or conditional. In the first category, the local authority has no discretion in exercising the power conferred on it. "The absolute power may be said to cover all the necessary consequences of its direct operation even if such consequences amount to nuisance." On the other hand, a conditional power may only be exercised in such a way that the consequences do not constitute a nuisance.

It is the intention of the legislature which determines whether a power is absolute or conditional. . . . [As] there is the possibility that the social policy of the legislature may change from time to time, a power which in one era would be construed as being conditional, might in another era be interpreted as being absolute in order to further the policy of the Welfare State. This point is one which should be borne in mind when considering some of the older cases upon this aspect of the law of nuisance.[34]

It would seem desirable to summarize the burden of this long section. The problem which we face in dealing with actions which have harmful effects is not simply one of restraining those responsible for them. What has to be decided is whether the gain from preventing the harm is greater than the loss which would be suffered elsewhere as a result of stopping the action which produces the harm. In a world in which there are costs of rearranging the rights established by the legal system, the courts, in cases relating to nuisance, are, in effect, making a decision on the economic problem and determining how resources are to be employed. It was argued that the courts are conscious of this and that they often make, although not always in a very explicit fashion, a comparison between what would be gained and what lost by preventing

[33] See Sir Alfred Denning, Freedom Under the Law 71 (1949).

[34] M. B. Cairns, The Law of Tort in Local Government 28-32 (1954).

actions which have harmful effects. But the delimitation of rights is also the result of statutory enactments. Here we also find evidence of an appreciation of the reciprocal nature of the problem. While statutory enactments add to the list of nuisances, action is also taken to legalize what would otherwise be nuisances under the common law. The kind of situation which economists are prone to consider as requiring corrective Government action is, in fact, often the result of Government action. Such action is not necessarily unwise. But there is a real danger that extensive Government intervention in the economic system may lead to the protection of those responsible for harmful effects being carried too far.

VIII. Pigou's Treatment in "The Economics of Welfare"

The fountainhead for the modern economic analysis of the problem discussed in this article is Pigou's *Economics of Welfare* and, in particular, that section of Part II which deals with divergences between social and private net products which come about because

one person A, in the course of rendering some service, for which payment is made, to a second person B, incidentally also renders services or disservices to other persons (not producers of like services), of such a sort that payment cannot be exacted from the benefited parties or compensation enforced on behalf of the injured parties.[35]

Pigou tells us that his aim in Part II of *The Economics of Welfare* is

to ascertain how far the free play of self-interest, acting under the existing legal system, tends to distribute the country's resources in the way most favorable to the production of a large national dividend, and how far it is feasible for State action to improve upon 'natural' tendencies.[36]

To judge from the first part of this statement, Pigou's purpose is to discover whether any improvements could be made in the existing arrangements which determine the use of resources. Since Pigou's conclusion is that improvements could be made, one might have expected him to continue by saying that he proposed to set out the changes required to bring them about. Instead, Pigou adds a phrase which contrasts "natural" tendencies with State action, which seems in some sense to equate the present arrangements with "natural" tendencies and to imply that what is required to bring about these improvements is State action (if feasible). That this is more or less Pigou's position is evident from Chapter I of Part II.[37] Pigou starts by referring to "optimistic

---

[35] A. C. Pigou, The Economics of Welfare 183 (4th ed. 1932). My references will all be to the fourth edition but the argument and examples examined in this article remained substantially unchanged from the first edition in 1920 to the fourth in 1932. A large part (but not all) of this analysis had appeared previously in Wealth and Welfare (1912).

[36] *Id.* at xii.

[37] *Id.* at 127-30.

THE PROBLEM OF SOCIAL COST   29

followers of the classical economists"[38] who have argued that the value of production would be maximised if the Government refrained from any interference in the economic system and the economic arrangements were those which came about "naturally." Pigou goes on to say that if self-interest does promote economic welfare, it is because human institutions have been devised to make it so. (This part of Pigou's argument, which he develops with the aid of a quotation from Cannan, seems to me to be essentially correct.) Pigou concludes:

But even in the most advanced States there are failures and imperfections. . . . there are many obstacles that prevent a community's resources from being distributed . . . in the most efficient way. The study of these constitutes our present problem. . . . its purposes is essentially practical. It seeks to bring into clearer light some of the ways in which it now is, or eventually may become, feasible for governments to control the play of economic forces in such wise as to promote the economic welfare, and through that, the total welfare, of their citizens as a whole.[39]

Pigou's underlying thought would appear to be: Some have argued that no State action is needed. But the system has performed as well as it has because of State action. Nonetheless, there are still imperfections. What additional State action is required?

If this is a correct summary of Pigou's position, its inadequacy can be demonstrated by examining the first example he gives of a divergence between private and social products.

It might happen . . . that costs are thrown upon people not directly concerned, through, say, uncompensated damage done to surrounding woods by sparks from railway engines. All such effects must be included—some of them will be positive, others negative elements—in reckoning up the social net product of the marginal increment of any volume of resources turned into any use or place.[40]

The example used by Pigou refers to a real situation. In Britain, a railway does not normally have to compensate those who suffer damage by fire caused by sparks from an engine. Taken in conjunction with what he says in Chapter 9 of Part II, I take Pigou's policy recommendations to be, first, that there should be State action to correct this "natural" situation and, second, that the railways should be forced to compensate those whose woods are burnt. If this is a correct interpretation of Pigou's position, I would argue that the first recommendation is based on a misapprehension of the facts and that the second is not necessarily desirable.

[38] In *Wealth and Welfare*, Pigou attributes the "optimism" to Adam Smith himself and not to his followers. He there refers to the "highly optimistic theory of Adam Smith that the national dividend, in given circumstances of demand and supply, tends 'naturally' to a maximum" (p. 104).

[39] Pigou, op. cit. supra n. 35 at 129–30.

[40] *Id.* at 134.

Let us consider the legal position. Under the heading "Sparks from engines," we find the following in Halsbury's Laws of England:

If railway undertakers use steam engines on their railway without express statutory authority to do so, they are liable, irrespective of any negligence on their part, for fires caused by sparks from engines. Railway undertakers are, however, generally given statutory authority to use steam engines on their railway; accordingly, if an engine is constructed with the precautions which science suggests against fire and is used without negligence, they are not responsible at common law for any damage which may be done by sparks. . . . In the construction of an engine the undertaker is bound to use all the discoveries which science has put within its reach in order to avoid doing harm, provided they are such as it is reasonable to require the company to adopt, having proper regard to the likelihood of the damage and to the cost and convenience of the remedy; but it is not negligence on the part of an undertaker if it refuses to use an apparatus the efficiency of which is open to bona fide doubt.

To this general rule, there is a statutory exception arising from the Railway (Fires) Act, 1905, as amended in 1923. This concerns agricultural land or agricultural crops.

In such a case the fact that the engine was used under statutory powers does not affect the liability of the company in an action for the damage. . . . These provisions, however, only apply where the claim for damage . . . does not exceed £ 200, [£ 100 in the 1905 Act] and where written notice of the occurrence of the fire and the intention to claim has been sent to the company within seven days of the occurrence of the damage and particulars of the damage in writing showing the amount of the claim in money not exceeding £ 200 have been sent to the company within twenty-one days.

Agricultural land does not include moorland or buildings and agricultural crops do not include those led away or stacked.[41] I have not made a close study of the parliamentary history of this statutory exception, but to judge from debates in the House of Commons in 1922 and 1923, this exception was probably designed to help the smallholder.[42]

Let us return to Pigou's example of uncompensated damage to surrounding woods caused by sparks from railway engines. This is presumably intended to show how it is possible "for State action to improve on 'natural' tendencies." If we treat Pigou's example as referring to the position before 1905, or as being an arbitrary example (in that he might just as well have written "surrounding buildings" instead of "surrounding woods"), then it is clear that the reason why compensation was not paid must have been that the railway had statutory authority to run steam engines (which relieved it of liability for fires caused by sparks). That this was the legal position was

41 See 31 Halsbury, Laws of England 474–75 (3d ed. 1960), Article on Railways and Canals, from which this summary of the legal position, and all quotations, are taken.

42 See 152 H.C. Deb. 2622–63 (1922); 161 H.C. Deb. 2935–55 (1923).

THE PROBLEM OF SOCIAL COST   31

established in 1860, in a case, oddly enough, which concerned the burning of surrounding woods by a railway,[43] and the law on this point has not been changed (apart from the one exception) by a century of railway legislation, including nationalisation. If we treat Pigou's example of "uncompensated damage done to surrounding woods by sparks from railway engines" literally, and assume that it refers to the period after 1905, then it is clear that the reason why compensation was not paid must have been that the damage was more than £100 (in the first edition of *The Economics of Welfare*) or more than £200 (in later editions) or that the owner of the wood failed to notify the railway in writing within seven days of the fire or did not send particulars of the damage, in writing, within twenty-one days. In the real world, Pigou's example could only exist as a result of a deliberate choice of the legislature. It is not, of course, easy to imagine the construction of a railway in a state of nature. The nearest one can get to this is presumably a railway which uses steam engines "without express statutory authority." However, in this case the railway would be obliged to compensate those whose woods it burnt down. That is to say, compensation would be paid in the absence of Government action. The only circumstances in which compensation would not be paid would be those in which there had been Government action. It is strange that Pigou, who clearly thought it desirable that compensation should be paid, should have chosen this particular example to demonstrate how it is possible "for State action to improve on 'natural' tendencies."

Pigou seems to have had a faulty view of the facts of the situation. But it also seems likely that he was mistaken in his economic analysis. It is not necessarily desirable that the railway should be required to compensate those who suffer damage by fires caused by railway engines. I need not show here that, if the railway could make a bargain with everyone having property adjoining the railway line and there were no costs involved in making such bargains, it would not matter whether the railway was liable for damage caused by fires or not. This question has been treated at length in earlier sections. The problem is whether it would be desirable to make the railway liable in conditions in which it is too expensive for such bargains to be made. Pigou clearly thought it was desirable to force the railway to pay compensation and it is easy to see the kind of argument that would have led him to this conclusion. Suppose a railway is considering whether to run an additional train or to increase the speed of an existing train or to install spark-preventing devices on its engines. If the railway were not liable for fire damage, then, when making these decisions, it would not take into account as a cost the increase in damage resulting from the additional train or the faster train or the failure to install spark-preventing devices. This is the source of the di-

[43] Vaughan v. Taff Vale Railway Co., 3 H. and N. 743 (Ex. 1858) and 5 H. and N. 679 (Ex. 1860).

vergence between private and social net products. It results in the railway performing acts which will lower the value of total production—and which it would not do if it were liable for the damage. This can be shown by means of an arithmetical example.

Consider a railway, which is *not* liable for damage by fires caused by sparks from its engines, which runs two trains per day on a certain line. Suppose that running one train per day would enable the railway to perform services worth $150 per annum and running two trains a day would enable the railway to perform services worth $250 per annum. Suppose further that the cost of running one train is $50 per annum and two trains $100 per annum. Assuming perfect competition, the cost equals the fall in the value of production elsewhere due to the employment of additional factors of production by the railway. Clearly the railway would find it profitable to run two trains per day. But suppose that running one train per day would destroy by fire crops worth (on an average over the year) $60 and two trains a day would result in the destruction of crops worth $120. In these circumstances running one train per day would raise the value of total production but the running of a second train would reduce the value of total production. The second train would enable additional railway services worth $100 per annum to be performed. But the fall in the value of production elsewhere would be $110 per annum; $50 as a result of the employment of additional factors of production and $60 as a result of the destruction of crops. Since it would be better if the second train were not run and since it would not run if the railway were liable for damage caused to crops, the conclusion that the railway should be made liable for the damage seems irresistable. Undoubtedly it is this kind of reasoning which underlies the Pigovian position.

The conclusion that it would be better if the second train did not run is correct. The conclusion that it is desirable that the railway should be made liable for the damage it causes is wrong. Let us change our assumption concerning the rule of liability. Suppose that the railway is liable for damage from fires caused by sparks from the engine. A farmer on lands adjoining the railway is then in the position that, if his crop is destroyed by fires caused by the railway, he will receive the market price from the railway; but if his crop is not damaged, he will receive the market price by sale. It therefore becomes a matter of indifference to him whether his crop is damaged by fire or not. The position is very different when the railway is *not* liable. Any crop destruction through railway-caused fires would then reduce the receipts of the farmer. He would therefore take out of cultivation any land for which the damage is likely to be greater than the net return of the land (for reasons explained at length in Section III). A change from a regime in which the railway is *not* liable for damage to one in which it *is* liable is likely therefore to lead to an increase in the amount of cultivation on lands adjoining the railway. It will also, of course, lead to an increase in the amount of crop destruction due to railway-caused fires.

Let us return to our arithmetical example. Assume that, with the changed rule of liability, there is a doubling in the amount of crop destruction due to railway-caused fires. With one train per day, crops worth $120 would be destroyed each year and two trains per day would lead to the destruction of crops worth $240. We saw previously that it would not be profitable to run the second train if the railway had to pay $60 per annum as compensation for damage. With damage at $120 per annum the loss from running the second train would be $60 greater. But now let us consider the first train. The value of the transport services furnished by the first train is $150. The cost of running the train is $50. The amount that the railway would have to pay out as compensation for damage is $120. It follows that it would not be profitable to run any trains. With the figures in our example we reach the following result: if the railway is not liable for fire-damage, two trains per day would be run; if the railway is liable for fire-damage, it would cease operations altogether. Does this mean that it is better that there should be no railway? This question can be resolved by considering what would happen to the value of total production if it were decided to exempt the railway from liability for fire-damage, thus bringing it into operation (with two trains per day).

The operation of the railway would enable transport services worth $250 to be performed. It would also mean the employment of factors of production which would reduce the value of production elsewhere by $100. Furthermore it would mean the destruction of crops worth $120. The coming of the railway will also have led to the abandonment of cultivation of some land. Since we know that, had this land been cultivated, the value of the crops destroyed by fire would have been $120, and since it is unlikely that the total crop on this land would have been destroyed, it seems reasonable to suppose that the value of the crop yield on this land would have been higher than this. Assume it would have been $160. But the abandonment of cultivation would have released factors of production for employment elsewhere. All we know is that the amount by which the value of production elsewhere will increase will be less than $160. Suppose that it is $150. Then the gain from operating the railway would be $250 (the value of the transport services) minus $100 (the cost of the factors of production) minus $120 (the value of crops destroyed by fire) minus $160 (the fall in the value of crop production due to the abandonment of cultivation) plus $150 (the value of production elsewhere of the released factors of production). Overall, operating the railway will increase the value of total production by $20. With these figures it is clear that it is better that the railway should not be liable for the damage it causes, thus enabling it to operate profitably. Of course, by altering the figures, it could be shown that there are other cases in which it would be desirable that the railway should be liable for the damage it causes. It is enough for my purpose to show that, from an economic point of view, a situation in which there is "uncompensated damage done to surrounding woods by sparks from railway engines" is not necessarily undesirable. Whether it is desirable or not depends on the particular circumstances.

How is it that the Pigovian analysis seems to give the wrong answer? The reason is that Pigou does not seem to have noticed that his analysis is dealing with an entirely different question. The analysis as such is correct. But it is quite illegitimate for Pigou to draw the particular conclusion he does. The question at issue is not whether it is desirable to run an additional train or a faster train or to install smoke-preventing devices; the question at issue is whether it is desirable to have a system in which the railway has to compensate those who suffer damage from the fires which it causes or one in which the railway does not have to compensate them. When an economist is comparing alternative social arrangements, the proper procedure is to compare the total social product yielded by these different arrangements. The comparison of private and social products is neither here nor there. A simple example will demonstrate this. Imagine a town in which there are traffic lights. A motorist approaches an intersection and stops because the light is red. There are no cars approaching the intersection on the other street. If the motorist ignored the red signal, no accident would occur and the total product would increase because the motorist would arrive earlier at his destination. Why does he not do this? The reason is that if he ignored the light he would be fined. The private product from crossing the street is less than the social product. Should we conclude from this that the total product would be greater if there were no fines for failing to obey traffic signals? The Pigovian analysis shows us that it is possible to conceive of better worlds than the one in which we live. But the problem is to devise practical arrangements which will correct defects in one part of the system without causing more serious harm in other parts.

I have examined in considerable detail one example of a divergence between private and social products and I do not propose to make any further examination of Pigou's analytical system. But the main discussion of the problem considered in this article is to be found in that part of Chapter 9 in Part II which deals with Pigou's second class of divergence and it is of interest to see how Pigou develops his argument. Pigou's own description of this second class of divergence was quoted at the beginning of this section. Pigou distinguishes between the case in which a person renders services for which he receives no payment and the case in which a person renders disservices and compensation is not given to the injured parties. Our main attention has, of course, centred on this second case. It is therefore rather

THE PROBLEM OF SOCIAL COST 35

astonishing to find, as was pointed out to me by Professor Francesco Forte, that the problem of the smoking chimney—the "stock instance"[44] or "classroom example"[45] of the second case—is used by Pigou as an example of the first case (services rendered without payment) and is never mentioned, at any rate explicitly, in connection with the second case.[46] Pigou points out that factory owners who devote resources to preventing their chimneys from smoking render services for which they receive no payment. The implication, in the light of Pigou's discussion later in the chapter, is that a factory owner with a smokey chimney should be given a bounty to induce him to install smoke-preventing devices. Most modern economists would suggest that the owner of the factory with the smokey chimney should be taxed. It seems a pity that economists (apart from Professor Forte) do not seem to have noticed this feature of Pigou's treatment since a realisation that the problem could be tackled in either of these two ways would probably have led to an explicit recognition of its reciprocal nature.

In discussing the second case (disservices without compensation to those damaged), Pigou says that they are rendered "when the owner of a site in a residential quarter of a city builds a factory there and so destroys a great part of the amenities of neighbouring sites; or, in a less degree, when he uses his site in such a way as to spoil the lighting of the house opposite; or when he invests resources in erecting buildings in a crowded centre, which by contracting the air-space and the playing room of the neighbourhood, tend to injure the health and efficiency of the families living there."[47] Pigou is, of course, quite right to describe such actions as "uncharged disservices." But he is wrong when he describes these actions as "anti-social."[48] They may or may not be. It is necessary to weigh the harm against the good that will result. Nothing could be more "anti-social" than to oppose any action which causes any harm to anyone.

The example with which Pigou opens his discussion of "uncharged disservices" is not, as I have indicated, the case of the smokey chimney but the case of the overrunning rabbits: ". . . incidental uncharged disservices are rendered to third parties when the game-preserving activities of one occupier involve the overrunning of a neighbouring occupier's land by rabbits. . . ." This example is of extraordinary interest, not so much because the economic

[44] Sir Dennis Robertson, I Lectures on Economic Principles 162 (1957).

[45] E. J. Mishan, The Meaning of Efficiency in Economics, 189 The Bankers' Magazine 482 (June 1960).

[46] Pigou, op. cit. supra n. 35 at 184.

[47] *Id.* at 185–86.

[48] *Id.* at 186 n.1. For similar unqualified statements see Pigou's lecture "Some Aspects of the Housing Problem" in B. S. Rowntree and A. C. Pigou, Lectures on Housing, in 18 Manchester Univ. Lectures (1914).

analysis of the case is essentially any different from that of the other examples, but because of the peculiarities of the legal position and the light it throws on the part which economics can play in what is apparently the purely legal question of the delimitation of rights.

The problem of legal liability for the actions of rabbits is part of the general subject of liability for animals.[49] I will, although with reluctance, confine my discussion to rabbits. The early cases relating to rabbits concerned the relations between the lord of the manor and commoners, since, from the thirteenth century on, it became usual for the lord of the manor to stock the commons with conies (rabbits), both for the sake of the meat and the fur. But in 1597, in *Boulston*'s case, an action was brought by one landowner against a neighbouring landowner, alleging that the defendant had made coney-burrows and that the conies had increased and had destroyed the plaintiff's corn. The action failed for the reason that

> . . . so soon as the coneys come on his neighbor's land he may kill them, for they are ferae naturae, and he who makes the coney-boroughs has no property in them, and he shall not be punished for the damage which the coneys do in which he has no property, and which the other may lawfully kill.[50]

As *Boulston*'s case has been treated as binding—Bray, J., in 1919, said that he was not aware that *Boulston*'s case has ever been overruled or questioned[51]—Pigou's rabbit example undoubtedly represented the legal position at the time *The Economics of Welfare* was written.[52] And in this case, it is not far from the truth to say that the state of affairs which Pigou describes came about because of an absence of Government action (at any rate in the form of statutory enactments) and was the result of "natural" tendencies.

Nonetheless, *Boulston*'s case is something of a legal curiousity and Professor Williams makes no secret of his distaste for this decision:

[49] See G. L. Williams, Liability for Animals—An Account of the Development and Present Law of Tortious Liability for Animals, Distress Damage Feasant and the Duty to Fence, in Great Britain, Northern Ireland and the Common Law Dominions (1939). Part Four, "The Action of Nuisance, in Relation to Liability for Animals," 236–62, is especially relevant to our discussion. The problem of liability for rabbits is discussed in this part, 238–47. I do not know how far the common law in the United State regarding liability for animals has diverged from that in Britain. In some Western States of the United States, the English common law regarding the duty to fence has not been followed, in part because "the considerable amount of open, uncleared land made it a matter of public policy to allow cattle to run at large" (Williams, *op. cit. supra* 227). This affords a good example of how a different set of circumstances may make it economically desirable to change the legal rule regarding the delimitation of rights.

[50] 5 Coke (Vol. 3) 104 b. 77 Eng. Rep., 216, 217.

[51] See Stearn v. Prentice Bros. Ltd., (1919) 1 K.B., 395, 397.

[52] I have not looked into recent cases. The legal position has also been modified by statutory enactments.

THE PROBLEM OF SOCIAL COST   37

The conception of liability in nuisance as being based upon ownership is the result, apparently, of a confusion with the action of cattle-trespass, and runs counter both to principle and to the medieval authorities on the escape of water, smoke and filth. . . . The prerequisite of any satisfactory treatment of the subject is the final abandonment of the pernicious doctrine in *Boulston*'s case. . . . Once *Boulston*'s case disappears, the way will be clear for a rational restatement of the whole subject, on lines that will harmonize with the principles prevailing in the rest of the law of nuisance.[53]

The judges in *Boulston*'s case were, of course, aware that their view of the matter depended on distinguishing this case from one involving nuisance:

This cause is not like to the cases put, on the other side, of erecting a lime-kiln, dye-house, or the like; for there the annoyance is by the act of the parties who make them; but it is not so here, for the conies of themselves went into the plaintiff's land, and he might take them when they came upon his land, and make profit of them.[54]

Professor Williams comments:

Once more the atavistic idea is emerging that the animals are guilty and not the landowner. It is not, of course, a satisfactory principle to introduce into a modern law of nuisance. If A. erects a house or plants a tree so that the rain runs or drips from it on to B.'s land, this is A.'s act for which he is liable; but if A. introduces rabbits into his land so that they escape from it into B.'s, this is the act of the rabbits for which A. is not liable—such is the specious distinction resulting from *Boulston*'s case.[55]

It has to be admitted that the decision in *Boulston*'s case seems a little odd. A man may be liable for damage caused by smoke or unpleasant smells, without it being necessary to determine whether he owns the smoke or the smell. And the rule in *Boulston*'s case has not always been followed in cases dealing with other animals. For example, in *Bland v. Yates*,[56] it was decided that an injunction could be granted to prevent someone from keeping an *unusual and excessive* collection of manure in which flies bred and which infested a neighbour's house. The question of who owned the flies was not raised. An economist would not wish to object because legal reasoning sometimes appears a little odd. But there is a sound economic reason for supporting Professor Williams' view that the problem of liability for animals (and particularly rabbits) should be brought within the ordinary law of nuisance. The reason is not that the man who harbours rabbits is solely responsible for the damage; the man whose crops are eaten is equally responsible. And given that the costs of market transactions make a rearrange-

---

[53] Williams, op. cit. supra n. 49 at 242, 258.

[54] Boulston v. Hardy, Cro. Eliz., 547, 548, 77 Eng. Rep. 216.

[55] Williams, op. cit. supra n. 49 at 243.

[56] 58 Sol.J. 612 (1913–1914).

38   THE JOURNAL OF LAW AND ECONOMICS

ment of rights impossible, unless we know the particular circumstances, we cannot say whether it is desirable or not to make the man who harbours rabbits responsible for the damage committed by the rabbits on neighbouring properties. The objection to the rule in *Boulston*'s case is that, under it, the harbourer of rabbits can *never* be liable. It fixes the rule of liability at one pole: and this is as undesirable, from an economic point of view, as fixing the rule at the other pole and making the harbourer of rabbits always liable. But, as we saw in Section VII, the law of nuisance, as it is in fact handled by the courts, is flexible and allows for a comparison of the utility of an act with the harm it produces. As Professor Williams says: "The whole law of nuisance is an attempt to reconcile and compromise between conflicting interests. . . ."[57] To bring the problem of rabbits within the ordinary law of nuisance would not mean *inevitably* making the harbourer of rabbits liable for damage committed by the rabbits. This is not to say that the sole task of the courts in such cases is to make a comparison between the harm and the utility of an act. Nor is it to be expected that the courts will always decide correctly after making such a comparison. But unless the courts act very foolishly, the ordinary law of nuisance would seem likely to give economically more satisfactory results than adopting a rigid rule. Pigou's case of the overrunning rabbits affords an excellent example of how problems of law and economics are interrelated, even though the correct policy to follow would seem to be different from that envisioned by Pigou.

Pigou allows one exception to his conclusion that there is a divergence between private and social products in the rabbit example. He adds: ". . . unless . . . the two occupiers stand in the relation of landlord and tenant, so that compensation is given in an adjustment of the rent."[58] This qualification is rather surprising since Pigou's first class of divergence is largely concerned with the difficulties of drawing up satisfactory contracts between landlords and tenants. In fact, all the recent cases on the problem of rabbits cited by Professor Williams involved disputes between landlords and tenants concerning sporting rights.[59] Pigou seems to make a distinction between the case in which no contract is possible (the second class) and that in which the contract is unsatisfactory (the first class). Thus he says that the second class of divergences between private and social net product

cannot, like divergences due to tenancy laws, be mitigated by a modification of the contractual relation between any two contracting parties, because the divergence arises out of a service or disservice rendered to persons other than the contracting parties.[60]

[57] Williams, op. cit. supra n. 49 at 259.

[58] Pigou, op. cit. supra n. 35 at 185.

[59] Williams, op. cit. supra n. 49 at 244–47.

[60] Pigou, op. cit. supra n. 35 at 192.

THE PROBLEM OF SOCIAL COST   39

But the reason why some activities are not the subject of contracts is exactly the same as the reason why some contracts are commonly unsatisfactory— it would cost too much to put the matter right. Indeed, the two cases are really the same since the contracts are unsatisfactory because they do not cover certain activities. The exact bearing of the discussion of the first class of divergence on Pigou's main argument is difficult to discover. He shows that in some circumstances contractual relations between landlord and tenant may result in a divergence between private and social products.[61] But he also goes on to show that Government-enforced compensation schemes and rent-controls will also produce divergences.[62] Furthermore, he shows that, when the Government is in a similar position to a private landlord, e.g. when granting a franchise to a public utility, exactly the same difficulties arise as when private individuals are involved.[63] The discussion is interesting but I have been unable to discover what general conclusions about economic policy, if any, Pigou expects us to draw from it.

Indeed, Pigou's treatment of the problems considered in this article is extremely elusive and the discussion of his views raises almost insuperable difficulties of interpretation. Consequently it is impossible to be sure that one has understood what Pigou really meant. Nevertheless, it is difficult to resist the conclusion, extraordinary though this may be in an economist of Pigou's stature, that the main source of this obscurity is that Pigou had not thought his position through.

IX. The Pigovian Tradition

It is strange that a doctrine as faulty as that developed by Pigou should have been so influential, although part of its success has probably been due to the lack of clarity in the exposition. Not being clear, it was never clearly wrong. Curiously enough, this obscurity in the source has not prevented the emergence of a fairly well-defined oral tradition. What economists think they learn from Pigou, and what they tell their students, which I term the Pigovian tradition, is reasonably clear. I propose to show the inadequacy of this Pigovian tradition by demonstrating that both the analysis and the policy conclusions which it supports are incorrect.

I do not propose to justify my view as to the prevailing opinion by copious references to the literature. I do this partly because the treatment in the literature is usually so fragmentary, often involving little more than a reference to Pigou plus some explanatory comment, that detailed examination would be inappropriate. But the main reason for this lack of reference is that the doctrine, although based on Pigou, must have been largely the product of an oral tradition. Certainly economists with whom I have discussed these problems have shown a unanimity of opinion which is quite

---

[61] *Id*. 174–75.   [62] *Id*. 177–83.   [63] *Id*. 175–77.

remarkable considering the meagre treatment accorded this subject in the literature. No doubt there are some economists who do not share the usual view but they must represent a small minority of the profession.

The approach to the problems under discussion is through an examination of the value of physical production. The private product is the value of the additional product resulting from a particular activity of a business. The social product equals the private product minus the fall in the value of production elsewhere for which no compensation is paid by the business. Thus, if 10 units of a factor (and no other factors) are used by a business to make a certain product with a value of $105; and the owner of this factor is not compensated for their use, which he is unable to prevent; and these 10 units of the factor would yield products in their best alternative use worth $100; then, the social product is $105 minus $100 or $5. If the business now pays for one unit of the factor and its price equals the value of its marginal product, then the social product rises to $15. If two units are paid for, the social product rises to $25 and so on until it reaches $105 when all units of the factor are paid for. It is not difficult to see why economists have so readily accepted this rather odd procedure. The analysis focusses on the individual business decision and since the use of certain resources is not allowed for in costs, receipts are reduced by the same amount. But, of course, this means that the value of the social product has no social significance whatsoever. It seems to me preferable to use the opportunity cost concept and to approach these problems by comparing the value of the product yielded by factors in alternative uses or by alternative arrangements. The main advantage of a pricing system is that it leads to the employment of factors in places where the value of the product yielded is greatest and does so at less cost than alternative systems (I leave aside that a pricing system also eases the problem of the redistribution of income). But if through some God-given natural harmony factors flowed to the places where the value of the product yielded was greatest without any use of the pricing system and consequently there was no compensation, I would find it a source of surprise rather than a cause for dismay.

The definition of the social product is queer but this does not mean that the conclusions for policy drawn from the analysis are necessarily wrong. However, there are bound to be dangers in an approach which diverts attention from the basic issues and there can be little doubt that it has been responsible for some of the errors in current doctrine. The belief that it is desirable that the business which causes harmful effects should be forced to compensate those who suffer damage (which was exhaustively discussed in section VIII in connection with Pigou's railway sparks example) is undoubtedly the result of not comparing the total product obtainable with alternative social arrangements.

THE PROBLEM OF SOCIAL COST   41

The same fault is to be found in proposals for solving the problem of
harmful effects by the use of taxes or bounties. Pigou lays considerable stress
on this solution although he is, as usual, lacking in detail and qualified in
his support.[64] Modern economists tend to think exclusively in terms of
taxes and in a very precise way. The tax should be equal to the damage
done and should therefore vary with the amount of the harmful effect. As
it is not proposed that the proceeds of the tax should be paid to those suffering the damage, this solution is not the same as that which would force a
business to pay compensation to those damaged by its actions, although
economists generally do not seem to have noticed this and tend to treat the
two solutions as being identical.

Assume that a factory which emits smoke is set up in a district previously
free from smoke pollution, causing damage valued at $100 per annum.
Assume that the taxation solution is adopted and that the factory owner
is taxed $100 per annum as long as the factory emits the smoke. Assume
further that a smoke-preventing device costing $90 per annum to run is
available. In these circumstances, the smoke-preventing device would be
installed. Damage of $100 would have been avoided at an expenditure of
$90 and the factory-owner would be better off by $10 per annum. Yet the
position achieved may not be optimal. Suppose that those who suffer the
damage could avoid it by moving to other locations or by taking various
precautions which would cost them, or be equivalent to a loss in income of,
$40 per annum. Then there would be a gain in the value of production of
$50 if the factory continued to emit its smoke and those now in the district
moved elsewhere or made other adjustments to avoid the damage. If the
factory owner is to be made to pay a tax equal to the damage caused, it
would clearly be desirable to institute a double tax system and to make
residents of the district pay an amount equal to the additional cost incurred
by the factory owner (or the consumers of his products) in order to avoid
the damage. In these conditions, people would not stay in the district or
would take other measures to prevent the damage from occurring, when the
costs of doing so were less than the costs that would be incurred by the producer to reduce the damage (the producer's object, of course, being not so
much to reduce the damage as to reduce the tax payments). A tax system
which was confined to a tax on the producer for damage caused would tend to
lead to unduly high costs being incurred for the prevention of damage. Of
course this could be avoided if it were possible to base the tax, not on the
damage caused, but on the fall in the value of production (in its widest
sense) resulting from the emission of smoke. But to do so would require a
detailed knowledge of individual preferences and I am unable to imagine
how the data needed for such a taxation system could be assembled. Indeed,

[64] *Id.* 192–4, 381 and Public Finance 94–100 (3d ed. 1947).

the proposal to solve the smoke-pollution and similar problems by the use of taxes bristles with difficulties: the problem of calculation, the difference between average and marginal damage, the interrelations between the damage suffered on different properties, etc. But it is unnecessary to examine these problems here. It is enough for my purpose to show that, even if the tax is exactly adjusted to equal the damage that would be done to neighboring properties as a result of the emission of each additional puff of smoke, the tax would not necessarily bring about optimal conditions. An increase in the number of people living or of business operating in the vicinity of the smoke-emitting factory will increase the amount of harm produced by a given emission of smoke. The tax that would be imposed would therefore increase with an increase in the number of those in the vicinity. This will tend to lead to a decrease in the value of production of the factors employed by the factory, either because a reduction in production due to the tax will result in factors being used elsewhere in ways which are less valuable, or because factors will be diverted to produce means for reducing the amount of smoke emitted. But people deciding to establish themselves in the vicinity of the factory will not take into account this fall in the value of production which results from their presence. This failure to take into account costs imposed on others is comparable to the action of a factory-owner in not taking into account the harm resulting from his emission of smoke. Without the tax, there may be too much smoke and too few people in the vicinity of the factory; but with the tax there may be too little smoke and too many people in the vicinity of the factory. There is no reason to suppose that one of these results is necessarily preferable.

I need not devote much space to discussing the similar error involved in the suggestion that smoke producing factories should, by means of zoning regulations, be removed from the districts in which the smoke causes harmful effects. When the change in the location of the factory results in a reduction in production, this obviously needs to be taken into account and weighed against the harm which would result from the factory remaining in that location. The aim of such regulation should not be to eliminate smoke pollution but rather to secure the optimum amount of smoke pollution, this being the amount which will maximise the value of production.

X. A Change of Approach

It is my belief that the failure of economists to reach correct conclusions about the treatment of harmful effects cannot be ascribed simply to a few slips in analysis. It stems from basic defects in the current approach to problems of welfare economics. What is needed is a change of approach.

Analysis in terms of divergencies between private and social products concentrates attention on particular deficiencies in the system and tends to nourish the belief that any measure which will remove the deficiency is necessarily desirable. It diverts attention from those other changes in the system which are inevitably associated with the corrective measure, changes which may well produce more harm than the original deficiency. In the preceding sections of this article, we have seen many examples of this. But it is not necessary to approach the problem in this way. Economists who study problems of the firm habitually use an opportunity cost approach and compare the receipts obtained from a given combination of factors with alternative business arrangements. It would seem desirable to use a similar approach when dealing with questions of economic policy and to compare the total product yielded by alternative social arrangements. In this article, the analysis has been confined, as is usual in this part of economics, to comparisons of the value of production, as measured by the market. But it is, of course, desirable that the choice between different social arrangements for the solution of economic problems should be carried out in broader terms than this and that the total effect of these arrangements in all spheres of life should be taken into account. As Frank H. Knight has so often emphasized, problems of welfare economics must ultimately dissolve into a study of aesthetics and morals.

A second feature of the usual treatment of the problems discussed in this article is that the analysis proceeds in terms of a comparison between a state of laissez faire and some kind of ideal world. This approach inevitably leads to a looseness of thought since the nature of the alternatives being compared is never clear. In a state of laissez faire, is there a monetary, a legal or a political system and if so, what are they? In an ideal world, would there be a monetary, a legal or a political system and if so, what would they be? The answers to all these questions are shrouded in mystery and every man is free to draw whatever conclusions he likes. Actually very little analysis is required to show that an ideal world is better than a state of laissez faire, unless the definitions of a state of laissez faire and an ideal world happen to be the same. But the whole discussion is largely irrelevant for questions of economic policy since whatever we may have in mind as our ideal world, it is clear that we have not yet discovered how to get to it from where we are. A better approach would seem to be to start our analysis with a situation approximating that which actually exists, to examine the effects of a proposed policy change and to attempt to decide whether the new situation would be, in total, better or worse than the original one. In this way, conclusions for policy would have some relevance to the actual situation.

A final reason for the failure to develop a theory adequate to handle the problem of harmful effects stems from a faulty concept of a factor of production. This is usually thought of as a physical entity which the businessman acquires and uses (an acre of land, a ton of fertiliser) instead of as a right to perform certain (physical) actions. We may speak of a person owning land and using it as a factor of production but what the land-owner in fact possesses is the right to carry out a circumscribed list of actions. The rights of a land-owner are not unlimited. It is not even always possible for him to remove the land to another place, for instance, by quarrying it. And although it may be possible for him to exclude some people from using "his" land, this may not be true of others. For example, some people may have the right to cross the land. Furthermore, it may or may not be possible to erect certain types of buildings or to grow certain crops or to use particular drainage systems on the land. This does not come about simply because of Government regulation. It would be equally true under the common law. In fact it would be true under any system of law. A system in which the rights of individuals were unlimited would be one in which there were no rights to acquire.

If factors of production are thought of as rights, it becomes easier to understand that the right to do something which has a harmful effect (such as the creation of smoke, noise, smells, etc.) is also a factor of production. Just as we may use a piece of land in such a way as to prevent someone else from crossing it, or parking his car, or building his house upon it, so we may use it in such a way as to deny him a view or quiet or unpolluted air. The cost of exercising a right (of using a factor of production) is always the loss which is suffered elsewhere in consequence of the exercise of that right—the inability to cross land, to park a car, to build a house, to enjoy a view, to have peace and quiet or to breathe clean air.

It would clearly be desirable if the only actions performed were those in which what was gained was worth more than what was lost. But in choosing between social arrangements within the context of which individual decisions are made, we have to bear in mind that a change in the existing system which will lead to an improvement in some decisions may well lead to a worsening of others. Furthermore we have to take into account the costs involved in operating the various social arrangements (whether it be the working of a market or of a government department), as well as the costs involved in moving to a new system. In devising and choosing between social arrangements we should have regard for the total effect. This, above all, is the change in approach which I am advocating.

[6]

On Divergences between Social Cost and Private Cost*

By Ralph Turvey

The notion that the resource-allocation effects of divergences between marginal social and private costs can be dealt with by imposing a tax or granting a subsidy equal to the difference now seems too simple a notion. Three recent articles have shown us this. First came Professor Coase's " The Problem of Social Cost ", then Davis and Whinston's " Externalities, Welfare and the Theory of Games " appeared, and, finally, Buchanan and Stubblebine have published their paper " Externality ".[1] These articles have an aggregate length of eighty pages and are by no means easy to read. The following attempt to synthesise and summarise the main ideas may therefore be useful. It is couched in terms of external diseconomies, i.e. an excess of social over private costs, and the reader is left to invert the analysis himself should he be interested in external economies.

The scope of the following argument can usefully be indicated by starting with a brief statement of its main conclusions. The first is that if the party imposing external diseconomies and the party suffering them are able and willing to negotiate to their mutual advantage, state intervention is unnecessary to secure optimum resource allocation. The second is that the imposition of a tax upon the party imposing external diseconomies can be a very complicated matter, even in principle, so that the *a priori* prescription of such a tax is unwise.

To develop these and other points, let us begin by calling A the person, firm or group (of persons or firms) which imposes a diseconomy, and B the person, firm or group which suffers it. How much B suffers will in many cases depend not only upon the *scale* of A's diseconomy-creating activity, but also upon the precise *nature* of A's activity and upon B's *reaction* to it. If A emits smoke, for example, B's loss will depend not only upon the quantity emitted but also upon the height of A's chimney and upon the cost to B of installing air-conditioning, indoor clothes-dryers or other means of reducing the effect of the smoke. Thus to ascertain the optimum resource allocation will frequently require an investigation of the nature and costs both of alternative activities open to A and of the devices by which B can reduce the impact of each activity. The optimum involves that kind and scale of A's activity and that adjustment to it by B which maximises the algebraic sum of A's gain and B's loss as against the situation where A

* I am indebted to Professor Buchanan, Professor Coase, Mr. Klappholz, Dr. Mishan and Mr. Peston for helpful comments on an earlier draft.
[1] *Journal of Law and Economics*, Vol. III, October, 1960, *Journal of Political Economy*, June, 1962, and *Economica*, November, 1962, respectively.

pursues no diseconomy-creating activity. Note that the optimum will frequently involve B suffering a loss, both in total and at the margin.[1]

If A and B are firms, gain and loss can be measured in money terms as profit differences. (In considering a social optimum, allowance has of course to be made for market imperfections.) Now assuming that they both seek to maximise profits, that they know about the available alternatives and adjustments and that they are able and willing to negotiate, they will achieve the optimum without any government interference. They will internalize the externality by merger[2], or they will make an agreement whereby B pays A to modify the nature or scale of its activity.[3] Alternatively,[4] if the law gives B rights against A, A will pay B to accept the optimal amount of loss imposed by A.

If A and B are people, their gain and loss must be measured as the amount of money they respectively would pay to indulge in and prevent A's activity. It could also be measured as the amount of money they respectively would require to refrain from and to endure A's activity, which will be different unless the marginal utility of income is constant. We shall assume that it is constant for both A and B, which is reasonable when the payments do not bulk large in relation to their incomes.[5] Under this assumption, it makes no difference whether B pays A or, if the law gives B rights against A, A compensates B.

Whether A and B are persons or firms, to levy a tax on A which is *not* received as damages or compensation by B may prevent optimal resource allocation from being achieved—still assuming that they can and do negotiate.[6] The reason is that the resource allocation which maximises A's *gain less B's loss* may differ from that which maximises A's *gain less A's tax less B's loss*.

The points made so far can usefully be presented diagrammatically (Figure 1). We assume that A has only two alternative activities, I and II, and that their scales and B's losses are all continuously variable. Let us temporarily disregard the dotted curve in the right-hand part of the diagram. The area under A's curves then gives the total gain to A. The area under B's curves gives the total loss to B after he has made the best adjustment possible to A's activity. This is thus the direct loss as reduced by adjustment, plus the cost of making that adjustment.

If A and B could not negotiate and if A were unhampered by restrictions of any sort, A would choose activity I at a scale of OR. A scale of OS would obviously give a larger social product, but the optimum is clearly activity II at scale OJ, since area 2 is greater than area 1. Now B will be prepared to pay up to $(1a + 1b - 2a)$ to secure this result, while

[1] Buchanan-Stubblebine, pp. 380–1.
[2] Davis-Whinston, pp. 244, 252, 256; Coase, pp. 16–17.
[3] Coase, p. 6; Buchanan-Stubblebine agree, p. 383.
[4] See previous references.
[5] Dr. Mishan has examined the welfare criterion for the case where the only variable is the scale of A's activity, but where neither A nor B has a constant marginal utility of income; Cf. his paper " Welfare Criteria for External Effects ", *American Economic Review*, September, 1961.
[6] Buchanan-Stubblebine, pp. 381–3.

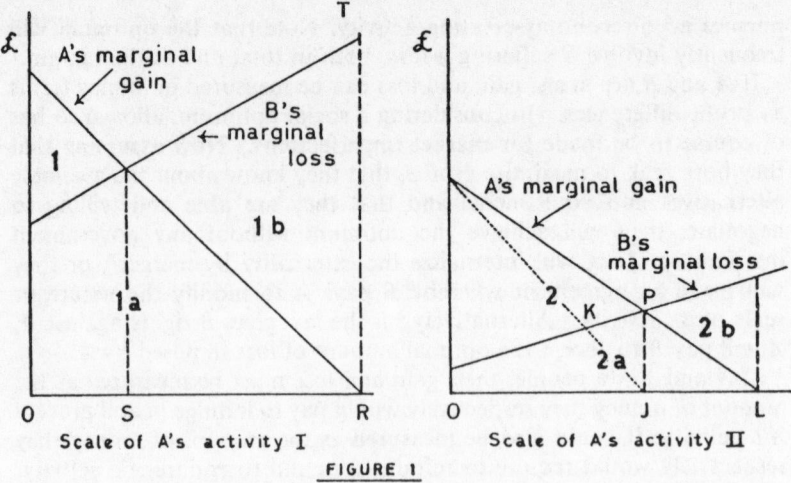

FIGURE 1

A will be prepared to accept down to $(1 + 1a - 2 - 2a)$ to assure it. The difference is $(1b - 1 + 2)$, the maximum gain to be shared between them, and this is clearly positive.

If *A* is liable to compensate *B* for actual damages caused by either activity I or II, he will choose activity II at scale *OJ* (i.e. the optimum allocation), pay $2a$ to *B* and retain a net gain of 2. The result is the same as when there is no such liability, though the distribution of the gain is very different: *B* will pay *A* up to $(1a + 1b - 2a)$ to secure this result. Hence whether or not we should advocate the imposition of a liability on *A* for damages caused is a matter of fairness, not of resource allocation. Our judgment will presumably depend on such factors as who got there first, whether one of them is a non-conforming user (e.g. an establishment for the breeding of maggots on putrescible vegetable matter in a residential district), who is richer, and so on. Efficient resource allocation requires the imposition of a liability upon *A* only if we can show that inertia, obstinacy, etc. inhibit *A* and *B* from reaching a voluntary agreement.[1]

We can now make the point implicit in Buchanan-Stubblebine's argument, namely that there is a necessity for any impost levied on *A* to be paid to *B* when *A* and *B* are able to negotiate. Suppose that *A* is charged an amount equal to the loss he imposes on *B*; subtracting this from his marginal gain curve in the right-hand part of the diagram gives us the dotted line as his marginal net gain. If *A* moves to point *J* it will then pay *B* to induce him to move back to position *K* (which is sub-optimal) as it is this position which maximises the *joint* net gain to *A* and *B* together.

There is a final point to be made about the case where *A* and *B* can negotiate. This is that if the external diseconomies are reciprocal, so

---

[1] Cf. the comparable argument on pp. 94–8 of my *The Economics of Real Property*, 1957, about the external economy to landlords of tenants' improvements.

that each imposes a loss upon the other, the problem is still more complicated.[1]

We now turn to the case where A and B cannot negotiate, which in most cases will result from A and/or B being too large a group for the members to get together. Here there are certain benefits to be had from resource re-allocation which are not privately appropriable. Just as with collective goods,[2] therefore, there is thus a case for collective action to achieve optimum allocation. But all this means is that *if* the state can ascertain and enforce a move to the optimum position at a cost less than the gain to be had, and *if* it can do this in a way which does not have unfavourable effects upon income distribution, then it should take action.

These two " ifs " are very important. The second is obvious and requires no elaboration. The first, however, deserves a few words. In order to ascertain the optimum type and scale of A's activity, the authorities must estimate all of the curves in the diagrams. They must, in other words, list and evaluate all the alternatives open to A and examine their effects upon B and the adjustments B could make to reduce the loss suffered. When this is done, if it can be done, it is necessary to consider how to reach the optimum. Now, where the nature as well as the scale of A's activity is variable, it may be necessary to control both, and this may require two controls, not one. Suppose, for instance, that in the diagram, both activities are the emission of smoke: I from a low chimney and II from a tall chimney. To induce A to shift from emitting OR smoke from the low chimney to emitting OJ smoke from the tall chimney, it will not suffice to levy a tax of PJ per unit of smoke.[3] If this alone were done, A would continue to use a low chimney, emitting slightly less than OR smoke. It will also be necessary to regulate chimney heights. A tax would do the trick alone only if it were proportioned to losses imposed rather than to smoke emitted, and that would be very difficult.

These complications show that in many cases the cost of achieving optimum resource allocation may outweigh the gain. If this is the case, a second-best solution may be appropriate. Thus a prohibition of all smoke emission would be better than OR smoke from a low chimney (since 1 is less than 1b) and a requirement that all chimneys be tall would be better still (giving a net gain of 2 less 2b). Whether these requirements should be imposed on existing chimney-owners as well as on new ones then introduces further complications relating to the short run and the long run.

There is no need to carry the example any further. It is now abundantly clear that any general prescription of a tax to deal with external diseconomies is useless. Each case must be considered on its own and

[1] Davis-Whinston devote several pages of game theory to this problem.
[2] Buchanan-Stubblebine, p. 383.
[3] Note how different PJ is from RT, the initial observable marginal external diseconomy.

there is no *a priori* reason to suppose that the imposition of a tax is better than alternative measures or indeed, that any measures at all are desirable unless we assume that information and administration are both costless.[1]

To sum up, then: when negotiation is possible, the case for government intervention is one of justice not of economic efficiency; when it is not, the theorist should be silent and call in the applied economist.

The London School of Economics.

---

[1] Coase, pp. 18, 44.

[7]

Prices *vs.* Quantities [1,2]

MARTIN L. WEITZMAN

Massachusetts Institute of Technology

I. INTRODUCTION

The setting for the problem under consideration is a large economic organization or system which in some cases is best thought of as the entire economy. Within this large economic organization resources are allocated by some combination of commands and prices (the exact mixture is inessential) or even by some other unspecified mechanism. The following question arises. For one particular isolated economic variable that needs to be regulated,[3] what is the best way to implement control for the benefit of the organization as a whole? Is it better to directly administer the activity under scrutiny or to fix transfer prices and rely on self-interested profit or utility maximization to achieve the same ends in decentralized fashion? This issue is taken as the prototype problem of central control which is studied in the present paper. There are a great many specific examples which fit nicely into such a framework. One of current interest is the question of whether it would be better to control certain forms of pollution by setting emission standards or by charging the appropriate pollution taxes.

When quantities are employed as planning instruments, the basic operating rules from the centre take the form of quotas, targets, or commands to produce a certain level of output. With prices as instruments, the rules specify either explicitly or implicitly that profits are to be maximized at the given parametric prices. Now a basic theme of resource allocation theory emphasizes the close connection between these two modes of control. No matter how one type of planning instrument is fixed, there is always a corresponding way to set the other which achieves the same result when implemented.[4] From a strictly theoretical point of view there is really nothing to recommend one mode of control over the other. This notwithstanding, I think it is a fair generalization to say that the average economist in the Western marginalist tradition has at least a vague preference toward indirect control by prices, just as the typical non-economist leans toward the direct regulation of quantities.

That a person not versed in economics should think primarily in terms of direct controls is probably due to the fact that he does not comprehend the full subtlety and strength of the invisible hand argument. The economist's attitude is somewhat more puzzling. Understanding that prices can be used as a powerful and flexible instrument for rationally allocating resources and that in fact a market economy automatically regulates itself in this manner is very different from being under the impression that such indirect controls are generally preferable for the kind of problem considered in this paper. Certainly a careful reading of economic theory yields little to support such a universal proposition.

[1] *First version received August* 1973; *final version accepted January* 1974 (*Eds.*).
[2] Many people have made helpful comments about a previous version of this paper. I would like especially to thank P. A. Diamond and H. E. Scarf for their valuable suggestions. The National Science Foundation helped support my research.
[3] Outside the scope of this paper is the issue of *why* it is felt that the given economic activity must be regulated. There may be a variety of reasons, ranging all the way from political considerations to one form or another of market failure.
[4] Given the usual convexity assumptions. Without convexity it may not be possible to find a price which will support certain output levels. In this connection it should be mentioned that non-convexities (especially increasing returns) are sometimes responsible for regulation in the first place.

478   REVIEW OF ECONOMIC STUDIES

Many economists point with favour to the fact that if prices are the planning instrument then profit maximization automatically guarantees total output will be efficiently produced, as if this result were of any more than secondary interest unless the prices (and hence total output) are optimal to begin with.[1] Sometimes it is maintained that prices are desirable planning instruments because the stimulus to obtain a profit maximizing output is built right in if producers are rewarded in proportion to profits. There is of course just as much motivation, e.g. to minimize costs at specified output levels so long as at least some fraction of production expenditures is borne by producers. With both modes of control there is clearly an incentive for self-interested producers to systematically distort information about hypothetical output and cost possibilities in the pre-implementation planning phase. Conversely, there is no real way to disguise the true facts in the implementation stage so long as actual outputs (in the case of price instruments) and true operating costs (in the case of quantity instruments) can be accurately monitored. For the one case the centre must ascertain *ceteris paribus* output changes as prices are varied, for the other price changes as outputs are altered.

A reason often cited for the theoretical superiority of prices as planning instruments is that their use allegedly economizes on information. The main thing to note here is that generally speaking it is neither easier nor harder to name the right prices than the right quantities because in principle exactly the *same* information is needed to correctly specify either. It is true that in a situation with many independent producers of an identical commodity, only a single uniform price has to be named by the centre, whereas in a command mode separate quantities must be specified for each producer. If such an observation has meaningful implications, it can only be within the artificial milieu of an iterative *tâtonnement* type of " planning game " which is played over and over again approaching an optimal solution in the limit as the number of steps becomes large. Even in this context the fact that there are less " message units " involved in each communication from the centre is a pretty thin reed on which to hang claims for the informational superiority of the price system. It seems to me that a careful examination of the mechanics of successive approximation planning shows that there is no principal informational difference between iteratively finding an optimum by having the centre name prices while the firms respond with quantities, or by having the centre assign quantities while the firm reveals costs or marginal costs.[2]

If there were really some basic intrinsic advantage to a system which employed prices as planning instruments, we would expect to observe many organizations operating with this mode of control, especially among multi-divisional business firms in a competitive

[1] An extreme example may help make this point clear. Suppose that fulfilment of an important emergency rescue operation demands a certain number of airplane flights. It would be inefficient to just order airline companies or branches of the military to supply a certain number of the needed aircraft because marginal (opportunity) costs would almost certainly vary all over the place. Nevertheless, such an approach would undoubtedly be preferable to the efficient procedure of naming a price for plane services. Under profit maximization, overall output would be uncertain, with too few planes spelling disaster and too many being superfluous.

[2] The " message unit " case for the informational superiority of the price system is analogous to the blanket statement that it is better to use dual algorithms for solving a programming problem whenever the number of primal variables exceeds the number of dual multipliers. Certainly for the superior large step decomposition type algorithms which on every iteration go right after what are presently believed to be the best instrument values on the basis of all currently available information, such a general statement has no basis. With myopic gradient methods it is true that on each round the centre infinitesimally and effortlessly adjusts exactly the number of instruments it controls, be they prices or quantities. But who can say *how many* infinitesimally small adjustments will be needed? Gradient algorithms are known to be a bad description of iterative planning procedures, among other reasons because they have inadmissably poor convergence properties. If the step size is chosen too small, convergence takes forever. If it is chosen too large, there is no convergence. As soon as a finite step size is selected on a given iteration to reflect a desire for quick convergence, the " message unit " case for prices evaporates. Calculating the *correct* price change puts the centre right back into the large step decomposition framework where on each round the problem of finding the best iterative prices is formally identical to the problem of finding the best iterative quantities. For discussion of these and various other aspects of iterative planning, see the articles of Heal [4], Malinvaud [5], Marglin [7], Weitzman [9].

environment. Yet the allocation of resources within private companies (not to mention governmental or non-profit organizations) is almost never controlled by setting administered transfer prices on commodities and letting self-interested profit maximization do the rest.[1] The price system as an allocator of internal resources does not itself pass the market test.[2]

Of course, all this is not to deny that in any *particular* setting there may be important *practical* reasons for favouring either prices or quantities as planning instruments. These reasons might involve ideological, political, legal, social, historical, administrative, motivational, informational, monitoring, enforcing, or other considerations.[3] But there is little of what might be called a system-free character.

In studying such a controversial subject, the only fair way to begin must be with the tenet that there is no *basic* or *universal* rationale for having a general predisposition toward one control mode or the other. If this principle is accepted, it becomes an issue of some interest to abstract away all " other " considerations in order to develop strictly " economic " criteria by which the comparative performance of price and quantity planning instruments might be objectively evaluated. Even on an abstract level, it would be useful to know how to identify a situation where employing one mode is relatively advantageous, other things being equal.

II. THE MODEL

We start with a highly simplified prototype planning problem. Amount q of a certain commodity can be produced at cost $C(q)$, yielding benefits $B(q)$.[4] The word " commodity " is used in an abstract sense and really could pertain to just about any kind of good from pure water to military aircraft. Solely for the sake of preserving a unified notation, we follow the standard convention that goods are desirable. This means that rather than talking about air pollution, for example, we instead deal with its negative—clean air.

Later we treat more complicated cases, but for the time being it is assumed that in effect there is just one producer of the commodity and no ambiguity in the notion of a cost curve. Benefits are measured in terms of money equivalents so that the benefit function can be viewed as the reflection of an indifference curve showing the trade-off between amounts of uncommitted extra funds and output levels of the given commodity. It is assumed that $B''(q)<0$, $C''(q)>0$, $B'(0)>C'(0)$, and $B'(q)<C'(q)$ for q sufficiently large.

---

[1] Strictly speaking, this conclusion is not really justified because there may be important externalities or increasing returns within an organization (they may even constitute its *raison d'être*). Nevertheless, the almost universal absence of internal transfer pricing within private firms strikes me as a rather startling contradiction with the often alleged superiority of indirect controls.

[2] About a decade ago, Ford and GM performed a few administrative trials of a limited sort with some decentralization schemes based on internal transfer prices. The experiments were subsequently discontinued in favour of a return to more traditional planning methods. See Whinston [10].

[3] As one example, if it happens to be the case that it is difficult or expensive to monitor output on a continuous scale but relatively cheap to perform a pass-fail litmus type test on whether a given output level has been attained or not, the price mode may be greatly disadvantaged from the start. The pollution by open-pit mining operations of nearby waterways presents a case in point. It would be difficult or impossible to record how much pollutant is seeping into the ground, whereas it is a comparatively straightforward task to enforce the adoption of one or another level of anti-pollution technology. Another realistic consideration arises when we ask who determines the standards under each mode. For example, if an agency of the executive branch is empowered to regulate prices but the legislature is in charge of setting quantities, that by itself may be important in determining which mode is better for controlling pollution. The price mode would have greater flexibility, but might carry with it more danger of caving in to special interest groups. As yet another realistic consideration, equity arguments are sometimes put forward in favour of price (the supposed " justice " of a uniform price to all) or quantity (equal sharing of a deficit commodity) control modes.

[4] It might be thought that an equivalent approach would be to work with demand and supply curves, identifying the consumers' (producers') surplus area under the demand (supply) curve as benefits (costs) or, equivalently, the demand (supply) curve as the marginal benefit (cost) function. The trouble with this approach is that it tends to give the misleading impression that the market left to itself could solve the problem, obscuring the fact that some key element of the standard competitive supply and demand story is felt to be missing in the first place.

The planning problem is to find that value q^* of q which maximizes

$$B(q) - C(q).$$

The solution must satisfy

$$B'(q^*) = C'(q^*).$$

With

$$p^* \equiv B'(q^*) = C'(q^*),$$

it makes no difference whether the planners announce the optimal price p^* and have the producers maximize profits

$$p^*q - C(q)$$

or whether the centre merely orders the production of q^* at least cost. In an environment of complete knowledge and perfect certainty there is a formal identity between the use of prices and quantities as planning instruments.

If there is any advantage to employing price or quantity control modes, therefore, it must be due to inadequate information or uncertainty. Of course it is natural enough for planners to be unsure about the precise specification of cost and benefit functions since even those most likely to know can hardly possess an exact account.

Suppose, then, that the centre perceives the cost function only as an estimate or approximation. The stochastic relation linking q to C is taken to be of the form

$$C(q, \theta),$$

where θ is a disturbance term or random variable, unobserved and unknown at the present time. While the determination of θ could involve elements of genuine randomness,[1] it is probably more appropriate to think primarily in terms of an information gap.

Even the engineers most closely associated with production would be unable to say beforehand precisely what is the cheapest way of generating various hypothetical output levels. How much murkier still must be the centre's *ex ante* conception of costs, especially in a fast moving world where knowledge of particular circumstances of time and place may be required. True, the degree of fuzziness could be reduced by research and experimentation but it could never be truly eliminated because new sources of uncertainty are arising all the time.[2]

Were a particular output level really ordered in all seriousness, a cost-minimizing firm could eventually grope its way toward the cheapest way of producing it by actually testing out the relevant technological alternatives. Or, if an output price were in fact named, a profit maximizing production level could ultimately be found by trial and error. But this is far from having the cost function as a whole knowable *a priori*.

While the planners may be somewhat better acquainted with the benefit function, it too is presumably discernable only tolerably well, say as

$$B(q, \eta)$$

with η a random variable. The connection between q and B is stochastic either because benefits may be imperfectly known at the present time or because authentic randomness may play a role. Since the unknown factors connecting q with B are likely to be quite different from those linking q to C, it is assumed that the random variables θ and η are independently distributed.

As a possible specific example of the present formulation, consider the problem of air pollution. The variable q could be the cleanliness of air being emitted by a certain type of source. Costs as a function of q might not be known beyond doubt because the technology, quantified by θ, is uncertain. At a given level of q the benefits may be unsure since they depend among other things on the weather, measured by η.

---

1 Like day-to-day fluctuations.
2 For an amplification of some of these points, see Hayek [3].

Now an *ideal* instrument of central control would be a contingency message whose instructions depend on which state of the world is revealed by θ and η. The ideal *ex ante* quantity signal $q^*(\theta, \eta)$ and price signal $p^*(\theta, \eta)$ are in the form of an entire schedule, functions of θ and η satisfying

$$B_1(q^*(\theta, \eta), \eta) = C_1(q^*(\theta, \eta), \theta) = p^*(\theta, \eta).$$

By employing either ideal signal, the *ex ante* uncertainty has in effect been eliminated *ex post* and we are right back to the case where there is no theoretical difference between price and quantity control modes.

It should be readily apparent that it is infeasible for the centre to transmit an entire schedule of ideal prices or quantities. A contingency message is a complicated, specialized contract which is expensive to draw up and hard to understand. The random variables are difficult to quantify. A problem of differentiated information or even of moral hazard may be involved since the exact value of θ will frequently be known only by the producer.[1] Even for the simplest case of just *one* firm, information from different sources must be processed, combined, and evaluated. By the time an ideal schedule was completed, another would be needed because meanwhile changes would have occurred.

In this paper the realistic issue of central control under uncertainty is considered to be the " second best " problem of finding for each producer the single price or quantity message which optimally regulates his actions. This is also the best way to focus sharply and directly on the essential difference between prices and quantities as planning instruments.

The issue of prices *vs.* quantities has to be a " second best " problem by its very nature simply because there is no good *a priori* reason for limiting attention to just these two particular signals. Even if stochastic contingency messages were eliminated on *ad hoc* grounds as being too complicated, there would still be no legitimate justification for not considering, say, an entire expected benefits schedule, or a " kinked " benefit function in the form of a two-tiered price system, or something else. The reason we specialize to price and quantity signals is that these are two *simple* messages, easily comprehended, traditionally employed, and frequently contrasted.[2]

The optimal quantity instrument under uncertainty is that target output $\hat{q}$ which maximizes expected benefits minus expected costs, so that

$$E[B(\hat{q}, \eta) - C(\hat{q}, \theta)] = \max_q E[B(q, \eta) - C(q, \theta)],$$

where $E[.]$ is the expected value operator. The solution $\hat{q}$ must satisfy the first order condition

$$E[B_1(\hat{q}, \eta)] = E[C_1(\hat{q}, \theta)]. \qquad \qquad ...(1)$$

When a price instrument p is announced, production will eventually be adjusted to the output level

$$q = h(p, \theta)$$

which maximizes profits given p and θ. Such a condition is expressed as

$$ph(p, \theta) - C(h(p, \theta), \theta) = \max_q pq - C(q, \theta),$$

implying

$$C_1(h(p, \theta), \theta) = p. \qquad \qquad ...(2)$$

---

[1] So that it may be inappropriate, for example, to tell him to produce less if costs are high unless a very sophisticated incentive scheme goes along with such a message. For an elaboration of some of these points see Arrow [1], pp. 321-322.

[2] There are real costs associated with using more complicated signals. At least implicitly, we are assuming that the magnitude of such costs is sufficiently large to make it uneconomical to consider messages other than prices or quantities. It would be nice to incorporate these costs explicitly into the model, but this is hard to do in any meaningful way.

If the planners are rational, they will choose that price instrument $\tilde{p}$ which maximizes the expected difference between benefits and costs given the reaction function $h(p, \theta)$:

$$E[B(h(\tilde{p}, \theta), \eta) - C(h(\tilde{p}, \theta), \theta)] = \max_{p} E[B(h(p, \theta), \eta) - C(h(p, \theta), \theta)].$$

The solution $\tilde{p}$ must obey the first order equation

$$E[B_1(h(\tilde{p}, \theta), \eta) . h_1(\tilde{p}, \theta)] = E[C_1(h(\tilde{p}, \theta), \theta) . h_1(\tilde{p}, \theta)],$$

which can be rewritten as

$$\tilde{p} = \frac{E[B_1(h(\tilde{p}, \theta), \eta) . h_1(\tilde{p}, \theta)]}{E[h_1(\tilde{p}, \theta)]}. \qquad \ldots(3)$$

Corresponding to the optimal *ex ante* price $\tilde{p}$ is the *ex post* profit maximizing output $\tilde{q}$ expressed as a function of θ,

$$\tilde{q}(\theta) \equiv h(\tilde{p}, \theta). \qquad \ldots(4)$$

In the presence of uncertainty, price and quantity instruments transmit central control in quite different ways. It is important to note that by choosing a specific mode for implementing an intended policy, the planners are at least temporarily locking themselves into certain consequences. The values of η and θ are at first unknown and only gradually, if at all, become recognized through their effects. After the quantity $\hat{q}$ is prescribed, producers will continue to generate that assigned level of output for some time even though in all likelihood

$$B_1(\hat{q}, \eta) \neq C_1(\hat{q}, \theta).$$

In the price mode on the other hand, $\tilde{q}(\theta)$ will be produced where except with negligible probability

$$B_1(\tilde{q}(\theta), \eta) \neq C_1(\tilde{q}(\theta), \theta).$$

Thus neither instrument yields an optimum *ex post*. The relevant question is which one comes closer under what circumstances.[1]

In an infinitely flexible control environment where the planners can continually adjust instruments to reflect current understanding of a fluid situation and producers instantaneously respond, the above considerations are irrelevant and the choice of control mode should be made to depend on other factors. Similar comments apply to a timeless *tâtonnement* milieu where iterations are costless, recontracting takes place after each round, and in effect nothing real is presumed to happen until all the uncertainty has been eliminated and an equilibrium is approached. In any less hypothetical world the consequences of an order given in a particular control mode have to be lived with for at least the time until revisions are made, and real losses will be incurred by selecting the wrong communication medium.

Note that the question usually asked whether it is better to control prices or quantities for *finding* a plan is conceptually distinct from the issue treated in this paper of which mode is superior for *implementing* a plan. The latter way of posing the problem strikes me as more relevant for most actual planning contexts—either because there is no significant informational difference between the two modes in the first place, or because a step in the *tâtonnement* planning game cannot meaningfully occur unless it is really implemented, or because no matter how many iterations have been carried out over time there are always spontaneously arising changes which damp out the significance of knowing past history. In the framework adopted here, the planners are at the decision node where as much information as is feasible to gather has already been obtained by one means or another and an operational plan must be decided on the basis of the available current knowledge.

1 We remark in passing that the issue of whether it is better to stabilize uncertain demand and supply functions by pegging prices or quantities can also be put in the form of the problem analysed in this paper if benefits are associated with the consumers' surplus area under the demand curve and costs with the producers' surplus area under the supply curve.

III. PRICES *vs.* QUANTITIES

It is natural to define the *comparative advantage of prices over quantities* as

$$\Delta \equiv E[(B(\tilde{q}(\theta), \eta) - C(\tilde{q}(\theta), \theta)) - (B(\hat{q}, \eta) - C(\hat{q}, \theta))]. \qquad \ldots(5)$$

The loss function implicit in the definition of Δ is the expected difference in gains obtained under the two modes of control. Naturally there is no real distinction between working with Δ or with $-\Delta$ (the comparative advantage of quantities over prices).

The coefficient Δ is intended to be a measure of *comparative* or *relative* advantage only. It goes without saying that making a decision to use price or quantity control modes in a specific instance is more complicated than just consulting Δ. There are also going to be a host of practical considerations formally outside the scope of the present model. Although such external factors render Δ of limited value when isolated by itself, they do not necessarily diminish its conceptual significance. On the contrary, having an objective criterion of the *ceteris paribus* advantage of a control mode is very important because conceptually it can serve as a benchmark against which the cost of " non-economic " ingredients might be measured in reaching a final judgment about whether it would be better to employ prices or quantities as planning instruments in a given situation.

As it stands, the formulation of cost and benefit functions is so general that it hinders us from cleanly dissecting equation (5). To see clearly what Δ depends on we have to put more structure on the problem. It is possible to be somewhat less restrictive than we are going to be, but only at the great expense of clarity.

In what follows, the amount of uncertainty in marginal cost is taken as sufficiently small to justify a second order approximation of cost and benefit functions within the range of $\tilde{q}(\theta)$ as it varies around $\hat{q}$.[1] Let the symbol " $\cong$ " denote an " accurate local approximation " in the sense of deriving from the assumption that cost and benefit functions are of the following quadratic form within an appropriate neighbourhood of $q = \hat{q}$:

$$C(q, \theta) \cong a(\theta) + (C' + \alpha(\theta))(q - \hat{q}) + \frac{C''}{2}(q - \hat{q})^2 \qquad \ldots(6)$$

$$B(q, \eta) \cong b(\eta) + (B' + \beta(\eta))(q - \hat{q}) + \frac{B''}{2}(q - \hat{q})^2. \qquad \ldots(7)$$

In the above equations $a(\theta)$, $\alpha(\theta)$, $b(\eta)$, $\beta(\eta)$ are stochastic functions and C', C'', B', B'' are fixed coefficients.

Without loss of generality, $\alpha(\theta)$ and $\beta(\eta)$ are standardized in (6), (7) so that their expected values are zero:

$$E[\alpha(\theta)] = E[\beta(\eta)] = 0. \qquad \ldots(8)$$

Since θ and η are independently distributed,

$$E[\alpha(\theta) . \beta(\eta)] = 0. \qquad \ldots(9)$$

Note that the stochastic functions

$$a(\theta) \cong C(\hat{q}, \theta)$$

$$b(\eta) \cong B(\hat{q}, \eta)$$

translate different values of θ and η into pure vertical shifts of the cost and benefit curves.

Differentiating (6) and (7) with respect to q,

$$C_1(q, \theta) \cong (C' + \alpha(\theta)) + C'' . (q - \hat{q}) \qquad \ldots(10)$$

$$B_1(q, \eta) \cong (B' + \beta(\eta)) + B'' . (q - \hat{q}). \qquad \ldots(11)$$

---

[1] Such an approximation can be rigorously defended along the lines developed by Samuelson [8].

Employing the above equations and (8), the following interpretations are available for the fixed coefficients of (6), (7):

$$C' \cong E[C_1(\hat{q}, 0)]$$

$$B' \cong E[B_1(\hat{q}, \eta)]$$

$$C'' \cong C_{11}(q, 0)$$

$$B'' \cong B_{11}(q, \eta).$$

From (1),

$$B' = C'. \qquad \ldots(12)$$

It is apparent from (8) and (10) that stochastic changes in $\alpha(\theta)$ represent pure unbiased shifts of the marginal cost function. The variance of $\alpha(\theta)$ is precisely the mean square error in marginal cost

$$\sigma^2 \equiv E[(C_1(q, \theta) - E[C_1(q, \theta)])^2] \cong E[\alpha(0)^2]. \qquad \ldots(13)$$

Analogous comments hold for the marginal benefit function (11) where we have

$$E[(B_1(q, \eta) - E[B_1(q, \eta)])^2] = E[\beta(\eta)^2].$$

From (10) and (2),

$$h(p, 0) \cong \hat{q} + \frac{p - C' - \alpha(0)}{C''} \qquad \ldots(14)$$

implying

$$h_1(p, \theta) \cong \frac{1}{C''}. \qquad \ldots(15)$$

Substituting from (15) into (3) and cancelling out C'' yields

$$\tilde{p} \cong E[B_1(h(\tilde{p}, \theta), \eta)]. \qquad \ldots(16)$$

Replacing q in (11) by the expression for $h(\tilde{p}, 0)$ from (14) and plugging into (16), the following equation is obtained after using (8)

$$\tilde{p} \cong B' + \frac{B''}{C''}(\tilde{p} - C'). \qquad \ldots(17)$$

From (12) and the condition $B'' < 0 < C''$, (17) implies

$$\tilde{p} \cong C'. \qquad \ldots(18)$$

Combining (4), (14), and (18),

$$\tilde{q}(\theta) \cong \hat{q} - \frac{\alpha(\theta)}{C''}. \qquad \ldots(19)$$

Now alternately substitute $q = \hat{q}$ and $q = \tilde{q}(\theta)$ from (19) into (6) and (7). Then plugging the resulting values of (6), (7) into (5), using (8), (9), and collecting terms,

$$\Delta \cong \frac{\sigma^2 B''}{2C''^2} + \frac{\sigma^2}{2C''}. \qquad \ldots(20)$$

Expression (20) is the fundamental result of this paper.[1] The next section is devoted to examining it in detail.

---

[1] In the supply and demand context B'' is the slope of the (linear) demand curve, C'' is the slope of the (linear) supply curve, and σ^2 is the variance of vertical shifts in the supply curve.

IV. ANALYSING THE COEFFICIENT OF COMPARATIVE ADVANTAGE

Note that the uncertainty in benefits does not appear in (20).[1] To a second-order approximation it affects price and quantity modes *equally* adversely. On the other hand, Δ depends linearly on the mean square error in marginal cost. The *ceteris paribus* effect of increasing σ^2 is to magnify the expected loss from employing the planning instrument with comparative disadvantage. Conversely, as σ^2 shrinks to zero we move closer to the perfect certainty case where in theory the two control modes perform equally satisfactorily.

Clearly Δ depends critically on the curvature of cost and benefit functions around the optimal output level. The first thing to note is that the sign of Δ simply equals the sign of $C'' + B''$. When the sum of the " other " considerations nets out to a zero bias toward either control mode, quantities are the preferred planning instrument if and only if benefits have more curvature than costs.

Normally we would want to know the magnitude of Δ and what it depends on, as well as the sign. To strengthen our intuitive feeling for the meaning of formula (20), we turn first to some extreme cases where there is a strong comparative advantage to one control mode over the other. In this connection it is important to bear in mind that when we talk about " large " or " small " values of B'', C'', or σ^2, we are only speaking in a relative sense. The absolute measure of any variable appearing in (20) does not really mean much alone since it is arbitrarily pegged by selecting the units in which output is reckoned.

The coefficient Δ is negative and large as either the benefit function is more sharply curved or the cost function is closer to being linear. Using a price control mode in such situations could have detrimental consequences. When marginal costs are nearly flat, the smallest miscalculation or change results in either much more or much less than the desired quantity. On the other hand, if benefits are almost kinked at the optimum level of output, there is a high degree of risk aversion and the centre cannot afford being even slightly off the mark. In both cases the quantity mode scores a lot of points because a high premium is put on the rigid output controllability which only it can provide under uncertainty.

From (20), the price mode looks relatively more attractive when the benefit function is closer to being linear. In such a situation it would be foolish to name quantities. Since the marginal social benefit is approximately constant in some range, a superior policy is to name it as a price and let the producers find the optimal output level themselves, after eliminating the uncertainty from costs.

At a point where the cost function is highly curved, Δ becomes nearly zero. If marginal costs are very steeply rising around the optimum, as with fixed capacity, there is not much difference between controlling by price or quantity instruments because the resulting output will be almost the same with either mode. In such a situation, as with the case $\sigma^2 = 0$, " non-economic " factors should play the decisive role in determining which system of control to impose.

It is difficult to refrain from noticing that although there are plenty of instances where

---

[1] This is because the *expected* benefit function (see equation (7)) does not depend on the variance of marginal benefits so long as costs and benefits are independently distributed. If they are *not*, so that

$$\sigma_{bc}^2 \equiv E[\{C_1(q, \theta) - E[C_1(q, \theta)]\}.\{B_1(q, \eta) - E[B_1(q, \eta)]\}] = E[\alpha(\theta).\beta(\eta)] \neq 0,$$

(20) must be replaced by: $\Delta \triangleq \dfrac{\sigma^2 B''}{2C''^2} + \dfrac{1}{2C''}(\sigma^2 - 2\sigma_{bc}^2)$. The sole effect of having costs and benefits correlated with each other is embodied in the term σ_{bc}^2. When marginal costs are positively correlated with marginal benefits, the *ceteris paribus* comparative advantage of the quantity mode is increased. If prices are used as a control mode, the producer will tend to cut back output for high marginal costs. But with σ_{bc}^2 positive, this is the very same time that marginal benefits tend to be high, so that a cutback may not really be in order. In such situations the quantity mode has better properties as a stabilizer, other things being equal. The story is the other way around when σ_{bc}^2 is negative. In that case high marginal costs are associated with low marginal benefits, so that the price mode (which decreases output for high marginal costs) tends to be a better mode of control other things being equal.

the price mode has a good solid comparative advantage (because $-B''$ is small), in some sense it looks as if prices can be a *disastrous* choice of instrument far more often than quantities can. Using (20), $\Delta \to -\infty$ if either $B'' \to -\infty$ or $C'' \to 0$ (or both). The only way $\Delta \to +\infty$ is under the thin set of circumstances where simultaneously $C'' \to 0$, $B'' \to 0$, and $C'' > -B''$. In a world where C'' and B'' are themselves imperfectly known it seems hard to avoid the impression that there will be many circumstances where the more conservative quantity mode will be preferred by planners because it is better for avoiding very bad planning mistakes.[1]

Having seen how C'' and B'' play an essential role in determining Δ, it may be useful to check out a few of the principal situations where we might expect to encounter cost and benefit functions of one curvature or another. We start with costs.

Contemporary economic theory has tended to blur the distinction between the traditional marginalist way of treating production theory with smoothly differentiable production functions and the activity analysis approach with its limited number of alternative production processes. For many theoretical purposes convexity of the underlying technology is really the fundamental property.

However, there are very different implications for the efficacy of price and quantity control modes between a situation described by classically smooth Marshallian cost curves and one characterized by piecewise linear cost functions with a limited number of kinks. In the latter case, the quantity mode tends to have a relative advantage since $\Delta = -\infty$ on the flats and $\Delta = 0$ at the elbows. Of course it is impossible to use a price to control an output at all unless some hidden fixed factors take the flatness out of the average cost curve. Even then, Δ will be positive only if there are enough alternative techniques available to make the cost function have more (finite difference) curvature than the benefit function in the neighbourhood of an optimal policy.

What determines the benefit function for a commodity is contingent in the first place on whether the commodity is a final or intermediate good. The benefit of a final good is essentially the utility which arises out of consuming the good. It could be highly curved at the optimum output level if tastes happen to be kinked at certain critical points. The amount of pollution which makes a river just unfit for swimming could be a point where the marginal benefits of an extra unit of output change very rapidly. Another might be the level of defence which just neutralizes an opponent's offence or the level of offence which just overcomes a given defence. There are many examples which arise in emergencies or natural calamities. Our intuitive feeling, which is confirmed by the formal analysis, is that it doesn't pay to " fool around " with prices in such situations.

For intermediate goods, the shape of the benefit function will depend among other things on the degree of substitutability in use of this commodity with other resources available in the production organization and upon the possibilities for importing this

---

[1] This idea could be formalized as follows. Consider two generalizations of formulae (6) and (7):

$$C(q, \theta) \triangleq a(\theta) + (C' + \alpha(\theta))(q - \hat{q}) + \frac{C''}{2f(\theta)} (q - \hat{q})^2$$

$$B(q, \eta) \triangleq b(\eta) + (B' + \beta(\eta))(q - \hat{q}) + \frac{B''g(\eta)}{2} (q - \hat{q})^2.$$

The only difference with (6), (7) is that now $1/C_{11}(q, \theta)$ and $B_{11}(q, \eta)$ are allowed to be uncertain. The change in the profit maximizing output response per unit price change is now stochastic, $h_1(p, \theta) = f(\theta)/C''$. Without loss of generality we set

$$E[f(\theta)] = E[g(\eta)] = 1.$$

Note that increasing the variance of $f(g)$ is a mean preserving spread of C_{11} (B_{11}). Suppose for simplicity that f and α are independent of each other. Then we can derive the appropriate generalization of (20) as

$$\Delta \triangleq \frac{B''\sigma^2(1 + \delta^2)}{2C''^2} + \frac{\sigma^2}{2C''}$$

where $\delta^2 \equiv E[\{f(\theta) - E[f(\theta)]\}^2]$ is the variance of $f(\theta)$. The above formula can be interpreted as saying that other things being equal, greater uncertainty in $1/C_{11}(q, \theta)$ increases the comparative advantage of the quantity mode.

commodity from outside the organization. These things in turn are very much dependent on the planning time horizon. In the long run the benefit function probably becomes flatter because more possibilities for substitution are available, including perhaps importing. Take for example the most extreme degree of complete " openness " where any amount of the commodity can be instantaneously and effortlessly bought (and sold) outside the production organization at a fixed price. The relevant benefit function is of course just a straight line whose slope is the outside price.

There is, it seems to me, a rather fundamental reason to believe that quantities are better signals for situations demanding a high degree of coordination. A classical example would be the short run production planning of intermediate industrial materials. Within a large production organization, be it the General Motors Corporation or the Soviet industrial sector as a whole, the need for balancing the output of any intermediate commodity whose production is relatively specialized to this organization and which cannot be effortlessly and instantaneously imported from or exported to a perfectly competitive outside world puts a kink in the benefit function. If it turns out that production of ball bearings of a certain specialized kind (plus reserves) falls short of anticipated internal consumption, far more than the value of the unproduced bearings can be lost. Factors of production and materials that were destined to be combined with the ball bearings and with commodities containing them in higher stages of production must stand idle and are prevented from adding value all along the line. If on the other hand more bearings are produced than were contemplated being consumed, the excess cannot be used immediately and will only go into storage to lose implicit interest over time. Such short run rigidity is essentially due to the limited substitutability, fixed coefficients nature of a technology based on machinery.[1] Other things being equal, the asymmetry between the effects of overproducing and underproducing are more pronounced the further removed from final use is the commodity and the more difficult it is to substitute alternative slack resources or to quickly replenish supplies by emergency imports. The resulting strong curvature in benefits around the planned consumption levels of intermediate materials tends to create a very high comparative advantage for quantity instruments. If this is combined with a cost function that is nearly linear in the relevant range, the advantage of the quantity mode is doubly compounded.[2]

V. MANY PRODUCTION UNITS

Consider the same model previously developed except that now instead of being a single good, $q = (q_1, ..., q_n)$ is an n-vector of commodites. The various components of q might represent physically distinct commodities or they could denote amounts of the same commodity produced by different production units. Benefits are $B(q, \eta)$ and the cost of producing the ith good is $c^i(q_i, \theta_i)$. As before, for each i the two random variables η and θ_i are distributed independently of each other.

Suppose the issue of control is phrased as choosing either the quantities $\{\hat{q}_i\}$ which maximize

$$E\left[B(q, \eta) - \sum_1^n c^i(q_i, \theta_i) \right],$$

---

[1] The existence of buffer stocks changes the point at which the kink occurs, but does not remove it. For a more detailed treatment of this entire topic, see Manove [6].

[2] Note that in the context of an autarchic planned economy, such pessimistic conclusions about the feasibility of using Lange-Lerner price signals to control short run output do not carry over to, say, agriculture. The argument just given for a kinked benefit function would not at all pertain to a food crop, which goes more or less directly into final demand. In addition, the cost function for producing a given agricultural commodity ought to be much closer to the classical smooth variety than to the linear programming type with just a few kinks.

or the prices $\{\tilde{p}_i\}$ which maximize

$$E[B(h(p,\,0),\,\eta) - \Sigma c^i(h_i(p_i,\,0_i),\,0_i)],$$

where $\{h_i(p_i,\,0_i)\}$ are defined analogously to (2).

Naturally the coefficient of comparative advantage is now defined as

$$\Delta_n \equiv E\left[\left\{B\left(\tilde{q}(0),\,\eta\right) - \sum_1^n c^i(\tilde{q}_i(0_i),\,0_i)\right\} - \left\{B(\hat{q},\,\eta) - \sum_1^n c^i(\hat{q}_i,\,0_i)\right\}\right].$$

Assuming locally quadratic costs and benefits, it is a straightforward generalization of what was done in Section III to derive the analogue of expression (20),

$$\Delta_n \underset{\simeq}{\simeq} \sum_{i=1}^n \sum_{j=1}^n \frac{B_{ij}\sigma_{ij}^2}{2c_{11}^i c_{11}^j} + \sum_{i=1}^n \frac{\sigma_{ii}^2}{2c_{11}^i}, \qquad \dots(21)$$

where

$$\sigma_{ij}^2 \underset{\simeq}{\simeq} E[\{c_1^i(q_i,\,0_i) - E[c_1^i(q_i,\,0_i)]\}\{c_1^j(q_j,\,0_j) - E[c_1^j(q_j,\,0_j)]\}]. \qquad \dots(22)$$

To correct for the pure effect of n on Δ_n, it is more suitable to work with the transformed cost functions

$$C^i(x_i,\,0_i) \equiv nc^i(x_i/n,\,0_i). \qquad \dots(23)$$

The meaning of C^i is most readily interpreted for the situation where n different units are producing the same commodity or a close substitute with similar cost functions. Then C^i is what total costs would be as a function of total output if each production unit were an identical replica of the ith unit. When " other things being equal " n is changed, it is more appropriate to think of C^i being held constant rather than c^i.

With C^i defined by (23), we have

$$C_1^i = c_1^i \qquad \dots(24)$$

$$C_{11}^i = \frac{c_{11}^i}{n}. \qquad \dots(25)$$

Relation (24) means that in the quadratic case the coefficients of the marginal cost variance-covariance matrix for the $\{C_1^i\}$ are the same as those given by (22) for the $\{c_1^i\}$. Substituting (25) into (21),

$$\Delta_n \underset{\simeq}{\simeq} \frac{1}{n^2} \sum_{i=1}^n \sum_{j=1}^n \frac{B_{ij}\sigma_{ij}^2}{2C_{11}^i C_{11}^j} + \frac{1}{n} \sum_{i=1}^n \frac{\sigma_{ii}^2}{2C_{11}^i}. \qquad \dots(26)$$

The above formula shows that in effect the original expression for Δ holds *on the average* for Δ_n when there is more than one producer. Naturally the generalization (26) is more complicated, but the interpretation of it is basically similar to the diagnosis of (20) which was just given in the previous section.

There is, however, a fundamental distinction between having one and many producers which is concealed in formula (26). With some degree of independence among the distributions of individual marginal costs, less weight will be put on the first summation term of (26). Other things being equal, in situations with more rather than fewer independent units producing outputs which substitute for each other in yielding benefits, there is a correspondingly greater relative advantage to the price mode of control. Although this point has general validity, it can be most transparently seen in the special regularized case of one good being produced by many micro-units with symmetrical cost functions. In such a case

$$B_{ij} = B'' \qquad \dots(27.\text{i})$$

$$C_{11} = C'' \qquad \dots(27.\text{ii})$$

$$\sigma_{ii}^2 = \sigma^2 \qquad \qquad ...(27.\text{iii})$$

$$\sigma_{ij}^2 = \rho\sigma^2, \quad i \neq j, \quad -1 \leqq \rho \leqq 1. \qquad ...(27.\text{iv})$$

The coefficient ρ is a measure of the correlation between marginal costs of separate production units. If all units are pretty much alike and are using a similar technology, ρ is likely to be close to unity. If the cost functions of different units are more or less independent of each other, ρ should be nearly zero. While in theory the correlation coefficient can vary between plus and minus unity, for most situations of practical interest the marginal costs of two different production units will have a non-negative cross correlation.

Using (27), (26) can be rewritten as

$$\Delta_n \stackrel{\circ}{=} \rho\left(\frac{B''\sigma^2}{2C''^2} + \frac{\sigma^2}{2C''}\right) + (1-\rho)\left(\frac{1}{n}\frac{B''\sigma^2}{2C''^2} + \frac{\sigma^2}{2C''}\right). \qquad ...(28)$$

If the marginal costs of each identical micro-unit are perfectly correlated with each other so that $\rho = 1$, it is as if there is but a single producer and we are exactly back to the original formula (20). With $n > 1$, as ρ decreases, Δ_n goes up. A *ceteris paribus* move from dependent toward independent costs increases the comparative advantage of prices, an effect which is more pronounced as the number of production units is larger. If there are three distinctly different types of sulphur dioxide emitters with independent technologies instead of one large pollution source yielding the same aggregate effect, a relatively stronger case exists for using prices to regulate output.

When it is desired to control different units producing an identical commodity by setting prices, only a single price need be named as an instrument. The price mode therefore possesses the *ceteris paribus* advantage that output is being produced efficiently *ex post*. With prices as instruments

$$c_1^i(\tilde{q}_i, \theta_i) = c_1^j(\tilde{q}_j, \theta_j) = \tilde{p},$$

whereas with quantities

$$c_1^i(\hat{q}_i, \theta_i) \neq c_1^j(\hat{q}_j, \theta_j)$$

except on a set of negligible probability.

Using prices thus enables the centre to automatically screen out the high cost producers, encouraging them to produce less and the low cost units more. This predominance in efficiency makes the comparative advantage of the price mode go up as the number of independent production units becomes larger, other things being equal. The precise statement of such a proposition would depend on exactly what was held equal as n was increased—the variance of *individual* costs or the overall variance of *total* costs. For simplicity consider the case of completely independent marginal costs, $\rho = 0$. Then (28) becomes

$$\Delta_n \stackrel{\circ}{=} \frac{1}{n}\frac{B''\sigma^2(n)}{2C''^2} + \frac{\sigma^2(n)}{2C''}, \qquad ...(29)$$

where $\sigma^2(n)$ is implicitly some (given) function of n. If the " other thing " being equal is the constant variance of marginal costs for each individual producing unit, then $\sigma^2(n) \equiv \sigma^2$. If the variance of total costs is held constant as n varies, $\sigma^2(n) \equiv n\sigma^2$. Either way Δ_n in (29) increases monotonically with n and eventually becomes positive.

It is important to note that such *ceteris paribus* efficiency advantages of the price mode as we have been considering for large n are by no means enough to guarantee that Δ_n will be positive in a particular situation for any *given* n. True, what aggregate output is forthcoming under the price mode will be produced at least total cost. But it might be the wrong overall output level to start with. If the $\{-B_{ij}\}$ are sufficiently large or the $\{C_{11}^i\}$ sufficiently small, it may be advantageous to enjoy greater control over total output by setting individual quotas, even after taking account (as our formula for Δ_n does) of the losses incurred by the *ex post* productive inefficiency of such a procedure.[1]

Returning to the general case with which this section began, we note that the basic difference between benefits and costs becomes somewhat more transparent in the n commodity vector formulation. Only the centre knows benefits. Even if it could be done it would not help to transmit $B(.)$ to individual production units because benefits are typically a non-separable function of *all* the units' outputs, whereas a particular unit has control only over its *own* output. In any well formulated mode of decentralized control, the objective function to be maximized by a given unit must depend in some well-defined way on *its* decisions alone. For the purposes of our formulation B need not be a benefit and the $\{c^i\}$ need not be costs in the usual sense, although in many contexts this is the most natural interpretation. The crucial distinction is that B is in principle knowable only by the centre, whereas c^i is best known by firm i.[2]

When uncertainties in individual costs are unrelated so that the random variables θ_i and θ_j are independently distributed, the decision to use a price or quantity instrument to control q_i alone is decentralizable. Suppose it has already been resolved by one means or another whether to use price or quantity instruments to control q_j for each $j \neq i$. To a quadratic approximation, the comparative advantage of prices over quantities for commodity i is

$$\Delta^i \gtreqqless \frac{\sigma_{ii}^2 B_{ii}}{2c_{11}^{i^2}} + \frac{\sigma_{ii}^2}{2c_{11}^i}, \qquad \qquad ...(30)$$

which is exactly the formula (20) for this particular case.

In some situations, " mixed " price-quantity modes may give the best results. As a specific example, suppose that q_1 is the catch of a certain fish from a large lake and q_2 from a small but prolific pond. Let q_1 be produced with relatively flat average costs but q_2 have a cost function which is curved at the optimum somewhat more than the benefit function. The optimal policy according to (30) will be to name a quota for q_1 and a price for q_2.

REFERENCES

[1]   Arrow, K. J.   " Research in Management Controls: A Critical Synthesis ", pp. 317-327, in Bonini, Jaedicke and Wagner (eds.), *Management Controls* (New York: McGraw-Hill, 1964).

[2]   Dales, J. H.   *Pollution, Property and Prices* (Toronto: University of Toronto Press, 1968).

[1] An even better procedure from a theoretical point of view in the case where an identical output is produced by many firms would be to fix *total* output by command and subdivide it by a price mechanism. This kind of solution is proposed by Dales [2] who would set up a market in " pollution rights ", the fixed supply of which is regulated by the goverrment. In effect, such an approach aggregates the individual cost functions, and we are right back to a single cost function. Note that a basic question would still remain: is it better to fix the total amount by a quantity or price control mode?

[2] An interesting application of the ideas of this section is provided by the problem of choosing a control mode for best distributing a deficit commodity in fixed supply (say gasoline). In this case what we have been calling an individual cost function, $c^i(q_i, \theta_i)$, would really be the negative of a user's benefit function (as measured by the area under his demand curve). Our B function (of total demand) would just reflect the opportunity loss of having a surplus or shortage of the implied amount when only a fixed supply is available. All the considerations of this section would apply in determining the coefficient of comparative advantage. Accurately characterizing the B function seems especially difficult in the present context. If the commodity can be bought from or sold to the outside world, the B function would just embody the terms of this opportunity (in particular, it would be flat if any amount of the commodity could be bought or sold at some fixed price). Under autonomy, the shape of the B function would depend on what is done in a surplus or deficit situation. With a surplus (from naming too high a price), it would depend on the value to future allocation possibilities of the excess supply, relative to what welfare was lost at the present

[3] Hayek, F. A. " The Use of Knowledge in Society ", *American Economic Review*, **35**, 4 (September 1945), pp. 519-530.

[4] Heal, G. " Planning Without Prices ", *Review of Economic Studies*, **36** (1969), pp. 347-362.

[5] Malinvaud, E. " Decentralized Procedures for Planning ", ch. 7 in Malinvaud (ed.), *Activity Analysis in the Theory of Growth and Planning* (New York: Macmillan, 1967).

[6] Manove, M. " Non-Price Rationing of Intermediate Goods in Centrally Planned Economies ", *Econometrica*, **41** (September 1973), pp. 829-852.

[7] Marglin, S. " Information in Price and Command Systems of Planning ", in Margolis (ed.), *Conference on the Analysis of the Public Sector* (Biarritz, 1966), pp. 54-76.

[8] Samuelson, P. A. " The Fundamental Approximation Theorem of Portfolio Analysis in Terms of Means, Variances and Higher Moments ", *Review of Economic Studies*, **37** (October 1970), pp. 537-542.

[9] Weitzman, M. " Iterative Multilevel Planning with Production Targets ", *Econometrica*, **38**, 1 (January 1970), pp. 50-65.

[10] Whinston, A. " Price Guides in Decentralized Institutions ", Ph.D. thesis, Carnegie Institute of Technology, 1962.

---

time from having demand less than supply. With a deficit (from naming too low a price), the loss of welfare hinges on how shortages are actually distributed among consumers. If shortages result in some people doing completely without the product, the overall welfare losses may be very great and $|B''|$ could be large. If there is some inherent reason to believe that shortages will automatically be evenly distributed, then $|B''|$ may not be so big. In addition to redistribution losses, there will always be waiting time losses in a shortage. Finally, note that if the amount of the fixed supply is known, a superior policy to naming prices or quantities is to distribute ration tickets (instead of quantities), allowing them to be resold at a competitively determined market price.

[8]

JOURNAL OF ENVIRONMENTAL ECONOMICS AND MANAGEMENT 3, 178–188 (1976)

Uncertainty and the Choice of Pollution Control Instruments

ZVI ADAR

Department of Economics, Tel Aviv University, Tel Aviv, Israel

AND

JAMES M. GRIFFIN

Department of Economics, University of Pennsylvania, Philadelphia, Pennsylvania 19174

Received January 12, 1976

This paper compares the relative efficiencies of pollution taxes, pollution standards, and the auctioning of pollution rights when the marginal damage function or marginal control cost are subject to uncertainty. In the first case, we find that all instruments yield the same expected social surplus. In the latter case, the choice of the optimal instrument depends, in general, on the relative elasticities of the marginal damage and marginal expected cost functions, on the way in which uncertainty enters the model, and on the distribution of the error term. Policy conclusions are derived.

I. INTRODUCTION

The choice between alternative pollution control instruments typically centers on comparisons of transaction costs, and administrative and policy costs.[1] While such cost comparisons are no doubt important, we question why the role of uncertainty is generally omitted in welfare calculations. Practitioners in the field of environmental quality recognize that uncertainty concerning the nature of the marginal damage function and the marginal control cost function are major stumbling blocks to selecting Pareto-efficient policies.[2] Perhaps the omission of uncertainty in the instrument choice discussion is due to an implicit assumption that uncertainty, while pervasive, is simply neutral to the instrument choice question. A notable exception is Lerner [6] who recognized that the relative slopes of the marginal damage and control cost functions should affect the choice between price and quantity controls.

As an extension to Lerner's conjecture, this paper delimits the circumstances under which uncertainty does and does not affect the choice between the following three policy instruments: taxes (a flat excise tax per unit of pollution); standards (quantitative controls on the amount of pollution generated by each source or firm[3]); and the Dale's proposal [3] for the auctioning of a fixed quantity of transferable pollution

---

[1] For example, see [3, 5].

[2] For an example concerning SO_2 taxes, see [4], where major uncertainty about the availability of flue-gas desulphurization is a problem.

[3] Note that throughout, we assume standards are set such that the marginal cost of abatement is equalized across firms, i.e., they are Pareto-efficient. Later, we return to this assumption.

POLLUTION CONTROL UNDER UNCERTAINTY 179

rights. This paper shows that certain types of uncertainty can affect our choice between the three instruments while other types should not.

In order to delimit the circumstances under which uncertainty matters, it is necessary to distinguish the types and sources of uncertainty. Uncertainty permeates environmental policy-making in terms of the calculations of both marginal damages and marginal control costs. Uncertainty can manifest itself to the individual firm's decision makers and/or to the pollution control agency. At the firm level, uncertainty enters through the firm's marginal control cost function and through uncertainty induced by the control agency. Uncertainty concerning the firm's marginal cost function for pollution abatement is partially technology-induced as the control technology may be unproven or so new that future cost reductions due to potential scale economies, learning-curve phenomena, or technology diffusion rates are uncertain. In addition, uncertainty about future input prices introduces added uncertainty to the firm's marginal control cost function. As firms are well aware, the actions of the control agency can introduce an added source of disturbance. Examples include frequent changes in the pollution tax rate, changes in the pollution standards, or variations in the auction price for tickets.

Uncertainty at the level of the pollution control agency includes many of the same phenomena facing the firm, such as the uncertainty attached to the firm's marginal cost functions which in turn imparts uncertainty to the aggregate marginal control cost function facing the agency (society). Technologic and input price uncertainties prevail at either level of disaggregation. While the agency is presumably free of the uncertainty it confers on the firm through policy changes, it faces two additional sources of uncertainty. First, even if the firm's marginal cost functions are known, the marginal control cost function facing the agency may not be known. Baumol [1] has considered these uncertainties and found them so pervasive that he favors policies which effectively disregard Pareto-efficiency criteria.[4]

A second and perhaps the most perplexing form of additional uncertainty is that the agencies have only vague ideas about the social marginal damage function. The standard errors attached to estimates of health and real estate costs of air pollution are indeed large. Thus a type of measurement uncertainty is connected with the marginal damage function owing to the difficulties of measuring social damage from pollution. Even with correctly measured marginal damage functions, a stochastic component would still enter through ambient air conditions which change continuously depending on climatic conditions. In the case of air pollution, factors varying daily, such as wind velocity and direction, affect the social damage of a given pollutant discharge.

In opposition to Baumol's policy advice, this paper posits that the purpose of policy in the face of uncertainty is to maximize expected welfare. In Section II, we begin by examining uncertainty at the level of the control agency. First, we contrast the expected welfare losses of all three policy instruments when uncertainty enters the marginal damage function. Second, we contrast the three instruments assuming the marginal control cost function is subject to uncertainty. These exercises reveal a fundamental asymmetry in the effects of uncertainty. In Section III, we consider how uncertainty combined with risk aversion by firms might change the previous results. Section IV explores differential uncertainty effects between standards and auctions. In Section V, we recapitulate the major policy implications.

_____

[4] Also see [2].

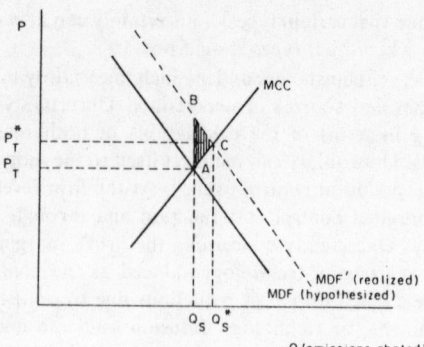

FIG. 1. Uncertain marginal damage function.

II. UNCERTAINTY AT THE AGENCY LEVEL

This section illustrates that there is a basic asymmetry in the effects of uncertainty associated with the marginal damage function *vis-à-vis* the marginal control cost function on the choice between taxes, standards, and auctions. First, consider the case where the marginal control cost function (MCC) is known, and only the marginal damage function (MDF) is subject to uncertainty. In Fig. 1, we measure along the quantity axis, the pollution abated; corresponding to the origin of 0 reductions is the uncontrolled discharge of Q_{max}. Policies based on the hypothesized marginal damage function would result in a tax of P_T, the abatement of Q_S units under a standards policy, or the auction of $Q_{max} - Q_S$ tickets. Due to uncertainty, the realized marginal damage function (MDF) deviated from the hypothesized MDF function in Fig. 1. Equivalent welfare losses will occur under a tax, standards, or an auction. With a tax policy, where the tax is set at P_T, emissions abated will only be Q_S and the welfare loss from a tax is given by the shaded area ABC. Under a standards or auction policy, the emissions abated are again only Q_S, while the optimal reduction is Q_S^*. Likewise, the welfare loss associated with these policies is the area ABC. Thus all three policies yield similar welfare losses. The explanation for this equivalency is that the quantities discharged, irrespective of the instrument, depend solely on the marginal control cost function, which is certain in this case, thereby resulting in identical quantities discharged, irrespective of the policy instrument. Thus the introduction of uncertainty in the damage function has nothing to say about the choice of policy instruments.

While intuition might suggest that similar results hold for the case in which the marginal control cost function is uncertain, this is not the case. Figure 2 illustrates a case in which the optimal tax, P_T, and the equivalent optimal quantity, Q_S, are assigned based upon the hypothesized shape of the marginal control cost function (MCC). However, the actual marginal control cost function turns out to be MCC′ as marginal costs are much higher than anticipated.

With a tax of P_T, only Q' emissions were abated, even though at Q' the marginal damage rate $(Q'B)$ exceeds the marginal costs $(Q'A)$. An optimal tax, P_T^*, would have provided for emission abatement of Q_S^* and would have avoided the welfare loss given by the shaded area (ABC).

With perfect hindsight, the optimal standard would have been Q_S^*. The resulting welfare loss from a standards policy is given by the shaded area CDE. Similarly, since

POLLUTION CONTROL UNDER UNCERTAINTY   181

for an auction only $Q_{max} - Q_S$ tickets would be auctioned, the level of pollution is reduced to Q_S and the welfare loss is equivalent to that of a standards policy (CDE). As Fig. 2 illustrates for the case depicted, the welfare loss from a tax clearly exceeds the welfare loss for either a standards or auction policy. Therefore, we observe a fundamental asymmetry between uncertainty in the MDF, which leads to equivalent welfare losses, and uncertainty in the MCC curve which produces dichotomous results between taxes and quantitative restrictions (either in the form of an auction or standards). The explanation is that in the former case the MCC is known, thus price or quantitative controls are equivalent, while, with a stochastic marginal control cost functions, this uniqueness between prices and quantities no longer holds since quantity under a tax varies with shifts in MCC.

Clearly, the welfare loss, CDE is not equal to the welfare loss ABC. In the case plotted in Fig. 2, the former is smaller, indicating the superiority of quantity restrictions. This, of course, is not a general result; the welfare loss from setting the tax P_T can be approximated by the area of the triangle ABE less the area ACE, and can be expressed by

$$WL_T - ACE = \tfrac{1}{2}\Delta P_T \Delta Q_T, \tag{1}$$

where

$$\Delta P_T = AB \quad \text{and} \quad \Delta Q_T = Q_S - Q'.$$

Substituting the elasticity (e_d) of the MDF curve, (1) can be also written as

$$WL_T - ACE = -(\tfrac{1}{2})(P/Q)(\Delta Q_T)^2(1/e_d). \tag{2}$$

The welfare loss associated with a quantitative restriction can be viewed graphically in Fig. 2 as the triangle ADE less the area ACE. The new welfare loss can be approximated as

$$WL_q - ACE = \tfrac{1}{2}\Delta P_S \Delta Q_S, \quad \text{where} \quad \Delta P_S = DE \quad \text{and} \quad \Delta Q_S = Q_S - Q'. \tag{3}$$

Equation (3) can be restated in terms of price, quantity, and the elasticity of the control cost function (e_c).

$$WL_q - ACE = (\tfrac{1}{2})(P/Q)(\Delta Q_s)^2(1/e_c). \tag{4}$$

Combining Eqs. (2) and (4), and using the fact that $\Delta Q_s = \Delta Q_T$, yields

$$WL_T - WL_q = -(\tfrac{1}{2})(P/Q)(\Delta Q)^2[(1/e_d) + (1/e_c)]. \tag{5}$$

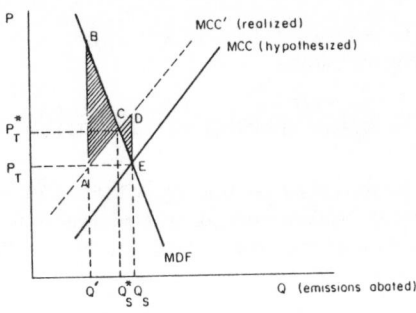

FIG. 2. Uncertain marginal control cost function.

Equation (5) suggests that tax and standards policies will have identical welfare loss properties only when (a) the damage and control cost elasticities are equal in absolute value, or (b) $\Delta Q = 0$, i.e., actual equals the hypothesized marginal control cost function implying zero welfare losses. An important implication of (5) is that standards are preferable when e_d approaches zero and a tax policy is preferable when e_c approaches zero, *ceteris paribus*.

This result suggests a fundamental asymmetry between the uncertainty in the damage function and in the control cost function on the relative effectiveness of tax, standards, and auction policies of abating pollution. When MDF deviates from its hypothesized value, all policies will generate the same deadweight loss. With (vertical) variations in MCC, we should expect welfare losses which depend on the slopes, or elasticities of the MDF and MCC curves. The marginal control cost function forms a behavioral relation for the firm under a tax. If MCC is known, taxes and quantitative instruments yield equivalent reductions in pollution, irrespective of movements in the marginal damage function. In contrast, the actual, as opposed to the hypothesized, marginal damage function, evinces no quantitative response irrespective of the instrument. Thus variations in MDF produce no dichotomy between price (tax) and quantitative (standards or auction) policies.

This asymmetry between uncertainty in the damage and control cost functions carries over to the problem of selecting the optimal policy instrument as well as the level of control under uncertainty.

First, consider the case where MDF is random, and the goal of the agency is to maximize *expected* welfare (i.e., minimizing the expected area ABC in Fig. 2).

Let MDF be given by the relationship

$$\text{MDF}(q, u), \tag{6}$$

where q is the quantity abated and u is a random variable with known density $dF(u)$. By assumption, MCC is a known function depending only on the level of abatement

$$\text{MCC}(q), \tag{7}$$

with quantitative restrictions of either a standards or auction type. An agency attempting to maximize the expected welfare gain will set Q_S such that expected consumers' and producers' surplus is maximized as follows.

$$\operatorname*{E}_{u} \int_{0}^{Q_s} [\text{MDF}(q, u) - \text{MCC}(q)]dq. \tag{8}$$

Under a tax policy, the agency will again set a tax, P, so as to maximize the expected consumers' and producers' surplus

$$\operatorname*{E}_{u} \int_{0}^{Q_s(P)} [\text{MDF}(q, u) - \text{MCC}(q)]dq. \tag{9}$$

Since $Q_s(P)$ is the single valued relation $Q_s = \text{MCC}^{-1}(P)$, which is known with certainty, maximizing (8) with respect to Q is equivalent to maximizing (9) with respect to P_T. The optimal quantity corresponding to P^* (i.e., Q_S^* or $Q_s(P^*)$] is given by the first-order condition

$$\operatorname*{E}_{u} \text{MDF}(Q_S^*, u) = \text{MCC}(Q_S^*). \tag{10}$$

POLLUTION CONTROL UNDER UNCERTAINTY   183

The second-order condition invariably holds since we assume a negatively sloped MDF curve and a positively sloped MCC. Substituting optimal Q_s^* into (8) we can find the value of the maximized expected welfare gain. In the linear case with an additive error term shown in Fig. 2, where

$$MDF = a - bq + u, \tag{11}$$

where $E(u) = 0$ and

$$MCC = \alpha + \beta q_s. \tag{12}$$

Note that (10) reduces to

$$Q_s^* = (a - \alpha)/(b + \beta) \quad \text{and} \quad P^* = \alpha + \beta(a - \alpha)/(b + \beta). \tag{13}$$

The expected welfare gain (EWG) depends only on the parameters a, α, b, and β, and is independent of the distribution of u.

$$EWG = \frac{1}{2}\frac{(a - \alpha)^2}{(b + \beta)}. \tag{14}$$

We conclude that when MDF is uncertain and the agency is risk neutral, expected MDF should be used in the selection of optimal control levels. Moreover, taxes, standards, and auctions have the same resulting performance.[5]

Next, consider the case where MDF is known with certainty, but MCC is subject to a stochastic disturbance as given by

$$MCC(q, u), \tag{15}$$

where again u has known density of $dF(u)$. With quantitative controls, we obtain results similar to the previous case. Maximizing with respect to Q_s the expectation

$$\mathop{E}_{u} \int_0^{Q_s} [MDF(q) - MCC(q, u)]dq = \mathop{E}_{u}(z), \tag{16}$$

we conclude that the risk neutral agency should again select Q_s^* to satisfy

$$E[MDF(Q_s^*) - MCC(Q_s^*, u)] = 0, \tag{17}$$

i.e., that Q_s^* where MDF equals expected MCC. This result is independent of $dF(u)$ and of the particular form of uncertainty in MCC.

When a tax policy is used, the quantity of pollution abated with a given tax rate P_T is a random variable

$$\tilde{Q}_s = MCC^{-1}(P_T, u). \tag{18}$$

Writing the expression for expected welfare gain

$$EWG = \mathop{E}_{u} \int_0^{MCC^{-1}(P_T, u)} [MDF(q) - MCC(q, u)]dq, \tag{19}$$

we realize that this source of uncertainty compounds the uncertainty of producer surplus for a given Q_s, and that in general the frequency distribution of u and the form in which it enters MCC will affect both the optimal tax, P_T^*, and the expected welfare gain, EWG. To illustrate this conclusion, consider first the generalization of Fig. 3, which depicts a linear MDF and MCC, and u enters MCC additively. While an additive

---

[5] This is not to say they are equivalent in other respects.

stochastic error term facilitates the exposition, it has considerable economic content since factor price variations in inputs subject to a Leontief production technology would produce additive errors. Specifically, we assume

$$\text{MCC} = \alpha + \beta Q_s + u, \qquad E(u) = 0. \tag{20}$$

Optimal P_T can be derived by solving

$$\frac{d}{dP} \mathop{E}_u \int_0^{\tilde{Q}(P)} [(a - bq) - (\alpha + \beta q + u)]dq = \frac{d}{dP} \mathop{E}_u (\tilde{z}) = 0, \tag{21}$$

where

$$\tilde{Q}(P) = (1/\beta)[P - \alpha - u]. \tag{22}$$

Differentiating, and substituting (22) into (21) we find the optimum condition to be

$$(P^* - \alpha)/\beta = \mathop{E}_u \tilde{Q}(P^*, u) = (a - \alpha)/(b + \beta), \tag{23}$$

which means that P^* should be selected such that MDF equals *expected* MCC at the optimal level of abatement. Note the similarity to our general result for quantity (i.e., standards/auction) setting policy, but note also a difference: substituting into (16) an MCC with an additive error term, the expected welfare gain for the optimal standards or auction policy is

$$E(\tilde{z}) = \frac{1}{2} \frac{(a - \alpha)^2}{b + \beta}. \tag{24}$$

Substituting (23) into the expectation in (21), we find that with a tax policy, the expected welfare gain for a tax $[E(\tilde{z})]$ is

$$E(\tilde{z}) = (a - \alpha) \mathop{E}_u \tilde{Q} - \left(\frac{b + \beta}{2} \right) \mathop{E}_u \tilde{Q}^2 - \mathop{E}_u u\tilde{Q},$$

$$= \frac{1}{2} \frac{(a - \alpha)^2}{(b + \beta)} - \frac{b - \beta}{2\beta^2} \mathop{E}_u u^2, \tag{25}$$

and since $\mathop{E}_u \tilde{Q}(P^*, u)$ for the tax policy equals Q^* for the standards policy,

$$E(\tilde{z}) - E(\tilde{z}) = E u^2[(b - \beta)/2\beta^2]. \tag{26}$$

This is a generalization of the result in (5). It indicates that when the slope of the expected MCC is steeper than MDF, a tax policy is preferred to quantity restrictions, and vice versa. Note that for given MCC and MDF, the difference in performance between the two policies is proportional to the variance of u,[6] but the choice of optimal policy is independent of it.

A multiplicative disturbance term in the marginal control cost function is interesting to contemplate since, like a heteroscedastic error term, its variance increases with marginal costs. This is not unrealistic as technology for high cost, low abatement technology is no doubt subject to greater uncertainty. When MCC contains a multi-

---

[6] If MCC were nonlinear, it would depend on higher moments of $dF(u)$ as well.

plicative error term, i.e.,

$$M\tilde{C}C = (\alpha + \beta q)u, \qquad E(u) = 1,$$
$$\tilde{C}(q) = \alpha u q + \tfrac{1}{2}(\beta u)^2 q^2,$$

(27)

our conclusions change. The expected welfare gain of standards or an auction is

$$\underset{u}{E}(\tilde{z}) = \underset{u}{E}\int_0^Q [(a - bq) - (\alpha + \beta q)u]\,dq,$$

(28)

and maximizing $\underset{u}{E}(\tilde{z})$ with respect to Q still yields the familiar first-order condition

$$Q_s{}^* = (a - \alpha)/(b + \beta).$$

(29)

Again, the quantity should be selected where MDF equals *expected* MCC.

However, when a tax policy is used, this result should be modified. Differentiating (28) with respect to P where the upper bound of the integral is

$$\tilde{\tilde{Q}}(P, u) = (P - u\alpha)/u\beta$$

(30)

yields the first-order condition

$$\underset{u}{E}[(a/u) - \alpha] = \underset{u}{E}\{\tilde{Q}(P, u)[(b/u) + \beta]\},$$

(31)

or

$$\underset{u}{E}\frac{\partial Q}{\partial P}MDF(Q) = \underset{u}{E}\frac{\partial Q}{\partial P}MCC(\tilde{Q}, u),$$

(32)

which is different, of course, from the quantity conditions. Nevertheless, we can still maintain that the economic meaning of the optimal condition is equating *expected* marginal damage to *expected* marginal cost, but in this case, with respect to price rather than quantity.

In a manner similar to the additive case, we can now compare the maximized expected welfare gain under a tax policy and a standards/auction policy. Not surprisingly, the result depends again on parameters of MCC and MDF,

$$\underset{u}{E}(\tilde{z}) - \underset{u}{E}(\tilde{z}) = \frac{a\beta + \alpha b}{2\beta}\left[\underset{u}{E}\tilde{Q} - \frac{a - \alpha}{b + \beta}\right] = \frac{a\beta + \alpha b}{2\beta}[\underset{u}{E}\tilde{Q} - Q^*],$$

(33)

where $E_u\tilde{Q}$ is expected quantity abated under the optimal tax, and Q^* is the optimal quantity abated under a standards/auction scheme. Since $\tilde{Q} = (P - \alpha u)/\beta u$, the choice of optimal policy depends on $dF(u)$.

We conclude that when MCC is random, the effects of taxes and quantity controls of pollution will differ, and that the choice of the optimal instrument depends on (a) the parameters of MDF and *expected* MCC, (b) the particular way in which the random element u enters the MCC, and (c) the frequency distribution of u.

Admittedly, the difference in the expected welfare gains is more cumbersome to calculate for policy analysis than the simple case where the disturbance is additive and we need only measure the relative elasticities, or slopes and the variance of u. Nevertheless, we believe such calculations are possible and instructive. Policy analysts definitely have some knowledge about the parameters of MDF and MCC [point (a)], since this is presumably the basis for current decision making. By the types of economic rationales offered here for additive and multiplicative disturbance terms, we feel that policy analysts can distinguish the types of uncertainty [point (b)] most relevant to the case at hand. Finally, as for the frequency distribution of u [point (c)], our suggestion is simply to test for sensitivity using several alternative distributions as the policy implications may turn out to be quite robust with respect to distributional changes in u.

III. UNCERTAINTY AT THE FIRM LEVEL AND RISK AVERSION

The results of the previous section hold for cases in which (1) uncertainty exists only at the agency level or (2) uncertainty exists both at the agency and firm level and firms are risk neutral. The first situation is obvious, but the second involves the critical question of whether the expected marginal control cost function evinces a behavioral relationship as well as the social costs of abatement. Throughout this paper, we treat the private and social costs of abatement as equivalent. If the expected MCC does in fact measure private abatement costs, we will face the question of whether it describes a behavioral relation. For the risk neutral firm, it is well known that decisions are based on expected marginal costs. Therefore, under risk neutrality, the expected marginal control cost curve facing the agency is nothing more than the summation of firms' expected marginal cost functions for abatement.

For the risk averse firm, the agency's expected marginal control cost curve describes the relevant expected social costs; however, it does not represent a behavioral relationship. The introduction of risk aversion in firm behavior complicates our results and adds another interesting asymmetry. We introduce risk aversion in the firm's behavior by hypothesizing that firms behave as if they possess a well-behaved utility of profits function, $U(\pi)$ with $U'(\pi) > 0$, $U''(\pi) < 0$, and act to maximize the mathematical expectation of utility.[7] Thus, when the firm knows only the frequency distribution of P_T when making its pollution decision it is assumed to maximize with respect to Q the following expected utility of profits:

$$\mathop{E}_{\tilde{P}_T} U[\tilde{P}_T Q - C(Q)]. \tag{34}$$

When P_T is certain but $C(Q)$ is uncertain, we replace $C(Q)$ by the random cost relationship $C(Q, u)$. The firm maximizes

$$\mathop{E}_{u} U[P_T Q - C(Q, u)]. \tag{35}$$

Analysis of the first- and second-order conditions of these maximization problems usually reveals that the firm will not operate where its expected marginal cost equals the expected price as we established for the risk neutral firm.

When P_T is uncertain, Sandmo has shown that the firm will produce the output, where $\tilde{P}_T > C'(Q)$. In a similar manner, when marginal costs are stochastic, the first-order condition

$$EU'(\tilde{\pi})[P_T - C'(Q, u)] = 0, \qquad \tilde{\pi} = P_T Q - C(Q, u), \tag{36}$$

implies that under risk aversion,

$$P_T > \mathop{E}_{u} C'(Q, u). \tag{37}$$

[7] See [7] for a model of the competitive firm facing an uncertain price. This assumption has been widely used in other studies of the economics of the firm under uncertainty.

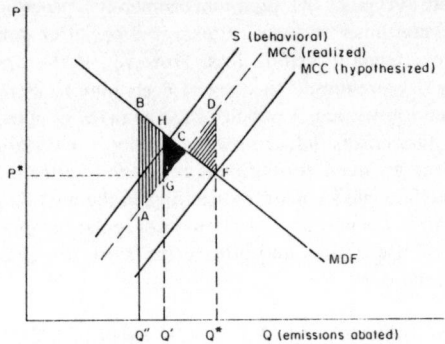

FIG. 3. Uncertain marginal control costs and risk aversion.

As a consequence of the fact that $P > C'(Q, u)$ and $\bar{P} > C'(Q)$, we can no longer use the expected MCC curve to evaluate both the social cost of pollution abatement and to determine the supply response of the polluting firm to a given policy.

For example, in Fig. 3, MDF and the expected MCC curve still have the same normative meaning as in Section II above, but now we represent the firm's behavior by the "supply" curve S. In order to maximize the expected welfare, the agency concludes that price P^* and quantity Q^* are optimal. Following the exposition in Fig. 2, we assume that the actual MCC differs from the expected MCC. Under risk neutrality, the tax P^* would have resulted in the abatement of Q' with welfare loss of CHG; however, risk aversion lead to a reduction of Q'' and a welfare loss of ABC. Note however, that the quantitative restriction (either standards or an auction) resulted in a loss of CDF, the same loss as under risk neutrality. In sum, the asymmetry between taxes and quantitative restrictions for uncertain MCC still holds. The expected welfare loss in Eq. (26) between taxes and quantitative standards would, however, need to be altered for the effects of risk aversion.

IV. SOME CAVEATS AND ADDITIONAL INSIGHTS

Up until now the careful reader might ask why the analysis has been concluded in terms of three policy instruments when the affects of uncertainty have so far fallen into two dichotomous groups—price controls (taxes) and quantity controls (standards and auctions). The answer is that despite the above, standards and auctions are not identical with respect to uncertainty. One of the primary motivations for auctions in place of standards is that they reduce the information requirements of the agency since for standards to be applied efficiently, the agency must know the individual firm's expected marginal cost function for abatement. Obviously, the auction reveals this information in a much cheaper manner to the agency. As a consequence, the auction avoids the uncertainty attendant to the more complex informational requirements of standards.

While auctions have less informational uncertainty attached to them than standards, it is conceivable that under certain conditions some offsetting welfare effects may exist. In the case where the sole source of uncertainty is being induced by the auction via large price variation, the expected auction price will lie above the expected marginal control costs for the risk averse firms. If the difference between the auction price and marginal control costs (a type of risk premium) is merely a pecuniary payment to risk, then expected MCC continues to measure expected social abatement costs and the auction generates no attendant welfare loss. However, if the firm expends real resources to avoid this risk premium,[8] then social costs may be increased in an auction relative to more certain government policies such as taxes or standards. We feel that in most cases the welfare effects induced by the auction's uncertain price are likely to be small relative to the greater informational uncertainty attached to standards. On the other hand, the welfare effects of large variations in the auction price would appear to offer some explanation for why auctions could not replace standards on offshore oil production, nuclear reactor design, and other cases where the price for tickets might be subject to large variations.

V. SUMMARY AND POLICY IMPLICATIONS

This paper reaches the following three major conclusions regarding differential welfare effects between taxes, standards, and auctions.

(1) Uncertainty in the marginal damage function has absolutely no effect on the choice between the three policy instruments.

(2) Uncertainty in the marginal control cost function will yield different expected welfare losses between taxes or quantitative restrictions (standards or auctions) depending on the variance of the stochastic error term and the slopes or elasticities of the MDF and MCC functions.

(3) Even under risk aversion, this asymmetry still holds, however, now the welfare loss also depends on the degree of risk aversion.

In conclusion, in situations of uncertain marginal control costs where the marginal damage function tends to be very price elastic, such as believed to occur for SO_2 emissions, a strong case can be made for taxes. On the other hand, where the marginal damage function is very inelastic, quantitative restrictions of an auction or standards type appear desirable.

In cases where quantity restrictions are appropriate, auctions and standards are not equivalent. Unlike auctions, standards introduce added informational uncertainty, which seems likely to dominate possible welfare losses due to wide variations in the auction price.

REFERENCES

1. W. J. Baumol, On taxation and the control of externalities, *Amer. Econ. Rev.* 62, 307–322 (1972).
2. W. J. Baumol and W. E. Oates, The use of standards and pricing for protection of the environment, *Swed. J. Econ.* 73, 42–54 (1971).
3. J. H. Dales, "Pollution, Property and Prices," Univ. of Tronto Press, Toronto (1968).
4. J. M. Griffin, An econometric evaluation of sulphur taxes, *J. Polit. Econ.* 82, 669–688 (1974).
5. A. V. Kneese and B. T. Bower, "Managing Water Quality: Economics, Technology, Institutions," Johns Hopkins Press, Baltimore (1968).
6. Abba P. Lerner, The 1971 report of the President's Council of Economic Advisers: Priorities and efficiency, *Amer. Econ. Rev.* 61, 527–530 (1971).
7. Agnar Sandmo, On the theory of the competitive firm under price uncertainty, *Amer. Econ. Rev.* 61, 65–73 (1971).

[8] For example, to avoid the losses associated with wide variations in ticket prices, the firm might install more flexible abatement equipment providing a flatter short-run cost function over a wider range. Such a technology may not, however, be of least cost at the abatement level corresponding to the standard.

[9]

Journal of Public Economics 5 (1976) 193–208. © North-Holland Publishing Company

EFFLUENT CHARGES AND LICENSES UNDER UNCERTAINTY*

Marc J. ROBERTS and Michael SPENCE**

Harvard University, Cambridge, MA 02138, U.S.A.

Received September 1974, revised version received November 1975

This paper is concerned with pollution control when the regulators are uncertain about firms' cleanup costs. Under these circumstances, the regulatory authority can reduce expected total social costs (consisting of damages from pollution and cleanup costs) below the levels achievable with either effluent fees or licenses. The reduction is achieved by the use of licenses supplemented by an effluent subsidy and a finite penalty, when effluents are below or above the levels permitted by licenses. The mixed system retains the property of efficiently distributing cleanup among firms.

1. Introduction

The purpose of this paper is to explore, in the context of a simple model, what kind of policy might be used to control pollution, when the regulatory authority is uncertain what the actual costs of pollution control will be. In posing the problem as we do, we are rejecting the idea that the government can iteratively 'feel out' the 'optimum' by successively announcing and revising its policies in light of the responses of waste sources. Much of the investment that will be made in any pollution control program will take several years to plan and complete and will be largely irreversible once in place. Thus the response to all subsequent policies will be heavily dependent on previous history. Indeed the cycle time may be so great as to prevent convergence, since the 'correct' solution will be constantly changing. Given these circumstances, we have chosen to explore the once-and-for-all problem, where the government seeks to achieve a comparative static maximum in expected utility terms.

The principal point of the paper is that a mixed system, involving effluent charges and restrictions on the total quantity of emissions via marketable licenses, is preferable to either effluent fees or the licenses used separately.[1]

*This work was supported by National Science Foundation Grant GS-39004 and by the Ford Foundation, Office of Resources and Environment. The authors are grateful to Robert Dorfman, Charles Untiet and the referees for helpful comments.
**Department of Economics, Stanford University, Stanford, CA 94305, U.S.A.
[1]Some of the previous treatments of effluent fees and marketable licenses include Kneese and Bower (1968), Jacoby, Schaumberg, and Gramlech (1972) and Montgomery (1972).

This follows because a mixed system permits the implicit penalty function imposed upon the private sector to more closely approximate the expected damage function for pollution at each level of total waste output.

In setting up this model, we are fully conscious of the differences between the formal structures we will use and real situations, and we will call attention to some of them as we proceed. The point of this exercise is not to 'prove' one or another approach 'better.' Rather, by exploring and manipulating some simplified conceptualizations, we hope to develop some insights and formulations which will prove to be useful in formulating policy.

The problem is posed as one of choosing a control scheme so as to minimize expected total social costs, these being the sum of (1) expected damages from pollution and (2) cleanup costs. In order to actually implement any policy, the regulatory authority must quantify its uncertainty about cleanup costs in the form of subjective probabilities. Given these probabilities, the calculation of the optimal parameters for the sort of mixed scheme we will develop is sufficiently straightforward that we believe it could be made even with limited analytical resources.

Effluent charges and marketable licenses have the virtue of inducing the private sector to minimize the costs of cleanup. But in the presence of uncertainty, they differ in the manner in which the ex post achieved results differ from the socially optimal outcome. Effluent charges bring about too little cleanup when cleanup costs turn out to be higher than expected, and they induce excessive cleanup when the costs of cleanup turn out to be low. Licenses have the opposite failing. Since the level of cleanup is predetermined, it will be too high when cleanup costs are high and too low when costs are low.

Given that effluent charges and license outcomes deviate from the optimum in opposite ways, which kind of imperfection is preferable? It turns out, plausibly enough, that the answer depends upon the curvature of the damage function. When the expected damage function is linear, an effluent charge equal to the slope of the damage function always leads to optimal results, regardless of what costs turn out to be, while licenses do not. On the other hand, if *marginal* damages increase sharply with effluents, licenses are relatively more attractive and yield lower expected total costs than the fee system.

Licenses and effluent charges can be used together further to reduce expected total costs. Each can protect against the failings of the other. Licenses can be used to guard against extremely high levels of pollution while, simultaneously, effluent charges can provide a residual incentive to clean up more than the licenses required, should costs be low.

In what follows, the model is described and the mixed effluent fee license scheme set forth and analyzed. In an appendix, we argue that one can come arbitrarily close to minimum expected total costs with the use of multiple licenses supplemented by a carefully constructed schedule of effluent fees.

2. Notation

To simplify the exposition we assume all waste dischargers have the same impact on ambient conditions at the one point we monitor. We will not consider multiple monitoring points, or substances, though the analysis could be generalized in that direction.[2] Thus we can use a single variable, x, to indicate both the total pollution discharged and the resulting quality of the environment. Damages from pollution are measured in dollars. Expected total damages are denoted by $D(x)$. There are, of course, significant uncertainties associated with damages. And if risk aversion were assumed, the monetary equivalents of the damages associated with various policies would rise. The analysis to follow, which focuses upon costs and cleanup, could be amended to account for risk aversion. For expositional clarity, we will deal only with expected damages.

The current level of output of the pollutant of firm i is $\bar{x}_i$. The costs of cleanup for firm i are uncertain from the point of view of the regulators. This uncertainty is summarized by a random variable, ϕ. The costs of cleanup for firm i are stated as a function of its output of pollution, x_i, and the random variable ϕ, and are denoted by $c^i(x_i, \phi)$. These costs represent reductions in total profits. Adjustment in cleanup may be accompanied by changes in the levels of outputs and inputs of the firm. Our assumption here is that this reduction in profits accurately reflects the social cost of cleanup, which can be shown to be correct if markets are competitive.[3] By definition, when there is no cleanup, $x_i = \bar{x}_i$ and $c^i(\bar{x}_i, \phi) = 0$.

Total cleanup costs, $c(x, \phi)$, are simply the sum of the individual firm costs. Again we can simply use ϕ to parameterize our uncertainty. However, in what follows, whenever we write c, we do so only to refer to circumstances where the cleanup is distributed among firms in a cost minimizing manner, so that by definition,

$$c(x, \phi) = \sum_i c^i(x_i, \phi),$$

[2]Montgomery (1972) considers the problem of multiple points of concern.
[3]The argument is as follows. Let $P(q)$ be the inverse demand for the firm, and $d(q, x)$ its costs. The effluent charge is e. The surplus generated by the market is

$$T = \int_p^q P(s)\, ds - d(q, x) - ex.$$

Differentiating with respect to x, we have

$$\frac{dT}{dx} = (P - d_q)\frac{dq}{dx} - (d_x + e).$$

A profit maximizing firm will set $d_x + e = 0$. At that point $dT/dx = 0$ only if either $P = d_q$ (price equals marginal cost – the industry is competitive) or $dq/dx = 0$. The latter occurs when $d_{xq} = 0$. Therefore, when a competitive industry maximizes profits or costs or profit losses, the social optimum is achieved. But if the firm has market power $p > d_q$, there will be too much or too little cleanup depending on the sign of dq/dx.

where $x = \sum_i x_i$, and for all i and j,

$$c_x^i(x_i, \phi) = c_x^j(x_j, \phi).$$

The following assumptions are carried throughout: $D''(x) > 0$, so that $D(x)$ is convex, and $c_x < 0$, $c_{xx} > 0$; marginal cleanup costs increase at an increasing rate. The random variable ϕ represents 'states of the world.' It simply captures all the relevant uncertainty about cleanup costs. It can be thought of as an exhaustive labeling of the possible cleanup cost functions for all polluters. The reader may find it easier to think in terms of a large, but finite, exhaustive list. However, to facilitate the following analysis, we will assume that $c_\phi > 0$ and that $c_{x\phi} < 0$. This means that as ϕ shifts, both absolute and marginal costs shift in the same directions for all values of x. In particular, members of the family of aggregate costs do not cross.

The regulatory authority's decision problem is to choose a pollution control scheme to minimize expected total costs. Their subjective distribution for ϕ is represented by $f(\phi)$. Expected total costs are

$$T = \int [D(x) + c(x, \phi)] f(\phi) \, d\phi = E[D(x) + c(x, \phi)].$$

In general, x will be a function of ϕ. The function will vary with the scheme being used for controlling pollution. It is assumed that firms know or can find out their cleanup cost functions. The uncertainty therefore attaches to the regulatory authority.

3. Controlling via mixed effluent charges and licenses

The control mechanism we want to put forward has three components. First there is a finite set of transferable licenses that are issued by the regulatory authority, and are bought and sold in a market. The quantity of licenses is l. The number of licenses held by firm i is denoted by l_i. Second, there is a unit effluent subsidy, denoted by s. It is paid to any firm whose license holdings, l_i, exceed its emissions, x_i. Thus if $l_i > x_i$, the firm receives $s(l_i - x_i)$. Finally, if a firm's emissions exceed its holdings of licenses, so that $x_i > l_i$, then it is assessed a per unit penalty of p, or a total penalty of $p(x_i - l_i)$. The three components then are licenses, l, an efficient subsidy, s, and an effluent penalty, p.

We want to demonstrate that this approach has several properties. First, it allocates cleanup among polluting firms efficienctly.[4] Second, it is preferable to either a pure effluent fee or a pure license scheme. Expected total costs

---

[4] If there is just one polluter, one could set a nonlinear effluent charge equal to marginal damages, $D'(x)$. This would lead to the optimum. But when there is more than one polluter, a nonlinear effluent charge is inconsistent with either decentralization or cost minimization, and possibly both.

M.J. Roberts and M. Spence, Effluent charges under uncertainty 197

(cleanup and damages from pollution) are lower. Third, the system operates as if there were just one polluting firm confronted with a piecewise linear penalty function with one kink in it. This is demonstrated below.

The economic rational for this scheme is the following. One wants to limit effluents; this is done by issuing marketable licenses. But if cleanup costs have been significantly overestimated, one wants a residual incentive to cleanup. This is provided by the subsidy, s. On the other hand, if cleanup costs turn out to be very high, one wants an escape valve from the restriction imposed by the licenses. This escape valve is provided by having a finite penalty, p, for exceeding levels of effluents permitted by licenses. It is assumed that $p \geq s$.

Formally, the functioning of the system is represented as follows. Let q be the market price of the licenses. It is determined as part of the equilibrium in the market for licenses. The total costs for firm i consist of (1) cleanup costs, (2) license costs, and (3) penalties or subsidies when applicable. These costs are

$$c^i(x_i, \phi) + ql_i - s(l_i - x_i) \quad \text{if} \quad x_i \leq l_i, \tag{1}$$

and

$$c^i(x_i, \phi) + ql_i + p(x_i - l_i) \quad \text{if} \quad x_i \geq l_i. \tag{2}$$

The firm minimizes these by selecting x_i and l_i appropriately. In addition, in an equilibrium,

$$\sum_{i=1}^{N} l_i = l.$$

We turn now to the properties of the equilibrium. Suppose first that $q < s$. Then from (1) every firm could reduce costs indefinitely by buying licenses. This is clearly inconsistent with equilibrium in the license market. Thus q cannot be less than s. Now suppose that $q > p$. Then from (2), every firm would set $l_i = 0$, and this is inconsistent with equilibrium in the license market. Therefore, q cannot exceed p. The subsidy s and the penalty p place bounds on the equilibrium value of q: $s \leq q \leq p$.

The next step is to show that $c_x^i(x_i, \phi)$ is always equal to $-q$. Suppose first that $s = q$. Then the firm will set $l_i \geq x_i$ (in fact it is indifferent about the level); and then set $c_x^i(x_i, \phi) = -s = -q$. Next suppose $s < q < p$. Then from (1) and (2) firm i will set $x_i = l_i$. Thus its costs are

$$c^i(x_i, \phi) + qx_i.$$

These are minimized when $c_x^i(x_i, \phi) + q = 0$. Finally if $q = p$, the firm will set $l_i \leq x_i$, and then minimize with respect to x_i by setting $c_x^i(x_i, \phi) + q = 0$. Thus in all possible cases, $c_x^i(x_i, \phi) + q = 0$. This fact has the immediate implication that $c_x^i(x_i, \phi) = c_x^j(x_j, \phi)$ for all i and j, so that cleanup is efficiently distributed among polluters.[5] In addition q is bounded by the effluent subsidy s and the penalty p.

Since marginal cleanup costs are minimized, the condition

$$c_x(x, \phi) + q = 0 \tag{3}$$

is always satisfied.

The remaining question is what determines the levels of q and x? If $s < q < p$, then $x_i = l_i$ for all i, and hence $x = l$. Condition (3) will be satisfied if

$$s < -c_x(l, \phi) < p. \tag{4}$$

Inequality (4) will hold for some intermediate range of costs of cleanup. If cleanup costs are very high, then q will be driven up to the level of the penalty p. At that point, effluents will exceed licenses: $x > l$. The equilibrium condition is

$$c_x(x, \phi) + p = 0. \tag{5}$$

Finally if costs are low, so that $c_x(l, \phi) + s < 0$, then $x < l$ and $q = s$. The level of effluents actually achieved will be given by

$$c_x(x, \phi) + s = 0. \tag{6}$$

In summary: (1) if $c_x(l, \phi) + s > 0$, then $c_x(x, \phi) + s = 0$ and $q = s$; (2) if $s < -c_x(l, \phi) < p$, then $x = l$ and $q = -c_x(l, \phi)$; and (3) if $c_x(l, \phi) + p < 0$, then $c_x(x, \phi) + p = 0$ and $q = p$.

The interesting feature of the mixed effluent–license is that it produces levels of the effluents, conditional on costs, that reproduce exactly the effluents that would occur if (1) the polluting firms were merged (and made cleanup decisions centrally) and (2) they faced a piecewise linear penalty function of the form,

$$P(x) = sx + p \, \text{Max} \, (x - l, 0).$$

If the firms collectively were to minimize the sum of penalties and cleanup costs, $P(x) + c(x, \phi)$, they would act as follows: if $s < -c_x(l, \phi) < p$, they would set $x = l$; if $-c_x(l, \phi) < s$, they would set $c_x(x, \phi) + s = 0$; and if $-c_x(l, \phi) > p$, they would set $c_x(x, \phi) + p = 0$. But this is exactly what the decentralized system does.

The pure efficient fee and pure license systems are special cases of the mixed system. The pure effluent fee is obtained by setting $s = p$, at which point the

[5]Note that $c_x(x, \phi) = c_x^i(x_i, \phi)$, for all i, when x is distributed among polluters in a cost minimizing manner.

M.J. Roberts and M. Spence, Effluent charges under uncertainty 199

level of *l* becomes irrelevant. The implicit penalty function is then linear. If $s = 0$ and $p = +\infty$, then we have a pure license system. It is not therefore surprising that the more flexible mixed system can achieve lower expected total costs.

The mixed system implicitly approximates the expected damage function by a piecewise linear penalty (see fig. 1). The same point can be seen in the context

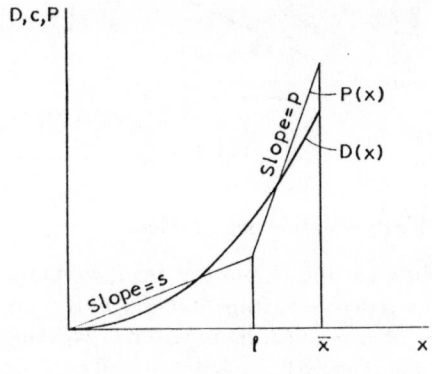

Fig. 1

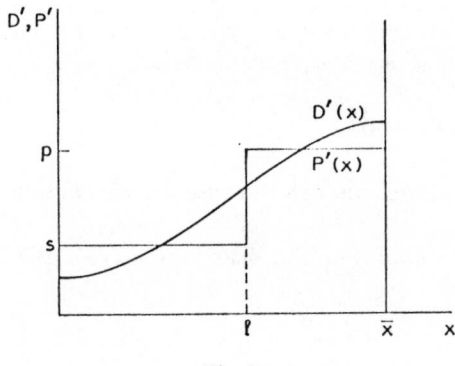

Fig. 2

of the marginal damages (see fig. 2). The mixed effluent–license system approximates the marginal damage function with a step function.

It is worth noting that the implicit penalty function $P(x)$, does *not* correspond exactly to the payments by firms for licenses, plus or minus penalties and subsidies. The actual payments depend upon the parameter ϕ that determines costs, and not just upon x, the final level of effluents. But if we plot ex post payments as a function of effluents, the result is as in fig. 3.

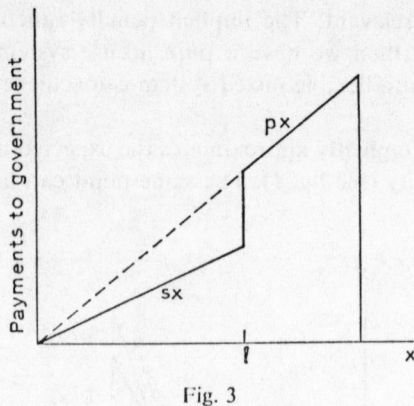

Fig. 3

4. The regulatory authority's optimizing problem

The decision variables for the regulators are s, p, and l. The objective is to minimize expected total costs, consisting of damages from pollution and cleanup costs. For given levels of s, p and l, there will be two critical levels of the cost determining parameter ϕ. The first, ϕ_1, is the level of cost such that

$$c_x(l, \phi_1) = s = 0. \tag{7}$$

Here the marginal cleanup costs are just equal to the effluent subsidy when $x = l$. The second value, $\phi_2 > \phi_1$, is defined by

$$c_x(l, \phi_2) + p = 0. \tag{8}$$

Here costs are almost high enough to cause the system to have effluents exceed licenses.

Let $[0, b]$ be the support of the distribution $f(\phi)$. We define $x_1(\phi, s)$ and $x_2(\phi, p)$ by

$$c_x(x_1(\phi, s), \phi) + s = 0,$$

and

$$c_x(x_2(\phi, p), \phi) + p = 0.$$

Expected total costs are

$$T(s, p, l) = \int_0^{\phi_1} [D(x_1(\phi, s)) + c(x_1(\phi, s), \phi)] f(\phi) \, \mathrm{d}\phi$$

$$+ \int_{\phi_1}^{\phi_2} [D(l) + c(l, \phi)] f(\phi) \, \mathrm{d}\phi$$

$$+ \int_{\phi_2}^{b} [D(x_2(\phi, p)) + c(x_2(\phi, p), \phi)] f(\phi) \, \mathrm{d}\phi.$$

These expected total costs are minimized when the partial derivatives, T_s, T_p and T_l, are zero, or when the following conditional expectations hold:

$$E\left(\frac{D'(x_1)-s}{c_{xx}(x_1, \phi)}\,\middle|\,\phi \le \phi_1\right) = 0, \tag{9}$$

$$E(D'(l)+c_x(l, \phi)|\phi_1 \le \phi \le \phi_2) = 0, \tag{10}$$

$$E\left(\frac{D'(x_2)-p}{c_{xx}(x_2, \phi)}\,\middle|\,\phi \ge \phi_2\right) = 0. \tag{11}$$

With perfect information about costs, the authority would set

$$D'(x)+c_x(x, \phi) = 0, \tag{12}$$

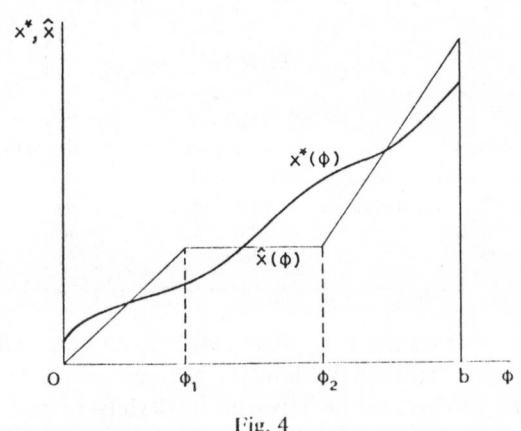

Fig. 4

for all ϕ. Let the optimal schedule of effluents, defined by (12), be $x^*(\phi)$. Let $\hat{x}(\phi)$ be the effluent levels achieved with the optimal mixed system described above. The relationship between $x^*(\phi)$ and $\hat{x}(\phi)$ is depicted in fig. 4. The schedule $\hat{x}(\phi)$ crosses $x^*(\phi)$ three times, once in each interval.

The optimizing conditions, (9) through (11), are simply conditions for optimal pure effluent fees or licenses on each of the three intervals. For example, eq. (9) is the condition for s to be the optimal pure effluent fee assuming costs vary only on the interval $[0, \phi_1]$. A pure effluent fee schedule crosses the optimal schedule once. Hence, the mixed schedule crosses $x^*(\phi)$ once in each of three intervals. Notice that pure effluent fees induce excessive cleanup when costs are low and too little cleanup when costs are high. This occurs because at low levels of pollution the effluent fee exceeds marginal damages, and conversely. The pure license scheme has the opposite property. It is insensitive to variations in clean-up costs.

The superiority of the mixed scheme is simply a result of its ability to better approximate the optimal relationship between pollution levels and damages. The exception occurs when the damage function is linear. In that case, $\phi_1 = 0$, $\phi_2 = b$ and $p = s$. The pure effluent fee system is optimal.

5. Expected gains from using a mixed system

It is not possible in a short paper to comment extensively on the quantitative benefits of the mixed scheme. However, one can isolate the circumstances under which it is likely to yield significant gains. There are two conditions which make the mixed schemed attractive. First, the marginal damages must vary considerably with total effluents. Otherwise the pure effluent fee performs quite well. Second, there must be significant uncertainty about the cleanup costs. Otherwise, the pure license scheme performs well. It is perhaps worth noting that when

Table 1

Control scheme	Expected total costs	Percentage above the optimum
Optimum (also mixed system)	12.416	0
Pure effluent fee	20.6	66
Pure licenses	18.25	46

marginal cleanup costs do not vary greatly with quantity, an effluent fee system performs poorly even with small amounts of uncertainty. The reason is that actual levels of cleanup may vary wildly with small shifts in the cost function.

The following numerical example illustrates the potential benefits of the mixed system. It assumes there is a threshold level of pollution, l, below which marginal damages are one, and above which they are six. Costs are assumed to have the form $(\phi/2)(\bar{x}-x)^2$, where ϕ takes on the values 0.12 and 2.0 with probabilities of one half. A mixed system yields the optimum for this kind of damage function. Table 1 summarizes the results for the various control schemes.

6. Conclusions

When the regulatory authority is uncertain about pollution control costs, the usefulness of monetary incentives to decentralize pollution control decisions is limited by our inability to pick the correct price. That price should be equal to marginal damages and thus depends upon the level of pollution. But it is not known exactly what pollution will be as a function of price because control costs are known only imperfectly. With a nonlinear damage function, and uncertain irreversible costs, we would like to find some way of confronting each firm with incentives to cleanup that in fact depend upon marginal damages, and hence on total waste output. The combination of the license scheme with subsidies and penalties permits one simultaneously to ensure that all firms face the same marginal costs, but to have that cost vary (within limits) depending on what the aggregate costs of cleanup actually turn out to be. The level of pollution also varies with the aggregate cleanup costs.

The authority has three parameters to manipulate: the subsidy, the penalty and the stock of licenses. The authority knows that pollution will equal the stock of licenses provided the market price turns out to be between the subsidy and the penalty. The subsidy provides a residual incentive for firms to clean up even more when costs are low. The finite penalty provides an escape valve in case costs are very high. The aggregate damage function is approximated by a piecewise linear penalty function. But once the equilibrium in license prices is established, each firm effectively faces a linear penalty function whose slope is the price of the license. As a result, marginal cleanup costs are equalized and total cleanup costs are minimized.

How useful is this formulation in the real world? First, we do not believe that limiting our attention to regions of increasing marginal damages is a major practical limitation. There are real cases in which marginal damages may decline – adding more waste to a river which is already an open sewer may have few environmental costs. But in general, even damage functions which exhibit such regions also often appear to be characterized by other regions in which marginal costs are increasing. For example, as the organic material in a river increases, and dissolved oxygen levels decline, we appear to move successively through several thresholds as we lose additional species and human uses. And, intuition suggests that output controls are more likely to be favorable in a region of increasing, rather than decreasing, marginal damages.

In practice, the scheme amounts to setting an ambient target (similar to the ambient standards widely used today) and working back to the magnitude of the discharges allowed by that constraint. Then the regulatory authority has to develop some notion about marginal damages in the regions above and below that point in order to set the subsidy and the penalty fee. Even if the regulatory authority does not quantify its uncertainty and compute an optimal schedule, the rough and ready approach should lead to a reasonable set of policies. After all, in a second-best world with imperfectly maximizing waste sources, the formal optimality of a policy scheme is not necessarily proof of what its actual impact will be.

Like any decentralized approach to pollution control, our scheme has certain serious limitations. It will not provide for efforts to act directly on the environment as opposed to on a waste source. Nor does it ensure that all economies of scale in treatment will be exhausted unless waste sources agree to appropriate joint ventures among themselves. We have also not discussed what should be done in the face of natural variations in climate which make it uncertain what damages will in fact result from any waste discharge.[6] All this suggests that a good deal of detailed work would be required to develop a viable set of policies and institutions for any specific circumstances. For example, could we vary policy seasonally or with actual natural conditions?

In theory, we would want a separate system of licenses to control each polluting substance we are concerned with at each geographic point of interest. Since administrative costs will rise with the complexity of the entire scheme, at some point we will need to make a (perhaps crude) compromise between the costs and benefits of additional elaboration and fine-tuning of the system. Note too that we have to construct our markets such that each has enough participants to ensure relatively competitive functioning. Nevertheless, even viewed as a practical measure designed to move us into a better, if not the best, position, we believe the mixed scheme we have proposed has significant merit. Perhaps the next important step is to consider how to set the penalty function in the presence of risk-aversion relative to damages.

Appendix: A generalized decentralization proposition

In the body of the paper, it was argued that expected total costs could be reduced by the use of both licenses and effluent fees, while maintaining the property of efficiently distributing cleanup among polluters. It was pointed out that the system operated as if the firms made a centralized decision against a penalty function with two facets and one kink. We want to argue now that if one is prepared to introduce more than one kind of license, the penalty function can be made to approximate any convex damage function arbitrarily closely. More precisely, by the use of multiple licenses, the system can be made to efficiently distribute costs and implicitly respond to a penalty function with as many kinks as there are types of licenses.

Let l^j be the number of licenses of type j. Assume that $l^0 \leq l^1 \leq l^2 \leq \ldots \leq l^n$ and that $l^0 = 0$. Let $s_0, s_1, \ldots, s_{n+1}$, be an increasing sequence of numbers with $s_0 = 0$. Define a penalty function $P(x)$, in the following way:

$$P(x) = \sum_{j=0}^{n} (s_{j+1} - s_j) \, \text{Max} \, (x - l^j, 0). \tag{A.1}$$

The function $P(x)$ is depicted in fig. 5. It is piecewise linear with kinks at $l^1, \ldots, l^n$. The slopes of the facets are $s_1, \ldots, s_{n+1}$, respectively.

The question then, is whether a system of licenses and effluent subsidies and penalties can induce the firms to act collectively as if the penalty function $P(x)$

---

[6] For a discussion of some of those issues, see Roberts (1975).

M.J. Roberts and M. Spence, *Effluent charges under uncertainty*   205

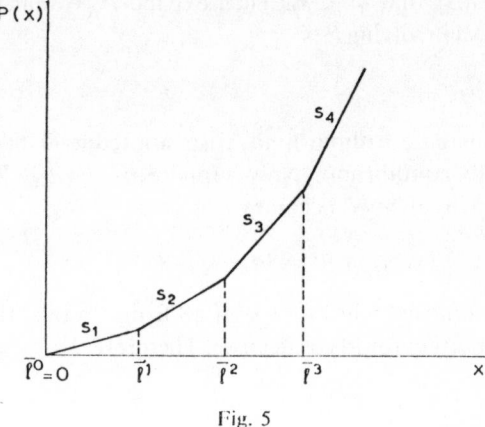

Fig. 5

had been imposed. Let q_j ($j = 1, \ldots, n$) be the market price of the jth type of license. Let x_i be the ith firm's effluents, let l_i^j be the holdings of the jth type of license by the ith firm, and let $c_i(x_i)$ be the cleanup cost function for the ith firm. Having identified the ith firm's variables, we shall suppress the subscript i in what follows. It should be remembered that the following formulae apply to single firms.

The required technique is to confront each firm with the following total cost function:

$$c(x) + \sum_{j=1}^{n} (q_j - s_j)l_j + \sum_{j=0}^{n} (s_{j+1} - s_j) \, \mathrm{Max} \, (x - l^j, 0). \qquad (\text{A}.2)$$

The last term looks very much like the earlier penalty function. The first term represents cleanup costs. The second term is special. The cost function can be interpreted as follows. The firm pays for cleanup. It also pays for the licenses it purchases, but it receives a rebate of s_j per license of type j that it holds. Then, having selected the licenses, the firm pays a penalty given by the piecewise linear function,

$$\hat{P}(x) = \sum_{j=0}^{n} (s_{j+1} - s_i) \, \mathrm{Max} \, (x - l^j, 0).$$

The locations of the kinks in this function are determined by the firm, through its license purchases. It is the second term in (A.2) that is crucial, for as we shall see, it has the effect of placing bounds on the license prices, q_j.

It remains to show that firms, in maximizing (A.2), efficiently distribute costs and act as if they were one firm facing the penalty function (A.1).

The first step to show that

$$s_j \leqq q_j \leqq s_{j+1} \qquad (\text{A}.3)$$

for all j. Suppose first that $q_j < s_j$. Then expand l^j so that $l^j > x$. It follows that the term in (A.2) involving l^j is

$$(q_j - s_j)l_j.$$

By allowing l^j to increase without limit, costs are reduced indefinitely. But that is inconsistent with equilibrium. Now suppose $q_j > s_{j+1}$. Reduce l^j so that $l^j < x$ and the term involving l^j becomes

$$(q_j - s_j)l^j - (s_{j+1} - s_j)l^j = (q_j - s_{j+1})l^j.$$

Hence costs are minimized when $l^j = 0$. If all firms do this, there cannot be an equilibrium in the market for j-type licenses. Therefore

$$s_j \leqq q_j \leqq s_{j+1},$$

for all $j = 1, \ldots, n$.

The next step is to show that if $q_j < s_{j+1}$, then $q_{j+1} = s_{j+1}$. Suppose that $q_j < s_{j+1}$. We show that $l^j \leq x$. Suppose to the contrary that $l^j > x$. Then the part of costs involving l^j is, from (A.2),

$$(q_j - s_{j+1})l^j.$$

Hence l^j should be contracted. Therefore if $q_j < s_{j+1}$, then $l^j \geq x$, and $l^{j+1} > l^j \geq x$, so that x is less than l^{j+1}. But if $l^{j+1} > x$, then q_{j+1} must equal s_{j+1}. For if $q_{j+1} > s_{j+1}$, then the part of costs involving l^{j+1} is

$$(q_{j+1} - s_{j+1})l^{j+1},$$

and l^{j+1} would be reduced. Hence if $l^{j+1} > x$, then $q_{j+1} = s_{j+1}$. This proves the assertion that if $q_j < s_{j+1}$, then $q_{j+1} = s_{j+1}$.

These arguments tell us a considerable amount about the equilibrium. Only one license price q^j can be in the interior of $[s_j, s_{j+1}]$. The remainder are on the boundaries – upper or lower depending upon whether the corresponding license has a lower or higher index than j, respectively.

We now take a typical interval $[s_j, s_{j+1}]$ and assume q_j is the interior of $[s_j, s_{j+1}]$. From the preceding argument, we know that $l^j = x$, that $q_k = s_{k+1}$ for $k < j$, and that $q_k = s_k$ for $k > j$. Thus the costs for the firm are, from (A.2),

$$c(x) + \sum_{k=0}^{j-1}(s_{k+1} - s_k)l^k + \sum_{k=j+1}^{n}(s_{k+1} - s_k)l^k$$

$$+ \sum_{k=0}^{j-1}(s_{k+1} - s_k)(x - l^k) + (q_j - s_j)x + (s_{j+1} - s_j)(0)$$

$$= c(x) + q_j x.$$

Similarly, if $q_j = s_j$, or $q_j = s_{j+1}$, and if $q_k = s_{k+1}$ for $k < j$ and $q_k = s_k$ for $k > j$, then (A.2) implies that the firm's costs (with licenses optimized out) are

$$c(x) + q_j x.$$

In an equilibrium, the costs for every firm will be

$$c(x) + q_j x,$$

for some j and some equilibrium value q_j. Thus when firms minimize, with respect to x, they set

$$c'(x) + q_j = 0. \tag{A.4}$$

In particular, marginal cleanup costs, $c'(x)$, are the same for every firm. Therefore cleanup costs are efficiently distributed in an equilibrium. Let $C(x)$ be the aggregate cost function, where x is now the sum of the effluents from all firms. In an equilibrium, (A.4) implies that

$$C'(x) + q_j = 0.$$

Moreover, if $s_j < q_j < s_{j+1}$, then $x = l^j$, where l^j is the fixed total number of j-type licenses. If $q_j = s_j$, then $l^{j-1} < x \leq l^j$, and if $q_j = s_{j+1}$, then $l^j < x \leq l^{j+1}$. The equilibrium level of x is therefore determined by the level of costs. If

$$s_j < -C''(l^j) < s_{j+1}, \tag{A.5}$$

then $x = l^j$ in an equilibrium. If $-C'(l^j) < s_j$ and $-C'(l^{j-1}) > s_j$, then $C'(x) = s_j$ in the equilibrium.[7]

The system therefore simply acts so as to minimize

$$C(x) + \sum_{j=1}^{n} (s_{j+1} - s_j) \,\text{Max}\,(x - l^j, 0).$$

This is what we set out to show.

The implication of the preceding argument is that any convex damage function can be approximated to any desired degree of accuracy through the introduction of markets for different kinds of licenses. The private sector can be confronted with a nonlinear damage function without sacrificing efficiency in the distribution of cleanup.

[7]Note that (A.5) can only hold for one type of license because as j increases, and $-C'(l^j)$ falls, s_{j+1} rises.

B

As a practical matter, in the pollution context, the cost of the additional license markets may not be justified by the reduction in expected total cost. But it is perhaps a matter of some intellectual interest, both here and in other decentralization problems, that a carefully designed set of markets for options to buy or sell commodities at various prices can solve the problem of reconciling the competing demands of efficiency and decentralization. This subject is probably worthy of further investigation.

References

Jacoby, H., G. Schaumberg and F. Gramlech, 1972, Marketable pollution rights (M.I.T., Cambridge, MA) unpublished.

Kneese, A.V. and B. Bower, 1968, Managing water quality (Resources for the Future, Johns Hopkins Press, Baltimore).

Montgomery, W.C., 1972, Markets in licenses and efficient pollution control programs, Journal of Economic Theory 5, no. 3, 395–418.

Roberts, M.J., 1975, Environmental protection: The complexities of real policy choice, in: Fox and Swainson, eds., Water quality management: The design of institutional arrangements (University of British Columbia Press, Vancouver).

Part III
The Design and Implementation of
Environmental Policy

[10]

THE USE OF STANDARDS AND PRICES FOR PROTECTION OF THE ENVIRONMENT

William J. Baumol and Wallace E. Oates*

Princeton University, Princeton, N.J., USA

Summary

In the Pigouvian tradition, economists have frequently proposed the adoption of a system of unit taxes (or subsidies) to control externalities, where the tax on a particular activity is equal to the marginal social damage it generates. In practice, however, such an approach has rarely proved feasible because of our inability to measure marginal social damage.

This paper proposes that we establish a set of admittedly somewhat arbitrary standards of environmental quality (e.g., the dissolved oxygen content of a water-way will be above x per cent at least 99 per cent of the time) and then impose a set of charges on waste emissions sufficient to attain these standards. While such *resource-use prices* clearly will not in general produce a Pareto-efficient allocation of resources, it is shown that they nevertheless do possess some important opti-mality properties and other practical advantages. In particular, it is proved that, for any given vector of final outputs such prices can achieve a specified reduction in pollution levels at minimum cost to the economy, even in the presence of firms with objectives other than that of simple profit maximization.

In the technicalities of the theoretical discussion of the tax-subsidy approach to the regulation of externalities, one of the issues most critical for its application tends to get the short end of the discussion. Virtually every author points out that we do not know how to calculate the ideal Pigouvian tax or subsidy levels in practice, but because the point is rather obvious rarely is much made of it.

This paper reviews the nature of the difficulties and then proposes a sub-stitute approach to the externalities problem. This alternative, which we shall call the environmental pricing and standards procedure, represents what we consider to be as close an approximation as one can generally achieve in practice to the spirit of the Pigouvian tradition. Moreover, while this method does not aspire to anything like an optimal allocation of resources, it will be shown to possess some important optimality properties.

---

* The authors are members of the faculty at Princeton University. They are grateful to the Ford Foundation whose support greatly facilitated the completion of this paper.

Swed. J. of Economics 1971

1. Difficulties in Determining the Optimal Structure of Taxes and Subsidies

The proper level of the Pigouvian tax (subsidy) upon the activities of the gene-rator of an externality is equal to the marginal net damage (benefit) produced by that activity.[1] The difficulty is that it is usually not easy to obtain a reasonable estimate of the money value of this marginal damage. Kneese & Bower report some extremely promising work constituting a first step toward the estimation of the damage caused by pollution of waterways including even some quantitative evaluation of the loss in recreational benefits. However, it is hard to be sanguine about the availability in the foreseeable future of a comprehensive body of statistics reporting the marginal net damage of the various externality-generating activities in the economy. The number of activities involved and the number of persons affected by them are so great that on this score alone the task assumes Herculean proportions. Add to this the intangible nature of many of the most important consequences—the damage to health, the aesthetic costs—and the difficulty of determining a money equivalent for marginal net damage becomes even more apparent.

This, however, is not the end of the story. The optimal tax level on an ex-ternality generating activity is not equal to the marginal net damage it gener-ates *initially*, but rather to the damage it would cause if the level of the activity had been adjusted to its *optimal* level. To make the point more specifically, suppose that each additional unit of output of a factory now causes 50 cents worth of damage, but that after the installation of the appropriate smoke-control devices and other optimal adjustments, the marginal social damage would be reduced to 20 cents. Then a little thought will confirm what the appropriate mathematics show: the correct value of the Pigouvian tax is 20 cents per unit of output, that is, the marginal cost of the smoke damage *corresponding to an optimal situation*. A tax of 50 cents per unit of output corresponding to the current smoke damage cost would lead to an excessive reduction in the smoke-producing activity, a reduction beyond the range over which the marginal benefit of decreasing smoke emission exceeds its marginal cost.

The relevance of this point for our present discussion is that it compounds enormously the difficulty of determining the optimal tax and benefit levels. If there is little hope of estimating the damage that is currently generated, how much less likely it is that we can evaluate the damage that would occur in an optimal world which we have never experienced or even described in quantitative terms.

There is an alternative possibility. Instead of trying to go directly to the optimal tax policy, one could instead, as a first approximation, base a set of

---

[1] We will use the term marginal *net* damage to mean the difference between marginal social and private damage (or cost).

44   *W. J. Baumol and W. E. Oates*

taxes and subsidies on the current net damage (benefit) levels. Then as outputs and damage levels were modified in response to the present level of taxes, the taxes themselves would in turn be readjusted to correspond to the new damage levels. It can be hoped that this will constitute a convergent, iterative process with tax levels affecting outputs and damages, these in turn leading to modifications in taxes, and so on. It is not clear, however, even in theory, whether this sequence will in fact converge toward the optimal taxes and resource allocation patterns. An extension of the argument underlying some of Coase's illustrations can be used to show that convergence cannot always be expected. But even if the iterative process were stable and were in principle capable of yielding an optimal result, its practicality is clearly limited. The notion that tax and subsidy rates can be readjusted quickly and easily on the basis of a fairly esoteric marginal net damage calculation does not seem very plausible. The difficulty of these calculations has already been suggested, and it is not easy to look forward with equanimity to their periodic revision, as an iterative process would require.

In sum, the basic trouble with the Pigouvian cure for the externalities problem does not lie primarily in the technicalities that have been raised against it in the theoretical literature but in the fact that we do not know how to determine the dosages that it calls for. Though there may be some special cases in which one will be able to form reasonable estimates of the social damages, in general we simply do not know how to set the required levels of taxes and subsidies.

2. The Environmental Pricing and Standards Approach

The economist's predilection for the use of the price mechanism makes him reluctant to give up the Pigouvian solution without a struggle. The inefficiencies of a system of direct controls, including the high real enforcement costs that generally accompany it, have been discussed often enough; they require no repetition here.

There is a fairly obvious way, however, in which one can avoid recourse to direct controls and retain the use of the price system as a means to control externalities. Simply speaking, it involves the selection of a set of somewhat arbitrary standards for an acceptable environment. On the basis of evidence concerning the effects of unclean air on health or of polluted water on fish life, one may, for example, decide that the sulfur-dioxide content of the atmosphere in the city should not exceed x percent, or that the oxygen demand of the foreign matter contained in a waterway should not exceed level y, or that the decibel (noise) level in residential neighborhoods should not exceed z at least 99 % of the time. These acceptability standards, x, y and z, then amount to a set of constraints that society places on its activities. They represent the decision-maker's subjective evaluation of the minimum standards that must be met in order to achieve what may be described in persuasive terms as "a reasonable quality of life". The defects of the concept will immediately be clear to the reader, and, since we do not want to minimize them, we shall examine this problem explicitly in a later section of the paper.

For the moment, however, we want to emphasize the role of the price system in the implementation of these standards. The point here is simply that the public authority can levy a uniform set of taxes which would in effect constitute a set of prices for the private use of social resources such as air and water. The taxes (or prices) would be selected so as to achieve specific acceptability standards rather than attempting to base them on the unknown value of marginal net damages. Thus, one might tax all installations emitting wastes into a river at a rate of $t(b)$ cents per gallon, where the tax rate, t, paid by a particular polluter, would, for example, depend on b, the BOD value of the effluent, according to some fixed schedule.[1] Each polluter would then be given a financial incentive to reduce the amount of effluent he discharges and to improve the quality of the discharge (i.e., reduce its BOD value). By setting the tax rates sufficiently high, the community would presumably be able to achieve whatever level of purification of the river it desired. It might even be able to eliminate at least some types of industrial pollution altogether.[2]

Here, if necessary, the information needed for iterative adjustments in tax rates would be easy to obtain: if the initial taxes did not reduce the pollution of the river sufficiently to satisfy the preset acceptability standards, one would simply raise the tax rates. Experience would soon permit the authorities to estimate the tax levels appropriate for the achievement of a target reduction in pollution.

One might even be able to extend such adjustments beyond the setting of the tax rates to the determination of the acceptability standards themselves. If, for example, attainment of the initial targets were to prove unexpectedly inexpensive, the community might well wish to consider making the standards stricter.[3] Of course, such an iterative process is not costless. It means that at least some of the polluting firms and municipalities will have to adapt their

---

[1] BOD, biochemical oxygen demand, is a measure of the organic waste load of an emission. It measures the amount of oxygen used during decomposition of the waste materials. BOD is used widely as an index of the quality of effluents. However, it is only an approximation at best. Discharges whose BOD value is low may nevertheless be considered serious pollutants because they contain inorganic chemical poisons whose oxygen requirement is nil because the poisons do not decompose. See Kneese and Bower on this matter.
[2] Here it is appropriate to recall the words of Chief Justice Marshall, when he wrote that "The power to tax involves the power to destroy" (McCulloch vs. Maryland, 1819). In terms of reversing the process of environmental decay, we can see, however, that the power to tax can also be the power to restore.
[3] In this way the pricing and standards approach might be adapted to approximate the Pigouvian ideal. If the standards were revised upward whenever there was reason to believe that the marginal benefits exceeded the marginal costs, and if these judgments were reasonably accurate, the two would arrive at the same end product, at least if the optimal solution were unique.

46   *W. J. Baumol and W. E. Oates*

operations as tax rates are readjusted. At the very least they should be warned
in advance of the likelihood of such changes so that they can build flexibility
into their plant design, something which is not costless (See Hart). But, at
any rate, it is clear that, through the adjustment of tax rates, the public
authority can realize whatever standards of environmental quality it has
selected.

3. Optimality Properties of the Pricing and Standards Technique

While the pricing and standards procedure will not, in general, lead to Pareto-
efficient levels of the relevant activities, it is nevertheless true that the use
of unit taxes (or subsidies) to achieve the specified quality standards does
possess one important optimality property: it is the least-cost method to
realize these targets.[1] A simple example may serve to clarify this point. Suppose
that it is decided in some metropolitan area that the sulfur-dioxide content of
the atmosphere should be reduced by 50 %. An obvious approach to this matter, and the one that often recommends itself to the regulator, is to require
each smoke-producer in the area to reduce his emissions of sulfur dioxide by
the same 50 %. However, a moment's thought suggests that this may constitute
a very expensive way to achieve the desired result. If, at existing levels of
output, the marginal cost of reducing sulfur-dioxide emissions for Factory A
is only one-tenth of the marginal cost for Factory B, we would expect that
it would be much cheaper for the economy as a whole to assign A a much
greater decrease in smoke emissions than B. Just how the least-cost set of
relative quotas could be arrived at in practice by the regulator is not clear,
since this obviously would require calculations involving simultaneous relationships and extensive information on each polluter's marginal-cost function.

It is easy to see, however, that the unit-tax approach can *automatically*
produce the least-cost assignment of smoke-reduction quotas without the need
for any complicated calculations by the enforcement authority. In terms of
our preceding example, suppose that the public authority placed a unit tax
on smoke emissions and raised the level of the tax until sulfur-dioxide emissions
were in fact reduced by 50 %. In response to a tax on its smoke emissions, a
cost-minimizing firm will cut back on such emissions until the marginal cost
of further reductions in smoke output is equal to the tax. But, since all economic
units in the area are subject to the same tax, it follows that the marginal cost
of reducing smoke output will be equalized across all activities. This implies
that it is impossible to reduce the aggregate cost of the specified
decrease in smoke emissions by re-arranging smoke-reduction quotas: any
alteration in this pattern of smoke emissions would involve an increase in

---

[1] This proposition is not new. While we have been unable to find an explicit statement of
this result anywhere in the literature, it or a very similar proposition has been suggested
in a number of places. See, for example, Kneese & Bower, Chapter 6, and Ruff, p. 79.

smoke output by one firm the value of which to the firm would be less than
the cost of the corresponding reduction in smoke emissions by some other firm.
For the interested reader, a formal proof of this least-cost property of unit
taxes for the realization of a specified target level of environmental quality
is provided in an appendix to this paper. We might point out that the
validity of this least-cost theorem does not require the assumption that firms
are profit-maximizers. All that is necessary is that they minimize costs for
whatever output levels they should select, as would be done, for example,
by a firm that seeks to maximize its growth or its sales.

The cost saving that can be achieved through the use of taxes and subsidies
in the attainment of acceptability standards may by no means be negligible.
In one case for which comparable cost figures have been calculated, Kneese &
Bower (p. 162) report that, with a system of uniform unit taxes, the cost of
achieving a specified level of water quality would have been only about half
as high as that resulting from a system of direct controls. If these figures are
at all representative, then the potential waste of resources in the choice
between tax measures and direct controls may obviously be of a large order.
Unit taxes thus appear to represent a very attractive method for the realization of specified standards of environmental quality. Not only do they require
relatively little in the way of detailed information on the cost structures of
different industries, but they lead automatically to the least-cost pattern of
modification of externality-generating activities.

4. Where the Pricing and Standards Approach is Appropriate

As we have emphasized, the most disturbing aspect of the pricing and standards
procedure is the somewhat arbitrary character of the criteria selected. There
does presumably exist some optimal level of pollution (i.e., quality of the air
or a waterway), but in the absence of a pricing mechanism to indicate the value
of the damages generated by polluting activities, one knows no way to determine accurately the set of taxes necessary to induce the optimal activity levels.

While this difficulty certainly should not be minimized, it is important at
the outset to recognize that the problem is by no means unique to the
selection of acceptability standards. In fact, as is well known, it is a difficulty
common to the provision of nearly all public goods. In general, the market will
not generate appropriate levels of outputs where market prices fail to reflect
the social damages (or benefits) associated with particular activities. As a
result, in the absence of the proper set of signals from the market, it is typically necessary to utilize a political process (i.e., a method of collective
choice) to determine the level of the activity.[1] From this perspective, the selec-

---

[1] As Coase and others have argued, voluntary bargains struck among the interested parties
may in some instances yield an efficient set of activity levels in the presence of externalities. However, such coordinated, voluntary action is typically possible only in small
groups. One can hardly imagine, for example, a voluntary bargaining process involving
all the persons in a metropolitan area and resulting in a set of payments that would
generate efficient levels of activities affecting the smog content of the atmosphere.

48   *W. J. Baumol and W. E. Oates*

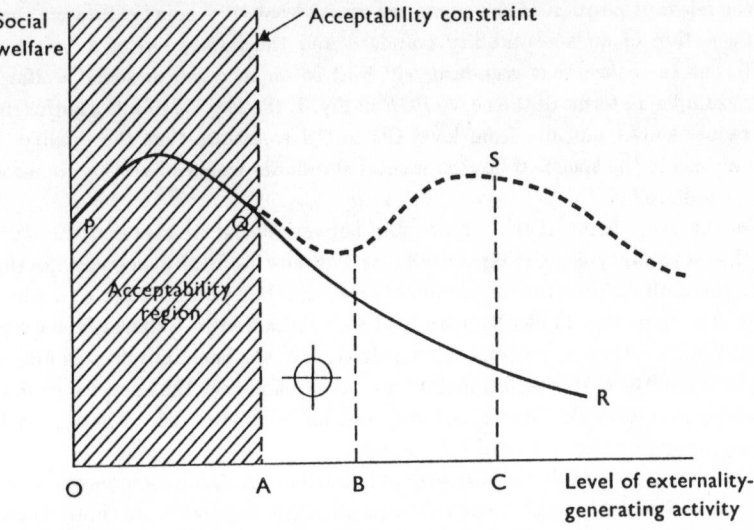

Fig. 1

tion of environmental standards can be viewed as a particular device utilized in a process of collective decision-making to determine the appropriate level of an activity involving external effects.

Since methods of collective choice, such as simple-majority rule or decisions by an elected representative, can at best be expected to provide only very rough approximations to optimal results, the general problem becomes one of deciding whether or not the malfunction of the market in a certain case is sufficiently serious to warrant public intervention. In particular, it would seem to us that such a blunt instrument as acceptability standards should be used only sparingly, because the very ignorance that serves as the rationale for the adoption of such standards implies that we can hardly be sure of their consequences.

In general, it would seem that intervention in the form of acceptability standards can be utilized with any degree of confidence only where there is clear reason to believe that the existing situation imposes a high level of social costs *and* that these costs can be significantly reduced by feasible decreases in the levels of certain externality-generating activities. If, for example, we were to examine the functional relationship between the level of social welfare and the levels of particular activities which impose marginal net damages, the argument would be that the use of acceptability standards is justified only in those cases where the curve, over the bulk of the relevant range, is both decreasing and steep. Such a case is illustrated in Fig. 1 by the curve *PQR*. In a case of this kind, although we obviously will not have an accurate knowledge of the relevant position of the curve, we can at least have some assurance that the selection of an acceptability standard and the imposition of a unit tax sufficient to realize that standard will lead to an increase in social welfare. For example, in terms of the curve PQR in Fig. 1, the levying of a tax sufficient to reduce smoke outputs from level OC to OA to ensure that the quality of the air meets the specified environmental standards would obviously increase social welfare.[1]

On the other hand, if the relationship between social welfare and the level of the externality-generating activity is not monotonically decreasing, the changes resulting from the imposition of an acceptability standard (e.g., a move from S to Q in Fig. 1) clearly may lead to a reduction in welfare. Moreover, even if the function were monotonic but fairly flat, the benefits achieved might not be worth the cost of additional intervention machinery that new legislation requires, and it would almost certainly not be worth the risk of acting with highly imperfect, inconclusive information.

In some cases, notably in the field of public utility regulation, some economists have criticized the employment of acceptability standards on both these grounds; they have asserted that the social costs of monopolistic misallocation of resources are probably not very high (i.e., the relevant portion of the social-welfare curve in Fig. 1 is not steep) and that the regulation can itself introduce inefficiencies in the operations of the regulated industries.

Advocacy of environmental pricing and standards procedures for the control of externalities must therefore rest on the belief that in this area we do have a clear notion of the general shape of the social welfare curve. This will presumably hold true where the evidence indicates, first that a particular externality really does have a substantial and unambiguous effect on the quality of life, if, for example, it makes existence very unpleasant for everyone or constitutes a serious hazard to health; and second that reductions in the levels of these activities do not themselves entail huge resource costs. On the first point, there

---

[1] The relationship depicted in Fig. 1 is to be regarded as an intuitive device employed for pedagogical purposes, not in any sense as a rigorous analysis. However, some further explanation may be helpful. The curve itself is not a social-welfare function in the usual sense; rather it measures in terms of a numeraire (kronor or dollars) the value, summed over all individuals, of the benefits from the output of the activity minus the private *and* net social costs. Thus, for each level of the activity, the height of the curve indicates the *net* benefits (possibly negative) that the activity confers on society. The acceptability constraint indicates that level of the activity which is consistent with the specified minimum standard of environmental quality (e.g., that level of smoke emissions from factories which is sufficiently low to maintain the quality of the air in a particular metropolitan area). There is an ambiguity here in that the levels of several different activities may jointly determine a particular dimension of environmental quality, e.g., the smoke emissions of a number of different industries will determine the quality of the air. In this case, the acceptable level of pollutive emissions for the firm or industry will clearly depend on the levels of emissions of others. If, as we discussed earlier, unit taxes are used to realize the acceptability standards, there will result a least-cost pattern of levels of the relevant externality-generating activities. If we understand the constraint in Fig. 1 to refer to the activity level indicated by this particular solution, then this ambiguity disappears.

50   W. J. Baumol and W. E. Oates

is growing evidence that various types of pollutants do in fact have such unfortunate consequences, particularly in areas where they are highly concentrated. [On this see, for instance, Lave & Seskin]. Second, what experience
we have had with, for example, the reduction of waste discharges into waterways suggests that processes involving the recycling and reuse of waste materials can frequently be achieved at surprisingly modest cost.[1] In such cases
the rationale for the imposition of environmental standards is clear, and it
seems to us that the rejection of such crude measures on the grounds that they
will probably violate the requirements of optimality may well be considered
a kind of perverse perfectionism.

It is interesting in this connection that the pricing and standards approach
is not too different in spirit from a number of economic policy measures that
are already in operation in other areas. This is significant for our discussion,
because it suggests that regulators know how to work with this sort of approach
and have managed to live with it elsewhere. Probably the most noteworthy
example is the use of fiscal and monetary policy for the realization of macroeconomic objectives. Here, the regulation of the stock of money and the
availability of credit along with adjustments in public expenditures and tax
rates are often aimed at the achievement of a selected target level of employment or rate of inflation. Wherever prices rise too rapidly or unemployment
exceeds an "acceptable" level, monetary and fiscal variables are readjusted in
an attempt to "correct" the difficulty. It is noteworthy that this procedure is
also similar to the pricing and standards approach in its avoidance of direct
controls.

Other examples of this general approach to policy are not hard to find.
Policies for the regulation of public-utilities, for instance, typically utilize a
variety of standards such as profit-rate ceilings (i.e., "fair rates of return")
to judge the acceptability of the behavior of the regulated firm. In the area
of public education, one frequently encounters state-imposed standards (e.g.,
subjects to be taught) for local school districts which are often accompanied
by grants of funds to the localities to help insure that public-school programs
meet the designated standards. What this suggests is that public administrators
are familiar with this general approach to policy and that the implementation
of the pricing and standards technique should not involve insurmountable
administrative difficulties. For these reasons, the achievement of specified
environmental standards through the use of unit taxes (or subsidies) seems to
us to possess great promise as a workable method for the control of the quality
of the environment.

---

[1] Some interesting discussions of the feasibility of the control of waste emissions into
waterways often at low cost are contained in Kneese & Bower. In particular, see their
description of the control of water quality in the Ruhr River in Germany.

5. Concluding Remarks

It may be useful in concluding our discussion simply to review the ways in which the pricing and standards approach differs from the standard Pigouvian-prescription for the control of externalities.

(1) Under the Pigouvian technique, unit taxes (or subsidies) are placed on externality-generating activities, with the level of the tax on a particular activity being set equal to the marginal net damage it generates. Such taxes (if they could be determined) would, it is presumed, lead to Pareto-efficient levels of the activities.

(2) In contrast, the pricing and standards approach begins with a predetermined set of standards for environmental quality and then imposes unit taxes (or subsidies) sufficient to achieve these standards. This will not, in general, result in an optimal allocation of resources, but (as is proved formally in the appendix) the procedure does at least represent the least-cost method of realizing the specified standards.

(3) The basic appeal of the pricing and standards approach relative to the Pigouvian prescription lies in its workability. We simply do not, in general, have the information needed to determine the appropriate set of Pigouvian taxes and subsidies. Such information is not, however, necessary for our suggested procedure.

(4) While it makes no pretense of promising anything like an optimal allocation of resources, the pricing and standards technique can, in cases where external effects impose high costs (or benefits), at least offer some assurance of reducing the level of these damages. Moreover, the administrative procedures—the selection of standards and the use of fiscal incentives to realize these standards—implied by this approach are in many ways quite similar to those used in a number of current public programs. This, we think, offers some grounds for optimism as to the practicality of the pricing and standards technique for the control of the quality of the environment.

References

1. Bohm, P.: Pollution, Purification, and the Theory of External Effects. *Swedish Journal of Economics* 72, no. 2, 153–66, 1970.
2. Coase, R.: The Problem of Social Cost. *Journal of Law and Economics 3*, 1–44, 1960.
3. Hart, A.: Anticipations, Business Planning, and the Cycle. *Quarterly Journal of Economics 51*, 273–97, Feb. 1937.
4. Kneese, A. & Bower, B.: *Managing Water Quality: Economics, Technology, Institutions*. Baltimore, 1968.
5. Lave, L. & Seskin, E.: Air Pollution and Human Health. *Science 21*, 723–33 Aug. 1970.
6. Portes, R.: The Search for Efficiency in the Presence of Externalities. *Unfashionable Economics: Essays in Honor of Lord Balogh* (ed. P. Streeten), pp. 348–61. London, 1970.
7. Ruff. L.: The Economic Common Sense of Pollution. *The Public Interest*, Spring 1970, 69–85.

52   *W. J. Baumol and W. E. Oates*

APPENDIX

In the text, we argued on a somewhat intuitive level that the appropriate use of unit taxes and subsidies represents the least-cost method of achieving a set of specified standards for environmental quality. In the case of smoke-abatement, for instance, the tax-subsidy approach will automatically generate the cost-minimizing assignment of "reduction quotas" without recourse to involved calculations or enforcement.

The purpose of this appendix is to provide a formal proof of this proposition. More precisely, we will show that, to achieve *any* given vector of final outputs along with the attainment of the specified quality of the environment, the use of unit taxes (or, where appropriate, subsidies) to induce the necessary modification in the market-determined pattern of output will permit the realization of the specified output vector at minimum cost to society.

While this theorem may seem rather obvious (as the intuitive discussion in the text suggests), its proof does point up several interesting properties which are noteworthy. In particular, unlike many of the propositions about prices in welfare analysis, the theorem does not require a world of perfect competition. It applies to pure competitors, monopolists, or oligopolists alike so long as each of the firms involved seeks to minimize the private cost of producing whatever vector of outputs it selects and has no monopsony power (i.e., no influence on the prices of inputs). The firms need not be simple profit-maximizers; they may choose to maximize growth, sales (total revenues), their share of the market, or any combination of these goals (or a variety of other objectives). Since the effective pursuit of these goals typically entails minimizing the cost of whatever outputs are produced, the theorem is still applicable. Finally, we want simply to emphasize that the theorem applies to whatever set of final outputs society should select (either by direction or through the operation of the market). It does not judge the desirability of that particular vector of outputs; it only tells us how to make the necessary adjustments at minimum cost.

We shall proceed initially to derive the first-order conditions for the minimization of the cost of a specified overall reduction in the emission of wastes. We will then show that the independent decisions of cost-minimizing firms subject to the appropriate unit tax on waste emissions will, in fact, satisfy the first-order conditions for overall cost minimization.

Let

x_{iv} represent the quantity of input i used by plant v $(i=1, ..., n)$, $(v=1, ..., m)$,

z_v be the quantities of waste it discharges,

y_v be its output level,

$f_v(x_{1v}, ..., x_{nv}, z_v, y_v)=0$ be its production function,

p_i be the price of input i, and

k the desired level of $\sum z_v$, the maximum permitted daily discharge of waste.

The use of standards and prices for environment protection 53

In this formulation, the value of k is determined by the administrative authority in a manner designed to hold waste emissions in the aggregate to a level consistent with the specified environmental standard (e.g., the sulphuric content of the atmosphere). Note that the level of the firm's waste emissions is treated here as an argument in its production function; to reduce waste discharges while maintaining its level of output, the firm will presumably require the use of additional units of some other inputs (e.g., more labor or capital to recycle the wastes or to dispose of them in an alternative manner).

The problem now becomes that of determining the value of the x's and z's that minimize input cost

$$c = \sum_i \sum_v p_i(x_{iv})$$

subject to the output constraints

$$y_v = y_v^* = \text{constant} \qquad (v = 1, ..., m)$$

and the constraint on the total output of pollutants

$$\sum_v z_v = k.$$

It may appear odd to include as a constraint a vector of given outputs of the firms, since the firms will presumably adjust output levels as well as the pattern of inputs in response to taxes or other restrictions on waste discharges. This vector, however, can be *any* vector of outputs (including that which emerges as a result of independent decisions by the firms). What we determine are first-order conditions for cost-minimization which apply to *any* given vector of outputs no matter how they are arrived at. Using $\lambda_v(v=1, ..., m)$ and λ as our $(m+1)$ Lagrange multipliers, we obtain the first-order conditions:

$$\left.\begin{aligned}
\lambda_v f_{vz} + \lambda &= 0 & (v = 1, ..., m) \\
p_i + \lambda_v f_{vi} &= 0 & (v = 1, ..., m)\,(i = 1, ..., n) \\
y_v &= y_v^* & (v = 1, ..., m)
\end{aligned}\right\} \qquad (1)$$

where we use the notation $f_{vz} = \partial f_v / \partial z_v$, $f_{vi} = \partial f_v / \partial x_{iv}$.

Now let us see what will happen if the m plants are run by independent managements whose objective is to minimize the cost of whatever outputs their firm produces, and if, instead of the imposition of a fixed ceiling on the emission of pollutants, this emission is taxed at a fixed rate per unit, t. So long as its input prices are fixed, firm v will wish to minimize

$$c = tz_v + \sum_i p_i x_{iv}$$

subject to

$$y_v = y_v^*.$$

54   *W. J. Baumol and W. E. Oates*

Direct differentiation of the m Lagrangian functions for our m firms immediately yields the first-order conditions (1)—the same conditions as before, provided t is set equal to λ. Thus, if we impose a tax rate that achieves the desired reduction in the total emission of pollutants, we have proved that this reduction will satisfy the necessary conditions for the minimization of the program's cost to society.[1]

---

[1] In this case, λ (and hence t) is the shadow price of the pollution constraint. In addition to satisfying these necessary first-order conditions, cost-minimization requires that the production functions possess the usual second-order properties. An interesting treatment of this issue is available in Portes. We should also point out that our proof assumes that the firm takes t as given and beyond its control. Bohm discusses some of the problems that can arise where the firm takes into account the effects of its behavior on the value of t.

[11]

LAND, WATER, AND OWNERSHIP*

J. H. DALES   *University of Toronto*

Rôle des droits de propriété du sol et de l'eau dans l'allocation des ressources. Le mécanisme des prix ne peut conduire à une allocation efficace des ressources qui ne font pas l'objet de propriété. C'est ce que nous constatons en comparant l'histoire de l'utilisation du sol et de l'eau en amérique du Nord. La même conclusion va d'ailleurs pour l'utilisation de l'air.

Dans cet article, l'auteur défend la thèse selon laquelle les problèmes de la pollution des eaux seraient réglés plus facilement en établissant une grille des droits d'usage de l'eau plutôt que par l'institution de systèmes complexes de prix témoins. Une solution qui s'impose d'elle-même consiste dans le paiement de droits d'usage des biens libres. On parvient ainsi à la mise sur pied d'un système de prix pour l'utilisation des biens libres dans le cas où l'usage conduit à leur détérioration ou leur destruction. L'auteur n'accepte pas l'idée selon laquelle le système des prix témoins se justifie par l'existence des économies ou des déséconomies externes, et cela pour deux raisons. D'abord l'existence d'un système de prix réels permet de transformer les externalités technologiques nuisibles en externalités pécuniaires acceptables pour la société. En second lieu, la thèse des externalités ignore la mobilité des individus tout en reconnaissant celle des agents de pollution. Enfin l'auteur conclut que, dans le cadre des certains choix collectifs, l'établissement d'un marché des ressources dite libres est non seulement économiquement rentable, mais se traduit par des réductions considérables des frais d'administration.

I

Increasing public concern about the pollution of natural water systems in North America has confronted governments with a new problem in resource administration, and challenged economists to devise an artificial pricing system for water that will itself promote wise use of the resource, thereby greatly simplifying the lives of water administrators. The pricing problem turns out, not unexpectedly, to be a deliciously complex tangle of joint uses, externalities, and peak-load problems. The administrative problem of approximating optimum shadow prices by actual user charges promises to be a nightmare.

The economic and administrative complexity of water problems is commonly explained as being inherent in the nature of a fluid resource. Because of the self-mixing quality of a fluid, one use of water at a given point may affect other uses at the same point; and because water flows through space, use at one point may also affect uses at other points. Opportunity cost pricing is accordingly very complex because of the number of alternative opportunities that may be affected by any one use at any one point, not to mention the complications introduced by time of use, varying stream flow, different rates of self-regeneration of different

*Presented at the First Annual Meeting of the Canadian Economics Association, Calgary, June, 1968.

I am grateful to colleagues for comments on earlier versions of this paper. My main debt, however, is to Mr. J. C. McManus, who has spent much time discussing the paper with me and has done his best to prevent me from making errors. The paper has been written during a sabbatical year financed in part by the Canada Council.

Canadian Journal of Economics/Revue canadienne d'Economique, I, no. 4
November/novembre 1968

stretches of water, and the chemical interactions of different types of waste after they have been discharged into a natural water system.

Before we submit to this incubus of complexity, however, we might seek comfort in the reflection that the great virtue of a pricing system is that it solves, avoids, mediates, or somehow manages to dispel, all sorts of complexities, particularly those that arise from various interdependencies between uses and users of goods. Yet the existence of a natural pricing system depends crucially on the institution of ownership. What is not owned cannot be priced since prices are payments for property rights or rights to the use of an asset.[1] In the course of allocating property rights to assets among different owners, the price system in fact transforms most potential "technological externalities" into "pecuniary externalities," a synonym for prices. Thus we hear very little about externalities of land use, precisely because property rights to land use are well established and allocated by the price system. It is quite otherwise where water is concerned.

We can now re-formulate the water problem and blame its complexity not on nature and the laws of fluids, but on man and his failure to devise property rights to the use of natural water systems. Economists tend to assume implicitly that it is impossible to own water and therefore seek to devise artificial price systems that are identical to what prices "would be" if ownership were possible. The alternative strategy is to devise an ownership system and then let a price system develop. The purpose of this article is to suggest that there are very considerable advantages to attacking our water problems by means of a system of explicit ownership rather than by a system of shadow prices.

A geographical reflection is also in order. Despite the large numbers of people who live on the St. Lawrence, the Fraser, and the St. John, most Canadians live on lakes, or on rivers that flow into lakes, rather than into oceans, whereas most Americans, despite the large population around the southern rim of the Great Lakes, live on river systems that discharge into salt water. Lakes are much less "mobile" and much less "self-mixing" than rivers. Most of the water in lakes *stays* there for prolonged periods, and recent research has shown that during much of the year the shallow, inshore waters of large lakes are effectively isolated from the very large volumes of water in their deep centres.[2] (Similar propositions apparently apply to oceans; otherwise the serious pollution problems of coastal cities such as San Francisco, New York, and Vancouver would not exist.)

People who live on river systems, as most Americans do, tend to pass on their pollution to the next downstream community, thereby creating vexing externality problems. American literature on pollution has been strongly influenced by the uni-directional flow of rivers, which makes it relatively easy to solve the

[1]One never owns physical assets, but only the rights to use physical assets. Professor Ronald Coase writes that a factor of production "is usually thought of as a physical entity which the businessman acquires and uses (an acre of land, a ton of fertilizer) instead of as a right to perform certain (physical) actions. We may speak of a person owning land and using it as a factor of production but what the land-owner in fact possesses is the right to carry out a circumscribed list of actions. The rights of a land-owner are not unlimited." See his "The Problem of Social Cost," *Journal of Law and Economics*, Oct. 1960, 1–44, reprinted in W. Breit and H. M. Hochman, eds., *Readings in Micro-Economics*, (New York, 1968), 423–56; the quotation is from p. 456.

identification problem of who pollutes whom. River pollution therefore lends itself to economic analysis in terms of externalities, and shadow-pricing schemes to offset them. People who live on lake systems (most Canadians) tend to pollute themselves; because inshore lake water, far from being uni-directional, tends to slosh up and down the shoreline, lake pollution tends to be a sort of Hobbesean war of all against all. It therefore requires economic analysis in terms of social decision-making and social welfare functions rather than in terms of the effects of autonomous upstream communities on autonomous downstream communities. The economics of Canadian water pollution is therefore quite different from the economics of American water pollution.

II

Rent theory has been the traditional vehicle for studying the economics of natural resources, and a review of some of the effects of the ownership-rental system as applied to land highlights the opposite effects induced by the absence of an ownership-rental system as applied to water. Following normal practice, we shall speak of the supply of land (or water) available to any society as fixed by nature. Though fixed in supply when measured in natural units (acres or gallons), the *quality* of land and water can be changed by human action. (Were we to measure the quantity of land in efficiency units of a given quality, its supply would be variable; we conduct the present argument, however, in terms of natural units, fixed supplies, and variable qualities.) Imagine a society where all land is being used and even the poorest of it commands a positive rent (this assumption allows us to avoid those not very illuminating discussions about no-rent land and the relationships between the extensive and intensive margins) and suppose that an initial state of equilibrium exists, and in particular that at existing land values and rents there is neither investment nor disinvestment in the quality of the soil. Population growth when superimposed on this initial state will lead to increases in land values and rents; these increases in turn will lead to economies in the use of soil by means of the substitution of manufactured fertilizers and other intensive farming practices against inputs of natural soil fertility. The process may be described as one of investing in soil fertility, and the equilibrium stock of soil fertility will accordingly rise (or its rate of decline will fall). In a general form, the conclusion is that *the level of rent determines the quality of the soil that it is economic to maintain*. It is also clear, as Ricardo showed, that when man-made inputs are substituted for natural inputs in the food-producing industry the real cost of food increases and the standard of living in terms of food falls. Rising rents, therefore, tend to slow down population growth and lessen the population pressure that produces them.

The working out of these processes in the historical development of the United

²See G. K. Rodgers and D. V. Anderson, "The Thermal Structure of Lake Ontario," *Proceedings Sixth Conference Great Lakes Research*, 1963, University of Michigan publication 10, 59–69; P. F. Hamblin and G. K. Rodgers, *The Currents in the Toronto Region of Lake Ontario*, publication (PR 29) of the Great Lakes Institute of the University of Toronto, 1967; and G. K. Rodgers, "Thermal Regime and Circulation in the Great Lakes," in Claude E. Dolman, ed., *Water Resources of Canada* Royal Society of Canada, studia varia 11, (Toronto, 1967), 87–95.

States has been brilliantly described by Bunce.[3] In the early history of the country there was a high ratio of soil fertility to the human demands on it, and rent was accordingly low; "high farming" practices on the European model were therefore rejected, and economic use necessitated soil-depleting practices. In the course of time the man-soil fertility ratio rose, as a result both of population growth and of soil depletion; rents rose; more intensive farming practices became economic, and the rate of soil depletion was thereby reduced. A slowing down in the rate of population growth after 1900 further reduced pressure on the land; it is possible that in general soil depletion has now been brought to a halt in the United States and Canada, and that soil erosion and soil-depleting practices in some areas are balanced by soil-building investments in others.

The contrast between the history of land and of water use on this continent is eloquent. Property rights were established in land, with rent being the payment for the right to use the soil fertility; there were no water rents because property rights to water use were not established. Rising land rents led to more intensive land use and after 350 years there is no problem of population pressure on the land in North America. Water rents were zero; over-use of the water led to continuous reduction in water quality; and there is now a growing problem of population pressure on North American water resources. If we accept a simple dynamic extension of rent theory and assume a direct relationship between the level of rent and the development of improved technologies, the land-water comparison is again suggestive. Rising land rents have been associated with phenomenal improvements in land-use technology; zero rents for water have been associated with virtually zero improvement in water-use technology so far as quality-depleting uses are concerned.

The short-run function of land rent, of course, is to allocate parcels of land among different users and different uses. What is interesting is that potential externalities of land use, for example, the operation of a pig farm in the centre of a choice residential area, seldom materialize. Land being immobile, the ownership-rental system seems to work in such a way as to produce "natural zoning" in land use. Differential rents provide the mechanism for such zoning, and the result is that potential technological externalities are continuously transformed into pecuniary externalities, or prices. It should also be noted that a formal economic description of this process depends on a recognition of space, and particularly of the socially "insulating" quality of space. So long as space exists—and we must remember that in most economic analysis it does not—"zoning" solutions to externalities, or what Mishan has recently called "separate facilities" solutions,[4] are possibilities. Given space, there is no need for pig farmers and business executives to live as neighbours, and therefore no need to devise a system of bribes to compensate one or the other party for damages suffered.

The absence of an ownership-rental system for water has meant that water use has in fact been determined by such things as historical priority, gall, and force and fraud; it cannot be otherwise when property rights do not exist and when the price for the use of a valuable asset is zero. When no pricing process

[3]A. C. Bunce, *The Economics of Soil Conservation* (Ames, Iowa, 1945).
[4]E. J. Mishan, *The Costs of Economic Growth* (New York, 1967), chap. 8.

exists, there is no mechanism to transform technological externalities into pecuniary externalities. Accordingly we *do* observe striking examples of externalities in water use; stinking streams flow through choice residential areas, and anglers experience a mixture of rage and resignation as their favourite streams are polluted by industrial wastes. And then there are the externalities of all against all—householders help to destroy swimming beaches by their use of detergents (which promote algal growth), motorists pollute the air they breathe, and we all promote municipal and industrial pollution by insisting on cheap products and low taxes.

These considerations suggest the enormous social benefits that have resulted from applying an ownership-rental system to land, and, by contrast, the enormous social friction and economic waste that result from not applying an ownership-rental system to water. It has, of course, been relatively "easy" to apply property rights to land because land is both divisible and immobile. The awkward problem remains: is it *possible* to apply an ownership-rental system to the use of our water resources?

III

To speak of owning an asset is to use a convenient abbreviation for a complex interaction between a legal concept and an economic concept. An asset may be thought of as "a bundle of potential utility-yielding services that can be used in alternative ways." In the same vein, ownership consists of "a bundle of legally-defined user rights to an asset." As Coase has pointed out, it is rights, never objects, that are owned, and the rights themselves are always limited by law; "outright" ownership can never, by definition, extend to the use of an asset for illegal purposes.[5]

From the whole spectrum of possible ownership arrangements, we shall pick four major types for brief comment. What we shall call *common-property* ownership is, from an economic point of view, virtually non-ownership. A common-property asset is one that can be used by everyone, for almost any purpose, at zero cost. Examples are the mediaeval commons, the high seas, wild game, freeways, and (until recently in this country) air and water. Common-property ownership is justified economically *only* when the costs of enforcing a more restricted form of property-rights would be greater than the benefits of doing so. H. S. Gordon has shown that, neglecting enforcement costs, common-property ownership of an asset is economically inefficient in that the asset will be over-used by comparison with assets that are subject to more restrictive property rights.[6] Empirically it is clear that if the asset is depletable it will be continuously depleted on the grounds that "everybody's property is nobody's property": mediaeval commons were overstocked; modern freeways (but not toll-ways) quickly become congested; wild animals (but never domestic animals) become scarce or extinct; and the deteriorating quality of our air and water resources has become a matter of widespread concern. The concept of a

[5]See Coase, "The Problem of Social Cost."
[6]H. S. Gordon, "The Economic Theory of a Common-Property Resource: The Fishery," *Journal of Political Economy*, April 1954, 124–42.

free good has always been a contradiction in terms; it is time we appreciated its sardonic overtones, for anything that is treated as a free good is indeed likely to become a valueless thing.

In general common-property assets are nominally owned by some public body, usually a government, and the owner may restrict use of the property in a variety of ways. Some roads may be used by motorists but not by cyclists or pedestrians; some wild animals may be photographed, but not shot; on some lakes canoes and sailboats may be used, but not motor-boats. It seems reasonable to refer to such property as *restricted common-property;* though the type of use is restricted, it is still common-property in the sense that everyone can use it for designated purposes at zero cost. If uses that deplete the asset in a physical sense are banned, the quality of the asset can be maintained, though "congestion" problems may reduce its value to other users.

When the use of an asset is restricted by law to particular persons, or a particular person, we have what can conveniently be called *status-tenure* or *fixed-tenure* ownership. Such ownership guarantees exclusivity of use to the parties authorized to use the property, but these user rights are not transferable. Though secure right of access to an asset by a limited group of people is valuable, the absence of the right of transferability prevents an explicit price system from developing. Nevertheless implicit prices are likely to appear. If the right to send one's children to a particularly good school is limited to those who live in a particular area, the value of the rights are likely to become reflected in the value of real estate in the area concerned. The "regulatory" branches of modern governments create an enormous variety of valuable property rights that are imperfectly transferable, and that tend to be capitalized and monetized in ways that are usually unsuspected by their creators. The value of tariff protection, a quota to grow tobacco, a licence to transport milk or to operate a taxicab, are reflected in the values of tariff-protected businesses, tobacco farms, milk routes, and taxi fleets.[7] Though the indirect monetization of such rights is seldom illegal, contemporary populations choose to be as hypocritical about the process as mediaevel populations were about the evasions of prohibitions on the payment of interest; social inhibitions about a rational approach to property and prices have outlived social inhibitions about rational approaches to astronomy and sex.

From status-tenure to full *ownership,* in the usual contemporary sense of the term, is but a short step. Once the property right is separated from the person, it becomes transferable, and transfers of assets (rights) then take place at explicit prices. *Transferable* property rights stand in a one-to-one relationship to prices; everything that is owned is priced, and everything that is priced is owned—which is to say nothing about either the form of ownership (transferable property rights to assets may be owned by individuals, corporations, or governments) or about the precise functional relationship between ownership and prices. Ideological hang-ups on concepts of property rights and ownership are understandable because such concepts touch the very roots of society. We have not yet learned to discuss such matters unemotionally. Though we are inclined to take a condescending view of mediaeval man's distrust of full property rights

[7]On this general question, see Charles A. Reich, "The New Property," *Yale Law Journal,* 73, no. 5 (April 1964), 733–87.

to land, we tend to become quite agitated when valuable government-granted rights (licences to import, for example) are traded in the market place, or when suggestions to extend property rights to air and water are put forward for discussion. Property and prices still raise ancient fears that "the rich will eat out the poor."

IV

Since the right to use water is valuable, and since ownership consists of user rights, it should in principle be possible to devise an ownership-rental system for water. As is well known, however, certain characteristics of a natural water system create special problems in ownership.

The characteristics of an ownership system reflect in part the "divisibility" of the asset to which it is applied. Let us define an *asset-unit* as the smallest physical amount of the asset to which it is practicable to apply property rights, i.e., for which it is practicable to enforce exclusivity of use. In land, the asset-unit is very small, perhaps a few square yards; when the asset-unit is small compared to the quantity of the asset available, the asset can be held by a large number of individual owners. In such cases a "private property" form of ownership is likely to work well; decisions about the use of the asset will be decentralized among many owners, and a reasonably competitive market in asset-units will emerge.

In water, the asset-unit is very large. If water were completely "self-mixing," no one would pay anything to own Lake Ontario unless he could also own the whole Great Lakes drainage basin above the St. Lawrence river. As we have seen, however, water, especially in large lakes, mixes only slowly and imperfectly; because of this, and because of the self-purifying characteristic of water, the quality of water in the eastern end of Lake Ontario may be effectively independent of the uses made of the water at the western end of the lake. Even so, it is clear that the asset-unit is very large. It might be possible to divide the Great Lakes water system into, say, a dozen "regions" each of which would be self-contained for practical purposes, but it would certainly be impossible to divide them into a thousand such regions. In a democratic society it would be unacceptable to allow as few as a dozen, or even a score, of owners to control such an immense property as the Great Lakes drainage system. The only sensible alternative is the one actually adopted, namely, monopoly ownership by government. The reverse side of this coin is that the government must decide how its property is to be used and must enforce its decisions—assuming that it wishes to avoid the horrors of the common-property approach to resource management.

The decision about how water shall be used must be an arbitrary one from the standpoint of economics. Let me argue this point on the basis of a simple (but seemingly realistic) classification of water uses.

If we ignore such uses as navigation and the generation of hydroelectric power, which have insignificant effects on water quality, it seems reasonable to classify other uses into two categories: waste disposal, and "all other" uses, which we shall call amenity use. These two uses are competitive. Though it is not true that fishermen, swimmers, industries that use water for processing purposes, and municipal authorities responsible for residential water supplies all have the same quality demands, it is true that some of these users would be benefited, and none would be harmed, by an improvement in water quality. Waste disposers, on the other hand, would be harmed by such an improvement since it could only occur if less waste were discharged into the water. We thus reduce the many uses of water to two: amenity use and waste disposal. The social problem is then to decide on the division of water services between these two conflicting uses. In principle, the division should be made in such a way that the value of a marginal increment in the one good is equal to the value of a marginal decrement in the other. But since the value of a marginal change in amenity use cannot be measured, the optimum amount of waste disposal cannot be identified. In practice, the decision is made on a political rather than an economic calculus. Once there is a political demand for "pollution control," anti-pollution measures tend to be instituted incrementally until complaints about their cost outweigh complaints about pollution! That sort of solution, applied also to such things as education, road systems, and various social welfare schemes, seems to me to be eminently sensible, *faute de mieux.*

In water quality problems, however, it is important to keep in mind that, within limits, water can be "regionalized" for practical purposes, and that "zoning" solutions to quality problems are therefore possible in some cases. In practice it would probably be wise to provide for different ratios of amenity use to waste disposal use in different water "regions"; the socially insulating quality of space should be utilized wherever possible. People are mobile, and if they can consume the amenity services of water in the upper reaches of a river and the waste disposal services of the same river in its lower reaches, there is no need to force them to decide on the optimum division between amenity uses and waste disposal uses of the water in both the upper and lower parts of the river. But again, alas, economics has little to say about a feasible or desirable delimitation of water "regions"; a sensible "mapping" of water must be left to the good judgment of physical scientists and politicians.

The contention that there exists no economically optimum division between amenity and pollution uses of water will be resisted by exponents of damage-cost pricing.[8] In the classic example of an upstream community polluting a downstream community, an allegation of damage to the downstream user seems to rest on three assumptions: that the downstream community owns its water and in particular owns the right not to have its water polluted by others; that the downstream community gains no advantage from the upstream pollution, i.e., that its residents buy no goods from their upstream neighbours at prices that are lower than they would be if the upstream community were forced to reduce its pollution; and that the upstream residents suffer no disadvantages from the downstream pollution because they never visit the downstream area for fishing, swimming, or other recreational purposes. The property rights assumption has not generally been true in the past in North America, and even to-day it is far from clear that a downstream community has any more right to use the river water for swimming and drinking than the upstream community has to use it for waste disposal purposes. The other two assumptions about the inter-community

[8] A good exposition of damage-cost pricing is to be found in Allen V. Kneese, *The Economics of Regional Water Quality Management* (Baltimore, 1964).

immobility of goods and people are, in general, untenable. The "polluter-pollutee" view of the problem that underlies the recommendation of damage-cost pricing derives from the apparently easy identification of the two parties on a river. Once the mobility of goods and people up and down a river is taken into account, however, identification becomes much more difficult and the problem appears much like the "war of all against all" that is characteristic of lake and ocean pollution.

Even if everyone is at once a polluter and a pollutee, however, the optimum amount of pollution could be achieved if the value of a marginal dose of pollution could be measured. But it cannot be measured, because its value is the value of the amenity use forgone, which cannot be measured. Attempts have been made to measure the recreational value of particular land and water areas, but all such measurements are made on the partial equilibrium assumption that the recreational use of neighbouring areas is held constant. In general, however, a reduction in the amenity capacity of one river or lake will result in increased pressure on the amenity capacities of other rivers and lakes in the same general area. So far as I know, no one has been able to measure the amenity value of an acre-foot of water under general equilibrium assumptions. All we can be reasonably sure about is that the recreational value of water rises as population grows and the standard of living increases.

In brief, it seems to me that it is unrealistic to view water management as a problem in externalities, and that the question of how water should be used is purely a matter of collective decision-making. Economics cannot be of any significant help in making this decision. Even the principle that property rights should be set so as to maximize social product is of no use in the case of water because the values of amenity uses of water—recreation, and the simple aesthetic satisfaction that most of us gain from looking at, or even merely contemplating the existence of, clean water—cannot be measured, though such values are certainly part of any society's gross national welfare. Social welfare functions, community indifference curves, and benefit-cost analysis are ways of visualizing the social decision-making problem, but not of solving it.

What is special about the ownership of water, therefore, is that the owner must decide, without the benefit of economics, how his asset is to be divided among different uses. (When asset-units are small relative to the amount of the asset available, as in land, decentralized ownership is possible and the amount of the asset devoted to different uses is, for practical purposes, determined by market forces.) But this special quality of water (and air) ownership does not make it impossible to apply a rental system to water management.

V

If economics has nothing useful to say about the ownership decision of how water should be used, it has a great deal to say about how the decision, once made, should be implemented. What the government-owner of a natural water system must decide is how many equivalent tons of wastes may be discharged into the waters of each water region. The decision has at least three arbitrary components. Since in given circumstances a ton of one waste is likely to be more

800   J. H. DALES

injurious than a ton of another, some equivalence must be established between different waste products, and since circumstances differ widely I assume that some average equivalence is chosen for each region in order to simplify the problem and reduce administrative difficulties. The other two sources of arbitrariness from the economic point of view, the mapping of regions and the choice of the amount of pollution in each region, have already been discussed. Let us now suppose that the owner has decided that during the next five years no more than x equivalent tons of waste per year are to be dumped into the waters of region A, and that x represents a 10 per cent reduction from the amount of waste that is currently being discharged into the region's waters. How can the government-owner enforce this decision?

The government can enforce its decision in one of six main ways. It can *regulate*: (1) a waste quota can be assigned to each waste discharger and set so that the sum of the quotas does not exceed x; or (2) an across-the-board regulation that each discharger must reduce his waste discharge by 10 per cent may be promulgated. It can *subsidize*: (3) dischargers can be subsidized to reduce their wastes, either individually or (4) on an across-the-board basis of so much per ton of waste discharge reduced. It can *charge*: (5) an effluent charge can be levied on dischargers, either individually, or (6) on an across-the-board basis of so much per ton of waste discharged.

I suggest that it is intuitively obvious that the *individual*, or point-by-point, procedures would involve staggering administrative costs. Yet it should be noted that politicians and civil servants seem to favour point-by-point *regulation*, and that economists who recommend damage-cost pricing favour point-by-point *charging* schemes. It seems intuitively obvious that in practice no point-by-point procedure could distribute the cost of reducing pollution among polluters in an economically optimal way, i.e., in a way that would minimize the total cost of reducing pollution by 10 per cent. To suppose that optimality in this sense is possible is to suppose that the administrative authority is able to solve a set of thousands of simultaneous equations, when the information required to write the equations in numerical form is not only not available, but also often unobtainable. It is also obvious that an across-the-board regulation to the effect that all dischargers must reduce their wastes by 10 per cent would results in a non-optimal distribution of the cost burden.[9]

Let us then examine the across-the-board schemes of subsidization and charging. Both possess the advantages of low administrative costs relative to the point-by-point schemes, and both would result in an optimum distribution of costs among dischargers; all dischargers would reduce their wastes up to the point where the marginal cost of doing so equalled the subsidy provided, or the charge levied. Both schemes have two disadvantages: a certain amount of experimentation would be necessary to establish the level of subsidy, or charge, that would produce a 10 per cent reduction in waste discharge; and the levels

[9]Paul A. Bradley, "Producers' Decisions and Water Quality Control" (Background Paper D 29–3 in *Pollution and Our Environment*, papers presented at a conference held in Montreal, Oct. 31 to Nov. 4, 1966, by the Canadian Council of Resource Ministers) discusses various possible reactions of individual firms to the regulation of effluent standards and to a system of effluent charges. Standards, charges, and subsidies are discussed extensively in Kneese, *Economics of Regional Water Quality Management*, chaps. 4 and 8.

would have to be varied annually to take account of industrial and demographic growth (or decline) in the region in order to keep to the target of x equivalent tons of waste discharge. The subsidy scheme, however, has two disadvantages that the charging scheme does not have. First, if a subsidy of so much per ton of waste reduced is set, extra profits will accrue to those firms that can reduce their wastes at a cost per ton that is less than the subsidy provided, and no change in relative prices of goods is necessary. In the charging scheme excess profits will not be generated, and there will necessarily be a change in relative prices of goods, which in turn will result in a socially desirable adjustment of consumption patterns to reflect the differential costs of waste disposal as between different goods. Second, the subsidization scheme provides no incentive to choose production methods that reduce the amount of waste generated (and may indeed have the opposite effect!), whereas the charging scheme provides incentives both to reduce waste and improve the technology of treating waste before it is discharged. The across-the-board charging scheme is therefore clearly the best of the six possible ways of implementing the government's decision.

Its victory is made decisive by the fact that it lends itself easily to a market mechanism, whereas the subsidy scheme does not. The government's decision is, let us say, that for the next five years no more than x equivalent tons of waste per year are to be discharged into the waters of region A. Let it therefore issue x pollution rights and put them up for sale, simultaneously passing a law that everyone who discharges one equivalent ton of waste into the natural water system during a year must hold one pollution right throughout the year. Since x is less than the number of equivalent tons of waste being discharged at present, the rights will command a positive price—a price sufficient to result in a 10 per cent reduction in waste discharge. The market in rights would be continuous. Firms that found that their actual production was likely to be less than their initial estimate of production would have rights to sell, and those in the contrary situation would be in the market as buyers. Anyone should be able to buy rights; clean-water groups would be able to buy rights and not exercise them. A forward market in rights might be established. The rights should be for one year only, the price of one right for one year representing the annual rental value of the water for waste disposal purposes.[10] (There is no reason, though, why speculators should not gamble in one year on the price of rights in later years.) The virtues of the market mechanism are that no person, or agency, has to *set* the price—it is set by the competition among buyers and sellers of rights—and that the price in the market automatically "allows for" the regional growth (or decline) factor. If the region experiences demographic or industrial growth the price of rights will automatically rise and induce existing dischargers to reduce their wastes in order to make room for the newcomers. The government should make it clear that it reserves the right to alter the allowable level of pollution (the number of rights it issues) at stated time intervals (say, every five or ten years). All that is required to make the market work is the inflexible resolve of the government not to change the rights issue during the interval, no matter

[10]Professor Neufeld has suggested that it would be desirable to issue rights of different durations; more complicated schemes than the one outlined in the text could easily be arranged.

what the political pressures to do so may be, and to enforce rigidly the requirement that a ton-year of waste discharge *must* be paid for by the holding of one pollution right for one year. Pollution rights are fully transferable property rights, and any welching on the enforcement of the right would be a breach of trust.

The automaticity of the market mechanism reduces administrative costs by relieving administrators of the necessity of setting the charge for rights and changing it periodically to reflect economic growth or decline. The administrative costs of enforcement would remain, of course, but they would be no greater than the costs of enforcing any of the other implementation schemes that we have considered. Technological change in the form of automatic monitoring devices to measure the volume of effluents from discharge points promises to reduce the costs of policing for all anti-pollution schemes.

Compliance with any point-by-point regulatory or subsidization scheme of pollution control establishes a sort of *status-tenure* property right. The right inheres to the discharger that earns it, and is only transferable (at the capitalized value of its implicit price) when the property to which it applies is sold. The market mechanism of the across-the-board charging scheme separates the property right to water use from the other assets of the discharger, and thereby makes the property right *fully transferable*. Full transferability and explicit prices are, as has been noted, considered preferable to status tenure and implicit prices by contemporary populations in Western democratic societies.

VI

Having puffed the merits of the across-the-board *cum* market mechanism scheme of pollution control, I must now take note of its deficiencies. There are four arbitrary elements: the mapping of water regions; the setting of waste equivalents; the choice of the allowable amount of waste discharge; and the choice of time interval during which the number of pollution rights is fixed. By comparison with some ideal, Pareto-optimal scheme laid up in Heaven, each of these decisions is bound to introduce elements of non-optimality into the arrangements I have proposed. In each case, however, I suggest that the saving in administrative costs is likely to outweigh the loss in terms of resource misallocation, measured from some theoretical optimum that ignores administrative and other transactions costs—notably the cost of acquiring enough information to administer an optimal pricing system.[11]

The question of the possible effects of pollution charges on the location of industries (and population) requires special comment. It is often suggested in the literature that waste discharged into a large, lightly populated river system does less damage than if it is discharged into a small, thickly populated river system, and that accordingly pollution charges for use of the former ought to be lower than for use of the latter. This reasoning assumes that the only costs of

[11]A referee for this paper wrote that my scheme requires "that the questions of how much pollution, where pollution is to be allowed, how it is to be measured . . . etc., are all answered beforehand. But *these* are the really big questions." I agree. I don't think that economic analysis can answer these questions; it can, however, point to the best means of implementing the given answers.

waste discharge are the objective, measurable, costs to residents in the area, or more generally—if people are allowed to live in one area and vacation in another —that the damage done to amenities by an extra ton of waste is everywhere the same. A system of charging that equalized marginal measurable costs as between water systems would then minimize the objective costs of disposing of a given tonnage of wastes over all the water systems in an area. But this argument does *not* hold if the goal is to minimize *total* costs of disposing of a given tonnage of wastes.

In general, as one river system (or one part of a lake) becomes more polluted, the amenity value of neighbouring unpolluted waters rises. Moreover, when pollution reaches a level that is inconsistent with all recreational uses, added waste discharge has no recreational cost, while added pollution (that destroys swimming even if not, say, boating) in a popular vacation area probably has a very high recreational cost. The demand for amenity uses of water is certainly not a continuous function of water quality. Not enough is known, or perhaps knowable, about the demand for amenity uses of water to devise a fully optimal use of water in an "*n*-region system." In general, though, when congestion problems arise—when people begin to realize the existence of a spatially generalized pollution problem—it is clear that as pollution levels in one area rise the amenity value of relatively clean water in neighbouring areas rises; thus the opportunity cost of using such waters for waste disposal purposes also rises. This consideration by itself, therefore, suggests that pollution charges should be *higher* in areas where pollution is currently at low levels than in areas where it is at high levels —the reverse of the pricing system usually recommended. The system of low pollution charges for a low pollution level tends to spread pollution evenly over the countryside. I prefer the opposite system of high pollution charges for a low pollution level; it tends to create the separate facilities recommended by Mishan.

In any event, in the present state of knowledge about amenity values of water, it is obvious that the spatial pattern of pollution, or the price differentials between regions for pollution rights, will reflect an arbitrary decision by government. In the scheme outlined in this paper initial differentials in the prices of pollution rights will probably not be large if waste disposal were to be reduced by 10 per cent in each region. As time goes on, however, price differentials will tend to change as other forces lead to the centralization or decentralization of industries and populations. These tendencies can be offset, or encouraged, by the government's decision about the absolute and relative numbers of rights made available for sale in different regions. Thus the government-owner of a water (or air) system must decide not only the over-all quality of his asset, but also the quality of the asset in each region.

It should be noted, finally, that the market in pollution rights is not a "true" or "natural" market. In natural markets price creates two-way communication between sources of supply and demand and affects amounts supplied as well as amounts demanded. (Where supply is fixed in natural units, as in the land market, price affects the equilibrium quality of the asset, and mediates between the users of land on the one hand and the users of the products of land on the other.) My market provides only for one-way communication. It transmits the government-owner's decisions about the use of water to the users of the asset, but there is no feedback from the users to the owner. A rise in the price of a pollution right signals that the waste disposal use of water is becoming more valuable; but this does *not* mean that the supply of allowable waste disposal capacity should be increased, for the value of the competing amenity use of water is also likely to be increasing under the impact of the same growth forces that make the waste disposal use more valuable. The price signals that the government gets from the market are "false," in the sense that they are largely echoes of its own arbitrary decision about the supply of rights. The market proposed in this paper is therefore nothing more than an administrative tool. But administrative tools that have some *prima facie* claim to efficiency should not be ignored in an increasingly administered society.

[12]

JOURNAL OF ECONOMIC THEORY 5, 395–418 (1972)

Markets in Licenses and Efficient Pollution Control Programs*

W. David Montgomery

Division of the Humanities and Social Sciences, California Institute of Technology, Pasadena, California 91109

Received May 19, 1972

1. Introduction

Artificial markets have received some attention as a means of remedying market failure and, in particular, dealing with pollution from various sources. Arrow [1] has demonstrated that when externalities are present in a general equilibrium system, a suitable expansion of the commodity space would lead to Pareto optimality by bringing externalities under the control of the price system. Since his procedure is to define new commodities, each of which is identified by the type of externality, the person who produces it and the person who suffers it, his conclusion is pessimistic. Each market in the newly defined commodities involves but one buyer and one seller, and no forces exist to compel the behavior which would bring about a competitive equilibrium.

On the other hand, many forms of pollution are perfect substitutes for each other. Sulfur oxide emissions from one power plant trade off in the preferences of any sufferer with sulfur oxide emissions from some other power plant at a constant rate. This fact leads to the possibility of establishing markets in rights (or "licenses") which will bring together many buyers and sellers. Dales [2] has discussed a wide variety of such arrangements.

Unfortunately, because of the elements of public goods present in most environmental improvements, it appears unlikely that markets in rights, containing many sufferers from pollution as participants, will lead to overall Pareto optimality. They can only serve the more limited, but still

* Parts of this article appeared in my Ph.D. dissertation "Market Systems for the Control of Air Pollution," submitted to the Department of Economics at Harvard University in May, 1971. Research on this thesis was partly supported under Grant No. AP-00842 from the Environmental Protection Agency to Walter Isard. I am also indebted to Kenneth Arrow and James Quirk for valuable advice. Needless to say, all errors are solely the responsibility of the author.

395

valuable, function of achieving specified levels of environmental quality in an efficient manner. An example of this function is found in a proposal by Jacoby and Schaumburg [6] to establish a market in licenses (or "BOD bonds") to control water pollution from industrial sources in the Delaware estuary. The purpose of the present article is to provide a solid theoretical foundation for such proposals. Markets such as those proposed by Jacoby and Schaumburg will be characterized in a general fashion, and it will be proved that even in quite complex circumstances the market in licenses has an equilibrium which achieves externally given standards of environmental quality at least cost to the regulated industries.

Two types of license are discussed: a "pollution license," and an "emission license." The emission license directly confers a right to emit pollutants up to a certain rate. The pollution license confers the right to emit pollutants at a rate which will cause no more than a specified increase in the level of pollution at a certain point. Since a polluter will in general affect air or water quality at a number of points as a result of his emissions, he will be required to hold a portfolio of licenses covering all relevant monitoring points. All such licenses are free transferable. A main thesis of this article is that the market in pollution licenses will be more widely applicable than the market in emission licenses.

1.1. *The Applicable Pollution Control Problem*

Consider the following problem of pollution control: In a certain region there is a set of n industrial sources of pollution, each of which is fixed in location and owned by an independent, profit-maximizing firm. The prices of the inputs and outputs of these firms are fixed, because the region is small relative to the entire economy. Therefore any change in the level of output of a firm or industry in the region will have only a negligible impact on the output of the economy as a whole, and prices will be unaffected by output changes in the region. These firms are represented by a set of integers $I = \{1,..., n\}$.

Some regional standard of environmental quality in terms of a single pollutant has been chosen as a goal by a resource management agency. This standard is denoted by a vector $Q^* = (q_1^*,..., q_m^*)$. If air pollution is the particular area of interest, q_j^* might be an annual average concentration of sulfur dioxide at point j in an air basin. If water pollution is involved, q_j^* might be a measure of dissolved oxygen deficit at point j on a river. Since there is only one pollutant present in the region, the elements of Q^* represent concentrations of the one pollutant at various locations. The development of a decentralized system for achieving environmental goals at a number of different locations is the most important contribution of this article.

All pollution in the region arises from the industrial sources, each of which emits a single pollutant at the rate e_i. The emission vector $E = (e_1, ..., e_n)$ is mapped into concentrations by a semipositive matrix H, so that $E \cdot H = Q$. The standard Q^* imposes constraints on allowable emission rates of the form $E \cdot H \leqslant Q^*$. The problem of pollution control is to achieve Q^* at least cost to the polluters.

Some discussion of the limitations which the model places on the results presented is in order. The assumption that concentrations are a linear function of emissions is the only part of this problem which does not generalize easily. Therefore, the market in licenses to be described must be construed as applicable only in situations in which the assumption is approximately true. Fortunately, there are at least two important problems of pollution control in which it is true. One such is the management of dissolved oxygen deficit in a river. The DOD at a point downstream of a source releasing BOD (bacteriological oxygen demand) effluent is proportional to the BOD released [6, 8].

Management of concentrations of nonreactive atmospheric pollutants is another problem in which linearity is approximately true, as long as the variables to be related are average emission rates and average concentrations [5]. In this case, which will be used in this article as the source of illustrative examples, a meteorological diffusion model provides the means of relating long-run average concentrations to average rates of emission. As formulated by Martin and Tikvart [11], the model is based on an equation describing the shape of a smoke plume from an elevated source emitting at a constant rate with a wind of constant direction and speed. From this equation, the contribution of any source to concentration at any receptor can be calculated for given wind direction and speed. By taking the frequency distribution of wind direction and speed and appropriately modifying the predicted concentrations, one arrives at a theoretical relationship between average rates of emission and average concentrations [14].

The results of the diffusion model can be conveniently represented as an $m \times n$ matrix of unit diffusion coefficients, denoted

$$H = \begin{pmatrix} \vdots \\ \cdots h_{ij} \cdots \\ \vdots \end{pmatrix}.$$

The typical element states the contribution which one unit of emission by firm i makes to average pollutant concentration at point j.

The assumption that only one pollutant is present in the region can be justified by appeal to the external decision on desired air quality. If desired air quality in terms of one pollutant is independent of desired air quality in terms of any other so that, for example, the decision on the desirability of a certain concentration of sulfur dioxide is independent of the concentration of particulates permitted in the region, then nothing is lost. The management problem can be generalized by adding constraints representing emission vectors which achieve desired levels of many pollutants and joint production of pollution. In principle, it is solved in the same way as the one-pollutant system developed here.

The assumption that all prices (except those associated with pollution) are unaffected by measures undertaken to control pollution is a common one in economic analysis of environmental problems. It is necessary to allow consideration of problems in isolation, and to avoid full-sized (and nonoperational) general-equilibrium models [9].

When this assumption is made, it is possible to define for each firm a single-valued function which associates a cost with any emission rate adopted by the firm.

1.2. *The Cost Function*

The purpose of this section is to construct a function relating each level of emission which might be adopted by the firm to its cost and to establish that the profit-maximizing firm will minimize this function. Moreover, it will be argued that no firm will ever choose a level of emission greater than that which is observed in the complete absence of regulation.

Consider the typical multiproduct firm i. Let

$$G_i(y_{i1}, ..., y_{iR}, e_i)$$

represent the minimum total cost of producing a vector of output $(y_{i1}, ..., y_{iR})$ and emissions e_i. This is the cost incurred when inputs are optimally adjusted for that output and emission level. For the static analysis with which we deal, we can assume that both operating costs and an annual capital cost are included. Profit then will be

$$\pi_i = \sum_r p_r y_{ir} - G_i(y_{i1}, ..., y_{iR}, e_i).$$

Assume that G_i is convex and twice differentiable and that its domain is the positive orthant of the $r + 1$-dimensional space of real numbers. Define $(\bar{y}_{i1}, ..., \bar{y}_{ir}, \bar{e}_i)$ by

$$\sum_r p_r \bar{y}_{ir} - G_i(\bar{y}_{i1}, ..., \bar{y}_{iR}, \bar{e}_i) = \max_{y_{ir}, e_i} \left[\sum_r p_r y_{ir} - G_i(y_{i1}, ..., y_{iR}, e_i) \right].$$

Now consider the case in which the firm must adopt an emission level e_i and adjusts its output in order to obtain maximum profit for the fixed level of emission. Define $\tilde{y}_{ir}$ by

$$\sum_r p_r \tilde{y}_{ir} - G_i(\tilde{y}_{i1},...,\tilde{y}_{iR},e_i) = \max_{y_{ir}} \left[\sum_r p_r y_{ir} - G_i(y_{i1},...,y_{iR},e_i) \right].$$

The cost to firm i of adopting emission level e_i is defined as the difference between its unconstrained maximum of profit and its maximum of profit when emissions equal e_i. That is,

$$F_i(e_i) = \sum_r p_r(\bar{y}_{ir} - \tilde{y}_{ir}) - [G_i(\bar{y}_{i1},...,\bar{y}_{iR},\bar{e}_i) - G_i(\tilde{y}_{i1},...,\tilde{y}_{iR},e_i)].$$

$$\tag{1.1}$$

This cost is composed of two terms: the change in gross income from altering the output vector and the change in costs from setting emissions at a nonoptimal level (with an optimal adjustment of output).[1]

Consider the variation in $F_i(e_i)$ when a small change is made in e_i. Differentiating totally with respect to e_i, we find

$$dF_i(e_i) = -\sum_r \left(p_r - \frac{\partial G_i}{\partial y_{ir}} \right) \frac{dy_{ir}}{de_i} de_i + \frac{\partial G_i}{\partial e_i} de_i. \tag{1.2}$$

We have assumed that output levels adjust to maximize profit for a given level of e_i. That is, y_{ir} adjusts so that

$$p_r - \partial G_i/\partial y_{ir} = 0$$

for $j = 1,...,r$. Therefore [13],

$$dF_i(e_i)/de_i = \partial G_i/\partial e_i. \tag{1.3}$$

It can further be shown that the convexity of $G_i(y_{i1},...,y_{iR},e_i)$ implies the convexity of $F_i(e_i)$.

THEOREM 1.1.   *If $G_i(y_{i1},...,y_{iR},e_i)$ is convex, $F_i(e_i)$ is also convex.*

Proof.   The proof is immediate from the definition of convexity.

It is convenient to be able to use a single-valued function $F_i(e_i)$ to associate with any emissions level its cost. The properties of $F_i(e_i)$ proved above allow us to conclude that any relevant conditions which are satisfied

---

[1] Three general classes of techniques of emission reduction are available. First, emissions can be reduced by reducing the scale of output, or by altering the product mix of the firm. Second, the production process or the inputs used, such as fuels, can be altered. Finally, "tail-end" cleaning equipment can be installed to remove pollutants from effluent streams before they are released into the environment. All three of these techniques will commonly be found in combination.

by the partial derivative of G_i with respect to e_i will be satisfied by the derivative of F_i. In particular, we can conclude that if the profit-maximizing firm has any choice of e_i, it will minimize $F_i(e_i)$ subject to whatever costs or constraints we impose on it. Moreover, if G_i is convex, it follows that the conditions under which $\sum_i F_i(e_i)$ is minimized are the same as the conditions under which the total economic cost to firms of emissions control is minimized.

2. The Characterization of an Efficient Emission Vector

The goal of management is limited to bringing about an emission vector which will result in air of quality Q^* at least total cost to the region. Such an emission vector is called efficient, and designated E^{**}. The concept of least cost to the community is also given a specific meaning: it is the minimum of the sum $\sum_i F_i(e_i)$. With some risk of ambiguity, this sum is called "joint total cost."

To provide a reference to which later results can be compared, a general solution for the efficient emission vector can now be derived. The problem is to choose the vector $E = (e_1,..., e_n)$ to minimize $\sum_i F_i(e_i)$ subject to the constraints

$$E \geqslant 0 \quad \text{and} \quad EH \leqslant Q^*,$$

where $Q^* \geqslant 0$, $h_{ij} \geqslant 0$ for all i, j. We will label this the "total joint cost minimum problem." Our exploration will proceed throughout this article on the assumption that G_i is convex. This implies that $F_i(e_i)$ is convex, and therefore that $\sum_i F_i(e_i)$ is also convex. It is also assumed that H is semipositive. The typical shape of $F_i(e_i)$ is illustrated in Fig. 1.

Minimizing a convex function subject to linear constraints and non-negativity constraints is equivalent to finding the saddle point of an associated Lagrangean. Formally, $(E^{**}, U^{**}) = (e_1^{**},..., e_n^{**}, u_1^{**},..., u_m^{**})$ will be a saddle point of the expression

$$- \sum_i F_i(e_i) + \sum_j u_j \left(q_j^* - \sum_i h_{ij} e_i \right)$$

with $E^{**} \geqslant 0$, $U^{**} \geqslant 0$. The differential Kuhn–Tucker conditions for this saddle point are

$$F_i'(e_i) + \sum_j u_j h_{ij} \geqslant 0, \quad \sum_i \left[e_i \left(F_i'(e_i) + \sum_j u_j h_{ij} \right) \right] = 0, \quad (2.1)$$

$$q_j^* - \sum_i h_{ij} e_i \geqslant 0, \quad \sum_j \left[u_j \left(q_j - \sum_i h_{ij} e_i \right) \right] = 0. \quad (2.2)$$

These conditions are necessary and sufficient [7]. Moreover, it is easy to show that the minimum does in fact exist.

THEOREM 2.1. *E^{**} and U^{**} satisfying (2.1) and (2.2) exist.*

Proof. Since $\sum_i F_i(\bar{e}_i) = 0$ and $\sum_i F_i(e_i) \geqslant \sum_i F_i(\bar{e}_i)$, for $e_i \geqslant 0$, $\sum_i F_i(e_i)$ is bounded from below. By hypothesis, the set

$$\Psi = \{E \mid EH \leqslant Q^*, E \geqslant 0\}$$

is not empty. Therefore, $\sum_i F_i(e_i)$ is defined on a nonempty closed set and bounded from below; therefore, it attains a minimum over the set Ψ for some element of Ψ.

If $\sum_i F_i(e_i)$ is not strictly convex, then E^{**} need not be unique. Since, however, $\min_{E \in \Psi} \sum_i F_i(e_i)$ is unique, it does not matter what particular minimizer is chosen. Therefore, I shall refer to the vector which minimizes costs; the reader may interpret this reference as meaning "any element of the set of E which minimizes $\sum_i F_i(e_i)$."

The following theorem is true if $\sum_i F_i(e_i)$ is strictly convex.

THEOREM 2.2. *If E^{**} minimizes $\sum_i F_i(e_i)$ subject to $EH \leqslant Q^*$ and $E \geqslant 0$, then $E^{**} \leqslant \bar{E}$.*

Proof. Assume *per contra* that $e_i^{**} > \bar{e}_i$ for some $i = i'$. Then $F_{i'}(e_{i'}^{**}) > F_{i'}(\bar{e}_{i'})$ and $h_{ij}e_i^{**} > h_{ij}\bar{e}_{i'}$. Therefore

$$\sum_{i \neq i'} F_i(e_i^{**}) + F_i(\bar{e}_{i'}) < \sum_i F_i(e_i^{**}) \tag{2.3a}$$

and

$$\sum_{i \neq i'} h_{ij}e_i^{**} + h_{i'j}\bar{e}_i < \sum_i h_{ij}e_i^{**}. \tag{2.3b}$$

By (2.3b) the vector $(e_1^{**},..., \bar{e}_{i'},..., e_n^{**})$ satisfies $EH \leqslant Q^*$ and by (2.3a) E^{**} does not minimize $\sum_i F_i(e_i)$.

3. MARKETS IN LICENSES

We can now proceed to the construction of markets which, in equilibrium, lead to emission rates which satisfy the conditions of Theorem 2.1. A set of licenses are defined, such that the possession of licenses confers the right to carry out a certain average rate of emission.

Consider the function

$$\Lambda(H_i, L_i),$$

where H_i is the i-th row of the matrix H and $L_i = (l_{i1}, ..., l_{ik})$. We define l_{ik} as the number of licenses of type k held by firm i. This function defines the right to emit which is generated by holding a portfolio of licenses L_i. Then firm i can maximize profits by minimizing direct emission costs plus the cost of purchasing licenses, subject to the constraint that emissions not exceed $\Lambda(H_i, L_i)$. We assume throughout that some initial allocation of licenses l_{ik}^0, is made. Then the firm's problem is to minimize

$$F_i(e_i) + \sum_k p_k(l_{ik} - l_{ik}^0)$$

subject to $e_i \leqslant \Lambda(H_i, L_i)$.

A market equilibrium will exist if there exist nonnegative prices P^* such that when $e_i{}^*, L_i$ solve the firm's minimization problem for $p_k{}^*$, the following market clearing conditions hold:

$$\sum_i (l_{ik}^* - l_{ik}^0) \leqslant 0, \qquad \sum_k p_k{}^* \left[\sum_i (l_{ik}^* - l_{ik}^0) \right] = 0. \qquad (3.1a)$$

That is, there is some set of prices of licenses such that when each firm minimizes the sum of the cost of reducing emissions and the net cost of buying licenses, excess demand for licenses is nonpositive, and excess supply of a license drives its price to zero.

The market equilibrium is efficient if $e_i{}^*$ represents equilibrium emissions and in any equilibrium

$$\sum_i F_i(e_i{}^*) = \sum_i F_i(e_i^{**}). \qquad (3.1b)$$

Note that when all licenses are allocated to firms, (3.1a) implies that any expenditure on licenses by one firm is a revenue to another firm. Therefore total expenditure among all firms, associated with the control of pollution, just equals the total cost of emission control. That is,

$$\sum_i \left[F_i(e_i{}^*) + \sum_k p_k(l_{ik}^* - l_{ik}^0) \right] = \sum_i F_i(e_i{}^*) + \sum_k p_k \left[\sum_i (l_{ik}^* - l_{ik}^0) \right]$$

$$= \sum_i F_i(e_i{}^*).$$

These three properties do not exhaust the set of desirable properties of a market system. It might be that an equilibrium exists, or is efficient, only under strong conditions on the initial allocations of licenses which can be adopted. The more variation which is possible in the choice of initial allocations, the more freedom the management agency will have to pursue such goals as equity of the treatment, subsidization of "deserving" industries, and so on. We begin by defining a licensing system which has an efficient equilibrium for all distributions of a fixed total of licenses.

Analogously to the distinction between ambient standards and emission standards, we must differentiate between emission licenses and pollution licenses. Emission licenses are perhaps the most natural to think of trading, but there are great problems in using them when quality at many locations is a matter of concern. In particular, it is not possible to allow the licenses to be traded on a one-for-one basis [12].

Suppose there are two sources of pollution and one monitoring point, that each source is assigned licenses which allow it to emit 5 units of pollutant, and that $h_{11} = 1$ and $h_{21} = 2$. Under these circumstances, there will be $5 \cdot 1 + 5 \cdot 2 = 15$ units of pollution at the monitoring point. The marginal rate of substitution between emissions at source 2 and emissions at source 1 which keeps air quality constant is 2. If licenses are exchanged on a one-for-one basis, the transfer of one license from firm 1 to firm 2 will result in air quality being degraded to 16 units of pollution. If there is a second monitoring point, and $h_{22}/h_{12} \neq 2$, the marginal rate of substitution between emissions at sources 1 and 2 will change, depending on which monitoring point imposes the *operative* constraint on emissions. By defining rights to *cause* pollution at each of the monitoring points, we can avoid these problems completely, although they can be resolved with emission licenses if certain restrictions on trades are observed.

3.1. *The Market in Licenses to Pollute*

In this section we establish the existence and efficiency of equilibrium in a system of transferable licenses to pollute. Let l_{ij} represent the quantity of licenses allowing pollution at point j held by firm i, and let

$$L_i = (l_{i1}, ..., l_{im})$$

be the "portfolio" of licenses held by firm i. The licensing function can have the form

$$\Lambda(H_i, L_i) = \min_j \frac{l_{ij}}{h_{ij}},$$

which implies that each firm faces the constraints

$$h_{ij}e_i \leqslant l_{ij} \qquad j = 1, ..., m.$$

That is, the relevant element of the diffusion matrix is taken to be a correct predictor of the amount which an average rate of emission at point i contributes to pollutant concentration at point j. Each firm is allowed to have an average rate of emission which produces no more pollution at any point than the amount which the firm is licensed to cause at that point. The firm will minimize $F_i(e_i) + \sum_j p_j(l_{ij} - l_{ij}^0)$ subject to the licensing constraint.

In the theorems which follow we use the convention that l_j is a scalar, a total number of licenses allowing pollution at point j. Thus $\sum_i l_{ij} = l_j$. When $L_i = (l_{i1}, ..., l_{im})$ and $L = (l_1, ..., l_m)$, $\sum_i L_i = L$.

The strategy of proof is to define a market equilibrium relative to an initial allocation of licenses and to derive necessary and sufficient conditions for its existence. A subsidiary construction, called a "license-constrained joint cost minimum," is defined and shown to exist. It generates a second set of necessary and sufficient conditions. It is shown that the emission vector and shadow prices which satisfy the conditions of a license-constrained joint cost minimum for given totals of licenses also satisfy the conditions of competitive equilibrium relative to any initial allocation of licenses in which the given totals are completely distributed among firms. An equilibrium license portfolio for each firm is constructed, and shadow prices on each firm's licensing constraints are identified. To prove that a competitive equilibrium achieves the joint cost minimum defined in Section 2, we show that when license totals equal desired air qualities any emission vector and price vector which satisfy the equilibrium conditions also satisfy the conditions for efficiency. In the course of the proof the efficient emission vector is identified as the equilibrium emission vector and shadow prices on the air quality constraints in the overall joint cost minimum are identified as the prices of licenses. The equilibrium license portfolio has each element just equal to the pollution caused by the efficient rate of emission for the corresponding firm. The proof itself is rigorous and abstract.

DEFINITION. A market equilibrium is an $n + 2$ tuple of vectors $L_i^* \geq 0$, $E^* \geq 0$, and $P^* \geq 0$ such that L_i^* and E^* minimize

$$F_i(e_i) + \sum_j p_j^*(l_{ij} - l_{ij}^0)$$

subject to $l_{ij} - h_{ij}e_i \geq 0$, $j = 1, ..., m$, for all i and which also satisfy the market clearing conditions

$$\sum_i (l_{ij}^* - l_{ij}^0) \leq 0, \qquad \sum_j p_j^* \left[\sum_i (l_{ij}^* - l_{ij}^0) \right] = 0. \qquad (3.1a)$$

LEMMA 3.1.   *A market equilibrium exists if and only if there exist vectors*

$$(u_{i1}^*,..., u_{im}^*) \geqslant 0 \qquad i = 1,..., n,$$
$$(p_1^*,..., p_m^*) \geqslant 0$$

such that

$$F_i'(e_i^*) + \sum_j u_{ij}^* h_{ij} \geqslant 0, \qquad e_i^* \left[F_i'(e_i^*) + \sum_j u_{ij}^* h_{ij} \right] = 0, \quad (3.2a)$$

$$p_j^* - u_{ij}^* \geqslant 0, \qquad \sum_j l_{ij}^* [p_j^* - u_{ij}^*] = 0, \quad (3.2b)$$

$$l_{ij}^* - h_{ij} e_i^* \geqslant 0, \qquad \sum_j u_{ij}^* [l_{ij}^* - h_{ij} e_i^*] = 0, \quad (3.2c)$$

for all i and

$$\sum_i (l_{ij}^* - l_{ij}^0) \leqslant 0, \qquad \sum_j p_j^* \left[\sum_i (l_{ij}^* - l_{ij}^0) \right] = 0. \quad (3.2d)$$

Proof.   First we characterize the vectors L_i^* and e_i^* which minimize cost for the firm. Minimizing a function is equivalent to maximizing its negative; and the negative of a convex function is concave. Therefore, we can state the problem of the firm as one of maximizing the concave function

$$-F_i(e_i) - \sum_j p_j^* (l_{ij} - l_{ij}^0).$$

Form the Lagrangean

$$\phi_i(l_{i1},..., l_{im}, e_i, u_{i1},..., u_{im})$$
$$= -F_i(e_i) - \sum_j p_j^* (l_{ij} - l_{ij}^0) + \sum_j u_{ij}(l_{ij} - h_{ij} e_i).$$

From the Kuhn–Tucker theorem the following conditions are necessary and sufficient for the constrained maximum; where $\phi_i(l_{i1}^*,..., l_{in}^*, e_i^*, u_{i1}^*,..., u_{in}^*) = \phi_i^*.$

$$\partial \phi_i^* / \partial e_i \leqslant 0, \qquad e_i^* \cdot (\partial \phi_i^* / \partial e_i) = 0,$$

$$\partial \phi_i^* / \partial l_{ij} \leqslant 0, \qquad \sum_j l_{ij}^* \cdot (\partial \phi_i^* / \partial l_{ij}) = 0,$$

$$\partial \phi_i^* / \partial u_{ij} \geqslant 0, \qquad \sum_j u_{ij}^* \cdot (\partial \phi_i^* / \partial u_{ij}) = 0.$$

Performing the indicated differentiation gives 3.2a to 3.2c which must be satisfied for all i. Equation (3.2d) repeats the market clearing condition.

DEFINITION.   A license-constrained joint cost minimum is a vector E^{**} which minimizes

$$\sum_i F_i(e_i)$$

subject to $EH \leqslant L^0$ and $E \geqslant 0$.

In making this definition we assume that some arbitrary vector of licenses L^0 is issued by the management agency. We must assume that the set $\{E \mid EH \leqslant L^0 \text{ and } E \geqslant 0\}$ is not empty. Then the same argument used in Section 2 to establish the existence of a joint cost minimum will establish the existence of a license-constrained minimum. We now can use the following lemma to prove existence of an equilibrium on the pollution license market.

LEMMA 3.2.   *An emission vector E^{**} is a license-constrained joint cost minimum if and only if there exists a vector $(u_1^{**},..., u_m^{**}) \geqslant 0$ such that*

$$F_i'(e_i^{**}) + \sum_j u_j^{**} h_{ij} \geqslant 0, \qquad \sum_i e_i^{**} \left[F_i'(e_i^{**}) + \sum_j u_j^{**} h_{ij} \right] = 0, \quad (3.3a)$$

$$l_j^0 - \sum_i h_{ij} e_i^{**} \geqslant 0, \qquad \sum_j u_j^{**} \left[l_j^0 - \sum_i h_{ij} e_i^{**} \right] = 0. \quad (3.3b)$$

Proof.   The proof is as in Lemma 3.1.

The market equilibrium will exist for any distribution of licenses such that $l_{ij}^0 \geqslant 0$ and $\sum_i l_{ij}^0 = l_j^0$.

THEOREM 3.1.   *A market equilibrium of the pollution license system exists for $\sum_i l_{ij}^0 = l_j^0$.*

Proof.   We proceed constructively by using (3.3a) and (3.3b) to show that $e_i^* = e_i^{**}$, $l_{ij}^* = h_{ij} e_i^{**}$, $p_j^* = u_j^{**}$ and $u_{ij}^* = u_j^{**}$ for all i satisfy (3.2a)–(3.2d).

Equation (3.2a).   Since $F_i'(e_i^{**}) + \sum_j u_j^{**} h_{ij} \geqslant 0$ for all i, and $e_i^{**} \geqslant 0$, it follows from

$$\sum_i e_i^{**} \left[F_i'(e_i^{**}) + \sum_j u_j^{**} h_{ij} \right] = 0$$

that

$$e_i^{**} \left[F_i'(e_i^{**}) + \sum_j u_j^{**} h_{ij} \right] = 0$$

for all i. Therefore, e_i^{**} and u_j^{**} satisfy 3.2a for all i.

Equation (3.2b). If $p_j{}^* = u_j{}^{**}$ and $u_{ij}^* = u_j{}^{**}$, $p_j{}^* - u_{ij}^* = 0$ for all i and j, and (3.2b) is satisfied by any l_{ij}^*.

Equation (3.2c). If $l_{ij}^* = h_{ij}e_i{}^{**}$ for all i and j, clearly l_{ij}^* and $e_i{}^{**}$ satisfy (3.2c) for any u_{ij}^*, and in particular for $u_j{}^{**}$.

Equation (3.2d). Let $\sum_i l_{ij}^0 = l_j{}^0$ and $l_{ij}^* = h_{ij}e_i{}^{**}$. Then, (3.3b) gives by substitution

$$\sum_i l_{ij}^0 - \sum_i l_{ij}^* \geqslant 0 \qquad \text{and} \qquad \sum_j u_j{}^{**}\left[\sum_i l_{ij}^0 - \sum_i l_{ij}^*\right] = 0.$$

Therefore, $p_j{}^* = u_j{}^{**}$ and l_{ij}^* satisfy (3.2d).

Thus we conclude that for any choice of license totals which imply a feasible air quality vector, a market equilibrium exists. If we choose the license totals correctly, we can show that any market equilibrium is a joint cost minimum. The joint cost minimum was defined in Section 2 as a vector E^{**} which minimizes $\sum_i F_i(e_i)$ subject to $EH \leqslant Q^*$ and $E \geqslant 0$. First we prove that any emission vector which results from a market equilibrium with $\sum_i l_{ij}^0 = l_j{}^0$ minimizes $\sum_i F_i(e_i)$ subject to $EH \leqslant L^0$ and $E \geqslant 0$.

THEOREM 3.2. *Any emission vector which satisfies the conditions of a market equilibrium with $\sum_i L_i{}^0 = L^0$ is a license-constrained joint cost minimum.*

Proof. We show that any $e_i{}^*$ which satisfies (3.2a)-(3.2d) satisfies (3.3a) and (3.3b) with $u_j{}^{**} = p_j{}^*$.

Equation (3.3a). By (3.2b), either $u_{ij}^* = p_j{}^*$ or $l_{ij}^* = 0$. By (3.2c), $l_{ij}^* \geqslant h_{ij}e_i{}^*$; therefore, whenever $p_j{}^* \neq u_{ij}^*$, $l_{ij}^* = 0$, and it follows that $e_i{}^* = 0$, or $h_{ij} = 0$. Whenever $h_{ij} = 0$, $p_j{}^* h_{ij} = u_{ij}^* h_{ij} = 0$. Therefore, $e_i{}^*[F_i'(e_i{}^*) + \sum_j p_j{}^* h_{ij}] = 0$ holds whether or not $p_j{}^* = u_{ij}^*$.

Since $u_{ij}^* \leqslant p_j{}^*$, $\sum_j u_{ij}^* h_{ij} \leqslant \sum_j p_j{}^* h_{ij}$ and $F_i'(e_i{}^*) + \sum_j u_{ij}^* h_{ij} \geqslant 0$ imply $F_i'(e_i{}^*) + \sum_j p_j{}^* h_{ij} \geqslant 0$. Therefore, $e_i{}^*$ and $p_j{}^*$ satisfy the inequality in (3.3a).

Equation (3.3b). Since $\sum_i l_{ij}^0 = l_j{}^0$, (3.2d) implies that $l_j{}^0 = \sum_i l_{ij}^0 \geqslant \sum_i l_{ij}^*$. Since, by (3.2c), $l_{ij}^* - h_{ij}e_i{}^* \geqslant 0$, $\sum_i l_{ij}^* - \sum_i h_{ij}e_i{}^* \geqslant 0$. If $l_j{}^0 \geqslant \sum_i l_{ij}^*$, then it must be true that $l_j{}^0 - \sum_i h_{ij}e_i{}^* \geqslant 0$ and the inequality in (3.3b) is satisfied by $e_i{}^*$.

Substitute $l_j{}^0$ for $\sum_i l_{ij}^0$ in (3.2d) giving $\sum_j p_j{}^*[l_j{}^0 - \sum_i l_{ij}^*] = 0$. If $l_{ij}^* = h_{ij}e_i{}^*$ for all i and all j, clearly $\sum_j p_j{}^*[l_j{}^0 - \sum_i h_{ij}e_i{}^*] = 0$. Assume that $l_{ij}^* - h_{ij}e_i{}^* > 0$ for some i and j. Then, by (3.2c), $u_{ij}^* = 0$. If $p_j{}^* \neq 0$,

(3.2b) implies that $l_{ij}^* = 0$ for that i and j, and since $l_{ij}^* > h_{ij}e_i^*$ for that i and j, e_i^* must be negative. Since this is impossible, we must have either $l_{ij}^* = h_{ij}e_i^*$ for all i or $p_j^* = 0$; and the alternative holds for each j. Therefore,

$$p_j^* \left[\sum_i h_{ij}e_i^* - l_j^0 \right] = 0,$$

and p_j^*, e_i^* satisfy (3.3b).

Thus, if we take the totals of each type of license distributed to firms we will find that firms exchange licenses so as to minimize joint total cost subject to the constraint that concentrations of pollutants at each monitoring point be no greater than the total of licenses issued for that point. The following corollary is immediate.

COROLLARY. *If $L^0 = Q^*$, the equilibrium emission vector is a joint cost minimum.*

Proof. If $L^0 = Q^*$, by Theorem 3.2 an equilibrium emission vector minimizes $\sum_i F_i(e_i)$ subject to $EH \leqslant Q^*$ and $E \geqslant 0$.

Theorem 3.1 can now be restated as "an efficient emission vector can be achieved as a competitive equilibrium" and 3.2 as "any competitive equilibrium with appropriate license distribution achieves an efficient vector." We can also prove an interesting theorem on the initial allocation of licenses.

THEOREM 3.3. *If $l_{ij}^0 \geqslant 0$ and $\sum_i l_{ij}^0 = q_j^*$, then E^*, P^*, and L_i^* are independent of L_i^0.*

Proof. Equations (3.2a)–(3.2c) depend in no way on L_i^0. In (3.2d) L_i^0 appears, but only in the form of the sum $\sum_i L_i^0$.

This result is somewhat unusual, in that the particular equilibrium achieved in a system usually depends on the initial allocations. The reason that this system is independent of the initial allocation is that the firm's behavior is independent of its asset position. Any redistribution which preserves totals of each type of license does not change the equilibrium. A graphical depiction of the equilibrium of the firm when a system of pollution licenses is imposed reveals the independence of initial allocations. The equilibrium is depicted in Fig. 1.

In the course of proving Theorem 3.1 it was noted that $p_j^*(h_{ij}e_i^* - l_{ij}^*) = 0$, so that $\sum_j p_j^*(h_{ij}e_i^* - l_{ij}^*) = 0$. Any emission level chosen by the firm implies that the firm purchases certain quantities of licenses, so that we can associate with any emission rate a cost equal to $\sum_j p_j^* h_{ij}e_i^*$. The minimization of cost (of emission control plus net purchases of licenses) can then be represented as the minimization of the sum $F_i(e_i) + \sum_j h_{ij} p_j{}^* e_i$. The emission rate $e_i{}^*$ in Fig. 1 is the minimizer of this sum. Theorem 3.1 states that there exist prices which clear markets for licenses when each firm chooses license holdings, and emission rates $e_i{}^*$, to minimize cost.

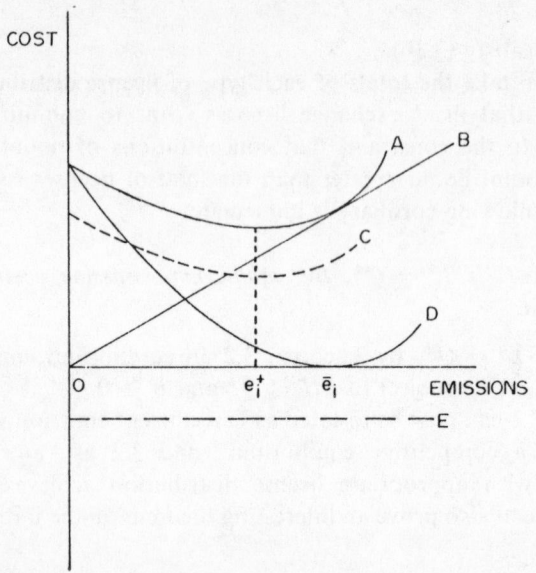

FIG. 1. A—$F_i(e_i) + \sum_j p_j h_{ij} e_i$; B—$\sum_j p_j h_{ij} e_i$; C—$F_i(e_i) + \sum_j p_j h_{ij} e_i - \sum_j p_j l_{ij}^0$; D—$F_i(e_i)$; E—$\sum_j p_j l_{ij}^0$.

The initial allocation of licenses is equivalent to a lump sum subsidy, and is independent of emission level. Therefore, this subsidy can be represented as a horizontal line, $\sum_j p_j{}^* l_{ij}^0$, in Fig. 1. The curve $F_i(e_i) + \sum_j p_j{}^* h_{ij} e_i - \sum_j p_j{}^* l_{ij}^0$ is the net cost function which represents the actual cost of emission control and licenses. Note that $e_i{}^*$ is independent of the size of the subsidy. Because of this result, the management agency can distribute licenses as it pleases. Considerations of equity, of administrative convenience, or of political expediency can determine the allocation. The same efficient equilibrium will be achieved.

It should, however, be noted that in assuming the convexity of $F_i(e_i)$ we impose certain conditions relating to nonnegative profits. Let $\bar{\pi}_i$ be the (maximal) profit earned before the introduction of a licensing system, and let $\tilde{\pi}_i(e_i)$ be the profit earned when emissions are set at rate e_i. Then by (1.1) we have $\tilde{\pi}_i(e_i) = \bar{\pi}_i - F_i(e_i)$. In the long run the firm will only stay in business if $\tilde{\pi}_i(e_i) \geqslant 0$. In this case the cost function will have the form $F_i(e_i) = \min(\bar{\pi}_i - \tilde{\pi}_i(e_i), \bar{\pi}_i)$. An upper bound, equal to $\bar{\pi}_i$, is placed on costs incurred by the firm. This upper bound destroys the convexity of the cost function unless $F_i(0) \leqslant \bar{\pi}_i$. Such an assumption is implicit in the assumption that $F_i(e_i)$ is convex.

It would appear that the need to purchase licenses imposes a cost on the firm additional to the cost of emission control $F_i(e_i)$. Even though this cost sums to zero for all firms taken together, it may be positive for some individual firms and negative for others. Fortunately, we can prove the following theorem, namely, that if $F_i(0) \leqslant \bar{\pi}_i$, then even if a firm is allocated no licences initially (i.e., $l_{ij}^0 = 0$ for some i and all j), it can still earn nonnegative profits at any levels of emissions and license holding.

THEOREM 3.4.   *If* $F_i(0) \leqslant \bar{\pi}_i$, $F_i(e_i^*) + \sum_j p_j^* l_{ij}^* \leqslant \bar{\pi}_i$.

Proof.   We have proved that

$$F_i(e_i^*) + \sum_j p_j^* l_{ij}^* = F_i(e_i^*) + \sum_j p_j^* h_{ij} e_i^*.$$

If $F_i(e_i^*) + \sum_j p_j^* h_{ij} e_i^* > \bar{\pi}_i$, then $F_i(e_i^*) + \sum_j p_j^* h_{ij} e_i^* > F_i(0)$. But $e_i = 0$ and $l_{ij} = 0$ satisfy $e_i \leqslant \Lambda(H_i, L_i)$, so that e_i^* does not minimize cost subject to the licensing constraint. This contradiction establishes the theorem.

This demonstration completes the discussion of pollution licenses. We began by showing that for any vector of licenses L^0 which implies feasible concentration levels at each monitoring point there exists a competitive equilibrium in the license market. We then showed that the concentrations which result from the equilibrium will be less than or equal to the levels permitted by the vector of licenses and that joint total costs are minimized subject to this constraint. Finally we showed that when $L^0 = Q^*$, the problem of achieving desired air quality standards at minimum cost is solved by the market in pollution licenses.

The major generalization provided by this theorem is that it establishes the possibility of achieving environmental goals at a *number* of geographic points while maintaining the advantages of a market system. Thus one important objection to the use of economic incentives, that they could lead to change in the pattern of emissions such that although air quality improvements at one point are achieved, it is at the expense of deteriorating air quality elsewhere, is laid to rest. Moreover, we discovered that the fixed totals could be allocated arbitrarily among firms.

Overall convexity and the possibility, for each firm, of absorbing all costs of abatement in profits were assumptions necessary for the operation of the system when no information on cost functions is available.

We turn now to an alternative licensing system. It will turn out that this system of emission licenses is interesting because it provides a means of linking up the proposal to issue transferable licenses with other proposals for achieving efficient solutions in a decentralized manner.

3.2. *The Market in Emission Licenses*

The effluent charge is a tax which a firm must pay on each unit of pollutant which it emits into a water course. A corresponding charge for air pollution control might be called an emission charge. In order to calculate a charge which will lead to efficiency in air pollution control, the manager must solve in advance the overall cost-minimization problem. It is not difficult to show that the correct tax on emission by firm i is equal to the shadow price on its emissions determined by the minimization of joint total cost. The tax is $\sum_j u_j^* h_{ij}$, where u_j^* is the value of the Lagrange multiplier on the j-th quality constraint evaluated at the optimum. But in order to calculate such a tax the manager must know the cost functions of each firm. It is, of course, possible to obtain that information in an iterative process by varying the tax. This is a cumbersome and politically unattractive procedure, and it has been shown by Marglin [10] that the information transferred to the regulatory authority by such a procedure is as great as the information needed to set quantity standards for each firm. That is, whenever it is possible to calculate the correct tax it is possible to achieve E^{**} in the initial allocation.

A licensing scheme does not require such prior or iterative gathering of information. The market makes the necessary calculations independently in the course of reaching equilibrium. For this reason we are led to consider licensing schemes as superior to taxation. The natural correlate of emission charges is a system of emission licenses.

An emission license confers on the firm holding it the right to emit pollutants at a certain rate. It is not always desirable to allow such rights to be transferred on a one-for-one basis: the desirable rule governing exchange of emission rights is that a firm may be allowed to emit up to a level which causes pollution equal to that which would be caused if each firm from which it obtained rights emitted to the maximum extent permitted by the rights which it has given up. We must differentiate rights to emit by the location at which they permit emissions to take place. Then l_k , $k = 1,..., n$, is a quantity of licenses to emit at location k. It is sufficient to allow k to run over the set of firms I since each firm is in a fixed location. Let l_{ik} represent the quantity of licenses allowing emissions at location k held by firm i.

If the exchange of such licenses between polluters at different locations is to be permitted, some rule must be stated regarding the right to emit which a license to emit at location k confers on a firm at location i. Consider a firm i which emits at a rate $e_i = h_{kj}l_{ik}/h_{ij}$. Then the pollution which firm i causes at point j is precisely the pollution which firm k would cause if it emitted at the rate $e_k = l_{ik}$, since $h_{ij}e_i = h_{kj}l_{ik} = h_{kj}e_k$. The licensing function can have the form

$$\Lambda(H_i, L_i) = \min_j \left(\sum_k h_{kj}l_{ik}/h_{ij} \right),$$

which implies that each firm faces the constraints

$$h_{ij}e_i \leqslant \sum_k h_{kj}l_{ik} \qquad j = 1,..., m,$$

and will minimize

$$F_i(e_i) + \sum_k p_k(l_{ik} - l_{ik}^0)$$

subject to those constraints.

A restriction on the initial allocation of licenses is needed if the market equilibrium with emission licenses is to be efficient. It is that $\sum_i l_{ik}^0 \geqslant 0$ and $\sum_k h_{kj} \sum_i l_{ik}^0 = q_j^*$ for all j. Note that this assumption is equivalent to the assumption that there exists a nonnegative emission vector E^0 such that

$$E^0 \cdot H = Q^*.$$

This is quite a strong condition, since even if the matrix H is of full rank, for arbitrary semipositive H and Q^* the equations

$$E \cdot H = Q^*$$

will not in general have nonnegative solutions.

If $\sum_k h_{kj}l_k^0 < q_j^*$ for some j it may not be possible to achieve the minimum of joint total cost without prior knowledge of cost functions. Suppose that the joint cost minimum vector E^{**} satisfies

$$\sum_i h_{ij}e_i^{**} = q_j^*$$

for some j, and that $\sum_k h_{kj}l_k^0 < q_j^*$ for the same j. Then since the equilibrium emission vector E^* satisfies

$$\sum_i h_{ij}e_i^* \leqslant \sum_k h_{kj}l_k^0,$$

it follows that

$$\sum_i h_{ij} e_i{}^* < \sum_i h_{ij} e_i{}^{**}$$

and $e_i{}^* \neq e_i{}^{**}$, so that the market equilibrium is inefficient.

DEFINITION. A market equilibrium in emission licenses is an $n + 2$-tuple of vectors $L_i{}^* \geqslant 0$, $E^* \geqslant 0$ and $P^* \geqslant 0$ such that $L_i{}^*$ and E^* minimizes

$$F_i(e_i) + \sum_k p_k{}^*(l_{ik} - l_{ik}^0)$$

subject to

$$\sum_k h_{kj} l_{ik} - h_{ij} e_i \geqslant 0 \qquad j = 1,..., m$$

and

$$e_i \geqslant 0; \qquad l_{ik} \geqslant 0$$

for all i and which also satisfy the market clearing conditions

$$\sum_i (l_{ik}^* - l_{ik}^0) \leqslant 0, \qquad \sum_k p_k{}^* \left[\sum_i (l_{ik}^* - l_{ik}^0) \right] = 0.$$

LEMMA 3.3. *A market equilibrium exists if there exist vectors*

$$\begin{aligned}(u_{i1}^*,..., u_{im}^*) &\geqslant 0 \qquad i = 1,..., n, \\ (p_1{}^*,..., p_n{}^*) &\geqslant 0,\end{aligned} \tag{3.4}$$

such that

$$F_i'(e_i{}^*) + \sum_j u_{ij}^* h_{ij} \geqslant 0, \qquad e_i{}^* \left[F_i'(e_i{}^*) + \sum_j u_{ij}^* h_{ij} \right] = 0, \quad \text{(3.5a)}$$

$$p_k{}^* - \sum_j u_{ij}^* h_{kj} \geqslant 0, \qquad \sum_k \left[l_{ik}^* \left(p_k{}^* - \sum_j u_{ij}^* h_{kj} \right) \right] = 0, \quad \text{(3.5b)}$$

$$\sum_k h_{kj} l_{ik}^* - h_{ij} e_i{}^* \geqslant 0, \qquad \sum_j \left[u_{ij}^* \left(\sum_k h_{kj} l_{ik}^* - h_{ij} e_i{}^* \right) \right] = 0, \quad \text{(3.5c)}$$

for all i and

$$\sum_i (l_{ik}^* - l_{ik}^0) \leqslant 0, \qquad \sum_k p_k{}^* \left[\sum_i (l_{ik}^* - l_{ik}^0) \right] = 0. \quad \text{(3.5d)}$$

Proof. The proof is as in Lemma 3.1.

THEOREM 3.5. *A market equilibrium in emission licenses exists.*

Proof. In Theorem 2.2 it was shown that an emission vector minimizing joint total costs subject to the air quality constraints exists, and that in consequence E^{**} and U^{**} satisfying (2.1) and (2.2) exist. Let licenses be issued initially so that

$$\sum_k h_{kj} \sum_i l_{ik}^0 = q_j^*$$

for all j. Then we show that E^{**} is an emission vector and U^{**} a price vector satisfying (3.5a)–(3.5d).

We begin by proving the following proposition:

P.1. *If* $\sum_k h_{kj} l_k^0 \geqslant \sum_t h_{ij} e_i^{**}$, *then there exist* l_{ik}^* *such that* $\sum_i l_{ik}^* \leqslant l_k^0$, $l_{ik}^* \geqslant 0$, *and* $\sum_k h_{kj} l_{ik}^* \geqslant h_{ij} e_i^{**}$ *for all* i *and* k. *Letting* $L_i = (l_{i1}, ..., l_{in})$ *and* H_i *be the i-th row of the matrix H we may write the inequalities which must have a nonnegative solution in matrix form as*

$$(L_1^*, ..., L_n^*) \begin{bmatrix} -H & & I \\ & \ddots & \vdots \\ & & -HI \end{bmatrix} \leqslant (-H_1 e_1^{**}, ..., -H_n e_n^{**}, L^0).$$

It is a theorem [3] *that either these inequalities or the following inequalities have a nonnegative solution*:

$$\begin{bmatrix} -H & & I \\ & \ddots & \vdots \\ & & -HI \end{bmatrix} \begin{bmatrix} X_1 \\ \vdots \\ X_n \\ X_{n+1} \end{bmatrix} \geqslant 0, \tag{1}$$

$$(-H_1 e_1^{**}, ..., -H_n e_n^{**}, L) \begin{bmatrix} X_1 \\ \vdots \\ X_n \\ X_{n+1} \end{bmatrix} < 0. \tag{2}$$

We can write (1) as

$$- \sum_{j=1}^m h_{ij} x_{1j} + x_{n+1i} \geqslant 0 \qquad (i = 1, ..., n)$$

$$\vdots$$

$$- \sum_{j=1}^m h_{ij} x_{nj} + x_{n+1i} \geqslant 0 \qquad (i = 1, ..., n)$$

and (2) as

$$- \sum_{i=1}^{n} \sum_{j=1}^{m} h_{ij}e_i^*x_{ij} + \sum_i l_i^0 x_{n+1i} < 0.$$

We assume that there do exist nonnegative solutions denoted with superscript 0's to (1) and (2). Let us multiply each line of (1) through by l_i^0 and sum the result over i, giving

$$- \sum_{j=1}^{m} \sum_{i=1}^{n} h_{ij}l_i^0 x_{kj} + \sum_i l_i^0 x_{n+1i} \geqslant 0$$

for all k.

Comparing this inequality with (2) we find

$$- \sum_{i=1}^{n} \sum_{j=1}^{m} h_{ij}e_i^*x_{ij} < - \sum_{i=1}^{n} \sum_{j=1}^{m} h_{ij}l_i^0 x_{kj} .$$

Since $\sum_i h_{ij}e_i^* \leqslant \sum_i h_{ij}l_i^0$ by hypothesis,

$$- \sum_j x_{kj}^0 \sum_i h_{ij}l_i^0 \leqslant - \sum_j x_{kj}^0 \sum_i h_{ij}e_i^*,$$

and

$$- \sum_{i=1}^{n} \sum_{j=1}^{m} h_{ij}e_i^*x_{ij}^0 < - \sum_{i=j}^{n} \sum_{j=1}^{m} h_{ij}e_i^*x_{kj}^0$$

for all k. We remove the minus signs and reverse the inequality, giving

$$\sum_i e_i^* \sum_j h_{ij}x_{ij}^0 > \sum_i e_i^* \sum_j h_{ij}x_{kj}^0$$

for all k. Therefore it must be true for some i that

$$\sum_j h_{ij}x_{ij}^0 > \sum_j h_{ij}x_{kj}^0$$

for all k. Therefore, it must be true for $k = i$, which implies

$$h_{i1}x_{i1}^0 + \cdots + h_{in}x_{in}^0 > h_{i1}x_{i1}^0 + \cdots + h_{in}x_{in}^0 .$$

This contradiction establishes that there is no nonnegative solution to inequalities (1) and (2) and P.1 is proved.

We can now proceed line by line to show that E^{**} and U^{**} satisfying (2.1) and (2.2) also satisfy (3.5a)–(3.5d).

Equation (3.5a). From (2.1), e_i^{**} and u_j^{**} satisfy (3.5a) for all i.

Equation (3.5b). Let $p_k^* = \sum_j u_j^{**} h_{kj}$ and $u_{ij}^* = u_j^{**}$ for all i. Then they satisfy (3.5b) since $p_k^* - \sum_j u_{ij}^* h_{kj} = 0$ for all i and k.

Equation (3.5c). Let $\sum_k h_{kj} \sum_i l_{ik}^0 = q_j^*$. Then by (2.2),

$$0 \leqslant \sum_k h_{kj} \sum_i l_{ik}^0 - \sum_i h_{ij} e_i^{**},$$

and by P.1 there exist $l_{ik}^* \geqslant 0$ such that

$$\sum_i l_{ik}^0 \geqslant \sum_i l_{ik}^* \quad \text{and} \quad \sum_k h_{kj} l_{ik}^* - h_{ij} e_i^{**} \geqslant 0$$

for all i. If $>$ holds for some i and j,

$$q_j^* = \sum_k h_{kj} \sum_i l_{ik}^0 \geqslant \sum_k h_{kj} \sum_i l_{ik}^* > \sum_i h_{ij} e_i^{**},$$

and $u_j^{**} = 0$. Therefore, (3.5c) is satisfied with $u_{ij}^* = u_j^{**}$.

Equation (3.5d). If $\sum_i l_{ik}^0 > \sum_i l_{ik}^*$ for some k and $h_{kj} > 0$,

$$q_j^* = \sum_k h_{kj} \sum_i l_{ik}^0 > \sum_k h_{kj} \sum_i l_{ik}^* \geqslant \sum_i h_{ij} e_i^{**},$$

and $u_j^{**} = 0$ for all j. If $h_{kj} = 0$ for that k and some j, then for the corresponding j, $u_j^{**} h_{kj} = 0$. In either case $p_k^* = \sum_j u_j^{**} h_{kj} = 0$ and (3.5d) is satisfied.

We reverse the direction of inference to prove that if $\sum_i h_{ij} l_i^0 = q_j^*$, the competitive equilibrium emission vector is efficient. We assume in addition that the rank of H is m: this involves no significant loss of generality since any constraint matrix can be made to satisfy the condition by striking out redundant constraints. The operation of eliminating redundant constraints does not change the set Ψ of emission vectors which satisfy the constraints.

THEOREM 3.6. *If* $\sum_k h_{kj} l_k^0 = q_j^*$, E^* *minimizes* $\sum_i F_i(e_i)$ *subject to* $EH \leqslant Q^*$, $E \geqslant 0$.

Proof. First we note that in proving Theorem 3.4 we established that (3.5a)–(3.5d) are satisfied, for all i, by $u_{ij}^* = u_j^{**}$, and that the rank of H

equals m. Therefore, the matrix of partial derivatives of the licensing constraints for each firm also has rank m, and the multipliers on those constraints are unique [4]. Since the Kuhn–Tucker conditions are satisfied by identical multipliers for each firm, they are *only* satisfied by identical multipliers. Let u_j^{**} be equal to any of the u_{ij}^*, identical for all i. Then,

Equation (2.1). e_i^* and u_j^{**} as defined satisfy (2.1) whenever they satisfy (3.5a).

Equation (2.2).   By (3.5d)

$$\sum_i l_{ik}^0 \geqslant \sum_i l_{ik}^*, \qquad \text{and} \qquad q_j^* = \sum_k h_{kj} \sum_i l_{ik}^0 \geqslant \sum_k h_{kj} \sum_i l_{ik}^*.$$

By (3.5c)

$$\sum_k h_{kj} \sum_i l_{ik}^* \geqslant \sum_i h_{ij} e_i^*.$$

Therefore $q_j^* - \sum_i h_{ij} e_i^* \geqslant 0$. If $q_j^* > \sum_i h_{ij} e_i^*$, either $\sum_i l_{ik}^0 > \sum_i l_{ik}^*$ for some k with $h_{kj} \neq 0$, or $\sum_k h_{kj} l_{ik}^* > h_{ij} e_i^*$ for some i and that j. If the latter, $u_{ij}^* = 0$ and $u_j^{**} = 0$. If the former, $p_k^* = 0$ and since by (3.5b) $p_k^* - \sum_j u_{ij}^* h_{kj} \geqslant 0$, $\sum_j u_{ij}^* h_{kj} = 0$ and $u_{ij}^* = 0$, so that $u_j^{**} = 0$. Therefore, $u_j^{**}(q_j^* - \sum_i h_{ij} e_i^*) = 0$ when $u_j^{**} = u_{ij}^*$.

This completes the proof that a competitive equilibrium, satisfying the conditions of joint cost minimization, exists in the market for emission licenses. An integral part of the proof was the assumption that the total of each type of license is determined by solving the *equations*

$$\sum_k h_{kj} l_k^0 = q_j^*.$$

If the management agency is restricted to assigning all licenses of type i which it issues to firm i, then its ability to redistribute costs will be severely limited by the necessity of choosing l_i^0 to satisfy the air quality constraints with equality if indeed such a solution exists in the problem at hand.

REFERENCES

1. K. J. ARROW, The organization of economic activity: Issues pertinent to the choice of market versus non-market allocation, *in* "The Analysis and Evaluation of Public Expenditures: The PPB System," pp. 47–64, U.S. Congress, Joint Economic Committee, U.S. Government Printing Office, Washington, DC, 1969.
2. J. H. DALES, "Pollution, Property, and Prices," University of Toronto Press, Toronto, Canada, 1968.

3. D. GALE, "The Theory of Linear Economic Models," p. 47, McGraw-Hill, New York, 1960.

4. G. HADLEY, "Nonlinear and Dynamic Programming," p. 190, Addison-Wesley Publ. Co., Inc., Reading, MA, 1964.

5. H. W. HERZOG, The air diffusion model as an urban planning tool, *Socio-Econ. Plan. Sci.* 3 (1969), 329–349.

6. H. JACOBY AND G. SCHAUMBURG, "Administered Markets in Water Quality Control: A Proposal for the Delaware Estuary," unpublished.

7. S. KARLIN, "Mathematical Methods and Theory in Games, Programming and Economics," Vol. I, pp. 203–204, Addison-Wesley Publ. Co., Inc., Reading Mass., 1962.

8. A. KNEESE AND B. BOWER, "Managing Water Quality: Economics, Technology, Institutions," Chapter 2, Johns Hopkins Univ. Press, Baltimore, 1968.

9. S. MARGLIN, Objectives of water resources development: A general statement, *in* "Design of Water Resource Systems" (A. Maass *et al.*, Eds.), p. 23, Harvard Univ. Press, Cambridge, MA, 1962.

10. S. MARGLIN, Information in price and command systems of planning, *in* "Public Economics" (J. Margolis, Ed.), St. Martin's Press, New York, 1969.

11. D. O. MARTIN AND J. A. TIKVART, A general atmospheric diffusion model for estimating the effects on air quality of one or more sources, APCA Paper No. 68-148, presented at the Annual Meeting of the Air Pollution Control Association, June 1968.

12. W. D. MONTGOMERY, Artificial markets and the theory of games, Social Science Working Paper No. 8, California Inst. of Technol., March 1972.

13. P. SAMUELSON, "Foundations of Economic Analysis," pp. 34–35, Harvard Univ. Press, Cambridge, MA, 1966.

14. TRW Systems Group, "Regional Air Pollution Analysis, Phase I: Status Report," pp. 4.3–4.15, U.S. Department of Health, Education and Welfare and National Air Pollution Control Administration, Washington, DC, 1969.

[13]

Transferable Discharge Permits and the Control of Stationary Source Air Pollution: A Survey and Synthesis

Thomas H. Tietenberg

I. INTRODUCTION

Background

Recently, in the United States, there has been an increasing interest in the use of economic incentives to achieve environmental quality goals, particularly for air pollution.[1] Though there are a range of such possible economic incentives two have received the most analytical attention—effluent or emission charges and transferable discharge permits. In this paper attention is focused on the latter approach.[2]

Although the central concept involved can be traced at least back to Alfred Marshall and Henry George, it seems fair to attribute much of the revival of interest to Dales (1968*a*; 1968*b*) for water and Crocker (1966) for air. The concept is a disarmingly simple and powerful one. Its intellectual genesis is to be found in the realization that the behavioral sources of the pollution problem could be traced to an ill-defined set of property rights. The right to discharge pollutants had historically, in the absence of government intervention, been allocated at a zero price to all potential users. While this allocation process *can* be cost justified when the costs of controlling pollution (including the administrative and enforcement costs) exceed the costs of pollution damage incurred by the absence of control, it *cannot* be justified when the level of pollution damage indicates that some form of control is appropriate. One natural outcome of using this perspective to characterize the nature of the pollution problem is that it suggests a particular policy approach—the establishment of a correctly defined right to discharge.

The current appeal of this concept for air pollution in the United States is based upon several considerations. First, and probably foremost, is the realization that a movement from the current purely regulatory system of control to a system based on transferable discharge permits promises the potential for achieving a better quality of air than currently enjoyed with a substantially lower commitment of resources to pollution control. Secondly, for air pollution, the transferable discharge permit (henceforth TDP) system would be compatible with

Professor Tietenberg is with the Department of Economics at Colby College, Waterville, Maine. The author wishes to acknowledge the benefit of helpful comments from Barbara Ingle, William Baumol, Scott Atkinson, Cliff Russell and two anonymous referees as well as to acknowledge the research assistance provided by Alison Jones and Cynthia Keating. An earlier version of this paper was delivered at the International Institute for Environment and Society, Berlin, West Germany in September, 1979.

[1] See, for example, the examples provided in Yandle (1978).

[2] This approach is characterized by a variety of different names. The policy instrument has been referred to as a marketable emission permit, a pollution right and a transferable discharge permit. I have chosen in this paper to use the last of these exclusively.

Land Economics, Vol. 56, No. 4, November 1980
0023-7639/80/0004-0391 $1.00/0

the existing legislation. It would represent a modification of, rather than a radical departure from, the current regulatory approach. In addition, the transferable discharge permit system is administratively flexible, yet feasible. It avoids many of the most costly rigidities in the current approach and, yet, the implementation requirements are realistic. Finally, unlike the current system the TDP system provides an incentive for emitters to adopt new control techniques which can clean up more emissions at lower cost (since they can sell the resulting excess permits), which in turn stimulates the development of these techniques.

The Policy Context

Although the existing regulatory approach to air pollution control is exceedingly complex, it is possible to capture briefly the essence both of the basic approach and the recent reforms which have moved it further in the direction of an increasing reliance on economic incentives. This synopsis can then serve as a point of departure and benchmark for the discussion of the possibilities for moving toward a less restrictive transferable discharge permit system.

The existing system of air pollution control relies on ambient standards (or concentration targets) defined by the Environmental Protection Agency (EPA) and implementation plans submitted by the states (SIPs) to detail the procedures by which the states intend to meet those standards.[3] In addition, for several classes of new and modified polluting sources, the EPA has issued emission standards directly.[4]

This basic approach does little to control the degradation of the air quality in regions where the air is cleaner than the ambient standards. Therefore, prodded initially by a court suit[5] and, subsequently, the amendments to the Clean Air Act of 1977[6] the EPA moved to define a policy (referred to as the PSD policy) to prevent the significant deterioration of the air in areas not currently in violation of the air quality standards. The approach taken was to designate allowable pollution increments and ceilings (either of which could serve as the binding constraint) for three separate types of regional classifications. Those increments are currently allocated on a first come, first served basis although a market approach, such as discussed in this paper, is clearly an option for the future.

The other two major reforms which have taken place recently and which have the effect of moving current policy closer to a market approach are the alternative emission reduction approach[7] (known popularly as the "bubble" concept) and the emissions offset policy[8] applied to nonattainment areas[9] and to certain sources in attainment areas if they could be expected to contribute pollution to nonattainment areas[10] or to cause an attainment area to exceed the standard.[11]

---

[3] The procedures to be followed by states are detailed in 40 CFR 51 and the EPA approval procedures are spelled out in 40 CFR 52.

[4] See 40 CFR 60 for criteria pollutants and 40 CFR 61 for hazardous pollutants.

[5] Sierra Club v. Ruckelshaus, 334 Supp. 253 (DDC 1972) which was later affirmed by the Supreme Court, 412 U.S. 541.

[6] 91 Stat 731. The details of the policy can be found in 40 CFR 51.24 and 40 CFR 52.21. Proposed amendments to that policy resulting from a successful court suit against EPA (Alabama Power Company v. Costle, 13 ERC 1225) are located in 44 FR 41924 (5 September 1979).

[7] See 44 FR 71780 (11 December 1979).

[8] See 40 CFR 51 Appendix S, originally presented in 44 FR 3274 (16 January 1979).

[9] Nonattainment areas are designated geographic areas which have not yet attained air as clean as required by the ambient standards. See 40 CFR 81.300 et seq.

[10] See 44 FR 3283, §IIE (16 January 1979).

[11] See 44 FR 3884, §III (18 January 1979).

The "bubble" concept specifically allows existing emitters to propose modifications of their emission standards based on the substitution of a more relaxed degree of control for one source for a more stringent degree of control of another source of the same pollutant. These substitutions can, under certain circumstances, occur between plants or even between firms. This design feature carries the bubble policy a long way toward a fully transferable permit system. The object, of course, is to allow a firm to meet its emission reduction goal as flexibly and cheaply as possible while insuring that air quality is not degraded by the substitution. This concept replaced an established procedure based upon the levying of a separate emission standard on each source. Both the business community[12] and EPA[13] expect the costs of pollution control to be considerably reduced by this method.

The emission offset policy was originally designed as a means for allowing economic growth in nonattainment areas while insuring no further degradation of their air quality. It allows potential new entrants to a nonattainment area to procure sufficient reductions from existing firms (over and above their previous legal requirements) so as to offset the increases in pollution which would otherwise occur upon their initiation of production in the area without the compensating reduction. The significance of this program is that it allows the transfer of emission reductions from existing sources to new sources, whereas the bubble concept allows transfers only among existing emitters.

These reforms are important because they introduce into the basic system two additional degrees of transferability that can serve to reduce the costs of compliance significantly. They both allow limited interfirm transfers, to be approved on a case by case basis as long as total emissions do not increase and air quality is not adversely affected. In addition, the bubble concept allows an existing emitter to actually exceed the SIP emission standards for some of its sources as long as it compensates with sufficient emission reductions from the other sources in the plant. Thus, the bubble concept establishes the very important principle (for existing sources, but not for new sources) that the SIP standards are not inviolable, a principle which expands the set of trading possibilities (and, hence, the cost reduction possibilities) considerably.

The key difference between the existing system and a TDP system with full transferability lies in the fact that in the latter the control authority allows all sources to participate in the trades and allows all emission reductions to be traded in a regularized market. In contrast the bubble and offset policies have restrictions on what emission reductions can be traded (e.g., only those additional reductions above the standard in the offset policy) and on what sources can participate in trades (e.g., only existing sources in areas demonstrating attainment in the bubble policy).

An Overview of the Paper

On a purely ideological level the move to this more general system is clearly merited. On a more pragmatic level, however, the implementation of an unrestricted TDP market faces a number of technical, legal and administrative challenges.

The purpose of this paper is to examine the prospects for moving toward this

---

[12] See Nulty (1979).
[13] 40 CFR 71780.

less restrictive TDP system by surveying and synthesizing the most prominent published English language literature on the subject. While the focus will be on air pollution the relevant water pollution literature will be included insofar as it yields insights which are pertinent to controlling air pollution. The objective is to draw together what is known and is not known about this form of control and to assess the implications of this research for the design of an operating TDP market.

The paper opens with a discussion of design criteria and the implications of these criteria for the design of the permit itself and for the design of the market within which the TDPs can be transferred. This is followed by a brief survey of the requirements for such a system to be enforceable. The final section briefly surveys the rather sparse literature dealing with simulations of hypothetical TDP markets.

II. ENVIRONMENTAL GOALS AND DESIGN OF THE MARKET

Rudiments of a TDP Approach

The current regulatory approach to air pollution control involves the specification of emission standards for each emitter. Any emissions above these standards are in noncompliance and therefore the responsible emitter is subject to some kind of sanction. The problem with this approach is that there is no guarantee that the particular allocation of emission standards chosen by the control authority will achieve the air pollution goals at anything approaching minimum cost. Indeed much available empirical evidence suggests that the typical allocations are significantly more expensive than the minimum cost allocation.[14]

The bubble concept and the offset strategies are partial responses to this deficiency, but they fall somewhat short of a marketable permit system. They rely on a case by case approach to transferability and impose severe restrictions on the conditions under which transfers can take place. In essence they are the administratively easiest modifications to make from the current system but the existing restrictions on trades prevent the system from approaching a minimum cost system.

The transferable discharge permit system responds to these deficiencies in the current system by establishing a regular market for discharge permits with few restrictions on transferability. This approach is both legally and philosophically compatible with the existing legislative framework. The allocation problem is handled by the remarkably simple device of making the emission standards (legitimized by the discharge permit) completely transferable. In this way those emitters facing very steep control costs can purchase permits from emitters having less costly options, thereby subsidizing the more intensive control of their own emissions by these low cost emitters. Remarkably, as the discussion of the literature below reveals, under competitive conditions the reallocation of permits which takes place by virtue of making them transferable can cause substantial reductions in the amount of resources committed to pollution control while meeting the air quality standards.

Specifying the Objective

The first step in designing a less restrictive TDP system is specifying the

---

[14] See, for example, the studies cited in Kneese (1977, pp. 195–202), Atkinson and Lewis (1974), and Anderson et al. (1979).

objective the system is supposed to accomplish. There are two objectives commonly discussed in the economics literature—efficiency and cost-effectiveness.

Ignoring implementation costs the efficiency criterion clearly dominates. Intuitively, the efficient allocation balances, at the margin, the damage cost incurred from remaining uncontrolled pollution with the costs of avoiding the damage. It is the allocation which minimizes the sum of damage costs and avoidance costs.[15]

The problem with this objective from a policy point of view is that it is difficult to achieve. For the control authority to achieve this objective it would have to know the control costs and the damage costs associated with each emitter. Given the large number of emitters that is a tall order and one not likely to be fulfilled. Various conceptual schemes are currently being developed to overcome some of the theoretical hurdles for (example, the public good problems associated with the incorrect revelation of preferences) but at this stage it seems clear that these schemes are not yet sufficiently developed to permit them to be used as a basis for policy.[16]

For these pragmatic reasons there has been a reluctant acceptance of a cost-effectiveness criterion.[17] This criterion is based upon a dichotomization of the control problem—the specification of a policy target and the establishment of a system to assure that target is met. Cost-effectiveness deals only with the second component. It provides no guidance for choosing the appropriate policy target or the appropriate level of that target, but it provides a good deal of guidance in selecting among the various ways of meeting that target. It suggests that the "best" allocation is the one which achieves the target at minimum cost. If the target happens to be efficient,

then a cost-effective allocation will also be efficient. There is nothing in the cost-effectiveness criterion, however, which would guarantee that result.

Choice of Policy Targets

The key to applying the cost-effectiveness criterion involves choosing the target which is to be met at minimum cost. Two candidate targets have received prominence in the literature, either explicitly or implicitly. The first, an aggregate emissions target, focuses on the total weight of emissions placed into the receiving medium (air or water) in a particular geographic area during some period of time. The aggregate emissions cost-effectiveness (ECE) criterion envisions the establishment of some legal ceiling (the standard) on the allowable weight of emissions and then allocating the responsibility for meeting that standard among the emitters in such a fashion as to cause it to be met with the smallest possible commitment of control resources. The chief virtue of this criterion is its administrative simplicity. It is relatively easy to monitor and the contribution of each emitter to the policy target is not difficult to define.

This policy target also has a substantial disadvantage for local pollutants—it is not uniquely related to the level of damages caused.[18] The reason is quite clear. For local pollutants the damage they cause is related to their ground level concentration in the air. Their concentration,

---

[15] A formal mathematical characterization of this allocation in the context of a general equilibrium model can be found in Tietenberg (1973*b*).

[16] See, for example, Bohm (1972), Clarke (1971), Randall et al. (1974), Scherr and Babb (1975), and Barnett and Yandle (1973).

[17] See, for example, Baumol and Oates (1975).

[18] Local pollutants can be contrasted with global pollutants for which the damage depends solely on the aggregate volume of residuals emitted. For a discussion of

in turn, is based upon the proximity of the emitters to each other, and the process of accumulation within the environmental medium, as well as upon the amount emitted. Thus while the aggregate level of emissions is important, many other factors are as well.

To compensate for these problems a second policy target, the ambient standard, has emerged and it is this target which is mandated by the Clean Air Act. The ambient standard represents a target concentration level measured at a specific location for specific averaging times (for example, one hour, daily, annually). This standard has the virtue that it is closely related to damage caused, but it has the disadvantage that the relationship of each emitter to this standard is no longer as clear cut. Because this target involves a threshold concentration level, if each emitter in an area were to hypothetically and sequentially reduce its emission rate by a constant amount, the effect on air quality in those areas where the thresholds have been exceeded would be much more dramatic for some emitters than for others. The contribution of any single emitter to air quality at a particular receptor location depends upon the location of the emitter vis à vis the monitoring site, and the flow characteristics of the environmental medium between the monitoring site and the emission site, as well as upon the level of emissions. The ambient cost effectiveness (ACE) criterion requires that the responsibility for cutting back emissions be allocated among emitters so as to minimize the cost of meeting the ambient standard as measured at specific monitoring stations.[19]

Geographic Extent of the Market

Geographic considerations enter the design of a TDP system in two main ways: the geographic domain of the policy targets and the area of applicability of the permits.[20] The most natural domain for the policy targets is the local airshed while the most desirable area of applicability for the permits includes all territory with emitters contributing pollutants to that airshed.

Unfortunately, a local airshed is rarely a well-defined physical entity. Any sub-planet partitioning of the air space must be plagued by a certain degree of arbitrariness. Yet it is equally clear that some local partitioning is absolutely necessary. To illustrate this consider what would happen if the aggregate emissions target were defined on a national domain. Permits would then be issued or sold to emitters. Since there are no geographic constraints, it is quite possible that a disproportionate share of those permits might end up in urban areas (e.g., Los Angeles) with particularly harsh existing pollution problems. This would cause the damage in these areas to be unacceptably high. The basic point is that an aggregate emissions target has a weak connection with damage caused under any circumstance, but the weakness is exacerbated as the geographic area covered by the definition of this target is expanded.

The air quality targets are, by their very nature, defined in terms of concentration measurements at specific locations. The issue for this set of targets is the number of such locations needed to adequately cover a particular airshed. It

the distinction between these two types of pollutants in terms of their mathematical specification and the policy implications of those specifications, see Tietenberg (1978*a*).

[19] The Clean Air Act requires that the standards be met everywhere, which means that the monitoring stations have to be sufficiently numerous and sufficiently dispersed to provide adequate coverage of the geographic area.

[20] Geographic considerations also affect the design of the permit itself. This is discussed in the next section.

is not possible to come up with a specific suggestion without reference to the characteristics of the particular airshed, but it is possible to suggest some of the considerations which would affect such a choice. The danger of an inadequate number of such locations is that the permit system will be designed to insure compliance with the measured concentrations only, leaving the distinct possibility of air quality deterioration in other unmonitored parts of the airshed. In practice, because of the flow of pollutants within the airshed, it is probably possible to gain an adequate description of the state of an airshed with a relatively few monitoring stations. To my knowledge there have been no empirical studies devoted to this critical design question.

Thus the notion of a local airshed, while lacking a precise, unambiguous means of defining its boundaries, appears both necessary and workable as a basis for defining the policy targets.[21] It would be tempting and administratively simple to project the boundaries of this airshed, however defined, on the land area underlying it and call this the area of applicability of the permit market.[22]

This definition of the area of applicability would present problems for two reasons: it would not, in all likelihood, correspond to existing political boundaries and it would omit from consideration many emitters which contributed to the degradation of the air in that airshed, but are located some distance downwind from it. Each of these places important constraints on the ability of any control authority to achieve the desired policy targets at minimum cost.

An example of the former problem is provided by the Northeast corridor of the United States. The New York metropolitan airshed, under any reasonable definition, overlies parts of at least three

states (New Jersey, New York and Connecticut). For a coordinated TDP market to be established in these regions a regional political authority has to be established with sufficient authority to implement the system.[23]

To make matters even worse there is accumulating evidence that some pollutants are transported rather long distances.[24] As a result the initial sources of the pollutants may be quite far removed from the airshed and well beyond the jurisdiction of the control authority unless the jurisdiction of that authority extends well beyond the perimeter established by the airshed.

The long distance transport of pollutants also makes quite likely the possibility that any given emitter will contribute to pollution problems in more than one airshed. Conceptually this presents no problem as long as that emitter is forced to have permits from all control authorities whose airsheds that emitter affects. Legally, however, this notion of overlapping jurisdictions may well be troublesome. The current approach involves a procedure for source states to identify multistate sources and to notify recipient states, and a procedure for recipient states to petition the administrator for disapproval of the implementation plan involving that source.[25] This is a far cry from what the theoretical optimum would suggest.

---

[21] The Clean Air Act follows this route with the establishment of air quality control regions. See 42 USC 7407.

[22] An area of applicability is defined as the jurisdictional range of the permit market. Emitters within the area of applicability have to have permits issued by the control authority governing that area while those emitters outside the area do not.

[23] The United States has made a start in this direction with the establishment of multistate air quality control regions, but these entities have not, as yet, been endowed with sufficient authority to implement a TDP system. See 42 USC 7407.

[24] See, for example, Cleveland and Graedel (1979).

[25] See 91 Stat 724.

The considerations do not eliminate the desirability of a TDP system (they plague all other local control systems as well), but they do suggest caution in relying exclusively on this approach. For example, a TDP system should be complemented by legislation which rules out various control options that solve the local pollution problem by exporting the pollution to other airsheds. The most obvious current example of such a system is the use of a tall stack to inject the polluting substance into the atmosphere at such a penetrating height and velocity that there is no effect on ground level concentrations in the immediate area, but the effect is pronounced at more distant locations.[26]

Coverage of Emitters

Once the area of applicability of the permit system is established it remains to determine whether or not all emitters within that area are required to have permits. The major concern is whether emitters who individually represent a very small contribution to the pollution (e.g. residences or automobile owners) in an airshed ought to be forced to purchase rights.

Macintosh (1974, p. 65) suggests that they should and devises a special branch of the control authority to deal with the purchase and sale of permits denominated in especially small units. The analogy he draws is the odd-lot trading system employed by the major stock exchanges.

Tietenberg (1974, p. 283) on the other hand, argues that some emitters should be excluded on the grounds that the costs of monitoring and enforcing the permits on each small emitter may far outweigh the benefits derived from the reduced pollution which results from their inclusion.

One useful test which emerges from these divergent views is to allow exemptions when the *collective* reduction in air pollution from the class of emitters being considered does not justify the additional expenditures on monitoring and enforcement. In addition this discussion suggests that different market designs may be appropriate for these different types of sources.[27] Small emitters will be included when collectively they are an important source of pollution in that airshed and the enforcement costs of inclusion under the most favorable market design do not seem to outweigh those benefits. The current reforms focus almost exclusively on large sources.[28]

Initial Distribution of Permits

It is useful to distinguish between the initial distribution of the permits and some ultimate distribution at a later date. The control authority has a good deal of control over the initial allocation while the market will handle the ultimate allocation.

It is one of the desirable properties of an appropriately designed[29] transferable discharge permit system that the ultimate

---

[26] Some steps in this direction have already been taken. The law already rules out stacks which are taller than "good engineering practice" as a means of meeting air quality standards. Yet the law specifically prohibits the administrator from regulating stack height. See 91 Stat 721.

[27] These alternative market designs are explored in what follows on p. 407.

[28] In the Alabama Power decision the court provided that EPA may exempt from review those situations determined to be *de minimis*. The administrator exercises this authority by establishing emission or air quality thresholds and exempting or limiting the review of sources falling below these thresholds. Interestingly, the court limited the administrator's discretion in setting these thresholds by ruling out the use of a cost-effectiveness rationale. See 44 FR 41937, §10 (5 September 1979).

[29] The question of what permit designs are compatible with cost-effectiveness is treated in section III.

allocation of these permits among emitters will be cost-effective regardless of their initial allocation as long as the permit market is competitive. This is formally proven by Montgomery (1972). Intuitively, this follows from the transferability of the right. Those emitters which can control their pollution most cheaply will have an incentive to sell to those emitters which have higher clean up costs. This does not imply that the initial allocation of these permits is unimportant; on the contrary, it is quite important because it affects the level of costs faced by the emitters and the amount of revenue generated by the control authority.

Conceptually the initial distribution possibilities can be arrayed on a spectrum where on one end of the spectrum the entitlement to discharge is reserved for the control authority (and granted to emitters only upon receipt of their payment) while on the other it is reserved for the emitters (and granted to the control authority only upon receipt of adequate compensation). Each of these imply different behavior on the part of the control authority and different allocations of the cost burden for meeting the community air quality goals.

On one end of the spectrum is the "government pays" principle. If the entitlements are considered to be currently held by the existing set of emitters, then in order to improve the quality of air the control authority would have to buy back some of the permits. As long as they were bought at a market price (as opposed to a government dictated price) the local community would end up paying for the improvement in air quality through the tax system.

A rather different cost incidence is obtained when the entitlements are considered vested in the state. In this "polluter pays" case the emitters must not

only pay for the pollution control equipment, they must also purchase the permits from the control authority. In this case, the cost falls on the consumers of the product, the owners of the emitting firms and the employees of the emitting firms. While members of the local community may end up paying the costs of increasing the quality of air under this scheme as well, they will do so in their role as employee, employer or consumer, not as taxpayer.

There is a middle ground of this spectrum which does not seem to have been explored systematically. In one possibility entitlements could be vested in the state, but the control authority could choose to give them at no cost to the existing emitters on some rational allocative basis. This makes the public sector budgetary impact rather small while holding the costs down to the emitters. While they must pay for the costs of the pollution control equipment, the emitters do not have to pay for their initial allocation of permits (although they do have to purchase any additional permits beyond their initial allocation).

It should be realized, however, that this middle part of the spectrum requires that the control authority define the initial allocation. With either the "government pays" case or the "polluter pays" case the initial allocation can be handled by the market. When the permits are given away, some basis for allocating them must be determined. Some criterion for allocation must therefore be developed.

One of the key determinants of whether the expanded market system is politically feasible is whether the various participants (for example, employers, employees, taxpayers, etc.) view it as "better" than the existing system. One traditional measure of whether a policy change is "better" is whether the new policy is Pareto superior to the old policy.[30] It is a rather remarkable characteristic of this transferable discharge permit system that it provides an opportunity to implement a Pareto superior policy change.[31]

The existing system has assigned emission control responsibility via the state implementation plans. Presumably this assignment is consistent with achieving the ambient standards. If the permits in an expanded system are initially allocated to the emitters so as to allow each polluter the right to pollute as much as was previously allowed by the implementation plans, then any transfers among emitters which take place after the initial allocation, because they are voluntary, will result in mutual gains for those trading. Since this choice guarantees that no emitter faces higher costs than it otherwise would, this implies that consumers and employees should be as well off. Thus this particular allocation has the potential to be a minimum disruption means of moving from the current system to a full market system, should such a move be deemed desirable.[32]

If there were perfect foresight on the part of all emitters and a competitive market structure for the TDPs, the control authority would not have to worry about the intertemporal allocation of TDPs. All current emitters would foresee the future demands for the permits as well as their effect on prices and choose their control investments accordingly.[33] New emitters would simple bid the TDPs away from existing emitters prior to their entry into the market.

Both a lack of perfect foresight, however, and a noncompetitive market structure can create problems, although probably not serious problems, with this harmonious view. The lack of perfect foresight could cause existing firms to underinvest in pollution control if they underestimate the future prices of the permits or overinvest if they overestimate future prices. This is due to the fact that the permit can subsequently be sold for a profit in the right circumstances. Underinvestment could arise because many of the methods of emission reduction involve durable equipment purchases. Prior to the purchase emitters have a choice of any point on their long run marginal cost of control function. If they expect a heavy demand for permits from new emitters, they might rationally choose to purchase some temporarily idle capacity. However, once the equipment is purchased an emitter must operate on its associated short run marginal cost function. This built-in lack of *ex post* flexibility could create problems for growth when all existing emitters systematically underinvest. This is, however, a problem new firms face in many markets whenever a resource is in fixed supply. Since they seem to handle it in these other markets, there is reason to believe they can handle it in this one too.

---

[30] A Pareto superior reallocation is one in which no one is made worse off and at least one of the participants is made better off.

[31] The careful reader might argue that it is Pareto superior for existing emitters but not for potential new emitters. Since the current system forces new emitters to purchase offsets (as would the market system), this initial reaction is not valid for these areas. It is valid for attainment areas, however, since the allowable increments are currently given, free of charge, to the first requestors.

[32] The one caveat to this proposition that has to be kept in mind is that it ignores the change in administrative costs which would accompany the transition to an expanded market system. If administrative costs rise by a sufficient amount the new policy will not be Pareto superior. One study which has examined this question concludes that a TDP system would probably result in *lower* administrative costs than the current system. See Anderson, et al. (1979, chap. 6, p. 71; chap. 7, p. 38).

[33] The EPA currently allows a firm to bank excess emission reductions for later use (i.e., during an expansion or for transfer as on offset). See 44 FR 51935 (5 September 1979) and 44 FR 3280 (16 January 1979).

Noncompetitive markets can also potentially create problems. If the holders of the permits are few in number, they might, through collusion, charge higher than competitive prices for the transfer of a permit to a new emitter. This could stifle growth and create windfall profits for the sellers. This is a likely problem, however, only when the number of sellers is small and there are no alternative locations the buyer could choose. Therefore this is a problem to be confronted in few (if any) markets and can be dealt with in those few with additional constraints on the transferability of the permits.

If the control authority concludes that the existing incentives do not provide for an adequate reserve of permits for new emitters, two distinct approaches are available. The first assigns a very large role to the control authority while the latter assigns more of the responsibility to the private sector. The public sector approach envisions the analytical derivation of the annual optimal stockpile of permits to be held by the control authority to accomodate future growth. To operationalize this notion the public sector would attempt to simulate the operation of the market under various growth scenarios. Then decision theory could be used to derive the supply of permits for each year which maximizes the present value of expected social benefits. While this is a conceptually easy model to construct, the data requirements are somewhat formidable.

An alternative approach, suggested by Roberts and Spence (1976) for a slightly different problem than the one considered here, could be used to shift some of the uncertainty onto the emitters while keeping their incentives compatible with cost-minimization for the system as a whole. Their system envisions comple-

menting a TDP system with a subsidy for unused TDPs and a penalty for exceeding the emission level permitted by the TDP. For our purposes here the interesting facet of this approach is the subsidy for holding unused permits. This subsidy creates an additional incentive for the emitter (above the normal incentive of holding the permit for higher future prices) to retain some capability to trade permits to other emitters in the future. This capability can be achieved by constructing a pollution control capacity larger than current needs and stockpiling the permits or by constructing control facilities which provide rather more *ex post* flexibility than would be achieved with competing, presumably cheaper, alternative facilities.[34]

This subsidy approach has the virtue that it will encourage emitters to retain the capability to sell permits in the future when the cost of doing so is relatively low, but not when it is high because the subsidy in this latter case will not be sufficient to make these actions profitable. It has the undesirable feature that it requires larger expenditures by the control authority.

Enforcing the Permit System

The enforcement of this kind of permit system depends on the technical ability to detect violations and the legal ability to deal with the violations once detected. The ability to monitor emissions is a key aspect of the system because without it emitters do not have to worry whether they have the appropriate number of permits or not and the incentive properties of the system are lost. Simi-

---

[34] In this context *ex post* flexibility refers to situations where some increases in the degree of emissions control can be accomplished without sharply increasing marginal cost.

larly, violators should be sufficiently penalized to make violations under normal circumstances an unattractive option, but not so harsh as to make them lack credibility.

The state of the act in monitoring pollution from a policy perspective has recently been surveyed by Anderson et al. (1977, pp. 90–106). A transferable discharge permit system designed to achieve ambient standards requires both ambient concentration monitoring and emission monitoring. Since emissions monitoring is the most difficult component of an enforcement policy, we shall concentrate on it. Anderson et al. (1977) summarize:

Direct, continuous monitoring may be feasible for larger installations where suitable instruments are available, and their cost is small relative to the overall cost of operating the plant. But . . . instrument technology does not provide solutions for every monitoring problem (p. 101).

The article goes on to conclude, however, that direct continuous monitoring of emissions is not essential to the success of the program. There are a number of techniques available for sampling or estimating the emissions flow. These may lack the precision and completeness of direct continuous monitoring, but in the absence of that alternative they may be acceptable.

One such approach would use a production function relationship to relate various input and output combinations to the emission rate. These could be estimated econometrically on the basis of initial sampling. Once these relationships were validated they could be used instead of direct continuous monitoring. The records on inputs and outputs would be used to estimate emission rates. These empirical estimating relationships could be subjected to periodic validation.

When new pollution control measures are adopted by the emitter, the relationships would be reestimated.[35] What is sacrificed by this approach is the monitoring of circumstances such as the temporal deterioration of the equipment or deviations from normal operating practice (for example, accidents or shutting the equipment off).

Anderson and his coauthors (1977) also address the question of whether the responsibility for the initial burden of monitoring should fall on the discharger or the pollution control authority. Appealing to the income tax system as a viable example they suggest that a self-reporting system complemented by punitive fines for false reports could play a significant role. As to the constitutionality of such a system they point out that it has survived constitutional challenges in at least one (unidentified) state (p. 93, n. 1).

In the longer run several promising technologies (e.g., lasers) are on the drawing board for remote sensing.[36] The development of this capability would significantly increase the feasibility of a self-reporting system by providing a random, surprise audit capability for the control authority. No doubt the implementation of control systems for which such capabilities would be useful would hasten the development of such systems by providing an obvious market for them.

Monitoring, however, is only the first of the requirements for an effective enforcement strategy. The second is the legal authority to deal with noncom-

---

[35] Anderson et al. (1974, pp. 103–04) point out that this method is already being used for water pollution monitoring in both Germany and Czechoslovakia.

[36] For an extensive discussion of the possibilities see Staff of Research and Education Association (1978, chap. 18, pp. 49–65).

pliance including effective sanctions. The most complete treatment of the legal issues is found in Irwin and Lirhoff (1974), although some pertinent insights are contained in Anderson et al. (1977), deLucia (1974) and Jaffe et al. (1978).

There are several legal constraints which might potentially inhibit an effective enforcement policy. The first is federal preemption. If there is a federal preemption, then states may not venture into what becomes, with preemption, a national jurisdiction. On this issue Irwin and Lirhoff (1974) conclude:

The states and their subdivisions are not preempted from adopting disincentives applicable to other than new motor vehicles, aircraft or the use of fuels or fuel additives (p. 75).

The general constitutional constraints on state action are derived from the Fourth, Fifth and Fourteenth Amendments to the U. S. Constitution. The general impression given by Irwin and Lirhoff's extensive review is that a carefully conceived economic disincentive program (such as a transferable discharge permit system) would survive constitutional tests.[37]

Effective enforcement also requires the availability of legal sanctions which can be invoked when emitters fail to comply with the terms of the permits. Noncompliance can occur either when the emitter delays in installing the pollution control procedures and equipment or when the conditions of the permit are exceeded during the normal operation of these procedures and equipment either intentionally or unintentionally.

The most complete early work on the economics of air enforcement of air pollution control policies can be found in Downing and Watson (1973). They conduct a theoretical and (limited) empirical

analysis of the air pollution control enforcement system as it currently exists and as it might exist if alternative approaches were pursued. Unfortunately, they do not consider transferable discharge permit systems, but they do introduce a number of ideas which are relevant to such a system.[38]

One of these ideas concerns the type of sanction to be employed. Downing and Watson (1973, p. 26) point out that there are three basic types of sanctions which can be imposed: (1) cease and desist orders, (2) financial penalties of various types and (3) a shutdown order. The first of these typically is insufficient since it provides no penalty for past noncompliance and therefore weakens the compliance incentives in the future. The shutdown order suffers the opposite kind of problem; it is such a harsh response that emitters do not expect it to be invoked. It does not represent a credible threat.[39]

Most attention therefore has focused on using some sort of monetary penalty to induce compliance. These penalties can take several forms. They can be predetermined or determined after the fact and tailored to the circumstances of the permit violation. They can represent a charge per unit of emissions, more or less

---

[37] One of the legal issues involving a TDP system involves the constitutionality of particular permit designs. These issues are reserved for the next section which discusses permit design.

[38] One of the other useful insights of this document (p. 6) is the demonstration that an effective control policy is not very sensitive to the accuracy of monitoring devices as long as the measurement error is known. They conclude that research and development money should be spent on extending the number of pollutants which can be monitored rather than improving the accuracies of existing systems.

[39] A good example of sanction overkill is the repeated failure of the EPA to stand firm in the face of repeated successful demands of the automobile manufacturers to delay the implementation dates for the new car emission standards. See Grad et al. (1975, p. 375).

continuously imposed, or a lump sum compensation imposed in infrequent judicial proceedings.

Spence and Weitzman (1978) focus on the predetermined charge-per-pound sanction. They recommend that the predetermined fee be set equal to the "marginal damages at the level of effluents prior to the imposition of regulation" (Spence and Weitzman 1978, p. 213). Thus the emitter is assessed a penalty which is crudely related to the damages that would be caused if the conditions of the permit are violated. The emitter knows precisely what the unit cost of noncompliance will be prior to its occurrence.

Quite a different approach has been developed in what is known as "the Connecticut plan." This plan (described by Clark 1978 and Drayton 1978), which has currently been adopted by Connecticut, relates the noncompliance penalty imposed to the costs of pollution control avoided by the emitter who is not in compliance. This approach obviously is designed to remove any financial advantages to the emitter from noncompliance.[40]

The philosophical differences between these two approaches can be summarized as being an argument between optimal noncompliance and complete compliance. The Spence and Weitzman approach attempts to relate compliance costs to the damages incurred. When compliance costs are higher than the damages, noncompliance will be the expected (even desired) outcome. The Connecticut plan, on the other hand, attempts to insure that noncompliance will never be in the interest of the emitter.

The former approach has much to recommend it; it can be handled administratively with a minimum of cost. As Anderson et al. (1977, pp. 123–28) point out,

however, it is not clear that the courts would allow the administrative imposition of a charge as being consistent with the due process requirement of the constitution. There are two issues involved. The first deals with the constitutionality of executive (as opposed to judicial) imposition of noncompliance fees while the second involves the procedural safeguards involved in various forms of assessment. These are important issues because they have a drastic effect on the rapidity with which the system can be enforced and the amount of resources that would have to be committed to enforcement.

A court determination that these fees were criminal penalties would prompt the need for procedural safeguards that present serious obstacles to an effective enforcement policy. Thus the feasibility of this approach rests with the court system and remains to be established. Unfortunately as long as the statutes require the "Connecticut plan approach" that test will not be forthcoming.

III. DESIGNING PERMIT ENTITLEMENTS

Taxonomy of Permit Entitlement Choices

There are three basic permit designs discussed in the literature. In this section these designs will be described and the differences among them clarified. In the next section the relationships of these various designs to the achievement of the two goals will be discussed. The succeeding sections will then treat other matters which impinge on the permit design.

---

[40] This is the basic approach that the 1977 amendments require. The amendments require the penalty to be set at "the economic value of noncompliance." See 91 Stat 715.

The major difference among permit designs concerns whether the permits are differentiated or not. An undifferentiated discharge permit (UDP) is one which conveys the same entitlement to emit to every emitter. Transfers among emitters take place on a one for one basis. Total emissions are unaffected by the trade.

In contrast to this stands the various types of differentiated permits. The first, an ambient differentiated permit (ADP) allows each permit holder to discharge one standardized unit of emissions in the air for each permit held.[41] The standardization procedure is specific to the receptor location. A number of key receptor locations are identified and the air quality control region is divided into a number of source zones. A separate permit system is created for each of these key receptor sites. A source has to have sufficient permits in each of these markets to justify its emissions. The trades within each zone take place on a one for one basis. The standardization procedure defines the exchange ratio for interzonal trades. It is worth noting that this standardization procedure has to be accomplished only once when the system is established. This contrasts sharply with current offset policy procedure which has to be reaccomplished every time a trade is proposed.[42]

Yet it is true that a separate permit system for each key receptor site is more administratively cumbersome than a single permit market. Therefore some attempts have been made to define a single permit market which will have desirable allocative properties. One of these, the emission discharge permit (EDP), was mentioned by Rose-Ackerman (1977) and developed in more detail by Montgomery (1972). Its legal implications are explored in Jaffe et al. (1978). It allows a fixed number of permits to be allocated to each of several zones within an airshed. These permits are freely transferable on a one for one basis within zones, but no transfers are permitted between zones. This system represents an attempt to gain the advantages of a single market while maintaining the cost reduction possibilities to be derived from a spatially differentiated permit system. As we shall see in the next section it is possible only in a limited sense.

Properties of Alternative Permit Designs

As Baumol and Oates (1975) and Hamlen (1977) have shown formally, under competitive conditions the UDP system can fulfill the ECE criterion. The transferability of the permits insures that they will be reallocated by the market until the marginal costs of control are equalized across emitters. This in turn guarantees that the responsibility for achieving the aggregate emission target will be allocated among emitters so as to insure that the target is met with a minimum commitment of pollution control resources. This conclusion is an important one because it implies that a UDP system is a cost-effective means of dealing with global pollutants.[43]

As Tietenberg (1973a) has demonstrated formally, a UDP system will not fulfill the ACE criterion. Furthermore

---

[41] The standardization procedure is described in some detail in Tietenberg (1974, pp. 288–89). It is a quantity standardization procedure. Anderson et al. (1979, pp. 7–11) suggest a price differentiation process. Mathematically they are equivalent, but administratively they have rather different properties.

[42] Since legal challenges can arise every time a new standardization procedure is proposed (which is with every proposed trade under the current system), this could be a significant advantage of the ADP system.

[43] The Rand Corporation is currently engaged in the examination of the feasibility of a TDP market for fluorocarbons.

the magnitude of the cost increase from using a UDP system to achieve an ACE criterion is apparently substantial (Tietenberg 1978a) and there is reason to believe that the cost advantage of differentiated permit systems over the undifferentiated systems will be even larger in the future than it is currently. This is due to the effect of each system on location incentives. With a UDP system the location of the emitter within the airshed does not affect its pollution control cost while for the differentiated permit systems it does. With differentiated permit systems emitters have the incentive to consider the air quality impacts of their location decision while with UDPs they do not. The long run cost-effective achievement of the ambient standards requires that both relocation and the adoption of pollution control equipment be considered as ways to reduce the costs of achieving the standards. While clearly no wholesale relocation of emitters should or will take place, for some emitters, particularly new entrants to the area, the choice of location may greatly affect both their costs and the costs of other emitters in the area.[44]

As Montgomery (1972) has demonstrated both the ADP permit design and the EDP permit design can fulfill the ACE criterion at any point in time, but in order to do so the EDP system requires much more information on the part of the control authority and this particular design allows much less flexibility to the control authority in its capacity to influence the distribution of the costs. The ADP design allows the control authority to choose any initial allocation of permits and therefore to use this allocation as a means of choosing an agreeable distribution of the costs. Regardless of what initial allocation is chosen, because of the complete transferability of the permit across zones, the ultimate allocation will be cost-effective. This cost-effective allocation of permits will imply a particular distribution of emissions across the airshed. If the control authority were to allocate the permits in an EDP system so that the initial allocation was consistent with this distribution of emissions, then that EDP system would fulfill the ACE criterion as well.

However, two aspects of this conclusion are worth pointing out. First, for the initial allocation to fulfill the ACE criterion in the EDP system the control authority would have to know the control costs for every emitter in the airshed. This information is not required for an ADP system to be cost-effective. Secondly, even if the control authority possessed that rather unrealistically large amount of information it would have only *one* distribution of permits which would be consistent with the ACE criterion (as opposed to the infinite number of ADP initial allocations which are consistent with the ACE criterion).[45] Even in the rather unlikely event that the control authority was able to discover this one initial EDP allocation it would have no flexibility in trying to distribute the costs fairly.

All of these differentiated systems are based upon source zones. The number of these zones and their size is one variable which can be manipulated by the control authority when the system is designed. Since the administrative complexity of the system rises with the number of

---

[44] See, for example, the empirical work presented in Kohn (1974).

[45] It would be pure coincidence if this unique allocation coincided with the minimum disruption allocation discussed above. Therefore it is not likely that an EDP system could fulfill the ACE criterion while simultaneously guaranteeing no emitter would be worse off by leaving the current system. The ADP system can simultaneously achieve those goals.

zones, it is tempting to use very large zones (and hence only a few of them) to characterize a particular geographic area. This temptation should be resisted, however, since an increase in the size of the zone will introduce the possibility that "hot spots" or high pollution levels will occur within the zone, since one-for-one transfers within zones could result in a clustering of emitters. On the other hand, in the EDP system smaller zones reduce the transferability of permits, a prime source of cost reduction.

These types of permit designs should not be considered as either/or choices. It may well be that for small sources a UDP system is appropriate when these sources are relatively ubiquitous. In this case the additional complexity of spatial differentiation is not warranted. On the other hand, for large sources, where their location makes a big difference, one of the differentiated permit systems could be used.[46]

Incorporating the Temporal Dimension

Although it would be possible to define an aggregate emission standard with a time dimension the use of an aggregate emission standard as the policy target normally implies that the temporal pattern of emissions is not important and, therefore, is of no consequence in the design of the permit. This is not true when an ambient standard policy target is pursued using an ADP system. Both the emission intensity of contributing sources and meteorological conditions have a temporal component that can be integrated into the design of an ADP system. Several options exist for the manner of integration, each incurring quite different public control costs. In general, the most complete control over the system requires the largest outlay of

funds; therefore, some trade-off between completeness and minimizing costs appears in order.

For the integration of a changing meteorology into the control process a continuum of options is available, at one end of which would be a control policy based on current meteorological conditions. Here the standardization coefficients (which determine the exchange rate between emission in one zone and emission in another) would have to be changed at least daily. Although this policy would increase the degree of control over the process in the sense that air-quality forecasts would be based on actual rather than annual average conditions, it would also incur significant and, at present, even prohibitive costs both for the public and private sectors. Public costs would be high because of the necessity for continuously updating the table and transmitting this information to the firm; private costs would be high because it would be very difficult to plan production schedules.

The opposite end of the control spectrum in terms of temporal complexity, a system of controls that does not vary over time, is much easier to implement, administer, and enforce. Such constant control is implemented by using annual average meteorological conditions in constructing the table of equivalences and choosing a level of control such that even under somewhat adverse conditions the desired concentration level would not appreciably exceed the standard. The problem with this approach is that it contains no special provisions for handling those rare, but devastating, occasions when thermal inversions prevent

---

[46] This multiple-tiered approach in which a UDP system for small emitters is combined with an ADP approach for large emitters was suggested to me by Barbara Ingle in a telephone conversation.

the normal dispersion and dilution of the pollutants. The damage that can occur on these occasions to humans, animals, materials, and vegetation is so severe as to warrant a special procedure for such days. One solution is to establish a two-tier kind of control in which the permits allow two different emission rates—one for days characterized by thermal inversions and one for all other days. The emission rates allowed during thermal inversions would be substantially less.

One other element in the temporal nature of the meteorological processes can be integrated into the design of an ADP: the regular periodic nature of wind patterns. The conditions that go into the derivation of the equivalency remain relatively constant within seasons but tend to change as the seasons change. Since accurate records are kept by the weather bureau for wind patterns, it is possible to derive a separate set of equivalences for each season. With this table of equivalences defined the administrator could either design specific permits to be sold in four seasonal markets, or sell an annual permit that would be adjusted for each season. As long as these permits were transferable among emitters, the allocation could change over the seasons without the need for different permits in each season.

One benefit of incorporating meteorological seasonality into the design is that it provides incentives to emitters to shift their emissions to time periods and locations where they will do the least harm. Consider a hypothetical firm, moving into a metropolitan area, that emits only during the winter months because of a large space-heating need then. If a seasonal ADP market is operative, the firm will have an incentive to locate where its costs per unit of emissions is the lowest. According to the design of

the market, this location is where winter emissions do the least harm in terms of meeting the desired air-quality standards. On the other hand, if a nonseasonal, annual ADP market is in existence, the firm will still locate where the ADPs are the cheapest, but this will no longer coincide with the location where *winter* emissions do the least damage. Rather it will coincide with the location where a steady emission rate all year would do the least damage. Because of the quite large differences in seasonal wind patterns, these locations will not generally coincide.

Another temporal pattern exists for emissions. Our society concentrates its economic activity into the daylight hours, resulting in higher concentrations during the daytime. The impact of this on the design of the ADP is that if the permits were made specific to an eight-hour period then presumably the price of the permit during the 12:00 A.M.–8:00 A.M. period would be much lower than those for the two other shifts. This would provide an incentive for emitters to shift their emissions to this period, partly offsetting some existing incentives in the opposite direction, such as the higher wage rates required for the "graveyard" shift. If this incentive were successful in shifting some production into these hours, a beneficial result may be observed on automobile-produced pollutants as well. The portion of the rush-hour traffic representing the workers affected by this shift would be channeled into a less active period.

The current legislation would appear to rule these refinements out. The Clean Air Act Amendments of 1977 state unambiguously:

The degree of emission limitation required for control of any air pollutant under an applicable implementation plan under this title shall not be affected in any manner by . . . any other dispersion technique. . . . For the purposes of this section, the term "dispersion technique" includes any intermittent or supplemental control of air pollutants varying with atmospheric conditions.[47]

Unlike many other characteristics of an expanded TDP system this refinement, if implemented, would require new legislation.

Duration of the Permit

The TDP could be designed either to entitle the owner to discharge a specified emission rate into the air in perpetuity or for some finite time period. In theory, either option is acceptable, because their transferability would insure that they were reallocated in response to a changing environment. New firms would bid them away from firms who no longer had need for them, and the government would have to set up the auction market only once if the TDPs were perpetuities.

David et al. (forthcoming), deLucia (1974) and Tietenberg (1974) argue for a limited term permit on the grounds that it provides more administrative flexibility in changing the allowed level of pollution. However, even with perpetual rights the control authority can increase or decrease the level of pollution by entering the market as a buyer of existing permits or a seller of new permits. The increased flexibility to the control authority offered by a limited duration permit is offset by an increase in the uncertainty of the emitter.[48]

The upshot of the argument is that it probably makes sense for the control authority to issue permits with different terms. Those emitters who feel the need for a long-term permit and are willing to pay for that security can purchase those permits. Conversely those polluters who

prefer lower cost permits and less security can purchase the shorter term permits. Staggered expiration dates would allow the control authority an annual option to increase or decrease the number of permits in the market.

Coverage of Pollutants

Administratively it would be desirable if all the different types of pollutants in a particular airshed could be handled within the context of a specific market. This would be possible with the aggregate emissions target as long as the target is defined in terms of equivalent emissions. Macintosh (1973, pp. 66–68) suggests this approach. He suggests choosing the weights for determining the equivalency on the basis of some historical contribution to pollution in the local area.

In general, however, a single market with temporally fixed weights is not consistent with the cost-effective achievement of the ambient air quality standards. The cost-effective weights will necessarily change over time since some pollutants will be cheaper to clean up than others and will be subject to different growth pressures due to the entry and exit of emitters. The differential costs of control faced by emitters would, with a single multipollutant market, cause the permits to be used for pollutants which were expensive to control, rather than for others. When some historical basis for choosing the weights is used, this will lead to a situation in which the ambient air quality standard for those pollutants which are less expensive to control will be met easily, but the standards for the

---

[47] 91 Stat 721.

[48] Anderson et al. (1979) also suggest that governments lease the permits for limited durations rather than sell them.

other pollutants will be violated. To compensate for this the control authority would have to reduce the number of permits until the ambient air quality standards were met for all pollutants, but this would generally result in a very expensive, excessive control of the other pollutants. The problem with this approach is that the final amount of each pollutant in the air is determined by the emitters; the control authority will have lost the capability to control each pollutant. The retention of that capability, in the absence of detailed knowledge on control costs, requires a separate market for each pollutant.[49]

Administrative Feasibility of ADP and EDP Systems

The ADP system and some versions of the EDP system require the use of air diffusion modeling. The ADP system uses these models to define the exchange rate between the permissible emission rates allowed by a permit in any two zones. This is essential to insure that regardless of which emitters use the permits the air quality standards will be met. It is the mechanism which makes complete transferability compatible with the achievement of the air quality standards at minimum cost. The EDP system may use it to define an initial allocation of permits which is compatible with the air quality standards. If the state of the art in diffusion modeling is not equal to the task, then, by default, alternative "second best" strategies become attractive.

The adequacy of the state of the art of diffusion modeling for policy purposes cannot definitively be affirmed; reasonable people may disagree. Yet, on balance, for nonreactive and relatively nonreactive pollutants it does seem adequate, particularly in light of the tremendous reductions in cost which can be achieved with its use. For highly reactive pollutants such as volatile organic compounds this conclusion clearly is not warranted.

The most common perception of those who know nothing about diffusion modeling is that the task is hopeless because air flow is such a complicated dynamic process. To be sure it is a complicated process, but annual average air flow patterns show a striking regularity—and annual averages are all that are needed to implement the ADP and EDP systems![50] The diffusion models which predict annual averages are, on the whole, quite accurate.[51] They are already authorized by the Environmental Protection Agency for use in developing state implementation plans and more important for our purposes they are authorized for defining permissible offset trades.

Administratively the ADP system requires only one type of information to implement it over and above that required to implement a UDP system—a matrix defining the amount of emissions a permit allows depending on where the emissions are injected into the airshed. The data requirements for deriving this matrix are available in urban areas and rural areas served by an airport.[52] Because of the stability of annual averages from year to year, the matrix need only be constructed once. The cost of the exercise, therefore, when compared to

[49] It is worth noting that the offset policy explicitly rules out interpollutant trades. See 44 FR 3284, §4.A.3. (16 January 1979).

[50] The method for relating annual averages to the standards is given in Tietenberg (1974, p. 285).

[51] A survey of the state of the art in air diffusion modeling is provided in Staff of Research and Education Association (1978, chap. 2). Some evidence on the accuracy of these models is also provided in Grad (1975, pp. 220–24).

[52] The data requirements are described in Grad (1975, pp. 217–19).

the saving to be achieved by conducting it, is trivial.

The ultimate test is, of course, whether the state of the art is sufficiently well-developed to withstand effective legal challenge. Local areas would invoke these permit systems under their general police power to protect public health and welfare. The legal challenge, if it were to be mounted, would probably question whether an ADP or an EDP system violated the equal protection clause of the Constitution. The equal protection clause precludes discriminating among persons or organizations in the same classification. The question of interest is whether or not a differentiated permit system would violate this requirement. If the classification system is not arbitrary or capricious and is consistent with some broader social purpose it can survive. While no direct precedent of the ability of a differentiated permits system to meet this test exists, it does appear that air dispersion models are now sufficiently well developed to allow them to serve as the basis for an acceptable classification system within an airshed. Pierce and Gutfreund (1975), for example, conclude that air dispersion models are likely to be admissible provided they are used by trained professionals and are based upon the best available data and methodology.[53] Similarly, for the EDP system Jaffe et al. (1978, p. 95) conclude:

The developing law in land-use controls does not yet provide all the answers to these problems, but it does suggest that careful implementation of an emission quota strategy can escape constitutional challenge except in extreme cases.

It is much less clear that the models used to forecast the long range transport of pollutants and those forecasting the concentrations of the highly reactive pollutants would be similarly admissible.

IV. EMPIRICAL RESULTS

There are only four studies of an empirical nature which are directly concerned with the effect of implementing a transferable discharge permit system.[54] Two of these, deLucia (1974) and David et al. (forthcoming), deal with water pollution while Macintosh (1973) and Anderson et al. (1979) deal with air pollution. Other studies by Atkinson and Lewis (1974) and Teller (1970), while not explicitly related to TDP systems, have some pertinent insights. All of these studies deal with hypothetical computer simulations of what would happen if a transferable discharge permit system were implemented; none deal with the results of an actual implementation.

The Macintosh study deals with the implementation of a hypothetical air rights market in the New Orleans Air Quality Control District. The permits in the study cover particulates, sulphur oxides and carbon monoxide. A single market is used to control all three by defining the permit entitlement in terms of equivalent tons; the equivalency among the three pollutants is determined by a temporally constant weighting system which is based on the historical importance of the three pollutants in the area. The simulation covers a ten year period.

In the simulation the price of the permit rises from $542 per equivalent ton in 1970 to $803 per equivalent ton in 1980. The supply of permits is fixed and the price rise mainly represents the hypothesized growth in demand from the arrival of new emitters and expansion of production by old ones. Since the per-

---

[53] Interestingly enough, the legal issues for spatially differentiated air pollution emission charges are more complicated. See Tietenberg (1978*b*).

[54] A number of other studies are currently under way, but were not available as this was written.

mits are auctioned off, the market generates $1,768,052 in revenue for the control authority.

It should also be noted what this simulation does not do. It does not simulate an ambient standard TDP system; it is rather a simulation employing an aggregate emission standard. Since the study did not include any air dispersion modeling, it is not clear that the simulation results were in compliance with air quality standards.

The UDP system could, of course, be used to pursue air quality goals in spite of the fact that it would not be cost-effective; that is, an optimum would not be achieved. It is legitimate, however, to ask how much costs are increased by using this administratively simpler system. If they are not raised very much, then the simpler system might be preferable, all things considered.

Two studies which specifically examine this question focus on different pollutants in different cities. In the first study using data for St. Louis, Atkinson and Lewis (1974) compared the costs of meeting a particulate ambient standard at several receptor locations with a UDP and ADP system.[55] They concluded that the cost saving which would result from substituting the ADP system for the UDP system was approximately 50% (p. 237). While we have a right to be skeptical of the exact magnitude of this differential, it is certainly large enough to suggest that spatial differentiation of the permits is important.

Similar results were achieved by another recent study (Anderson et al. 1979) focusing on nitrogen dioxide concentration in Chicago. Using a short-term ambient standard of 250 mg./m.[3] the study found that the least cost allocation would result in an annualized cost of $21 million. A control system based upon

RACT (reasonably available control technologies) plus a least cost solution to achieve the additional emission reduction necessary to meet the standard would result in an annualized cost of $44 million. A roll-back strategy that ignores the location of the emitters was estimated to require 90% control for all sources, which resulted in an annualized cost of $254 million, or some twelve times the least cost solution (chap. 5, p. 34). This study reinforces the notion that spatial differentiation of the permits results in significantly lower costs and that enforcing some minimum threshold of control for all sources causes a not insignificant increase (in this case about 100%) in those costs.

These studies leave two empirically important questions unanswered. (1) What is the cost saving from substituting an ADP system for an EDP system when various rules of thumb are used to make the initial allocation of permits among the zones? (2) What is the optimum number of receptor locations and emitter zones for an airshed?

The first question is important in establishing a cost comparison between the EDP and ADP systems. Conceptually it is not clear whether an EDP system is more or less cost-effective than a UDP system. The EDP system incorporates locational considerations which certainly have the effect of reducing costs. On the other hand, in contrast to the UDP system the EDP system does not allow interzonal transfers, which eliminates a major source of cost reduction. The relative importance of these two factors is an empirical question resolvable only through an appeal to the data.

---

[55] Strictly speaking their comparison was for emission charge structures, but the results are valid for the comparison made above as well.

The second question is important because it will determine the complexity of
the ADP system. In an ADP system the
number of separate permit markets required to cost-effectively achieve the
ambient standards at several receptor locations is equal to the number of receptor
locations. Therefore the more receptor
locations that are needed to adequately
characterize an airshed the more complex (and administratively difficult) the
system.

Another early study examined a question of some relevance to TDP system
design. Using data for Nashville, Tennessee, Teller (1970) compared the costs
of a temporally constant form of control
with a scheme which tailored the degree
of control to the forecasted conditions.
The study indicated that forecasted control was substantially less expensive than
constant abatement. This provides important empirical support for having a
TDP system which differentiates between episode control and normal control as discussed in section III. The question of whether a two-tiered system, as
proposed, is superior to a three- or four-
tiered control system involving successively more stringent degrees of emission
reduction awaits further empirical work.

While there have been a number of
studies accomplished for water pollution,[56] only two have dealt specifically
with the use of a TDP system. The first,
conducted by deLucia (1974), used the
Mohawk River in New York as the focal
point of the study. The permit system
was designed to influence the polluting
behavior of eight municipalities. Some of
the most significant conclusions of the
study are:

The permit systems, by and large, provide for
waste treatment at a cost level that is less than
one-half of 1% greater than the least-cost method
(p. 119).

This applies to an aggregate emission
type target as no differentiated permits
were considered.

Permit costs are significant; they are often the same
order of magnitude as treatment costs (p. 119).

This makes the method of initial allocation very important as a way to distribute
costs.

The constraint that all polluters must achieve a
level of waste reduction equivalent to secondary
waste treatment markedly limits the efficiency
savings that can be achieved by a permit system
(p. 121).

The effectiveness of a TDP system is
undermined when that system is complemented by additional regulations
compelling some high minimum level of
treatment on the part of all emitters. This
is a very relevant concern for air pollution since the Clean Air Act mandates
minimum standards for certain large,
new or modified emitting production
facilities. Unless firms are able to violate
those standards the cost advantages of a
TDP system may significantly diminish.

Hence at the high minimum level of waste reduction called for in this model, total costs are simply
not affected by the model's reallocation of waste
treatment among discharges (p. 122).

When very high degrees of control are
necessary, the cost reductions which can
be expected from a TDP permit system
are smaller because all emitters have to
control their emissions extensively and
there are fewer possibilities for trading
emissions reductions.

The dangers of market distortions and manipu-
lations are greater with fewer participants. It is encouraging to note, however, that with the eight

---

[56] See Kneese (1977, chap. 7) for a careful review.

414   *Land Economics*

cities of the Mohawk there appears to be little danger of price manipulation by a single polluter (p. 131).

This provides empirical support for the proposition advanced earlier that the anticompetitive effects of a TDP system are not likely to be very important in general.

The final study, conducted by David et al. (forthcoming) concerns the use of a TDP system to control phosphorous influent into Lake Michigan. This simulation includes 52 large polluters and is designed mainly to show how a particular initial distribution of permits (allocating permits in proportion to average daily flow) affects the distribution of the permit costs. The study shows this particular allocation would result in a small net financial gain (from selling the permits) to most permit holders, a large net gain to one (Milwaukee) and large financial losses (from buying additional permits) to another (Kenosha). No attempt was made in this simulation to use an ambient standard so the effects of differentiated permits were not considered.

V. CONCLUSIONS

The use of a transferable discharge permit control system would appear to offer real potential for achieving our air quality goals at a minimum cost both in allocating the offsets in nonattainment regions and in allocating the PSD increments in attainment regions. The current reforms embodied in the bubble concept and the offset policy represent substantial moves in this direction, but they contain important restrictions on transferability. How much is accomplished by these reforms in practice will only be determined after we have sufficient experience with them to see how constraining these restrictions turn out to be.

Similarly, it would be a mistake to ignore the host of issues which must be resolved if the current system is to be replaced by a regularized TDP market. In this paper I have tried to survey those issues and what we know both theoretically and empirically about them. What has emerged is not only a menu of approaches which can be taken, but also a sense that the general approach can be usefully tailored to individual circumstances.

It has also been pointed out that the ultimate success of the current reforms as well as any potential further reforms will depend on future events at present only dimly perceived. These include legal issues, the development of monitoring instrumentation and further empirical work toward defining a balanced compromise between administrative complexity and cost-effectiveness.

The theoretical and empirical case for transferable discharge permit systems is extensive and persuasive; it is also incomplete. Simulations are suggestive, not conclusive; many small details that could serve to undermine the central strengths of the proposal are omitted by assumption from these simulations. We should not let the enthusiasm built up by these initial positive results blind us to potential flaws as TDP systems move closer to becoming operational.

References

Anderson, Frederick R. et al. 1977. *Environmental Improvement through Economic Incentives.* Baltimore, Md.: Johns Hopkins University Press.
Anderson, Robert J., Jr. et al. 1979. *An Analysis of Alternative Policies for Attaining and Maintaining a Short Term No₂ Standard.* Report to

the Council on Environmental Quality. Princeton, N.J.: MATHTECH, Inc.

Atkinson, Scott E. and Lewis, Donald H. 1974. "A Cost-Effective Analysis of Alternative Air Quality Control Strategies." *Journal of Environmental Economics and Management* 1 (Nov.): 237–50.

Barnett, Andy H. and Yandle, Bruce, Jr. 1973. "Allocating Environmental Resources." *Public Finance* 28(1): 11–19.

Bath, C. R. 1978. "Alternative Cooperative Arrangement for Managing Transboundary Air Resources along the Border." *Natural Resources Journal* 18: 181–98.

Baumol, William J. and Oates, Wallace E. 1975. *The Theory of Environmental Policy*. Englewood Cliffs, N.J.: Prentice-Hall, Inc.

Bohm, Peter. 1972. "Estimating Demand for Public Goods: An Experiment." *European Economic Review* 3(2): 111–30.

Buchanan, James M. 1969. "External Diseconomies, Corrective Taxes and Market Structure." *American Economic Review* 59 (March): 174–77.

Clark, Edwin H., II. 1978. "Regulatory Strategies for Pollution Control: Comment." In *Approaches to Controlling Air Pollution*, ed. Ann Friedlander. Cambridge, Mass.: The MIT Press.

Clarke, E. H. 1971. "Multipart Pricing of Public Goods." *Public Choice* (Feb.): 17–33.

Cleveland, William S. and Graedel, T. E. 1979. "Photochemical Air Pollution in the Northeast United States." *Science* 204 (June): 1273–78.

Crocker, Thomas D. 1966. "The Structuring of Atmospheric Pollution Control Systems." In *The Economics of Air Pollution*, ed. Harold Wolozin. New York: W. W. Norton.

Dales, J. H. 1968a. "Land, Water, and Ownership." *Canadian Journal of Economics* 1 (Nov.): 797–804.

Dales, J. H. 1968b. *Pollution Property and Prices*. Toronto: University Press.

David, Martin H. et al. Forthcoming. "Marketable Effluent Permits for the Control of Phosphorous Influent into Lake Michigan." *Water Resources Research*.

deLucia, R. J. 1974. *Evaluation of Marketable Effluent Permit Systems*. Office of Research and Development, U.S. Environmental Protection Agency. Washington D.C.: Government Printing Office.

Downing, Paul B. and Watson, William D., Jr. 1973. *Enforcement Economics in Air Pollution Control*. U.S. Environmental Agency, EPA-600/5-73-014.

Drayton, William, Jr. 1978. "Regulatory Strategies for Pollution Control: Comment." In *Approaches to Controlling Air Pollution*, ed. Ann Friedlander. Cambridge, Mass.: The MIT Press.

Grad, Frank P. et al. 1975. *The Automobile and the Regulation of Its Impact on the Environment*. Norman, Okla.: University of Oklahoma Press.

Hamlen, William A. 1977. "The Quasi-Optimal Price of Undepletable Externalities." *The Bell Journal of Economics* 8 (Spring): 324–34.

Irwin, William A. and Lirhoff, Richard A. 1974. *Economic Disincentives for Pollution Control: Legal, Political and Administrative Dimensions*. U.S. Environmental Protection Agency, EPA 600/5-74-026 (July).

Jaffe, Martin et al. 1978. *Legal Issues of Emission Density Zoning*. U.S. Environmental Protection Agency, EPA 450/3-78-049 (September).

Kneese, Allen V. 1977. *The Economics of the Environment*. New York: Penguin Books.

Kneese, Allen V. and Bower, Blair T. 1968. *Managing Water Quality: Economics, Technology and Institutions*. Baltimore, Md.: Johns Hopkins University Press/Resources for the Future.

Kneese, Allen V. and Schultz, Charles L. 1975. *Pollution Prices and Public Policy*. Washington D.C.: The Brookings Institution.

Kohn, Robert E. 1974. "Industrial Location and Air Pollution Abatement." *Journal of Regional Science* 14 (April): 55–63.

Mar, B. W. 1971. "A System of Waste Discharge Rights for the Management of Water Quality." *Water Resources Research* 7 (Oct.): 1079–86.

Macintosh, Douglas R. 1973. *The Economics of Airborne Emissions: The Case of an Air Rights Market*. New York: Praeger Publishers.

Mishan, Ezra J. 1967. *The Costs of Economic Growth*. New York: Frederick A. Praeger.

Montgomery, David W. 1972. "Markets in Licenses and Efficient Pollution Control Programs." *Journal of Economic Theory* 5 (Dec.): 395–418.

Nulty, Peter. 1979. "A Brave Experiment in Pollution Control." *Fortune* 99 (Feb. 12): 120–23.

Pierce, D. F. and Gutfreund, P. D. 1975. "Evidentiary Aspects of Air Dispersion Modeling and Air Quality Measurements in Environmental Litigation and Administrative Proceedings." *Federation of Insurance Council Quarterly* 25 (Spring): 341–53.

Randall, A. et al. 1974. "Bidding Games for Valuation of Aesthetic Environmental Improvements." *Journal of Environmental Economic Management* 1 (Aug.): 132–49.

Rassin, A. David and Roberts, John J. 1972. "Episode Control Criteria and Strategy for Carbon Monoxide." *Journal of the Air Pollution Control Association* 20 (April): 254–59.

Roberts, Marc and Spence, Michael. 1976. "Effluent Charges and Licenses Under Uncertainty." *Journal of Public Economics* 95 (April/May): 193–208.

Rose-Ackerman, Susan. 1977. "Market Models for Water Pollution Control: Their Strengths and Weaknesses." *Public Policy* 25 (Summer): 283–406.

Rose, Marshal. 1973. "Market Problems in the Distribution of Emission Rights." *Water Resources Research* 5 (Oct.): 1132–44.

Scherr, B. A. and Babb, E. M. 1975. "Pricing Public Goods: An Experiment with Two Proposed Pricing Systems." *Public Choice* 23 (Fall): 35–48.

Spence, A. Michael and Weitzman, Martin L. 1978. "Regulatory Strategies for Pollution Control." In *Approaches to Controlling Air Pollution*, ed. Ann Friedlander. Cambridge, Mass.: The MIT Press.

Staff of Research and Education Association. 1978. *Modern Pollution Control Technology: Vol. 1, Air Pollution Control*. New York: Research and Education Association.

Teller, Azriel. 1970. "Air Pollution Abatement: Economic Rationality and Reality." In *America's Changing Environment*, eds. Roger Revelle and Hans H. Landsberg. Boston, Mass.: Beacon Press.

Tietenberg, Thomas H. 1973a. "Controlling Pollution by Price and Standards Systems: A General Equilibrium Analysis." *Swedish Journal of Economics* 75 (June): 193–203.

———. 1973b. "Specific Taxes and the Control of Pollution: A General Equilibrium Analysis." *Quarterly Journal of Economics* 87 (Nov.): 503–22.

———. 1974. "Design of Property Rights for Air Pollution Control." *Public Policy* 22 (Summer): 275–92.

———. 1978a. "The Quasi-Optimal Price of Undepletable Externalities: Comment." *The Bell Journal of Economics* 9 (Spring): 287–91.

———. 1978b. "Spatially Differentiated Air Pollutant Emission Charges: An Economic and Legal Analysis." *Land Economics* 54 (Aug.): 265–77.

Yandle, Bruce. 1978. "The Emerging Market in Air Pollution Rights." *Regulation* (July/August): 21–29.

[14]

JOURNAL OF ENVIRONMENTAL ECONOMICS AND MANAGEMENT 10, 346–355 (1983)

Transferable Discharge Permits and Economic Efficiency: The Fox River

WILLIAM O'NEIL, MARTIN DAVID,[1] CHRISTINA MOORE, AND ERHARD JOERES

Department of Economics, Colby College, Waterville, Maine 04901; Department of Economics, University of Wisconsin at Madison, Wisconsin 53706; Anderson–Nichols, Boston, Massachusetts; and Department of Civil and Environmental Engineering, University of Wisconsin, Madison, Wisconsin 53706.

Received September 31, 1981; revised December 1982

Recent emphasis on reforms of environmental regulation has led to suggestions for strategies which maintain environmental standards but allow the needed flexibility and cost effectiveness. The transferable discharge permit (TDP) is one such strategy for water pollution control recently adopted in Wisconsin. In this article, the potential for substantial cost savings from trading TDPs is demonstrated using data on the Fox River in Wisconsin. A simulation model of water quality (Qual-III) and a linear programming model of abatement costs determine the optimum pattern of discharge. Reaching that optimum from proposed pollution abatement orders is shown to be feasible. Varying conditions of flow and temperature can be accommodated using trade coefficients which can be accurately estimated through interpolation. The calculations demonstrate the value and feasibility of flexible regulations governing water pollution abatement.

I. INTRODUCTION

The Wisconsin Department of Natural Resources approved regulations in March of 1981 which allow dischargers to transfer permits by approved contracts. This makes the Fox River in Wisconsin the first body of water in the United States where cost savings in abatement may be achieved using transferable discharge permits. This paper addresses two of the concerns exposed in the course of discussions about whether or not to adopt this option.

The potential for more cost-effective regulation to modify strict control directives has been discussed in the economics literature starting with Crocker [1] and Dales [2]. The EPA has been actively discussing and developing such policies for air pollution control, but to date there has been no parallel concern in water pollution control. This paper documents the feasibility of using one option for increasing the cost effectiveness of water pollution regulation.

Although the economic efficiency of the market mechanism has been recognized in theory [3], and has been used for the control of air pollution, it has not been used as a water pollution control strategy in the United States prior to its adoption in Wisconsin. This paper provides an evaluation of transferable discharge permits based on a water quality simulation model of the Fox River (Qual-III) to determine water quality effects and a linear programming model to estimate cost effects. Similar studies of the Delaware Estuary were completed by Kneese and Bower [4] and by Ackerman *et al.* [5]. Although those studies did not explicitly evaluate

[1] To whom correspondence should be addressed: 1180 Observatory Dr., Madison, Wis. 53706.

transferable permits, many of the political obstacles to efficient pollution control that were discussed by Ackerman are addressed in the present paper. In particular, the case of the Fox River illustrates how a small number of governmental bodies were able to cooperate in the development of a cost-effective river basin management plan.

II. THE SETTING

The Wisconsin Department of Natural Resources (DNR) has classified the lower Fox River between Lake Winnebago and Green Bay as "water quality limited." This means that the assimilative capacity of the stream is inadequate to maintain water quality standards when industries and municipalities are discharging at the federal maximum uniform treatment requirements—best practicable treatment (BPT) for industries and secondary treatment levels for municipalities. The additional point source abatement needed to meet the water quality standards was handled initially by a central directive requiring proportionate reductions of effluent discharge (biochemical oxygen demanding wastes or BOD) starting from the federal uniform requirements for each discharger. The transferable permit comes into play once this initial allocation of daily pollution discharge has been made.

III. THE WATER QUALITY MODEL

Ten pulp and paper mills and four municipalities discharge effluent into a 22-mile reach of the lower Fox River. The natural effluent decomposition process uses available concentrations of dissolved oxygen (DO) in the stream; and under conditions of low flow and high temperature this process may cause the DO levels to fall below the water quality standard of 6.2 mg/liter.

As an aid in exploring alternative abatement strategies, the state water regulatory agency (DNR) developed a simulation model of the river which allows estimation of the relations between discharger and DO levels at various locations along the stream.

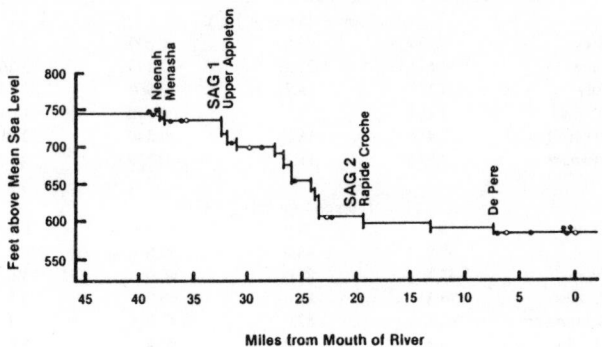

● Paper Mills
○ Sewage Treatment Plants

FIG. 1. Location of dams and dischargers on the lower Fox River.

The current version of the model, Qual-III, is a one-dimensional model that accounts for the most important factors influencing the levels, or profile, of DO in a flowing stream. The model simulates levels of DO, via two different rates of BOD decomposition, total phosphorus, organic nitrogen, ammonia, nitrates, nitrites, chlorophyll *a*, and sediment oxygen demand; it can be run in either a steady-state or a dynamic mode [6]. The accuracy with which Qual-III predicts DO levels given input data on flow, temperature, and BOD loadings was tested in several ways [7]. Comparison of Qual-III predictions with actual monitoring data and with the predictions of an ARIMA time-series model convinced both dischargers and regulators that the average prediction error was small enough for political acceptability.

Preliminary simulation analyses confirmed the observation that, because of the location of dischargers, dams, and pools in the lower Fox, effluent discharges cause two local minimums or "sag points" in the levels of dissolved oxygen. Figure 1 depicts the lower Fox showing the location of dischargers, dams, and sag points.

Any allocation of effluent limits which results in the meeting of water quality standards at those sags leads to acceptable water quality throughout the river. Economic analysis of feasible wasteload allocations (WLAs) entails estimation of a 2×14 matrix of linear impact coefficients H from the Qual-III model. H was generated by simulating a series of DO levels associated with increased individual effluent loadings and calculating the changes in the DO at the sag points. Sensitivity analysis confirmed the accuracy of using linear approximation to define the effluent/water quality relationship at different combinations of stream flow and stream temperature [8]. In this analysis linear relations among impact coefficients and flow and temperature were estimated using ordinary least-squares regression techniques. The appropriate model was chosen by examination of the forecast errors.

As Table I shows, historically there have been large variations in the flow and water temperature of the river. These variations cause the impact coefficients to vary

TABLE I

Flow[a] and Temperature[b] Data for the Lower Fox River (May 1 to October 31, 1934 to 1977)

Month	Mean	Maximum	Minimum	Standard deviation
		Flow data (cfs $\times 10^3$)		
May	5.596	23.6	1.200	3.783
June	4.621	21.3	0.598	3.268
July	3.142	16.2	0.660	2.146
August	2.283	8.1	0.138	1.018
September	2.452	18.0	0.544	2.013
October	2.843	18.2	0.530	2.123
		Temperature data (°F)		
May	58.3	78.0	42.0	6.0
June	69.9	83.0	50.0	4.9
July	75.7	87.0	66.0	3.6
August	74.3	87.0	60.0	3.9
September	65.8	82.0	47.0	5.3
October	54.3	70.0	40.4	5.6

[a]Measurements taken at the Rapide Croche Dam power station.
[b]Measurements taken at Appleton and the Bergstrom Paper Company.

significantly from day to day, as illustrated in Fig. 2 for one discharger. An additional complication is that each of the 14 dischargers has different impact coefficients because their wastes decay at different rates. A system which allows one discharger to offset another's pollution has to take these differences into account to be sure that the water quality standards are maintained under any configuration of permissible discharges and any set of flow and temperature conditions in the river.

These observations, together with the knowledge that individual abatement costs differ among dischargers, imply that a fixed central directive is unlikely to be the least-cost approach to maintaining minimum water quality.

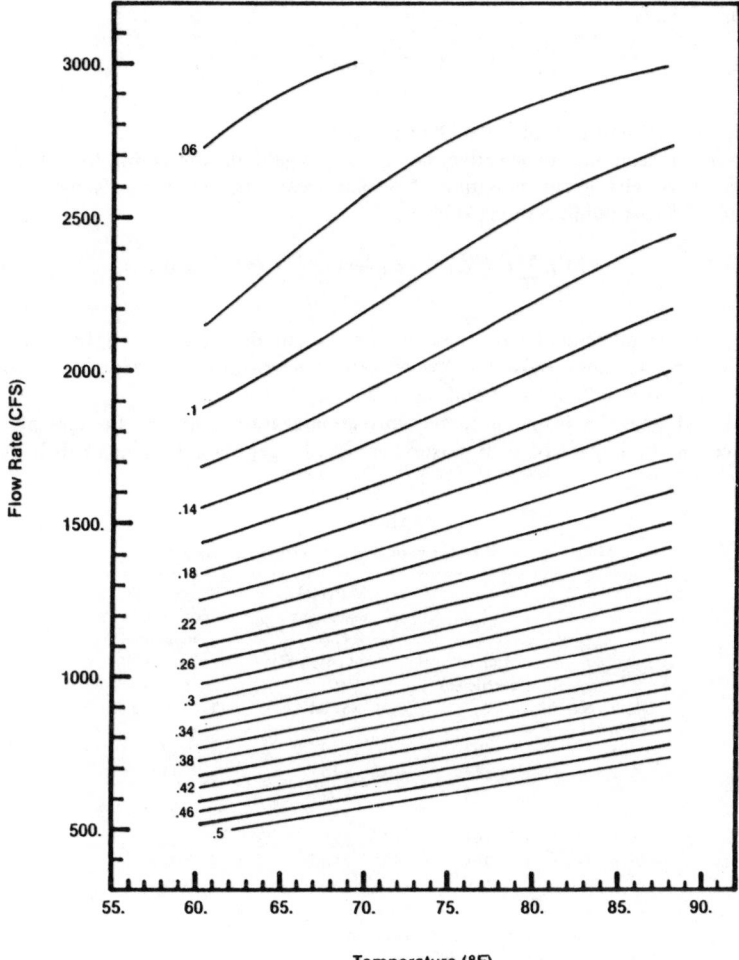

FIG. 2. $h_{31}(F, T)$, impact coefficient for discharger 3, sag 1.

IV. THE ECONOMIC MODEL

Having derived linear impact coefficients h_{ij} for the dischargers, the abatement problem can be characterized mathematically as follows. Let e_i^0 represent federal (BPT) discharge levels, X_i represent additional abatement in pounds of BOD, and q_j^S represent the quantities of DO available for assimilating the effluent at the sag points. The effluent demand for DO at sag j corresponding to federal BPT requirements is

$$q_j^D = \sum_i h_{ij} e_i^0 \tag{1}$$

Abatement, in addition to BPT, is needed if $q_j^D > q_j^S$. Any set of abatement activities X_i which yields

$$\sum_i h_{ij} X_i \geqslant \Delta q_j \equiv \sum_i h_{ij} e_i^0 - q_j^S \qquad \forall j \tag{2}$$

would be sufficient to achive the DO standard.

From an economic perspective, however, it would be preferable to induce an allocation of abatement activities X^* which solves the following "steady-state," constrained cost-minimization problem:

$$\underset{X_i}{\text{Min}} \sum_i C_i(X_i) \qquad \text{subject to (2) and } X_i \geqslant 0 \tag{3}$$

$C_i(X_i)$ is the abatement cost function for the ith discharger. This form of the problem implies that steady-state "worst case" stream flow and temperature conditions are used to determine H and the level of q_j^S [9].

Table II provides insight into the cost minimization problem. Because of differences in the impact of their wastes, one discharger (No. 3) is more than three

TABLE II

Marginal Cost of Increases in Dissolved Oxygen at Sag $j = 1$

Discharger	Impact[a] coefficient h_{i1}	Marginal abatement cost "end-of-pipe" C_i ($/lb)	Marginal cost of DO increase "at sag" C_i/h_{i1} ($/0.001 mg/l)
1	107	7.20	72
2	189	2.10	11
3	373	1.90[b]	5[b]
4	231	3.10	14
5	184	1.80	11
6	214	7.90	37
7	101	2.60	·27

Source. Moore [8, page 32]; O'Neil [9, page 67].

[a]For F, T values 950 cfs, 80°F.

[b]Plant is operating at maximum abatement capacity; the numbers shown in the table are costs for the last unit treated.

times more effective in achieving increased DO than an equal abatement by another (No. 7). In addition, marginal abatement costs differ among dischargers by a factor of four. As a consequence, the cost of increasing DO at the first sag point (the product of the physical impact and the marginal abatement cost) varies sevenfold across the dischargers. This is shown in column 3. (Column 3 is also the "shadow price" of pollution abatement generated from the linear programming problem. It shows that the most effective procedure to reduce abatement cost is to assign more abatement activity to discharger 5 and less to discharger 1, if possible.)

Montgomery [3] has shown that a properly specified market in effluent permits (or DO permits) can yield the least cost allocation as a competitive market equilibrium. The basic conditions of market operation are that all available DO must be allocated initially to permit holders in any feasible WLA scheme, and that subsequent trades of effluent permits must be adjusted according to the ratio of the seller's and buyer's impact coefficients so as to assure no net decrease in dissolved oxygen in the river. (The costs of contracting and supervising the market are assumed zero.) To bound the value of the market option in the case of the Fox River, H from Qual-III was incorporated into (2) and X^* minimizing (3) was determined. This analysis generated estimates of the total and individual abatement costs associated with the initial distribution of permits, by central directive, and with X^*.

Table III, part A, presents these cost results for various water quality standards and stream flow and temperature (F, T) conditions. Columns 3 and 4 list the total annual expenses, including capital costs, of achieving the water quality targets shown in column 1 under the flow–temperature conditions shown in column 2. For example, given a DO target of 6.2 ppm, a stream flow of 950 cfs, and water temperature of 80°F, annual expenditures of $16.8 million would be required with TDP trading allowed. Under the same conditions, the central directive, with no TDP market, would require expenditures of $23.6 million. Thus the TDP market could allow annual savings of about $6.8 million in this case for the Fox River. As can be seen in the table, the potential cost savings vary depending on the DO target and river conditions.

TABLE III

Abatement Cost (Annual Expense)

	Flow/ temperature (cfs/°F)	TDP market ($ million)	Central rule ($ million)
A DO target (ppm)			
2.0	950/80	5.4	11.1
4.0	950/80	10.3	16.1
6.2	950/80	16.8	23.6
6.2	1500/72	9.0	16.5
6.2	2500/64	2.3	6.8
B w/v^a			
0.95	950/80	17.0	23.6
0.90	950/80	17.2	23.6
0.85	950/80	18.0	23.6
0.80	950/80	19.3	23.6

^{a}DO target = 6.2 ppm, flow temperature 950 cfs, 80°F.

V. ADMINISTRATION OF A TDP MARKET

The potential value of TDPs has been demonstrated by the optimization. The problem is to implement a mechanism for trading when H varies. The problem can be divided into two parts: estimating H for any given flow and temperature condition and devising a simple mechanism to ensure that the constraint (2) is met.

Knowing that the estimation of H with Qual-III for the full range of possible river conditions (F, T) would be expensive for the dischargers, we approximated $H(F, T)$ by a cubic function

$$h_{ij}(F, T) = a_{ij} + b_{ij}F + c_{ij}T + d_{ij}F^2 + e_{ij}FT + g_{ij}F^3 \qquad (4)$$

The resulting equations fit the data well and showed no systematic forecast error when applied to the range of river conditions for which the approximation was estimated [8].[2] Table IV provides information on the residuals. The last two rows show that extrapolation to other conditions may be precarious.

Devising a mechanism to ensure that the constraint (2) is met is somewhat more complex. Let X_i^p represent the level of abatement entailed by the permit issued to the ith discharger before trading. The difference $(X_i^* - X_i^p)h_{ij}$ reflects the potential supply of DO due to i's activities at the jth sag when the term is positive and the potential demand when the term is negative. A viable sale under fixed F, T of $(X_i^* - X_i^p)$ to buyer k implies that k may decrease abatement by

$$\Delta X_k = (h_{ij}/h_{kj})(X_i^* - X_i^p) \equiv \mathrm{TC}_{ik}(X_i^* - X_i^p) \qquad (5)$$

TC_{ik} is the "trading coefficient" relating the two dischargers. It is clear from Eq. (4) that TC_{ik} is a rational polynomial and is easily computed from 12 coefficients. Figure 3 depicts trading coefficient level curves for a pair of dischargers.

TABLE IV

$|h_{ij}(F, T) - \hat{h}_{ij}(F, T)|$ Residuals from the Polynomial Approximation to Qual-III

Flow/temp[a]	Number of observations within residual ranges (mg/l DO)				
	0.00–0.0020	0.0021–0.0040	0.0041–0.0060	0.0061–0.0100	> 0.0101
	A. Within sample space				
1200/68	8	2	1	2	1
1200/76	7	2	1	2	2
2000/68	2	4	2	1	5
2000/76	0	4	4	2	4
	B. Outside sample space				
3000/68	1	0	1	1	11
3000/76	0	0	1	1	12
Total	18	12	10	9	35

[a] Flow in cfs/temperature in °F.

[2] A multiperiod optimization model was also developed to analyze the case of a time-varying H and q_j^s associated with changes in F, T. See O'Neil [9].

A strategy for trading might then entail one of two alternatives: (A) *Daily computation* of (4) by buyer and seller to assure that DO offsets are equal; (B) *Periodic computation* in which the level of trading is constrained by choosing $TC_{ik} \equiv TCM_{ik}$ for the *likely* river conditions. Augmenting k's discharges will then not exceed the assimilative capacity under those conditions. Choice of an appropriate boundary trading coefficient depends on the damage expected from violation of the DO target. Since no explicit damage function for the Fox River exists, we present only an illustrative analysis of the implications of periodic computation of trading coefficients.

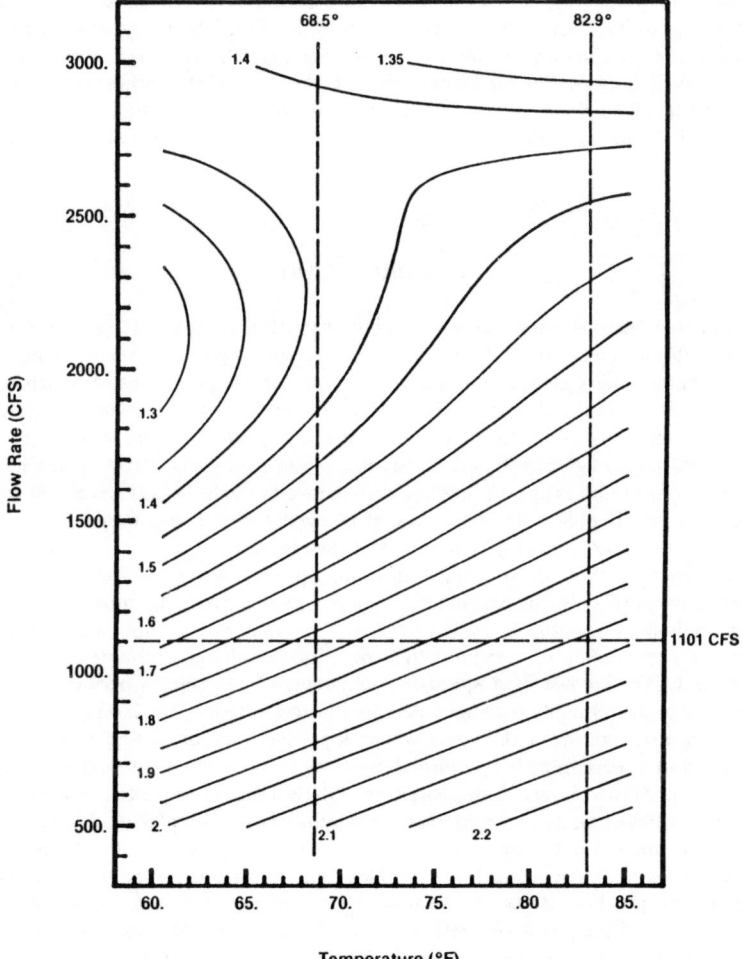

FIG. 3. $TC_{3,5}$, Trading coefficient when discharger 5 buys from discharger 3. The dotted lines bound an area corresponding to flows exceeding the 7-day low flow in 20 years and temperatures expected to occur with a probability of 0.95.

354   O'NEIL ET AL.

Moore [8] has demonstrated that given the appropriate information, TCM_{ik} can be found and provides a computational algorithm to determine its value on a monthly basis. However, the limit on trading imposed by TCM_{ik} will prevent realization of the full benefits of X^*. Some insight to this problem comes from a recomputation of the programming problem on the assumption that buyers have an impact $vh_{kj}, v > 1$, and sellers have an impact $wh_{ij}, w < 1$. Then $TCM_{ik} \equiv (w/v)TC_{ik} < TC_{ik}$. While w/v can be chosen to transform TCM_{ik} into $\overline{TCM_{ik}}$, it is not the case that those values will define the $\overline{TCM_{i'k'}}$, for another pair of traders i', k'. Hence the solution of the program for a particular v, w is only suggestive of the limitation imposed by periodic computation.

Table III, part B illustrates the cost effects of imposing adjustments of trading coefficients by the factors $w/v = \{0.95, 0.90, 0.85, 0.80\}$. These adjustments clearly decrease the cost savings achievable by trading permits. However, even a safety margin of 20% ($w/v = 0.80$) leaves the cost of the market solution substantially lower with TDPs than the initial centrally determined allocation. These results suggest that the market mechanism may be useful even in restricted trading scenarios.

VI. CONCLUSION

This paper demonstrates that water pollution control strategies allowing transfers between dischargers can be both cost effective and capable of maintaining any desired water quality standard. It shows that transferable permits can be used even in situations where the characteristics of the effluent differ between dischargers and the river conditions vary. The conclusion is that a regulatory system which does not permit and encourage transfers is substantially and needlessly costly. Transferable permits appear to be as appropriate for national water quality as offsets and bubbles have been for air policy. Those interested in regulatory reforms would do well to encourage the development and adoption of these options.

To summarize, there is no obstacle to trading permits *even when* the permit itself varies in proportion to the assimilative capacity of the river. The most straightforward method of trading, a daily trade, requires that buyer and seller make an elementary calculation to determine their permitted discharge. Variants of the daily trade might be the sale of a specified percentage of the seller's permit. Such an arrangement would imply that the seller would need to reduce the level of the initial permit by a fraction while the buyer would apply the relevant trading coefficient to that fraction to determine his permitted discharge. Since both buyer and seller need to review permitted levels of discharge on a daily basis in any case, trading adds flexibility without an excessive increase in administrative complexity. Although use of a permit market does imply increased information requirements for dischargers, conversations with managers have revealed that in the relatively simple market structure of the Fox River transactions costs are not expected to be large in comparison with the potential abatement cost savings. For other cases the design of the market may not be so simple. Clearly the choice of trading rules and particularly the size of the trading area will crucially affect the cost of administering and using the market. Since the potential transactions costs associated with the Fox River market were not estimated explicitly, the Wisconsin DNR wrote the relevant administrative rules so that dischargers have the option to trade permits or not as they see fit. The optional nature of the system was sufficient to neutralize most political arguments opposing the experiment (see Acknowledgments).

ACKNOWLEDGMENTS

We gratefully acknowledge financial support of the Wisconsin Sea Grant Institute, and the cooperation of the Wisconsin Department of Natural Resources in assessing Qual-III.

REFERENCES

1. T. D. Crocker, "The Structuring of Atmospheric Pollution Control Systems", *in* "The Economics of Air Pollution", (Harold Wologin, Ed.), Norton, New York (1966).
2. J. W. Dales, "Pollution, Property and Prices", University Press, Toronto (1968).
3. W. Montgomery, Markets in licenses and efficient pollution control programs, *J. Econ. Theory* 5, 395 (1972).
4. A. V. Kneese and B. T. Bower, "Managing Water Quality: Economics Technology and Institutions", John Hopkins Univ. Press, Baltimore (1968).
5. B. Ackerman *et al.*, "The Uncertain Search for Environmental Quality", Free Press, New York (1974).
6. D. Patterson, "Water Quality Modelling of the Lower Fox River for Wasteload Allocation Department", Wisconsin Department of Natural Resources, Madison (1980).
7. M. Gregory, "Qual-III Model used as a Management Tool", Department of Civil Engineering, University of Wisconsin, Madison (1979).
8. C. Moore, "Implementation of Transferable Discharge Permits When Permit Levels Vary According to Flow and Temperature: A Study of the Fox River, Wisconsin", Department of Civil and Environmental Engineering, University of Wisconsin, Madison (1980).
9. W. B. O'Neil, "Pollution Permits and Markets for Water Quality", unpublished Ph.D. dissertation, University of Wisconsin, Madison (1980).

[15]

JOURNAL OF ENVIRONMENTAL ECONOMICS AND MANAGEMENT 10, 112–124 (1983)

An Empirical Analysis of Economic Strategies for Controlling Air Pollution*

EUGENE P. SESKIN

Bureau of Economic Analysis, U.S. Department of Commerce, Washington, D.C. 20230

ROBERT J. ANDERSON, JR.

MATHTECH, Inc., Princeton, New Jersey, 08540

AND

ROBERT O. REID

Energy and Environmental Analysis, Inc., Arlington, Virginia, 22209

Received April 21, 1981; revised March 1982 and October 1982

In evaluating current environmental protection policy, economists often note that current regulations are more costly than necessary to meet environmental quality standards. While the *a priori* case is strong that current regulatory approaches are resulting in higher-than-necessary costs to attain environmental standards, there is relatively little empirical evidence to support this claim. The purpose of this paper is to supply some of the missing evidence by presenting the results of one study that assesses some of the potential savings associated with implementing economic, rather than command-and-control, regulatory approaches to abate one type of air pollution in one region of the country. Specifically, the paper examines the costs of meeting a prospective short-term standard for nitrogen dioxide under a range of alternative emissions control strategies for stationary sources of nitrogen oxide emissions in the Chicago Air Quality Control Region. The alternative strategies that are considered range from those that might result under current regulatory policy to those that economic policy approaches (such as emissions charges or marketable permits) are designed to implement. The analysis shows that the most efficient program of emissions controls may be more than an order of magnitude less costly than current regulatory strategies, and that economic approaches have additional advantages over more conventional regulatory approaches.

1. INTRODUCTION

In their evaluation of current environmental protection policy, economists have sometimes noted that current regulations are far more costly than strictly necessary to meet environmental quality standards.[2] This conclusion derives, in part, from the

---

*Correspondence should be addressed to: Seskin, BE-52, Bureau of Economic Analysis, U.S. Department of Commerce, Washington, D.C. 20230.

[1] A more detailed and technical presentation of the analysis may be found in [2]. In preparing that study, the authors benefited from the patient and constructive criticism from a number of people including David Tundermann, the Technical Monitor, as well as Allen Basala, Tayler Bingham, Alan Carlin, Alex Christofaro, Toby Clark, John Hoffman, Barbara Ingle, Skip Luken, Willard Smith, Paul Stolpman, and Larry White. The study was subsequently used by EPA together with additional work in [10]. The empirical work reported in the present paper reflects additions made by EPA in the Report to Congress; however, it should not be inferred that EPA necessarily endorses the conclusions expressed in the present paper. Any errors are, of course, the responsibility of the current authors. The opinions and conclusions expressed in this paper are not necessarily those of the organizations with which the authors are affiliated.

[2] See, for example, Kneese and Schultze [5].

ECONOMIC STRATEGIES FOR AIR POLLUTION CONTROL   113

observation that regulations often fail to exploit opportunities for polluters to reduce costs while achieving required emissions standards.

The causes adduced for this failure are many. For example, the procedural requirements of current regulatory approaches result frequently in protracted seriatim (source-by-source) negotiations. The standards ensuing from this process are unlikely to reflect a careful balancing of abatement costs with abatement effectiveness. Additional impediments may be imposed politically by legislated environmental laws, especially in cases where little scientific support was available. As a result, sources may be required to adopt specific emissions standards based on proven (or potential) technologies and processes. This, in turn, leaves sources with little incentive to exceed mandated requirements.

While the *a priori* case is strong that current regulatory approaches are resulting in higher-than-necessary costs to attain environmental quality standards, there is relatively little empirical evidence to support this claim. One previous study undertaken by Atkinson and Lewis [3] employed data for the St. Louis Air Quality Control Region (AQCR) to look at alternative strategies to control particulate emissions from 27 major sources of air pollution. Using a somewhat simplified version of the methodology applied in this study, it was found that an air quality control strategy representative of those developed by states in preparing State Implementation Plans (SIPs) was six to ten times as costly as a strategy designed to achieve a prescribed ambient particulate standard at minimum cost.

The purpose of this paper is to supply further empirical evidence of how economic measures could be used to control stationary-source air pollution emissions. Specifically, the paper examines the cost of meeting a prospective "short-term" standard for nitrogen dioxide (NO_2) under a range of alternative emissions control strategies.[3] An "emissions control strategy" refers to any plan specifying emissions limitations to be achieved by the specific sources in a region. The alternative strategies that are considered range from those that might result under current regulatory policy to those that economic policy approaches are designed to implement. The results are strikingly similar to those of Atkinson and Lewis [3]: The most efficient program of emissions controls may be more than an order of magnitude less costly than controls corresponding to current regulatory strategies. Furthermore, economic approaches have several inherent advantages over more conventional regulatory approaches for implementation.

2. METHOD OF ANALYSIS

In proceeding with the analysis, the first question to be answered is: What effect does a control strategy have on ambient concentrations of NO_2? In addressing this question, it is taken as given that an acceptable plan must be effective in meeting and maintaining an ambient short-term, 1-hour standard for NO_2.[4] The second

---

[3]Short-term here refers to an air quality standard based on pollution concentrations averaged over a period of one hour. The EPA has been evaluating alternative short-term, 1-hour NO_2 standards in the range of 250 to 1000 $\mu g/m^3$ because of potential adverse health effects from corresponding exposures.

[4]It should be noted that the results of this analysis will differ according to the standard that is finally set (see below). Furthermore, if the environmental objective was maintenance and attainment of a *long-term* standard based on annual average concentrations, the conclusions would be expected to change because elevated concentrations of NO_2 during short averaging periods occur only sporadically.

question to be addressed is: What effect does the choice of strategy have on the costs of controlling nitrogen oxides? In answering this question, primary emphasis is on the costs incurred by polluters to control their emissions; however, consideration is also given to the costs incurred by polluters to administer their programs and to monitor their emissions as well as costs incurred by the public sector to administer, monitor, and enforce programs.

The Analytical Model

The starting point of the analysis of plans for the control of stationary-source emissions of nitrogen oxides is an examination of alternative emissions control strategies and their effects on the control expenditures necessary to achieve a specified ambient short-term, 1-hour NO_2 standard. Basically, the approach used for this exercise involves the application of a mathematical programming model to the problem.

The specific type of mathematical programming model adopted for the analysis was an integer programming model. This model is basically a variation of what is known in operations research as the Knapsack Problem.[5]

The basic elements of the programming model are as follows:

- Emissions—$E_{i_k} \geqslant 0$ representing nitrogen oxide emissions of the ith source using control technology level k.
- Cost functions—$C_{i_k}(E_{i_l}) \geqslant 0$ representing the costs of controlling emissions at the ith source using control technology level k.

Given these elements, the model estimates the total technological costs of emissions controls across all N_s sources:

$$\sum_{i=1}^{N_s} C_{i_k}(E_{i_k})$$

and the corresponding 1-hour ambient concentrations of NO_2 at each of N_r receptors:

$$\sum_{i=1}^{N_s} d_{i_k,j} E_{i_k} \quad j = 1,\dots, N_r,$$

where $d_{i_k,j}$ is the contribution of the ith source (with control technology level k in place) of nitrogen oxide emissions to concentrations of NO_2 at the jth receptor.

Using this notation, the least cost optimization problem can be characterized as:

$$\text{minimize} \sum_{i=1}^{N_s} C_{i_k}(E_{i_k})$$

$$\text{subject to} \sum_{i=1}^{N_s} d_{i_k,j} E_{i_k} \leqslant Q \quad j = 1,\dots, N_r,$$

---

[5]See, for example, Senju and Toyoda [7], Toyoda [8], and Zanakis [12].

ECONOMIC STRATEGIES FOR AIR POLLUTION CONTROL   115

where $Q \geqslant 0$ represents the short-term NO_2 air quality standard that must be met at each of N_r receptors.

For each strategy analyzed, the model simultaneously produces two types of estimates. It computes the total costs of emissions control of nitrogen oxides for all sources on an annual basis. This provides a means for comparing strategies on the basis of these costs. At the same time, it calculates the 1-hour ambient NO_2 concentrations that would result at each receptor. This provides a means for comparing the strategies on the basis of effectiveness in reducing pollution.

The Data

The analysis was performed using data characterizing the Chicago Air Quality Control Region (AQCR) which represents an area approximately 150 by 80 kilometers and includes the following counties: Cook, Lake, Dupage, McHenry, Kane, and Will. Chicago was selected not only because data were available, but also because peak 1-hour NO_2 levels in Chicago were among the highest concentrations observed in any urban area of the United States [9, pp. 22–27].

Because only four continuous monitors of nitrogen oxides existed at the time of the study in the Chicago AQCR, it was necessary to develop an air quality assessment model to evaluate further the extent of the short-term NO_2 problem in the region. For this purpose, a multiple point- and area-source model known as RAM was used.[6] To implement, the model requires data on point sources, area sources, mobile sources, and meteorological conditions.

Point-source information for the Chicago AQCR was obtained and augmented with data from EPA's National Emissions Data System (NEDS) point-source subfile and from the Illinois EPA.[7] For each point source, data included: location, level of nitrogen oxide emissions and associated activity (capacity of unit, hours of operation per year), and characteristics of emissions point (stack height and diameter, exhaust gas temperature and volume). When required data were unavailable, default values typical of normal operating practice were used. Area-source data on small stationary sources emitting less than 10 pounds per hour of nitrogen oxides and mobile-source data primarily on automobiles were apportioned to 634 five-kilometer-square grid cells and entered into the area-source subroutine of RAM. Meteorological data on wind direction, wind speed, stability class, and mixing height were obtained from the National Weather Service and covered stations located in Greenbay, Peoria, Flint, and Dayton.

In addition to the above information, receptor locations were selected to "monitor" the impact of nitrogen oxide emissions across the Chicago AQCR. Their locations were difficult to determine because the pollution concentration at any point is a complex function of meteorological parameters, source locations and

---

[6]RAM is an EPA-approved, Gaussian steady-state model capable of predicting short-term ambient concentrations of relatively stable pollutants from multiple point and area sources. Since NO_2 is primarily a secondary pollutant formed by oxidation of nitric oxide (NO), a dynamic model of NO_2 formation was developed and used in conjunction with RAM to predict nitrogen oxide concentrations at receptors due to point sources and to translate them into NO_2 concentrations.

[7]Specifically, 472 point sources in 1975 were "updated" to 534 sources in 1984. "Point source" here is equivalent to a source classification code (SCC) source. Thus, several "point sources" may be found in a given plant. Since EPA deemed 1984 as the earliest possible date for implementing a short-term NO_x control strategy, EPA "updated" the 1975 source inventory to represent 1984 conditions; see [10, p. A2].

emissions, source overlaps, and so on. Several preliminary analyses revealed the presence of two distinct types of point sources: (1) large plants with tall stacks such as power plants, and (2) plants with a large number of smaller sources with short stacks such as steel mills and refineries. It was found that the diffusion characteristics of emissions from the second category were similar to those of area sources and that together these sources were the dominant cause of high short-term NO_2 concentrations in Chicago. Thus, for the final analyses, 200 high-impact receptors selected by RAM, along with approximately 400 other receptors "blanketing" the region were used.

Finally, information on specific nitrogen oxide control technologies and their associated costs was needed. EPA has identified roughly three hundred separate source categories that emit nitrogen oxides. Nine such categories were sufficient to characterize the important point sources in the Chicago AQCR. These were:

1. Utility Coal-fired Boilers
2. Utility Oil- and Gas-fired Boilers
3. Industrial Coal-fired Boilers
4. Industrial Oil- and Gas-fired Boilers
5. Gas Turbines
6. Large Internal Combustion Engines
7. Industrial Process Units
8. Nitric Acid Plants
9. Municipal Incinerators

For purposes of the analysis that follows, the control technologies applicable to these sources can be categorized in terms of *combinations* of the following techniques: combustion process modification, fuel modification, removal of nitrogen oxides from stack gases (flue gas treatment), and alternative combustion processes. The costs of implementing these controls as well as their effectiveness in terms of reducing emissions of nitrogen oxides were estimated by using data from a number of sources. Information on source size was used to estimate capital costs, while information on source utilization (annual hours of operation) was used to estimate operating and maintenance costs.[8] It is important to note that most of these data were based on engineering analyses of hypothetical plants with only limited "field" experience; hence, the actual cost-effectiveness of these control technologies could vary by a wide margin when applied to individual sources.

3. COMPARING CONTROL STRATEGIES

The relative efficiency (measured in terms of annual emissions control costs) and effectiveness (measured in terms of resulting ambient concentrations) of four basic emissions control strategies were compared. The strategies were:

1. No Control Baseline—which considers only those emissions controls already in place.

---

[8] The interested reader is referred to chapter 2 of [2] for further details.

ECONOMIC STRATEGIES FOR AIR POLLUTION CONTROL   117

TABLE 1

Analysis of Alternative Emissions Control Strategies for Chicago

Strategy	Number of sources controlled	Number of receptors in violation of $250 \mu g/m^3$ standard	Areawide point-source emission rate reductions (percent)	Annual control costs (millions of dollars)
No Control Baseline	0	36	0	0
SIP (State Implementation Plan)	472	0	21	130
Least Cost	100	0	3	9
Source Category Emissions Controls	472	0	18	66

2. SIP (State Implementation Plan)—which requires similar categories of major polluting sources to meet specific technology-based uniform levels of emissions control.

3. Least Cost—which establishes emissions limits by source based on each source's control costs and impact on ambient air quality.

4. Source Category Emissions Controls—which establishes uniform emissions limits for each source *category* consistent with the air quality objective.

The results of the comparison of these strategies are reported in Table 1.

No Control Baseline

To analyze this case, the model was run under the assumption that no *new* emissions controls were put in place. That is, the 1975 source inventory characteristics updated to 1984 conditions (see Fn. 7) were adopted.[9] As can be seen from Table 1, 36 of the receptor locations used in the final analysis indicated potential violations of a $250 \mu g/m^3$ short-term, 1-hour NO_2 standard. Since no new emissions controls were added it was assumed that no further reduction in nitrogen oxides emissions would take place and no additional costs would be borne under this strategy.

SIP (State Implementation Plan)

This strategy, which simulates the "traditional" approach to pollution control,[10] applies the highest level of emissions control to *all* sources in the three source

---

[9] Presumably, these characteristics account for any existing pollution controls required to ensure attainment of the current *annual* standard for ambient concentrations of NO_2.

[10] If EPA promulgates a short-term NO_2 standard, many existing State Implementation Plans (SIPs) would have to be revised. Such revisions would involve state regulations prescribing emissions limitations for specific source categories and timetables for compliance. Under the Clean Air Act, states are allowed nine months after a standard is issued to develop their plans, which must demonstrate attainment within three years. Until the area attains the standard, the applicable emissions regulation for an existing source is termed Reasonably Available Control Technology (RACT) and for a new source it is termed Lowest Achievable Emissions Rate (LAER) achieved in practice for that source category, or the most stringent emissions limitation contained in any SIP (whichever is more stringent).

categories that were the major stationary-source polluters in Chicago. The three source categories were: industrial coal-fired boilers, industrial oil- and gas-fired boilers, and industrial process units. Table 1 indicates that for this simulation, controls were placed on 472 sources in these categories, and that these controls were sufficient to attain the ambient standard at all receptor locations. It can also be seen that areawide point-source emissions rates would be reduced by 21% under this strategy. The incremental costs associated with implementing SIP (over and above the No Control Baseline) were estimated to be $130 million per year.

Least Cost

The Least Cost strategy was found by using the programming model described in Section 2 to find a set of emissions controls that simultaneously minimize control costs and meet the short-term 1-hour NO_2 standard at all receptor locations. By definition, under the Least Cost strategy, no receptors would be in violation of the 250 $\mu g/m^3$ standard. Furthermore, as seen in Table 1, only 100 of the point sources would require emissions controls *over and above* those controls associated with the No Control Baseline. These emitters were all from the three most polluting source categories noted above: industrial coal-fired boilers, industrial oil- and gas-fired boilers, and industrial process units.[11] It is also interesting to note that a reduction of only 3% in the areawide emissions rates would be sufficient to attain the short-term standard at all receptor locations. Finally, it can be seen that the annual costs associated with the Least Cost strategy were estimated to be only $9 million more than the No Control Baseline.

Source Category Emissions Controls

This strategy requires the application of a uniform set of emissions controls across all sources in a particular source category. As such, it circumvents the need for the source-by-source emissions limitations necessary to implement the Least Cost option and represents a relatively sophisticated use of current regulatory planning methods. The emissions control level specified for a given source category was that control level—for example, dry selective catalytic reduction (flue gas treatment)—required to ensure that no emitter in the class would violate the short-term, 1-hour ambient standard at any receptor.[12] Again, the three source categories requiring controls were: industrial coal-fired boilers, industrial oil- and gas-fired boilers, and industrial process units. As defined, under this strategy all receptors would be in compliance with the short-term, 1-hour NO_2 standard. The reduction in areawide emissions rates was estimated to be 18% and the total control costs were estimated to be $66 million annually over and above the No Control Baseline (see Table 1).

---

[11] It should be stressed that this does not mean that other sources were not *contributing* to violations of the short-term, 1-hour standard, only that it was not cost-effective to control those sources.

[12] Note, this differs from the SIP strategy in that it does not require that the most stringent control level be applied to each source category in question.

ECONOMIC STRATEGIES FOR AIR POLLUTION CONTROL   119

Summary of Findings

The preceding analyses demonstrate that abatement strategies designed to exploit differences in sources' emissions control costs as well as associated meteorological-dispersion characteristics are significantly less costly than those that do not account for such factors. For example, the results for Chicago indicate that a Least Cost strategy is less than one-tenth as costly as a strategy that reflects a more traditional regulatory approach (SIP) and less than one-seventh as costly as a strategy that represents a relatively sophisticated version of current regulatory approaches (Source Category Emissions Controls). In absolute terms, a policy that would lead to the adoption of a scenario approximating the Least Cost strategy to meet a short-term, 1-hour NO_2 standard could save more than $100 million annually in technological control costs in the Chicago Air Quality Control Region alone.

4. IMPLEMENTATION: POLICY INSTRUMENTS AND RELATED ISSUES

It would be premature to conclude that the less costly strategies described would necessarily be superior *in practice* to more traditional regulatory approaches. This follows from the fact that the policy instruments needed to implement the less costly strategies may be unavailable because of legal or political constraints, or may be so costly to administer as to offset the potential savings in emissions control costs. One category of policy instruments—emissions charges—can be examined briefly to shed more light on these issues.[13] In doing so, alternative emissions charge plans will first be described. This will be followed by an examination of informational requirements, their associated costs, and some legal considerations.

Alternative Emissions Charge Plans

The results of a mathematical programming analysis of the type discussed above can be used to formulate emissions charge schemes. In particular, charges were set at the minimum amounts required to ensure that the ambient standard would be achieved at all receptors when the sources acted in their economic self-interest to minimize the sum of annual control costs plus charge payments. It should be noted that the charges were applied to emissions *rates* rather than simply to emissions. This is necessary because a charge scheme based on total emissions would not ensure attainment of a 1-hour standard since sources could reduce their charge liabilities simply by reducing their hours of operation without reducing their *rate* of emissions. The resulting source-by-source charge levels (and the associated annual liabilities for charge payments) were found to vary considerably by source. Total annual liabilities for the charge payments amounted to $4 million or almost 50% of the total control expenditures estimated under the Least Cost option.

---

[13] No explicit consideration is given here to a system of marketable emissions permits for implementing efficient control strategies. However, such policy instruments were analyzed in [2, Chapter 7] and in [10], and were shown to have many favorable attributes and in some ways were thought to be easier to implement and superior to emissions charge systems.

120   SESKIN, ANDERSON, JR., AND REID

TABLE 2

Effects of Alternative Charge Systems for Chicago

Plan	Number of sources controlled	Areawide point-source emissions rate reductions (percent)	Annual control costs (millions of dollars)	Annual charge payments (millions of dollars)	Annual control costs + charge payments (millions of dollars)
Least cost (source-by-source) charge levels (see text)	100	3	9	4	13
Uniform charge levels ($15,800 per year per pound per hour)	534	84	305	414	719
Source category charge levels[a]	472	18	66	89	155

[a] Industrial coal-fired boilers = $15,800 per year per pound per hour; industrial oil- and gas-fired boilers = $15,300 per year per pound per hour; and industrial process units = $3500 per year per pound per hour.

The marked differences in charge levels and liabilities together with the preceding comparison of control strategies reaffirm that a system based on uniform treatment of sources or even uniform treatment by source classification is not consistent with the implementation of an efficient control program. Nevertheless, it is recognized that there may be practical difficulties in implementing a system in which "seemingly similar" sources are treated differently.[14]

In order to more fully explore the "excess" control costs associated with establishing more uniform charge systems, two alternative schemes were examined. Under the first system, denoted the Uniform Charge plan, a single charge level was levied on all sources. The magnitude of the charge was set at the lowest amount that would ensure compliance with the short-term, 1-hour NO_2 standard at all receptors. That amount was equal to $15,800 per year (per pound of nitrogen oxides per hour).

Under the second system, designated the Source Category Charge plan, three different charge rates were set, one for each of the three source classes that were controlled under the Least Cost strategy.[15] The magnitudes of these charges were set equal to the highest *average* annual control costs (per pound of nitrogen oxides per hour) in each source category under the Least Cost option. The resulting charge levels were $15,800 per year (per pound of nitrogen oxides per hour) for industrial coal-fired boilers, $15,300 for industrial oil- and gas-fired boilers, and $13,500 for industrial process units.

Table 2 presents the results of implementing these alternative schemes together with the basic results from the Least Cost Charge plan (described above). As can be seen, the Uniform Charge plan is associated with estimated nitrogen oxide emissions

[14] For example, it is quite conceivable that the Least Cost strategy would require two plants producing competing brands of the same product to meet substantially different emissions limitations because their locations (and impacts on ambient air quality) differed.

[15] The reader will note similarities between the Source Category Charge plan and the Source Category Emissions Control strategy discussed above.

rate reductions of more than 80% below the levels corresponding to the Least Cost Charge plan, but estimated annual emissions control costs exceed the costs under the Least Cost Charge plan by almost $300 million; annual charge payments are $410 million greater. Under the Source Category Charge plan, emissions rates are reduced by approximately 15% below the levels corresponding to the Least Cost Charge plan but estimated annual emissions control costs are about $57 million greater than those associated with the Least Cost Charge plan and annual charge payments are about $85 million greater. Thus, while the more uniform plans do reduce nitrogen oxide emissions rates substantially below emissions rates under the Least Cost Charge plan, these reductions are exceedingly costly and represent overcontrol in that all figures are based on minimum charge levels necessary to ensure attainment of the short-term, 1-hour NO_2 standard. At the same time, the Least Cost Charge plan appears to impose the smallest *overall* burden on sources (and ultimately society).

Informational Requirements, Associated Costs, and Legal Considerations

As alluded to above, it is sometimes suggested that despite possible Control cost savings associated with economic approaches to pollution control, implementation costs of such approaches would more than offset the potential savings. Therefore, it is useful to explore the feasibility and costs of implementing these approaches.

The Appendix details estimates for the range of administration, monitoring, and enforcement (AME) activities required to implement a regulatory system and a charge system in Chicago. There it is shown that the costs directly attributable to the administration, monitoring, and enforcement of a charge system to control stationary sources of nitrogen oxide emissions are of the same order of magnitude as the costs associated with implementing an effective regulatory policy.[16] The main reason for this is that effective regulation is likely to involve more investigation, negotiation, and litigation than would an equally effective incentive system. At the same time, it is recognized that existing legislation may need to be amended explicitly to allow implementation of such incentive systems. Nevertheless, it does not appear that legal considerations pose serious barriers to the implementation of economic approaches to pollution control such as emissions charge systems. While such approaches and the requisite supporting legislation represent a somewhat new regulatory framework and, as such, have not been fully tested in the courts, a thorough examination of the possible legal bases for implementing these types of economic inventive systems led one study to the conclusion that "[m]any different sources of government power could be invoked to legitimatize the legislature's imposition of charge plans,..." [1, p. 144].

5. CONCLUSIONS

The quantitative analysis of emissions control strategies for Chicago shows that approaches designed to account for differences in sources' incremental costs of

---

[16]While the cost estimates forming the basis for this conclusion are, at best, approximate, it is unlikely that further refinement would change the qualitative results.

controls and incremental contributions to ambient pollution concentrations can achieve a short-term ambient NO_2 standard at significantly lower costs than strategies that do not account for these differences. While acknowledging some of the practical difficulties in implementing such strategies as well as legal and political considerations, these problems do not appear to be insurmountable.

The analysis also suggests that emissions charge plans can provide profit-and-loss incentives to firms sufficient to induce the degree of emissions controls required to attain the short-term NO_2 standard in an economically efficient manner. Furthermore, a charge system provides an effective stimulus to the development and application of new emissions control technology. This, too, is an important practical advantage of the emissions charge approach. It is especially apparent if one recognizes that in the simulation study of Chicago, the emissions control technologies required to meet a short-term, 1-hour NO_2 standard of 250 $\mu g/m^3$ were technologies that are only *projected* to become available (at the earliest) between 1981 and 1985. Clearly, efficient and effective environmental policy must provide incentives for technological development, and economic approaches—in the form of emissions charges or marketable emissions permits—do exactly this. Taken as a whole, then, the magnitude of the potential cost savings associated with simulating such a system in only one region, together with the attributes just noted, appear to provide adequate justification for further experimentation and analysis of economic approaches to control environmental pollution.

APPENDIX: ADMINISTRATION, MONITORING, AND ENFORCEMENT ESTIMATES FOR THE CHICAGO AQCR

To effectively implement the economic strategies described above, the regulatory authority must know sources' emissions rates, the impact of these emissions on ambient air quality, the effects of abatement controls on emissions, and the costs of these controls.[17] One of the most important aspects concerning these informational requirements is the ability of existing monitoring techniques to provide adequate and reliable data. It appears that technically adequate nitrogen oxide emissions monitoring systems are currently available at a cost that is considerably smaller than the total costs of abatement associated with meeting a short-term, 1-hour NO_2 standard of 250 $\mu g/m^3$.[18] This is true even under the Least Cost emissions control strategy in which the average annual control cost per controlled source is approximately $90,000 ($9 million divided by 100; see Table 1). Under the conservative assumption that each controlled source would require a separate monitoring system,[19] annual monitoring costs were estimated to be on the order of $25,000 per source.

It was also noted that under any policy approach to pollution control, sources will bear the burden of some costs of monitoring and reporting their emissions. Thus, one would not expect the costs of these activities to differ very much between a

[17]While it has been discussed in the theoretical literature that a regulatory agency could achieve air quality objectives under a "standard-and-charges" program without knowledge of sources' control costs by adjusting charge rates until the desired objectives were achieved (see, for example, [4, p. 144]), in practice, the rigidities imposed by economic, political, and legal constraints make this seem unlikely.

[18]For details see [2], especially Section 2.5.

[19]The assumption is conservative in that many sources are co-located and could therefore share some or all parts of the monitoring system.

ECONOMIC STRATEGIES FOR AIR POLLUTION CONTROL 123

TABLE 3

Administration, Monitoring, and Enforcement Estimates for the Chicago AQCR

Activity	Regulatory system		Charge system	
	Person-years	thousands of dollars[a]	Person-years	thousands of dollars
Initial (one-time) efforts:				
Dispersion modelling	0.24	5	0.24	5
Determining emissions control cost functions	—	—	0.32	6
Equipment expenditures	—	150	—	150
Total	0.24	155	0.56	161
Recurring (annual) efforts:				
Administration	26 to 30	376 to 445	29 to 37	370 to 489
Monitoring	9 to 15	104 to 207	8 to 15	108 to 207
Enforcement	27 to 110	441 to 1950	19 to 44	280 to 631
Total	62 to 155	921 to 2602	56 to 96	758 to 1327

[a] All expenditures in 1978 dollars. Salary information was obtained from [11, p. 40]; estimates do not include overhead and fringe benefits.

regulatory approach and one based on an economic approach such as an emissions charge plan. The main difference would be related to some additional accounting and record-keeping activities necessary under a charge system. Following an examination of alternatives for carrying out these activities, it was concluded that they could be relatively easily and inexpensively integrated into the hardware and software associated with emissions monitoring systems that would be required under conventional regulatory approaches. Specifically, the incremental annual cost was estimated to be on the order of, at most, $2500 per source.[20]

Table 3 details the complete personnel and cost estimates for the range of administration, monitoring, and enforcement (AME) activities required to implement a regulatory system and a charge system in Chicago. Note that there are essentially two stages of effort. Initially, estimates of transfer coefficients (the $d_{i,j}$ described on p. 114), background concentrations of pollutants, and (in the case of a charge system) engineering-based emissions control cost functions would be derived. Subsequently, there would be less intense, on-going efforts to improve this information as well as the recurring costs associated with operating the systems.

These estimates were derived by using the format developed in an EPA "manpower planning model" [6]. However, since the model focuses only on state and local agencies, it was necessary to include supplementary information on Federal involvement.[21] Specifically, it was found that in the Chicago AQCR, a major portion of Federal activity involves case development; that is, bargaining and negotiating with sources on acceptable compliance schedules. Since sources can realize substantial economic benefits from delaying compliance, they often challenge agency-desired

[20] Details on system configurations and estimated development and system costs can be found in Section 6.8 of [2].

[21] Much of this information was obtained through conversations and correspondence with Tom Donaldson, USEPA, Control Program Section, Research Triangle Park; Ron Shafer, USEPA, Washington, D.C.; Pat Reape, Enforcement Division, USEPA, Region V; Wayne Jones, Division of Air Pollution Control, Illinois EPA; and Mr. Kason of the Department of Environmental Control, City of Chicago.

124   SESKIN, ANDERSON, JR., AND REID

control techniques or the time frame for compliance. Thus, the agency must have
resources available for intensive negotiating sessions as well as for courtroom
appearances in formal legal proceedings. It was estimated that such activities could
require between 7 and 45 person-years at a cost of between $100,000 and $700,000
annually.[22] The estimated range of total AME costs under a regulatory system were
$900,000 to $2.6 million annually, with personnel effort ranging between 62 and 155
person-years.

The specific charge system used in the development of corresponding AME costs
estimates was based on the Least Cost Charge plan discussed above. Again,
calculations were made using the framework in the EPA manpower planning model.
Table 3 indicates that a Least Cost emissions charge program could be implemented
in the Chicago AQCR with AME costs running between $750,000 and $1.3 million
annually and with personnel effort ranging between 56 and 96 person-years.[23]

REFERENCES

1. F. R. Anderson, A. V. Kneese, P. D. Reed, S. Taylor, and R. B. Stevenson, "Environmental
   Improvement Through Economic Incentives," Johns Hopkins Univ. Press, Baltimore, 1977.
2. R. J. Anderson, Jr., R. O. Reid, and E. P. Seskin, "An Analysis of Alternative Policies for Attaining
   and Maintaining a Short-term NO_2 Standard," prepared for the U.S. Environmental Protection
   Agency, U.S. Council on Environmental Quality, and Council of Economic Advisers, September
   17, 1979.
3. S. E. Atkinson and D. H. Lewis, A cost-effective analysis of alternative air control strategies, *J.
   Environ. Econ. Manag.* 1 (1974), 237–250.
4. W. J. Baumol and W. E. Oates, "The Theory of Environmental Policy," Prentice-Hall, Englewood
   Cliffs, New Jersey, 1975.
5. A. V. Kneese and C. L. Schultze, "Pollution, Prices, and Public Policy," The Brookings Institution,
   Washington, D.C., 1975.
6. D. A. Lynn and G. L. Deane, "Manpower Planning Model," Office of Air and Waste Management,
   Office of Air Quality Planning and Standards, U.S. Environmental Protection Agency, Research
   Triangle Park, North Carolina, EPA 450/3-75-034, March 1975.
7. S. Senju and Y. Toyoda, An approach to linear programming with 0-1 variables, *Manag. Sci.* 15
   (1968), 196–207.
8. Y. Toyoda, A simplified algorithm for obtaining approximate solutions to 0-1 programming problems, *Manag. Sci.* 21, (1975), 1417–1427.
9. U.S. Council on Environment Quality, "Environmental Quality: The Ninth Annual Report of the
   Council on Environmental Quality," U.S. Government Printing Office, Washington, D.C., 1978.
10. U.S. Environmental Protection Agency, "An Analysis of Economic Incentives to Control Emissions
    of Nitrogen Oxides from Stationary Sources," Report to Congress, January 1981.
11. U.S. Environmental Protection Agency, "Methodology Report, Air Pollution Strategy Resource
    Estimator" 2, 1975.
12. S. H. Zanakis, Heuristic 0-1 linear programming: An experimental comparison of three methods,
    Manag. Sci. 24 (1977), 91–104.

[22] These figures are incorporated in the category of recurring annual enforcement costs of the
regulatory system.

[23] It should be noted that these numbers do not reflect Federal-level case development activities, since
it is assumed that no compliance schedules are required under a charge system.

[16]

Journal of Public Economics 24 (1984), 29-46. North-Holland

EFFLUENT FEES AND MARKET STRUCTURE

Wallace E. OATES

Bureau of Business and Economic Research, University of Maryland, College Park, MD 20742, USA

Diana L. STRASSMANN*

Rice University, Houston, TX 77001, USA

Received May 1982, revised version received May 1983

This paper explores the efficiency properties of a system of effluent fees in a mixed economy in which polluting agents take a variety of organizational forms: private monopoly, the managerial firm, regulated firms, and public bureaus. The analysis, including some crude empirical estimates, suggests that the welfare gains from pollution control are likely to dwarf in magnitude the potential losses from the various imperfections in the economy. The tentative conclusion is that the case for a system of fees that is invariant with respect to organizational form is not seriously compromised by likely deviations from competitive behavior.

1. Introduction

The formal analysis of a Pigouvian tax on polluting activities typically proceeds in terms of perfectly competitive firms whose productive pursuits impose external costs on other agents in the economy. Moreover, the optimality properties of the Pigouvian measure depend upon this assumption of perfect competition. A cursory inspection of the real world, however, reveals that the major sources of pollution encompass a wide variety of institutional structure. The public sector, for example, is itself a major polluter [see Oates and Strassmann (1978)]. Municipal waste-treatment plants dump enormous quantities of wastes into our waterways, and publicly-owned power plants are heavy contributors to air pollution. The largest single sulfur polluter in the United States is the Tennessee Valley Authority (TVA), which accounts for 16 percent of sulfur emissions in the nation [see King (1977)]. In addition, private but publicly-regulated firms (including utilities that provide electrical power) are among the very largest of polluters. Finally, many of the large factories that emit massive quantities of wastes are owned and operated by huge firms in highly concentrated

*We are grateful for many helpful comments on earlier drafts of this paper to Peter Altroggen, William Baumol, Richard Caves, Robert Dorfman, Joseph Kalt, Margaret Lewis, Robert Mackay, Albert McGartland, Lee Preston, Eugene Seskin, Jeffery Smisek, and anonymous referees. We are also indebted for the support of parts of this work to the National Science Foundation and the Sloan Foundation.

industries like steel, chemicals, and automobile manufacturing. The application of the competitive model with its myriad of small firms acting as price-takers is thus suspect for many classes of polluters.

The economic analysis of market incentives for pollution control must, therefore, push beyond the simple competitive model. We must ask how polluters with widely varying sets of objectives are likely to respond to these incentives. In this paper, we seek to determine what some standard models of organizational behavior tell us about how decision-makers in different institutions would respond to the introduction of a set of effluent charges.[1] We then use these results to evaluate the implications of these responses for efficient resource allocation, taking explicit account of the distortions that market imperfections, bureaucratic behavior, and public regulation of private firms themselves introduce.

2. The problem of 'allocative efficiency'

2.1. The conceptual issue

We begin the analysis with the standard monopoly model under which a profit-maximizing firm has some discretion over the price it charges for its output. We assume that the firm has a production function of the form:

$$Q = Q(L, E), \tag{1}$$

where L (which we shall call 'labor') represents a vector of all inputs other than E, the firm's level of waste emissions. We thus treat the source of pollution, namely waste emissions, as a productive input from the perspective of the firm. If factor markets are perfectly competitive and if the environmental authority confronts the firm with a Pigouvian charge on its emissions equal to marginal social damage (MSD), it follows that the firm, in the process of minimizing its costs, will select what from society's point of view is the cost-minimizing combination of factor inputs for whatever level of output it chooses. In short, cost-minimizing behavior ensures 'technical efficiency' in the use of all inputs including the services of the environment. A corollary is that, for the case where units of emissions from all sources are equally damaging, a uniform effluent fee will lead cost-minimizing polluters to equate their marginal abatement costs and hence to achieve the desired level of environmental quality at the minimum aggregate abatement cost (our 'least-cost theorem').

---

[1]The analysis also has relevance for systems of marketable pollution permits. However, it would need to be extended to account for any imperfections in the permit market itself [Hahn (1981)]. The assumption here is that, under a system of effluent fees, individual polluters take the fee structure as given.

The problem in this case concerns allocative distortions in the pattern of final outputs. As Buchanan (1969) has pointed out, the monopolist's sub-optimal level of output is the source of a basic dilemma for the formulation of policy to regulate externalities. An effluent fee provides an incentive for needed pollution abatement, but, at the same time, raises the firm's marginal cost and thereby induces a reduction in output. The result is some gain in efficient resource allocation from reduced waste emissions, but some loss in efficiency from the contraction in output; the *net* effect on social welfare is uncertain. In short, an effluent fee (Pigouvian or otherwise) may represent too much of a good thing.

The analysis must, therefore, take explicit account of Buchanan's tradeoff between pollution abatement and monopolistic output restriction. Following Baumol and Oates (1975, ch. 6), we depict the nature of this tradeoff in fig. 1. Let DD' represent the industry demand curve confronting a monopolist, with DMR being the corresponding marginal-revenue curve. We assume that the monopoly can produce at constant cost (PMC=private marginal cost), but that its production activities impose costs on others. In particular, in the absence of any fees, the monopolist's (private) cost-minimizing technique of production generates pollution costs per unit equal to AB so that the SMC_0 (social marginal cost) curve indicates the true cost to society of each unit of output. To maximize profits, the monopolist would produce OQ_m.

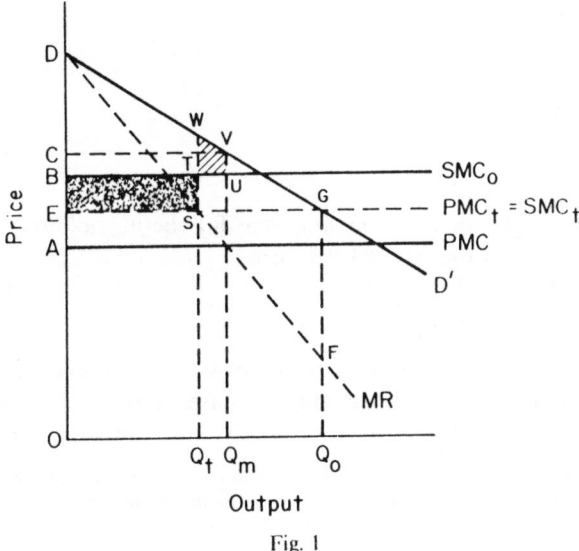

Fig. 1

Suppose next that we subject the monopolist to a pollution tax, a fee per unit of waste emissions. This will provide an incentive to alter the production process in a way that yields lower emissions per unit of output. In fig. 1 this would have two effects: it would raise the *PMC* curve and, over some range, would tend to lower *SMC*. This second effect results from the choice of what, from society's standpoint, is a lower-cost method of production (taking into account the costs of pollution). The minimum social cost of production will be reached when the pollution costs are wholly internalized so that $PMC_t = SMC_t$ (where the subscript t refers to costs in the presence of a Pigouvian tax). At this point, the firm's selection of a production process will be based upon a set of input prices (including a price of waste emissions) that reflects true social opportunity costs.

Since there exist two distinct sources of allocative distortions, a full resolution of the problem will, in general, require two policy actions: a Pigouvian tax on waste emissions equal to *MSD* *and* a subsidy per unit of output equal to *GF* (the difference between marginal cost and marginal revenue at the Pareto-efficient level of output). A typical environmental agency, however, will have neither the authority nor the inclination to offer subsidies to monopolists.

In this constrained setting, the problem of the environmental authority takes on a second-best character: the determination of the effluent fee which balances, at the margin, the social gain from increased abatement against the social loss from reduced output from the monopolist. Lee (1975), and more recently Barnett (1980), have derived formally the first-order conditions for this second-best optimal fee. Although the Lee–Barnett results take a slightly different form, they can be expressed as:

$$t_j = t^* - \frac{C_j}{|\eta_j|}, \tag{2}$$

where

t_j = optimal tax per unit of waste emissions for the jth polluter,
t^* = Pigouvian tax on the competitive firm,
C_j = marginal abatement cost, and
η_j = price elasticity of demand.

The second term on the RHS of eq. (2) reflects the marginal welfare loss from reduced output associated with a unit increase in the tax.[2] For a perfectly competitive firm, this term is zero so that $t_j = t^*$. But for a firm with some

[2]It is easy to see, incidentally, that in accord with intuition this term is equal to the marginal welfare loss per unit of reduced output (i.e. price minus marginal cost) multiplied by the reduction in output associated with an additional unit of abatement. More formally:

$$\frac{C_j}{|\eta_j|} = \frac{P_j}{|\eta_j|} \cdot \frac{\partial Q_j}{\partial a_j} = (P_j - MR_j)\frac{\partial Q_j}{\partial a_j} = (P_j - MC_j)\frac{\partial Q_j}{\partial a_j},$$

where a_j is the level of abatement activity and where profit maximization implies that $MR_j = MC_j$. The marginal cost of abatement, $P_j(\partial Q_j/\partial a_j)$ is expressed in terms of the value of forgone output.

control over market price, the optimal unit tax on emissions will vary inversely with marginal abatement cost and directly with the price elasticity of demand for the firm's output.

In principle, therefore, we can determine the optimal set of effluent fees on all polluters, be they competitive firms or monopolists. However, this is not, in fact, very comforting. First, such a determination would require an enormous amount of information encompassing both the price elasticities of demand *and* the abatement costs for each polluter. And second, even if the environmental authority were able to assemble all these data, it is difficult to envision a legal and political setting in which such a discriminatory set of fees would be acceptable.

At the policy level, the real choice may well be that between a single fee applicable both to perfect and imperfect competitors or the abandonment of a system of pricing incentives for environmental protection. From this perspective, the important issue is the *extent* of the welfare loss associated with the pattern of reductions in output induced by the charge on waste emissions. There is a substantial empirical literature suggesting that the magnitude of the overall allocative losses in the economy attributable to monopolistic distortions is quite small.[3] Since the large estimated welfare gains from pollution abatement would seem to dwarf the apparently small welfare losses from effects on the pattern of industry outputs, it is tempting simply to conclude that concern over monopolistic distortions represents, in this case, a theoretical nicety that we can safely ignore in the design of environmental policy.

This, however, will not quite do. The proper question is: *Given the existing pattern of monopolistic distortions* (i.e. existing divergences between price and marginal cost), do the *additional* reductions in monopoly outputs generate efficiency losses of a substantial magnitude?

2.2. A rough estimate

In order to get some feel for just how damaging the existence of monopolistic elements in the economy is to the case for an effluent fee that is invariant with respect to industry structure, we have undertaken some admittedly quite crude, partial-equilibrium calculations making use of a representative polluter.[4] Our procedure involves a comparison of two

---

[3]The seminal paper presenting this result is Harberger (1954). Several later studies support Harberger's general finding [e.g. Schwartzman (1960)]. However, for a dissenting view, see Cowling and Mueller (1978) who have criticized the earlier work on methodological grounds and have calculated their own estimates of allocative losses from monopoly for both the United States and the United Kingdom. Their estimates for these losses are much more sizable.

[4]The shortcoming of a partial-equilibrium approach is clear. A full, general-equilibrium treatment of the problem would take into account the interaction between markets; the outcome in this setting would depend not only on the magnitude of the initial distortion and the own price elasticity of demand, but also on cross elasticities.

equilibrium positions: the first involves no control over the externality (and hence no abatement), and the second is the outcome under a system of effluent fees where the fee does not vary with industry structure. In moving from the former to the latter, we compare the welfare gains from reduced pollution *net* of abatement costs to the *increment* of new allocative losses associated with monopoly elements in the existing market structure. We use existing environmental programs in the United States as a (rough) benchmark for overall abatement efforts.

Proceeding in terms of a 'representative polluter', we assume that the social marginal cost of production associated with each level of abatement activity is approximately constant over the relevant range. We can then approximate the welfare gain from reduced pollution net of abatement costs by:

$$W_g = Q[SMC_0 - SMC_t], \tag{3}$$

where SMC_0 and SMC_t are, respectively, social marginal cost before and after the introduction of a set of Pigouvian taxes. The welfare gain is simply the reduced cost (private plus external) per unit times the level of output (area $EBTS$ in fig. 1). Likewise, we can approximate the welfare loss from reduced output by:

$$W_1 = \Delta Q(P - SMC_0). \tag{4}$$

Welfare loss is the loss per unit (equal to the difference between price and *social* marginal cost) times the change in output (an approximation to area $TWVU$ in fig. 1). To determine the relative sizes of these two effects, we divide (4) by (3) to obtain:

$$W_r = \frac{\Delta Q}{Q} \frac{[P - SMC_0]}{[SMC_0 - SMC_t]}. \tag{5}$$

It will facilitate the numerical comparisons to divide both numerator and denominator by P:

$$W_r = \frac{\Delta Q}{Q} \frac{[P - SMC_0]/P}{[SMC_0 - SMC_t]/P}. \tag{6}$$

The next step is to try to make some educated guesses as to the orders of magnitude of the various terms in eq. (6). To do this, we construct a profile of a representative polluter that incorporates reasonable estimates of the parameters. In each instance we lean in the direction of magnitudes that are favorable to the finding of a relatively large welfare loss associated with monopolistic distortions.

W.E. Oates and D.L. Strassmann, *Effluent fees and market structure*   35

The first term in eq. (6) is the percentage change in quantity, which we can express as the percentage change in price times the price elasticity of demand (η). There are available for the United States fairly detailed data on abatement expenditures by sector, and we make use of a careful ongoing study by H. David Robison (1983) in which he uses these data and a large input–output model to estimate existing abatement costs per dollar of output for 78 sectors in the U.S. economy. Using 1977 data, Robison finds, for example, the following percentage increases in costs attributable to abatement expenditures: 2.0 for the paper industry, 2.1 for ferrous metals, 2.3 for copper, and 3.3 for electric utilities. He assumes that these costs are passed forward in terms of higher prices. Deriving a 'representative' increase in prices under a fee system from these estimates is problematic, since the effect of a set of fees on costs would differ in two important respects from the existing command-and-control system. First, as existing studies indicate, a fee system would tend to reduce abatement costs significantly through more cost-efficient patterns of abatement and technology, but, second, such savings in abatement costs must be balanced against the effluent fees that sources would have to pay. We take as a 'typical' increase in price for our representative polluter a figure of 5 percent, where we assume that this cost increase to our polluter (and the consequent rise in price) is constituted in equal parts of control costs (2.5 percent) and effluent fees (2.5 percent).[5] A best estimate for a representative price elasticity of demand is also uncertain, but for the major industries of concern, including power generation, chemicals, pulp and paper, etc., a typical value of two is probably a generous assumption. This gives us a value of $\Delta Q/Q$ for our representative polluter of:

$$\frac{\Delta Q}{Q} = |\eta| \frac{\Delta P}{P} = 2(0.05) = 0.1. \tag{7}$$

We thus assume a 10 percent reduction in output for our representative polluter attributable to the adoption of the fee program.

Turning next to the numerator of the second term in (6), we note that $[P - SMC_0]$ is equal to that portion of the difference between price and private marginal cost that is not offset by the marginal social damage of waste emissions; that is:

$$\frac{[P - SMC_0]}{P} = \frac{[P - (PMC + MSD)]}{P}, \tag{8}$$

where MSD is the marginal external cost associated with polluting emissions. Finding appropriate magnitudes for these variables is somewhat

[5] This distinction is important, because control costs represent actual social costs, while fee payments are, from the perspective of society, a transfer payment.

more conjectural. However, we can make a very rough guess by noting that existing estimates of the benefits from air pollution control in the United States are about twice the level of abatement costs; Lave and Seskin (1977, p. 230), for example, offer a conservative estimate of health benefits alone from meeting standards for ambient air quality of about $16 billion as compared to EPA's estimate of $9.5 billion for abatement costs.[6] If we double our representative estimate for abatement costs of 2.5 percent and add on another 2.5 percent for residual damages, we reach a figure of 7.5 percent of marginal cost for our estimate of marginal social damages in the absence of any control program.[7]

Next we need a figure for monopolistic markup over marginal cost. There exists an empirical literature that has estimated the relationship between price–cost margins and industry concentration [e.g. Shepard (1972)]; these studies find that the margin of price over cost rises by about one percentage point for every increase of ten percentage points in the four-firm industry concentration ratio (C_4). If we assume that 'competition' involves a C_4 of about 20 and that 'monopolistic' industries have a typical C_4 of 70, we would have a level of monopolistic prices that exceeds competitive prices by about 5 percent. Leaning in the direction of a more generous estimate, we take 10 percent as our representative monopolistic markup over private marginal cost. This leaves us with an estimate of 2.5 for the difference between price and social marginal cost as a percentage of price.[8]

The denominator of the second term in eq. (6) follows directly from the preceding profile of our representative polluter. The representative reduction in marginal social damages from the control program is 5 percent of price (since we assume benefits equal to twice the level of abatement costs); from this, we subtract 2.5 percent of price for abatement costs leaving us with a net reduction in social marginal cost of 2.5 percent of price.

Pulling together our results for the various terms in (6), we arrive at:

$$W_r = (0.1)\frac{0.025}{0.025} = 0.1. \tag{9}$$

---

[6]These figures admittedly refer to total, rather than marginal, benefits and costs. However, since we are considering the entire increment from the introduction of a program of effluent fees, we take them as a reasonable approximation.

[7]Our estimate thus implies that the fee program reduces the representative marginal damages from pollution by about two-thirds. This seems to us a relatively conservative figure, since abatement efforts have typically led sources to reduce emissions by well over 50 percent (in excess of 90 percent in several cases); such reductions in the presence of increasing marginal damages (the typical case) would suggest reductions in damages from pollution far in excess of one-half.

[8]Note that if the markup were only 5 percent, then social marginal cost for our representative polluter would actually exceed the monopoly price so that a contraction in output would raise, rather than lower, social welfare. Such may well be the case in some instances.

We thus estimate the monopolistic welfare loss from a program of effluent fees to be roughly an order of magnitude smaller than the welfare gain from reduced pollution (net of abatement costs). While this estimate obviously depends on our choice of values for the various parameters, we believe that the 'representative calculation' is relatively generous to the magnitude of the potential welfare loss from reduced monopoly outputs and that 'reasonable' parameter values are unlikely to suggest that this loss can rival in size the gains from improved environmental quality. In view of the range of policy options available to the environmental authority, our conclusion is that it is probably safe to ignore the issue of incremental output distortions associated with a system of effluent fees.

3. The problem of technical efficiency

In the preceding section, the assumption of simple profit-maximizing behavior with its corollary of cost minimization allowed us to ignore the issue of technical efficiency: faced with a Pigouvian fee, cost-minimizing agents will select the socially least-cost combination of inputs and will operate along their minimum cost curves. In this section of the paper we drop this assumption and explore the implications of technical inefficiencies for the efficacy of a system of effluent fees. We examine a series of models in which the failure to minimize costs comes from either of two sources: a more complex objective function that incorporates variables other than (or in addition to) the level of profits, or some type of regulatory constraint that provides the decision-maker with an incentive to choose something other than the cost-minimizing pattern of factor inputs.

3.1. Managerial models of maximizing firms

For our purposes, the Williamson (1963) model captures the spirit of the results that emerge when a firm's managers maximize an objective function that contains variables other than simply short-run profits. In particular, Williamson formulates a managerial utility function that incorporates 'expense preferences' for expenditures on staff (S), managerial emoluments (M) (extra salary and perquisites), and 'discretionary profits' consisting of the difference between actual profits and the minimum profits demanded. The firm thus maximizes:

$$U = U[S, M, \pi_R - \pi_0 - T] \quad \text{subject to} \quad \pi_R > \pi_0 + T \tag{10}$$

or

$$U = U\{S, M, (1-t)[R(X) - C(X) - S - M] - \pi_0\}, \tag{11}$$

where

$R = \text{revenue} = P \cdot X; \quad \partial^2 R / \partial X \partial S \geq 0,$

$P = \text{price} = P(X, S; \varepsilon); \quad \partial P / \partial X < 0; \quad \partial P / \partial S \geq 0; \quad \partial P / \partial \varepsilon > 0,$

$X = \text{output},$

$S = \text{staff (in money terms) or (approximately) general}$
  $\quad \text{administrative and selling expense};$

$\varepsilon = \text{a demand shift parameter},$

$C = \text{costs of production} = C(X),$

$M = \text{managerial emoluments},$

$\pi = \text{actual profits} = R - C - S,$

$\pi_R = \text{reported profits} = \pi - M,$

$\pi_0 = \text{minimum (after-tax) profits demanded},$

$T = \text{taxes, where } t = \text{tax rate, and}$

$\pi_R - \pi_0 - T = \text{discretionary profits}.$

To treat waste emissions and the effluent fee explicitly, we amend the Williamson model to distinguish between these emissions (E) and all other inputs (L). Eq. (11) thus becomes:

$$U = U\{S, M, (1-t)[R(g(L,E)) - P_l L - fE - S - M] - \pi_0\}, \qquad (12)$$

where P_l is the price of other inputs and f denotes the effluent fee. Maximization of this utility function yields as one of the first-order conditions the familiar result:

$$\frac{P_l}{f} = \frac{\partial X / \partial L}{\partial X / \partial E}. \qquad (13)$$

This is the usual condition for the cost-minimizing combination of factor inputs: marginal products proportional to factor prices. It may seem surprising at first glance to find that firms that are technically inefficient (i.e. do not produce at minimum cost *overall*) are effectively cost-minimizers with regard to pollution abatement. However, the rationale is quite straightforward: since abatement activities contribute nothing to staff or emoluments and reduce discretionary profits, the firm's managers have an incentive to minimize the expenditure on abatement (consisting of effluent fees plus pollution-control costs) by extending abatement activity to the point where marginal abatement cost equals the effluent fee. We can thus extend our cost-minimization theorem to encompass certain managerial models of maximizing firms: a world of such firms subject to an effluent fee can, in principle, achieve the desired standard of environmental quality at the minimum aggregate abatement cost.[9]

[9]As one potential qualification to this result, we note that abatement activities could, under certain circumstances, enter directly into the managerial utility function. The firm's managers might perceive, for example, that activities to curtail pollution produce some valuable 'good-will' for the firm. In such instances, the firm might well extend abatement activities beyond the point at which marginal abatement cost equals the effluent fee.

3.2. Organizational models of firm behavior

Organizational models of firm behavior treat managerial decisions in the context of the firm's internal structure and environment. Firm behavior in these models cannot be characterized by an explicit objective function. These models include both the Carnegie Tech type that emphasizes internal coalitions, information costs, limited time, and bounded rationality [e.g. Cohen and Cyert (1962)] and the Harvard Business School variety that focus on the internal dynamics and structure of the firm [e.g. Chandler (1962) and Bower (1970)]. Without probing in detail into these alternative views of managerial decision-making, we wish to note in passing that both of these approaches imply the possible presence of a degree of 'managerial slack'.

Such slack may well have some implications for the effectiveness of a system of effluent fees. In particular, the case for effluent fees rests on the presumption that an increase in the price of effluents will induce firms to use less effluents relative to other inputs; over the longer haul, fees will induce firms to engage in R&D that will allow them to develop cheaper abatement technologies. However, the incentives to change production policies quickly in response to relative price changes may be quite weak in a managerial context. Changes in production methods (particularly to less pollution-intensive methods) may involve major changes in equipment. If an important perquisite is 'ease of management', the firm might conceivably employ some of the fat in its budget to avoid the effort and possible complications associated with the adoption and development of new abatement techniques. There are, in fact, some investigations of the diffusion of knowledge and new technologies that have found that firms in concentrated industries do not respond as quickly to price changes and the availability of new innovations as do firms in more competitive industries [see Kamien and Schwartz (1975)]. The evidence on this issue, however, is not conclusive; yet the lack of consensus certainly provides some justification for skepticism about the belief that effluent fees will work as well in highly concentrated industries as they might in more competitive cases.

We shall return to this issue again in our discussion of bureaucratic leanings toward 'ease of management'. What we can say is that all of the models of imperfectly competitive firm behavior that we have discussed establish some presumption that effluent fees will induce firms to pollute less; how closely the outcomes approach a cost-minimizing solution is less clear.

3.3. Public bureaus

Since models of bureaucratic behavior typically posit neither profit maximization nor cost minimization, the response of public agencies to pricing incentives is problematic [see Oates and Strassmann (1978)]. To explore the impact of effluent fees on public decision-makers, we first examine a variant of the Niskanen (1977) model of bureaucratic behavior. As we shall see, the model and its implications for abatement activities bear a strong resemblance to our analysis in the Williamson framework of private managerial maximization. We then discuss the implications of Wilson et al.'s (1980) richer study of public agencies.

In our varient of the Niskanen model, we postulate that the bureau's decision-makers seek to maximize an objective function that contains as arguments the bureau's output (Q) and its level of perquisites (P):

$$U = U(Q, P).$$ (14)

Bureaucrats desire an increased output (or 'size'), for this enhances the bureau's power and prestige and with these its capacity to influence the course of events. Migue and Belanger (1974) have contended that agency officials also place a premium on the bureau's 'discretionary budget', the excess of the bureau's funding above its necessary costs. This 'fat' in the budget can be employed for a variety of perquisites ranging from higher salaries and expanded staff to additional facilities or, perhaps, reduced effort.

As earlier, we assume that the production function for the bureau's output depends on waste emissions, E, and a vector of other outputs, L:

$$Q = Q(L, E).$$ (15)

Moreover, the bureau is subject to a budget constraint:

$$B = wL + fE + cP,$$ (16)

where B is the bureau's budget, w is the price of 'other' inputs (given to the bureau), f is the effluent fee per unit of waste emissions, and c is the (constant) marginal cost of perquisites. Note that L is defined to include only the minimally necessary quantity of other inputs such as labor to provide a given output; likewise, w can be thought of as the lowest wage that will keep employees. Extra salary and labor are viewed as perquisites.

The budget-determination process is the remaining issue. Here we follow Niskanen and assume that the bureau possesses a kind of monopoly power in its dealings with the legislative agency that provides its funding. In particular, the bureau submits (and obtains) a budget of an all-or-nothing character that extracts the entire area under the legislature's demand curve up to the bureau's proposed level of output. In short, the bureau behaves much like a perfectly discriminating monopolist; for whatever level of output it selects, say $\hat{Q}$, the bureau's budget equals:

$$B = \int_0^{\hat{Q}} D(Q)\,dQ,$$ (17)

where $D(Q)$ is the legislature's inverse demand function for the bureau's output.[10]

In this framework the bureaucrat's problem becomes that of maximizing the utility function in eq. (14) subject to its budget constraint:

$$M = U[Q(L, E), P] + \left[wL + fE + cP - \int_0^Q D(Q)\,dQ \right].$$ (18)

Solving for the stationary values of (18) yields (among other results):

$$\frac{\partial Q/\partial E}{\partial Q/\partial L} = \frac{f}{w}.$$ (19)

This result is essentially the same as that obtained from our analysis of the Williamson model. Eq. (19), like that for the managerial model of the maximizing firm, implies cost minimization in only a limited sense: the bureau minimizes pollution abatement and other costs that do not generate perquisites. Effluent fees are effectively lost dollars; they provide no utility to the bureaucrat. By minimizing pollution-abatement costs, the bureau maximizes the remaining budget for the procurement of perquisites. Like cost-minimizing firms, a bureau behaving according to this model has an incentive to extend pollution-abatement activities to the point where marginal abatement cost equals the effluent fee.

An important qualification to this result introduces an indeterminacy similar to that in the satisficing models of firm behavior. Bureaucrats, like the employees of firms, are likely to have some preferences for the perquisite 'ease of management'. Just how pervasive such behavior is in public agencies is unclear; however, it could introduce some inefficiencies in the allocation of abatement quotas among polluters. Although, as the analysis suggests, bureaucrats are likely to have some incentive to economize on abatement costs, the discussion in the previous section on diffusion of innovations is also likely to apply to bureaus. Bureaus, like firms protected by managerial slack, do not need to respond as quickly to price changes and to the availability of new technologies as do competitive firms, since the survival of a bureau does not, in general, depend on an aggressively tight management.

The model is admittedly a very simplistic one that cannot begin to encompass the diversity in circumstances and particular objectives of different public agencies. In a recent series of case studies of bureaucratic behavior, Wilson et al. (1980) criticize such simplistic approaches to the characterization of public agencies. Their studies find that the behavior of these agencies is 'complex and changing' (p. 373); it is not subject, for

[10]Alternatively, we might simply assume that the budget is, for our purposes, some predetermined sum [see Oates and Strassmann (1978)]. This would not alter the results.

example, to the broad generalization of the 'captive theory', that, as a rule, 'Regulation is acquired by the industry and is designed and operated primarily for its benefit' [Stigler (1971, p. 3)]. Instead, Wilson et al. suggest that 'We view these agencies as coalitions of diverse participants who have somewhat different motives' (p. 373). Wilson et al. find that the studies reveal public agencies to '...prefer security to rapid growth, autonomy to competition, stability to change... Government agencies are more risk averse than imperialistic' (p. 376). This serves to underline our earlier observations on the potential for public agencies to respond sluggishly to incentives for change.

We note of particular interest the general similarity of the findings and qualifications of the behavior of managers of public and (imperfectly competitive) private enterprises. In a set of case studies of several electric utilities, Roberts and Bluhm (1981) can likewise find no systematic differences in behavior between publicly and privately owned concerns; they conclude that 'The mere fact of public or private ownership by itself does not tell us very much about the kind of behavior to expect' (p. 335).

In summary, although the formal model in this section predicts minimization of abatement costs by public agencies, the interpretation of this result and the broadening of our perspective on bureaucratic behavior suggest some basic reservations. We surely cannot, in a simplistic way, extend the umbrella of our cost-minimization theorem to encompass public agencies. At the same time, the analysis does suggest that an explicit price on pollution activities will present managers (public or private) with a real incentive for abatement. Managers are obviously not entirely oblivious to the costs of alternatives; Roberts and Bluhm, for example, in describing the history of the huge publicly-owned utility, TVA, found that 'Despite the agency's broad responsibility for conservation and regional development, most of its engineering decisions have reflected a continuing attempt to minimize the cost of power' (p. 63).

3.4. Regulated firms

The presence of regulated firms introduces, in principle, another source of technical inefficiency: a regulatory constraint that effectively distorts the relative prices of inputs to the firm. By setting some maximum 'fair' rate of return to capital inputs, the regulatory authority creates an incentive for the firm to extend its use of capital, for by using more capital, the firm is able to enlarge the base upon which its profit constraint is determined. All this is well known and has been described in terms of the Averch and Johnson (1962) (A–J) model; the distortion in factor inputs involving an excessive use of capital is the A–J effect.[11]

---

[11]For excellent, comprehensive treatments of the analytics of the A–J model, see Baumol and Klevorick (1970) and Bailey (1973).

It is fairly straightforward exercise to take the standard version of the A–J model (in which the regulated firm maximizes profits subject to a rate-of-return constraint), to introduce waste emissions into the production function as earlier, and then to examine the first-order conditions for profit maximization in the presence of an effluent fee. We shall not go through the mechanics here, but wish simply to note that the results of this exercise indicate that the regulated firm will not, in general, be a cost minimizer with respect to abatement activity.[12] It would be quite plausible, for example, for such a firm to extend abatement activity beyond the level at which marginal abatement cost equals the effluent fee, if by doing so the firm could expand its capital stock through the use of pollution-control equipment. The rationale from the perspective of the firm is the higher level of absolute profits that the expanded capital stock would allow. But from society's vantage point, this represents, of course, an excessive level of abatement. Under these circumstances, a system of effluent fees could not be expected to generate the least-cost set of pollution-abatement quotas among sources.

More generally, we cannot even conclude that an increase in the effluent fee will lead to a reduction in the waste emissions of the regulated firm. Bailey (1973, pp. 135–137) shows that for the two-factor case, a rise in the wage rate need not lead to reduced labor input; although there must surely be a strong presumption of this result, the outcome is formally indeterminate. Likewise, in his two-factor formulation of the A–J model, Cowing (1976) finds that the sign of the derivative of waste emissions with respect to the effluent fee is ambiguous.

While these results are, *in principle*, disturbing, there remains the important practical question of the actual magnitude of the A–J effect. The literature has not produced any compelling evidence of a widespread A–J effect [e.g. Baron and Taggart (1977), Spann (1974)]. Not only is there an absence of empirical support for 'over-capitalization' by regulated firms, but there is evidence that the rate-of-return constraint may often not even be binding.

In addition to the empirical studies, recent theoretical work casts further doubt on the applicability of the A–J theorem. Peles and Stein (1976) show that the theorem is 'highly sensitive' to the treatment of uncertainty; if uncertainty is multiplicative in form, the A–J effect is reversed! Perhaps even more basic is the issue of the interaction between the regulated firm and the regulating authority [e.g. Stigler (1971), Peltzman (1976), Joskow (1972, 1973)]. In the A–J model, the firm simply takes the rate-of-return constraint as exogenous. In the real world, however, the regulated firm must typically make application for any price changes, and, as Joskow (1972) shows, the determination of the allowed rate of return appears to involve a fairly complicated process of interaction between the regulator and the regulated firm.

---

[12]We would be happy to provide the formal analysis to any interested readers.

The industrial-organization literature thus establishes some compelling reasons for being quite skeptical about the A–J description of the behavior of the regulated firm. However, it does not, at this juncture, provide a straightforward alternative framework for our analysis of the regulated firm's response to an effluent fee. Some of the literature notes (as does our treatment of managerial models of the firm and of public agencies) the presence of other variables in the objective function in addition to profit maximization; for example, Roberts and Bluhm (1981) conclude that 'Our studies have shown that regulated firms are not pure incentive-oriented profit maximizers. To varying extents, managers are sensitive — albeit within financial limits — to not harming the public and to doing "the right thing"' (p. 384). Moreover, to the extent that the costs associated with effluent charges can be passed along through viable requests for higher prices to the regulatory authority, there may be grounds for questioning a highly 'cost-conscious' response to a system of fees.

We emerge with the sense that our expectations for the regulated firm are much in the spirit of those for the 'managerial' firm and the public bureau. In all these cases, we envision a managerial utility function which contains a multiplicity of objectives as a consequence of which cost-minimization plays an important, but not a singular, role in the determination of behavior.

4. Conclusion

While the analysis in this paper cannot yield any firmly grounded conclusions about the effectiveness of a system of effluent fees in a mixed economy, it does, we think, suggest some tentative results. First, our admittedly crude calculations in section 2 suggest that any distortions in the vector of final outputs resulting from a system of effluent fees (or probably from other forms of pollution control) are unlikely to be the source of substantial welfare loss. The 'allocative' issue that has troubled Buchanan and others in the design of systems to regulate externalities appears to be relatively unimportant in terms of its magnitude.

Second, although it is more difficult to get a sense of the extent of the 'technical inefficiencies' associated with deviations from cost minimization, the analysis does indicate that even where profit maximization is not the sole or dominant objective of the source, there are other considerations that can make it in the interest of polluters to engage in (relatively) efficient levels of abatement activities in response to effluent charges. We found, for example, that in our versions of both the Williamson model of utility-maximizing managers of private firms and the Niskanen model of bureaucracy, there exist incentives promoting cost-minimizing behavior with respect to abatement activities. While these incentives are no doubt blunted somewhat by a certain amount of 'managerial slack', there is at least a real rationale for managers and bureaucrats to seek out cost-saving abatement techniques.

More generally, the central point is that the case for relying on pricing incentives for pollution control in a mixed economy is really little different from that for using prices to guide the allocation of other inputs. While there obviously exists some degree of technical inefficiency in the economy associated with departures from cost-minimizing behavior, there is little reason to believe that the extent of such inefficiencies in pollution control under a system of effluent fees (or marketable emission permits) will be any greater (or any less) than in the use of labor, capital, and other factor inputs.

The importance of introducing pricing incentives for pollution control is underscored by an emerging empirical literature that indicates that existing programs of direct controls are generating enormous waste: abatement costs on the order of two to ten times as large as needed to attain the designated standards of environmental quality [see, for example, Atkinson and Lewis (1974), Palmer et al. (1980), Seskin et al. (1983), and Kneese et al. (1971, appendix C)]. These estimates, moreover, refer only to savings based upon existing abatement technology; they do not address the important long-run issues of the stimulus such pricing incentives would provide for research and development of new techniques for the curtailment of emissions. Our judgement is that a least-cost solution over time to the achievment of our objectives for cleaner air and water would probably involve aggregate costs no larger than 20–25 percent of those under the command-and-control programs that have been adopted in the United States.

Even in the presence of a substantial amount of 'slippage' in the form of technical inefficiencies, it is our view that the likely gains from a system of pricing incentives are quite large. We doubt that the complications arising from the existence of a mixed economy compromise significantly the case for a system of pricing incentives for environmental management.

References

Atkinson, S. and D. Lewis, 1974, A cost-effectiveness analysis of alternative air quality control strategies, Journal of Environmental Economics and Management 1, 237–250.

Averch, H. and L. Johnson, 1962, Behavior of the firm under regulatory constraint, American Economic Review 52, 1052–1069.

Bailey, E., 1973, Economic theory of regulatory constraint (Heath, Lexington, Mass.).

Barnett, A., 1980, The Pigouvian tax rule under monopoly, American Economic Review 70, 1037–1041.

Baron, D. and R. Taggart, Jr., 1977, A model of regulation under uncertainty and a test of regulatory bias, Bell Journal of Economics 8, 151–167.

Baumol, W. and A. Klevorick, 1970, Input choices and rate of return regulation: An overview of the discussion, Bell Journal of Economics and Management 1, 162–190.

Baumol, W. and W. Oates, 1975, The theory of environmental policy (Prentice-Hall, Englewood Cliffs, N.J.).

Bower, J., 1970, Managing the resource allocation process (Harvard Business School, Cambridge, Mass.).

Buchanan, J., 1969, External diseconomies, corrective taxes, and market structure, American Economic Review 59, 174–177.

Chandler, Jr., A., 1962, Strategy and structure (MIT Press, Cambridge, Mass.).

Cohen, K. and R. Cyert, 1962, Theory of the firm: Resource allocation in a market economy (Prentice-Hall, Englewood Cliffs, N.J.).

Cowing, T., 1976, The environmental implications of monopoly regulation: A process analysis approach, Journal of Environmental Economics and Management 2, 207–223.

Cowling, K. and D. Mueller, 1978, The social costs of monopoly power, Economic Journal 88, 727–748.

Hahn, R., 1981, Market power and transferable property rights, unpublished paper.

Harberger, A., 1954, Monopoly and resource allocation, American Economic Review 44, 77–87.

Joskow, P., 1972, The determination of the allowed rate of return in a formal regulatory hearing, Bell Journal of Economics and Management Science 3, 632–644.

Joskow, P., 1973, Pricing decisions of regulated firms: A behavioral approach, Bell Journal of Economics and Management Science 4, 118–140.

Kamien, M. and N. Schwartz, 1975, Market structure and innovation: A survey, Journal of Economic Literature 13, 1–37.

King, W., 1977, T.V.A., a major polluter, faces suit to cut sulfur dioxide fumes, New York Times 76 (July 4).

Kneese, A., S. Rolfe and J. Harned, eds., 1971, Managing the environment (Praeger, New York).

Lave, L. and E. Seskin, 1977, Air pollution and human health (Johns Hopkins Press, Baltimore).

Lee, D., 1975, Efficiency of pollution taxation and market structure, Journal of Environmental Economics and Management 2, 69–72.

Migue, J. and G. Belanger, 1974, Toward a general theory of managerial discretion, Public Choice 17, 27–43.

Niskanen, Jr., W., 1977, Bureaucracy and representative government (Aldine, Chicago).

Oates, W. and D. Strassmann, 1978, The use of effluent fees to regulate public-sector sources of pollution: An application of the Niskanen model, Journal of Environmental Economics and Management 5, 283–291.

Palmer, A., et al., 1980, Economic implications of regulating chlorofluorocarbon emissions from nonaerosol applications (Rand, Santa Monica, California).

Peles, Y. and J. Stein, 1976, The effect of rate of return regulation is highly sensitive to the nature of uncertainty, American Economic Review 66, 278–289.

Peltzman, S., 1976, Toward a more general theory of regulation, Journal of Law and Economics 19, 211–240.

Roberts, M. and J. Bluhm, 1981, The choices of power: Utilities face the environmental challenge (Harvard University Press, Cambridge, Mass.).

Robison, H.D., 1983, Three essays on input–output analysis, unpublished Ph.D. dissertation, University of Maryland, College Park, Md.

Schwartzman, D., 1960, The burden of monopoly, Journal of Political Economy 68, 627–630.

Seskin, E., R. Anderson, Jr. and R. Reid, 1983, An empirical analysis of economic strategies for controlling air pollution, Journal of Environmental Economics and Management 10, 112–124.

Shepard, W., 1972, Elements of market structure: An inter-industry analysis, Southern Economic Journal 38, 531–537.

Spann, R., 1974, Rate of return regulation and efficiency in production: An empirical test of the Averch Johnson thesis, Bell Journal of Economics and Management Science 5, 38–52.

Stigler, G., 1971, The theory of economic regulation, Bell Journal of Economics and Management Science 2, 3–21.

Williamson, O., 1963, Managerial discretion and business behavior, American Economic Review 53, 1032–1057.

Wilson, J., et al., 1980, The politics of regulation (Basic Books, New York).

17

Journal of Economic Perspectives—Volume 3, Number 2—Spring 1989—Pages 95–114

Economic Prescriptions for Environmental Problems: How the Patient Followed the Doctor's Orders

Robert W. Hahn

One of the dangers with ivory tower theorizing is that it is easy to lose sight of the actual set of problems which need to be solved, and the range of potential solutions. As one who frequently engages in this exercise, I can attest to this fact. In my view, this loss of sight has become increasingly evident in the theoretical structure underlying environmental economics, which often emphasizes elegance at the expense of realism.

In this paper, I will argue that both normative and positive theorizing could greatly benefit from a careful examination of the results of recent innovative approaches to environmental management. The particular set of policies examined here involves two tools which have received widespread support from the economics community: marketable permits and emission charges (Pigou, 1932; Dales, 1968; Kneese and Schultze, 1975). Both tools represent ways to induce businesses to search for lower cost methods of achieving environmental standards. They stand in stark contrast to the predominant "command-and-control" approach in which a regulator specifies the technology a firm must use to comply with regulations. Under highly restrictive conditions, it can be shown that both of the economic approaches share the desirable feature that any gains in environmental quality will be obtained at the lowest possible cost (Baumol and Oates, 1975).

Until the 1960s, these tools only existed on blackboards and in academic journals, as products of the fertile imaginations of academics. However, some countries have recently begun to explore using these tools as part of a broader strategy for managing environmental problems.

■ *Robert W. Hahn is Senior Staff Economist, Council of Economic Advisers, Washington, D.C., and Associate Professor of Economics, Carnegie–Mellon University, Pittsburgh, Pennsylvania.*

This paper chronicles the experience with both marketable permits and emissions charges. It also provides a selective analysis of a variety of applications in Europe and the United States and shows how the actual use of these tools tends to depart from the role which economists have conceived for them.

The Selection of Environmental Instruments

In thinking about the design and implementation of policies, it is generally assumed that policy makers can choose from a variety of "instruments" for achieving specified objectives. The environmental economics literature generally focuses on the selection of instruments that minimize the overall cost of achieving prescribed environmental objectives.

One instrument which has been shown to supply the appropriate incentives, at least in theory, is marketable permits. The implementation of marketable permits involves several steps. First, a target level of environmental quality is established. Next, this level of environmental quality is defined in terms of total allowable emissions. Permits are then allocated to firms, with each permit enabling the owner to emit a specified amount of pollution. Firms are allowed to trade these permits among themselves. Assuming firms minimize their total production costs, and the market for these permits is competitive, it can be shown that the overall cost of achieving the environmental standard will be minimized (Montgomery, 1972).

Marketable permits are generally thought of as a "quantity" instrument because they ration a fixed supply of a commodity, in this case pollution. The polar opposite of a quantity instrument is a "pricing" instrument, such as emissions charges. The idea underlying emissions charges is to charge polluters a fixed price for each unit of pollution. In this way, they are provided with an incentive to economize on the amount of pollution they produce. If all firms are charged the same price for pollution, then marginal costs of abatement are equated across firms, and this result implies that the resulting level of pollution is reached in a cost-minimizing way.

Economists have attempted to estimate the effectiveness of these approaches. Work by Plott (1983) and Hahn (1983) reveals that implementation of these ideas in a laboratory setting leads to marked increases in efficiency levels over traditional forms of regulation, such as setting standards for each individual source of pollution. The work based on simulations using actual costs and environmental data reveals a similar story. For example, in a review of several studies examining the potential for marketable permits, Tietenberg (1985, pp. 43–44) found that potential control costs could be reduced by more than 90 percent in some cases. Naturally, these results are subject to the usual cautions that a competitive market actually must exist for the results to hold true. Perhaps more importantly, the results assume that it is possible to easily monitor and enforce a system of permits or taxes. The subsequent analysis will suggest that the capacity to monitor and enforce can dramatically affect the choice of instruments.

Following the development of a normative theory of instrument choice, a handful of scholars began to explore reasons why environmental regulations are actually selected. This positive environmental literature tends to emphasize the potential winners and losers from environmental policies as a way of explaining the conditions under which we will observe such policies. For example, Buchanan and Tullock (1975) argue that the widespread use of source-specific standards rather than a fee can be explained by looking at the potential profitability of the affected industry under the two regimes. After presenting the various case studies, I will review some of the insights from positive theory and see how they square with the facts.

The formal results in the positive and normative theory of environmental economics are elegant. Unfortunately, they are not immediately applicable, since virtually none of the systems examined below exhibits the purity of the instruments which are the subject of theoretical inquiry. The presentation here highlights those instruments which show a marked resemblance to marketable permits or emission fees. Together, the two approaches to pollution control span a wide array of environmental problems, including toxic substances, air pollution, water pollution and land disposal.

Marketable Permits

In comparison with charges, marketable permits have not received widespread use. Indeed, there appear to be only four existing environmental applications; three of them in the United States. One involves the trading of emissions rights of various pollutants regulated under the Clean Air Act; a second involves trading of lead used in gasoline; a third addresses the control of water pollution on a river; and a fourth involves air pollution trading in Germany and will not be addressed here because of limited information (see Sprenger, 1986). These programs exhibit dramatic differences in performance, which can be traced back to the rules used to implement these approaches.

Wisconsin Fox River Water Permits

In 1981, the state of Wisconsin implemented an innovative program aimed at controlling biological oxygen demand (BOD) on a part of the Fox River (Novotny, 1986, p. 11).[1] The program was designed to allow for the limited trading of marketable discharge permits. The primary objective was to allow firms greater flexibility in abatement options while still maintaining environmental quality. The program is administered by the state of Wisconsin in accord with the Federal Water Pollution Control Act. Firms are issued five-year permits which define their wasteload allocation. This allocation defines the initial distribution of permits for each firm.

Early studies estimated that substantial savings, on the order of $7 million per year, could result after implementing this trading system (O'Neil, 1983, p. 225).

---

[1]BOD is a measure of the demand for dissolved oxygen imposed on a water body by organic effluents.

However, actual cost savings have been minimal. In the six years that the program has been in existence, there has been only one trade. Given the initial fanfare about this system, its performance to date has been disappointing.

A closer look at the nature of the market and the rules for trading reveals that the result should not have been totally unexpected. The regulations are aimed at two types of dischargers: pulp and paper plants and municipal waste treatment plants. David and Joeres (1983) note that the pulp and paper plants have an oligopolistic structure, and thus may not behave as competitive firms in the permit market. Moreover, it is difficult to know how the municipal utilities will perform under this set of rules, since they are subject to public utility regulation (Hahn and Noll, 1983). Trading is also limited by location. There are two points on the river where pollution tends to peak, and firms are divided into "clusters" so that trading will not increase BOD at either of these points. There are only about 6 or 7 firms in each cluster (Patterson, 1987). Consequently, markets for wasteload allocations may be quite thin.

In addition, Novotny (1986) has argued that several restrictions on transfers may have had a negative impact on potential trading. Any transaction between firms requires modifying or reissuing permits. Transfers must be for at least a year; however, the life of the permit is only five years. Moreover, parties must waive any rights to the permit after it expires, and it is unclear how trading will affect the permit renewal process. These conditions create great uncertainty over the future value of the property right. Added to the problems created by these rules are the restrictions on eligibility for trades. Firms are required to justify the "need" for permits. This effectively limits transfers to new dischargers, plants which are expanding, and treatment plants that cannot meet the requirements, despite their best efforts. Trades that only reduce operating costs are not allowed. With all the uncertainty and high transactions costs, it is not surprising that trading has gotten off to a very slow start.

While the marketable permit system for the Fox River was being hailed as a success by economists, the paper mills did not enthusiastically support the idea (Novotny, 1986, p. 15). Nor have the mills chosen to explore this option once it has been implemented. Indeed, by almost any measure, this limited permit trading represents a minor part of the regulatory structure. The mechanism builds on a large regulatory infrastructure where permits specifying treatment and operating rules lie at the center. The new marketable permits approach retains many features of the existing standards-based approach. The initial allocations are based on the status quo, calling for equal percentage reductions from specified limits. This "grandfathering" approach has a great deal of political appeal for existing firms. New firms must continue to meet more stringent requirements than old firms, and firms must meet specified technological standards before trading is allowed.

Emissions Trading

By far the most significant and far-reaching marketable permit program in the United States is the emissions trading policy. Started over a decade ago, the policy attempts to provide greater flexibility to firms charged with controlling air pollutant emissions.[2] Because the program represents a radical departure in the approach to pollution regulation, it has come under close scrutiny by a variety of interest groups. Environmentalists have been particularly critical. These criticisms notwithstanding, the Environmental Protection Agency Administrator Lee Thomas (1986) characterized the program as "one of EPA's most impressive accomplishments."

Emissions trading has four distinct elements. Netting, the first program element, was introduced in 1974. Netting allows a firm which creates a new source of emissions in a plant to avoid the stringent emission limits which would normally apply by reducing emissions from another source in the plant. Thus, net emissions from the plant do not increase significantly. A firm using netting is only allowed to obtain the necessary emission credits from its own sources. This is called *internal trading* because the transaction involves only one firm. Netting is subject to approval at the state level, not the federal.

Offsets, the second element of emissions trading, are used by new emission sources in "non-attainment areas." (A non-attainment area is a region which has not met a specified ambient standard.) The Clean Air Act specified that no new emission sources would be allowed in non-attainment areas after the original 1975 deadlines for meeting air quality standards passed. Concern that this prohibition would stifle economic growth in these areas prompted EPA to institute the offset rule. This rule specified that new sources would be allowed to locate in non-attainment areas, but only if they "offset" their new emissions by reducing emissions from existing sources by even larger amounts. The offsets could be obtained through internal trading, just as with netting. However, they could also be obtained from other firms directly, which is called *external trading*.

Bubbles, though apparently considered by EPA to be the centerpiece of emissions trading, were not allowed until 1979. The name derives from the placing of an imaginary bubble over a plant, with all emissions exiting at a single point from the bubble. A bubble allows a firm to sum the emission limits from individual sources of a pollutant in a plant, and to adjust the levels of control applied to different sources as long as this aggregate limit is not exceeded. Bubbles apply to existing sources. The policy allows for both internal and external trades. Initially, every bubble had to be approved at the federal level as an amendment to a state's implementation plan. In 1981, EPA approved a "generic rule" for bubbles in New Jersey which allowed the state to give final approval for bubbles. Since then, several other states have followed suit.

Banking, the fourth element of emissions trading, was developed in conjunction with the bubble policy. Banking allows firms to save emission reductions above and beyond permit requirements for future use in emissions trading. While EPA action was initially required to allow banking, the development of banking rules and the administration of banking programs has been left to the states.

---

[2] Pollutants covered under the policy include volatile organic compounds, carbon monoxide, sulfur dioxide, particulates, and nitrogen oxides (Hahn and Hester, 1986).

Table 1
Summary of emissions trading activity

Activity		Estimated number of internal transactions	Estimated number of external transactions	Estimated Cost savings (millions)	Environmental quality impact
Netting		5,000 to 12,000	None	$25 to $300 in Permitting costs; $500 to $12,000 in emission control costs	Insignificant in individual cases; Probably insignificant in aggregate
Offsets		1800	200	See text	Probably insignificant
Bubbles:	Federally approved	40	2	$300	Insignificant
	State approved	89	0	$135	Insignificant
Banking		< 100	< 20	Small	Insignificant

Source: Hahn and Hester (1986)

The performance of emissions trading can be measured in several ways. A summary evaluation which assesses the impact of the program on abatement costs and environmental quality is provided in Table 1. For each emissions trading activity, an estimate of cost savings, the environmental quality effect, and the number of trades is given. In each case, the estimates are for the entire life of the program. As can be seen from the table, the level of activity under various programs varies dramatically. More netting transactions have taken place than any other type, but all of these have necessarily been internal. The wide range placed on this estimate, 5000 to 12,000, reflects the uncertainty about the precise level of this activity. An estimated 2000 offset transactions have taken place, of which only 10 percent have been external. Fewer than 150 bubbles have been approved. Of these, almost twice as many have been approved by states under generic rules than have been approved at the federal level, and only two are known to have involved external trades. For banking, the figures listed are for the number of times firms have withdrawn banked emission credits for sale or use. While no estimates of the exact numbers of such transactions can be made, upper bound estimates of 100 for internal trades and 20 for external trades indicate the fact that there has been relatively little activity in this area.

Cost savings for both netting and bubbles are substantial. Netting is estimated to have resulted in the most cost savings, with a total of between $525 million to over $12 billion from both permitting and emissions control cost savings.[3] By allowing new or modified sources to locate in areas that are highly polluted, offsets confer a major

---

[3]The wide range of this estimate reflects the uncertainty which results from the fact that little information has been collected on netting.

economic benefit on firms which use them. While the size of this economic benefit is not easily estimated, it is probably in the hundreds of millions of dollars. Federally approved bubbles have resulted in savings estimated at $300 million, while state bubbles have resulted in an estimated $135 million in cost savings. Average savings from federally approved bubbles are higher than those for state approved bubbles. Average savings from bubbles are higher than those from netting, which reflects the fact that bubble savings may be derived from several emissions sources in a single transaction, while netting usually involves cost savings at a single source. Finally, the cost savings from the use of banking cannot be estimated, but is necessarily small given the small number of banking transactions which have occurred.

The performance evaluation of emissions trading activities reveals a mixed bag of accomplishments and disappointments. The program has clearly afforded many firms flexibility in meeting emission limits, and this flexibility has resulted in significant aggregate cost savings—in the billions of dollars. However, these cost savings have been realized almost entirely from internal trading. They fall far short of the potential savings which could be realized if there were more external trading. While cost savings have been substantial, the program has led to little or no net change in the level of emissions.

The evolution of the emissions trading can best be understood in terms of a struggle over the nature and distribution of property rights. Emissions trading can be seen as a strategy by regulators to provide industry with increased flexibility while offering environmentalists continuing progress toward environmental quality goals. Meeting these two objectives requires a careful balancing act. To provide industry with greater flexibility, EPA has attempted to define a set of property rights that places few restrictions on their use. However, at the same time, EPA has to be sensitive to the concerns of environmentalists and avoid giving businesses too clear a property right to their existing level of pollution. The conflicting interests of these two groups have led regulators to create a set of policies which are specifically designed to deemphasize the explicit nature of the property right. The high transactions costs associated with external trading have induced firms to eschew this option in favor of internal trading or no trading at all.

Like the preceding example of the Fox River, emissions trading is best viewed as an incremental departure from the existing approach. Property rights were grandfathered. Most trading has been internal, and the structure of the Clean Air Act, including its requirement that new sources be controlled more stringently, was largely left intact.

Lead Trading

Lead trading stands in stark contrast to the preceding two marketable permit approaches. It comes by far the closest to an economist's ideal of a freely functioning market. The purpose of the lead trading program was to allow gasoline refiners greater flexibility during a period when the amount of lead in gasoline was being significantly reduced. (For a more detailed analysis of the performance of the lead trading program, see Hahn and Hester, 1987.)

Unlike many other programs, the lead trading program was scheduled to have a fixed life from the outset. Interrefinery trading of lead credits was permitted in 1982. Banking of lead credits was initiated in 1985. The trading program was terminated at the end of 1987. Initially, the period for trading was defined in terms of quarters. No banking of credits was allowed. Three years after initiating the program limited banking was allowed, which allowed firms to carry over rights to subsequent quarters. Banking has been used extensively by firms since its initiation.

The program is notable for its lack of discrimination among different sources, such as new and old sources. It is also notable for its rules regarding the creation of credits. Lead credits are created on the basis of existing standards. A firm does not gain any extra credits for being a large producer of leaded gasoline in the past. Nor is it penalized for being a small producer. The creation of lead credits is based solely on current production levels and average lead content. For example if the standard were 1.1 grams per gallon, and a firm produces 100 gallons of gasoline, it would receive rights entitling it to produce or sell up to 110 (100 × 1.1) grams of lead. To the extent that current production levels are correlated with past production levels, the system acknowledges the existing distribution of property rights. However, this linkage is less explicit than those made in other trading programs.[4]

The success of the program is difficult to measure directly. It appears to have had very little impact on environmental quality. This is because the amount of lead in gasoline is routinely reported by refiners and is easily monitored. The effect the program has had on refinery costs is not readily available. In proposing the rule for banking of lead rights, EPA estimated that resulting savings to refiners would be approximately $228 million (U.S. EPA, 1985a). Since banking activity has been somewhat higher than anticipated by EPA, it is likely that actual cost savings will exceed this amount. No specific estimate of the actual cost savings resulting from lead trading have been made by EPA.

The level of trading activity has been high, far surpassing levels observed in other environmental markets. In 1985, over half of the refineries participated in trading. Approximately 15 percent of the total lead rights used were traded. Approximately 35 percent of available lead rights were banked for future use or trading (U.S. EPA, 1985b, 1986). In comparison, volumes of emissions trading have averaged well below 1 percent of the potential emissions that could have been traded.

From the standpoint of creating a workable regulatory mechanism that induces cost savings, the lead market has to be viewed as a success. Refiners, though initially lukewarm about this alternative, have made good use of this program. It stands out amidst a stream of incentive-based programs as the "noble" exception in that it conforms most closely to the economists' notion of a smoothly functioning market.

Given the success of this market in promoting cost savings over a period in which lead was being reduced, it is important to understand why the market was successful.

---

[4]One of the reasons EPA set up the allocation rule in this way was to try to transfer some of the permit rents from producers to consumers. This will not always occur, however, and depends on the structure of the permits market as well as the underlying production functions.

The lead market had two important features which distinguished it from other markets in environmental credits. The first was that the amount of lead in gasoline could be easily monitored with the existing regulatory apparatus. The second was that the program was implemented after agreement had been reached about basic environmental goals. In particular, there was already widespread agreement that lead was to be phased out of gasoline. This suggests that the success in lead trading may not be easily transferred to other applications in which monitoring is a problem, or environmental goals are poorly defined. Nonetheless, the fact that this market worked well provides ammunition for proponents of market-based incentives for environmental regulation.

New Directions for Marketable Permits

An interesting potential application for marketable permits has arisen in the area of nonpoint source pollution.[5] In 1984, Colorado implemented a program which would allow limited trading between point and nonpoint sources for controlling phosphorous loadings in Dillon Reservoir (Elmore et al., 1984). Firms receive an allocation based on their past production and the holding capacity of the lake. At this time, no trading between point and nonpoint sources has occurred.

As in the case of the Fox River program, point sources are required to make use of the latest technology before they are allowed to trade. The conventional permitting system is used as a basis for trading. Moreover, trades between point and nonpoint sources are required to take place on a 2 for 1 basis. This means for each gram of phosphorous emitted from a point source under a trade, two grams must be reduced from a nonpoint source. Annual cost savings are projected to be about $800,000 (Kashmanian et al., 1986, p. 14); however, projected savings are not always a good indicator of actual savings, as was illustrated in the case of the Fox River.

EPA is also considering using marketable permits as a way of promoting efficiency in the control of chlorofluorocarbons and halons which lead to the depletion of stratospheric ozone.[6] In its notice of proposed rulemaking, EPA suggested grandfathering permits to producers based on their 1986 production levels, and allowing them to be freely traded. This approach is similar to earlier approaches which the agency adopted for emissions trading and lead trading.

The applications covered in this section illustrate that there are a rich array of mechanisms that come under the heading of marketable permits. The common element seems to be that the primary motivation behind marketable permits is to provide increased flexibility in meeting prescribed environmental objectives. This flexibility, in turn, allows firms to take advantage of opportunities to reduce their expenditures on pollution control without sacrificing environmental quality. However, the rules of the marketable permits can sometimes be so restrictive that the flexibility they offer is more imaginary than real.

[5] Point sources represent sources which are well-defined, such as a factory smokestack. Nonpoint sources refer to sources whose emission points are not readily identified, such as fertilizer runoff from farms.
[6] EPA's decision to use a market-based approach to limit stratospheric ozone depletion is examined in Hahn and McGartland (1988).

Charges in Practice

Charge systems in four countries are examined. Examples are drawn from France, Germany, the Netherlands, and the United States. Particular systems were selected because they were thought to be significant either in their scope, their effect on revenues, or their impact on the cost effectiveness of environmental regulation. While the focus is on water effluent charges, a variety of systems are briefly mentioned at the end of this section which cover other applications.

Charges in France

The French have had a system of effluent charges on water pollutants in place since 1969 (Bower et al., 1981). The system is primarily designed to raise revenues which are then used to help maintain or improve water quality. Though the application of charges is widespread, they are generally set at low levels.[7] Moreover, charges are rarely based on actual performance. Rather, they are based on the expected level of discharge by various industries. There is no explicit connection between the charge paid by a given discharger and the subsidy received for reducing discharges (Bower et al., 1981, p. 126). However, charges are generally earmarked for use in promoting environmental quality in areas related to the specific charge. The basic mechanism by which these charges improve environmental quality is through judicious earmarking of the revenues for pollution abatement activities.

In evaluating the charge system, it is important to understand that it is a major, but by no means dominant, part of the French system for managing water quality. Indeed, in terms of total revenues, a sewage tax levied on households and commercial enterprises is larger in magnitude (Bower et al., 1981, p. 142). Moreover, the sewage tax is assessed on the basis of actual volumes of water used. Like most other charge systems, the charge system in France is based on a system of water quality permits, which places constraints on the type and quantity of effluent a firm may discharge. These permits are required for sources discharging more than some specified quantity (Bower et al., 1981, p. 130).

Charges now appear to be accepted as a way of doing business in France. They provide a significant source of revenues for water quality control. One of the keys to their initial success appears to have been the gradual introduction and raising of charges. Charges started at a very low level and were gradually raised to current levels (Bower et al., 1981, p. 22). Moreover, the pollutants on which charges are levied has expanded considerably since the initial inception of the charge program.[8]

Charges in Germany

The German system of effluent charges is very similar to the French system. Effluent charges cover a wide range of pollutants, and the charges are used to cover

---

[7]Charges cover a wide variety of pollutants, including suspended solids, biological oxygen demand, chemical oxygen demand, and selected toxic chemicals.

[8]For example, Brown (1984, p. 114) notes that charges for nitrogen and phosphorous were added in 1982.

administrative expenses for water quality management and to subsidize projects which improve water quality (Brown and Johnson, 1984, p. 934, 939, 945). The bills that industry and municipalities pay are generally based on expected volume and concentration (Brown and Johnson, 1984, p. 934). Charges vary by industry type as well as across municipalities. Charges to industries and municipalities depend on several variables, including size of the municipality, desired level of treatment, and age of equipment (Brown and Johnson, 1984, pp. 934, 938).

Charges have existed in selected areas of Germany for decades (Bower et al., 1981, p. 299). Management of water quality is delegated to local areas. In 1981, a system of nationwide effluent charges was introduced (Bower et al., 1981, p. 226). The federal government provided the basic framework in its 1976 Federal Water Act and Effluent Charge Law (Brown and Johnson, 1984, p. 930). Initially, industry opposed widespread use of charges. But after losing the initial battle, industry focused on how charges would be determined and their effective date of implementation (Brown and Johnson, 1984, p. 932). While hard data are lacking, there is a general perception that the current system is helping to improve water quality.

Charges in the Netherlands

The Netherlands has had a system of effluent charges in place since 1969 (Brown and Bresssers, 1986, p. 4). It is one of the oldest and best administered charge systems, and the charges placed on effluent streams are among the highest. In 1983, the effluent charge per person was $17 in the Netherlands, $6 in Germany, and about $2 in France (Brown and Bressers, 1986, p. 5). Because of the comparatively high level of charges found in the Netherlands, this is a logical place to examine whether charges are having a discernible effect on the level of pollution. Bressers (1983), using a multiple regression approach, argues that charges have made a significant difference for several pollutants. This evidence is also buttressed by surveys of industrial polluters and water board officials which indicate that charges had a significant impact on firm behavior (Brown and Bressers, 1986, pp. 12–13). This analysis is one of the few existing empirical investigations of the effect of effluent charges on resulting pollution.

The purpose of the charge system in the Netherlands is to raise revenue that will be used to finance projects that will improve water quality (Brown and Bressers, 1986, p. 4). Like its counterparts in France and Germany, the approach to managing water quality uses both permits and effluent charges for meeting ambient standards (Brown and Bressers, 1986, p. 2).[9] Permits tend to be uniform across similar discharges. The system is designed to ensure that water quality will remain the same or get better (Brown and Bressers, 1986 p. 2). Charges are administered both on volume and concentration. Actual levels of discharge are monitored for larger polluters, while small polluters often pay fixed fees unrelated to actual discharge (Bressers, 1983, p. 10).

---

[9]Emission and effluent standards apply to individual sources of pollution while ambient standards apply to regions such as a lake or an air basin.

Charges have exhibited a slow but steady increase since their inception (Brown and Bressers, 1986, p. 5). This increase in charges has been correlated with declining levels of pollutants. Effluent discharge declined from 40 population equivalents in 1969 to 15.3 population equivalents in 1980, and it was projected to decline to 4.4 population equivalents in 1985 (Brown and Bressers, 1986, p. 10). Thus, over 15 years, this measure of pollution declined on the order of 90 percent.

As in Germany, there was initial opposition from industry to the use of charges. Brown and Bressers (1986, p. 4) also note opposition from environmentalists, who tend to distrust market-like mechanisms. Nonetheless, charges have enjoyed widespread acceptance in a variety of arenas in the Netherlands.

One final interesting feature of the charge system in the Netherlands relates to the differential treatment of new and old plants. In general, newer plants face more stringent regulation than older plants (Brown and Bressers, 1986, p. 10). As we shall see, this is also a dominant theme in American regulation.

Charges in the United States

The United States has a modest system of user charges levied by utilities that process wastewater, encouraged by federal environmental regulations issued by the Environmental Protection Agency. They are based on both volume and strength, and vary across utilities. In some cases, charges are based on actual discharges, and in others, as a rule of thumb, they are related to average behavior. In all cases, charges are added to the existing regulatory system which relies heavily on permits and standards.

Both industry and consumers are required to pay the charges. The primary purpose for the charges is to raise revenues to help meet the revenue requirements of the treatment plants, which are heavily subsidized by the federal government. The direct environmental and economic impact of these charges is apparently small (Boland, 1986, p. 12). They primarily serve as a mechanism to help defray the costs of the treatment plants. Thus, the charges used in the United States are similar in spirit to the German and French systems already described. However, their size appears to be smaller, and the application of the revenues is more limited.

Other Fee-Based Systems and Lessons

There are a variety of other fee-based systems which have not been included in this discussion. Brown (1984) did an analysis of incentive-based systems to control hazardous wastes in Europe and found that a number of countries had adopted systems, some of which had a marked economic effect. The general trend was to use either a tax on waste outputs or tax on feedstocks that are usually correlated with the level of waste produced. Companies and government officials were interviewed to ascertain the effects of these approaches. In line with economic theory, charges were found to induce firms to increase expenditures on achieving waste reduction through a variety of techniques including reprocessing of materials, treatment, and input and output substitution. Firms also devoted greater attention to separating waste streams because prices for disposal often varied by the type of waste stream.

The United States has a diverse range of taxes imposed on hazardous waste streams. Several states have land disposal taxes in place. Charges exhibit a wide degree of variation across states. For example, in 1984, charges were \$14/tonne in Wisconsin and \$70.40/tonne in Minnesota (U.S. CBO, 1985, p. 82). Charges for disposal at landfills also vary widely. The effect of these different charges is very difficult to estimate because of the difficulty in obtaining the necessary data on the quantity and quality of waste streams, as well as the economic variables.

The preceding analysis reveals that there are a wide array of fee-based systems in place designed to promote environmental quality. In a few cases, the fees were shown to have a marked effect on firm behavior; however, in the overwhelming majority of cases studied, the direct economic effect of fees appears to have been small. Several patterns repeat themselves through these examples.

First, the major motivation for implementing emission fees is to raise revenues, which are then usually earmarked for activities which promote environmental quality.[10] Second, most charges are not large enough to have a dramatic impact on the behavior of polluters. In fact, they are not designed to have such an effect. They are relatively low and not directly related to the behavior of individual firms and consumers. Third, there is a tendency for charges to increase faster than inflation over time. Presumably, starting out with a relatively low charge is a way of testing the political waters as well as determining whether the instrument will have the desired effects.

Implementing Market-Based Environmental Programs

An examination of the charge and marketable permits schemes reveals that they are rarely, if ever, introduced in their textbook form. Virtually all environmental regulatory systems using charges and marketable permits rely on the existing permitting system. This result should not be terribly surprising. Most of these approaches were not implemented from scratch; rather, they were grafted onto regulatory systems in which permits and standards play a dominant role.

Perhaps as a result of these hybrid approaches, the level of cost savings resulting from implementing charges and marketable permits is generally far below their theoretical potential. Cost savings can be defined in terms of the savings which would result from meeting a prescribed environmental objective in a less costly manner. As noted, most of the charges to date have not had a major incentive effect. We can infer from this that polluters have not been induced to search for a lower cost mix of meeting environmental objectives as a result of the implementation of charge schemes. Thus, it seems unlikely that charges have performed terribly well on narrow efficiency grounds. The experience on marketable permits is similar. Hahn and Hester (1986)

---

[10]The actual application of fees is similar in spirit to the more familiar deposit-refund approaches that are used for collecting bottles and cans.

argue that cost savings for emissions trading fall far short of their theoretical potential. The only apparent exception to this observation is the lead trading program, which has enjoyed very high levels of trading activity.

The example of lead trading leads to another important observation; in general, different charge and marketable permit systems exhibit wide variation in their effect on economic efficiency. On the whole, there is more evidence for cost savings with marketable permits than with charges.

While the charge systems and marketable permit systems rarely perform well in terms of efficiency, it is important to recognize that their performance is broadly consistent with economic theory. This observation may appear to contradict what was said earlier about the departure of these systems from the economic ideal. However, it is really an altogether different observation. It suggests that the performance of the markets and charge systems can be understood in terms of basic economic theory. For example, where barriers to trading are low, more trading is likely to occur. Where charges are high and more directly related to individual actions, they are more likely to affect the behavior of firms or consumers.

If these instruments are to be measured by their effect on environmental quality, the results are not very impressive. In general, the direct effect of both charges and marketable permits on environmental quality appears to be neutral or slightly positive. The effect of lead trading has been neutral in the aggregate. The effect of emissions trading on environmental quality has probably been neutral or slightly positive. The direct effect of charges on polluter incentives has been modest, although the indirect environmental effect of spending the revenue raised by charges has been significant.

The evidence on charges and marketable permits points to an intriguing conclusion about the nature of these instruments. Charges and marketable permits have played fundamentally different roles in meeting environmental objectives. Charges are used primarily to improve environmental quality by redistributing revenues. Marketable permits are used primarily to promote cost savings.

The positive theory of instrument choice as it relates to pollution control has been greatly influenced by the work of Buchanan and Tullock (1975). They argue that firms will prefer emission standards to emission taxes because standards result in higher profits. Emission standards serve as a barrier to entry to new firms, thus raising firm profits. Charges, on the other hand, do not preclude entry by new firms, and also represent an additional cost to firms. Their argument is based on the view that industry is able to exert its preference for a particular instrument because it is more likely to be well-organized than consumers.

While this argument is elegant, it misses two important points. The first is that within particular classes of instruments, there is a great deal of variation in the performance of instruments. The second is that most solutions to problems involve the application of multiple instruments. Thus, while the Buchanan and Tullock theory explains why standards are chosen over an idealized form of taxes, it does little to help explain the rich array of instruments that are observed in the real world. In particular, under what situations would we be likely to observe different mixes of instruments?

Several authors have explored these different issues for instrument choice within this basic framework (Coelho, 1976; Dewees, 1983; Yohe, 1976). The basic insight of this work is that the argument that standards will be preferred to taxes depends on the precise nature of the instruments being compared.

Another weakness in the existing theory is that the instruments are not generally used in the way that is suggested by the theory. Most emissions charges, for example, are used as a revenue raising device for subsidizing abatement activity, but a few also have pronounced direct effects on polluters. Most marketable permit approaches are not really designed to create markets. Moreover, the different types of trading schemes perform with widely varying success.

The data from the examples given earlier can be used to begin to piece together some of the elements of a more coherent theory of instrument choice. For example, it is clear that distributional concerns play an important role in the acceptability of user charges. The revenue from such charges is usually earmarked for environmental activities related to those contributions. Thus, charges from a noise surcharge will be used to address noise pollution. Charges for water discharges will be used to construct treatment plants and subsidize industry in building equipment to abate water pollution. This pattern suggests that different industries want to make sure that their contributions are used to address pollution problems for which they are likely to be held accountable. Thus, industry sees it as only fair that, as a whole, they get some benefit from making these contributions.

The "recycling" of revenues from charges points up the importance of the existing distribution of property rights. This is also true in the case of marketable permits. The "grandfathering" of rights to existing firms based on the current distribution of rights is an important focal point in many applications of limited markets in pollution rights (Rolph, 1983; Welch, 1983). All the marketable permit programs in the United States place great importance on the existing distribution of rights.

In short, all of the charge and marketable permit systems described earlier place great importance on the status quo. Charges, when introduced, tend to be phased in. Marketable permits, when introduced, usually are optional in the sense that existing firms can meet standards through trading of permits or by conventional means. In contrast, new or expanding firms are not always afforded the same options. For example, new firms must still purchase emission credits if they choose to locate in a non-attainment area, even if they have purchased state-of-the-art pollution control equipment and will pollute less than existing companies. This is an example of a "bias" against new sources. While not efficient from an economic viewpoint, this pattern is consistent with the political insight that new sources don't "vote" while existing sources do.

Though the status quo is important in all applications studied here, it does not explain by itself the rich variety of instruments that are observed. For example, there has been heated controversy over emissions trading since its inception, but comparatively little controversy over the implementation of lead trading. How can economists begin to understand the difference in attitudes towards these two programs?

There are several important differences between emissions trading and lead trading. In the case of lead standards, there appears to be agreement about the distribution of property rights, and the standard that defined them. Refiners had the right to put lead in gasoline at specified levels during specified time periods. Lead in gasoline was reduced to a very low level at the end of 1987. In contrast to lead, there is great disagreement about the underlying distribution of property rights regarding emissions trading. Environmentalists continue to adhere to the symbolic goal of zero pollution. Industry believes and acts as if its current claims on the environment, without any emission reductions, represent a property right.

In the case of lead trading, output could be relatively easily monitored using the existing regulatory apparatus. This was not the case for emissions trading. A new system was set up for evaluating proposed trades. This was, in part, due to existing weaknesses in the current system of monitoring and enforcement. It was also a result of concerns that environmentalists had expressed about the validity of such trades.

The effect that emissions trading was likely to have on environmental quality was much less certain than that of the lead trading program. Some environmentalists viewed emissions trading as a loophole by which industry could forestall compliance, and Hahn and Hester (1986) found some evidence that bubbles were occasionally used for that purpose. The effects of lead trading were much more predictable. Until 1985, there was no banking, so the overall temporal pattern of lead emissions remained unchanged under the program. With the addition of banking in 1985, this pattern was changed slightly, but within well-defined limits.

To accommodate these differing concerns, different rules were developed for the two cases. In the case of lead trading, rights are traded on a one-for-one basis. In contrast, under emissions trading, rights are not generally traded on a one-for-one basis. Rather, most trades must show a net improvement in environmental quality. In the case of lead, all firms are treated equally from the standpoint of trading. In the case of emissions trading, new firms must meet stringent standards before being allowed to engage in trading.

This comparison suggests is that it is possible to gain important insights into the likely performance and choice of instruments by understanding the forces that led to their creation. Analyzing the underlying beliefs about property rights to pollution may be vital both for the political success of the measure and for how well it works in terms of pure economic efficiency.

This view of efficiency is similar to, but should not be confused with, the notion of efficiency advanced by Becker (1983). Becker argues that government will tend to choose mechanisms which are more efficient over those which are less efficient in redistributing revenues from less powerful to more powerful groups. To the extent that his argument is testable, I believe it is not consistent with the facts. For example, the U.S. currently has a policy that directs toxic waste dumps to be cleaned up in priority order. The policy makes no attempt to examine whether a greater risk reduction could be attained with a different allocation of expenditures. Given a finite budget constraint, this policy does not make sense from a purely economic viewpoint. However, it might make sense if environmentalists hoped that more stringent policies would emerge in the future. Or it might make sense if Congress wants to be perceived as doing the job "right," even if only a small part of the job gets done.

A second example can be drawn from emissions trading. It is possible to design marketable permit systems which are more efficient and ensure better environmental quality over time (Hahn and Noll, 1982; Hahn, 1987), yet these systems have not been implemented. Environmentalists may be reluctant to embrace market alternatives because they fear it may give a certain legitimacy to the act of polluting. Moreover, they may not believe in the expected results. Thus, for Becker's theory to hold in an absolute sense, it would be necessary to construct fairly complicated utility functions. The problem is that the theory does not explicitly address how choices are made by lobbyists, legislators and bureaucrats (Campos, 1987).

These choices may be made in different ways in different countries. How can it be explained, for example, that a large array of countries use fees, while only two countries use marketable permits (and the application of permits in Germany is fairly limited)? Noll (1983) has argued that the political institutions of different countries can provide important clues about regulatory strategy. In addition, the comparison of lead trading and emissions trading revealed that the very nature of the environmental problem can have an important effect on interest group attitudes.

Interest group attitudes can be expected to vary across countries. In the Netherlands, Opschoor (1986, p. 15) notes that environmental groups tend to prefer charges while employer groups prefer regulatory instruments. Barde (1986, pp. 10–11) notes that the political "acceptability" of charges is high in both France and the Netherlands. Nonetheless, some French airlines have refused to pay noise charges because the funds are not being used (Barde, 1986, p. 12). In Italy, there has been widespread opposition from industry and interest groups (Panella, 1986, pp. 6, 22). While German industry has accepted the notion of charges, some industries have criticized the differential charge rates across jurisdictions. In the United States, environmentalists have shown a marked preference for regulatory instruments, eschewing both charges and marketable permits. These preferences may help to explain the choice of instruments in various countries as well as the relative utilization of different instruments. In addition, interest groups in different countries will share different clusters of relevant experiences, which will help to determine the feasible space for alternatives.

In short, existing theories could benefit from more careful analysis of the regulatory status quo, underlying beliefs about property rights, and how political choices are actually made in different countries.

The review of marketable permits and charge systems has demonstrated that regulatory systems involving multiple instruments are the rule rather than the exception. The fundamental problem is to determine the most appropriate mix, with an eye to both economic and political realities.

In addition to selecting an appropriate mix of instruments, attention needs to be given to the effects of having different levels of government implement selected policies. It might seem, for example, that if the problem is local, then the logical choice for addressing the problem is the local regulatory body. However, this is not always true. Perhaps the problem may require a level of technical expertise that does not reside at the local level, in which case some higher level of government involvement may be required. What is clear from a review of implementing environmental policies is that the level of oversight can affect the implementation of policies. For example, Hahn and Hester (1986) note that a marked increase in bubble activity is associated with a decrease in federal oversight.

Because marketable permit approaches have been shown to have a demonstrable effect on cost savings without sacrificing environmental quality, this instrument can be expected to receive more widespread use. One factor which will stimulate the application of this mechanism is the higher marginal costs of abatement that will be faced as environmental standards are tightened. A second factor which will tend, to stimulate the use of both charges and marketable permits is a "demonstration effect." Several countries have already implemented these mechanisms with some encouraging results. The experience gained in implementing these tools will stimulate their use in future applications. A third factor which will affect the use of both of these approaches is the technology of monitoring and enforcement. As monitoring costs go down, the use of mechanisms such as direct charges and marketable permits can be expected to increase. The combination of these factors leads to the prediction that greater use of these market-based environmental systems will be made in the future.

■ *This research was funded by the National Science Foundation and the Program for Technology and Society at Carnegie Mellon University. I would like to thank Gordon Hester, Dan Nagin, and the editors for helpful comments. The views expressed herein are those of the author and do not necessarily reflect the views of the Council of Economic Advisers.*

References

Barde, J., "Use of Economic Instruments for Environmental Protection: Discussion Paper," ENV/ECO/86.16, Organization for Economic Cooperation and Development, September 9, 1986.

Baumol, W. and Oates, W. *The Theory of Environmental Policy.* Englewood Cliffs, NJ: Prentice-Hall, 1985.

Becker, G., "A Theory of Competition Among Pressure Groups for Political Influence," *Quarterly Journal of Economics*, 1983, *XCVII*, 371–400.

Boland, J., "Economic Instruments for Environmental Protection in the United States," ENV/ECO/86.14, Organization for Economic Cooperation and Development, September 11, 1986.

Bower, B. et al., *Incentives in Water Quality Management: France and the Ruhr Area.* Washington, D.C.: Resources for the Future, 1981.

Bressers, J., "The Effectiveness of Dutch Water Quality Policy," Twente University of Technology, Netherlands, mimeo, 1983.

Brown, G., Jr., "Economic Instruments: Alternatives or Supplements to Regulations?" *Environment and Economics*, Issue Paper, Environment Directorate OECD, June 1984, 103–120.

Brown, G., Jr. and J. Bresser, "Evidence Supporting Effluent Charges," Twente University of Technology, The Netherlands, mimeo, September 1986.

Brown, G., Jr. and R. Johnson, "Pollution Control by Effluent Charges: It Works in the Federal Republic of Germany, Why Not in the U.S.," *Natural Resources Journal*, 1984, *24*, 929–966.

Buchanan, J. and G. Tullock, "Polluters' Profits and Political Response: Direct Controls Versus Taxes," *American Economic Review*, 1975 *65*, 139–147.

Campos, J., "Toward a Theory of Instrument Choice in the Regulation of Markets," California Institute of Technology, Pasadena, California, mimeo, January 26, 1987.

Coelho, P., "Polluters' and Political Response: Direct Control Versus Taxes: Comment," *American Economic Review*, 1976, *66*, 976–978.

Dales, J., *Pollution, Property and Prices*. Toronto: University Press, 1968.

David, M. and E. Joeres, "Is a Viable Implementation of TDPs Transferable?" In Joeres, E. and M. David, eds., *Buying a Better Environment: Cost-Effective Regulation Through Permit Trading*. Madison: University of Wisconsin Press, 1983, 233–248.

Dewees, D., "Instrument Choice in Environmental Policy," *Economic Inquiry, 1983, XXI, 53–71*.

Elmore, T. et al., "Trading Between Point and Nonpoint Sources: A Cost Effective Method for Improving Water Quality," paper presented at the 57th annual Conference/Exposition of the Water Pollution Control Federation, New Orleans, Louisiana, 1984.

Hahn, R., "Designing Markets in Transferable Property Rights: A Practitioner's Guide." In Joeres, E. and M. David, eds., *Buying a Better Environment: Cost Effective Regulation Through Permit Trading*. Madison: University of Wisconsin Press, 1983, 83–97.

Hahn, R., "Rules, Equality and Efficiency: An Evaluation of Two Regulatory Reforms," Working Paper 87-7, School of Urban and Public Affairs, Carnegie Mellon University, Pittsburgh, Pennsylvania, 1987.

Hahn, R. and G. Hester, "Where Did All the Markets Go?: An Analysis of EPA's Emission Trading Program," Working Paper 87-3, School of Urban and Public Affairs, Carnegie Mellon University, Pittsburgh, Pennsylvania, 1986. Forthcoming in the *Yale Journal on Regulation*.

Hahn, R. and G. Hester, "Marketable Permits: Lessons for Theory and Practice," *Ecology Law Quarterly*, forthcoming.

Hahn, R. and A. McGartland, "The Political Economy of Instrument Choice: An Examination of the U.S. Role in Implementing the Montreal Protocol," Working Paper 88-34, School of Urban and Public Affairs, Carnegie Mellon University, Pittsburgh, Pennsylvania, 1988.

Hahn, R. and Noll, R., "Designing a Market for Tradable Emissions Permits." In Magat, W. ed., *Reform of Environmental Regulation*. Cambridge, MA: Ballinger, 1982, 119–146.

Hahn, R. and Noll, R., "Barriers to Implementing Tradable Air Pollution Permits: Problems of Regulatory Interaction," *Yale Journal on Regulation*, 1983, *1*, 63–91.

Kashmanian, R. et al., "Beyond Categorical Limits: The Case for Pollution Reduction Through Trading," paper presented at the 59th Annual Water Pollution Control Federation Conference, Los Angeles, CA, October 6–9, 1986.

Kneese, A. and Schultze, C., *Pollution, Prices, and Public Policy*. Washington, D.C.: The Brookings Institution, 1975.

Montgomery, W. D., "Markets in Licenses and Efficient Pollution Control Programs," *Journal of Economic Theory*, 1972, *5*, 395–418.

Noll, R., "The Political Foundations of Regulatory Policy," *Zeitschrift fur die gesamte Staatswissenschaft*, 1983, *139*, 377–404.

Novotny, G., "Transferable Discharge Permits for Water Pollution Control In Wisconsin," Department of Natural Resources, Madison, Wisconsin, mimeo, December 1, 1986.

O'Neil, W., "The Regulation of Water Polllution Permit Trading under Conditions of Varying Streamflow and Temperature." In Joeres, E. and M. David, eds., *Buying a Better Environment: Cost-Effective Regulation Through Permit Trading*. Madison, Wisconsin: University of Wisconsin Press, 1983, 219–231.

Opschoor, J., "Economic Instruments for Environmental Protection in the Netherlands," ENV/ECO/86.15, Organization for Economic Cooperation and Development, August 1, 1986.

Panella, G., "Economic Instruments for Environmental Protection in Italy," ENV/ECO/86.11, Organization for Economic Cooperation and Development, September 2, 1986.

Patterson, D., Bureau of Water Resources Management, Wisconsin Department of Natural Resources, Madison, Wisconsin, telephone interview, April 2, 1987.

Pigou, A., *The Economics of Welfare*, fourth edition. London: Macmillan and Co., 1932.

Plott, C., "Externalities and Corrective Policies in Experimental Markets," *Economic Journal*, 1983, *93*, 106–127.

Rolph, E., "Government Allocation of Property Rights: Who Gets What?," *Journal of Policy Analysis and Management*, 1983, *3*, 45–61.

Sprenger, R., "Economic Instruments for Environmental Protection in Germany," Organization for Economic Cooperation and Development, October 7, 1986.

Thomas, L., memorandum attached to Draft Emissions Trading Policy Statement, Environmental Protection Agency, Washington, D.C., May 19, 1986.

Tietenberg, T., *Emissions Trading: An Exercise in Reforming Pollution Policy.* Washington, D.C.: Resources for the Future, 1985.

U.S. Congressional Budget Office, *Hazardous Waste Management: Recent Changes and Policy Alternatives,* Washington, D.C.: U.S. G.P.O., May 1985.

U.S. Environmental Protection Agency, "Costs and Benefits of Reducing Lead in Gasoline, Final Regulatory Impact Analysis," Office of Policy Analysis, February 1985a.

U.S. Environmental Protection Agency, "Quarterly Reports on Lead in Gasoline," Field Operations and Support Division, Office of Air and Radiation, July 16, 1985b.

U.S. Environmental Protection Agency, "Quarterly Reports on Lead in Gasoline," Field Operations and Support Division, Office of Air and Radiation, March 21, May 23, July 15, 1986.

Welch, W., "The Political Feasibility of Full Ownership Property Rights: The Cases of Pollution and Fisheries," *Policy Sciences,* 1983, *16,* 165–180.

Yohe, G., "Polluters' Profits and Political Response: Direct Control Versus Taxes: Comment," *American Economic Review,* 1976, *66,* 981–982.

Part IV
Measuring the Benefits and Costs of Environmental Amenities

[18]

*Methods of Measuring
the Demand for and Value of*

OUTDOOR RECREATION

By Marion Clawson

For several reasons, in recent years there has been a greatly increased interest in the measurement of demand for and value of outdoor recreation. At the same time, there has been a general dissatisfaction with the existing state of knowledge and methods of analysis. This statement is offered in that hope that it may contribute to a better understanding of several important related issues affecting outdoor recreation.

The use of outdoor recreation has been increasing rapidly for many years. For the period since the war, the rate of increase from year to year has run around 10 per cent for many types of areas—higher for some, lower for others.[1] Where records are available for comparatively long periods, it is evident that this rate of increase has been operative for many years. Thus, both national parks and national forests show growth curves approximating this rate. During the war, under the impact of gasoline rationing and other travel restrictions, use of the more distant areas fell off sharply. But use does not decline sharply during depression, and in some minor depressions and for some types of areas it has actually continued to increase, though at a slower rate. The major factors behind the persistent, steady, relatively rapid rise in use of outdoor recreation areas have been increased total population, higher real incomes per capita, greater leisure, and more travel. Since each of these factors is expected to show higher values for the future than today, the trend toward still greater use of outdoor recreation areas presumably will continue. Thus far, there is no evidence at all of a slackening in the rate of growth; at some future date, presumably the growth curve will begin to flatten out, but there is no sign of that now.

The competition for land and water resources for all major

[1] Marion Clawson, *Statistics on Outdoor Recreation* (Washington: Resources for the Future, Inc.), April 1958.

1

2

uses is also increasing. After all, the area of land and the volume of water are essentially fixed, although their usefulness can be increased through capital investment and in other ways. The proper role of recreation as a user of land and water, or as one use in a multiple-purpose program for either, is not easy to measure. In the case of water developments particularly, but also to a degree in management of land, it is customary to measure the economic or monetary gains and costs of each use of land or water. If this process is to be carried to its conclusion, and if recreation is to be considered in the same manner as alternative uses of the resources, then a value must be put on the amount of recreation provided.

If we could place an accurate and acceptable value on outdoor recreation, this would be valuable in resource management in several ways. First of all, it would provide a means for comparing the importance of recreation with that of other uses of the same resources—water in multiple-use water projects, land under multiple-use management programs. As I shall point out later, factors other than comparative values might well be decisive in decisions about use of resources, yet such values would be helpful. Secondly, the value of the recreation to be provided by a proposed recreation project, such as a new park, would provide one measure of the desirability of making the necessary investment in the project. Thirdly, the value of the recreation would provide a ceiling to any fees that might be charged for its use. An accurate estimate of the demand for recreation, in the economist's sense of the term, would permit advance estimates of the level of entrance fees which would just pay operating and maintenance costs, if it were desired to charge fees at this level. Other uses for accurate and detailed estimates of values of recreation probably exist also.

It is for the foregoing reasons that there has been a good deal of pressure for the development of monetary measures of the value of outdoor recreation. Many arguments can be advanced in favor of such a process.[2] The chief argument is that any reasonable estimate of value is better than none at all. Those who advance this argument assume that recreation must in some way be compared, and the more directly the better, with other land and water uses. They argue that not placing a value on recreation is, in this context, equivalent to placing a zero value on it. It might be pointed

    [2] Albert M. Trice and Samuel E. Wood, "Measurement of Recreation Benefits," *Land Economics*, Vol. xxxiv No. 3, August 1958. See also the discussion of their article in the succeeding issue of the same journal.

3

out to those who maintain this position that an estimate which was more than twice the true figure—however the latter is defined —would introduce more error than a zero figure. But there is considerable merit in the position that rational planning of resource development requires a value on recreation wherever it is one of the major uses of land or water.

On the other hand, many have argued against trying to place specific monetary values on outdoor recreation. Arguments against trying to put a value on outdoor recreation fall into two general categories: (1) it can't be done,[3] and (2) it is undesirable to try.[4] Those who argue that an accurate value cannot be put on outdoor recreation may base their objections on theoretical or practical grounds. Some argue that the whole valuation process is inapplicable to essentially subjective experiences. They will ask how one can put a value on the unique and highly personal experience of viewing the Big Trees or the Grand Canyon or some other outstanding spectacle for the first time. They will stress the unique character of such experiences, their emotional content, their intensely personal character, and argue that placing a monetary value on such experiences is a little like placing a monetary value on a mother's love for her child. The present author has found some of the statements about the best outdoor areas and their values, reminiscent of the statements made by the early economists who strove to explain the value of goods such as rare pictures, which had a value but provided no tangible service. Those who argue against monetary valuation of subjective experiences overlook the fact that we do this all the time, not only for such exotics as masterpieces of painting but also for schooling, medicine, and many other aspects of life.

A different type of argument is also employed against monetary values for outdoor recreation—namely, that the practical difficulties of measuring value are too great, even if the theoretical difficulties are solved. Surely something must be conceded to this viewpoint; it would probably be difficult to get fully satisfactory

[3] This is essentially the conclusion of the most formal study of the subject to date: Roy A. Prewitt, *The Economics of Public Recreation - an Economic Study of the Monetary Evaluation of Recreation in the National Parks,* National Park Service, Department of the Interior, 1949. ". . . there is no acceptable standard of evaluation that can be used to place a monetary value on recreation that is not arbitrary." (P. 27).

[4] That the record may be clear, let me admit that I took essentially this position in *Uncle Sam's Acres* (New York: Dodd, Mead, 1951).

4

data on which to measure the value of outdoor recreation. But
perhaps these difficulties have been exaggerated.

The second major argument against trying to place a monetary value on outdoor recreation is that it may be unwise to compute specific monetary values for something on which the major
decisions will be, or should be, based on other grounds. Those
who support outdoor recreation as a healthful activity—or as a
socially necessary one—would deny that the monetary values
should be the chief criterion, no matter how accurately such values could be defined and measured. They would support certain
areas for certain types of outdoor recreation, regardless of monetary
values, and could surely cite strong arguments for their position.
In this regard, such advocates of outdoor recreation are in a position analogous to those who support universal education—while
its value may be great, exceeding its cost, the real arguments for
it are different, and not much conditioned by estimates of monetary value.

The major premise of this paper is that it is both theoretically
possible and practically manageable to put monetary values on
outdoor recreation. The conceptual and theoretical problems,
while somewhat novel, are not insurmountable nor perhaps un-
usually difficult; the problem of getting accurate and dependable
data is serious, but still manageable. On the other hand, while
such monetary valuation can be useful for sound resource planning, too heavy reliance should not be placed upon monetary values. In our modern affluent society, we both can and should concern ourselves with the composition of our economic output as
well as its amount, and with the kind of society we fashion for
ourselves to live in. In this regard, outdoor recreation may be in
the same category as education, health, and several other major
aspects of our modern society.

Some Common Concepts Applied to Outdoor Recreation

Before attempting to measure the net rent or value of the recreation opportunity as such, let us examine four concepts applied
more or less frequently to outdoor recreation. They are:

1. The gross volume of business generated by reason of the
outdoor recreation opportunities. Estimates of this amount
have been made in many instances, are widely popular, and
even have been used as in some way, usually indefinitely, related to the value of the recreation opportunity itself.

5

2. The value added by local business, in the above estimated gross expenditures. Since only part of the gross expenditures represent a local contribution, an obvious step is to try estimating the part of total expenditures which represents local economic activities.

3. The demand for outdoor recreation, in the strict economic sense of the word "demand." This should measure a willingness of users to pay measurable or definable sums of money for specified volumes of outdoor recreation.

4. Consumer's surplus arising from specific outdoor recreation opportunity. When some people get recreation free or at low cost, when they would be willing to pay relatively large sums rather than do without it, then some measure of consumer surplus exists. How may it be defined more precisely, and how measured?

We shall now examine each of these concepts in greater detail, to see more exactly what each tries to measure, how each may be estimated, and what usefulness each may have if accurately estimated.

GROSS VOLUME OF BUSINESS FROM RECREATION

People who partake of outdoor recreation, especially that located relatively long distances away from their homes, necessarily spend money in so doing. These expenditures are for many purposes, and are likely to be made in many places. Estimates of such gross expenditures have been made by many groups—those interested in travel to national parks, those interested in travel of all kinds, those interested in tourist promotion within specific states or districts thereof, local Chambers of Commerce, and many others.[5] The same approach has been used for specific types of

[5] *Yosemite National Park Travel Survey,* National Park Service, California Division of Highways, and Bureau of Public Roads, 1953; *Glacier National Park Tourist Survey,* Montana State Highway Commission, Bureau of Public Roads, and National Park Service, 1951; *Grand Canyon Travel Survey,* Arizona Highway Department, Bureau of Public Roads, and National Park Service, 1954; *Shenandoah National Park Tourist Survey,* Virginia Department of Highways, National Park Service, and Bureau of Public Roads, 1952; *Vacation Survey, Rogue River Basin,* National Park Service, 1950; *The Great Smoky Mountains National Park Travel Study,* North Carolina State Highway and Public Works Commission, Tennessee State Department of Highways and Public Works, and United States Bureau of Public Roads, 1956; *Americans on the Highway, A Report on Habits and Patterns in Vacation Travel,* American Automobile Association, sixth edition, 1956; *The Travel Market among U. S. Families with*

6

outdoor activities, such as fishing and hunting.[6]

Such estimates of gross expenditures for outdoor recreation are very popular, in many quarters. For one thing, they are likely to yield large figures, even if accurate—and they have at times been suspected of exaggeration. If one can say that the tourist business leads to the expenditure of billions of dollars within a the state, and that this sum is exceeded only by the gross output of automobile manufacture, or farming, or some other activity, then one is likely to be able to impress most listeners with the importance of the tourist business. Such large figures are likely to give the impression of a large and profitable business. Indeed, this is one of their chief purposes. If visitors to Y national park spent Z millions of dollars in such visits and the trips necessary thereto, then Y national park must be an important part of the economic life of the state in which it is located.

Such gross expenditure estimates have at times been used in planning multiple-purpose water developments, as an indication of the value of the recreation opportunity provided by the specific projects. It has been argued that those persons making such expenditures must have gotten value received, or they would not have made them, and especially would not have continued to do so year after year. If the gross value of recreation was M millions of dollars, while the gross value of electric power produced was N million dollars, then the ratio of M to N somehow suggests the relative importance of the two.

But no one can be very happy about these estimates of gross expenditures on recreation. They are probably subject to considerable error of estimate, but a more important limitation is their meaning. In the first place, it is obvious that not all the reported expenditure is actually new or increased expenditure—some of it is merely "credited" here when otherwise it would have shown up somewhere else. Food bought while on vacation, for instance, re-

Annual Incomes of $5,000 or More, Research Department, The Curtis Publishing Company, 1955; and *How States Find Out About Their Tourist Trade*, by Robert S. Friedman, Bureau of Governmental Research, University of Maryland. These are only some of the references that have come to the author's attention; many others exist, especially for local areas and of an informal kind.

[6] *National Survey of Fishing and Hunting*, Fish and Wildlife Service, Department of the Interior, Circular 44, 1955; and *An Evaluation of Wildlife Resources in the State of Washington*, by Robert F. Wallace, Bulletin No. 28, Bureau of Economic and Business Research, State College of Washington, 1956. This latter publication lists and analyzes some eight other publications in this general field.

places food that would otherwise have been bought at home. In total, of course, it might be argued that people would have spent as much of their total incomes if they had not gone to enjoy outdoor recreation as they did while enjoying it. But, even within categories, expenditures associated with the outdoor recreation experience are not new or additional, but rather to a greater or lesser degree are substitutes.

In the second place, whatever may be the amount of the total expenditure, and whether it is all new or partly substitute, the full effect of the expenditure is not felt in the area where the outdoor recreation opportunity lies, in many cases. Some of what the family spends will be spent in its own home community. Food, gasoline, and most other items are often bought in the home community. Perhaps a boat will be rented at the park, or other minor expenditures made there. But it is precisely because expenditures for this type of recreation are typically not made in the local area, that units of local government are often unenthusiastic over hordes of outside visitors to a local recreation attraction. Moreover, of what is spent in the local area, much must in turn be spent outside to buy the goods or service sold to the vacationer.

Although the gross expenditure estimates have their greatest appeal as an indicator of total business opportunity, it is not possible to go from them to any firm estimate of the volume and incidence of local business created thereby.

Another serious shortcoming of the gross expenditure data is the lack of comparablity between them and estimates of gross output in other activities, especially other activities related to the same resources. If the gross expenditures by vacationers were equal to the gross value of the output of electric power, for instance, one could not thereby assume that each was equally significant in any economic sense. However, the inputs of labor, capital, management, other production materials, etc., might be greatly different in the two cases. The gross output of a highly integrated industry is not directly comparable with that of an industry which typically buys most of its production materials in a highly fabricated state. The beef cattle feeder who buys both feeder steers and feed, for instance, has a very high volume of business; yet his net income, and his contribution to the national product, may be no greater than that of a dairy farmer who produces all his feed, and has a gross volume of business only one tenth as great. Gross volume data are useful, if at all, only for comparisons with other business of a closely similar structure.

8

VALUE ADDED BY OUTDOOR RECREATION EXPENDITURES

An obvious refinement of the gross expenditure approach is to employ the device used to measure the economic output of many industries—the value added by the particular industry or plant. This approach recognizes that part of what a business receives for its product must be spent for raw materials and finished or semi-finished production materials. The costs of these are deducted from gross output; the difference is the value added by the plant or industry, by use of labor, capital, managerial ability, etc. A summation of value added by industries or regions will give a reasonable total for a nation, whereas a summation of gross business involves a major degree of double counting.

For outdoor recreation, this approach would deduct what had to be spent by the supplier of the vacationist services in order to get the materials to make such a service possible. For instance, the service stations in a local area do contribute some value added to the recreationist's expenditures, even though much of what he spends for gas must be sent outside the locality to buy gasoline. Similarly, the local grocery store earns part of what the vacationer spends, by buying at wholesale and providing the usual range of retail services. The same process applies to all other aspects of the recreation expenditures.

Use of the value-added approach would at least localize the impact of the gross expenditures made by those seeking outdoor recreation. One could then say that so and so much was spent by vacationers and used to support business and payrolls within the town, county, state, or region in question. The value added by the recreation "industry" obtained in this way could reasonably be compared with value added by other industries, or from other uses of the same land and water resources. On the other hand, even value added would not deal directly with the value of the recreation opportunity as such, as we shall point out below.

The value-added approach has been used in one unpublished New Mexico study.[7] By means of questionnaires, data were obtained from fishermen as to total expenditures, by classes of goods or services bought, and within the states as well as elsewhere, while engaged in sport fishing in the state. For each type of ex-

---

[7] A general study of water use in northern New Mexico has been made under the direction of Nathaniel Wollman of the University of New Mexico, by means of a grant from Resources for the Future, Inc. The study is not yet published. An appendix section deals with recreational use of water.

9

penditure made, estimates were made as to value added within the state for that type of good or service. The authors of this report conclude that their estimates of value added from sport fishing are comparable to estimates of value added in agriculture, mining, or industry; and that these value-added data from different economic actvities can be summed to obtain estimates of gross state output.

Value-added estimates of this kind meet some of the major objections levelled at gross expenditure data. They do indicate the volume of business within the state or local area; they are more directly comparable with similar data from other economic activities. However, it still remains true that these amounts are spent, not for the provision of the recreation opportunity as such, but for the provision of other services connected with the use of the recreation opportunity.

DEMAND CURVES FOR OUTDOOR RECREATION

While the value-added concept is a distinct improvement over the gross expenditure concept, at least for most purposes, yet even this does not really come to grips with a major problem: what is the outdoor recreation opportunity really "worth" in a price or market sense? For the other alternative uses of land and water, some approximation of a market price is usually calculated and used in the evaluation process, even when value added is estimated. Can we go this one step further, for outdoor recreation?

Let us start with a brief and elementary review of the demand curve of neoclassical economic theory, as shown in figure 1. The data for this are purely imaginary, but along the X-axis I have placed numbers of visits to a specific outdoor recreation area. On the Y-axis are costs of using this recreation opportunity, or prices in the economist's sense. Let us postpone for the present defining what these prices or costs mean. On the basis of this chart, if the cost of the recreation visit is as low as $1.00, then as many as 400 persons will use the area on a typical summer Sunday; as the price rises, the number of persons who will use it declines, until at the point where the price is $4.00, only 100 persons will use it. This is the typical Marshallian demand curve of elementary economic theory.

Let us review for a moment further some of the assumptions which underlie this curve. It is essentially a static concept; it assumes that numbers of people in the tributary area, their incomes,

10

their means of travel, their tastes as to outdoor recreation, all continue unchanged. A further assumption is that the marginal value of money will remain unchanged, no matter how much of the product or service is bought; that is, that the amounts spent by any single purchaser (user, in this case) will be small enough that he can disregard how large a portion of his total funds he has spent for this product or service. When any of these or other major basic factors change, then the position and shape of the demand curve in turn may change. In this case, we speak of a shift in the curve.

In this illustration, it is most unlikely that the same person would come into the area twice in a single day, especially since entrance fees are typically on a daily basis. But if we were to put the estimates of volume on a seasonal basis, then increased usage of the area could come from a more frequent use by a relatively small number of persons, or by spreading use among a larger circle of people, or by some of both. More volume, in the typical demand curve, thus may mean more intensive use of the commodity by the same people or a widened circle of users.

Economists speak of the elasticity of a demand curve—of the changes in volume purchased relative to the changes in price charged. If the decline in volume is exactly proportional to the increase in price, as in our hypothetical example, then the elasticity is -1.0, and the total sum spent remains constant. In this case, total expenditures are $400 a day, regardless of the price. If the demand were more inelastic, then use would not fall off so much as price was raised, and a relatively high price would bring in more revenue than a low one. On the other hand, if demand were more elastic, then comparatively small increases in price would lead to major shifts in use; raising price would lower total revenue, lowering it would increase total revenue.

Implicit in this kind of demand curve is the assumption that access to the good or service is unimpeded, and that it is only price which limits the volume of goods sold or the number of customers served. On this basis, the last buyer or user would regard the service as worth *to him* only just the amount he had to pay for it. If the price were raised just the least bit, this last purchaser or user would conclude that the good or service wasn't worth the price, and would refrain from buying. Conversely, were the price to be lowered the least bit, another buyer or customer would conclude that the good or service was at last just worth his while, and he would buy. To this last buyer, the price he must pay just meas-

11

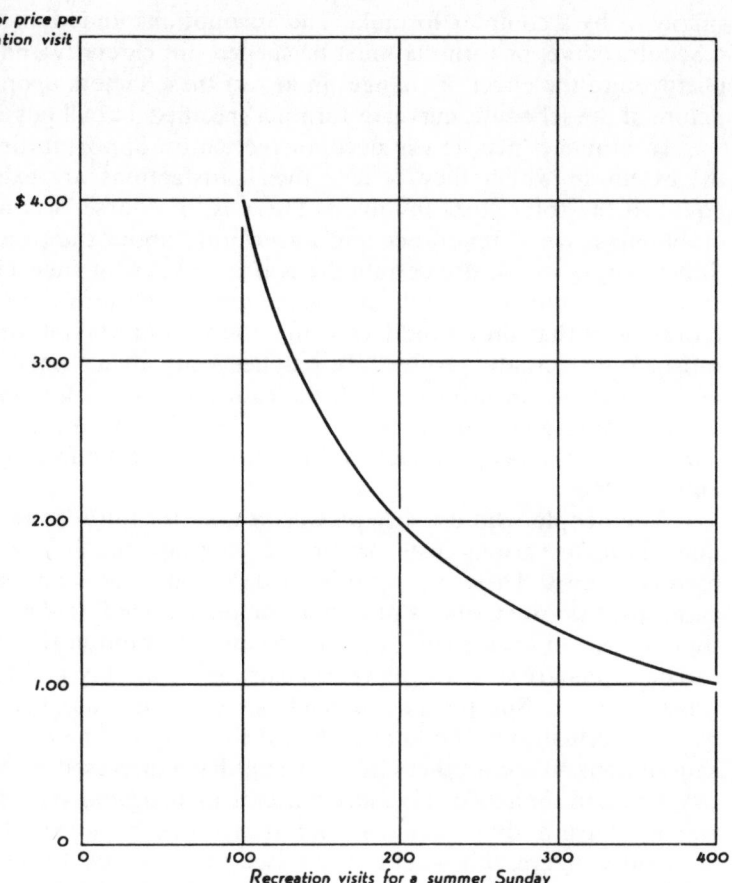

*Figure 1. Hypothetical demand curve for an imaginary outdoor rec-
reation area.*

ures the satisfactions to him from the good or service; the last drop
of utility or satisfaction is needed to make it worth while.

In this economist's use of "demand," it is impossible to conceive of demand by price alone; volume is always a necessary dimension of demand. In our example, the demand for outdoor recreation is not $1.00, nor $2.00, nor $3.00, nor $4.00, nor some intermediate point; it is measured at each of these points, in terms
of the number of persons who are willing to pay these prices. Demand, in this sense, is a schedule of volumes or amounts and of
prices; it may be possible to express it in mathematical form, either

12

simply or by a complex formula. The assumptions underlying the
schedule, curve, or formula must be spelled out carefully and explicitly, and the effect of changes in any of these factors upon the
nature of the schedule, curve, or formula specified if at all possible.

In practice, people use outdoor recreation opportunities to
the extent to which they believe their satisfactions are exactly
equal to the total costs involved. There is, of course, a considerable measure of ignorance and uncertainty about the process.
Some people would use certain areas if they knew of their existence or characteristics; and some make uses which turn out to be
more costly that they would knowingly have undertaken for the
satisfactions actually received. In practice, only a very small part
of the total cost of using outdoor recreation areas is found in the
entrance fees charged. In deciding how often, if at all, to go to
particular areas, people certainly take into account the free or low
entrance fees.

The people who use any particular area for outdoor recreation will incur various costs in doing so—perhaps small ones, perhaps large ones. These costs will be made up on many items, some
cash, some on time, others of a more subjective kind. If they continue to use an area, then it is a reasonable assumption that their
satisfactions are as great as their costs, and possibly greater in
some instances. But, for the marginal user or for the marginal visit
by the habitual user, the total costs just equal his estimate of total
satisfactions. Were it otherwise, he would have increased his visits
or decreased them. To this marginal user or marginal visit, there
was no margin above costs. Had entrance fees been raised to a
substantial figure, this would have raised the total cost of the recreation experience, and surely would have affected the amount of
use made of the area:

The early economists considered certain commodities as "free
goods"; they generally put air, sunshine, and water in this class.
They recognized that such goods had very great utility for man,
yet they were free of cost, for all to enjoy. Later economists pointed
out that it was the marginal utility or marginal value of these products which set their price. While some quantity of air is vital for
life, beyond a certain point additional quantities of air have no
value at all—man has all he can use, and more is valueless. People,
acting through their governments, can artificially place a zero value on a commodity, and thus make it a free good. Unlimited supplies of pure wholesome water piped into homes without charge
becomes a free good to the user. He is perfectly free to use it in

13

such quantity that the marginal value is zero. The same can be true of outdoor recreation. If provided in as great a quantity as wanted, free of charge, the recreation opportunity *at the point of supply* becomes valueless in monetary terms. People can use it until the marginal value falls to zero. In fact, this is what seems to have been done. There is nothing left, at the margin, as value for the recreation opportunity as such.

Where the public, acting through various levels of government, has established the price of recreation at zero, or relatively close to it, then use of the area has increased to the point where some users find the satisfactions, in relation to the other costs of using the area, worth zero or close to it. The calculus of the average user is not as precise as has been suggested; yet, in the long run and for the average of many users and potential users, the price of entrance to the recreation area certainly has entered into calculations of cost, and comparisons of cost with probable satisfactions.

How might one go about trying to estimate a genuine demand curve or schedule for outdoor recreation? It has been suggested that prices charged for private recreation of comparable character might provide a guide.[8] However, if the facilities on private land and those on public land were exactly comparable in every respect, including location with respect to users, then no more could be charged by the private owner than the user would have to pay on the public land. As far as the user is concerned, the price on the public areas is a supply price or cost to him, however much it may have been subsidized. Prices (entrance fees) are paid for private recreation areas, while public areas are available free, precisely because they are not fully comparable. The private facilities may not be as crowded, or may be better located, or the improvements may be better; physical similarity of the basic resources is not enough for economic comparability.

Estimation of the demand curve for a recreation area must, we believe, proceed in two stages: one curve for the *total recreation experience,* a second one for the *recreation opportunity per se.* The first can be estimated from the actual experiences of considerable numbers of people engaged in outdoor recreation; the second can be derived from the first.

In general, most outdoor recreation is engaged in by family

* If I understand it accurately, this is the approach currently used by the National Park Service in estimating the recreation benefits from water development projects.

14

groups. This means, first of all, that the family as a whole must consider and decide which, if any, outdoor recreation areas to visit. This involves comparisons between individuals as to their interests and desires—interpersonal comparisons. Their gains from outdoor recreation take the form of anticipations before the experience actually begins, the realization of the experience, and recollections afterward. They need not be equal for each member of the family, nor equal at the time and later. In retrospect, a trip may seem enjoyable which did not seem so at the time, for instance. The experiences might be grouped as those in preparation, in travel to the site, at the site, and in return.

In theory, each family in the United States has the alternative of using every public outdoor recreation area in the entire nation. In practice, of course, its alternatives are much narrower. Many families will know of only a few alternative spots, and perhaps imperfectly of these. Their interests will be conditioned to a major degree by their past experiences. If they have never been camping, for instance, they may be unenthusiastic about doing so for the first time. In addition to their knowledge and their interests, other limiting factors will be the cost of a particular opportunity in relation to what they can afford to spend, and the time they have available. To some extent, time and money are substitutes. With more money, they can afford quicker means of travel and thus reach more distant places, or they may be able to secure a longer vacation. If time is ample, cheaper means of travel may be possible. Travel of some form and distance is ordinarily necessary, and sometimes extensive travel is involved. Should this be regarded as a cost or as a benefit of the recreation experience? Some families may regard it one way, others differently.

The gains from the recreation experience are wholly subjective—attitudes of the various members of the family. If they regard the experience as a whole, or any parts of it, as pleasurable, then they have had a large gain, or "output." On the other hand, another family might regard their experiences as unenjoyable or as only moderately so; then the output of the recreation experience has been less, even though in physical terms it was identical with that of the first family. The costs of outdoor recreation experiences are partly subjective, partly material. Some cash will have to be spent for travel, food, lodging if more than one day is involved, and for other purposes. The use of equipment such as the automobile is usually included also. But there will be some work before, during, and perhaps after the actual recreation experience. The time and energy spent in travel will be a cost, which may or may not be offset by pleasures from the actual travel experience.

The whole outdoor recreation experience is, to a large extent, a package deal; it must be viewed as a whole, in terms of costs, satisfactions, and time, for all members of the family as a group. It was a consideration of these facts that led to my earlier assertion that demand curves must be derived first for the whole experience.

The demand curve for the whole experience of outdoor recreation, like the demand curves for other services and commodities, is applicable to considerable numbers of people, rather than to individuals. That is, any single individual may have a demand curve that is extreme in some form or other, but a large number of people will have a predictable and measurable reaction to an outdoor recreation opportunity. If we can measure the demand curve for a large group of people, then it is probable that another large group, chosen more or less at random but with similar characteristics to the first group, will respond in similar fashion to costs and other characteristics of the recreation experience. This assumption as to predictability or stability of reaction to similar factors of cost and value is basic to all demand curve analysis, and in fact to all studies of human action. It is an assumption of rationality, not of irrationality of response.

In the discussion which follows certain national parks are used as illustrations because certain data could be found for these parks. The method would work equally well for any outdoor area for which data were available. I shall try to show later that the requisite data could be obtained for any area.

If one is to estimate a demand schedule, some measure of volume is needed. This may be sought in terms of the proportions of a total population which actually took advantage of a known recreation opportunity. Thus, if there were 100,000 people in a city, what proportion of them went to the local city park, what proportion went to the nearest state park, what proportion went to a particular national park? Or, looking at it from the point of the recreation area, what proportion of each 100,000 population in each potential tributary zone visited this particular area? How did the proportion visiting the area vary, depending upon their location and the time and cost of getting to the area? One can estimate a number of participants per 100,000 base population; this is roughly analogous to per capita consumption data for food or other products.

16

These ideas can be illustrated by the actual available data for Yosemite. In 1953 there were roughly 35,000 visits to Yosemite by people who lived in nearby Merced County (table 1). Since the 1950 Census shows about 70,000 people in the county, there were about 50,000 visits per 100,000 population in that county, that year. This is a measure of volume of this kind of recreation taken by these people. From a group of four counties lying slightly more distant from the park, there were somewhat more than 110,000 visits; however, the population of these counties is much larger, about 640,000, so that per 100,000 of the population there were slightly less than 18,000 visits. Similarly, the numbers of visits and numbers of base population can be calculated for groups of California counties and for groups of states, in each case within rather well-defined distance zones from the park. For each distance zone, based upon certain data contained in the report, and some rather heroic assumptions as to other costs, a total monetary cost figure per visit can be estimated. For the nearby people of Merced County, this averages about $16 per visit; for the distant people of the Atlantic seaboard, it runs to nearly $300 per visit. In addition to this monetary cost, there was a time cost which ran from about one and one-half to over fifteen days per visit. Perhaps the travel was a cost, at least to some people; perhaps to others it was a source of satisfaction.

The data in table 1 are the basic data for a demand curve or schedule—a volume or quantity consumed or bought, and a cost incurred or a price paid. Accordingly, we can plot them and construct an approximation to a demand curve. Because of the very great variation in quantity and a somewhat less but still large variation in price, these data are more clearly presented on double log than on simple arithmetic graph paper (figure 2). The dots for the various distance zones fall into rather regular patterns, for the California counties and for the other states, separately. The correspondence is not perfect, but high. If the curves are valid, then values for intermediate points can be read off. Since our concern is with monetary values, we plot the monetary costs. Under the methods of estimating necessary because of data limitations, money, time, and distance are highly correlated. If more precise data were available, each might be considered separately.

It is clear from the chart that each curve has an elasticity greater than unity for at least part of its length. For the more distant states, the elasticity is close to unity; for the nearer states,

TABLE 1.—NUMBER OF VISITORS TO YOSEMITE IN RELATION TO TOTAL POPULATION, AND EXPENDITURES PER VISIT, BY DISTANCE ZONES

Distance Zones[1]	Average one-way distance[2] (miles)	Population of group of counties or states, 1950 (1,000)	Visits to Yosemite, 1953[3]		Estimated time required to complete a visit[4] (days)	Estimated cost per visit[5] $
			Total number	Per 100,000 of population		
1. Groups of California counties[6]						
less than 100 miles	81	70	35,250	50,500	1.4	16.65
100-150 miles	120	641	114,500	17,850	1.6	20.40
150-200 miles	190	1,588	143,400	9,030	1.95	27.05
200-250 miles	211	1,624	119,400	7,340	2.06	29.05
300 and more miles	350	5,206	245,000	4,710	2.75	42.25
2. Groups of states[7]						
300-500 miles	500	3,120	25,520	824	3.5	66.50
500-1,000 miles	800	5,856	19,030	325	5.0	85.00
1,000-1,500 miles	1,300	14,448	34,610	239	7.5	132.50
1,500-2,000 miles	1,800	38,649	66,450	172	10.0	180.00
2,000-2,500 miles	2,300	32,330	39,750	123	12.5	227.50
2,500 and more miles	2,900	44,910	51,400	114	15.5	284.50

[1] For California counties, calculated from road maps as distance from county seat to valley floor of Yosemite, via west entrance; for other states, airline distances.

[2] For California counties, weighted by total population in each county within group; for other states, estimated on basis of common routes of travel and population distribution within states.

[3] Calculated from data in YOSEMITE NATIONAL PARK TRAVEL SURVEY, National Park Service, California Division of Highways, and U.S. Bureau of Public Roads.

[4] Estimated on basis of 1 day per 400 miles of travel plus 1 day in park.

[5] Estimated at average cost of $9.00 per day (reported cost, minus transportation $8.47); plus 10 cents per mile for car for double one-way distance, divided by four on assumption of 4 passengers per car.

[6] Counties in each group are as follows: Merced; Madera, Stanislaus, Fresno, San Joaquin; Tulare, Monterey, Sacramento, Santa Clara, Alameda; San Francisco, San Mateo, Marin, Kern; San Bernardino, Los Angeles, Orange, San Diego. There were no counties, for which data were reported, that were 250 to 300 miles distant.

[7] States in each group were as follows: Oregon, Nevada, Utah, Arizona; Washington, Idaho, Montana, Wyoming, Colorado, New Mexico; North Dakota, South Dakota, Nebraska, Kansas, Oklahoma, Texas; Minnesota, Wisconsin, Iowa, Illinois, Missouri, Kentucky, Tennessee, Indiana, Arkansas, Mississippi, Louisiana; Michigan, Ohio, West Virginia, Virginia, North Carolina, South Carolina, Georgia, Alabama; Maine, New Hampshire, Vermont, Massachusetts, Connecticut, Rhode Island, New York, New Jersey, Pennsylvania, Delaware, Maryland, Florida.

18

much more elastic. It is above unit elasticity for all California
counties, and becomes greater for the nearer ones where the costs
are lower.

One major assumption entered the calculations of the average
cost per visit—that the trip to Yosemite was the chief purpose of
the trip, that it should therefore bear the costs of travel from home
to the park as well as within the park, and that other sightseeing
or recreation on the trip need bear only its direct or marginal cost.
More than half of the visitors interviewed stated that the principal
reason for their trip was to visit Yosemite, so this assumption is
not too far from the fact. Although exact data are missing, presumably the more distant visitors would most frequently include
other purposes on their trips, so that if some form of trip cost allocation to different objectives were made, presumably it would be
the more distant and costly visits which would be reduced most in
price. If so, this might well change the nature of the curve somewhat, to make it more elastic at the low volume—high price end.

In this table and figure, it should be recognized that the nature
and the content of the whole recreation experience of which the
visit to Yosemite was the crowning goal, differ according to distance from the park. Nearby visitors are able to come in a day or
two, are likely to come often, and perhaps derive some of their enjoyment from their familiarity with the scene. Distant visitors require several days to come, usually come only infrequently, and
for many it is the first experience with much of their enjoyment
deriving from its novelty. But in this respect the demand curve for
the whole recreation experiénce to Yosemite is not unique. The
housewife who buys four dozen eggs a week for her family surely
uses them in different ways than the housewife who buys half a
dozen. One of the common characteristics of a demand curve is
that the uses of the commodity change with the volume bought.

It is the contention here that the curve in figure 2 is an approximation to the demand curve of theory *for the recreation experience as a whole.* Although it is referred to as a visit to Yosemite, actually the whole trip from home to the park and back
again is included, for time, travel, cost, pleasure. It is a package
deal. Yosemite may have been the chief objective, but it is only
part of the total experience; it has been only a kind of shorthand
that has led me to describe the whole in terms of its chief feature.

The *approximation* aspect of the above statement is emphasized for several reasons. In the first place, the data at my disposal

19

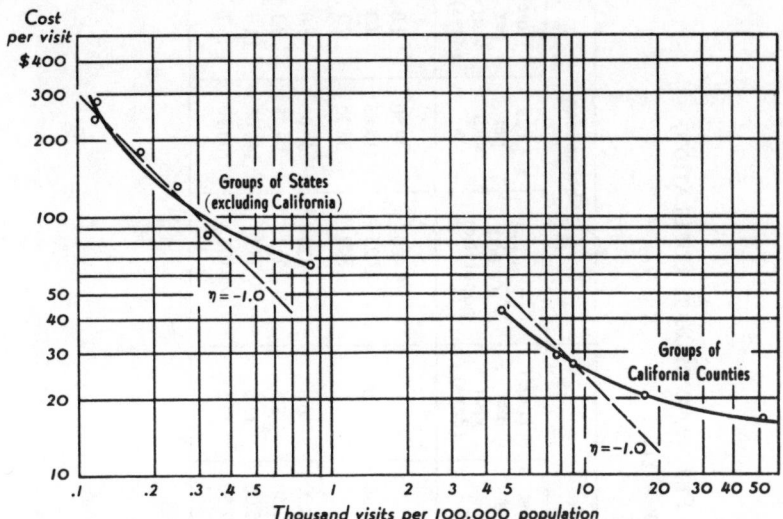

Figure 2. Estimated costs per visit to Yosemite, in relation to number of visits per 100,000 population, 1953.

were faulty for this purpose. It was necessary to make some rather major assumptions about costs of visits from different distance zones; while average costs are about the same as the average costs in the reference source, yet the true relation of distance to cost may be considerably different from what has been estimated. In the second place, it was necessary to make a cost allocation among possible, but largely unknown, other purposes of the trips, which may be at variance with the facts. It was assumed that the visit to Yosemite had to bear all the costs of the trip, allocating to other activities on the trip only those costs additional to the main trip.

The visitors to Yosemite may have made a much different allocation of costs in their own (perhaps subconscious) calculations. In the third place, the population in the various distance zones may differ considerably in terms of average income or of income distribution, as well as perhaps in other socio-economic characteristics. We made no attempt to include this in our calculations. Lastly, the money cost of visiting Yosemite may have not been the only cost involved. If the average visitor regards as onerous the travel experience as such, then distance as such should be entered into the formula. Our estimates of cost were built so directly on distance that there was no sense in trying to isolate the

20

TABLE 2.—VISITS TO SPECIFIED NATIONAL PARKS PER 100,000 OF BASE POPULATION, AND AVERAGE COSTS PER VISIT

Distance zone	Grand Canyon			Glacier			Shenandoah		
	Visits per 100,000 population	Cost per visit $	Time per visit (days)	Visits per 100,000 population	Cost per visit $	Time per visit (days)	Visits per 100,000 population	Cost per visit $	Time per visit (days)
Up to 100 miles	2,085	63.50	3.5	4,680	42.50	3.5	10,480	9.50	1.0
100 to 300 miles							2,025	15.85	1.3
300 to 500 miles							849	32.15	2.7
500 to 1,000 miles	1,033	116.00	6.0	547	80.00	6.0	428	60.00	5.0
1,000 to 1,500 miles	570	168.50	8.5	241	117.50	8.5	213	99.75	8.3
1,500 to 2,000 miles	402	221.00	11.0	97	155.00	11.0	112	144.00	12.0
2,000 or more miles	207	273.50	13.5	45	192.50	13.5	108	200.20	16.7

influence of distance from our data, but more refined data might permit such measurement. The time required to visit Yosemite might well be a major cost to many potential visitors, and this was not included directly. For many people, time equals money, and vice versa. A paid vacation is one resource, but the opportunity to take additional time without income may also exist. If time is limited, money may permit flying or other time-saving methods. These limitations are those of the data available, not of the method of the analysis. They could be cured by obtaining more precise and relevant data, as will be discussed later. In that case, more refined results would be possible.

The apparent correspondence between cost per visit and number of visits per 100,000 base population may thus include some variables indirectly, and to this extent not represent a pure demand curve showing the net relation between price and volume. However, an approximation such as this may have great empirical usefulness. This is not to argue against making every effort to secure better data, but merely to say that imperfect data may yield usable results.

Generally similar data can be calculated and thus similar total experience demand curves or schedules derived for three other major national parks (table 2 and figure 3). In each case, the dots fall into a rather regular pattern. For Grand Canyon national park, the curve approaches unit elasticity at the end toward lowest costs and largest volumes; there is not the increase in elasticity here that was found for California. The lack of a considerable local residential population may be one explanation. On the other hand, the curve for this park gets much more elastic at the end toward fewer visits and higher costs. The curve for Glacier national park is highly elastic throughout. That for Shenandoah is roughly unit elasticity for the half with lower volumes and higher prices, but gets much more elastic for the higher volumes and lower prices.

Too much significance should not be attached to the precise form, shape, and location of these curves. While data were available on numbers of people by states of origin (by counties within California, for Yosemite), this is a crude measure of the location of their residences. Distances travelled had to be estimated from such general location data; actual road distances may have been different. Average cost for all persons visiting the park was given in the reports, but was usually confined to estimates of costs incurred in or near the park; in no case was it differentiated accord-

22

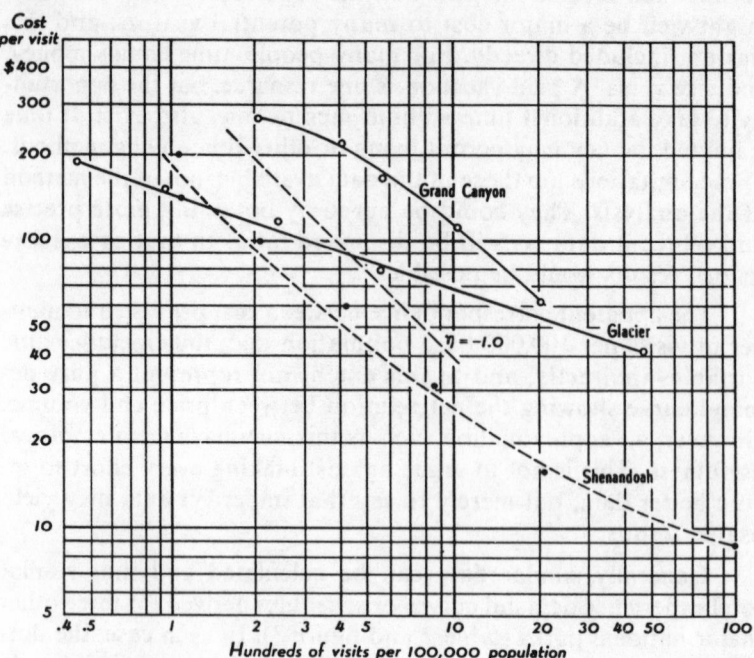

Figure 3. Estimated costs per visit in relation to number of visits per 100,000 of population, Grand Canyon, Glacier, and Shenandoah national parks.

ing to the costs incurred by the more distant and the nearby visitors. I have estimated the costs per visit from data on average costs per day and on distances travelled. Days involved in travel had also to be estimated. To a lesser extent the numbers of visitors per unit of resident population had to be estimated. Others more familiar with the original studies might have done a more accurate job on all these estimates; perhaps the original data could be tabulated in ways that would answer some of these questions; certainly, studies could have been devised which would have yielded data more directly applicable to the problem. In spite of these limitations, it is possible that the curves do in fact give a reasonable idea as to the nature of the demand curve for these parks for the year in question—one in the early 1950's in each case.

One major discrepancy is apparent in figure 2; the experience for California does not seem to join up with the experience for

23

other states. There is no logical reason why state boundaries should make any difference. Sufficient detail to calculate a zone of origin between the most distant counties shown in table 1 and the nearest adjacent states was not given in the source report. Had there been a distance zone volume and price for this intermediate area, its dot would have determined the shape of the curve between the two discontinuous curves now shown. There is no logical reason for two separate curves, but there is insufficient data now to bridge the gap with confidence.

The demand curves for these four national parks probably are not at all representative of the demand curves for other types of outdoor recreation areas. These are four of the largest, best known, most popular national parks; some of their use is by persons at relatively great distances. Certainly, relatively commonplace state parks have a very different clientele. And the potential users for the average city park come from an even more closely circumscribed area. However, it is our contention that total recreation experience demand curves such as these could be derived for any outdoor recreation area, given data on numbers of visitors from distance or use zones, statistics on total population within the same zones, and average costs of using the recreation area by people coming in from each zone. The location and shape of the curves might be different than for these outstanding national parks, but the method of estimation may be equally applicable.

It will be noted that no direct mention has been made thus far of the entrance fees to these parks. In each study, part of the visitor costs were classed as "other," or in addition to food, lodging, transportation. Presumably entrance fees were included here. While precise information is lacking from these studies, it is known from other sources that entrance fees at the time averaged less than $1.00 per person, at least for short visits.

The foregoing approximations to demand curves for the total recreational experience still do not directly answer the question, what is the value of the recreation opportunity per se? The costs incurred for the total recreation experience are for items other than rent on the recreation site, except as the latter finds small expression in the entrance fees. The costs are for food, lodging, travel, and miscellaneous items. I have suggested that the use of these various areas has expanded to the point where the value of the recreation site, *at the margin,* is zero, or as near to it as the entrance fees are to zero. This is one point on the demand curve for the site itself. How may the demand curve for the recreation site

24

per se be derived from the demand curve for the total recreation experience?

To estimate this we must make two assumptions. First, we assume that users of the parks would view an increase in entrance fees rationally—that is, that they would regard it as no more serious than any other equally large increase in total cost of visiting the park. At the same time it is recognized that since most parks, including the national parks, are publicly owned, many users might attempt to influence the level of entrance fees by political or other methods that they would not try to employ against an increase in the price of gasoline, or of meals, or of lodging. Second, we assume that the experience of users from one location zone provides a measure of what people in other location zones would do if costs in money and time were the same. That is, in the Yosemite case, we assume that the people in Los Angeles county would use Yosemite to the extent the people in Merced county

TABLE 3.—ESTIMATED EFFECT OF RAISING

Area of origin	Actual visits, 1953 (1,000)	Estimated cost per visit, pres. entrance fees $	Entrance fees raised by $3 per person	
			Estimated visits [1] (1,000)	Added fee revenue [2] ($1,000)
California Zone 1	35	16.65	14	42
2	114	20.40	77	231
3	143	27.05	119	357
4	119	29.05	111	333
5	245	42.25	234 [3]	702
Subtotal	656		555	1,665
Other states				
Zone 1	26	66.50	22	66
2	19	85.00	23	69
3	35	132.50	31	93
4	66	180	59	177
5	40	227.50	42	126
6	51	284.50	48 [3]	144
Subtotal	237		225	670
Total [4]	893		780	2,335

[1] These were calculated from figure 2 and table 1. The estimated number of visits for a specified entrance fee was estimated from the appropriate curves in figure 2, and this number multiplied by the number of people in the distance zone as shown in table 1.

[2] This ignores the small decrease in revenue due to fewer visitors at the original entrance fee.

actually now use it, were money and time costs the same. Demand curve analysis almost always requires a transfer of experience from one group of people to another, or from one time to another, and in this respect our demand curve is no different than one for eggs or oranges. In a country with as large a degree of common culture and as much mobility of individuals as the United States, an assumption of similar response to time and money costs is highly reasonable. If the cost of visiting Yosemite were to fall to $20.00 for residents of New York City, it would take them a little time to make the same response as people in nearby California counties now do, but one might hazard the guess their adjustment would be fairly prompt.

On the basis of these two assumptions, the effect of an increase in fees can be estimated for Yosemite from the data in figure 2 and table 1 (table 3). At the existing level of fees, the people in California zone 1 could visit the park for an average cost per visit of

ENTRANCE FEES TO YOSEMITE NATIONAL PARK, 1953

Entrance fee raised by $5 per person		Entrance fee raised by $10 per person		Entrance fee raised by $20 per person	
Estimated visits [1] (1,000)	Added fee revenue [2] ($1,000)	Estimated visits [1] (1,000)	Added fee revenue [2] ($1,000)	Estimated visits [1] (1,000)	Added fee revenue [2] ($1,000)
11	55	7	70	4	80
64	320	47	470	33	660
108	540	90	900	68 [3]	1,360
102	510	86	860	67 [3]	1,340
224 [3]	1,120	208 [3]	2,080	161! [3]	3,220
509	2,545	438	4,380	333	6,660
20	100	17	170	13	260
22	110	20	200	17	340
30	150	30	300	27	540
59	295	59	590	57	1,140
41	205	41	410	39	780
48 [3]	240	48 [3]	480	46 [3]	920
220	1,100	215	2,150	199	3,980
729	3,645	653	6,530	532	10,640

[3] Since these estimates involve extrapolation beyond the extent of the curves, they perhaps have a larger margin of error than the other estimates.

[4] Total of these areas only. In addition, there were some visits from other California counties and from outside of the continental United States.

26

$16.65; if the fees were $3.00 per visit higher, then the average cost
would rise to $19.65, the number of visitors per 100,000 of base
population would fall from 50,000 to 20,000 (not shown in table
3), and the total number of visitors from this zone would fall to
about 14,000. The new estimated number of visitors at this cost
per visit was estimated from figure 2. If the entrance fee were
raised by $5.00 per visit, total cost per visit would be $21.65; the
number of visits per 100,000 base population would fall to about
15,700, and total visits would be 11,000. A comparable lot of estimates could be made for each other distance zone, and for each
other increase in fees.

The new number of visits per 100,000 population, after fees
are raised, in each case must be multiplied by the base population
of each distance zone to get a new number of visits. An increase
of $3.00 in the entrance fee per person would reduce total visits to
Yosemite about 13 per cent; one of $5.00, nearly 19 per cent; one
of $10.00, 27 per cent; and one of $20.00 about 40 per cent. The
reduction is greatest, relatively and in absolute terms, from California; and within California, most from the nearer areas. This is
because the various increases in fees are relatively greater, compared to other costs of visiting the park, the nearer one lives to
the park.

Revenue from entrance fees continues to mount as the fee is
increased. This is because the increase in fee is, generally speaking,
such a small percentage of the total cost of visiting the park.

From the data on estimated numbers of visits at each level of
increased fees, it is possible to construct a new demand curve
(figure 4). This measures the relation between number of visits and
entrance fees. It is my contention that this approximates the true
demand curve for the recreation opportunity itself. It shows the
relationship between price per unit and number of units, all other
factors remaining unchanged. It is, of course, subject to all the in-
adequacies of the data on which it is based, which have been discussed. Yet, it is possible that this curve is closer to the true one
than the previous curves are to their true demand curve; if the
relationship among the various cost and use factors is at all as has
been estimated, then the demand curve for the recreation site per
se may be fairly accurate.

Similar estimates can be made for the other three national
parks considered (table 4). The curves for the four parks are markedly similar; each is highly inelastic. The entrance fees are such a
small part of the total cost that relatively large increases in them
are still only small increases in the total cost of the total recrea-

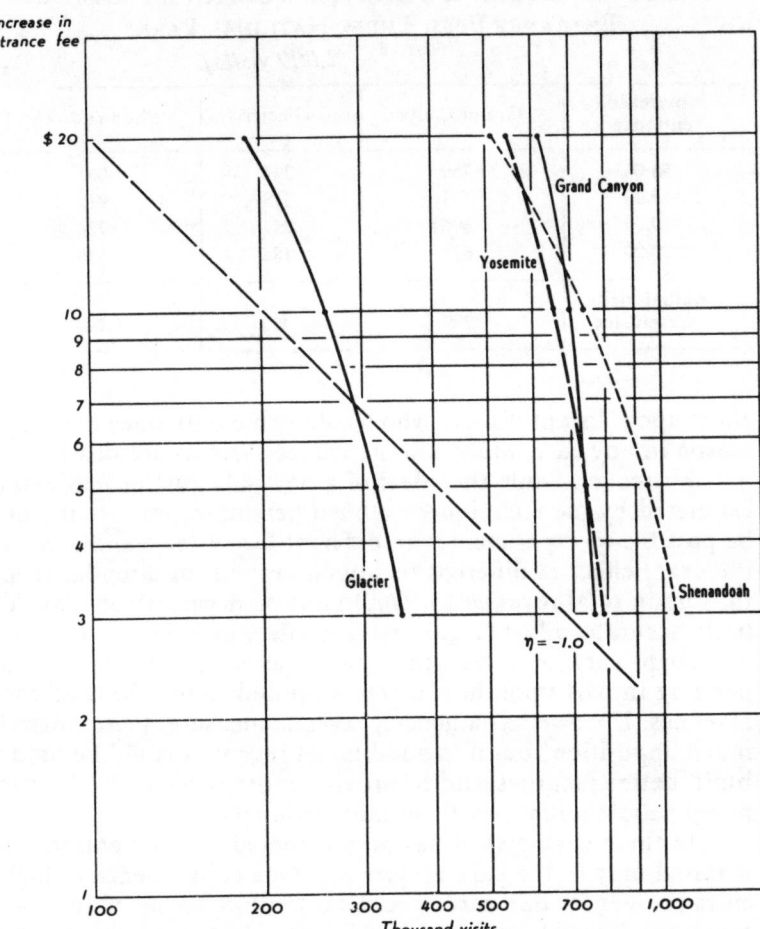

Figure 4. Estimated effect of entrance fees on visits to selected national parks.

tion experience. This is, I repeat, on the assumption that users view these fee increases rationally.

    In this example it has been assumed that the entrance fee per visit is raised by the assumed amount. It would be possible to have much more complex systems of entrance fees. For instance, a season admission at a price not much above a single admission would greatly lower the cost per visit for nearby residents who might visit a park several times a year, while having little or no

28

TABLE 4.—Estimated Visits for Specified Increases in
Entrance Fees, Three National Parks
(1,000 visits)

Increase in entrance fee	Grand Canyon	Glacier	Shenandoah
$3.00	759	344	1,065
5.00	737	318	926
10.00	696	257	728
20.00	617	185	518
Actual visits, present fee	799	403	1,499

effect upon distant visitors who would come only once during the
season in any case. Many alternative fee systems are possible.

Moreover, while the effect of a new schedule of fees can be
estimated by the techniques outlined herein, in practice it would
be possible to experiment with different fee systems and ascertain
the exact effect of different fees upon amount of attendance and
thus upon total revenues. It would not be necessary to make entirely accurate, advance guesses. The effect of different fee schedules might vary, or at least their public acceptance might vary, depending in part upon how it was proposed to use the additional
revenues. If viewed as a general revenue measure, there might be
much opposition; but if the additional revenues could be used to
build better facilities and to provide more services in the park,
many people might pay them more willingly.

In these examples, it has been assumed that the entrance fee
is raised only in the park in question. One consequence of higher
entrance fees for one park would be to shift some of its use to
other nearby park or recreational areas. If the entrance fee to
Yosemite national park were raised, some of those who would no
longer use it would turn to other national parks, to national forests,
to state parks, or other areas not too distant. If the entrance fees for
all outdoor areas were raised at the same time, and to more or less
the same degree, this substitution of one area for another would
not occur, or would be less. There would some tendency to substitute other forms of recreation for such recreation.

It is impossible to estimate the point at which the fees for
these four national parks would produce the maximum total revenue. This is because we do not know what will happen when
costs are raised much above our past experience with them; in

29

tables 3 and 4, it has been necessary to extrapolate the data to some extent, and this would grow more serious if estimates were made for much higher fees. It does seem clear, however, that if the objective were maximum revenues to the owner of the park then fees should be well above the $20.00 per visit level.

It should also be pointed out that as fees were raised and visits to the park decreased, gross expenditures by visitors, and presumably also the value added locally, would decline about in proportion to the decrease in numbers of visits. Those who sell goods and supply services to park visitors obviously want to see the maximum volume of business, and this means entrance fees as near zero as possible. However, if it is desired to make the park self-supporting, in the sense that entrance fees pay for costs of administration, then fees at a higher level are necessary. If the objective were to yield a monopolist's profit on the park—which presumably it never would be for a publicly owned area—then fees at a much higher but unknown level would be required.

Caution about the possible inaccuracies in the curves of figures 2, 3, and 4 should be re-emphasized at this point; but even if these curves are fully accurate, the results for these areas do not necessarily apply to other areas. In fact, one would expect that other areas, with other tributary populations, other appeals to the general public, other costs of reaching them, might have a very different relationship between level of fees and expected revenue.

It is well to remind ourselves again of such demand curves, assuming that the very best ones have been estimated. They apply to a single point, or year, in time. In a few years, the basic factors underlying them might change considerably. The numbers of people might rise, perhaps unevenly in the various distance zones; average per capita real incomes might also rise; better roads might reduce travel time and otherwise lower costs; and more leisure would permit a higher volume of visits. It is more than possible that tastes or desires of the population for a particular recreation experience will change also. If by some miracle the cost of getting to Yosemite of any other national park fifty years ago could have been reduced, in real terms, to its present-day level, the expansion in use to present levels would not have occurred so rapidly. It takes time for people to learn about specific recreation opportunities, as well as about recreation in general.

However, it might well be possible to make studies of the same area at intervals of a few years, and ascertain the extent of the shift in the demand curve. By studying areas of generally similar characteristics, economic as well as physical, but in different

30

stages of development, it might be possible to form some idea of the extent of the shift in demand as more people live in tributary area, as their incomes rise, as transportation improves, or as other factors change.

Moreover, it should not be asumed that these curves are so fixed as to be beyond influence. Through more investments in facilities the whole recreation experience might be improved, and thus more people come to the area, or those who come might be willing to pay higher entrance fees, or some of both. Better roads and other travel facilities would have the same general effect. The total recreational experience might be upgraded by various measures outside of the chief recreation area, and thus make the whole experience more enjoyable and its participants willing to pay more for it. In some instances, advertising might bring the virtues of an area to the attention of more people, and thus lead to heavier uses or make higher fees possible.

CONSUMER'S SURPLUS IN OUTDOOR RECREATION

The fourth general idea to explore is that of consumer's surplus in outdoor recreation. Since some people would be willing to pay more for outdoor recreation than they in fact are forced to pay, they enjoy some measure of surplus.

The general nature of consumer's surplus is evident from figure 1. At any given price, the marginal unit purchased provides its purchaser with just enough satisfactions or benefits to make him consider it worthwhile. But some purchases yield satisfactions greater than their costs. In the figure, if the price is $1.00, the 400th unit returns just enough to make it worthwhile; but each previous unit has some surplus, the amount increasing to the earlier units. If the price is $2.00, then the 200th unit is just marginal, and earlier units have a surplus, but a smaller one than before. It is obvious, I hope, that consumer's surplus has meaning only in relation to a volume of purchases and only in relation to a demand curve.

Under a scheme of discriminatory pricing, a monopolist might somehow manage to separate his potential customers or market into groups or segments, and to exploit each to the limit of its willingness to pay. In the figure, it might be possible to sell 100 units at $4.00 each to some selected customers; another 100 units at $2.00 each to another 100 selected customers; a third 100 units at $1.33 to a third selected lot of customers; and the last 100 units for $1.00 each. Under these nearly ideal (from the monopolist's viewpoint) conditions, he would receive $600 in total *more* than if he sold the whole lot at the marginal price of $1.00 each—a truly handsome profit! To the extent that anything like this is possible, the monopolist would reap for himself the consumer surplus. In practice, pricing of this sort would probably but not always be illegal; perhaps more important, it would be extremely difficult if not impossible to separate the total market so neatly in segments from each other of which a different price could be extracted.

In the case of the Yosemite park relationships shown in figure 2, it appears that some people have a consumer's surplus. For instance, from Merced County there were about 50,000 visits per 100,000 of total population. We do not know how many different individuals this represents, but for the present purpose it does not matter—a visit other than marginal can yield a surplus whether it is to a different person or merely another visit for the same persons. This number of visits was possible only because the cost per visit was slightly less than $17.00. For the marginal visit, this was the total value. However, for the 40,000th visit, or for one of even higher priority, a larger total cost would have been incurred if necessary. For as few as 5,000 visits per 100,000 of population from this county, as much as $41.00 per visit would have been paid, if necessary, assuming again that Merced County people react as do people elsewhere. Some people could afford such a cost, but it would limit their visits greatly. The difference between the approximately $17.00 it did cost them and the $41.00 they would have paid if necessary, represents consumer's surplus for the smaller group of people. Other calculations could be made, for other prices or costs, other numbers of visits, etc. In general, consumer's surplus is equal to monopolist's possible gain; to the extent the latter is realized, it reduces consumer surplus. In practice, it is hard to see how consumer's surplus can be captured, by either public or private provider of recreation.

In fact, the usefulness of estimating consumer's surplus is questionable in any situation. Under almost any circumstances some users of outdoor recreation will gain more from it than they would have been willing to pay if necessary. This may be taken for granted; but how can you capture it, would public policy permit you to try, and what is to be gained from estimating its amount?

APPLICATION OF ECONOMIC ANALYSIS TO RECREATION

Suppose that the proposal were made to develop a multiple-purpose water project, and the recreational possibilities thereof were to be evaluated; or suppose that a proposal was made to acquire and develop a new park, and that an economic appraisal

32

was required. Assume further that we had ideal data, or that we had sufficient resources and time in which to collect the best possible data. What kinds of analyses would we make, and what kinds of results might we reasonably hope for? In what ways would our analyses aid decision makers? Let me briefly attempt to answer these questions.

First of all, the physical alternatives of the resources should be considered and described in some detail. If the reservoir is built, what kind of swimming, boating, fishing or other recreation would it provide? What would be especially attractive about the area, for recreation, and what would be least attractive, and how important is each? How much fluctuation will there be in water level? How much impurities will the water have, and of what kind? What about fishing? In what alternative ways might the area be developed? What would be the approximate costs of each? A clear but imaginative understanding of the area is the basis on which all later analysis must rest, and care should be taken by competent and experienced recreation specialists to get this understanding.

Second, the social and economic setting of the proposed recreation area should also be considered in detail. How many people, by distance or time zones, live in its probable tributary area? What are their average incomes, and what else of a socio-economic character is distinctive about them? What are the alternative recreation possibilities in the same general area, now or prospective, that are or might be competitive with the proposed new area? How far, and for what groups of potential users, are the alternative areas fully substitutes for the proposed new area? How far would the latter draw users from established areas, and to what extent would it have a distinctive and new clientele? These are the kinds of questions that should be examined, largely on a descriptive basis. The trends in all these factors, as well as their present levels, should be studied.

Thirdly, the cost of actually using the proposed new area, for different types of uses, should be estimated for users from different residence zones. Such estimates necessarily will be rough, but they should be as good as possible. Money costs are needed, of course, but also time and other costs and possible benefits. These estimates of cost should be prepared for relevant and distinguishable zones of potential users. Ideally, estimates should be prepared for perhaps as many as ten zones, estimated ultimately to have more or less equal numbers of potential users.

Fourth, demand curves must be estimated for the most nearly similar other areas that can be found. The similarity should be

33

both physical and economic, if possible. Since complete similarity is usually impossible, several moderately similar areas may have to be studied.

Demand curves for other similar recreation areas should proceed by the two-stage analysis illustrated herein—that is, first for the total recreational experience, then for the recreation site per se. To get the first, questionnaires should be used to obtain information from users of the similar areas. Such questionnaires should get enough information on monetary costs to permit calculation or estimation of the cost per family for the recreational experience as a whole, and from this an average cost per member of the family included in the recreational experience could be calculated. This information might be obtained directly and frontally, by simply asking the total spent on the trip, or asking it by major items of expense, or it might be approached indirectly by getting information as to number of days, kind of accommodations used, place of meals, kind of travel facilities, and the like, from which details summary estimates could be prepared. The number of persons per car greatly affects the travel cost per person. These data should surely be tabulated for visitors from each of several distance zones. In addition to averages, it might be enlightening to construct frequency distributions of cost per visitor per day, and to explain as far as possible some of the reasons for variations.

Data should surely be obtained as to the purpose of the visitors in undertaking the total recreational experience of which the visit to the particular study area was a part. Was it the sole reason, or the primary reason, or one among several approximately equally important reasons, or a minor reason, or largely an incident to the primary purposes of the trip? Surely questions could be devised that would throw considerable light on this matter. And the information could be analyzed according to the importance the user gave to the particular area.

Data should also be obtained on the socio-economic characteristics of the recreationists. The number of persons in the total family, their ages and sexes, the number who came on this trip, the occupation of the worker or workers, the approximate income level of the family, and perhaps other items of information are desirable. Frequency distributions of all of these data, by distance zones from the recreation area, should be constructed. And the relation of some of these data, such as income, to some of the previously described data, such as expenditure per day per person, should be explored.

Lastly, such studies should get as much data as reasonably convenient about time—time on this trip, total paid vacation time,

34

how other recreation time was used, etc. And information about travel would be desirable—total distance, average distances per day, and whether the family regarded the travel as enjoyable, merely tolerable, or endured only for the sake of later recreation, etc.

For any recreation demand studies of this general type, a necessary preliminary step is to define the potential tributary area, and to divide it into a number of zones with roughly equal total population. These zones should be readily distinguishable and definable—the kind of names and areas that respondents would either think of or recognize. Some compromise between easily definability and ideal numbers and populations may be necessary. Ideally, as many as ten zones, with roughly equal base populations, should be established, and all the data collected analyzed for each zone. One major disadvantage of some of the studies consulted in the present study is that state of residence is too crude a classification by distance.

On the basis of data collected, the two types of demand curves illustrated could be calculated for each area studied, following roughly the procedure outlined herein. The collection of necessary data may be time-consuming and expensive, but if the studies are properly designed, its analysis according to the present framework is relatively simple and inexpensive.

If data are collected as suggested, the relationship between cost per visit and number of visitors per 100,000 of population could be calculated. In addition, it would be possible to test for the effect of time and distance upon demand for the area. It is entirely possible that long distances and long travel times have an effect in addition to their cost in monetary terms. It would also be possible to estimate the effect of income and perhaps of other socio-economic characteristics of the visitors, upon demand for this particular recreation area. If the various socio-economic data were defined in ways similar to those used in the census and other massive sources of data, then it would be possible to go from the sample to the larger universe from which it was drawn.

One major question may be faced in the analysis of the data collected. For some kinds of areas, there will be little or no question; the visit to it was the chief purpose of the trip, and all costs and all gains, monetary and personal, are due to the one area. For the more distant and major areas, such as the larger national parks, some of the visitors, probably the more distant ones, visited other areas or had other purposes than to visit the area under study. It will be recalled that this problem was encountered in the study reported herein. Two possible methods of dealing with this situ-

35

ation exist. One would be to limit the analysis to those users who said their visit to the area was the principal purpose of their trip. Presumably, this would yield a clearly defined demand curve for them. If such people were half of the total visitors coming from a distant residence zone (the other half having supplemental purposes in mind), then the number of visits per 100,000 of base population should be calculated on the basis of half the base population. On the other hand, total demand would have to be calculated on the basis of the entire population in each zone. It could be argued that others, who took in other attractions, shared the costs in a way that made their visit to the area under study comparable to those with equal costs who made it the sole purpose of their trip. The other possibility would be to attempt some allocation of costs and values among the various areas visited on the trip as a whole, and to relate only those costs chargeable against the particular area to the numbers of persons who used it and other areas jointly.

Fifth, on the basis of these studies for the various sample areas, estimate both types of demand curves for the area being planned, and for different methods of developing and managing it. This necessarily must involve a large degree of judgment. If the other areas studied are closely similar, then the demand curves for them can be taken over with only minor modifications. If, as is more probable, they differ in one or more respects, then major modifications of other relationships are necessary. This problem of transferring known experience from one area and set of conditions to a new, and as yet untried area, is by no means peculiar to recreation planning. It certainly enters in agricultural planning. It is unavoidable. The only course is to do it as consciously and carefully as possible.

Lastly, for each major method of developing and managing the proposed new recreation area, and for a considerable range in entrance fees for each, calculate: the number of estimated visits, by zone of origin; the probable total expenditures by all visitors; the value added locally and within the state, by their expenditures; and the total fee revenue. There might be as many as four or five different methods of developing and operating the area, depending upon its physical possibilities, and as many as four or five different fee schedules for each. The latter would provide estimates of total revenues or total monetary values of the recreation per se. If the earlier steps have been carried out well, this type of estimating is neither particularly difficult nor very costly; it follows from the demand schedules and related data.

36

These alternative physical plans and alternative financial plans would provide several real alternatives for public action. This particularly would be the case when similar plans were available for other areas, so that the comparative advantage of developing one area could be compared with another.

From the second type of demand curve it might be possible to calculate the level of entrance fees and method of development and management of the area that would yield the maximum net revenue to the owner of the area. This would certainly provide one basis of comparison with other possible uses of water and other resources in the same area. It is true that these resources are not always used for other purposes in the way to produce the greatest possible revenue—power is frequently sold at less than the maximum revenue, irrigation water is made available at cost, flood control is nearly free, etc. It could be argued that, if entrance fees are lower than those that will produce maximum revenue, this difference is a cost of socially desired actions. Again, in this respect recreation would be similar to water, power, flood control, and other resource programs—in various of them, prices are established well below the maximum revenue point, for social objectives.

It is assumed that, in practice, entrance fees for a new recreation area will be established below the maximum rent point. Other criteria will be used. One objective might be to establish fees such that the revenues therefrom would pay the cost of maintenance and management of the area; this level of fees could be estimated by the procedure outlined. It would also be possible, whatever the level of fees advocated or adopted, to show who gained, and by how much, from fees other than at the maximum revenue point.

The steps outlined above do not result in a neat, single, unequivocal answer as to the "best" plan of development or management of the proposed new recreation opportunity. It is, in fact, highly unrealistic to expect any method of analysis to provide final answers to all the questions. More, it may be argued that those who ask (and reasonably so) for better methods of economic analysis of recreation, would be the first to reject a mechanical and unequivocal approach. What the above procedure would do is to provide reasonably clearcut alternatives of public policy and action, with a clear statement of costs and benefits from each. Policies and programs for recreation must still be decided on the basis of judgment and intangibles, but with tools such as these, imperfect as they may be, the decision maker will have a far better picture of the real alternatives and their costs than has been possible in the past.

[19]

Comparisons of Methods for Recreation Evaluation

Jack L. Knetsch and *Robert K. Davis**

Evaluation of recreation benefits has made significant headway in the past few years. It appears that concern is increasingly focusing on the hard core of relevant issues concerning the economic benefits of recreation and how we can go about making some useful estimates.

The underlying reasons for this sharpening of focus are largely pragmatic. The rapidly increasing demand for recreation, stemming from the often-cited factors of increasing population, leisure, incomes, mobility, and urbanization, calls for continuing adjustments in resource allocations. This is the case with respect to our land and water resources in general; but more specifically it bears on such matters as the establishment of national recreation areas, setting aside or preserving areas for parks and open spaces in and near expanding urban areas, and clearly on questions of justification, location, and operation of water development projects.

Recreation services have only recently been recognized as products of land and water resource use. As such, they offer problems that do not occur when resolving the conflicting uses of most goods and services— for example, steel and lumber. Conflicting demands for commodities such as these are resolved largely in the market places of the private economy, where users bid against each other for the limited supplies.

Outdoor recreation, however, has developed largely as a non-market commodity. The reasons for this are quite elaborate, but in essence out-

* Research Associates, Resources for the Future, Inc.

125

METHODS FOR RECREATION EVALUATION

door recreation for the most part is produced and distributed in the absence of a market mechanism, partly because we prefer it that way and have rejected various market outcomes, and partly because many kinds of outdoor recreation experience cannot be packaged and sold by private producers to private consumers. This absence of a market necessitates imputing values to the production of recreation services. Such economic benefits can be taken into account in decisions affecting our use of resources.

MISUNDERSTANDINGS OF RECREATION VALUES

Discussions of values of outdoor recreation have been beset by many misunderstandings. One of these stems from a lack of appreciation that the use of outdoor recreation facilities differs only in kind, but not in principle, from consumption patterns of other goods and services. Another is that the market process takes account of personal and varied consumer satisfactions.

It is, furthermore, the incremental values that are important in making decisions relative to resource allocations. The incremental values of recreation developments of various kinds are a manageable concept which can be used for comparisons, in spite of the very great aggregate value that some may want to attribute to recreation. Nothing is gained— and no doubt a great deal has been lost—by what amounts to ascribing the importance of a total supply of recreation to an added increment, rather than concentrating on the added costs and the added benefits.

A similar difficulty arises with respect to questions of water supply. That man is entirely dependent upon the existence of water is repeatedly emphasized. While true, the point does not matter. Decisions necessarily focus on increments and therefore on the added costs and the added benefits that stem from adding small amounts to the existing total.

Further, no goods or services are priceless in the sense of an infinite price. There is an individual and collective limit to how much we will give up to enjoy the services of any outdoor recreation facility or to preserve any scenic resource. The most relevant economic measure of recreation values, therefore, is willingness on the part of consumers to pay for outdoor recreation services. This set of values is comparable to economic values established for other commodities, for it is the willingness to give up on the part of consumers that establishes values throughout the economy.

Failure to understand these value characteristics results in two types of error. The first is the belief that the only values that are worth con-

KNETSCH AND DAVIS

sidering are those accounted for commercially. A second and related source of error is a belief that outdoor recreation experience is outside the framework of economics, that the relevant values have an aesthetic, deeply personal, and even mystical nature. We believe both of these to be incorrect. In particular, the notion that economic values do not account for aesthetic or personal values is fallacious and misleading. Economically, the use of resources for recreation is fully equivalent to other uses, and the values which are relevant do not necessarily need to be determined in the market place. This last condition does indicate that indirect means of supplying relevant measures of the values produced may be necessary. But this is an empirical problem, albeit one of some considerable dimension, and the primary concern of this paper.

The problem of using imputed values for value determination has been met with a considerable degree of success for some products of water resource development. Procedures have been developed to assess the value of the flood protection, irrigation, and power services produced by the projects, even though in many cases a market does not in fact exist or is inadequate for the actual benefit calculations. Without commenting on the adequacy of these methods, it is generally agreed that such measures are useful in evaluating the output of project services.

NATIONAL AND LOCAL BENEFITS

Discussions of these topics have often been further confused by failure to separate two types of economic consequences or benefit. This has led to improper recognition of relevant and legitimate economic interests, and to inferior planning and policy choices.

There are, first, what we may call primary benefits, or national benefits. Second, there are benefits we may refer to as local benefits, or impact benefits. Both sets of values resulting from investment in recreation have economic relevance, but they differ, and they bear differently on decision.

The primary recreation benefits, or values, are in general taken to be expressions of the consumers' willingness to pay for recreation services. These values may or may not register in the commerce of the region or in the commerce of the nation, but this does not make them less real. When appropriately measured, they are useful for guiding social choices at the national level. The other set of accounts is concerned with local expenditure of money for local services associated with recreation. While outdoor recreation is not marketed—in the sense that the services of parks, as such, are not sold to any great extent in any organized market—money

METHODS FOR RECREATION EVALUATION

does indeed become involved in the form of expenditures for travel, equipment, lodging, and so forth. The amount of money spent in connection with outdoor recreation and tourism is large and growing, making outdoor recreation expenditures of prime concern to localities and regions which may stand to benefit. Our concern is with measuring the more difficult of the two types of benefit just mentioned—national recreation benefits. While these are measured essentially by the consumers' willingness to pay, in some cases the benefits extend to the non-using general public.

ALTERNATIVE MEASUREMENT METHODS

There are obvious advantages to evaluating recreation benefits by market prices in the same manner as their most important resource competitors. However, as we have indicated, past applications have been hampered by disagreement on what are the meaningful values. In spite of growing recognition that recreation has an important economic value, economists and public administrators have been ill-prepared to include it in the social or public calculus in ways that lead to better allocations of resources.

The benefits of recreation from the social or community viewpoint are alleged to be many and varied. Some of the descriptions of public good externalities arising from recreation consumption are gross overstatements of the real values derived from the production of recreation services. But recreation benefits do in fact exist. Where externalities are real—as in cases of recreation in connection with visits to various historic areas or educational facilities, or where preservaton of unique ecological units has cultural and scientific values—they should be recognized in assigning values to the development or preservation of the areas. However, it is our view that, by and large, recreation is a consumption good rather than a factor of production, and the benefits to be enjoyed are largely those accruing to the individual consumer participating. This is even more likely to be the case with recreation provided by water projects. The large bulk of primary recreation benefits can be viewed as the value of the output of the project to those who use them. This view stems from the concept that recreation resources produce an economic product. In this sense they are scarce and capable of yielding satisfaction for which people are willing to pay. Finally, some accounting can be made of this economic demand.

As the desirability of establishing values for recreation use of resources has become more apparent over the past few years, a number of methods for measuring or estimating them have been proposed and to some extent used. Some of the measures are clearly incorrect; others attempt to measure appropriate values, but fall short on empirical grounds [ref. 1, 2, 3].

Gross Expenditures Method

The gross expenditures method attempts to measure the value of recreation to the recreationist in terms of the total amount spent on recreation by the user. These expenditures usually include travel expenses, equipment costs, and expenses incurred while in the recreation area. Estimates of gross recreation expenditures are very popular in some quarters; for one thing, they are likely to produce large figures. It is argued that persons making such expenditures must have received commensurate value or they would not have made them. The usual contention is that the value of a day's recreation is worth at least the amount of money spent by a person for the use of that recreation.

These values have some usefulness in indicating the amount of money that is spent on a particular type of outdoor recreation, but as justification for public expenditure on recreation, or for determining the worth or benefit of the recreation opportunity afforded, they are of little consequence.

The values we seek are those which show not some gross value, but the net increase in value over and above what would occur in the absence of a particular recreation opportunity. Gross expenditures do not indicate the value of the losses sustained if the particular recreation opportunity were to disappear, nor do they show the net gain in value from an increase in a particular recreation opportunity.

Market Value of Fish Method

A proposed method for estimating the recreation benefits afforded by fishing imputes to sport fishing a market value of the fish caught. The main objection to this procedure is the implied definition that the fish alone are the primary objective of the activity.

Cost Method

The cost method assumes that the value of outdoor recreation resource use is equal to the cost of generating it or, in some extreme applications, that it is a multiple of these costs. This has the effect of justifying any contemplated recreation project. However, the method offers no guide in the case of contemplated loss of recreation opportunities, and allows little or no discrimination between relative values of alternative additions.

METHODS FOR RECREATION EVALUATION

Market Value Method

Basic to the market value method measure is a schedule of charges judged to be the market value of the recreation services produced. These charges are multiplied by the actual or expected attendance figures to arrive at a recreation value for the services.

The method is on sound ground in its emphasis on the willingness of users to incur expenses to make choices. However, the market for outdoor recreation is not a commercial one, certainly not for much of the recreation provided publicly and only to a limited extent for private recreation. It is in part because private areas are not fully comparable with public areas that users are willing to pay the fees or charges. It seems, therefore, inappropriate to use charges paid on a private area to estimate the value of recreation on public areas. Also a single value figure or some range of values will be inappropriate for many recreation areas. Physical units of goods and services are not everywhere equally valuable, whether the commodity be sawtimber, grazing, or recreation. Location in the case of recreation affects value greatly. Moreover, differences of quality and attractiveness of recreation areas are not fully comparable or recognized by the unit values.

There are other methods, but few have received much attention. Where does this leave us? The only methods to which we give high marks are based on the concept of willingness to pay for services provided.

METHODS BASED ON WILLINGNESS TO PAY

We have alluded to two kinds of problems we face in measuring the benefits of outdoor recreation: the conceptual problems and the measurement problems.

Conceptually, we wish to measure the willingness to pay by consumers of outdoor recreation services as though these consumers were purchasing the services in an open market. The total willingness of consumers to pay for a given amount and quality of outdoor recreation (that is, the area under the demand curve) is the relevant measure we seek. Our conceptual problems are essentially that any measurement of effective demand in the current time period, or even an attempt to project effective demand in future time periods, must necessarily omit from the computation two kinds of demand which may or may not be important. These are option demand and demand generated by the opportunity effect.[1]

[1] These concepts are developed by Davidson, Adams, and Seneca in "The Social Value of Water Recreational Facilities Resulting from an Improvement in Water Quality: The Delaware Estuary," published in this volume.

KNETSCH AND DAVIS

Option demand is that demand from individuals who are not now consumers or are not now consuming as much as they anticipate consuming, and who therefore would be willing to pay to perpetuate the availability of the commodities. Such a demand is not likely to be measured by observance or simulation of market phenomena. The opportunity effect derives from those unanticipated increases in demand caused by improving the opportunities to engage in a recreational activity and thereby acquainting consumers with new and different sets of opportunities to which they adapt through learning processes. To our knowledge no methods have been proposed which might be used to measure these two kinds of demand for a good.

Notwithstanding the undoubted reality of these kinds of demand, our presumption is that effective demand is likely to be the predominant component of the aggregate demand for outdoor recreation of the abundant and reproducible sorts we have in mind. We further presume that this quantity can be estimated in a useful way, although by fairly indirect means, for we have no market guide of the usual sort. Two methods—a direct interview, and an imputation of a demand curve from travel cost data—currently appear to offer reasonable means of obtaining meaningful estimates.

Interview Methods

The essence of the interview method of measuring recreation benefits is that through a properly constructed interview approach one can elicit from recreationists information concerning the maximum price they would pay in order to avoid being deprived of the use of a particular area for whatever use they may make of it. The argument for the existence of something to be measured rests on the conception that the recreationist is engaged in the utility maximizing process and has made a rational series of allocations of time and money in order to participate in the recreation being evaluated. Since the opportunity itself is available at zero or nominal price, the interview provides the means for discovering the price the person would pay if this opportunity were marketed, other things being equal.

The chief problem to be reckoned with in evaluating interview responses is the degree of reliability that can be attached to the information the respondent provides the interviewer. Particularly on questions dealing with matters of opinion, the responses are subject to many kinds of bias.

One such bias of particular interest to economists stems from the gaming strategy that a consumer of a public good may pursue on the theory that, if he understates his preference for the good, he will escape being charged as much as he is wiling to pay without being deprived of

METHODS FOR RECREATION EVALUATION

the amount of the good he now desires. This may be a false issue, particularly when it comes to pursuing recreation on private lands or waters, because the consumer may be well aware that the owner could, through the exercise of his private property rights, exclude the user from the areas now occupied. An equally good case can be made that, on state and national park lands to which there is limited access, particularly when at the access points the authority of the state is represented by uniformed park patrolmen, recreationists would have no trouble visualizing the existence of the power to exclude them. This being the case, it is not unreasonable to expect the recreationist to be aware of some willingness to pay on his part in order to avoid being excluded from the area he now uses.

Counterbalancing the possibility that the recreationist may purposely understate his willingness to pay in order to escape charges is the possibility that he may wish to bid up his apparent benefits in order to make a case for preserving the area in its current use, a case equally appropriate on private or public lands and waters.

The problem, to continue the argument, is narrowed to one of phrasing the question in such a way that the recreationist is not asked to give his opinion on the propriety of charging for the use of recreation areas.

It has become something of a principle in survey methodology that the less hypothetical the question, the more stable and reliable the response. By this principle, the respondent ought to be a consumer of the product rather than a potential consumer, thus distinguishing the data collected as pertaining to effective demand rather than to option or potential demand. It may also be preferable to impose the conditions on the interview that it occur at a time when the respondent is engaged in the activity. This may contribute to the accuracy of the responses by reducing the requirement that he project from one situation to another. (Admittedly, it is desirable to experiment with the methodology on this question, as well as others, in order to determine its sensitivity to such variations.)

In sum then, we expect to discover the consumer's willingness to pay through a properly constructed interview, and further, we expect that this measure will be the same quantity as would be registered in an organized market for the commodity consumed by the respondent. In other words, we hold a deterministic view that something exists to be measured, and is a sufficiently real and stable phenomenon that the measurement is useful.

The Interview Procedure.   The wilingness to pay of a sample of users of a forest recreation area in northern Maine was determined in inter-

KNETSCH AND DAVIS

views on the site [ref. 4]. The interviews included a bidding game in which respondents could react to increased costs of visiting the area. Bids were systematically raised or lowered until the user switched his reaction from inclusion to exclusion or vice versa. At the beginning of the interview rapport was established with the respondents largely through objective questions inquiring into their recreation activities on the area, on other areas, and the details of their trips. The bidding questions were interspersed with a series of propositions for which the respondent was to indicate his opinion in the form of a positive, negative, or neutral reaction. His reactions to increased expenses connected with the visit constituted the essence of the bidding game. Personal questions regarding income, education, and the like were confined to the end of the interview.

The sampling procedure amounted to cluster sampling, since the procedure followed was to locate areas of use such as campgrounds and to systematically sample from the available clusters of users. The interviews were conducted from June through November by visiting areas in the privately owned forests of northern Maine and in Baxter State Park.

The data from the interviews is pooled to include hunters, fishermen, and summer campers. This pooling is defended largely on the grounds that no structural differences between identifiable strata were detected in a multiple regression analysis of the responses.

The procedure imputes a discontinuous demand curve to the individual household which may be realistic under the time constraints faced particularly by vacation visitors and other non-repeating visitors. This rectangular demand curve (Figure 1) reflects a disposition either to come at the current level of use or not to come at all if costs rise above a limiting value. Its realism is supported by a number of respondents whose reaction to the excluding bid was precisely that they would not come at all. It seems reasonable to view the use of remote areas such as northern Maine as lumpy commodities which must be consumed in five- or six-day lumps or not at all. Deriving an aggregate demand function from the

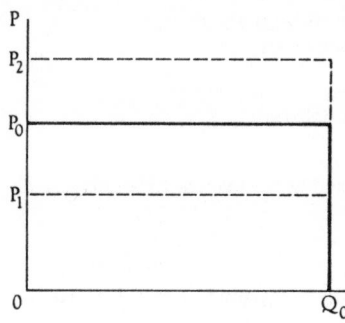

Figure 1. At prices in the range $0 - P_0$ the constant amount Q_0 will be demanded. Above P_0 demand will fall to zero. The individual may be in one of three states depending on the reigning price. Consider three individual cases with market price at P_0: The user paying P_1 is excluded; P_0 is associated with the marginal user; and P_2 is the willingness to pay of the third user who is included at the reigning price, P_0.

133

METHODS FOR RECREATION EVALUATION

individual responses so characterized is simply a matter of taking the distribution function of willingness to pay cumulated on a less-than basis. This results in a continuous demand schedule which can be interpreted for the aggregate user population as a conventional demand schedule.

For the sample of 185 interviews, willingness-to-pay-per-household-day ranges from zero to $16.66. Zero willingness to pay was encountered in only three interviews. At the other extreme, one or two respondents were unable to place an upper limit on their willingness to pay. The distribution of willingness to pay shows a marked skewness toward the high values. The modal willingness to pay occurs between $1.00 and $2.00 per day per household.

Sixty per cent of the variance of willingness to pay among the interviews is explained in a multiple regression equation with willingness-to-pay-per-household-visit a function of income of the household, years of experience by the household in visiting the area, and the length of the stay in the area. (See Equation 1.) While the large negative intercept of this equation necessitated by its linear form causes some difficulties of interpretation, the exhibited relation between willingness to pay, and income, experience, and length of stay appears reasonable. The household income not only reflects an ability to pay, but a positive income elasticity of demand for outdoor recreation as found in other studies. It is also significant that an internal consistency was found in the responses to income-related questions.

$$W = -48.57 + \underset{(1.52)}{2.85\,Y} + \underset{(0.58)}{2.88\,E} + \underset{(1.03)}{4.76\,L} \qquad \begin{matrix} R^2 \\ .5925 \end{matrix} \qquad (1)$$

$$W = \underset{(.13)}{.74\,L}^{.76} \; \underset{(.07)}{E}^{.20} \; \underset{(.17)}{Y}^{.60} \qquad\qquad .3591^* \qquad (2)$$

Standard errors of regression equations: (1) 39.7957; (2) 2.2007
Standard errors of coefficients are shown in parentheses.
W = household willingness to pay for a visit.
E = years of acquaintance with the area visited.
Y = income of the household in thousands of dollars.
L = length of visit in days.
F = ratios of both equations are highly significant.
* Obtained from arithmetic values of residual and total variances. (R^2 of the logarithmic transformation is .4309.)

The significance of years of experience in returning to the area may be interpreted as the effect of an accumulated consumer capital consisting

KNETSCH AND DAVIS

of knowledge of the area, acquisition of skills which enhance the enjoyment of the area, and in some cases use of permanent or mobile housing on the area.

The significance of length of stay in the regression equations is that it both measures the quantity of goods consumed and also reflects a quality dimension suggesting that longer stays probably reflect a greater degree of preference for the area.

Colinearity among explanatory variables was very low. The general economic consistency and rationality of the responses appear to be high. Respondents' comments indicated they were turning over in their minds the alternatives available in much the same way that a rational shopper considers the price and desirability of different cuts or kinds of meat. Both the success in finding acceptable and significant explanatory variables and a certain amount of internal consistency in the responses suggest that considerable weight can be attached to the interview method.

The Simulated Demand Schedule. While providing an adequate equation for predicting the willingness to pay of any user, the results of the interviews do not serve as direct estimates of willingness to pay of the user population, because the income, length of stay, and years' experience of the interviewed sample do not accurately represent the characteristics of the population of users. Fortunately, it was possible to obtain a reliable sample of the users by administering a questionnaire to systematically selected samples of users stopped at the traffic checking stations on the private forest lands. A logarithmic estimating equation, although not as well fitting, but free of a negative range, was used to compute the willingness to pay for each household in the sample. (See Equation 2.) The observations were then expanded by the sampling fraction to account for the total number of users during the recreation season.

The next step in the analysis consists of arraying the user population by willingness to pay, and building a cumulative distribution downward from the upper limit of the distribution. Table 1 shows the resulting demand and benefit schedule. The schedule accounts for the total of about 10,300 user households estimated to be the user population in a 450,000-acre area of the Maine woods near Moosehead Lake, known as the Pittston area.

The demand schedule is noticeably elastic from the upper limit of $60.00 to about $6.00, at which point total revenues are maximized. The interval from $60.00 to $6.00 accounts for the estimated willingness to pay of nearly half of the using households. Total benefits at $6.00 are

135

METHODS FOR RECREATION EVALUATION

TABLE 1.

Demand and Benefit Schedules for Pittston Area Based on Alternative
Estimates of Willingness to Pay

Price	Interview results		Willingness to drive (interview method)		Willingness to drive (travel cost method)	
	Household visits	Benefits[1]	Household visits	Benefits[1]	Household visits	Benefits[1]
$70.00	0	0				
60.00	11.36	$ 747.77				
50.00	15.35	983.56				
40.00	44.31	2,281.46				
30.00	150.22	6,003.19	11.36	$ 384.79	165	$ 3,800
26.00	215.80	7,829.71				
22.00	391.07	12,027.89				
20.00	536.51	15,099.31	76.96	1,890.12	422	12,134
18.00	757.86	19,275.95				
16.00	1,069.01	24,607.81				
14.00	1,497.75	31,027.17	392.29	7,287.06		
12.00	1,866.41	35,802.70				
10.00	2,459.70	42,289.68	2,157.91	28,921.93	1,328	26,202
8.00	3,100.99	48,135.01				
6.00	4,171.89	55,794.64				
4.00	5,926.94	64,436.36	5,721.06	53,531.68	3,459	44,760
2.00	7,866.02	70,222.66				
0.00	10,333.22	71,460.94	10,339.45	63,689.99	10,333	69,450

[1] Benefits are computed as the integral of the demand schedule from price maximum to price indicated. Willingness to drive computations are based on an assumed charge of 5¢ per mile for the one-way mileage.

$56,000. The price range below $6.00 accounts for the other half of the using households, but only for $15,000 in additional benefits. Benefits are estimated as the cumulative willingness to pay or the revenues available to a discriminating monopolist.

Willingness to Drive vs. Willingness to Pay. An alternative expression of the willingness of recreationists to incur additional costs in order to continue using an area may be found in their willingness to drive additional distances. This measure was first proposed by Ullman and Volk [ref. 5] although in a different version than is used here. (See also [ref. 6].)

Willingness to drive additional distances was elicited from respondents by the same technique used to elicit willingness to pay. If there are biases involving strategies to avoid paying for these recreation areas, then certainly willingness to drive is to be preferred over willingness to pay as an expression of value. Analysis of the willingness to drive responses shows that a partly different set of variables must be used to explain the re-

KNETSCH AND DAVIS

sponses. Equation 3 shows willingness to drive extra miles to be a function of length of stay and miles driven to reach the area.

$$Wm = 41.85 + 20.56L + .15M \tag{3}$$
$$(3.03) \quad (.04) \qquad\qquad (R^2 = .3928)$$

Wm = willingness to drive additional miles.
L = length of visit in days.
M = miles traveled to area.

The respondents thus expressed a willingness to exert an additional driving effort, just as they expressed a willingness to make an additional money outlay if this became a requisite to using the area. Moreover, there is a significant correspondence between willingness to pay and willingness to drive. The simple correlation coefficient between these two variables is .5. Because of the correlation with length of stay, the reduction in unexplained variance produced by adding either variable to the equation in which the other variable is the dependent one is not very high. However, willingness to pay was found to increase about 5¢ per mile as a function of willingness to drive additional miles. This result gives us a basis for transforming willingness to drive into willingness to pay.

We may now construct a demand schedule for the Pittston area on the basis of willingness to drive, and compute a willingness to pay at 5¢ per mile. The resulting demand and benefit schedules appear in Table 1. The estimated $64,000 of total benefits is very close to that developed from the willingness to pay interview. While one may quibble about the evaluation of a mile of extra driving and about the treatment of one-way versus round-trip distance, the first approximation using the obvious value of 5¢ and one-way mileage as reported by the respondents produces a result so close to the first result that we need look no further for marginal adjustments. The initial result strongly suggests that mileage measures and expenditure measures have equal validity as a measure of benefits in this particular case at least.

There are some differences between the respective demand schedules worth noting. The much lower price intercept on the willingness to drive schedule reflects the effect of the time constraint in traveling as well as our possibly erroneous constant transformation of miles to dollars when an increasing cost per mile would be more reasonable. The travel schedule is also elastic over more of its range than the dollar schedule—also perhaps a result of the constant transformation employed.

This initial success with alternative derivations of the benefits schedule now leads us to examine an alternative method for estimating the willingness to drive schedule.

METHODS FOR RECREATION EVALUATION

Travel-Cost Method of Estimating User-Demand Curve

The direct interview approach to the estimate of a true price-quantity relationship, or demand curve, for the recreation experience is one approach to the benefit calculations based on willingness to pay. An alternative approach has received some recognition and has been applied in a number of limited instances with at least a fair degree of success. This uses travel-cost data as a proxy for price in imputing a demand curve for recreation facilities. [Ref. 7, 8, 9, 10.] As with the direct interview approach, we believe that estimates derived from this approach are relevant and useful for measuring user benefits of outdoor recreation.

The travel-cost method imputes the price-quantity reactions of consumers by examining their actual current spending behavior with respect to travel cost. The method can be shown by using a simple, hypothetical example. Assume a free recreation or park area at varying distances from three centers of population given in Table 2.

TABLE 2.
Visits to a Hypothetical Recreation Area

City	Population	Cost of visit	Visits made	Visits/1,000 pop.
A	1,000	$1.00	400	400
B	2,000	3.00	400	200
C	4,000	4.00	400	100

The cost of visiting the area is of major concern and would include such items as transportation, lodging, and food cost above those incurred if the trip were not made. Each cost would vary with the distance from the park to the city involved. Consequently, the number of visits, or rather the rate of visits per unit of total population of each city, would also vary.

The visits per unit of population, in this case per thousand population, may then be plotted against the cost per visit. A line drawn through the three points of such a plot would have the relationship given by the equation of $C = 5 - V$, or perhaps more conveniently $V = 5 - C$, where C is cost of a visit and V is the rate of visits in hundreds per thousand population. This information is taken directly from the tabulation of consumer behavior. The linear relationship assumed here is for convenience. Actual data may very well show, for example, that $1.00 change in cost might have only a slight effect on visit rate where the visit is already high in cost, and a large effect on low-cost visits.

The construction of a demand curve to the recreation area, relating number of visits to varying cost, involves a second step. Essentially,

KNETSCH AND DAVIS

it derives the demand curve from the equation relating visit rates to cost, by relating visit rates of each zone to simulated increases in cost and multiplying by the relative populations in each zone. Thus we might first assume a price of $1.00, which is an added cost of $1.00 for visits to the area from each of the three different centers used in our hypothetical example. This would have the expected result of reducing the number of visitors coming from each of the centers. The expected reduction is estimated from the visit-cost relationship. The total visits suggested by these calculations for different prices or differing added cost are given as:

Price (added cost)	Quantity (total visits)
$0.00	1,200
1.00	500
2.00	200
3.00	100
4.00	0

These results may then be taken as the demand curve relating price to visits to the recreation area. While this analysis takes visits as a simple function of cost, in principle there is no difficulty in extending the analysis to other factors important in recreation demand, such as alternative sites available, the inherent attractiveness of the area in question or at least its characteristics in this regard, and possibly even some measure of congestion.

A difficulty with this method of benefit approximation is a consistent bias in the imputed demand curve resulting from the basic assumption that the disutility of overcoming distance is a function only of money cost. Clearly this is not so. The disutility is most likely to be the sum of at least three factors: money cost, time cost, and the utility (plus or minus) of driving, or traveling. The total of these three factors is demonstrably negative, but we do not know enough about the significance of the last two components. In all likelihood their sum—that is, of the utility or disutility of driving and the time cost—imposes costs in addition to money. To the extent that this is true the benefit estimate will be conservatively biased, for, as has been indicated, it is assumed that the only thing causing differences in attendance rates for cities located at different distances to a recreation area will be the differences in money cost. The method then postulates that if money cost changes are affected, the changes in rates will be proportional. What this bias amounts to is, essentially, a failure to establish a complete transformation function relating the three components of overcoming distance to the total effect on visitation rates. The resulting conservative bias must be regarded as an understatement of the recreation benefits which the approach is designed to measure.

METHODS FOR RECREATION EVALUATION

Application to Pittston Area.   The travel-cost method was applied to the same area as that used to illustrate the interview method of recreation benefit estimation. The same data were utilized to allow at least a crude comparison of the methods. In all, 6,678 respondents who said the Pittston area was the main destination of their trip were used in the analysis.

Visit rates of visitors from groups of counties near the area and from some states at greater distances were plotted against distance. The results were fairly consistent considering the rough nature of the approximations used in estimating distance. A curve was drawn through the points, giving a relationship between visit rates and distance. The demand curve was then calculated, giving a price-quantity relationship based on added distance (or added toll cost) and total visits. It was assumed initially that travel cost would be 5¢ per mile, using one-way distance to conform with our earlier analysis of travel cost by the interview method.

The results at this point were not comparable to the interview method because of a difference in the number of users accounted for. It will be recalled that in the analysis we are now describing only those respondents were used who had specifically stated that the visit to the Pittston area was the main destination of the trip. In order to make this number comparable to the total number of users accounted for in the interview estimate, we counted at half weight the 1,327 respondents who said that Pittston was *not* the primary destination of the trip, and also included in this group the non-response questionnaires and others with incomplete information. In this way we accounted for the same number of users as in the interview estimate. This very crude approximation points out the problems of the multiple-destination visit, but perhaps adequately serves the present purpose.

On the basis of these approximations, the benefit estimates on an annual basis were $70,000, assuming 5¢ per mile one-way distance. While the assumptions made throughout this analysis are subject to refinement, the exercise does seem to illustrate that the procedure is feasible from a practical standpoint and does produce results that are economically meaningful.

COMPARISON BETWEEN TRAVEL-COST AND
INTERVIEW METHODS

Having demonstrated that fairly close results are obtained from both the interview and imputation methods of estimating recreation benefits on the basis of reactions to travel costs, and further that the interview method of directly estimating willingness to pay agrees closely with both

KNETSCH AND DAVIS

estimates based on travel costs, we can now begin to assess the meaning of these results. In some ways the task would be easier if the results had not agreed so closely, for the three methodologies may imply different things about the users' reactions to increased costs. At least, it is not obvious without further probing as to why the agreement is so close.

The interview and imputation methods of estimating benefits on the basis of willingness to incur additional travel costs do not, for example, neatly imply the same relationship between distance traveled and willingness to incur additional travel costs. The estimating equation derived from the interviews (Equation 3) suggests that the farther one has traveled, the greater additional distance he will travel. Yet the imputation procedure implies that the willingness to drive by populations in the respective zones does not vary consistently with distance. Furthermore, according to the interviews, responses to the monetary measure of willingness to pay do not attribute any variance in willingness to pay to the distance factor, nor is an indirect relationship obvious. It seems relevant to inquire into the implied effects of these factors to discover why the alternative procedures appear to imply substantially different determinants of willingness to pay.

The superficial agreement in results may be upheld by this kind of further probing, but there are also some methodological issues which should not be overlooked. The travel-cost methods are obviously sensitive to such matters as the weighting given to multiple-destination visits and to the transformation used to derive costs from mileage values. Both methods are sensitive to the usual problems of choosing an appropriately fitting equation for the derivation of the demand schedule. The interview method has a poorly understood sensitivity to the various methodologies that might be employed in its use. Moreover, even the minimal use of interviews in studies of recreation benefits makes the method far more costly than the imputation method based on travel costs.

There are, however, complementarities in the two basic methods which may prove highly useful. In the first place, the two methods may serve as checks on each other in applied situations. One is certainly in a better position from having two methods produce nearly identical answers than if he has to depend on only one. There are also interesting possibilities that interviews may be the best way of resolving the ambiguities in the travel-cost method concerning the treatment of multiple-destination cases and for finding the appropriate valuation for converting distance into dollars. Much can be said for letting the recreationist tell us how to handle these problems.

In sum, we have examined three methods of measuring recreation benefits. All three measure recreationists' willingness to pay. This, we

141

METHODS FOR RECREATION EVALUATION

argue, is the appropriate measure of primary, or national, benefits. Furthermore, the measures are in rough agreement as to the benefits ascribable to an area of the Maine woods. This may be taken as evidence that we are on the right track. There are, however, some rough spots to be ironed out of each of the methods—an endeavor we believe to be worthy of major research effort if benefit-cost analysis is to contribute its full potential in planning decisions affecting recreation investments in land and water resources.

REFERENCES

[1] Lerner, Lionel. "Quantitative Indices of Recreational Values," in *Water Resources and Economic Development of the West*. Report No. 11. Proceedings, Conference of Committee on the Economics of Water Resources Development of Western Agricultural Economics Research Council with Western Farm Economics Association. Reno: University of Nevada, 1962.

[2] Merewitz, Leonard. "Recreational Benefits of Water-Resource Development." Unpublished paper of Harvard Water Program, 1965.

[3] Crutchfield, James. "Valuation of Fishery Resources," *Land Economics*, Vol. 38, No. 2 (1962).

[4] Davis, Robert K. "The Value of Outdoor Recreation: An Economic Study of the Maine Woods." Ph.D. thesis, Harvard University, 1963.

[5] Ullman, Edward, and Volk, Donald. "An Operational Model for Predicting Reservoir Attendance and Benefits: Implications of a Location Approach to Water Recreation," *Proceedings Michigan Academy of Sciences*, 1961.

[6] Meramec Basin Research Project. "Recreation," Chap. 5 in *The Meramec Basin*, Vol. 3. St. Louis: Washington University, December 1961.

[7] Clawson, Marion. *Methods of Measuring the Demand for and Value of Outdoor Recreation*. RFF Reprint No. 10. Washington: Resources for the Future, Inc., 1959.

[8] Knetsch, Jack L. "Outdoor Recreation Demands and Benefits," *Land Economics*, Vol. 39, No. 4 (1963).

[9] ——. "Economics of Including Recreation as a Purpose of Water Resources Projects," *Journal of Farm Economics*, December 1964. Also RFF Reprint No. 50. Washington: Resources for the Future, Inc.

[10] Brown, William G., Singh, Ajner, and Castle, Emery N. *An Economic Evaluation of the Oregon Salmon and Steelhead Sport Fishery*. Technical Bulletin 78. Corvallis: Oregon Experiment Station, 1964.

[20]

A METHOD OF ESTIMATING SOCIAL BENEFITS FROM POLLUTION CONTROL

Karl-Göran Mäler*

The Stockholm School of Economics, Stockholm, Sweden

I. Introduction

In an article in *Water Resources Research*, 1966 [3], Joe B. Stevens tried to estimate direct recreational benefits from water pollution control by using market demand curves for a sport fishery. The quality of the fishery was represented by the angling success per unit of effort. Water pollution would cause a deterioration in the quality, i.e. would decrease angling success. By estimating a demand function for the sport fishery, both as a function of the price of using the fishery and as a function of the quality variable, Stevens thought he could calculate the recreational benefits or the willingness to pay for maintaining constant quality, from various areas under the demand curves.

Stevens' idea, although a very sound one, was not developed in a rigorous way and his conclusions were therefore vague. The aim of this article is to develop a theory which can lend support to calculations such as those presented by Stevens.

The ideas in this article will first be presented intuitively in a non-rigorous way. Then Section III includes a brief review of elements from demand analysis and a statement of the marginal conditions for Pareto-optimality in an economy with public goods. A theoretical framework is developed in Section IV which enables derivation of the willingness to pay for public goods in certain cases on the basis of information on demand functions for private goods.

II. Intuitive Presentation of the Main Idea

It is natural to assume that if it is known that a public good is complementary to a private good, then it should be possible to calculate the demand for the public good if the demand for the private good is known. And if a public good is a perfect substitute for a private one, the consumers' preferences for the public good can be derived from the revealed preferences on the market.

A systematic study of the *a priori* conditions with regard to the preferences for a public good, obtained from complementariness and substitutability is

---
* I am very grateful to Professors P. Bohm, Clark Reynolds and Robert Solow for valuable comments and suggestions. This project was supported by the Ford Foundation and Stiftelsen Riksbankens Jubileumsfond.

122   *K.-G. Mäler*

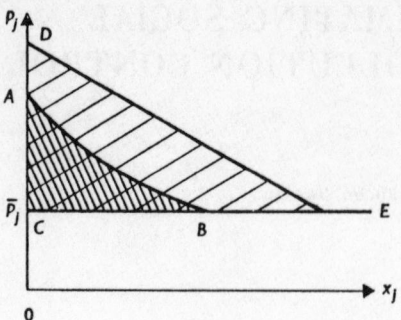

Fig. 1

required. We will not undertake this kind of study here, but instead discuss a single condition which seems realistic in some cases.

Consider a private good x_j, which can be produced in different qualities Y_k, but in only one quality at a time. The use of a fishery, for example, can be regarded as a private good. The quality of the fishery measured in terms of the catch of fish per unit of fishing time or the oxygen dissolved is a public good in the sense that all consumers using the fishery meet with the same quality. Those who do not use the fishery will generally be indifferent to quality changes. A single consumer will be indifferent to quality changes if the price of the corresponding private good is high enough to prevent him from using the fishery. This idea, simple as it is, provides an additional condition which can used for calculating the demand price for quality changes. (Note that if the private good can be supplied in different qualities at the same time, the quality ceases to be a public good. In this case we do not have one private good but many, each characterized by a certain quality.)

The condition can be stated mathematically in the following way: There exists a private good x_j and a public good Y_k such that

$$\frac{\partial u^h(x_1, \ldots, x_{j-1}, 0, x_{j+1}, \ldots, x_n, Y_1, \ldots, Y_m)}{\partial Y_k} = 0 \qquad (1)$$

where u^h is the utility function of consumer h.

Assumption (1) implies that the demand price for Y_k can be calculated from the demand function for x_j. This can be observed intuitively as follows.

Consider the compensated demand curve AB for good j in Fig. 1. At the price $p_j = \bar{p}_j$, the consumer demands $\bar{x}_j$ and the consumer surplus is the cross-shaded area ABC. The consumer is thus willing to pay ABC in order to prevent a fall in the supply from $\bar{x}_j$ to zero.

Now consider a change in Y_k. This will cause the compensated demand curve to shift to DE. The new consumer surplus becomes the area CDE

A method of estimating social benefits from pollution control 123

(provided the price does not change). How much is the consumer willing to pay for the change in Y_k, that is how much is he willing to pay for the induced movement from B to E?

This movement can be divided into three steps:

(a) a change in p_j from C to D. In order not to put the consumer in a worse position, he has to be compensated by ABC.

(b) a change in Y_k. If we apply assumption (1), this change will not cause any need for compensation.

(c) a change in p_j from D to E. In order not to put the consumer in a beter position, he has to pay the amount CDE.

The net result is $CDE - ABC$ or the area $BADE$. The amount the consumer is willing to pay to obtain the change in Y_k is thus $BADE$.

Note that this calculation is impossible without assumption (1). If (1) is not applicable, the appropriate transfer in step (b) cannot be estimated. If the consumer is willing to offer something in order to improve the quality of x_j even if he does not consume x_j, then nothing can be said about his willingness to pay for a change on quality on the basis of his demand curve for x_j.

III. Summary of Results from Demand Analysis

This section contains a brief review of some elementary parts of demand analysis which are relevant to this study.

We assume that there are H consumers, each equipped with a utility function

$$u^h(x^h, Y) \quad h = 1, ..., H$$

where x^h is the vector of net demand for private goods (there are n private goods in the economy) and Y is the vector of public goods supplied (there are m public goods and each public good is characterized by the condition that an increase in the supply of the public good for one person means an identical increase in the supply to all other persons). In this context environmental quality is interpreted as a public good because the quality of the water in a stream is the same for everyone.

We assume that $u^h(x^h, Y)$ is twice continuously differentiable and that u^h is quasi concave. We denote the partial derivatives by subscripts:

$$\frac{\partial u^h}{\partial x_i} = u_i^h$$

$$\frac{\partial u^h}{\partial Y_k} = u_k^h.$$

124   K.-G. Mäler

Given the lump sum income I^h and the price vector $p \in R^n$, the budget set for the h:th consumer is defined by

$$M^h = \{x^h \mid p^T x^h \leqslant I^h, x^h \geqslant 0\}.^1$$

We can now study the two "dual" problems

max $u^h(x^h, Y)$

s.t. $x^h \in M^h$

and

min $m^h = p^T x^h$

s.t. $u^h(x^h, Y) \geqslant \bar{u}^h$.

The first order conditions for the problems are

$$u_i^h = \lambda^h p_i \quad i = 1, ..., n \tag{2}$$

and

$$\alpha^h u_i^h = p_i \quad i = 1, ..., n \tag{3}$$

where λ^h and α^h, respectively, are Lagrange multipliers for the two problems.

Solving the first order conditions for the first problem yields:

$$x^h = x^h(p, I^h, Y)$$

$$u^h = u^h(x^h(p, I^h, Y), Y) = v^h(p, I^h, Y)$$

and for the second problem

$$x^h = x^{h+}(p, \bar{u}^h, Y)$$

$$m^h = p^T x^{h+}(p, \bar{u}^h, Y) = m^h(p, \bar{u}^h, Y).$$

x^h is the usual Marshallian demand function and v^h is called the indirect utility function. x^h is the Hicksian compensated demand function and m^h is called the expenditure function.

We need the following results (for proofs see e.g. Karlin, Ch. 8 [1])

(a) m^h is a concave function in p

(b) $x^h(p, m^h(p, \bar{u}^h, Y), Y) = x^{h+}(p, \bar{u}^h, Y)$, that is, if income is varied so that the consumer is always on the same indifference curve, then the compensated demand functions are obtained from the Marshallian demand functions.

---

[1] A vector x is interpreted as a column vector and transposition of a vector to a row vector will be denoted by the symbol $\top$. We use the following conventions for vector inequalities: $x \geqslant 0$ if $x_i \geqslant 0$ for all components x_i
$x \geqslant 0$ if $x \geqslant 0$ and $x \neq 0$
$x > 0$ if $x_i > 0$ for all components x_i.

A method of estimating social benefits from pollution control　125

(c) the Slutsky equations:

$$\frac{\partial^2 m^h}{\partial p_i \partial p_j} - \frac{\partial x_i^h}{\partial I^h} \frac{\partial m^h}{\partial p_j} - \frac{\partial x_i^h}{\partial p_j} = 0, \quad i,j = 1,...,n. \tag{4}$$

The Slutsky equations give the expenditure function as a solution to a system of (not independent) differential equations. The boundary conditions are

$$m^h(\bar{p}, \bar{u}^h, \overline{Y}) = I^h$$

$$\frac{\partial m^h(\bar{p}, \bar{u}^h, \overline{Y})}{\partial p_i} = x_i^h(\bar{p}, I^h, \overline{Y}) \quad i = 1,...,n$$

where $\bar{u}^h = v^h(\bar{p}, I^h, \overline{Y})$ and $\bar{p}, \overline{Y}$ are the prices and the supply of public goods in the initial situation.

If the Marshallian demand function $x^h(p, I^h, Y)$ are known, we can solve the Slutsky equations and determine m as a function of p. But without further assumptions m as a function of Y cannot be determined.

Let us now turn to the problem of aggregation of expenditure functions. The demand functions for consumer h are

$$x^h(p, I^h, Y).$$

The aggregate demand functions are

$$X(p, I^1, ..., I^H, Y) = \sum_{h=1}^{H} x^h(p, I^h, Y).$$

A necessary and sufficient condition for writing this aggregate demand function as a function of the aggregate income $I = \sum_{h=1}^{H} I^h$, instead of the individual incomes for arbitrary variations in income, is that all individuals have the same marginal propensity to demand out of income. Let us therefore assume that the individual demand functions are of the form

$$x_i^h = x_i^h(p, I^h, Y), \quad \frac{\partial x_i^h}{\partial I^h} = \frac{\partial x_i^k}{\partial I^k} = \beta_i; \quad h, k = 1,...,H, \quad i = 1,...,n.$$

We can then aggregate to

$$X_i = X_i(p, I, Y)$$

where

$$I = \sum_{h=1}^{H} I^h, \quad \frac{\partial X_i}{\partial I} = \beta_i.$$

Let us now define the aggregate expenditure function m as

$$m = \sum_{h=1}^{H} m^h.$$

126　*K.-G. Mäler*

Then

$$\frac{\partial m}{\partial p_i} = \sum_{h=1}^{H} \frac{\partial m^h}{\partial p_i}$$

and

$$\frac{\partial^2 m}{\partial p_i \partial p_j} = \sum_{h=1}^{H} \frac{\partial^2 m^h}{\partial p_i \partial p_j} = \sum_{h=1}^{H} \left\{ \frac{\partial x_i^h}{\partial I^h} \frac{\partial m^h}{\partial p_j} + \frac{\partial x_i^h}{\partial p_j} \right\} = \sum_{h=1}^{H} \left\{ \beta_i \frac{\partial m^h}{\partial p_j} + \frac{\partial x_i^h}{\partial p_j} \right\} = \beta_i \frac{\partial m}{\partial p_j} + \frac{\partial X_i}{\partial p_j}$$

and the aggregate expenditure function also satisfies the differential equations (4). Thus the condition for consistent aggregation of demand fumctions for arbitrary variations in individual incomes is also the conditions for consistent aggregation of expenditure functions. From now on it is assumed that this condition is fulfilled.

Samuelson [2] has shown that for a Pareto optimum in an economy with public goods, the following condition must be satisfied:

$$\sum_{h=1}^{H} \frac{\partial u^h}{\partial Y_k} \bigg/ \frac{\partial u^h}{\partial x_i^h} = MC_k^i$$

where MC_k^i is the social marginal opportunity cost of producing the public good Y_k in terms of production of the private good x_i.

Let the price of commodity 1 be p_1 and put

$$\delta_k^h = p_1 \frac{\partial u^h}{\partial Y_k} \bigg/ \frac{\partial u^h}{\partial x_1^h}.$$

δ_k^h will be interpreted as consumer h's demand price for the public good k. The purpose of this paper is to discuss one way of estimating the total demand price

$$\delta_k = \sum_{h=1}^{H} \delta_k^h$$

for the public good k.

Obviously, the total demand price will be a function of the price vector p, the incomes $I^1, \ldots, I^H$ and the vector of public goods supplied Y:

$$\delta_k = \sum_{h=1}^{H} \delta_k^h = \sum_{h=1}^{H} g_k^h(p, I^h, Y).$$

The expenditure function for consumer h is

$$m^h(p, \bar{u}^h, Y) = p^T x^{h+}.$$

If we differentiate the condition $u^h = \bar{u}^h$ with respect to Y_k we have

$$\sum_{i=1}^{n} u_i^h \frac{\partial x_i}{\partial Y_k} + \frac{\partial u^h}{\partial Y_k} = 0.$$

A method of estimating social benefits from pollution control 127

We also know that $\alpha^h u_i^h = p_i$ so that

$$\frac{\partial m^h}{\partial Y_k} = \sum_{i=1}^{n} p_i \frac{\partial x_i^{h+}}{\partial Y_k} = \alpha^h \sum_{i=1}^{n} u_i^h \frac{\partial x_i^{h+}}{\partial Y_k} = -\alpha^h \frac{\partial u^h}{\partial Y_k} = -p_1 \frac{\partial u^h}{\partial Y_k} \bigg/ \frac{\partial u^h}{\partial x_1^h} = -\delta_k^h.$$

The same relation holds for the total demand price

$$\frac{\partial m}{\partial Y_k} = -\delta_k.$$

The marginal willingness to pay or the demand price for the public good can therefore be estimated by estimating the expenditure function as a function of Y. But it was noted above that this is impossible if the only information we have consists of the demand functions for private goods. Thus further assumptions have to be added in order to solve our problem.

IV. Estimating Demand Prices for Public Goods

Note that assumption (1) is invariant for monotonic transformations of the utility function. In fact, let F be any monotonic increasing function. Then

$$\frac{\partial F(u^h(x_1, ..., 0, ..., x_n, Y))}{\partial Y_k} = F' \frac{\partial u^h(x_1, ..., 0, ..., x_n, Y)}{\partial Y_k}.$$

Note also that (1) is equivalent to

$$\frac{\partial m(p', \bar{u}, Y)}{\partial Y_k} = 0 \tag{5}$$

where p' is the price vector which causes a zero compensated demand for x_j, that is $x_j^+ = 0$ (for simplicity the superscript h is dropped).

Assume that there is a pair x_j, Y_k such that (1) is true. Let us now aggregate all other private goods to a composite good z with a price p_z and denote x_j by x. As the supply of all public goods except Y_k is going to be held constant, we can drop the corresponding variables and denote Y_k by Y.

The demand function for x can then be written

$$x = x(p_x, p_z, I, Y).$$

Consider the first equation in (3):

$$\frac{\partial^2 m}{\partial p_x^2} - \frac{\partial x(p_x, p_z, m, Y)}{\partial I} \frac{\partial m}{\partial p_x} - \frac{\partial x(p_x, p_z, m, Y)}{\partial p_x} = 0.$$

The general solution to this equation will have the form

$$m = \psi(p_x, p_z, Y, \varphi_1, \varphi_2) \tag{6}$$

128   *K.-G. Mäler*

where φ_1 and φ_2 are functions of p_z and Y.

The initial conditions are

$$\psi(\bar{p}_x, \bar{p}_z, \overline{Y}, \varphi_1, \varphi_2) = I$$

$$\frac{\partial \psi(\bar{p}_x, \bar{v}_z, \overline{Y}, \varphi_1, \varphi_2)}{\partial p_x} = x(\bar{p}_x, \bar{p}_z, I, \overline{Y})$$

where $\bar{p}_x$, $\bar{p}_z$, Y are the prices and supply of the public good in the initial situation. By solving the initial conditions the values of φ_1 and φ_2 in the initial situation can be obtained.

Note that the compensated demand function for x is given by

$$x^+ = \frac{\partial m}{\partial p_x} = \varkappa(p_x, p_z, Y, \varphi_1, \varphi_2).$$

Denote the inverse function by

$$p_x = h_x(x^+, p_z, Y, \varphi_1, \varphi_2).$$

Because the substitution effect is always negative, we know that this function always exists.

This function enables us to find those prices for which x^+ is zero:

$$p_x \geqslant p_x' = h_x(0, p_z, Y, \varphi_1, \varphi_2).$$

If we substitute this in (6) we obtain

$$m(p_x, p_z, Y) = m(p_x', p_z, Y) = \psi(h_x(0, p_z, Y, \psi_1, \varphi_2)) p_z, Y, \varphi_1, \varphi_2) \tag{7}$$

for $p_x \geqslant p_x'$.

Assumption (5) can now be applied. If assumption (1) or (5) holds, then the derivative of (7) with respect to Y is zero:

$$\frac{dm}{dY} = \frac{\partial \psi}{\partial p_x}\frac{\partial h_x}{\partial Y} + \frac{\partial \psi}{\partial Y} + \frac{\partial \psi}{\partial \varphi_1}\frac{\partial \varphi_1}{\partial Y} + \frac{\partial \psi}{\partial \varphi_2}\frac{\partial \varphi_2}{\partial Y} = 0. \tag{8}$$

This is a differential equation in the two unknown functions φ_1 and φ_2 .But (8) is an identity in p_z which implies that (8) can be differentiated with respect to p_z so as to obtain one more equation.

We thus have two differential equations in the two unknowns $\varphi_1(Y)$ and $\varphi_2(Y)$. By solving these two equations, m is determined wholly as function of p_x and Y. By utilizing standard theorems on the existence and uniqueness of solutions to differential equations we see that the solution obtained is the desired expenditure function.

This analysis has, however, been carried out under one implicit assumption, i.e. that the demand function for x has Y as an argument. If this is not the case, the differential equation (8) cannot be established. Later on it will be shown that this is an exception which is not likely to occur.

The following simple example will be used to clarify the procedure outlined above.

Suppose we have obtained estimates of the demand functions

$$x = I/2p_x - aY/2$$

$$z = I/2p_z + p_x aY/2p_z$$

where a is some positive constant.

The differential equations (3) become

$$\frac{\partial^2 m}{\partial p_x^2} - \frac{1}{2p_x}\frac{\partial m}{\partial p_x} + \frac{m}{2p_x^2} = 0$$

$$\frac{\partial^2 m}{\partial p_x \partial p_z} - \frac{1}{2p_z}\frac{\partial m}{\partial p_x} = \frac{aY}{2p_z}.$$

By substitution we see that

$$m = \varphi_1(p_z, Y)p_x^{\frac{1}{2}} + \varphi_2(p_z, Y)p_x$$

is a solution to the first equation. If this expression is substituted for m in the second equation, we obtain

$$\frac{1}{2}\frac{\partial \varphi_1}{\partial p_z}p_x^{-\frac{1}{2}} + \frac{\partial \varphi_2}{\partial p_z} - \frac{1}{4p_z}\varphi_1 p_x^{-\frac{1}{2}} - \frac{1}{2p_z}\varphi_2 = \frac{aY}{2p_z}.$$

Because both φ_1 and φ_2 are indepedent of p_x, this yields two equations

$$\frac{\partial \varphi_1}{\partial p_z} - \frac{1}{2p_z}\varphi_1 = 0$$

and

$$\frac{\partial \varphi_2}{\partial p_z} - \frac{1}{2p_z}\varphi_2 = \frac{aY}{2p_z}.$$

The solutions are

$$\varphi_1 = f(Y)p_z^{\frac{1}{2}}$$

$$\varphi_2 = C(Y)p_z^{\frac{1}{2}} - aY$$

where $f(Y)$ and $C(Y)$ are undetermined functions. However, if assumption (5) is applied, these functions can be determined.

The expenditure function is

$$m = fp_x^{\frac{1}{2}}p_z^{\frac{1}{2}} + Cp_x p_z^{\frac{1}{2}} - ap_x Y$$

and the compensated demand function for x is

$$x^+ = \frac{\partial m}{\partial p_x} = \frac{1}{2}fp_x^{-\frac{1}{2}}p_z^{\frac{1}{2}} + Cp_z^{\frac{1}{2}} - aY.$$

130   K.-G. Mäler

The compensated demand for x is zero when

$$p_x \geqslant p_x' = \frac{1}{4}\frac{f^2}{Y^2}\frac{p_z}{(a-p_z^{\frac{1}{2}}C/Y)^2}.$$

For $p_x \geqslant p_x'$ the expenditure function becomes

$$m(p_x,p_z,Y) = m(p_x',p_z,Y) = \frac{1}{2}\frac{f^2}{Y}\frac{p_z}{(a-p_z^{\frac{1}{2}}C/Y)}$$

$$+\frac{1}{4}\frac{f^2}{Y}\frac{p_z}{(a-p_z^{\frac{1}{2}}C/Y)^2}\frac{C}{Y}p_z^{\frac{1}{2}}-\frac{1}{4}\frac{f^2}{Y}\frac{p_z}{(a-p_z^{\frac{1}{2}}C/Y)}a = \frac{1}{2}\frac{f^2}{Y}\frac{p_z}{(a-p_z^{\frac{1}{2}}C/Y)}.$$

If assumption (5) is true, then $m(p_x, p_z, Y)$ with $p_x \geqslant p_x'$, has to be independent of Y for all p_z. This can only be true if

$$f(Y) = A Y^{\frac{1}{2}}$$

and

$$C(Y) = BY$$

This means that the expenditure function becomes

$$m = A\sqrt{p_x p_z\, Y} + (B\sqrt{p_z}-a)\,p_x\,Y.$$

The constants A and B can be determined from the initial conditions. If this is done, we find that

$$A = \frac{I+\bar{p}_x\overline{Y}}{\sqrt{\bar{p}_x\bar{p}_z\overline{Y}}}$$

$$B = 0$$

and

$$m = A\sqrt{p_x p_z\, Y} - ap_x\,Y.$$

It can easily be proved that A is the indirect utility function. Then

$$\frac{\partial A}{\partial I} = \frac{1}{\sqrt{\bar{p}_x\bar{p}_z\overline{Y}}} = \lambda$$

$$\frac{\partial A}{\partial p_x} = \frac{1}{\sqrt{\bar{p}_x\bar{p}_z\overline{Y}}}\left[\frac{I}{2\bar{p}_x}-\frac{aY}{2}\right] = -\lambda x$$

$$\frac{\partial A}{\partial p_z} = \frac{1}{\sqrt{\bar{p}_x\bar{p}_z\overline{Y}}}\left[\frac{I}{2\bar{p}_z}+\frac{a\bar{p}_x\overline{Y}}{2\bar{p}_z}\right] = -\lambda z$$

A method of estimating social benefits from pollution control   131

(where λ is the Lagrange multiplier in (2)) can be used to solve for $\bar{p}_x$, $\bar{p}_z$ and I in terms of x, z, λ and $\bar{Y}$:

$$\bar{p}_x = \frac{1}{\lambda} z^{\frac{1}{2}} Y^{-\frac{1}{2}} (x + aY)^{-\frac{1}{2}}$$

$$\bar{p}_z = \frac{1}{\lambda} z^{-\frac{1}{2}} Y^{-\frac{1}{2}} (x + aY)^{\frac{1}{2}}$$

$$I = (2x + aY) \frac{1}{\lambda} z^{\frac{1}{2}} Y^{-\frac{1}{2}} (x + aY)^{-\frac{1}{2}}.$$

By substituting these expressions back into A, the original utility function is obtained (if the demand functions are those of a single individual):

$$u = 2(x + aY)^{\frac{1}{2}} z^{\frac{1}{2}} Y^{-\frac{1}{2}}.$$

The utility function has thus been derived on the basis of the demand functions for private goods by only assuming (5).

This example illustrates the technique of using assumption (5) to derive the expenditure function as a function of the public good Y. But the method fails if the differential equations (3) cannot be established. If the demand for x is a function of Y, then we have shown that (8) can be obtained by means of a routine calculation. The theorems on uniqueness of solutions to differential equations guarantee that the expenditure function ultimately derived is the correct one. But in the case where x is not a function of Y, (8) cannot be established and there is no possible way of deriving the expenditure function as a function of Y. But I will argue here that when the utility function is such that x does not depend on Y, assumption (5) is not likely to be realistic.

First, let us investigate the conditions under which the demand for a commodity does not depend on the amount of the public good.

Differentiating the optimality conditions (2) with respect to Y yields

$$u_{11} \frac{\partial x}{\partial Y} + u_{12} \frac{\partial z}{\partial Y} - p_x \frac{\partial \lambda}{\partial Y} = -u_{13}$$

$$u_{21} \frac{\partial x}{\partial Y} + u_{22} \frac{\partial z}{\partial Y} - p_z \frac{\partial \lambda}{\partial Y} = -u_{23}$$

$$-p_x \frac{\partial x}{\partial Y} - p_z \frac{\partial z}{\partial Y} = 0.$$

Let D be the determinant of coefficients in this equation system. Then the solutions for $\partial x/\partial Y$ and $\partial z/\partial Y$ are

$$\frac{\partial x}{\partial Y} = \frac{p_z}{D} (p_z u_{13} - p_x u_{23})$$

$$\frac{\partial z}{\partial Y} = -\frac{p_x}{D} (p_z u_{13} - p_x u_{23}).$$

132   *K.-G. Mäler*

The condition for $\partial x/\partial Y = \partial z/\partial Y = 0$ is

$$p_z u_{13} - p_x u_{23} = 0.$$

Due to (2) and because this is an identity, it can be written as

$$\frac{u_1}{u_{13}} = \frac{u_2}{u_{23}}$$

or

$$\frac{\partial}{\partial Y} \log u_1 = \frac{\partial}{\partial Y} \log u_2$$

which gives us

$$\log u_1 = \log (B(x, z) u_2)$$

where $B(x, z)$ is an arbitrary function of x and z.
   This equation is equivalent to

$$u_1 - B(x, z) u_2 = 0$$

which is a partial differential equation of the first order, the characteristic of which is given by

$$dx + \frac{dz}{B(x,z)} = 0.$$

If B is differentiable, this equation has a solution which is given by

$$\varphi(x, z) = C$$

where C is an arbitrary integration constant.
   The general solution to the partial differential equation can now be written

$$u = f(\varphi(x, z), Y)$$

where φ satisfies

$$\frac{\partial z}{\partial x} = -B(x, z).$$

If assumption (1) is now applied we find that

$$f_2(\varphi(0, z), Y) = 0.$$

Since this relation holds for all z, by differentiating with respect to z we find that

$$f_{21} \varphi_2(0, z) = 0.$$

Swed. J. of Economics 1971

A method of estimating social benefits from pollution control   133

$f_{21} = 0$ is not a property which is invariant for monotone increasing transformations, so (if we want to stick to an ordinal approach)

$$\varphi_2(0, z) = 0$$

or

$$\frac{\partial}{\partial z} u(0, z, Y) = \frac{\partial}{\partial Y} u(0, z, Y) = 0.$$

This relation shows that if consumption of x is zero, then the consumer is indifferent to how much of the composite commodity z he consumes. This is a very strong statement about a certain complementariness between x and z. The assumption that the demand for private goods does not depend on the supply of the public good combined with (1) therefore yields a conclusion which is not likely to be realistic.

With respect to the type of analysis discussed here, cases where the demand for private goods does not depend on the supply of the public good can be disregarded with a high degree of confidence.

References

1. Karlin, S.: *Mathematical Methods and Theory in Games, Programming, and Economics*, Vol. I. Addison-Wesley, 1959.
2. Samuelson, P.: The pure theory of public expenditure. *Review of Econom-* ics *and Statistics XXXVI*, no. 4, November, 1954.
3. Stevens, J.: Recreation benefits from water pollution control. *Water Resources Research*, Vol. 2, Second Quarter, 1966.

[21]

THE DETERMINANTS OF RESIDENTIAL PROPERTY VALUES WITH SPECIAL REFERENCE TO AIR POLLUTION

Ronald G. Ridker and John A. Henning *

I Introduction

IN recent years there has been growing concern about the detrimental effects of air pollution. Evidence has been mounting that it can affect health, irritate the eyes, nose and throat, corrode metal and stone, discolor and dirty buildings outside and in, and in general make a neighborhood look shabby. There is also some evidence from questionnaires that people believe air pollution affects property values and that it sometimes figures in their calculations in planning to move.[1] While it is reasonable to assume that many of these detrimental effects are reflected in property values, reliable statistical evidence bearing on this hypothesis has been virtually non-existent. The main purpose of the research reported on in this paper has been to provide such evidence. This evidence consists of estimates of the effect of variations in air pollution levels on property values for single family dwelling units in an urban area and was obtained by applying least-squares regression methods to cross-sectional data from the St. Louis metropolitan area in 1960.

Since the focus of the study is on the estimation of the relevant regression coefficients rather than on the simple statistical explanation of variations in the dependent variable, the effects of multicollinearity (large non-zero correlations among the explanatory variables) cannot be ignored by arguing that the explanatory power of the fitted equation as a whole is not affected by its presence. With respect to the air pollution variable, the method of treating this problem involves the development of several alternative estimates of its effects, each based upon a different assumption concerning the independent contribution of pollution given other explanatory variables. These estimates have the property that they would be identical to the conventional ones if air pollution were completely uncorrelated with the remaining explanatory variables.

A discussion of the regression model and variables used is presented in section II. In section III, the methods used to handle the multicollinearity problems encountered in this study are discussed. The desired estimates are presented in the remaining section. As a by-product, a number of interesting results are derived for the effects of other variables on property values. In particular, we find ourselves in a position to say something about discrimination in the housing market and the importance of several neighborhood effects in the St. Louis metropolitan area.

II The Model and Variables Used

The form and content of this study are determined to a large extent by two considerations. First, the data available consist of a cross section of observations by census tracts within a single metropolitan area.[2] This leads

* While numerous persons gave advice and criticism on this paper, the authors are especially grateful to Dr. Hugh O. Nourse for his participation in the early phases of this study and to the referee for his comments on the penultimate draft. This study was supported by the United States Public Health Service under Contract PH-86-65-17 with partial payment for computer services by the National Science Foundation under Grant GP-1137.

[1] Public Administration and Metropolitan Affairs Program, Southern Illinois University, *"Public Awareness and Concern with Air Pollution in the St. Louis Metropolitan Area"* (Edwardsville, Ill.: Southern Illinois University, 1964) ; Walter S. Smith, Jean J. Schueneman, and Louis D. Zeidberg, "Public Reaction to Air Pollution in Nashville, Tennessee," *Journal of the Air Pollution Control Association*, 14, No. 10 (Oct. 1964), 418–423; and Peter Rossi, *Why Families Move* (Glencoe, Ill.: The Free Press, 1955), 82.

[2] Time-series data are not available, and cross-sectional data among cities present serious difficulties because of differences in measurement procedures as well as differences in the effects of pollution when meteorological conditions and the pollution "mix" are not held constant (to say nothing of the additional problems that would be involved in explaining property values).

Census tracts are used as the units of observation primarily for convenience. However, quite apart from the fact that most of the data are available in these units, there are some advantages in utilizing averages by census tracts instead of individual observations, assuming the sample size to be the same in both cases. Errors in estimating the value of individual houses tend to cancel out. Fewer explanatory variables, particularly those related to

PROPERTY VALUES — AIR POLLUTION 247

to the utilization of explanatory variables that pertain primarily to the physical and neighborhood characteristics of the property. A given residential unit is assumed to consist of a "bundle" of attributes present in varying degrees, each of which has an implicit market price (positive or negative), the market value of this unit being the sum of the values of these attributes.[3]

Since we can expect to find a good deal of matching of housing and family characteristics (e.g., larger families living in larger houses), variables of either type could be used to predict property values.[4] However, the market value of a given house is determined by the demand (for particular sets of attributes) of *all* potential buyers, not just the demand of its current occupants, and within a given market (assuming no discrimination) the determinants of this demand (aggregate income, the distribution of income, family size, etc.) are constant in cross-sectional data. If, therefore, we are interested in explaining differences in the values of properties available to the same set of purchasers, it should be done in terms of differ-

ences in the characteristics of the properties rather than in terms of differences in the characteristics of their owner-occupants. In the absence of adequate measures of property characteristics we may wish to utilize highly correlated occupant characteristics, but it should be understood that the latter are being used as proxies for the missing variables, not as direct determinants of property values. Explicit mention is made of this fact because in at least one case, we use an occupant characteristic (family income) in this way.

The situation is different, however, if the cross-sectional observations pertain to more than one market, for then the characteristics of the house as well as the characteristics of the potential purchasers may differ between census tracts. As a first approximation in some studies it may be sufficient to assume that the whole urban area comprises a single unified housing market. Particularly because the location of some submarkets in our case study tends to be associated with different levels of air pollution, we prefer to introduce some explicit recognition of the presence of these submarkets.

The second consideration that has significantly influenced this study has been our a priori expectation that the impact of air pollution on property value (as judged in terms of the partial correlation coefficients or the standardized beta weights) is likely to be small relative to that of other variables. This belief has led us, in most runs, to restrict the sample of observations to census tracts in which single family housing units as a percentage of total housing units is at least 60 per cent and the population density is at least one person per acre. These restrictions, which reduced the sample size from a total of 304 to 167[5], were introduced as constituting the only method available of separating predominantly rural, commercial, and industrial tracts from predominantly urban residential areas. By concentrating on the latter, considerable homogeneity with respect to market influences on single family housing units is obtained, while little is lost with respect to variations in the air pollu-

the idiosyncracies of individual houses and their owners, need be considered, and the air pollution data available are more accurate when applied to neighborhoods than when applied to individual houses within a neighborhood.

Since the census information is based upon owners' appraisals, there is, of course, the danger that large response errors are present. According to one study, however, this is not the case for averages. The difference between the means of appraisers' and owners' estimates for 568 homes was only $350. See Leslie Kish and John B. Lansing, "Response Errors in Estimating the Value of Homes," *American Statistical Association Journal*, 49 (1954), 520–532. Furthermore, errors in differences between average property values in different tracts are likely to be even smaller.

[3] This viewpoint may be contrasted with that of a study the purpose of which is to explain family housing expenditures with cross-sectional data. While the dependent variable may be the same, in this case the explanatory variables pertain to the characteristics of the owner-occupants of the property. This viewpoint may also be contrasted with that of a study using time-series data for a given house or group of houses. In this case determinants of market demand, which again mean mainly occupant characteristics, are the most important variables.

[4] Indeed, we have found that parsimony and convenience argue in favor of relying on only two variables, median family income (an occupant characteristic) and median number of rooms (a property attribute). With our data, it takes a regression equation containing ten different variables pertaining to property characteristics, some of which were measured specifically for this study, to approximately equal the explanatory value of an equation with these two variables.

[5] Actually, the 1960 census for St. Louis divides the area into 345 tracts, but data for median property values were not available for 17 tracts, and reasonable interpolation of air pollution data could not be made for an additional 24 of these tracts.

tion levels experienced.[6] For the purposes of comparison, one run using all census tracts has been included in the summary table of final results presented below.[7]

This belief has also led to the inclusion of a wider variety and number of variables than is generally included in property value studies. A useful rule of thumb is to include all variables that are likely to be at least as important as the variable of primary interest. It is then reasonably likely that the primary variable will not prove to be significant only because it happened to be correlated with some more important variable that was left out of the analysis.

On the basis of these considerations, data on the variables described below were gathered and tried in various runs. The variables have been roughly grouped into categories according to our judgment about the role they play in explaining property values, and hypotheses concerning the likely form of their relationship with the dependent variable are presented. A detailed description of the variables with sources and methods of measurement can be found in the appendix.

Air Pollution

To date there is no commonly accepted index for the general phenomenon called air pollution. In consultation with air pollution experts familiar with the St. Louis data, two measures of pollution were chosen for trial in this study. In both cases the annual geometric mean was used as the measure of central tendency. The

first, a measure of sulfation levels which for convenience is given the symbol *SUL*, is an index indicating the presence of SO_2, SO_3, H_2S, H_2SO_4 and in some instances dustfall.[8] SO_2 can damage freshly applied paint, making it dry more slowly, making it more permeable to water, and over its life-time causing it to flake off more rapidly. H_2S can also damage and discolor paints, and along with H_2SO_4, result in metal and stone corrosion. These compounds can also irritate the eyes, nose, and throat and cause damage to vegetation. The second measure of pollution tried is a measure of suspended particulates gathered by high-volume air samplers. In the absence of a sufficient number of sampling stations to permit use of dustfall measurements, hi-vol was used as an indicator of soiling. However, it is not by itself well suited for this purpose, since the particles it measures are sufficiently small that they are as likely to be blown off surfaces as to stick and cause damage.

After a number of trials utilizing both indexes, the second, hi-vol, was finally dropped. Statistically, it gave unsatisfactory results, the partial regression coefficients attaching it to property value generally being positive. It was not measured as accurately as sulfation, samples being collected from only 16 stations as compared to 41 for sulfation.[9] Furthermore, since a reasonably high correlation was found between the few measurements of dustfall available and sulfation, hi-vol proved to be less necessary as an index of soiling.

While air pollution is generally assumed to be negatively related to property values (other things being equal) there are no commonly accepted hypotheses about any more specific form that this relationship might take.

Characteristics Specific to the Property

As indicators of characteristics of the property itself, *median number of rooms (MNR)*, *percentage recently built (PRB)*, and *houses*

---

[6] In particular, the elimination of predominantly industrial tracts has the advantage of reducing the correlation between air pollution and other social "disamenities" associated with proximity to industry. It is less likely, therefore, that the pollution variable is picking up the effects of industrial noise, congestion, and eyesores. Furthermore, the elimination of tracts with a predominance of multifamily dwelling units makes variables such as median number of rooms per unit, which unfortunately is available only for all dwelling units, more representative of the true figures for single family units than they otherwise would be.

[7] A comparison of runs containing the same variables for the total and the restricted sample tend to bear out these contentions. For the total sample, the multiple R^2 as well as the F values for many regression coefficients were considerably lower, in spite of the larger sample size. While some coefficients were substantially different, curiously, that for *SUL*, the air pollution variable, was quite similar to those found for the restricted sample. Compare equation (5) with others, especially (1) and (2), given in table 1.

[8] Coal burning is the principle source of both dustfall and sulfation in the St. Louis area. The simple correlation coefficient between the two is .54.

[9] Measurements at specific stations are equally accurate, but they were used to obtain isopleth maps from which values for each census tract were obtained. Interpolation by this method from only 16 census tracts can result in very inaccurate estimates.

per mile (*HPM*) were utilized. *MNR* is assumed to be a proxy for house size and *HPM* for lot size.[10] Originally *percentage substandard* (*PSS*) was included, but the restrictions on the sample eliminated most of the tracts with high values for this variable and it was dropped from final runs. *PRB*, which is included as a general index of quality, probably picks up a good part of the influence of factors affecting *PSS* in any case. *MNR* and *PRB* should be positively related and *HPM* should be negatively related to median property values (*MPV*).

Location Characteristics

Four variables reflecting different aspects of locational advantages and disadvantages of the property were tried in early runs. The first is based upon a division of the metropolitan area into *time zones* (*TIZ*) depending upon express bus travel time during rush hour to the central business district. The other three are dummy variables reflecting *accessability to highways* (*HWA*), *shopping area accessability* (*SAA*) and *industrial area accessability* (*IAA*). Assuming that the central business district sufficiently dominates other transportation focal points, or that the dummy variables appropriately control for proximity to these points, *TIZ* should be negatively related to *MPV* throughout its whole range. The coefficients for the dummy variables should be positive.

Neighborhood Characteristics

Of the many neighborhood characteristics that may affect property values in addition to air pollution, we have been able to obtain data on *school quality* (*SCH*), *crime rates* (*CRR*), *persons per unit* (*PPU*), and *occupation ratio* (*OCR*). School quality is measured using dummy variables indicating residents' attitudes about quality. While data were collected on three categories for *SCH*, a dichotomous variable with above average in one category and average and below average in the other should

be sufficient since it is unlikely that finer distinctions are made by most people.[11]

Ideally, we should like to have information on *attitudes* about school quality and crime rates, although objective measurements may have to be used as proxies in the absence of information about them. It should be clear without elaboration that subjective evaluations more directly determine property values, but in addition, the influence of more objective measures is likely to be offset by associated financial changes, especially where residential property owners rather than businesses pay the bulk of the taxes. The effect on property values of increases in teachers' salaries or teacher student ratios — even if they do reflect actual quality — is likely to be offset by higher taxes (or lower quality of other services in order to finance better schools). Lower crime rates, which mean lower insurance rates, may also mean higher local taxes to support a more effective police force. While it proved possible to arrive at a simple consensus among knowledgeable persons about general attitudes towards school quality in different parts of the metropolitan area, it was unfortunately not possible to do so with crime rates.

Since we are controlling for houses per square mile, persons per unit (*PPU*) measures population density in residential areas. It is likely to be a better measure of this attribute than population per square mile because the measure of area includes some non-residential areas (despite our attempts to control for this by restrictions on the sample). Higher values of *PPU* are likely to be associated with larger numbers of children in the neighborhood, and consequently more wear and tear on property, more noise, nuisance (so far as others' children are concerned), possibly higher school taxes, and so on. However, this variable could also be considered another indication of the quality of the house itself, at least insofar as more persons per house generally means more depreciation on houses of the same age.[12]

---

[10] *HPM* serves as a proxy for lot size only in the restricted sample where rural, commercial and industrial tracts, with small values for *HPM* that do not necessarily reflect lot size, have been left out.

[11] This assumption corresponds with the real estate salesman's behavior in pointing out the good qualities, ignoring the mediocre and denying the existence of bad neighborhood characteristics, in talking to potential buyers.

[12] In a study of family housing expenditures this variable would be interpreted as an occupant characteristic reflect-

Occupation ratio (OCR) is one of the components of the Shevsky-Bell social area index.[13] It indicated the ratio of craftsmen, foremen, operatives and laborers to total numbers of employed persons. It is included as a measure of the homogeneity of a neighborhood, the underlying assumption being that, in general, people prefer to live in neighborhoods that are homogeneous with respect to broad occupational and social classes. Since high and low values for this variable would reflect such homogeneity, we expect to find property values higher for extreme than for intermediate values.

Taxes and Public Services

Taxes and the level and quality of public services provided by them are also likely to be capitalized in the value of the property. While an adequate introduction of these characteristics would require a special study lying beyond the scope of this research project, the most important differences between census tracts in these regards can easily be incorporated by including a dummy variable (ILL) indicating whether a census tract is in Illinois (one) or in Missouri (zero). This variable will certainly pick up the effect of differences in property taxes between the two states. Since these taxes are higher in Illinois than in Missouri, other things remaining equal, property values should be higher west of the Mississippi. However, this variable may also pick up the effects of other unknown differences between census tracts in the two states that are not accounted for by the other variables utilized in this study. Unfortunately, it also may pick up the effect of SUL and for this reason, as explained in the next section, is given special statistical treatment.

Submarket Variables

Of the various submarkets into which the housing market of the St. Louis area can be divided, the most important for our purposes is the non-white housing market. Since the dividing line between the white and non-white submarkets is not sharp, a dummy variable

cannot be used to make this distinction.[14] Instead, a continuous variable representing *percentage non-white* residents in a census tract (PNW) is utilized.

Previous studies have suggested that this variable has a significant impact on property values, but that the nature of the relationship varies from city to city and sometimes within cities, depending upon demand for and supply of houses for non-whites as compared with that for whites, the duration of time that a particular value of PNW has prevailed, and what is happening in adjacent neighborhoods.[15] Without additional information on each of these factors no a priori judgments about the form of the relationship of PNW with property values can be made.

A question can be raised as to why occupation ratio and percentage non-white are given separate treatments and different interpretations. Should not the former be treated as a submarket variable or the latter as a neighborhood characteristic? The distinction is justified because of the possibility of discrimination against non-whites. It is this possibility which generally takes the form of a prohibition against non-whites entering certain neighborhoods except at exorbitant prices, rather than merely a preference for living near members of one's own class or race, that makes it possible for demand and supply conditions to differ in different parts of the city.

This point can be emphasized by considering two groups, A and B, living side by side within a given urban boundary, both of which prefer to live with their own kind. If population in group A expands, additional housing for its members must be obtained by bidding houses away from members of group B, thereby raising the average price level. Other things remaining constant, if the perimeter of group A can expand in this way at will, there is no

[14] It is not sharp in our data since we are using census tracts as units of observation, the boundaries of which seldom coincide with the boundaries of these two markets. It is also our impression that in the St. Louis area the dividing line between such markets is in fact sometimes fuzzy.

[15] See Luigi Laurenti, *Property Values and Race* (Berkeley: University of California Press, 1960), 47–65; and Chester Rapkin and William G. Grigsby, *The Demand for Housing in Racially Mixed Areas* (Berkeley: University of California Press, 1960), 88–105.

ing family size, but it is not legitimate to do so here for reasons given earlier.

[13] E. Shevsky and W. Bell, *Social Area Analysis* (Stanford: Stanford University Press, 1955).

reason why the price of houses in A and B should differ. It is only when the perimeter of group A cannot expand — or can only do so at discriminatory prices — that the average price in A will increase relative to that in B.

Median Family Income (MFI)

This last variable must be given special treatment, for it does not fit into any one of the groups of variables specified above. As indicated, within one market, owner-occupant characteristics have no place in our model, except as proxies for property characteristics that could not be measured. The fact that income is highly correlated with some of the variables that have been included, leads us to believe it is also likely to be so correlated with many of the housing and neighborhood characteristics we have been unable to measure. However, this fact also leads us to prefer a "residulized" version of this variable (RMFI) that has been made orthogonal to the highly correlated variables included in our analysis. The procedure for obtaining this new variable is described below. It should be interpreted as a proxy for the housing and neighborhood characteristics that have not been included in this study.

III Adjustments for Multicollinearity

Because our principal goal is the estimation of specific regression coefficients (and their associated standard errors), it is necessary to assess and, if necessary, to make adjustments for, the effects of intercorrelation among the independent variables. In general, if the model has been properly specified, least squares estimates will be unbiased regardless of the extent of multicollinearity. If, however, a variable that a priori judgment suggests should be included in the analysis is omitted, the regression coefficients for the remaining variables with which it is correlated will be biased. This fact is well known. It is not so commonly recognized that biased estimates will also be obtained if a variable that a priori judgment suggested should be *excluded* is for some reason incorrectly *included* in the regression analysis. The extent of such biases due to incorrect specification of the model depends upon the degree of correla-

tion between the variable incorrectly excluded or included and the variables whose coefficients are critical to the analysis.

There are no cut and dried methods for detecting and treating the problem of multicollinearity.[16] Our procedures involved stepwise regressions to observe the effect on regression coefficients when new variables are included and, following a suggestion of Ferrar and Glauber, correlations of each independent variable against all others to observe the magnitudes of their multiple and partial correlation coefficients. From these observations, plus a consideration of the effects that changes in model specification could have on coefficients of principal interest, a number of areas were selected for special treatment. Such treatment must involve the injection of additional information, whether it be of an empirical or an a priori nature. In the absence of an additional sample of data in which such multicollinearity is negligible, the approach adopted here is to present alternative estimates of the coefficients of primary interest, each of which is based on a different assumption concerning the extent to which several possible explanatory variables should be included in the regression analysis. In doing so, we exploit two properties of least squares estimation methods: first, that calculated residuals from a least squares regression equation are orthogonal to the explanatory variables of that equation, and second, that the inclusion of a regressor that is orthogonal to previously included regressors will not bias their estimated coefficients.[17]

With respect to air pollution, a first estimate of its effect on property values is provided by equation (1). This estimate is a conventional one in the sense that no adjustments have been made for multicollinearity.

The second estimate results from a special treatment of the variable *ILL*. This dummy variable really reflects a number of differences between census tracts in Illinois and Missouri,

[16] See J. Johnston, *Econometric Methods* (New York: McGraw-Hill, 1963), 207; A. S. Goldberger, *Econometric Theory* (New York: John Wiley, 1964), 192–193; and D. E. Farrar and R. R. Glauber, "Multicollinearity in Regression Analysis: The Problem Revisited," this REVIEW, XLIX (Feb. 1967), 92.
[17] These and other properties of the methods used in this section are derived by — or easily derivable from — A. S. Goldberger, *op. cit.*, 194–197.

all of which should be included in our model, but at least one of which is already explicitly included. Since prevailing winds are from the west and northwest and most of the industry responsible for pollution is located along the Mississippi River, it is reasonable to assume that one such variable already included in the regression model is *SUL*. The partial correlation coefficient between *ILL* and *SUL* tends to support this contention. Its value is 0.35, the second largest observed between *ILL* and the explanatory variables.[18] To the extent that *ILL* does measure differences in air pollution, it is improper to include it since *SUL* is already present among the regressors. To leave it out would lead to an improper *exclusion* of other factors such as different tax rates that could explain differences in property values between the two states, as well as to biased estimates for the coefficients of other regressors.

A reasonable resolution of this problem is to replace *ILL* with another variable, *RILL*, that is orthogonal to *SUL*, but not to the other regressors. This new variable is obtained by subtracting from the actual values of *ILL* the computed values obtained from an auxiliary regression of *ILL* against *SUL*. *RILL*, in other words, is actual *ILL* "corrected for" *SUL*. The observations on *RILL* are, of course, simply the residuals from this auxiliary regression, and the adjustment may therefore be referred to as "residualization." The effect of this adjustment is to attribute to *SUL* whatever covariation exists between it and *ILL*. The coefficient of *SUL* is the same as it would have been had *ILL* not been included. The coefficients of all other variables, including that for *RILL*, are unaffected by this procedure. Equation (2) presents this estimate of the effect of *SUL* on *MPV*.

A third estimate of the effect of variations in the level of *SUL* is obtained by regressing "residualized" median property value (*RMPV*) against *SUL*. Observations on the variable *RMPV* are the residuals from an auxiliary regression of *MPV* on all the explanatory vari-

[18] The largest is that between *ILL* and *HWA*. Given the definition of *HWA* (see the appendix) there is no a priori reason for believing these variables are misspecified. For this reason as well as because *HWA* is not of major concern to us, no adjustment is made for this particular manifestation of multicollinearity.

ables other than *SUL*. The effect of this procedure is to attribute to the other regressors all the covariation between them and *SUL*. Accordingly, this estimate is the most conservative point estimate of the coefficient of the air pollution variable obtainable by these methods.

A fourth and final estimate has been obtained by first regressing *MPV* against all the independent variables for that subset of tracts for which *SUL* is constant at the lowest measured level. The coefficients so obtained were applied to the remaining tracts to obtain an estimate of what *MPV* *would* be in each of these tracts in the absence of air pollution. The difference between actual *MPV* and this conditional "prediction" of *MPV* was then explained by *SUL* in a regression of these differences on *SUL*.[19]

These are the most interesting of the alternative estimates of the effect of air pollution that were obtained.[20] Among them, we prefer

[19] This method is analogous to that employed in the construction of a Laspeyre's price index, the numerator of which indicates the present cost of the base period market basket of goods. Our analogs of the base period quantity weights are the regression coefficients for the base air pollution zone. Just as current quantities purchased are irrelevant to the interpretation of such a price index, so are the regression coefficients that actually apply in the moderate-to-high air pollution zones. Just as a Laspeyre's index would exactly agree with a Paasche price index if current and base period quantities were exactly the same, so would the results yielded by the method presently under discussion agree exactly with those obtained by taking the high pollution zone as the base if regression coefficients for all air pollution zones were exactly the same. Furthermore, this latter result would be identical to that obtained by the third method described above. Compare with Z. Griliches, "Hedonic price indexes for automobiles: An econometric analysis of quality change," U. S. Congress, Joint Economic Committee, *Government Price Statistics,* Hearings, January 24, 1961 (Washington: U. S. Government Printing Office, 1961).

A variation of this method would involve establishing a regression equation for *MPV* (against all variables other than *SUL*) for each different air pollution zone, weighting the coefficients together, and utilizing the weighted coefficients to obtain *RMPV* to be regressed against *SUL*. If weights used for this purpose are $\sum_r x_i^2 / \sum_1^m x_i^2$ where the denominator sum is taken over all observations and the numerator sum is taken over all observations for a given value of *SUL*, then it can be shown that the result is identical to that obtained from the conventional regression used in obtaining *RMPV*, as in equation (3).

[20] Still another estimate can be obtained by taking a simple regression between *MPV* and *SUL*. It can be shown that this represents an application extreme to that used for the second estimation above. It is equivalent to "residualizing" each independent variable against *SUL*, implying

the second one, namely −$245 per unit of *SUL* per household. This preference is based on the fact that the form of the regression equation in which this estimate appears accords most closely with the a priori model we have in mind. The fact that the first and fourth estimates are not too different from this result leads us to have more confidence in it. The third estimate, which has been deliberately made conservative, can be used as something of a lower bound for a range of reasonable point estimates.

A second area in which model specification is difficult because of multicollinearity pertains to the use of median family income in the regression equations. As in the case of *ILL*, it is useful to introduce this variable as a proxy for those neighborhood and property characteristics that could not be measured. But *MFI* is highly correlated with a number of variables explicitly included, with the consequence that estimates of their coefficients are biased by its inclusion. Two different treatments of this variable are presented, one in which income is included in conventional form, and a second in which it is "residualized" against *MNR*, *HPM*, and *OCR*, the variables whose coefficients are most likely to portray such a bias. In this latter form, it serves as a proxy only for those characteristics not explicitly included in the equation. The coefficient of air pollution is not affected by the inclusion of *RMFI* in place of *MFI*.[21]

The problem of multicollinearity also appeared when quadratic functions were fitted to allow for the possibility of curvilinear or parabolic relationships between *MPV* and a number of the independent variables. Simple correlations between a variable and its square were generally quite high, at times approaching unity. In order to fit such a function and at the same time avoid the possible misleading implications of large standard errors for the "true" significance of the variable, the *form* of

the parabola was first obtained in the usual way with the variable and its square as separate independent variables. The variable was then transformed to conform to this shape and employed as a single independent variable.[22] This transformation is of the form $(x - a)^2$, where a is the minimum point of the parabola obtained earlier. The statistical significance (or lack thereof) of the variable in question was judged by the standard error of the regression coefficient of this transformed variable.

IV Conclusions

Table 1 presents the most interesting equations derived in this study. Equation (2), which incorporated *ILL* and *MFI* in residualized form, is best in our judgment in that it most closely accords with our a priori beliefs. The other equations are presented for comparative purposes, the first being a conventional form of the second, the third providing the most conservative estimate of the effects of air pollution, the fourth representing a different method of adjusting for multicollinearity from that used in equation (2), and the last being based on all census tracts for which data were available.

The air pollution variable, *SUL*, turns out to be a relatively significant variable in explaining residential property values. Using equation (2) and judging in terms of the beta coefficients, it is almost as important as *HWA* and more important than *RILL*, *TIZ*, and

---

[21] It could be argued that *MFI* should be "residualized" against all property and neighborhood characteristics, including *SUL*, whether the covariance between them is high or not, since the presence of favorable characteristics "cause" families with higher incomes to move in, rather than the other way around. Since this treatment is virtually the same as leaving income out altogether, with the consequence that it could not serve as a proxy for anything, we do not favor this approach. It may, however, be of interest to note that the effect of omitting *MFI* on the regression coefficient of *SUL* is to lower it to −$259, with a standard error of $109.

[22] This transformation is accomplished by completing the square: Adding $\frac{b^2}{4c} - \frac{b^2}{4c} (= 0)$ to the right side of $Y = a + bX + cX^2$ and rearranging terms yields $Y = a - \frac{b^2}{4c} + c(X + \frac{b}{2c})^2$. It is clear that the coefficient of this transformed variable is simply the coefficient of X^2 in the original quadratic equation, and that the function attains a maximum or minimum value when $X = -\frac{b}{2c}$.

---

that their presence in the equation will bias the coefficient of *SUL* unless such an adjustment is made. The value obtained for this coefficient of *SUL* is −$1,716. This estimate can be interpreted as the impact on median property values of a unit increase in *SUL* on the assumption that all observed covariation between *SUL* and the other explanatory variables reflects the effects of air pollution. Since there are no a priori grounds for believing that this assumption is correct, this estimate is not defensible.

254   THE REVIEW OF ECONOMICS AND STATISTICS

TABLE 1. — ALTERNATIVE ESTIMATION EQUATIONS FOR MEDIAN PROPERTY VALUES OF
1960 CENSUS TRACTS FOR THE ST. LOUIS METROPOLITAN AREA *

Equation Number	(1)	(2)	(3)	(4)	(5)
Sample Size	167	167	167	93	304
Dependent Variable	MPV	MPV	RMPV	RSMPV	MPV
Constant	−1469.	−2800.	242.7	734.6	1384
SUL	−186.5 (91.9)	−245.0 (88.1)	−82.97 (59.65)	−248.1 (93.3)	−280.4 (92.9)
MNR	284.1 (46.1)	488.5 (41.1)			349.7 (33.9)
PRB	50.07 (7.02)	48.36 (7.20)			43.85 (7.26)
$(HPM - 2.42)^2$	64.97 (21.57)	116.6 (20.4)			38.39 (6.71)
$(TIZ - 3.82)^2$	337.1 (136.1)	320.2 (138.7)			112.4 (84.4)
HWA	920.0 (273)	922.5 (278.9)			73.98 (274.6)
SCH1	−1468. (808)	398.2 (302.2)			−1151. (531)
SCH2	−1923. (774)				−1254 (504)
$(OCR - 0.64)^2$	9847. (2889)	16940. (2840.)			32660. (2520)
PPU	−3385. (542)	−3210. (548.7)			−2013 (430)
$(PNW + 14)^2$	.1276 (.0655)	.1961 (.0623)			.0271 (.0598)
I11	−736.3 (361.4)				
RILL		−819.8 (369.1)			−1786. (368)
MFI	.9330 (.104)				
RMFI		.9374 (.1057)			.8512 (.121)
R^2	.939	.937	.012	.072	.870

* The variable names and their sources are given in the appendix.
The standard error of each partial regression coefficient is given in parentheses after the coefficient.
$RILL = ILL - \overline{ILL}$ where $\overline{ILL} = -0.1507 + 0.1396\ SUL$.
$RMFI = MFI - \overline{MFI}$ where $\overline{MFI} = -4396. + 226.7\ MNR + .3046\ (HPM - 2.42)^2 + 6.749\ (OCR - 0.64)^2$.
$RSMPV = MPV - SMPV$ where $SMPV = 9428. + 398.8\ MNR + 64.60\ PRB - 432.8\ HPM + 103.0\ (HPM)^2 - 4163.3\ TIZ + 484.8\ (TIZ)^2 + 67.45\ PNW - 0.5957\ (PNW)^2 - 14598.\ OCR + 13534.\ (OCR)^2 + 890.1\ HWA - 3308.\ PPU - 75.32\ ILL + .7611\ MFI, R^2 = .930$, using tracts with the lowest values for SUL.
$RMPV = MPV - \overline{MPV}$ where $\overline{MPV} = 444.3 + 286.4\ MNR + 49.29\ PRB + 66.42\ (HPM - 2.42)^2 + 328.0\ (TIZ - 3.82)^2 + 0.0908\ (PNW + 14)^2 + 1004.\ (SCH - .69)^2 + 11130.\ (OCR - 0.64)^2 + 854.5\ HWA - 1010.\ ILL - 3234.\ PPU + 0.9286\ MFI, R^2 = .937$.
R^2 is the coefficient of multiple determination for equations (1), (2) and (5), and the coefficient of partial determination linking SUL to (residualized) property values for equations (3) and (4).
The constants for variables of the form $(x - a)^2$ were obtained from the coefficients of three variables in standard quadratic form using the restricted sample.

SCH. Judging in terms of the coefficients of partial correlation, it explains 1.2 per cent of the variance in MPV. A linear fit appears to be best, and a value for the partial regression coefficient of −$245 per sulfation zone, which is significantly different from zero at the 0.3 per cent level, is reasonably well supported by the alternative estimates for this coefficient presented in table 1.

This information can be interpreted as meaning that if the sulfation levels to which any single-family dwelling unit is exposed were to drop by 0.25 mg./100cm²/day, the value of that property could be expected to rise by at least $83 and more likely closer to $245.[23] Using the latter figure and assuming the sulfation levels are reduced by 0.25 mg. but in no case below 0.49 mg. (taken as the background

[23] A 0.25 mg. change in sulfation can be compared with a mean of 0.85, a range of approximately 0.35 to 2.75 with a standard deviation of about 0.45 (all in mg. of SO₃/100 cm² per day) for observations in our sample. A reduction of this magnitude is probably quite feasible at the upper end of the scale but currently unfeasible at the lower end.

level) the total increase in property values for the St. Louis standard metropolitan statistical area could be as much as $82,790,000.[24] Invested at ten per cent, this sum amounts to a gain of over $8 million annually. If our model of the housing market is reasonably correct, householders should be willing to pay at least this amount for the specified reduction in pollution levels.

Currently available data do not permit a careful comparison between these benefits and the costs of bringing about such a reduction. A crude assessment suggests that a shift to low sulfur fuels would cut sulfation levels roughly in half and would cost $10 to $15 million per year.[25] This is a larger cut than envisioned in the above estimates, but extrapolating to this

[24] Assuming land use, lot size and other prices do not change. This is probably a reasonable assumption for the specified reduction in pollution levels.
[25] Conversation with Dr. Bernard Steigerwald, Robert A. Taft Sanitary Engineering Center, Cincinnati. Other methods such as stack cleaning processes might prove to be more economical.

PROPERTY VALUES — AIR POLLUTION 255

level would bring the annual benefit figure up to perhaps $15 million. However, three other considerations must be borne in mind. First, property values other than those for single family dwelling units would also rise, adding substantially to the above benefit estimate. Second, other benefits besides the increase in property values would also be derived from such a reduction.[26] Third, to bring about these property value and other benefits, it is probably necessary to reduce the levels of other pollutants (especially particulates) that are correlated with SO_3 levels, and this would substantially raise the cost estimates. Considerable work remains before an adequate comparison between the benefits and costs can be accomplished.

Characteristics specific to the property (MNR, PRB, and HPM) all turned out to be important explanatory variables. The sign and magnitudes of their coefficients are as expected.[27]

Of the four location characteristics tried, only TIZ and HWA are significant. This is a reasonable finding indicating that access to major thoroughfares is a more important locational characteristic than is contiguity to any one shopping or industrial concentration other than downtown St. Louis, the latter still appearing to dominate as an intraurban travel focal point.[28] The coefficients attached to TIZ, however, are not quite as expected. They indicate that MPV falls as travel time to the central business district increases up to about 28 minutes (a value of TIZ of 3.8 and — contrary to original expectations — increases thereafter. This finding can be explained in two ways. First TIZ may be picking up desirable property characteristics associated with suburbia, such as the presence of a view, that have not otherwise been accounted for (the dividing line between urban and suburban resi-

dential areas for many parts of St. Louis occurs at between 25 and 30 minutes bus time from downtown). Second, shopping areas and light industry tend to form a diffuse band around the city. TIZ may also be picking up the effect of being close to this band, an effect that is not picked up by SAA and IAA which identified only a small number of specific transportation focal points.

The neighborhood characteristics yielded mixed results. As predicted, OCR proved to be best estimated as a U-shaped function and PPU as a negative function of MPV. CRR, however, proved to be insignificant no matter what standard form was tried. The best explanation is probably that, as indicated at the outset, it was incorrectly measured in terms of its actual value instead of in terms of attitudes about it.

No such simple rationalization can explain the results obtained for school quality, however. In equation (2), school quality is represented as a dummy variable assigning a value of one for tracts lying in school districts believed to be of above average quality and a value of zero for all others. While the coefficient is of the right sign it is small and not significantly different from zero at conventional levels. Because we have no explanation for this result and continue to believe that in fact this variable is a significant one, it has been retained.[29]

Additional light is thrown on this variable by presenting the same information in a somewhat different way, as is done in equations (1) and (5). There, $SCH1$ is a dummy variable for which a value of one represents the presence of above-average school quality and $SCH2$ is a second dummy variable indicating the presence of average school quality (if both variables have zero values, below average school quality is indicated). While both variables are reasonably significant, this formulation leads to the curious result that property values are higher where school quality is above average than where it is average, but that they are higher yet where school quality is below aver-

---

[26] On this question, as well as on the question of what is being discounted in property values, see R. Ridker, *Economic Costs of Air Pollution Damage, Studies in Measurement* (New York: Frederick A. Praeger, 1967.

[27] Given the form in which HPM has entered into the equations and the fact that it is measured in thousands, a positive coefficient implies that HPM is negatively related to MPV up to 2,420 houses per square mile.

[28] Of course, it is also possible that the wrong secondary focal points were included in the dummy variables, or that they were included in the wrong way.

[29] It was inadvertently dropped from the equation used to obtain $RSMPV$. However, especially in the particular sample used in that calculation, its inclusion could not have made any difference.

age. In the restricted sample, only seven tracts are in poor school districts, so that only a few errors in measurement were necessary to lead to this result. However, it is interesting to speculate on the possibility that this variable reflects aspects of discrimination only partially accounted for by the variable *PNW*. This would be the case if there are a large number of persons (relative to the supply of houses in poor school districts) who cannot find housing outside the poor school districts. Support is lent to this hypothesis by observing that the coefficient attached to *PNW* falls from 0.196 in equation (2) to 0.128 in equation (1), while the only difference between these equations so far as this variable is concerned is the different way that *SCH* has been included.

The remaining variables yielded the expected results and are all significant. Of them, the most interesting is *PNW* which, given its coefficients, is positively related to *MPV* over its relevant range.[80] Using the coefficients of equation (2), *MPV* rises by about $780 as *PNW* increases from zero to 50 per cent and by another $1,775 as *PNW* increases to 100 per cent. Since both income and property characteristics have been held constant, this result clearly sug-

gests the presence of discrimination against non-whites in the St. Louis housing market. The fact that the coefficients for equation (5) are much smaller suggests that the discrimination against non-whites occurs mainly in predominantly residential tracts, that if they wish to live in predominantly commercial or industrial areas they can do so at less discriminatory prices.[81] The difference in the coefficients between equations (1) and (2) may be explained by the difference in the treatment of school quality, as explained above.

On the whole, therefore, the hypotheses underlying this study test out surprisingly well. The most important results are statistically significant and all are fairly reasonable within the context of the St. Louis metropolitan area. Especially important for this study is the fact that an estimate for the effect of air pollution on residential property values has been obtained that can be used with some confidence. However, these results cannot be generalized to other cities or times. Not only may the estimated values of the coefficients change, but different variables and functional forms for them may be necessary to provide similar evidence in other metropolitan areas.

---

[80] Since the minimum point of the parabola occurs at −14 per cent, only its positive tail starting at zero has relevance.

[81] Too few non-whites live in rural tracts to indicate anything about these areas.

APPENDIX

Description and Sources of Data

The following list describes the variables used in this study and indicates sources or methods of measurement. All data are by census tracts of the St. Louis standard metropolitan statistical area, and unless otherwise specified are for the year 1960.

Dependent Variable

MPV — Median value of owner-occupied single family housing units, estimated by owner as of April, 1960. From U. S. Bureau of the Census, *U. S. Censuses of Population and Housing: 1960, St. Louis, Missouri-Illinois*, Final Report PHC (1)-131 (Washington, D.C.: U. S. Government Printing Office, 1962), Table H-2. (Henceforth this publication is referred to by its final report number.)

Independent Variables Used in Final Equations

SUL — An index of annual geometric mean sulfation levels for the period February 20, 1963 to February

10, 1964. An index number running from one through eight was assigned to each census tract, a value of one representing levels equal to or less than 0.49 mg. of $SO_x/100cm^2/day$, a value of two for sulfation levels of 0.50 to 0.74 on the same scale, and so on up to a value of eight for those tracts having pollution levels equal to or greater than 2.0 mg. $SO_x/100\ cm^2/day$.

The figures were interpolated from an isopleth map developed from 41 stations by the Interstate Air Pollution Study. Measurements are made by measuring the amount of SO_x formed on the surface of a cylinder coated with lead dioxide and exposed for one month. See Jack R. Farmer, *Interstate Air Pollution Study, Air Quality Measurements* (Interstate Air Pollution Study, St. Louis-East St. Louis Metropolitan Area, February 1965), 6 and figure 75, p. 144.

MNR — Median number of rooms per housing unit, from PHC (1)-131, Table H-1.

PRB — Percentage recently built. Housing units built

PROPERTY VALUES — AIR POLLUTION   257

1950 to March 1960 as percentage of all housing units, from PHC (1)-131, Table H-1.

HPM — Total houses per square mile of tracts (in thousands). Total housing units from PHC (1)-131, Table H-1; area of tracts in square miles calculated from maps obtained from School of Architecture, Washington University, St. Louis.

TIZ — Time zone. The metropolitan area was divided into zones representing average time during rush hour (7:30 A.M., 1960) required for an express bus to reach the central business district, according to records provided by the St. Louis Metropolitan Transit Authority. Each census tract was assigned a number depending upon the zone within which it fell.

Zone	Minutes to CBD
1	0–10
2	11–20
3	21–30
4	31–40
5	more than 40

PNW — Percentage non-white housing units. Non-white owner and renter occupied units as a percentage of all occupied units.

SCH — School quality. The presence of *SCH*1 and *SCH*2 in an equation indicate the use of a three-fold ranking of a census tract according to the value its school district has in terms of selling a house. *SCH*1 is a one/zero dummy variable for above-average quality, and *SCH*2 is a similar variable for average quality. If only *SCH*1 appears in an equation, a two-fold classification of school quality has been used (above average, one, otherwise, zero). The judgments on school quality were based on interviews with educators who were asked how they believed that people in general evaluated the schools in 1960 and with real estate salesmen who were asked how advantageous different school districts were in selling a house in 1960. Close agreement was found among those interviewed.

OCR — Occupation ratio. Ratio of number of craftsmen, foremen, operatives and laborers to total number of employed persons, from David J. Pittman and Sarah L. Boggs, "An Analysis of Population, Housing, Crime and Delinquency Characteristics in the St. Louis Study Area" (mimeo., 1963).

HWA — Highway accessibility. One if census tract touched a highway or major thoroughfare, zero

otherwise. The thoroughfares included were the Daniel Boone Expressway, Chippewa-Route 66, Gravois, Lindbergh, Kingshighway, Broadway-Lemay Ferry-Bellfontain Rd., Big Bend, River Des Peres-McCausland-Skinker-Hodiamont, Mark Twain Expressway, and Riverview-Route 67 North.

ILL — Illinois/Missouri dummy variable: one/zero for in Illinois/Missouri.

PPU — Persons per unit. Population divided by all occupied units, from PHC (1)-131, Tables P-1 and H-2.

MFI — Median family income, 1959, from PHC (1)-131, Table P-1.

Independent Variables Used in Preliminary Equations Only

HIV — Index of annual geometric mean concentrations of suspended particulates gathered by high-volume air samplers for the period July 1, 1963 to July 1, 1964. The index numbers run from zero to ten, each higher number representing an increase of 10mg/m³ with an index of zero for 60mg/m³ or less, and ten for greater than 150 mg/m³. The figures for census tracts were interpolated from an isopleth map developed from 17 stations by the Interstate Air Pollution Study. See Jack R. Farmer, *op. cit.*, figure 11.

PSS — Percentage substandard. Percentage of all units dilapidated or lacking other plumbing facilities, from PHC (1)-131, Table H-1.

CRM — Crime rate. The number of criminal offenses (criminal homicide, rape, robbery, aggravated assault, burglary, larceny, and auto theft) per 10,000, rounded to hundreds. Information was gathered from individual policy districts and applied to census tracts.

SAA — Shopping area accessability. One/zero for include/exclude a major regional shopping district, based on U. S. Department of Commerce reports and personal knowledge of the area. Eleven regional centers were chosen for this designation.

IAA — Industrial area accessability. One/zero for include/exclude an industrial area, based on areas shown on U. S. Geological Survey Maps.

Social Area Analysis Indexes — Because of their availability the social rank, urbanization, and segregation indexes contained in the Pittman and Boggs study, *op. cit.*, were tried in one run. Since they did not work as well as the above variables, some of which are included in these indexes, and since the rationale for them is questionable, they were dropped after a preliminary trial.

[22]

Hedonic Prices and Implicit Markets: Product Differentiation in Pure Competition

Sherwin Rosen

University of Rochester and Harvard University

A class of differentiated products is completely described by a vector of objectively measured characteristics. Observed product prices and the specific amounts of characteristics associated with each good define a set of implicit or "hedonic" prices. A theory of hedonic prices is formulated as a problem in the economics of spatial equilibrium in which the entire set of implicit prices guides both consumer and producer locational decisions in characteristics space. Buyer and seller choices, as well as the meaning and nature of market equilibrium, are analyzed. Empirical implications for hedonic price regressions and index number construction are pointed out.

I. Introduction and Summary

This paper sketches a model of product differentiation based on the hedonic hypothesis that goods are valued for their utility-bearing attributes or characteristics. Hedonic prices are defined as the implicit prices of attributes and are revealed to economic agents from observed prices of differentiated products and the specific amounts of characteristics associated with them. They constitute the empirical magnitudes explained by the model. Econometrically, implicit prices are estimated by the first-step regression analysis (product price regressed on characteristics) in the construction of hedonic price indexes. With few exceptions, structural

The substance of this paper arose from conversations with H. Gregg Lewis several years ago. A multitude of other people have contributed advice and criticism. Among them are William Brock, Stanley Engerman, Robert J. Gordon, Zvi Griliches, Robert E. Lucas, Jr., Michael Mussa, and the referee. Remaining errors are my own responsibility. Financial support from the Center for Naval Analysis and the National Institute of Education is gratefully acknowledged.

34

interpretations of the hedonic method are not available.[1] Therefore, our primary goal is to exhibit a generating mechanism for the observations in the competitive case and to use that structure to clarify the meaning and interpretation of estimated implicit prices. It will be shown that these data generally contain less information than is commonly supposed. However, the model suggests a method that often can identify the underlying structural parameters of interest. Also, as a general methodological point, it is demonstrated that conceptualizing the problem of product differentiation in terms of a few underlying characteristics instead of a large number of closely related generic goods leads to an analysis having much in common with the economics of spatial equilibrium and the theory of equalizing differences.

The model itself amounts to a description of competitive equilibrium in a plane of several dimensions on which both buyers and sellers locate. The class of goods under consideration is described by n objectively measured characteristics. Thus, any location on the plane, is represented by a vector of coordinates $z = (z_1, z_2, \ldots, z_n)$, with z_i measuring the amount of the ith characteristic contained in each good. Products in the class are completely described by numerical values of z and offer buyers distinct packages of characteristics. Furthermore, existence of product differentiation implies that a wide variety of alternative packages are available. Hence, transactions in products are equivalent to tied sales when thought of as bundles of characteristics, suggesting applicability of the principle of equal advantage for analyzing market equilibrium.

In particular, a price $p(z) = p(z_1, z_2, \ldots, z_n)$ is defined at each point on the plane and guides both consumer and producer locational choices regarding packages of characteristics bought and sold. Competition prevails because single agents add zero weight to the market and treat prices $p(z)$ as parametric to their decisions. In fact the function $p(z)$ is identical with the set of hedonic prices—"equalizing differences"—as defined above, and is determined by some market clearing conditions: Amounts of commodities offered by sellers at every point on the plane must equal amounts demanded by consumers choosing to locate there. Both consumers and producers base their locational and quantity decisions on maximizing behavior, and equilibrium prices are determined so that buyers and sellers are perfectly matched. No individual can improve his position, and all optimum choices are feasible. As usual, market clearing prices, $p(z)$, fundamentally are determined by the distributions of consumer tastes and producer costs. We show how it is possible to recover,

---

[1] Excellent summaries of the hedonic technique are available in Griliches (1971, chap. 1) and Gordon (1973). Major exceptions to the statement in the text are those studies dealing with depreciation and obsolescence (see Griliches 1971, chaps. 7 and 8) and some recent models based on markup pricing (e.g., Ohta and Griliches 1972).

or identify, some of the parameters of these underlying distributions by a suitable transformation of the observations.

An early contribution to the problem of quality variation and the theory of consumer behavior has been made by Houthakker (1952). His analysis is designed to take account of the fact that consumers purchase truly negligible fractions of all goods available to them without having to deal with a myriad of corner solutions required by conventional theory. That virtue of Houthakker's treatment is preserved in the present model. More recently Becker (1965), Lancaster (1966), and Muth (1966) have extended Houthakker's methods to more explicit consideration of utility-bearing characteristics. Again, the emphasis is on consumer behavior and properties of market equilibrium have not been worked out, a gap we hope to fill, in part, here. The spirit of these recent contributions is that consumers are also producers. Goods do not possess final consumption attributes but rather are purchased as inputs into self-production functions for ultimate characteristics. Consumers act as their own "middlemen," so to speak. In contrast, the model presented below interposes a *market* between buyers and sellers. Producers themselves tailor their goods to embody final characteristics desired by customers and receive returns for serving economic functions as intermediaries. These returns arise from economies of specialized production achieved by specialization and division of labor through market transactions not available outside organized markets with self-production.

Section II discusses individual choices in the market and the nature of market equilibrium. Some simple examples of analytic solutions for general equilibrium are given in Section III. Section IV presents an empirical method for identifying the underlying structure from the observations, while Section V applies the model to price index number construction in the presence of legislated restrictions. To highlight essential features, the simplest possible specifications are chosen throughout. As a further appeal to intuition, use is made of geometrical constructions wherever possible.

II. Market Equilibrium

Consider markets for a class of commodities that are described by n attributes or characteristics, $z = (z_1, z_2, \ldots, z_n)$. The components of z are objectively measured in the sense that all consumers' perceptions or readings of the amount of characteristics embodied in each good are identical, though of course consumers may differ in their subjective valuations of alternative packages. The terms "product," "model," "brand," and "design" are used interchangeably to designate commodities of given quality or specification. It is assumed that a sufficiently large number of differentiated products are available so that choice among various combinations of z is continuous for all practical purposes. That is, there is a "spectrum of products" among which choices can be made. As will be apparent, this assumption represents an enormous simplification of the problem. It is obviously better approximated in some markets than others, and there is no need to belabor its realism.[2] To avoid complications of capital theory, possibilities for resale of used items in secondhand markets are ignored, either by assuming that secondhand markets do not exist, or alternatively, that goods represent pure consumption.

Each product has a quoted market price and is also associated with a fixed value of the vector z, so that products markets implicitly reveal a function $p(z) = p(z_1, \ldots, z_n)$ relating prices and characteristics. This function is the buyer's (and seller's) equivalent of a hedonic price regression, obtained from shopping around and comparing prices of brands with different characteristics. It gives the minimum price of any package of characteristics. If two brands offer the same bundle, but sell for different prices, consumers only consider the less expensive one, and the identity of sellers is irrelevant to their purchase decisions. Adopt the convention of measuring each z_i so that they all may be treated as "goods" (i.e., so that consumers place positive rather than negative marginal valuations on them) in the neighborhood of their minimum technically feasible amounts. Then firms can alter their products and increase z only by use of additional resources, and $p(z_1, \ldots, z_n)$ must be increasing in all its arguments. Assume $p(z)$ possesses continuous second derivatives. Since a major goal of the analysis is to present a picture of how $p(z)$ is determined, it is inappropriate to place too many restrictions on it at the outset. However, note that there is no reason for it to be linear as is typically the case. The reason is that the differentiated products are sold in separate, though of course highly interrelated, markets. This point is spelled out in some detail below.

A buyer can force $p(z)$ to be linear if certain types of arbitrage activities are allowed. Let z_a, z_b, and z_c be particular values of the vector z. (i) Suppose $z_a = (1/t)z_b$, and $p(z_a) < (1/t)p(z_b)$, where t is a scalar and $t > 1$. Then t units of a model offering z_a yield the same amount of characteristics as a model offering z_b, but at less cost, ruling out transactions in convex portions of $p(z)$. (ii) Suppose $z_a < z_b < z_c$ and $p(z_b) > \delta p(z_a) + (1 - \delta)p(z_c)$, where $0 < \delta < 1$ and z_b is defined by $z_b = \delta z_a + (1 - \delta)z_c$. Then characteristics in amount of z_b could be achieved by purchasing δ units of a model containing z_a and $(1 - \delta)$ units of a model containing z_c at lower cost than by direct purchase of a brand containing z_b, and products in concave portions of $p(z)$ would be uneconomical. Arbitrage is assumed impossible in what follows (at this point

[2] This assumption was first employed by L. M. Court (1941) and allows the use of marginal analysis rather than the programming methods required by Lancaster's (1966) formulation. Following the general rule, it is not without its costs, however (see below).

we depart from Lancaster [1966]) on the assumption of indivisibility. This amounts to an assumption that packages cannot be untied. For example, in terms of one characteristic, two 6-foot cars are not equivalent to one 12 feet in length, since they cannot be driven simultaneously (case [i]); while a 12-foot car for half a year and a 6-foot car for the other half is not the same as 9 feet all year round (case [ii]). Similarly, assume sellers cannot repackage existing products in this manner or do not find it economical to do so, as might not be the case with perfect rental markets and zero transactions and reassembly costs.

A. The Consumption Decision

To begin, suppose consumers purchase only one unit of a brand with a particular value of z. Write the utility function as $U(x, z_1, z_2, \ldots, z_n)$ assumed strictly concave, in addition to the other usual properties, where x is all other goods consumed. It would not be difficult to treat z as intermediate goods and relate them to yet more ultimate commodities through self-production functions, but that complication is ignored. Set the price of x equal to unity and measure income, y, in terms of units of x: $y = x + p(z)$. Maximization of utility subject to the nonlinear budget constraint requires choosing x and $(z_1, \ldots, z_n)$ to satisfy the budget and the first-order conditions $\partial p/\partial z_1 = p_i = U_{z_i}/U_x$, $i = 1, \ldots, n$. Optimality is achieved by purchasing a brand offering the desired combination of characteristics. Second-order conditions are fulfilled on the usual assumptions regarding U, so long as $p(z)$ is not sufficiently concave (for a general statement of these conditions under a nonlinear constraint see Intriligator [1971]).

To stress the essential spatial context of the problem, define a value or bid function $\theta(z_1, \ldots, z_n; u, y)$ according to

$$U(y - \theta, z_1, \ldots, z_n) = u. \tag{1}$$

The expenditure a consumer is willing to pay for alternative values of $(z_1, \ldots, z_n)$ at a given utility index and income is represented by $\theta(z; u, y)$. It defines a family of indifference surfaces relating the z_i with "money" (i.e., with x foregone), and has been widely used in urban economics (e.g., see Alonso 1964). Differentiate (1) to obtain

$$\theta_{z_i} = U_{z_i}/U_x > 0, \; \theta_u = -1/U_x < 0, \text{ and } \theta_y = 1, \tag{2}$$

$$\theta_{z_i z_i} = (U_x^2 U_{z_i z_i} - 2U_x U_{z_i} U_{xz_i} + U_{z_i}^2 U_{xx})/U_x^3 < 0, \tag{3}$$

where the inequality in (3) follows from the assumptions about the bordered Hessian matrix of U. Also, strict concavity of U implies that θ is concave in z. Equations (2) and (3) show that the value function is increasing in z_i at a decreasing rate. Alternatively, θ_{z_i} is the marginal rate of substitution between z_i and money, or the implicit marginal

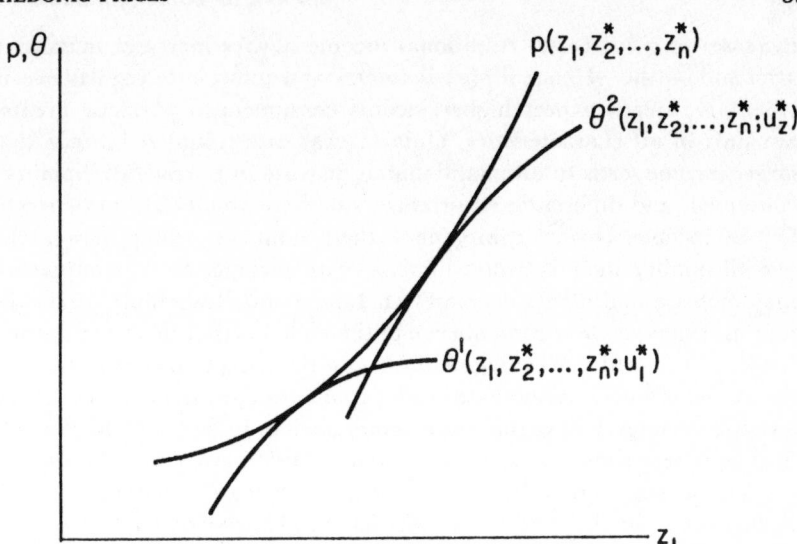

FIG. 1

valuation the consumer places on z_i at a given utility index and income. It indicates his reservation demand price for an additional unit of z_i, which is decreasing in z_i.

The amount the consumer is willing to pay for z at a fixed utility index and income is $\theta(z; u, y)$, while $p(z)$ is the minimum price he must pay in the market. Therefore, utility is maximized when $\theta(z^*; u^*, y) = p(z^*)$ and $\theta_{z_i}(z^*; u^*, y) = p_i(z^*), i = 1, \ldots, n$, where z^* and u^* are optimum quantities. In other words, optimum location on the z-plane occurs where the two surfaces $p(z)$ and $\theta(z; u^*, y)$ are tangent to each other. One dimension of consumer equilibrium is illustrated in figure 1, where the surfaces have been projected onto the $\theta - z_1$ plane cut at $(z_2^*, \ldots, z_n^*)$. A family of indifference curves, of which only one member (at u^*) is shown, is defined by $\theta(z_1, z_2^*, \ldots, z_n^*; u, y)$. Two different buyers are shown in the figure, one with value function θ^1 and the other with θ^2. The latter purchases a brand offering more z_1.[3]

In general, far less can be said than in the standard analysis about comparative statics, because the budget constraint is nonlinear. Differentiate θ_{z_i} with respect to u, $\theta_{z_i u} = (U_x U_{xz_i} - U_{z_i} U_{xx})/U_x^2$, the numerator of which is recognized as determining the sign of the income elasticity of demand for "good" z_i in standard theory when the other components of z are "held constant." If all these derivatives are positive (z_i is "normal" in this restricted sense for all i), the gradient of θ unambiguously

---

[3] Lewis (1969) employs a similar construction in analyzing the problem of hours of work as a tied sale. Jobs offer a fixed wage-hour package, which varies from job to job. The market establishes a function relating wages and hours on which both workers and employers base their decisions.

increases as u increases. Additional income always increases maximum attainable utility. Hence if $p(z)$ is convex and sufficiently regular everywhere, we might expect higher income consumers to purchase greater amounts of all characteristics. Only in that case would it be true that larger income leads to an unambiguous increase in the overall "quality" consumed, and differentiated products' markets would tend to be stratified by income. However, in general there is no compelling reason why overall quality should always increase with income. Some components may increase and others decrease (cf. Lipsey and Rosenbluth 1971). Be that as it may, a clear consequence of the model is that there are natural tendencies toward market segmentation, in the sense that consumers with similar value functions purchase products with similar specifications. This is a well-known result of spatial equilibrium models. In fact, the above specification is very similar in spirit to Tiebout's (1956) analysis of the implicit market for neighborhoods, local public goods being the "characteristics" in this case. He obtained the result that neighborhoods tend to be segmented by distinct income and taste groups (also, see Ellickson 1971). That result holds true for other differentiated products too.

Allowing a parameterization of tastes across consumers, the utility function may be written $U(x_1, z_1, \ldots, z_n; \alpha)$, where α is a parameter that differs from person to person. Equilibrium value functions depend on both y and α. A joint distribution function $F(y, \alpha)$ is given in the population at large, and equilibrium of all consumers is characterized by a family of value functions whose envelope is the market hedonic or implicit price function.

The model is easily expanded to include several quantities, so long as consumers are restricted to purchasing only one model. Following Houthakker (1952), the utility function becomes $U(x_1, z_1, \ldots, z_n, m)$, where m is the number of units consumed of a model with characteristics z. The constraint is $y = x + mp(z)$, and necessary conditions become

$$\frac{\partial U}{\partial m} = -p(z)U_x + U_m = 0, \tag{4}$$

$$\frac{\partial U}{\partial z_i} = -mp_i(z)U_x + U_{z_i} = 0. \tag{5}$$

The value function is still defined as the amount a consumer is willing to pay for z at a fixed utility index but now with the proviso that m is optimally chosen. That is, $\theta(z_1, \ldots, z_n)$ is defined by eliminating m from

$$u = U(y - m\theta, z_1, \ldots, z_n, m)$$
$$U_m/U_x = \theta.$$

Again, θ_{z_i} is proportional to U_{z_i}/U_x. The logic underlying figure 1 remains intact, and it can just as well serve for this case. However, second-order conditions are now more complex. For example, convexity of $p(z)$ is no longer sufficient for a maximum as it was in the case where m was restricted to be unity. Also, it is necessary to employ stronger assumptions than those used above if the value function θ is to be concave.

Note there is no question of monopsony involved here. Consumers act competitively in spite of the fact that marginal cost of quality, $p_i(z)$, is not necessarily constant—it is increasing in figure 1—because as many units as desired of any brand can be purchased without affecting prices. The function $p(z)$ is the same for all buyers and independent of m.

B. The Production Decision

Having set up the formal apparatus above, we give a symmetrical and consequently brief account of producers' locational decisions. What package of characteristics is to be assembled? Let $M(z)$ denote the number of units produced by a firm of designs offering specification z. The discussion is limited to the case of nonjoint production, in which each production establishment within the firm specializes in one design, and there are no cost spillovers from plant to plant. Thus a "firm" is an arbitrary collection of atomistic production establishments, each one acting independently of the others. Analytical difficulties arising from true joint production are noted in passing.

Total costs in an establishment are $C(M, z; \beta)$, derived from minimizing factor costs subject to a joint production function constraint relating M, z, and factors of production. The shift parameter β reflects underlying variables in the cost minimization problem, namely, factor prices and production function parameters. Assume C is convex with $C(0, z) = 0$ and C_M and $C_{z_i} > 0$. There are no production indivisibilities, and marginal costs of producing more units of a model of given design are positive and increasing. Similarly, marginal costs of increasing each component of the design are also positive and nondecreasing. (Ordinarily, there will be some technological constraints that limit the set of feasible locations on the plane.) Each plant maximizes profit $\pi = Mp(z) - C(M, z_1, \ldots, z_n)$ by choosing M and z optimally, where unit revenue on design z is given by the implicit price function for characteristics, $p(z)$.[4]

---

[4] Our inability to treat joint production nontrivially yet simply stems from the spectrum-of-commodities assumption. If a finite number (say v) of packages is available, it would be straightforward formally to specify a standard v-component multiple product cost function for the firm, and proceed on that basis. In the present case, firms engage in joint production only insofar as they own establishments specializing in different packages. However, genuine joint production requires cost dependencies between production units within the firm: the firm must choose a function $M(z)$ describing an entire "product line" offered in the market. The entire function $M(z)$ is an argument in each plant's costs and total costs in turn are the sum (or integral) over all production establishment costs. A complete treatment requires use of functional analysis and is beyond the scope of this paper.

Again, firms are competitors and not monopolists even though marginal costs of attributes $p_i(z)$ are not necessarily constant because all establishments observe the same prices and cannot affect them by their individual production decisions: $p(z)$ is independent of M.

Optimal choice of M and z requires

$$p_i(z) = C_{z_i}(M, z_1, \ldots, z_n)/M, \qquad i = 1, \ldots, n \tag{6}$$

$$p(z) = C_M(M, z_1, \ldots, z_n). \tag{7}$$

At the optimum design, marginal revenue from additional attributes equals their marginal cost of production per unit sold. Furthermore, quantities are produced up to the point where unit revenue $p(z)$ equals marginal production cost, evaluated at the optimum bundle of characteristics. As above, convexity of C does not assure second-order conditions due to nonlinearity of $p(z)$, and some stronger conditions, assumed to be satisfied in what follows, are required (see Intriligator 1971).

Symmetrically with the treatment of demand, define an *offer* function $\phi(z_1, \ldots, z_n; \pi, \beta)$ indicating unit prices (per model) the firm is willing to accept on various designs at constant profit when quantities produced of each model are optimally chosen. A family of production "indifference" surfaces is defined by ϕ. Then $\phi(z_1, \ldots, z_n; \pi, \beta)$ is found by eliminating M from

$$\pi = M\phi - C(M, z_1, \ldots, z_n) \tag{8}$$

and

$$C_M(M, z_1, \ldots, z_n) = \phi, \tag{9}$$

and solving for ϕ in terms of z, π, and β. Differentiate (8) and (9) to obtain $\phi_{z_i} = C_{z_i}/M > 0$ and $\phi_\pi = 1/M > 0$.

The marginal reservation supply price for attribute i at constant profit, assumed increasing in z_i, is ϕ_{z_i}. Again convexity of C does not always guarantee $\phi_{z_i z_i} > 0$. Since ϕ is the offer price the seller is willing to accept on design z at profit level π, while $p(z)$ is the maximum price obtainable for those models in the market, profit is maximized by an equivalent maximization of the offer price subject to the constraint $p = \phi$. Thus maximum profit and optimum design satisfy $p_i(z^*) = \phi_{z_i}(z_1^*, \ldots, z_n^*; \pi^*, \beta)$, for $i = 1, \ldots, n$, and $p(z^*) = \phi(z_1^*, \ldots, z_n^*; \pi^*, \beta)$. Producer equilibrium is characterized by tangency between a profit-characteristics indifference surface and the market characteristics–implicit price surface.

One dimension of the solution is depicted in figure 2, where

$$\phi(z_1, z_2^*, \ldots, z_n^*; \pi, \beta)$$

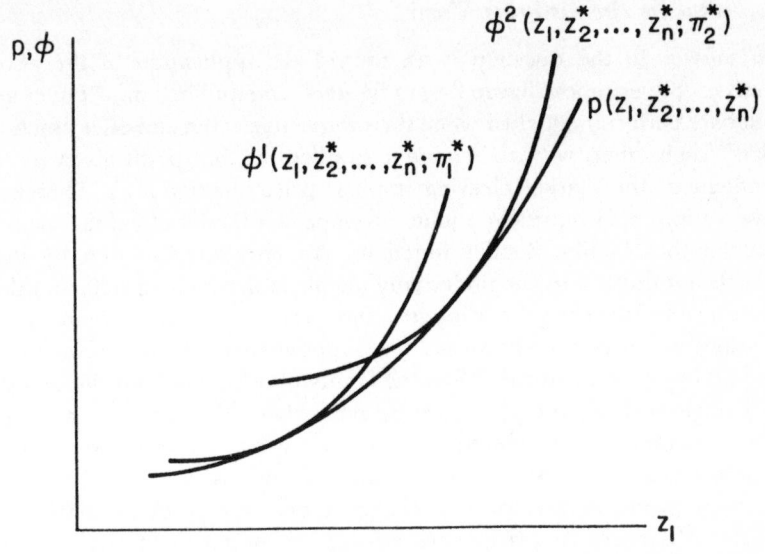

FIG. 2

defines a family of curves on the $z_1 - \phi$ plane cut through the indifference surface at the optimum values of the other attributes. Only one member is shown in the figure. The curve labeled ϕ^1 refers to a production unit possessing production and cost conditions making it well suited to produce lesser amounts of z_1, while the one labeled ϕ^2 refers to a firm with a comparative advantage at producing higher values of z_1. That is, the two plants have distinct values of the parameter β. More generally, there is a distribution of β across all potential sellers. Let $G(\beta)$ represent that distribution. Then producer equilibrium is characterized by a family of offer functions that envelop the market hedonic price functions.

What is the empirical content of β? It is anything that shifts cost conditions among firms. Thus, differences in factor prices are one possibility. For example, many products are produced in several countries and are traded on national markets (for examples, see Griliches [1971], chap. 5). There is no reason to assume equalization of factor prices in these cases. More generally, anything allowing identification of conventional multi-product production functions in cross-section data serves to provoke differences in β. Factor price differences across states or regions within a country often serve this purpose and do so here as well. Second, differences in "technology," as reflected by typically unmeasured, firm-specific factors of production, also act as supply shifters across firms. For example, agricultural production function research often treats education of the farm operator in this manner. Firm-specific R&D expenditure as well as the phenomena of progress-function-learning also serve these purposes.

C.   What Do Hedonic Prices Mean?

An answer to the question is an immediate application of the above analysis. Superimpose figure 2 onto figure 1. In equilibrium, a buyer and seller are perfectly matched when their respective value and offer functions "kiss" each other, with the common gradient at that point given by the gradient of the market clearing implicit price function $p(z)$. Therefore, observations $p(z)$ represent a joint envelope of a family of value functions and another family of offer functions. An envelope function by itself reveals nothing about the underlying members that generate it; and they in turn constitute the generating structure of the observations. Some qualifications are necessary however. (*a*) Suppose there is no variance in β and all firms are identical. Then the family of offer functions degenerates to a single surface, and $p(z)$ must be everywhere identical with a unique offer function. Price differences between various packages are exactly equalizing among sellers because offer functions are constructed at constant profit. A variety of packages appear on products markets to satisfy differences in preferences among consumers, and the situation persists because no firm finds it advantageous to alter the quality content of its products. (*b*) Suppose sellers differ, but buyers are identical. Then the family of value functions collapses to a single function and is identical with the hedonic price function. Observed price differences are exactly equalizing across buyers, and $p(z)$ identifies the structure of demand.

III. Existence of Market Equilibrium

Analysis of consumer and producer decisions has proceeded on the assumption of market equilibrium. This section demonstrates some details of equilibrium price and quantity determination. Market quantity demanded for products with characteristics z is $Q^d(z)$, and $Q^s(z)$ is market quantity supplied with those attributes. It is necessary to find a function $p(z)$ such that $Q^d(z) = Q^s(z)$ for all z, when buyers and sellers act in the manner described above. The fundamental difficulty posed by this problem is that $Q^d(z)$ and $Q^s(z)$ depend on the entire function $p(z)$. For example, suppose quantities demanded and supplied at a particular location do not match at prevailing prices. The effect of a change in price at that point is not confined to models with those particular characteristics but induces substitutions and locational changes everywhere on the plane. A very general treatment of the problem is found in Court (1941), and our discussion is devoted to some examples. These examples have been chosen for their simplicity but illuminate the problem and illustrate most of the basic issues. In contrast to the rest of the paper, discussion is specialized to the case where goods are described by exactly one attribute (i.e., $n = 1$). Therefore z_1 represents an unambiguous measure of "quality." When $n = 1$, the location surface degenerates to a line rather than a plane, and products are unequivocally ranked by their z content.

A. Short-Run Equilibrium

Consider a short-run equilibrium in which firms have geared up for the quality (z_1) of goods they can produce and are only capable of varying quantities. The horizon is sufficiently short so that new entry is precluded, and the distribution of firms by quality is given as an initial condition. The market reveals an implicit price function $p(z_1)$, and each firm determines the quantity it supplies to the market according to condition (7). Market supply in a small interval dz_1 near quality z_1 is found by weighting firm supply by the quality distribution function. Consumers differ in tastes and income, but all determine optimal quality and quantity as in (4) and (5). Market demand near any quality z_1 is found by using the conditions of consumer equilibrium to transform the distribution of tastes and income into a distribution of qualities demanded and weighting individual quantities demanded by the resulting distribution of qualities. Finally, setting demand equal to supply yields a differential equation in p and z_1 that must be satisfied by market equilibrium, subject to some boundary conditions.

To be specific, assume that $C(N, z) = (a/2)M^2z_1^2$ for all firms. Also, suppose firms are uniformly distributed by the characteristic z_1: $g(z_1)dz_1 = kdz_1$ for $z_{1s} \leq z_1 \leq z_{1l}$, where k is a constant and z_{1l} and z_{1s} are exogenously determined upper and lower limits of the product line. Apply equation (7) to obtain firm supply: $M(z_1) = p/az_1^2$, since qualities cannot be varied by assumption. Therefore,

$$Q^s(z_1)dz_1 = g(z_1)M(z_1)dz_1 = [(k/a)p(z_1)/z_1^2]dz_1. \qquad (10)$$

Assume a fixed number of consumers in the population and that only one unit per customer of the optimal model is purchased. Consumers have the same income, and utility is linear in x and z_1, with the marginal rate of substitution, ρ, varying from person to person. Maximize $U(x, z_1) = x + \rho z_1$ subject to $y = x + p(z_1)$. Each consumer purchases a brand for which $dp/dz_1 = p'(z_1) = \rho$. In this case the value functions of figure 1 are straight lines with a different slope, ρ, for each person. The marginal condition characterizes consumer choice so long as $p'' > 0$, which will be shown to be true. Suppose ρ is distributed uniformly, $f(\rho)d\rho = bd\rho$ for $\rho_s \leq \rho \leq \rho_l$, where b is a constant and ρ_l and ρ_s are, respectively, the largest and smallest marginal rates of substitution in the population. Use the marginal condition $p' = \rho$ to transform $f(\rho)d\rho$ into

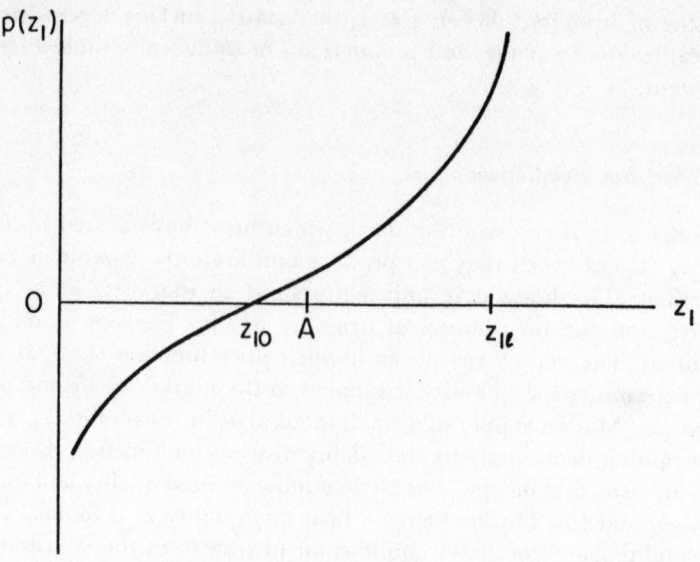

FIG. 3

a distribution of z_1. Then

$$Q^d(z)dz = f(z_1) \left| \frac{dp}{dz_1} \right| dz_1 = bp''(z_1)dz_1. \tag{11}$$

Price must clear the market at every quality. Equating (10) and (11), $p(z_1)$ must satisfy the differential equation

$$(k/ba)p/z_1^2 = d^2p/dz_1^2. \tag{12}$$

Equation (12) is a special case of what is called "Euler's equation" and has a known solution of the form

$$p = c_1 z_1^r + c_2 z_1^s, \tag{13}$$

where c_1 and c_2 are constants determined by the boundary conditions and r and s are defined by $r^2 - r - (a/bk) = 0$: $r = (1 + \sqrt{1 + 4a/bk})/2$ and $s = (1 - \sqrt{1 + 4a/bk})/2$. The parameters r and s are real numbers and $r > 0$ and $s < 0$. Furthermore, $p'(z_1)$ would not be positive throughout its range unless $c_1 > 0$ and $c_2 < 0$, and consumers could not be interior at those points. Equation (13) is graphed in figure 3 on that assumption. Note that p in (13) exhibits an inflection point at $z_{10} = (-c_1/c_2)^{1/(r-s)}$, and it so happens that $p(z_{10}) \equiv 0$. Therefore $p'' > 0$ for $z_1 > z_{10}$.

Boundary conditions.—Competition requires there be no masses of consumers at any quality, for there are few sellers located at any point and they would otherwise add nonzero weight to the market. As seen in Section II, consumers with high values of ρ buy higher-quality models, and it must be true that those for whom $\rho = \rho_l$ purchase the highest quality available. Otherwise prices of quality z_{1l} would fall, a great mass of consumers would switch over to them, driving the price back up and causing those buyers to relocate again. Therefore, one boundary condition is $p'(z_{1l}) = \rho_l$, or

$$\rho_l = rc_1 z_{1l}^{r-1} + sc_2 z_{1l}^{s-1}. \tag{14}$$

The other boundary condition is found by examining the lower end of the line. The following three cases cover all relevant possibilities:

1. $z_{1s} = 0$ and $\rho_s > 0$. Firms choose not to sell at negative prices (see fig. 3) and all plants geared to produce qualities less than z_{10} (to be determined) shut down. On the other hand, all consumers value z_1 at least as much as its minimum supply price (i.e., zero) and it must be true that they all buy some value of z_1. Individuals for whom $\rho = \rho_s$ consume the lowest qualities appearing on the market, for if they chose qualities greater than z_{10}, prices of models in the neighborhood of z_{10} would fall to zero, inducing low ρ customers to relocate there and driving their prices back up. Thus a second boundary condition is $p'(z_{10}) = \rho_s$, or

$$\rho_s = rc_1 z_{10}^{r-1} + sc_2 z_{10}^{s-1}. \tag{15}$$

The parameters z_{10}, c_1, and c_2 are determined by equations (14) and (15) plus the definition of z_{10}. It can be shown that $c_1 > 0$ and $c_2 < 0$, as required by the second-order conditions of consumer equilibrium. Therefore, the equilibrium hedonic price function appears as a portion of the curve in figure 3 in the interval (z_{10}, z_{1l}).

2. If $\rho_s = 0 = z_{1s}$, all producers must be in the market, and it follows that $z_{10} = 0$. This only is possible if $p'(0) = \rho_s = 0$ and c_2 must be zero. In this case price is a log-linear function of quality.

3. $z_{1s} > 0$ and $\rho_s = 0$. Now some consumers do not value z_1 very highly, and there is a definite limit to the smallest amount available. Clearly, $p(z_{1s})$ must exceed zero and some consumers must be driven out of the market, finding it optimal not to consume the product at all. If not, consumers with small values of ρ would mass on z_{1s} (there would be a corner solution there), adding finite weight to the market and causing $p(z_{1s})$ to explode. Using the budget constraint, the market rate of exchange between not buying at all and buying z_{1s} is $[y - p(z_{1s})]/z_{1s}$ and must equal the slope of the value function for buyers at that (extensive) margin. That is, the condition $[y - p(z_{1s})]/z_{1s} = p'(z_{1s})$ replaces equation (15)—after substituting for p and p' from (13)—in the determination of c_1 and c_2. The hedonic price function also can be illustrated in figure 3 as the portion of the curve between the points such as those marked $A(= z_{1s})$

and z_{1f}. Again, c_1 and c_2 have the correct signs and the second-order conditions are fulfilled.

A second type of short-run equilibrium could be considered in which existing firms can alter qualities as well as quantities of their products. When there is a distribution of cost functions, it is necessary to proceed analogously to the treatment of demand in the example above. For example, costs might be described by $(a/2)N^2z_1^\lambda$ with λ varying across firms. Then $(\lambda/2) = z_1 p'/p$ is used to transform the distribution of λ into a distribution of qualities supplied. The resulting distribution weights firm quantities supplied in the determination of market supply at any quality. A little experimentation will show that the differential equation resulting from setting $Q^d(z_1) = Q^s(z_1)$ is nonlinear in most cases, and closed solutions are not always feasible.

B. Long-Run Equilibrium

Firms may vary qualities at will and also construct establishments of optimum size. No entry restrictions imply the absence of profit ($\pi^* = 0$) and long-run offer price for each firm must satisfy $\phi(z; \beta) = C(M, z; \beta)/M$. Plants are constructed to produce models of quality z at minimum cost. Hence scale economies are exhausted under competition and the optimum production unit occurs where $C(M, z, \beta)$ is linear in M, variations of quantity being achieved by changes in the number of establishments. Let $h(z; \beta)$ represent minimum average cost of z for an establishment of optimum size. Then $C(M, z; \beta) = Mh(z; \beta)$ in the long run. Therefore $\phi = h(z; \beta)$ and $p(z) = h(z; \beta)$ is the equilibrium condition for maximum profit and $p(z)$ is completely determined by supply, or by the envelope of the family $h(z; \beta)$ with respect to β. Generalization to n characteristics is obvious in this case.

IV. An Identification Problem

Section III demonstrated that complete solutions for $p(z)$ and the distribution of qualities traded sometimes can be obtained if sufficient a priori structure is imposed on the problem. However, it is not always possible to proceed in that manner. In general, the differential equation defining $p(z)$ is nonlinear and it may not be possible to find closed solutions. Moreover, a great deal of structure must be imposed. For example, the distribution of income follows no simple law throughout its range, making it difficult to specify the problem completely. Finally, partial-differential equations must be solved when there is more than one characteristic. This section sketches an alternative and more efficient procedure, based on the analysis of Section II.

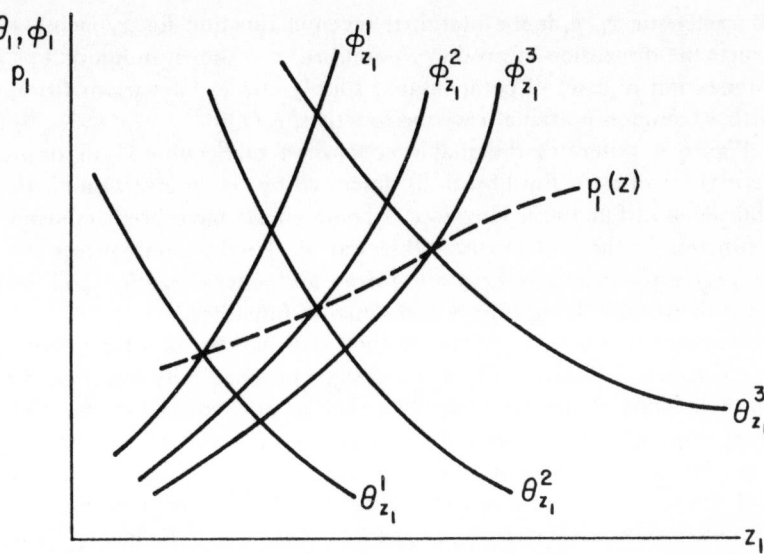

FIG. 4

As shown above, derivatives of a consumer's value function, θ_{z_i}, are proportional to marginal rates of substitution. They are reservation-demand prices for additional amounts of z_i at a constant utility index. Therefore $\{\theta_{z_i}(z)\}$ are the inverses of a set of ordinary compensated demand functions for the z_i's. The marginal cost of z_i to the consumer is $p_i(z)$, and optimal z is determined where marginal costs equal marginal values. One dimension of these marginal concepts is illustrated in figure 4. The curves labeled $\theta_{z_i}^j$ are derivatives of θ^j in figure 1 and reflect compensated demand functions for various buyers. The dashed line labeled $p_1(z)$ is the common marginal cost confronting all buyers. Consumer choice is given by the intersection of demand and marginal cost. It should be emphasized that the functions $\theta_{z_i}(z)$ are compensated demand prices (real income held constant) and can only be derived once equilibrium is determined, as in Section II. For example, a new equilibrium resulting from an exogenous shift in p would not always be given by the intersection of the new marginal costs, $p_1(z)$, and the initial compensated demand price functions. An exception occurs when $\theta_{z_i u} = 0$ and the family of surfaces $\theta(z; u)$, such as depicted in figure 1, are all parallel to each other: $\theta_{z_i u} = 0$ is equivalent to constant marginal utility of money and θ_{z_i} is unique and independent of u only in that case. If $\theta_{z_i u} \neq 0$, the shape and location of the $\theta_{z_i}^j$ functions are determined by the equilibrium conditions of Section II: tangency between $p(z)$ and $\theta^j(z, u^*)$.

A similar procedure applies to firms: θ_{z_i} is the reservation supply price of incremental z_i and reflects a profit-compensated supply function for characteristic z_i; p_i is the marginal revenue function for z_i facing each firm. One dimension of producer equilibrium is shown in figure 4 as the intersection of a set of compensated supply curves for various firms, θ_z^j, with a common marginal revenue function, $p_1(z)$.

Figure 4 reiterates the major conclusion of Section II in terms of derivatives of $p(z)$. Equlibrium is described by the intersection of supply and demand functions. However, income effects have been removed, in distinction to the typical case. Observed marginal hedonic prices merely connect equilibrium reservation prices and characteristics and reveal little about underlying supply and demand functions.

However, figure 4 suggests a method that can be used for estimation. In principle, data are available on designs purchased by buyers and also on their incomes and taste variables such as age, education, etc. Denote these empirical counterparts of α by a vector Y_1. Data are also potentially available on the characteristics' content of models produced by sellers and factor price and specific technological differences among them. Denote the empirical counterparts of β by a vector Y_2. Following figure 4, let $F_i(z, Y_1)$ represent the marginal demand price for z_i and $G_i(z, Y_2)$ represent the marginal supply price. Ignoring random terms, the model to be estimated can be written as

$$p_i(z) = F^i(z_1, \ldots, z_n, Y_1) \quad \text{(demand)}, \tag{16}$$

$$p_i(z) = G^i(z_1, \ldots, z_n, Y_2) \quad \text{(supply)}, \tag{17}$$

for $i = 1, \ldots, n$, where p_i and z_i are all jointly dependent variables and Y_1 and Y_2 are exogenous demand and supply shift variables. The $2n$ equations determine the $2n$ endogenous variables p_i and z_i. Estimation requires a two-step procedure. First, estimate $p(z)$ by the usual hedonic method, without regard to Y_1 and Y_2. That is, regress observed differentiated products' prices, p, on all of their characteristics, z, using the best fitting functional form. This econometrically duplicates the information acquired by agents in the market, on the basis of which they make their decisions. Denote the resulting estimate of the function $p(z)$ by $\hat{p}(z)$. Next, compute a set of implicit *marginal* prices, $\partial p(z)/\partial z_i = \hat{p}_i(z)$ for each buyer and seller, evaluated at the amounts of characteristics (numerical values of z) actually bought or sold, as the case may be. Finally, use estimated marginal prices $\hat{p}_i(z)$ as endogenous variables in the second-stage simultaneous estimation of equations (16) and (17). Estimation of marginal prices plays the same role here as do direct observations on prices in the standard theory and converts the second-stage estimation into a garden variety identification problem. There are four cases to consider:

1. There is no variance in β and cost conditions are identical across firms. The variables Y_2 drop out of equation (17) and $\hat{p}(z)$ identifies the

offer function. Similarly, the sample observations on $\hat{p}_i(z)$ and the z_i identify compensated supply functions. Suppose several cross sections for different years are available and firms' production functions have been subject to technical change. Then within-year hedonic price regressions identify supply conditions for each year. Changes in marginal prices and qualities induced by changing technology and cost conditions between years approximately sweep out the structure of preferences and compensated demand functions (with due qualification for the nonconstancy of the marginal utility of money).

2. If buyers are identical, but sellers differ, Y_1 drops out of (16) and single cross-sectional observations trace out compensated demand functions.

3. If buyers are identical and so are sellers, offer and value functions are tangent at a single point, and only one quality appears on the market. The observations degenerate to a single point; there is no product differentiation and no problem.

4. In general there is both a distribution of buyers and another distribution of sellers. Both Y_1 and Y_2 have nonzero variance, and the usual identifying rank and order conditions apply. A necessary prior condition for estimation is that $\hat{p}(z)$ be nonlinear at stage one. For if $\hat{p}(z)$ happens to be linear, $\hat{p}_i(z)$ are constants, independent of qualities traded, and display zero variance across sample observations. As shown above, linearity of $p(z)$ is unlikely so long as there is increasing marginal cost of attributes for sellers and it is not possible to untie packages. But it is obvious that the model does not apply if very few distinct products are actually traded.

V. Price Indexes, Economic Welfare, and Legislated Restrictions

This section uses the model to analyze the welfare consequences of quality-standards legislation, a problem not easily handled by conventional methods. The discussion clarifies issues in recent controversies regarding treatment of legislated standards in the construction of price indexes. For example, how should mandatory installation of seat belts and air bags affect the automobile price index? For expository convenience, discussion is confined to the case of one attribute. Generalization to several characteristics is immediate.

A minimum quality standard means that $z \geq \bar{z}$, and brands containing less than $\bar{z}$ are prohibited from the market. Assume constant returns to quantities (as in Section III B). Then the law is irrelevant for all consumers previously purchasing packages containing more than the legislated minimum. The situation for a buyer whose choice is affected by the law is shown in figure 5: z^* was the original choice, whereas $\bar{z}$ is chosen after the law has been passed, since z^* is no longer available. The

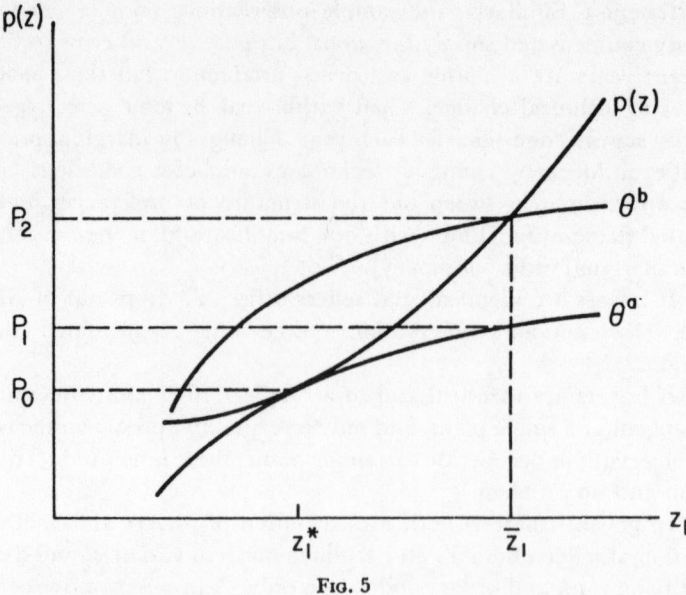

FIG. 5

minimum attainable value function has shifted from θ^a to θ^b, and the consumer is worse off (see eq. [2]).

Choose the distance $\Delta P = P_2 - P_1$ as a monetary measure of the loss in welfare. Since $\partial\theta/\partial y = 1$, ΔP is the bribe necessary for the consumer to purchase $\bar{z}$ when z^* was available. Clearly, this measure is not unique (i.e., if compensation is evaluated at a different amount of z) unless $\theta_{z_1 u} = 0$. The welfare loss can be estimated from the implicit price and bid functions. The distance $P_2 - P_0$ is given by

$$\int_{z_1^*}^{z_1} p_1(z)\,dz,$$

or the area under marginal cost from z^* to $\bar{z}$, and is shown in figure 6 as $z_1^* ab\bar{z}_1$. It represents the social opportunity cost of additional resources necessary to produce $\bar{z}$ instead of z^*. The integral

$$\int_{z^*}^{\bar{z}} \theta_1(z)\,dz,$$

or the area under a compensated demand function (compensated at the original level of real income) between z^* and $\bar{z}$ in figure 6 $(z_1^* ac\bar{z}_1)$ measures the amount the consumer would have paid for the increment $(\bar{z}_1 - z_1^*)$ at the unrestricted level of welfare. It measures $P_1 - P_0$ in figure 5 and represents the benefit of the restriction. The difference

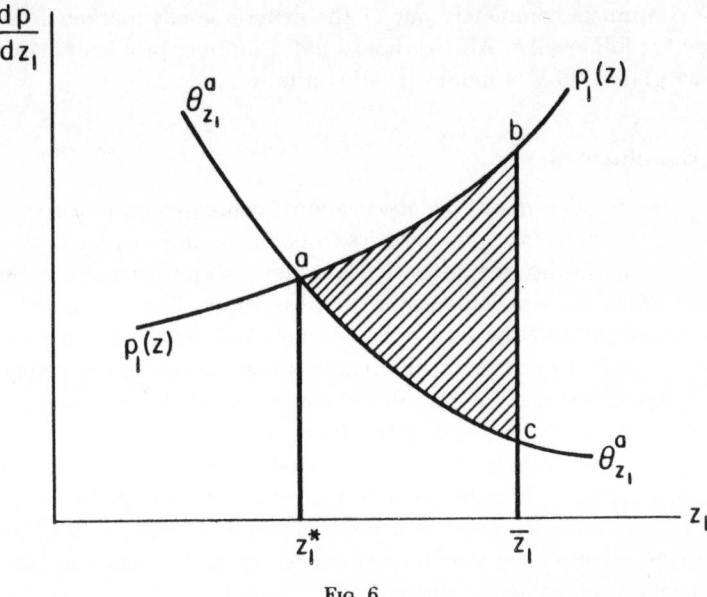

FIG. 6

between costs and benefits is given by $P_2 - P_1$, or the difference between the areas under the marginal cost and compensated demand functions, the shaded area in figure 6. In the general case of several attributes, ΔP must be measured by a line integral. Otherwise, everything else is unchanged.

When the marginal utility of money is constant, ΔP is unique and the price restriction is equivalent to an additive increase in implicit prices in amount ΔP everywhere. In figure 5, $\theta_{zu} = 0$ means that all value functions are parallel, and if the budget constraint was $y = x + p(z) + \Delta P$ instead of $y = x + p(z)$, the consumer would have arrived exactly at θ^b of his own free choice. The real price of the characteristic has risen because choices are restricted, and the price index should rise to reflect that fact. A natural measure of the real price increase imposed by the law is a weighted average of terms such as ΔP (including buyers for whom $\Delta P = 0$), where the weights are expenditure shares among all consumers.[5] This measure overstates the loss insofar as the restriction actually forces

[5] A complete assessment of the law and its effect on the price index requires balancing the costs calculated above against any externality-induced social benefits of the restriction. In our judgment, seat belts and air bags are in a different category than emission-control devices. In regard to the latter, the apparatus above can be used easily to analyze the effect of the European system of taxing engine displacement. An ad valorem tax increases average and marginal costs of packages with larger liter capacity, and the usual income and substitution effects apply: packages with smaller amounts of this and complementary characteristics (such as size of car) are purchased.

some consumers completely out of the generic goods market since they escape the full loss ΔP. Also, standard index number problems arise when the marginal utility of money is not constant.

VI. Conclusions

This paper has drawn out the observational consequences of the construct of implicit markets for characteristics embodied in differentiated products. When goods can be treated as tied packages of characteristics, observed market prices are also comparable on those terms. The economic content of the relationship between observed prices and observed characteristics becomes evident once price differences among goods are recognized as equalizing differences for the alternative packages they embody. Here, as elsewhere, price differences generally are equalizing only on the margin and not on the average. Hence, estimated hedonic price-characteristics functions typically identify neither demand nor supply. In fact, those observations are described by a joint-envelope function and cannot by themselves identify the structure of consumer preferences and producer technologies that generate them.

The formal analysis is complicated by the fact that budget constraints are nonlinear. Consequently, it is not surprising that far weaker theorems than usual apply. However, a feasible econometric procedure for estimating the underlying generating structure has been derived through the use of derivative transformations. When constraints are nonlinear, marginal prices serve the same role as average prices do in the linear case. Finally, the essential spatial context of the problem means that substitution and income effects must be more carefully distinguished than usual. Indeed, here is a major practical instance where compensated demand and supply functions become the relevant fundamental concepts. These compensated functions are estimated by the econometric method and measures of consumer and producer surplus can be derived directly from them. We anticipate that the basic conceptual framework outlined above will have a variety of applications to many practical problems involving equilibrium in cross-section data.

The analysis has been simplified by assuming divisibility in production. Generalization has to incorporate nonconvexities, and discontinuities must result. When nonconvexities are not small relative to the market, it is obvious that only isolated locations on the characteristics surface will be filled. In other words, such a generalization will naturally incorporate the case of monopolistic competition, and observed "distances" (in terms of characteristics) between differentiated products will be endogenously determined. The methods employed above do not carry through because certain nonmarginal decisions must be analyzed, and far more sophisticated techniques are required.

References

Alonzo, William. *Location and Land Use.* Cambridge, Mass.: Harvard Univ. Press, 1964.

Becker, Gary S. "A Theory of the Allocation of Time." *Econ. J.* 75 (September 1965): 493–517.

Court, Louis M. "Entrepreneurial and Consumer Demand Theories for Commodity Spectra." *Econometrica* 9, no. 1 (April 1941): 135–62; no. 2 (July–October 1941): 241–97.

Ellickson, Bryan. "Jurisdictional Fragmentation and Residential Choice." *A.E.R.* 61 (May 1971): 334–39.

Gordon, Robert J. "The Measurement of Durable Goods Prices." Mimeographed. Nat. Bur. Econ. Res., 1973.

Griliches, Zvi, ed. *Price Indexes and Quality Change.* Cambridge, Mass.: Harvard Univ. Press, 1971.

Houthakker, H. S. "Compensated Changes in Quantities and Qualities Consumed." *Rev. Econ. Studies* 19, no. 3 (1952): 155–64.

Intriligator, Michael D. *Mathematical Optimization and Economic Theory.* Englewood Cliffs, N.J.: Prentice-Hall, 1971.

Lancaster, Kelvin J. "A New Approach to Consumer Theory." *J.P.E.* 74 (April 1966): 132–56.

Lewis, H. Gregg. "Interes del empleador en las horas de Trabajo del empleado" [Employer interests in employee hours of work]. *Cuadernos de Economia,* Catholic Univ. Chile, 1969.

Lipsey, Richard G., and Rosenbluth, Gideon. "A Contribution to the New Demand Theory: A Rehabilitation of the Giffen Good." *Canadian J. Econ.* 4 (May 1971): 131–63.

Muth, Richard F. "Household Production and Consumer Demand Functions." *Econometrica* 34 (July 1966): 699–708.

Ohta, Makoto, and Griliches, Zvi. "Makes and Depreciation in the U.S. Passenger Car Market." Mimeographed. Harvard Univ., 1972.

Tiebout, Charles M. "A Pure Theory of Local Expenditure." *J.P.E.* 64 (October 1956): 416–24.

[23]

Welfare Measurement in the Household Production Framework

By Nancy E. Bockstael and Kenneth E. McConnell*

The household production approach to consumer behavior, developed from the work of Gary Becker, William Gorman, and Kelvin Lancaster, has considerable descriptive appeal in modelling the decisions of households. The approach derives from the observation that households frequently purchase market goods that do not yield utility directly, but are combined to produce commodity service flows which the household values. Thus observed behavior is determined by household production technology as well as by tastes. The advantage of this distinction is that we can pose reasonable hypotheses about characteristics of technology, though we rarely possess useful a priori information regarding tastes.

The putative advantages of the household production approach are questioned on empirical and conceptual grounds by Robert Pollak and Michael Wachter (1975). They show that jointness in production or nonconstant returns to scale cause implicit commodity prices to depend on both tastes and technology, raising serious econometric difficulties in the estimation of commodity demand functions. In addition, since commodity prices become functions of the commodity bundle consumed, the analogy to traditional demand theory breaks down.

Joint production occurs when a good enters several production processes simultaneously, or, equivalently, when a good in one production process also enters directly into the individual's utility function. The most common example is time, which provides the

context for all production processes and is often associated with the production of several commodities simultaneously. Since joint production in the household is likely to be pervasive, the critique by Pollak and Wachter cannot be ignored. In response to the comment by William Barnett, Pollak and Wachter (1977) suggest dispensing with the notion of commodity prices and treating the demand for commodities as a function of goods prices. This approach confounds tastes and technology, but it eliminates the troublesome concept of commodity prices as parameters when, in fact, they are likely to be endogenous.

In this paper we show that results from positive analysis, such as the critique by Pollak and Wachter, have implications for the use of the household production framework for welfare analysis. The household production function approach has had considerable appeal for measuring welfare effects of public actions in the environmental and natural resource areas (Gardner Brown, John Charbonneau, and Michael Hay; Elizabeth Wilman). Yet traditional approaches to welfare measurement are frequently inapplicable. We argue that welfare measurement in this framework is complicated by the difficulties of unravelling tastes and technology.

We extend Pollak and Wachter's results by demonstrating that Marshallian demand functions for commodities cannot be uniquely defined. Thus Marshallian functions cannot be used to derive exact compensated functions in the manner of Jerry Hausman, and of George McKenzie and I. F. Pearce, nor can compensating and equivalent variation measures be bounded by Marshallian consumer's surplus estimates following Robert Willig. In fact, duality results that normally allow us to move between Marshallian and Hicksian functions are not

*Assistant and Associate Professors, respectively, Department of Agricultural and Resource Economics, University of Maryland, College Park, MD 20742. This paper is Scientific Article No. A3404, Contribution No. 6476, of the Maryland Agricultural Experiment Station. We wish to thank Darrell Hueth, James Opaluch, V. Kerry Smith, and Elizabeth Wilman for comments on an earlier draft.

applicable for commodities in the household production framework.

Because Marshallian demand functions for household produced commodities are not unique, we are forced to develop welfare measures from observations on purchases of goods; that is, inputs into the household's production process. We show that under appropriate conditions, changes in the area under the demand curve for goods can serve as welfare measures for changes in the quantities of public goods. This finding is related to Hajime Hori's result that when all technology is known, the demand for public goods can be inferred from the purchases of private goods. However we develop a basis for measuring the value of public goods which, unlike Hori's measure, does not require that we know a priori the household technology. All the information that is required will be embodied in the derived demand for goods. Thus we show that the goods market is the only market which provides an indirect means of valuing changes in public goods.

The following three sections provide the three principal results of the paper. In Section I, we show that traditionally conceived Marshallian demands are not uniquely defined in this approach. In Section II, we show, in contrast, that utility-constant marginal value functions that are dependent only on preferences and not technology do exist and have the usual normative interpretation. Regardless of joint production or nonconstant returns to scale, the area behind the marginal value and marginal cost curves measures economic surplus. Changes in this area measure welfare effects associated with changes in the individual's economic environment. In Section III, we show that equivalent measures of welfare change can often be obtained in the market for goods which serve as inputs into the household production process. This result is analogous to the work by Richard Just, Darrell Hueth, and Andrew Schmitz, and by Just and Hueth, who show that in competitive markets, welfare changes can be measured in the markets for inputs or outputs. Additionally, we are able to obtain these measures of welfare without assuming that technology is known. Thus we provide a new conceptual basis for welfare measurement of nonmarket goods.

I. Positive Economics and the Household Production Function

An economic model is a useful positive tool if it implies theorems about behavior which can be tested. We argue that very little structure and a paucity of testable hypotheses emerge from the household production function. This argument is consonant with the results of Pollak and Wachter, who argue that commodity demand as a function of commodity price is not a meaningful concept. We expand their arguments by demonstrating that a unique Marshallian demand curve, as traditionally conceived, cannot be derived for commodities produced in the household production framework. In addition, we argue that commodity demands as a function of goods prices provide few qualitatively predictable results.

To characterize the household production approach, suppose that the consumer enjoys an m-dimensional bundle of commodities z which enters the quasi-concave preference function $u(z)$. Goods, denoted $x = (x_1, \ldots, x_n)$, are purchased at market prices, denoted $r = (r_1, \ldots, r_n)$, and are combined to produce the commodities according to the production process $t(z, x) = 0$. One of the x's will typically be time and can take some function of the wage rate as its price. Joint production occurs when the technology implied by $t(z, x)$ cannot be expressed in terms of separate production functions. We do not rule out joint production nor the possibility of nonconstant returns to scale.

Positive analysis derives from the solution to the representative household's income-constrained problem

$$(1) \qquad \max u(z),$$

subject to $C(z, r) - y = 0,$

where the joint cost function $C(z, r) = \min_x \{r \cdot x \mid t(z, x) = 0\}$ and y is money income. In general, the budget constraint will be nonlinear in the z's, and the marginal costs of commodities will be functions of the commodity bundle chosen.

Because the Marshallian demand curve has held such a central position in comparative statics and normative analysis, there have been strenuous efforts to derive this concept from the first-order conditions of problem (1). In its traditional formulation, the Marshallian demand function relates the quantity of a commodity purchased to the price of the commodity, with money income, prices of other commodities, and all other relevant variables assumed constant. The demand curve is traced out by recording the amount of the commodity the consumer would be willing to purchase at each price.

In the household production formulation, the marginal cost of producing the commodity is analogous to price in the traditional case. The marginal cost of producing a commodity is not in general constant, however, and as such does not encode all the necessary information required to ensure that all first-order conditions, including the budget constraint, will be satisfied. Holding income and other marginal cost functions constant, we attempt to trace out a Marshallian demand curve for a commodity by altering the cost of the final unit consumed of that commodity. This approach, however, cannot uniquely define the quantity consumed unless it incorporates knowledge of the entire cost function (and thus technology) or specific assumptions about how the cost function changes with changes in marginal costs.

By way of demonstration, consider the following expression for the cost function. Suppose that when no commodities are produced, costs are zero, $C(0, r) = 0$. Then there exists a θ in the unit interval such that

$$(2) \quad C(z, r) = \sum_i C_i(z, r) z_i$$
$$- \sum_i \sum_j C_{ij}(z(1 - \theta), r) z_i z_j / 2.$$

From this relationship, the first-order conditions of problem (1) become

$$(3) \quad u_i(z) - \lambda C_i(z, r) = 0 \ \forall i,$$
$$y - \sum_i C_i(z, r) z_i$$
$$+ \sum_i \sum_j C_{ij}(z(1 - \theta), r) z_i z_j / 2 = 0,$$

where λ is the multiplier associated with the budget constraint. Unless the production function is nonjoint and homogeneous of degree one, the C_{ij} in (3) will be nonzero.

Now suppose we attempt to trace out a Marshallian demand curve by asking the question: how much will be purchased at different levels of marginal cost (C_i)? If the hypothetical changes in marginal cost are generated by changes in input (goods) prices or other parameters of the cost function, they will, except in special instances, alter C_{ij} terms as well as other marginal cost functions through changes in the z vector. Changes in these additional terms in the budget constraint will make it impossible to define uniquely, at each marginal cost, a level of demand for which the income constraint holds.

A related and equally debilitating aspect of the household production function is that few qualitative comparative statics results are generated. In general, the decision function for a choice variable is obtained by differentiating the decision maker's indirect objective function with respect to an economic parameter. In such cases, appealing to second-order conditions (specifically, the curvature properties of the utility-constant expenditure function) allows us to sign the change in the choice variable with a change in the parameter.

In the household production approach, however, the expenditure function, defined as

$$m(r, u^0) = \min_z \{C(z, r) | u(z) = u^0\},$$

fails to yield comparative static results. The joint cost function $C(z, r)$ will not in general be linearly homogeneous in z. Thus, there will be no parameter β such that $\partial m / \partial \beta = z_k$ and ordinary envelope theorem derivations will not follow. As a consequence there are no a priori expectations on the sign of any $\partial z_i / \partial r_k$. Pollak and Wachter's suggestion that the demand for commodities be analyzed in terms of goods prices rather than commodity prices will yield constructs which are useful for prediction but which provide no hypotheses regarding the signs of any coefficients in commodity demand functions.

The nonlinearity of the cost function also prevents the Cournot and Engel aggregations from providing useful restrictions on demand systems. Analogous to these "adding-up" theorems, we can derive the following from the constraint $C(z, r) - y = 0$ and from the fact that $C(z, r) = r \cdot x$:

$$\sum_{i=1}^{m} z_i C_i \eta_i / y = 1$$

and

$$\sum_{k=1}^{n} \sum_{i=1}^{m} z_i C_i \varepsilon_{ik} / y = -1,$$

where $\varepsilon_{ik} = \partial \log z_i / \partial \log r_k$ and $\eta_i = \partial \log z_i / \partial \log y$. Unlike the standard neoclassical case with fixed prices, the ratios $z_i C_i / y$ depend on technology, do not in general sum to one, and do not possess the useful interpretation of budget shares. Only the homogeneity restrictions $\sum_{k=1}^{n} \varepsilon_{ik} = -\eta_i$ are retained.

Thus two conclusions arise in the positive economics setting. First, a unique Marshallian demand curve for commodities does not exist. Second, theory fails to provide useful prior restrictions on any function which relates consumption of the z's to parameters in the system.

II. Welfare Analysis in the Commodity Market

Pollak recognized that economists may wish to "use a household production framework to analyze the harm done by air pollution or the benefits of an outdoor recreation or child health project..." (1978, p. 286). This approach, depending as it does on the distinction between purchased goods and consumed commodities, has particular appeal for measuring nonmarket benefits derived from public goods (see, for example, Hori and Wilman). However the conceptual limitations discussed above preclude the straightforward application of well-known welfare measurement techniques in the household production framework.

Work by Willig, Hausman, and others employs duality results to demonstrate that, because of the link through the expenditure and utility functions, the unobserved compensated demand function can always be derived from knowledge of the observable Marshallian function. In the household pro-

duction function approach, the fact that Marshallian demands are not unique prevents us from using duality to derive the compensated demand function. It also suggests that the compensated function may be undefined.

In this section we demonstrate three results. First, we argue that unlike Marshallian demand curves, compensated demand curves which reflect households' marginal valuations of the commodity do exist, independent of the cost function for producing commodities. Second, we derive a measure of surplus associated with a commodity as the area between the marginal cost and marginal value curves in commodity space. Finally, we demonstrate that the well-established conditions for measuring the compensating variation of a change in an exogenous (for example, publicly supplied) factor are applicable in this framework.

When the household is viewed as minimizing the cost of obtaining a given utility level, independent marginal value and marginal cost functions are identifiable. Consider the utility-constrained, cost-minimization problem

$$\min_{z} \{ C(z, r) | u^0 = u(z) \}$$

which produces the first-order conditions

$$C_i(z, r) - \mu u_i(z) = 0 \, \forall i,$$

$$u^0 - u(z) = 0,$$

where μ is the multiplier associated with the constraint on utility. These first-order conditions could be solved for reduced-form demand functions for the z's as functions of goods prices, and technological and preference parameters. They also, however, allow for the determination of independent marginal cost and value functions. To see this, we need only recognize that the above problem is equivalent to one where an imaginary market with fixed parameter prices intervenes between the production and consumption activities of the household. Since the budget constraint is not required to hold along the compensated demand curve, the system of compensated curves is not dependent on the total cost function. Consequently the circumstances which cause the Marshallian curve to be ambiguous in this framework do not directly affect the compensated demand curve.

We are prevented from deriving the Marshallian curve from the compensated curve by the absence of exogenous prices. Both the utility and expenditure functions exist, but the absence of prices prevents the use of Roy's Identity to derive the Marshallian curve from the indirect utility function. Also, it is impossible to move from a compensated demand function to a unique expenditure function because of the nonlinearity of the cost function. Several different cost functions (generated by different technologies), and thus different expenditure functions, can be associated with the same values of marginal costs.

Nonetheless, theoretical welfare measures can be derived in commodity space but in a way which differs from the traditional approach. For simplicity we focus on a measure for z_1, though any z_i could be chosen. Partition the commodities such that $z = (z_1, \bar{z})$ where $\bar{z} = (z_2, \ldots, z_n)$. Derive an expenditure function conditional on the level of z_1 (as though z_1 were temporarily fixed) such that

(4) $E(z_1, r, u^0)$

$$= \min_{\bar{z}} \{ C(z_1, \bar{z}, r) | u^0 = u(z_1, \bar{z}) \}.$$

By the envelope theorem,

(5) $\partial E(z_1, r, u^0)/\partial z_1$

$$= -(\mu u_1(z_1, \bar{z}^*, u^0) - C_1(z_1, \bar{z}^*, r)),$$

where $\bar{z}^* = \bar{z}^*(z_1, r, u^0)$ are adjusted optimally as z_1, r, and u^0 change. The first term on the right is the compensated marginal value function for z_1.[1] The second term is the

marginal cost of producing z_1. Since expression (5) reflects the change in expenditures necessary to maintain utility level u^0 as z_1 increases, this expression will be negative for $z_1 < z_1^*$, the optimal quantity of z_1. Note that when z_1 is adjusted optimally, expression (5) equals zero and the conditional expenditure function in (4) reduces to the traditional expenditure function, since

(6) $E(z_1^*(r, u^0), r, u^0) = m(r, u^0).$

Using the function $E(z_1, r, u^0)$, we can compute the compensating variation associated with consuming z_1^*. This measure reflects the change in income which would keep the consumer at his initial utility level, a situation with no access to z_1, if he were subsequently given the opportunity to consume z_1^* at input prices, r, and given technology. The measure is calculated by integrating (5) from 0 to z_1^* yielding

(7) $\displaystyle\int_0^{z_1^*} \left[\partial E(z_1, r, u^0)/\partial z_1 \right] dz_1$

$$= E(z_1^*, r, u^0) - E(0, r, u^0).$$

This expression is the negative of the area between the compensated marginal value and marginal cost functions for z_1, where that area can be expressed as

(8) $A = \displaystyle\int_0^{z_1^*} \big[\mu u_1(z_1, \bar{z}^*, u^0)$

$$- C_1(z_1, \bar{z}^*, r) \big] dz_1.$$

Thus graphical measures of welfare exist in concept in the commodity market.

---

[1] It might be argued that one can integrate this inverse compensated demand function back to the distance function and then use the distance function to derive the Marshallian marginal value function (see, for example, Angus Deaton and John Muellbauer, ch. 2). Consider the distance function $d(z, u^0)$. Then

$$\partial d(z, u^0)/\partial z_i = MV_i(z, u^0),$$

where MV_i is the normalized marginal value function for z_i, i.e., the proportion of income one is willing to pay for

another unit of z_i. By letting $u^0 = u(z)$, we have

$$MV_i(z, u^0) = MV_i(z, u(z)).$$

The term MV_i changes with z_j as

$$dMV_i(z, u(z))/dz_j = MV_{ij}(z, u^0) + MV_{iu} u_j.$$

This equation is an Antonelli decomposition for price-dependent demand equations. The right-hand side is composed of a utility constant slope and real income effect. Note, however, that in the household production framework, $u_j = \lambda C_j(z, r)$, so that the decomposition implies

$$dMV_i(z, u(z))/dz_j = MV_{ij}(z, u^0) + MV_{iu} \lambda C_j(z, r).$$

Thus, each cost function $C(z, r)$ implies a different slope for the Marshallian demand function.

The ultimate task of this section is to evaluate a change in an exogenous factor in the household production framework. In our illustration, let the exogenous factor be a publicly supplied or regulated good, α, that affects the production or consumption of a household commodity. In keeping with standard welfare analysis, we interpret the compensation necessary to keep an individual at a given utility level after a change in α as a money measure of the associated welfare change.

Suppose that α is an environmental good, such as the water quality of a lake. Then it will enter the utility function directly and be complementary with some commodity which we shall denote z_1, such as lake recreation. In this case, utility will be a function of α and z. Alternatively, if α is a public health project or child care facility, it may be more appropriately viewed as an input into the production of some z_1, such as family health or child quality. Now α will enter the transformation function (i.e., $t(z, x)$ becomes $t(z, x, \alpha)$). In either case, the household's expenditure function will depend on α.

When u^0 is the initial welfare level, the compensating variation of a change in the parameter vector from α^0 to α' is given by

$$(9) \quad CV = m(r, u^0, \alpha') - m(r, u^0, \alpha^0).$$

Compensating variation is negative for an increase in α and positive for a decrease, when α is a desirable public good. Since the measure in (9) is not directly observable, we seek a means of evaluating the welfare effects of the changes in α from information on the production and consumption of the associated commodity z_1. The equivalence between compensating variation measures of z_1^* and areas in commodity space suggests a useful approach. From the results above, we know that the difference in the areas between the marginal value and marginal cost functions evaluated for α^0 and α' will be equivalent to

$$(10) \quad \int_0^{z_1^*(\alpha')} \left[\partial E(z_1, r, u^0, \alpha') / \partial z_1 \right] dz_1$$
$$- \int_0^{z_1^*(\alpha^0)} \left[\partial E(z_1, r, u^0, \alpha^0) / \partial z_1 \right] dz_1.$$

Expression (10) can be written as

$$(11) \quad E(z_1^*(\alpha'), r, u^0, \alpha') - E(0, r, u^0, \alpha')$$
$$- E(z_1^*(\alpha^0), r, u^0, \alpha^0) + E(0, r, u^0, \alpha^0).$$

However, analogous to equation (6), the conditional expenditure function $E(\cdot)$ evaluated at the optimal value of z_1 is equivalent to the usual expenditure function $m(\cdot)$, so that (11) becomes

$$(12) \quad m(r, u^0, \alpha') - m(r, u^0, \alpha^0)$$
$$- E(0, r, u^0, \alpha') + E(0, r, u^0, \alpha^0).$$

Thus when

$$(13) \quad E(0, r, u^0, \alpha') = E(0, r, u^0, \alpha^0),$$

the compensating variation associated with a change in α can be measured by changes in the area behind compensated demand and marginal cost curves for z_1. That is, expression (12) which equals this area collapses to the correct measure of welfare change given by expression (9).

When α enters the household's preference function directly, a sufficient condition for (13) to hold is that α be weakly complementary to z_1. Karl-Göran Mäler has defined weak complementary as follows: "If the demand for a private good is zero, then the demand for some environmental service [public good] will also be zero" (p. 183). Thus weak complementarity is consistent with the condition $\partial u(0, \bar{z}, \alpha) / \partial \alpha = 0$, which implies that the individual is indifferent to varying levels of the exogenous good when he does not consume z_1. Alternatively, when α serves as an input into the production process, condition (13) will hold automatically if α is only an input in the production of z_1.

This section demonstrates that the compensated marginal value and marginal cost functions generated by the household production approach have normative significance and can be used to capture the welfare effects resulting from a change in exogenous factors affecting either tastes or technology. However, these results are of minimal value if there is no means of observing utility-constant marginal value functions. The usual approximation by means of consumer's surplus as well as the possibility of deriving exact measures of compensating variation from the Marshallian demand curve are precluded as well since that curve is not uniquely defined.

III. Welfare Analysis in the Goods Market

While the commodity space of the household production framework provides conceptually valid welfare measures, our inability to observe Marshallian approximations of these measures makes normative analysis difficult. In this section we use goods space to derive equivalent and conceptually valid, but empirically feasible, measures of welfare change.

Recall that the expenditure function can be derived as

$$m(r, u^0, \alpha) = \min_x \{ r \cdot x | u^0 = u(z, \alpha) \}$$

where z for any x vector satisfies $t(z, x, \alpha) = 0$ and $m(r, u^0, \alpha') - m(r, u^0, \alpha^0)$ is a money measure of the welfare effects of a change in α. Since expenditures are linear in x's, the compensated demand for some input x_1 is the derivative of the expenditure function with respect to r_1:

$$\partial m(r, u^0, \alpha) / \partial r_1 = x_1(r, u^0, \alpha).$$

Define $\tilde{r}_1(\bar{r}, u^0, \alpha)$, where $\bar{r} = (r_2, \ldots, r_n)$, as the price that induces zero-compensated demand for x_1; that is, $x_1(\tilde{r}_1, \bar{r}, u^0, \alpha) = 0$. Note that $\tilde{r}_1$ depends on the utility level u^0, the level of the public good α, and prices $\bar{r}$, although these arguments will be supressed for simplicity. The area under the compensated demand curve for x_1 is therefore

$$(14) \quad A = \int_{r_1^0}^{\tilde{r}_1} x_1(r, u^0, \alpha) \, dr_1,$$

$$= m(\tilde{r}_1, \bar{r}, u^0, \alpha) - m(r_1^0, \bar{r}, u^0, \alpha),$$

where $(r_1^0, \bar{r})$ is the prevailing price vector.

By definition, compensating variation for a change in α is given by expression (9), but this expression is not directly observable.

Our task is to demonstrate the conditions under which expression (9) can be derived from the area in the goods market given by (14), an area which if not observable can be approximated from its Marshallian counterpart. The change in the area behind the compensated demand function for some x_1 caused by a change in α from α^0 to α' can be expressed as

$$(15) \quad \Delta A = \int_{r_1^0}^{\tilde{r}_1} x_1(r, u^0, \alpha') \, dr_1$$

$$- \int_{r_1^0}^{\tilde{r}_1} x_1(r, u^0, \alpha^0) \, dr_1.$$

If

$$(16) \quad m(\tilde{r}_1, \bar{r}, u^0, \alpha') = m(\tilde{r}_1, \bar{r}, u^0, \alpha),$$

then $\quad \Delta A = m(r, u^0, \alpha') - m(r, u^0, \alpha^0).$

Thus when (16) holds, the welfare effect of a change in α can be measured exactly in the goods market.

Expression (16) requires that the individual be indifferent among different levels of the public good when x_1 is not purchased. Sufficient conditions for (16) to hold are that

(i) α is complementary to a subset of z denoted z_A such that $\partial u / \partial \alpha = 0$ if $z_i = 0$, for all i in A;

(ii) x_1 is an essential input in the production of all z_i, for all i in A. Writing the transformation as a generalized production function for z_i implies $z_i = t^*(\bar{z}, x)$, where $\bar{z}$ is the vector of all other z's. The essentiality of x_1 implies $0 = t^*(\bar{z}, 0, x_2, \ldots, x_n)$ for all $\bar{z}$.

The intuition of condition (i) is that when the price vector induces no units of x_1 to be purchased, z_i cannot be produced, and with no z_i, the individual is indifferent among different levels of α. If α enters the preference function, condition (i) implies weak complementarity between α and z_i. If, instead, α enters the production function only, condition (i) holds trivially.

In addition, x_1 must be an essential input into the production of the z_i. Expression (16) can hold even when x_1 is nonessential in the production of commodities which are unrelated to α. However the measure is incom-

VOL. 73 NO. 4   BOCKSTAEL AND McCONNELL: WELFARE MEASUREMENT   813

plete if α is related to commodities, either through production or consumption, for which x_1 is nonessential. Consequently if we can conceptually measure the change in some commodity space, we can measure it in goods space as well, as long as an essential input to that commodity can be identified.

Welfare measurement in the household production framework gives further insight into the concept of weak complementarity which has played a crucial role in measuring the demand for public goods from market data. V. Kerry Smith argues that since weak complementarity describes a link between arguments of the preference function, it must be assumed and cannot be tested. He observes that behavior that appears to be consistent with weak complementarity between a public and a private good may instead be the result of technical links between these goods. However, in the household production framework, Smith's distinction between links of technology and tastes is unnecessary. Both technology and tastes affect the household's decisions regarding z and thus both affect demand for goods as inputs into the production of z. Conditions (i) and (ii) demonstrate that it does not matter whether the link between the public good and the produced commodity is through the preference or production function, as long as the public good is of no value when the commodity is not produced.

This approach represents an advancement in the art of valuing public goods in the household production framework on two counts. First, by focusing on goods rather than commodities, it avoids the ill-defined Marshallian commodity demands. Second, it does not require that technology be known as Hori's approach does. All information about technology necessary to derive the value of a public input is embodied in the derived demand functions for goods.

This section demonstrates that when certain conditions are met, the welfare changes resulting from the change in an exogenous variable can be measured as areas behind Hicksian demand curves for goods. This result is an important corollary to the general results of Just and Hueth, and of Just, Hueth, and Schmitz, who demonstrate the duality of

surpluses in factor and product markets for competitive firms. The equivalence of welfare measures in alternative markets depends on the input or output in question being "necessary." That is, when prices are such that the input is not hired or the output is not produced, the firm must be assumed to shut down. We show that parallel conditions on the essentiality of goods as inputs in the household technology allow us to value changes in public goods in the household production framework.

IV. Conclusion

This paper develops an approach for welfare measurement in the household production function framework. While the household production function offers almost no testable hypotheses involving the production and consumption of commodities, welfare measures in commodity space do exist. However because the Marshallian demand curve is not well defined, it is not possible to estimate this demand curve. As a consequence, the practice of approximating welfare changes as the area under Marshallian demand curves is precluded. Hence, welfare measurement using commodity demand functions is not feasible in the household production framework.

The use of purchased goods in the production of commodities provides an opportunity for measuring welfare changes. When a good is essential in the production of a commodity, and a publicly controlled resource is complementary to the commodity, changes in the area under the Hicksian demand curve for that good can be interpreted as welfare measures of changes in the public resource. Thus an alternative and feasible means of measuring welfare change is provided for the household production function framework.

REFERENCES

Barnett, William A., "Pollak and Wachter on the Household Production Function Approach," *Journal of Political Economy*, October 1977, *85*, 1073–82.

Becker, Gary S., "A Theory of the Allocation

of Time," *Economic Journal*, September 1965, *75*, 493–517.

Brown, Gardner, Jr., Charbonneau, John and Hay, Michael, "The Value of Wildlife Estimated by the Hedonic Approach," Working Paper No. 6, U. S. Department of Interior, Fish and Wildlife Service, 1978.

Deaton, Angus and Muellbauer, John, *Economics and Consumer Behavior*, Cambridge: Cambridge University Press, 1980.

Gorman, W. H., "A Possible Preference for Analysing Quality Differentials in the Egg Market," mimeo., 1956; reissued as Discussion Paper No. B4, London School of Economics Econometrics Program, 1976.

Hausman, Jerry A., "Exact Consumer's Surplus and Deadweight Loss," *American Economic Review*, September 1981, *71*, 662–76.

Hori, Hajime, "Revealed Preference for Public Goods," *American Economic Review*, December 1975, *65*, 978–91.

Just, Richard and Hueth, Darrell, "Welfare Measures in a Multimarket Framework," *American Economic Review*, December 1979, *69*, 947–54.

_____, _____, and Schmitz, Andrew, *Applied Welfare Economics and Public Policy*, Englewood Cliffs: Prentice-Hall, 1982.

Lancaster, Kelvin, J., "A New Approach to Consumer Theory," *Journal of Political Economy*, April 1966, *74*, 132–57.

McKenzie, George W. and Pearce, I. F., "Welfare Measurement—A Synthesis," *American Economic Review*, September 1982, *72*, 669–82.

Mäler, Karl-Göran, *Environmental Economics: A Theoretical Inquiry*, Baltimore: John Hopkins Press, 1974.

Pollak, Robert A., "Welfare Evaluation and the Cost-of-Living Index in the Household Production Model," *American Economic Review*, June 1978, *68*, 285–99.

_____ and Wachter, Michael, "The Relevance of the Household Production Function and Its Implications for the Allocation of Time," *Journal of Political Economy*, April 1975, *83*, 255–77.

_____ and _____, "Reply: Pollak and Wachter on the Household Production Function Approach," *Journal of Political Economy*, October 1977, *85*, 1083–86.

Smith, V. Kerry, "Introduction to Advances in Applied Microeconomics and Some Perspectives on Volume I," in his *Advances in Applied Micro-Economics*, Vol. 1, Greenwich: JAI Press, 1981.

Willig, Robert D., "Consumer's Surplus Without Apology," *American Economic Review*, September 1976, *66*, 589–97.

Wilman, Elizabeth, A., "Hedonic Prices and Beach Recreational Values," in V. K. Smith, ed., *Advances in Applied Micro-Economics*, Vol. 1, Greenwich: JAI Press, 1981.

[24]

JOURNAL OF URBAN ECONOMICS 25, 116–137 (1989)

The Economic Losses of a Waterborne Disease Outbreak

WINSTON HARRINGTON, ALAN J. KRUPNICK,
AND WALTER O. SPOFFORD, JR.

Resources for the Future, 1616 P Street, NW, Washington, DC 20036

Received July 29, 1986

I. INTRODUCTION

A safe, reliable, and inexpensive drinking water supply is one of the easiest aspects of modern life to take for granted. Yet, water supplies can and occasionally do become contaminated, in which case an exposed household is confronted with a dilemma: Either continued consumption of the contaminated water, risking illness thereby, or securing an alternative source, perhaps at great cost and inconvenience.

Preventing contamination is costly as well, and may involve tradeoffs with other social objectives. Thus, decisions on water treatment require economic analyses similar to those that arise with other water resource investments: a comparison of a stream of present and future costs with a stream of future benefits that are uncertain and difficult to quantify. Nonetheless, drinking water benefit estimation is underdeveloped methodologically. Previous studies of the economic losses or damages of a disease outbreak (such as Schwab [14], Levy and McIntire [11], Baker *et al.* [1]) have been ad hoc in their approach and were also forced to rely on data gathered for other purposes.[1]

An outbreak of a waterborne disease gives rise to two categories of damages for which methods are particularly underdeveloped. The first category consists of morbidity losses. Until recently, most health-related benefit estimates have been concerned with mortality. However, it is clear that morbidity losses can also be important, even in cases where mortality is the major interest. As we shall see, valuation of morbidity raises difficult issues regarding the valuation of time and the direct disutility of illness, issues that are irrelevant for mortality valuation.

---

[1] It should be kept in mind that the damages of a contamination episode are not the same as the benefits of an investment in water treatment technology. To transfer the former into the latter, one also needs to know the likelihood that a contamination episode will occur in the absence of any preventative action. In this paper, we are concerned exclusively with the damages of a contamination episode.

116

0094-1190/89 $3.00
Copyright © 1989 by Academic Press, Inc.
All rights of reproduction in any form reserved.

The second category consists of losses associated with the actions taken by individuals to reduce their exposure to environmental contaminants. While averting behavior can arise in a wide variety of contexts, it is particularly important for drinking water contamination, where the availability of close substitutes gives people an alternative to acceptance of illness. These substitutes can, however, be costly. The valuation of averting behavior requires the determination of a relationship between averting expenditures, which can be observed, and willingness to pay, which cannot.

This paper considers the valuation of consequences of a water contamination episode that arise in the household sector of the economy, that is, those directly related to individual illness or to the responses of individuals or households to a contaminated water supply. The incidence of these effects may be felt outside the household sector, as when illness-induced work loss affects the supply of goods and services through lost production and government through lost tax revenues.[2] In the next section, we describe methods for evaluating the economic damages of a waterborne disease outbreak, based on individual willingness to pay. These methods are then applied to the estimation of the losses resulting from an outbreak of waterborne giardiasis in Luzerne County, Pennsylvania in 1983–1984.

II. VALUATION THEORY

In this section, we describe a model of individual utility maximization from which we derive an expression for the losses due to an environmental pollution episode such as contaminated drinking water. Before discussing this model, however, we need to be clear about the relationship between individual losses and social welfare.

By definition, the social benefit associated with a change in the environment is the sum of each individual's willingness to pay for (or to avoid) the change. For most applications, it is sufficient to examine the effects on the individuals directly affected by the change. Thus, for example, the evaluation of a new recreation area can often be limited to consideration of the consumer surplus changes among recreation participants.

Evaluation of morbidity (or at least its employment effects) is not so simple, because illness affects the individual's contribution to social welfare through absence from work. The social value of lost work is greater than the individual's take-home wage, and affects not only the individual but also his employer, the customers, and the rest of society as well. Estimation of these losses and their distribution would mire us in a swamp of detail involving production and marketing relationships, as well as institutional considerations such as the availability of paid sick leave or medical insur-

---

[2] Other losses, arising from the responses of businesses and other institutions, will not be considered here, but are discussed in Harrington *et al.* [9].

ance. To avoid these complications, we assume that the individual is self-employed, so that the individual's interest and the employer's interest are identical, and that the before-tax wage is an adequate representation of the social value of lost work. The "before-tax" stipulation is made because the losses to the individual are based entirely on the after-tax wage. After we describe the losses to the individual we will make an adjustment to account for the broader social losses as represented by the lost tax revenue.

The model described below extends the earlier work of Harrington and Portney [10] to take into account the fact that illness may also affect worker productivity even on days when work is not missed. This element is important in estimating the losses associated with a lingering or intermittent illness.

Suppose an individual combines leisure time L and expenditure X on goods to produce satisfaction. Suppose also that the individual cannot control the level of contamination P, but can at least partially fend off its effects through defensive expenditures D, as in the utility function

$$U^*(X, L, D; P) = F(D, P)U(X, L),\qquad(1)$$

where F is one's "productivity" in producing utility, $0 \le F \le 1$. We assume $U_X, U_L > ; U_{XX}, U_{LL} < 0; F_D > 0, F_P < 0, F_{DD} < 0, F_{PP} < 0$. It is assumed that this productivity factor affects one's work performance and therefore wage income since the individual is assumed to be self-employed. In addition, it is possible for the contamination to make the individual sick enough to be completely incapacitated. During the time the individual is under this condition he is unavailable for either work or leisure. Denote this "sick time" by $S(D, P)$; as indicated, it is, like F, dependent on the level of defensive expenditures and the contamination level, where $S_D < 0, S_P > 0, S_{DD} > 0, S_{PP} > 0$.

The individual maximizes (1) subject to a time constraint

$$L + W + S = T,\qquad(2)$$

where W is work time and T is total time available, and a resource constraint

$$I + wF(D, P)W \ge mS + D + X.\qquad(3)$$

In (3) medical expenses mS are assumed proportional to duration of illness S, I represents nonwage income, and w is the rate at which income is produced from working in the absence of pollution-induced illness (which we refer to as the wage rate). In effect, we assume the individual is engaged in "piece work," and hence pay is adjusted by the productivity factor F. He may work as many or as few hours as he likes. Thus, the individual maximizes

$$\pounds = F(D, P)U(X, L)$$
$$+ \lambda[I + F(D, P)w(T - L - S) - D - X - mS], \qquad (4)$$

where the term in brackets is the "full income" constraint of Becker [3]. The first-order conditions are

$$\pounds_x = F(D, P)U_x - \lambda = 0 \qquad (5a)$$
$$\pounds_L = F(D, P)U_L - \lambda wF(D, P) = 0 \qquad (5b)$$
$$\pounds_D = F_DU + \lambda F_DwW - \lambda FwS_D - \lambda - \lambda mS_D = 0. \qquad (5c)$$

By considering the amount of additional income required to keep the individual on the same indifference curve, it can be easily shown that the individual's marginal willingness to pay (WTP) to avoid a small increase in contamination can be expressed in terms of the derivatives of the indirect utility function V:

$$\text{WTP} = -\frac{V_P}{V_I}. \qquad (6)$$

By the envelope theorem the derivatives of the indirect utility function are as follows:

$$V_I = \lambda \qquad (7a)$$
$$V_P = F_PU + \lambda F_PwW - \lambda FwS_P - \lambda mS_P. \qquad (7b)$$

Therefore willingness to pay can be written

$$\text{WTP} = -\left(\frac{F_DU}{\lambda} + F_DwW\right)\frac{F_P}{F_D} + (FwS_D + mS_D)\frac{S_P}{S_D}. \qquad (8)$$

Now consider the total change in sick time and productivity with a change in contamination:

$$\frac{dS}{dP} = S_DD_P + S_P, \qquad \frac{dF}{dP} = F_DD_P = F_P;$$

or

$$\frac{S_P}{S_D} = \frac{1}{S_D}\frac{dS}{dP} - D_P, \qquad \frac{F_P}{F_D} = \frac{1}{F_D}\frac{dF}{dP} - D_P.$$

120   HARRINGTON, KRUPNICK, AND SPOFFORD

Substituting these expressions into (8), we have

$$\text{WTP} = -\frac{U}{\lambda}\frac{dF}{dP} - wW\frac{dF}{dP} + Fw\frac{dS}{dP} + m\frac{dS}{dP}$$

$$+\left(\frac{F_D U}{\lambda} + F_D wW - FwS_D - mS_D\right)D_P. \tag{9}$$

From (5c), the bracketed expression in (9) is equal to 1. Also, by differentiating (2) we have $L_p + W_p + dS/dP = 0$. Therefore,

$$\text{WTP} = -\frac{U}{\lambda}\frac{dF}{dP} - wW\frac{dF}{dP} - FwW_p - FwL_p + m\frac{dS}{dP} + D_p. \tag{10}$$

As noted above, to obtain the social welfare losses associated with individual illnesses, we need to add to (10) the lost tax revenue associated with lost work. Hence, if G represents individual income taxes and SW social welfare, then

$$\frac{\partial\text{SW}}{\partial P} = \text{WTP} - \frac{dG}{dP}.$$

(The sign is negative because dG/dP represents the reduction in tax revenues.) If w^* is the wage rate before taxes (i.e., individual productivity in the absence of illness), then we can write taxes collected as

$$G = F(w^* - w)W,$$

so that

$$\frac{dG}{dP} = \frac{dF}{dP}(w^* - w)W + F(w^* - w)W_p.$$

The marginal loss of social welfare associated with individual response to increased contamination is therefore

$$\frac{\partial\text{SW}}{\partial P} = -\frac{U}{\lambda}\frac{dF}{dP} \qquad \text{(direct disutility of illness)}$$

$$-w^*W\frac{dF}{dP} \qquad \begin{array}{l}\text{(lost work productivity,}\\ \quad\text{evaluated at the before-tax wage rate)}\end{array}$$

$$-Fw^*W_p \qquad \begin{array}{l}\text{(lost work time evaluated at the}\\ \quad\text{before-tax wage rate)}\end{array}$$

$$-FwL_p \qquad \begin{array}{l}\text{(the value of lost leisure, evaluated}\\ \quad\text{at the after-tax wage rate)}\end{array}$$

$$+m\frac{dS}{dP} \qquad \text{(medical expenses)}$$

$$+D_p \qquad \text{(defensive expenditures).} \tag{11}$$

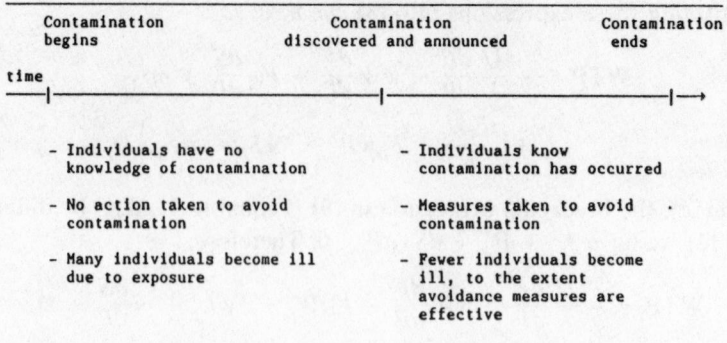

Fig. 1. Damages in a contamination episode depend on individual actions and knowledge.

One noteworthy aspect of this result is that there is no lost "leisure productivity" term corresponding to the lost "work productivity" term $w*WdF/dP$. In this model, the individual by assumption receives less satisfaction when illness strikes, but this effect is captured in the first term, the direct disutility of illness.

To apply this model to a contamination episode, we proceed as follows. The most important events in estimating losses to individuals are the time at which the water supply becomes contaminated, the time at which the contamination becomes known to the public, and the time at which contamination ends. These three events define two intervals during which individuals have different information, and hence behave differently. These differences, in turn, affect the nature of the damages incurred, as illustrated in the "time line" in Fig. 1.

In the first interval, individuals incur no incremental avoidance costs because they are unaware of anything to avoid. Therefore $D_P = 0$ in (11) above, and our estimate of losses is found by evaluating the other terms.[3]

In the second interval, individuals can avoid illness by taking averting action. Thus, the losses associated with reduced productivity or incapacity owing to illness are less important, and defensive expenditures correspondingly more important. Indeed, in the second interval, where near-perfect protection is possible, we assume that the only nonzero term of (11) is D_P.

---

[3]Caution is in order, however, because error may be introduced if these marginal conditions are used to evaluate a nonmarginal change. For example, inframarginal hours of leisure are in all likelihood more highly valued than those at the margin. For life-threatening or chronic illnesses requiring a lengthy convalescence or major life-style changes, this underestimate is likely to be a major source of error. However, for acute nonlethal infections, such as giardiasis, we believe that this effect is of minor importance.

122   HARRINGTON, KRUPNICK, AND SPOFFORD

Unfortunately, D_P is for two reasons an inadequate guide for estimating losses in the second interval.

First, the model suggests that there is a substance "D" that can be bought which protects against illness. In fact, people respond to water contamination by changing their consumption pattern—mainly substituting water from a safe source for that from the contaminated source. In this context, "averting behavior" consists of either securing water from an uncontaminated source or treating the contaminated tap water, for example, by filtering or boiling. Because consumption of some goods (bottled water, for example) changes from zero to some positive amount, the assumption of an interior maximum made in the preceding model is no longer valid. Second and more importantly, avoidance of contaminated water for drinking represents such a major change in household activities that extrapolation of willingness to pay from the marginal conditions does not seem justified.

By making two assumptions that do not seem unreasonable for the problem of drinking water contamination, we can derive an expression that gives observable upper and lower bounds for the willingness to pay to avoid environmental contamination. Those assumptions are (i) that the household adjusts its consumption so that there is no increase in exposure to the contaminating substance, and (ii) tap water and its alternative, bottled water, are perfect substitutes when contamination is not present.

With these assumptions, it can be shown that the damages A to a household when the contamination level increases from P_0 to P_1 can be bracketed as

$$(p_B - p_Z)(Z(P_0) - Z(P_1)) \geq A \geq (p_B - p_Z)B(P_1),$$

where p_B and p_Z denote the prices of bottled and tap water, respectively, and $Z(\cdot)$ and $B(\cdot)$ consumption of tap and bottled water as a function of the contamination level P. This result is demonstrated formally in Harrington *et al.* [9], but it can be understood informally by considering Fig. 2.

The bottom quadrant on the diagram in Fig. 2 shows the relationship between the concentration of contaminant P and tap water consumption Z. Initially it is assumed that bottled water consumption is zero; i.e., $B(P_0) = 0$. As the level of contamination increases, Z decreases as individuals act to avoid contamination (or to keep contamination constant). This decrease in Z is inconvenient, and people would therefore be willing to pay a price greater than the normal price of tap water, p_Z, in order to obtain additional safe water. The upper quadrant gives the relationship between tap water consumption Z and this price premium. As the contamination level increases, the price premium increases until it reaches $p_B - p_Z$, the price difference between bottled water and tap water. This occurs at the

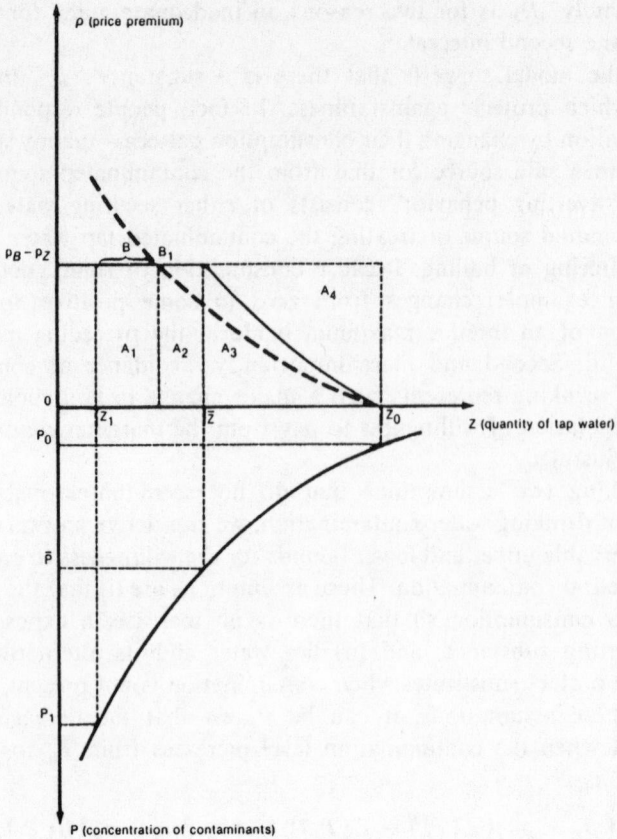

FIGURE 2.

contamination level $\bar{P}$, and water consumption $\bar{Z}$. With further increases in contamination, tap water consumption continues to fall. The premium does not increase, however, for the household does not have to pay more than p_B to purchase bottled water. With contamination at P_1, tap water consumption falls to Z_1. As shown in the figure, the bottled water consumption B may be less than the decrement in tap water consumption, $\bar{Z} - Z_1$.

The "true" willingness to pay to avoid a change from P_0 to P_1 is the area under the premium curve in the upper quadrant, or the areas marked A_1, A_2, and A_3. The lower and upper bounds mentioned above are, respectively, A_1 and $A_1 + A_2 + A_3 + A_4$.[4] For a linear demand curve, the WTP

[4] The premium curve is, in effect, the (Hicksian) demand curve for clean water. The Marshallian demand curve passes through the points Z_0 and B_1, as indicated by the dotted line in Fig. 2.

124   HARRINGTON, KRUPNICK, AND SPOFFORD

is found by averaging the upper and lower bounds. In the empirical work below, this is referred to as the "best estimate."

III. GIARDIASIS IN LUZERNE COUNTY, PENNSYLVANIA

Giardiasis, currently the most common waterborne disease in the United States, is caused by the protozoan parasite *Giardia lamblia*.[5] Although seldom fatal, giardiasis can be an unpleasant and temporarily debilitating diarrheal disease (Wolfe [18]). In a few rare cases, hospitalization for dehydration may be necessary. Although the acute stage generally is thought to last only 3 to 4 days, untreated giardiasis often develops into chronic infection, characterized by recurrent periods of acute illness lasting several days. This stage may last for months (Craun [6]). Indeed, it is the intermittent nature of giardiasis, together with the patient's failure to develop a fever, that distinguish giardiasis from many other gastroenteric illnesses.

The most serious public health problem associated with *Giardia* is its potential for contaminating public water supplies, for *Giardia* is notably resistant to chlorination. *Giardia* cysts in human and animal feces deposited in upland watersheds eventually find their way to watercourses where they are transported to water supply intakes. Once in the water distribution system, the cysts can be consumed by humans unless adequate water treatment is provided.

The Luzerne County Outbreak

During the late fall of 1983, an increase in the incidence of giardiasis among residents of a number of small communities near Wilkes-Barre, Pennsylvania was linked to drinking water.

By late winter, a total of 370 confirmed cases of giardiasis had been reported to the Pennsylvania Department of Health, making this outbreak one of the largest ever recorded in the United States in terms of confirmed cases. On December 23, 1983, about 25,000 households served by the contaminated reservoir were advised by the authorities to boil their drinking water until a safe drinking water supply could be made available. By reconfiguring the water distribution system, the water utility was eventually able to supply safe drinking water to the affected areas. For about half the

---

[5]Between 1965 and 1982, fifty-four outbreaks of giardiasis were reported in the United States, ranging in size from a few to as many as 5000 suspected cases. In 1980, the Center for Disease Control in Atlanta reported 11,000 cases of giardiasis. This was probably an underestimate because states with the strongest giardiasis detection programs report the largest number of cases. It is suspected that many cases, and even some outbreaks, go unreported. Nonetheless, both the number of outbreaks and the number of cases being reported have been on the rise since 1970. The extent to which this is due to an increased familiarity with the disease or a genuine increase in exposure and disease incidence is not known.

households, the boil-water advisory was lifted on March 30, 1984, after 99 days. The last households were removed from the advisory on September 21 (274 days), following completion of a new water supply line.

While on the advisory, households had other options beside boiling water. They could also buy bottled water at local supermarkets, or they could pick up free water supplied by some local governments at fire stations and other public facilities.

The theory described in Section II is used to estimate the welfare losses resulting from the Luzerne County episode. Corresponding to the two intervals in Fig. 1, two categories of losses are discussed—losses due to illness and losses due to actions taken by individuals to avoid drinking contaminated water. Estimates of losses are presented for three scenarios differing by the wage rates used to value loss of work and loss of leisure time activities due to illness, and by the time spent on averting activities, such as boiling water and obtaining bottled water.

IV. ESTIMATING LOSSES DUE TO ILLNESS

In September 1984, the Pennsylvania Department of Health (DOH) mailed a questionnaire designed by the authors to the 370 individuals in Luzerne County with confirmed cases of giardiasis. The purpose of the questionnaire was to gather data to estimate the costs incurred by those who were ill.

Description of Survey Data

Table 1 provides descriptive statistics for the 176 respondents in the sample that were used in the analysis of the costs of illness. Compared to the population of Luzerne County as a whole, the sample slightly overrepresents females and employed persons, but is otherwise fairly similar. As shown, an elevated incidence of giardiasis first was observed in October 1983 and peaked in December. A month after the issuance of the boil-water advisory, the occurrence of new cases practically disappeared.

Note that we asked for work lost not only of those in the labor market but also of persons doing household work. "Caretakers" are those who had to miss work to take care of sick children. Note that average work loss was twice as large for homemakers as for the employed (outside the home).[6] The "productivity loss" entries at the bottom of the table are related to the large discrepancy between duration of illness and work lost. Evidently people continued to go to work on most of the average of 63 days they

[6] This finding is not surprising. An employed worker, in contrast to a homemaker, foregoes either income or the opportunity to take future sick leave when he or she stays at home due to illness.

126   HARRINGTON, KRUPNICK, AND SPOFFORD

TABLE 1

Descriptive Statistics for Survey of Confirmed Cases of Giardiasis
in Luzerne County, Pennsylvania

Survey data	
Number surveyed[a]	370
Number returned by November 1, 1984	182
Number used in the analysis	176
Response rate (%)	49

Sample description	
Percentage male	42.4
Percentage female	57.6
Age distribution (%)	
0–6	6.7
7–12	2.8
13–20	6.7
21–30	19.2
31–40	25.3
41–50	16.9
51–60	11.2
> 60	11.2
	100.0
Status (%)	
Employed	58.7
Homemaker	15.7
Student	9.9
Preschool	4.7
Retired	6.4
Unemployed	4.6
	100.0
Pretax personal income (dollars per year)	
Median income group	7500–12,500
Maximum income in sample	75,000

Disease characteristics of sample	Average	Standard deviation	Maximum
Mean length of illness (days)	63.0		365
Median length of illness (days)	30.0		
Percentage with continuous symptoms	65.9		
Percentage with intermittent symptoms	34.1		
Mean length of illness			
If continuous (days)	41.6	45.5	310
If intermittent (days)	85.0	93.9	365
Well days	23.1		
Net sick days	61.9	76.6	300
Weight lost (pounds)[b]	9.0		34
Mean number of visits to doctor	2.0		11
Mean number of days in hospital	0.5		14

TABLE 1—Continued

Disease characteristics of sample		Average	Maximum
Percentage of confirmed cases first reported (by month)			
October, 1983		15.0	
November		10.8	
December		64.5	
December 1–23	54.8		
December 23–31	9.7		
January, 1984		8.6	
January 1–14	6.5		
January 15–31	2.1		
February		1.1	
Total		100.0	
Medication (prescriptions per confirmed case)			
Flagyl		1.1	3
Atebrine		0.1	3
Furoxone		0.04	2
Other		0.2	8

Economic effects[c]	Average	Maximum
Work loss days		
Employed	6.3	60
Homemakers	12.7	90
Caretakers		
Employed	0.4	
Homemakers	12.0	
Productivity loss (%)[d]		
Workers	30.4	
Homemakers	34.0	

[a]Questionnaires were mailed on September 13, 1984 to the 370 confirmed cases of giardiasis in Luzerne County.

[b]The questionnaire asked respondents how many pounds they lost as a result of their illness. It is possible that some respondents interpreted this question as asking for permanent weight loss, i.e., after taking into account any weight gain in the period following their illness. As the average weight loss of 9 lb in the RFF survey matches closely the 10-lb average offered in the clinical literature, we conclude that few respondents interpreted the question this way.

[c]Virtually all respondents reported that their leisure activities had also been affected.

[d]Average percentage loss in productivity for days ill but at work (subjective estimates).

reported symptoms. On the questionnaire, we asked respondents to estimate the extent to which their effectiveness as a worker suffered due to illness. While this procedure is subjective, it addresses a real economic consequence of illnesses of this sort.

Procedure Used to Estimate Losses

We estimated losses in nine categories: doctor visits, hospital visits, emergency room visits, laboratory tests, medication, time and travel losses associated with medical treatment, work loss, work productivity loss, and leisure time loss. The first six are costs associated with medical care. The last three correspond to terms in (11). (Of the remaining terms in (11), the direct disutility of illness is not estimated and defensive expenditures are zero.) Lost work time is estimated based on data in the survey. No questions were asked about lost leisure time, but it was assumed that one was as likely to be incapacitated during leisure time as during working hours.

The losses in many of these categories depend to a considerable extent on the value of time—mainly the time spent ill but also time spent seeking medical care. Following Becker [3], lost work time by those in the paid labor force was valued at the hourly wage rate before taxes for the sample of confirmed cases (on average, the rate was $8.09 per hour). The hourly

TABLE 2

Average Losses for Confirmed Cases of Giardiasis in Luzerne County, Pennsylvania
(1984 Dollars per Confirmed Case)

	Scenario[a]		
Loss category	A	B	C
Direct medical costs			
Doctor visits	36	36	36
Hospital visits	100	100	100
Emergency room visits	27	27	27
Laboratory tests	63	63	63
Medication	28	28	28
Subtotal	254	254	254
Time costs for medical care[b]	18	15	12
Value of work loss days	359	271	209
Cumulative subtotal	631	540	475
Loss of work productivity	371	316	278
Loss of leisure time	253	166	105
Total	1255	1022	858

[a]Assumptions for scenarios. Scenario A: Implicit after-tax wage rate of the unemployed, homemakers, and retirees equal to $6.39 per hour (average after-tax wage rate of employed persons in the sample). This estimate is not far from Cooper and Rice's 1977 estimate of the hourly value of household work ($6.08 in 1984 dollars) [5]. Scenario B: Implicit after-tax wage rate of the unemployed, homemakers, and retirees equal to $2.65 per hour (our estimate of the after-tax minimum wage). Scenario C: Implicit after-tax wage rate of the unemployed, homemakers, and retirees equal to $0. After-tax wages are the before-tax wages times 0.79 (see footnote 7).

[b]This includes both the value of time spent to obtain medical care and the costs of travel.

wage rate for employed persons in our sample was computed by dividing their reported before-tax annual (personal) income by the hours they worked per year. As explained above, leisure time losses were valued at the after-tax wage.[7]

Lost time of homemakers, retirees, and unemployed persons also has value, but for persons in these categories there is no labor market surrogate. We use three different values of time for such persons, denoting the resulting estimates by Scenarios A, B, and C. These values are given in Table 2. Losses of leisure time are estimated by multiplying three variables: the number of hours per day ordinarily available for leisure activitiès (the number of nonworking, nonsleeping hours), the real or implicit hourly wage rate, and the number of days a person was ill.

Estimates of Average Losses Due to Illness

Table 2 provides three estimates of the average losses for the confirmed cases of giardiasis in the sample. As shown, in all three scenarios the out-of-pocket costs for medical care are a small portion of the total. Time costs make up the rest, with the loss of productivity and leisure time accounting for more than half the loss.

V. ESTIMATING LOSSES DUE TO AVERTING ACTION

To obtain information on the actions taken by individuals in the outbreak area to avoid contaminated water, fifty telephone interviews were made during September and October, 1984, with households chosen at random from the telephone book.

Description of Survey Data

Table 3 provides descriptive statistics for the RFF random telephone survey. As shown, households in the affected area chose a wide variety of strategies to ensure a safe drinking water supply. About one-half of the households (46%) either hauled water or boiled water, but not both. Virtually no one (2%) in the affected area relied on bottled water alone. Mixed strategies were popular. The households that hauled water obtained the largest quantity per week. No household in the sample installed a filtration system.[8]

---

[7]Unfortunately, to convert before-tax to after-tax wage rates, we did not have the marginal tax rate of each household. In its stead we used the 1983 U.S. average tax rate on individual income (federal income tax, plus state and local income taxes, plus FICA) of 21% taken from the 1984 "Statistical Abstract" (U.S. Commerce Department, [17]).

[8]Although opportunistic entrepreneurs offered filtration systems for sale immediately following the outbreak, the Pennsylvania Department of Health refused to sanction such systems for either home or business use.

Procedures Used to Estimate Losses

We computed upper- and lower-bound estimates of the losses due to actions taken by the sample of 50 households to avoid drinking contaminated water and averaged them to obtain a "best estimate." As in the preceding section, time figured prominently in the damage estimates, and different assumptions regarding its value gave rise to alternative scenarios, again labeled A, B, and C. In this case, however, the scenarios involved another element, namely the degree to which avoidance activities were performed jointly with other activities. For example, the true cost of hauled water is much less if picked up on the way home from work than if a special

TABLE 3

Descriptive Statistics for Telephone Survey of Averting Behavior in
Luzerne County, Pennsylvania[a]

Strategy	Percentage of households	Frequency per week	Quantity (gallons per household per week)	Percentage nonjoint[b]
Strategy for obtaining water				
Haul water only	22.0	1.6	10.6	36
Boil water only	24.0	2.9	6.3	32
Purchase bottled water only	2.0	1.2	5.6	16
Haul and boil water	6.0			
Haul and purchase bottled water	18.0			
Boil and purchase bottled water	18.0			
Haul, boil, and purchase bottled water	8.0			
None of the above	2.0			
Total	100.0			
Substitution of other liquids	53.0			
Permanent change in water consumption	54.0			
Reports of undesirable changes in public water supply				
Pressure	17.0			
Odor	73.0			
Taste[c]	6.0			
Appearance	58.0			
Changes in dining out				
Increased	15.0			
Decreased	6.0			
No change	79.0			

Clinical attack rate 9.5% (14 cases out of a sample of 148 people)

[a] Number of households contacted = 50. Average number of persons per household = 2.96 (148 people in 50 households).
[b] The activity was not performed jointly with a nonaverting activity.
[c] This estimate may be low because few people drank the public water supply after the boil-water advisory was issued.

WATERBORNE DISEASE LOSSES

TABLE 4

Descriptions of Scenarios for Estimating Losses Due to Actions Taken by Individuals
to Avoid Contaminated Water

	Percentage of population in affected area[d]	Scenario		
		A	B	C
Value of time (dollars/hour)				
Status				
Working adults[a]	45.6	6.39	6.39	6.39
Homemakers	22.0	6.39[a]	2.65[b]	0
Retirees and disabled	19.5	6.39[a]	2.65[b]	0
Unemployed	5.0	6.39[a]	2.65[b]	0
Students[c]				
≥ 16 and working	4.4	2.65[b]	2.65[b]	2.65[b]
≥ 16 and not working	3.5	0	0	0
	100.0			
Weighted average value of time (dollars/hour)		6.00	4.26	3.03
Boil water is a joint activity[d]		No	Yes	Yes
Haul water is a joint activity[d]		No	No	No
Purchase of bottled water is a joint activity[e]		No	Yes	Yes
Pre-outbreak water consumption (gallons per capita per day)[f]		3.65	3.65	3.65

[a]Average after-tax wage rate for working adults in the outbreak area with confirmed cases of giardiasis (before-tax wage times 0.79), in 1984 dollars.

[b]After-tax minimum wage rate (before-tax wage times 0.79), in 1984 dollars.

[c]Children less than 16 years old are excluded from the analysis.

[d]"No" means the respondent's answer is used in the computation. "Yes" means the averting activity is assumed to be undertaken jointly with an ordinary activity.

[e]Bottled water is valued at \$.66/gallon when its purchase is assumed to be a joint event (Yes) and at \$1.17 when it assumed to be nonjoint (No).

[f]Based on information in Baker [2], Solley [15], and Denver Water Department [8].

trip must be made. During the interview, we asked whether averting activities were usually performed jointly with ordinary activities. In the scenarios we either took respondents at their word or we *assumed* all averting activity was jointly undertaken. The assumptions for the three scenarios are summarized in Table 4.

In all three scenarios, we do not value the aggravation and inconvenience of taking averting actions, nor do we value the fact that tap water is delivered under pressure or may have more (or less) acceptable odor, taste, or appearance than its alternatives. On the contrary, we assume that the alternative water obtained is equal in quality to uncontaminated tap water.

Table 5 presents lower-bound, upper-bound, and best estimates of the losses associated with actions taken by individuals to avoid contaminated water in Luzerne County, for the three scenarios.

132   HARRINGTON, KRUPNICK, AND SPOFFORD

TABLE 5

Average Costs of Actions Taken by Individuals to Avoid Contaminated Water
during the Outbreak in Luzerne County, Pennsylvania (1984 Dollars)

	Scenario		
	A	B	C
Lower-bound estimate[a]			
Total cost per household	776.4	182.8	169.6
Cost per person per day	1.81	0.43	0.40
Upper-bound estimate[b]			
Total cost per household	2304.4	852.4	800.0
Cost per person per day	5.37	1.99	1.86
Best estimate[c]			
Total cost per household	1540.4	517.6	484.8
Cost per person per day	3.59	1.21	1.13

[a] The lower-bound estimate is based on the actual cost of the substitute water used for drinking, food preparation, and personal hygiene.

[b] The upper-bound estimate is based on the cost of replacing with a substitute source of water the quantity of water for drinking, food preparation, and personal hygiene that would have been used had the municipal water supply not been contaminated.

[c] The best estimate is the average of the upper-bound and lower-bound estimates.

As shown, the "best estimate" of averting losses to the average household range from $485 to $1540 or from $1.13 to $3.59 per person per day for the duration of the outbreak.

Total Losses to Individuals in the Outbreak Area

Earlier in this section, we presented a range of estimates of average losses for the 176 people with confirmed cases of giardiasis who returned the questionaire and for the 50 households who responded to questions about the actions they took to avoid drinking the contaminated water. The final step in this analysis is to estimate the total losses to the 75,000 people at risk in the outbreak area.

The procedure used to estimate total losses due to actions taken to avoid contaminated water is straightforward. It assumes that the sample of 50 households is representative of the 25,000 households in the affected area and involves multiplying the average total cost per household by the 25,000 households at risk. Following this procedure, total lower-bound estimates of the losses due to averting activities for scenarios A, B, and C in Table 6 range from $4.2 to $19.4 million; total upper-bound estimates of the losses range from $20.0 to $57.6 million. Our best estimates range from $12.1 to $38.5 million.

Scaling up losses due to illness requires an estimate of the "attack rate," the fraction of the population that contracted giardiasis. When the outbreak

WATERBORNE DISEASE LOSSES   133

TABLE 6
Total Losses Due to Illness and to Actions Taken by Individuals to Avoid
Contaminated Water (1984 Millions of Dollars)

Loss category	Scenario[a]		
	A	B	C
Losses due to illness[b]			
Medical costs	1.07	1.05	1.03
Loss of work	2.15	1.63	1.25
Loss of productivity and leisure time	3.78	2.91	2.31
Total losses due to illness	7.00	5.59	4.59
Losses due to averting actions[c]			
Lower-bound estimate	19.41	4.57	4.24
Upper-bound estimate	57.61	21.31	20.00
Best estimate	38.51	12.94	12.12
Total losses			
Lower-bound estimate	26.41	10.16	8.83
Upper-bound estimate	64.41	26.90	24.59
Best estimate	45.51	18.53	16.71

[a]The scenarios are described in Tables 3 and 5.

[b]Estimated by multiplying average costs per confirmed case minus hospital costs by the 5630 clinical cases (6000 total cases − 370 confirmed cases = 5630 clinical cases) and adding to this product the total costs of the 370 confirmed cases.

[c]The lower-bound estimate is based on the actual costs to households of providing uncontaminated water for drinking, food preparation, and personal hygiene. This includes both out-of-pocket costs and some time costs (see Table 5). The losses due to individual averting actions are not likely to be less than this lower-bound. The upper-bound estimate is based on the opportunity costs of the tap water use foregone. This is a maximum estimate. The losses are not likely to be greater than this upper-bound. The quantity of uncontaminated water actually used is used to estimate the lower-bound. The quantity of water normally used for drinking, cooking, and dishwashing is used to estimate the upper-bound. The actual opportunity cost of tap water use foregone is likely to be between the upper and lower bounds. This is called the best estimate. The best estimate in this table is assumed to be the average of the upper and lower bounds and is computed as the lower-bound estimate plus one-half of the difference between the upper-bound and lower-bound estimates.

was discovered, the Pennsylvania Department of Health conducted a random telephone survey to determine the extent and cause of the outbreak. Respondents were asked whether any family members had recently suffered symptoms of giardiasis (10 days or more of diarrhea). Positive responses were defined to be "clinical" cases of giardiasis. Since the attack rate inside and outside the area served by the contaminated reservoir was found to be 9.5% and 1.5%, respectively, it was assumed that the incidence of giardiasis attributable to water supply contamination was the difference, 8% or 6000 cases of giardiasis.

Use of the attack rate to scale up illness losses from the losses reported in the confirmed case survey requires the assumption that the confirmed cases are typical of all cases. This might not be so because an average clinical case may be relatively less severe than an average confirmed case. An illness is confirmed only when a person is sick enough to seek medical attention and willing to provide one, two, and perhaps even three, stool samples. Thus, an illness may be unconfirmed simply because a person does not feel sick enough to visit a physician and to submit a stool sample for laboratory tests. On the other hand, some physicians apparently prescribe medication to patients with giardiasis-like symptoms without taking stool samples, particularly after an outbreak has been declared. Thus, a clinical case may be no less severe than a confirmed case.

Nevertheless, we assume that an average clinical case is just as severe and just as costly as an average confirmed case, with one exception: that anyone sick enough to be hospitalized for giardiasis-like symptoms would have been tested for *Giardia* cysts until a definite diagnosis was obtained. Therefore, before estimating losses to the clinical cases, we subtract hospital costs incurred by the confirmed cases and add them back after estimating the losses to the clinical cases.

Based on these data and procedures, the total losses due to illness range from $4.6 to $7.0 million, as summarized in Table 6. The total losses to households for the three composite scenarios range from $8.8 to $64 million. Additional, much smaller losses were also suffered by business and government.

VI. RESEARCH NEEDS

The usefulness of benefit analysis for policy applications depends in part on the accuracy of the estimates. Inasmuch as the estimates of total losses from the Luzerne County outbreak range, under various assumptions, between $11 and $68 million—approximately a sixfold difference—improvements in the accuracy of such estimates would seem to be indicated. The need for improved estimates in particular cases, however, depends on the estimates of the costs of water treatment and on other factors. In the case of Luzerne County, the need to improve estimates of benefits is not as compelling as it might be in other cases because the estimates of the costs of water treatment are in the vicinity of the lower range of benefit estimates (Harrington *et al.* [19]). It would not take much refinement in the estimates of benefits to determine whether the benefits of water treatment exceed the costs. In other cases and in other situations, however, the overlap in the ranges of benefits and cost estimates might require substantially more precise benefit estimates. In this section, we describe the major sources of uncertainty in estimates of losses from the Luzerne County outbreak and indicate the research needed to improve the accuracy of estimates.

The Economics of the Environment

We believe the following areas contributed most to the uncertainty in the estimates of losses, and hence are important candidates for future research:

- questionnaire design
- extrapolation of survey results to the affected population
- valuation of time
- valuation of illness
- valuation of anxiety.

Questionnaire Design

Although we were generally pleased with the results of the two main data-gathering instruments (the survey of confirmed cases and the survey of household averting behavior) there is room for improvement,

For one thing, one might question whether the "productivity loss" questions produced meaningful results. Respondents may have been telling us how they felt physically rather than the impairment of their performance. The questionnaire needs to be improved to obtain more useful information on losses in productivity.

In the household survey of averting behavior, we imposed time constraints on the interviews to avoid taxing the patience of the interviewees. As a result, the interviews may have led to an oversimplification of averting behavior. Also, we were unable to obtain data to estimate the consumption of water in the affected area by specific use prior to the outbreak. Instead, we were forced to use national per capita consumption data. Finally, we were unable to obtain much insight into the substitution of other liquids for drinking water after the public water supply was implicated.

Extrapolation of Survey Results

Problems were encountered in extrapolating the results of the two surveys to the total population in the affected area. The most troublesome was the use of the average loss due to illness (minus hospitalization costs) calculated from the losses incurred by the confirmed cases to estimate the losses incurred by the clinical cases. This procedure could be improved by having a sample of persons with clinical symptoms, but without a confirmed diagnosis, complete the same questionnaire sent to the confirmed cases. This procedure would establish if there were significant differences between the losses due to illness in the two groups.

Valuation of Time

A major portion of the losses resulting from Luzerne County outbreak arises from the imputed value of time, rather than from out-of-pocket expenses. Thus, the valuation of time is critical. For lack of any better information, we valued lost time at the individual's wage rate, appropriately adjusted for taxes. For lost work time, this requires the tenuous assumption that the wage rate equals the marginal value of an individual's labor.[9] Using the wage rate (after taxes) to value leisure time activities assumes that workers are free to choose the quantity of work, even though for most people the length of the work day is fixed. Moreover, even with this assumption, the wage rate applies only at the margin. It is not clear how to value the inframarginal leisure hours likely to be at stake. Finally, less than half of the population are wage-earners. Yet there is little guidance on how to value the time of homemakers, retirees, the unemployed, and children. Only for homemakers do we have even a remote market proxy.

Valuation of Illness

The effects of illness extend beyond the time taken away from other activities. Illness also imposes direct discomfort that individuals would presumably pay to avoid. While indirect measures of this "pain and suffering" component may eventually emerge, it is more likely that useful information on discomfort will be obtained from direct questioning, as in a contingent valuation (CV) study. We believe that this will require a redirection or expansion of current CV research on health impacts, which is for the most part concerned with the willingness to pay to reduce the risks of particular diseases, or the willingness to pay to take some policy action to reduce illness incidence. What is needed are estimates of the willingness to pay to avoid the actual consequences of a particular disease (rather than the increased probability of contracting it) (see Loehman and De [12] or Tolley *et al.* [16]).

Valuation of Anxiety[10]

One final area where further research is indicated was brought to our attention as an incidental outcome of the survey of individual averting behavior. Over one-half of those who responded to the survey reported a permanent change in drinking water habits, even though the water supply had been declared "safe" by the Pennsylvania Department of Environmental Resources. Whether such behavior is solely the result of the outbreak or whether, as some respondents suggested, the outbreak was "the last straw" in a series of incidents involving the local water supply would affect the

---

[9] A recent study of waiting in line at gas stations concluded that on average the value of time approximated the wage rate, but the variance was very high (Deacon and Sonstelie [7]).

[10] What we call "anxiety" is a little different from the effect discussed in the literature (see Schechter and Heiman [13]), which is the willingness to pay simply to resolve uncertainty. While that effect may be present here, what is more prominent is the lack of trust in water quality and also in local institutions such as the water supplier. Perhaps "valuation of distrust" would be a better term.

estimate of the losses. More important, the lack of faith in the safety of the local water supply is itself a costly outcome of the Luzerne County outbreak.

REFERENCES

1. E. L. Baker, W. Patterson, S. Van Allmen, and J. Fleming, Economic impact of a community-wide waterborne outbreak of gastrointestinal illness, *Public Health Briefs*, **69**, 501–502 (1979).
2. L. K. Baker, Experiences and benefits of the application of minimum flow water conservation hardware, *in* "Proceedings of the National Water Conservation Conference on Publicly Supplied Potable Water, April 14–15, 1981, Denver, Colorado," p. 282 (1982).
3. G. S. Becker, A theory of the allocation of time, *Econom. J.*, **75**, 493–517 (1965).
4. Bureau of the Census, "1980 Census of the Population: General Population Characteristics, Pennsylvania," U.S. Department of Commerce, U.S. Government Printing Office, Washington, DC (1982).
5. B. S. Cooper and D. P. Rice, The economic cost of illness revisited, *Social Security Bull.*, February, 21–36 (1976).
6. G. F. Craun, Waterborne outbreaks of giardiasis, *in* "Waterborne Transmission of Giardiasis" (W. Jakubowski and J. C. Hoff, Eds.), Environmental Protection Agency, Health Effects Research Laboratory and Municipal Environmental Research Laboratory, Cincinnati, OH (Available from National Technical Information Service, Springfield, VA, PB 299-265) (1979).
7. R. T. Deacon and J. Sonstelie, Rationing by waiting and the value of time: Results from a natural experiment, *J. Politic. Econom.*, **93**, No. 4 (1985).
8. Denver Water Department, "Hogwash," Denver, CO (undated).
9. W. Harrington, A. Krupnick, and W. Spofford, "The Benefits of Preventing an Outbreak of Giardiasis due to Drinking Water Contamination," Report prepared for EPA, Resources for the Future, Washington, DC (1985).
10. W. Harrington and P. Portney, Valuing the benefits of health and safety regulation, *J. Urban Econom.*, **22**, 101–112 (1987).
11. B. S. Levy and W. McIntire, The economic impact of a food-borne salmonellosis outbreak, *J. Amer. Med. Assoc.*, **230**, 1281–1282 (1974).
12. E. Loehman and Vo Hu De, Application of stochastic choice modeling to policy analysis of public goods: A case study of air quality improvements, *Rev. Econom. Statist.* **64**, 474–480 (1982).
13. M. Schechter and I. Heiman, "Anxiety, Value of Life and Environmental Episodes," unpublished paper, University of Haifa (undated).
14. P. M. Schwab, Economic cost of St. Louis encephalitis epidemic in Dallas, Texas, 1966, *Public Health Rep.* **83**, 860–866 (1968).
15. W. Solley, Water use in the United States, *Popular Publications of the U.S. Geological Survey*, No. 1001 (1980).
16. G. Tolley *et al.*, "Valuation of Reductions in Human Health Symptoms and Risks," Vol. 3, "Contingent Valuation Study of Light Symptoms and Angina," Report prepared for EPA, University of Chicago (1986).
17. U.S. Department of Commerce, Bureau of the Census, "The Statistical Abstract of the United States," U.S. Government Printing Office (1984).
18. M. S. Wolfe, Managing the patient with giardiasis: Clinical, diagnostic and therapeutic aspects, *in* "Waterborne Transmission of Giardiasis" (W. Jakubowski and J. C. Hoff, Eds.), Prepared for Environmental Protection Agency, Health Effects Research Laboratory and Municipal Environmental Research Laboratory, Cincinnati, OH (available from National Technical Information Service, Springfield, VA, PB 299-265) (1979).

[25]

COLLECTIVE-CONSUMPTION SERVICES OF INDIVIDUAL-CONSUMPTION GOODS *

Burton A. Weisbrod

Certain commodities of a pure individual-consumption variety also possess characteristics of a pure collective-consumption good, 471. — In certain cases when individual-consumption goods cannot be provided profitably by private enterprise, it may serve the social welfare to subsidize their production, 474. — Conclusion, 476.

It is customary to distinguish individual-consumption (private) goods from collective-consumption (public) goods. To be sure these are polar cases; but to distinguish between them is to imply that a particular commodity cannot be at both poles. The principal objectives of this paper are: (1) to point out that a number of significant commodities exist which are apparently of a pure individual-consumption variety, but which also possess characteristics of a pure collective-consumption good; and (2) to discuss some implications of this observation, in particular showing that even if some apparently individual-consumption goods cannot profitably be provided by private enterprise it may serve the social welfare to subsidize their production.

The main point to be made below involves (a) the infrequency and uncertainty of purchase of particular commodities, and (b) the cost (in time or resources) of expanding production once it has been curtailed. Thus, I begin by considering an extreme case of a commodity the purchase of which is infrequent and uncertain, and production of which cannot be reinitiated at any cost once it has been halted and the inputs devoted to other uses. The commodity is a visit to a particular national park, such as Sequoia. Other illustrations will be discussed later and generalizations will be developed.

Let us assume that the location of the park and its means of access are such that it is easy to charge an admission fee of all consumers (users, viewers). Assume further that the park is privately owned, at least to begin with. (This assumption is useful for the following exposition, but it is not essential to the argument.)

* I have benefited from comments by William Baumol and William Bowen on an earlier draft of this paper, and from discussions with T. Aldrich Finegan. This paper was written while I was Visiting Lecturer in Economics, and Associate in Research (Industrial Relations Section), Princeton University, 1962–63

Next assume that the entrepreneur practices price discrimination among all park visitors, but that even so, total costs cannot be covered. There are no external economies of either production or consumption, at least in the usual forms. Finally, the commodity (service) is not storable; it cannot be purchased prior to consumption. Under these circumstances, allocative-efficiency considerations would dictate "closing" the park, assuming that private and social rates of discount are equal. Total benefits (revenue) falling short of costs, the "firm" should close down in the interest of efficiency, and its resources (trees, minerals) should be devoted to alternative uses.[1] Needless to say, this recommendation disregards income distribution considerations and other social goals except allocative efficiency.[2]

Such may seem to be the result of the usual Marshallian analysis. It is certainly true that a profit-maximizing entrepreneur would cease operating if all costs could not be covered — that is, if the present value of future costs exceeded the present value of future revenue. But it may be unsound socially for him to do so. To see why, the reader need recognize the existence of people who anticipate purchasing the commodity (visiting the park) at some time in the future, but who, in fact, never will purchase (visit) it. Nevertheless, if these consumers behave as "economic men" they will be willing to pay something for the option to consume the commodity in the future. This "option value" should influence the decision of whether or not to close the park and turn it to an alternative use. But it probably will not exert any influence if the private market is allocating resources, because there may be no practical mechanism by which the entrepreneur can charge nonusers for this option. Schemes to charge them can be imagined, but noncoercive devices may be extremely difficult to implement.[3] In any event, the point to

1. This view, with specific respect to national parks, is held by Milton Friedman. See his *Capitalism and Freedom* (Chicago: University of Chicago Press, 1962), p. 31. While the discussion here is in terms of current costs and revenues, it should be clear that, in principle, what is relevant to the closing-down decision is the present value of expected future costs and revenues.

2. Strictly speaking, another requirement, generally unfulfilled, for recommending closing is that prices equal marginal costs throughout the economy.

3. Since the option demand is automatically satisfied when the park operates, it will pay every potential user to mask his preferences in order to minimize his private cost. This, of course, is the usual problem of getting consumers to reveal their preferences for pure public goods (such as the option).

Against this background of "uncooperative" consumers, the inability of a private entrepreneur to enforce payment by nonusers is likely to be a serious problem. An entrepreneur could conceivably tell people each year that they must pay a fee for the option of consuming in the future (at the sale price effective then); thus admission would be denied anyone who did not have

be emphasized is that user charges (admission fees) are an inadequate (understated) guide to the total value of the park. And of course, if revenue is insufficient, so that the park is closed and its trees cut down, the option demands of potential future users would not be satisfied.

Nor is the issue simply one of short period versus long period demand. A potential consumer may have an option demand throughout his lifetime, and yet he may die without ever having purchased the commodity.[4]

If actual users were willing to pay enough to provide adequate profit, the park would remain in business, and the option demand of persons who were *not* current consumers would be satisfied at zero marginal cost. That is, as long as the park operates, provision of the option is a pure collective good of standard type: it (the option to consume in the future) may be "consumed" (enjoyed) by all persons simultaneously, and the consumption by one person does not subtract from the consumption opportunities for others. But when the park is on the verge of closing down (or reducing its scale), the option to consume in the future ceases being a a costless byproduct of the park's operations; the option demand would not be met at all if the firm closed (or would be met less satisfactorily if the firm reduced its scale) assuming that it could not reverse its action — e.g., because its giant trees had been cut down. In the interest of economic efficiency it would be desirable to keep the firm in business if the total of fees potentially collectable from current consumers *and* fees potentially collectable from prospective future consumers — including those who, in fact, will not become consumers — are adequate to cover costs.[5]

The collective-good aspect of the commodity — in satisfying the option demand — may be viewed as an external economy from current production; that is, current production enters positively into

option-tickets for *each* year prior to the time of purchase of the commodity (visit to the park). Such a scheme would surely be costly and cumbersome because of the large number of persons and undoubtedly very small per capita annual fees, the need to make collections throughout the country (not merely at the park), and the problem of lost receipts or expensive record-keeping.

4. The analogy with insurance may be drawn. Loss (purchase) is infrequent, and a person may, as in the case of property insurance, never have a loss though he pays annual premiums for the protection for many years. The insurance was providing a service, protection against a large financial loss, though the protection was only of a stand-by nature and was, in fact, never "used."

5. Of course, the latter might equal zero if the consumption of park services went out of fashion permanently, for then the option value would be zero. At the same time there might be no demand for current use of the park, and yet the option value could be positive.

the utility functions of *prospective* users. Or the park may be thought of as producing two outputs: services of an individual-consumption sort to actual users, and stand-by, or option, services of a collective-consumption sort to nonusers. The latter is difficult to sell especially if some of its "consumers" do not become actual users.

Infrequency and uncertainty of purchase are not the only conditions bringing about a potential deviation of optimal private from optimal social behavior. In the present context there is another requirement: expansion or recommencement of production at the time any occasional-purchasers wish to make a purchase must be difficult (in time or resources) or impossible; this implies that storage of the commodity (service) must be expensive — at the limit, impossible. In the case of a natural phenomenon such as Sequoia National Forest, if the trees were destroyed (allocated to alternative use), centuries would be required to restore them.

But a national park is an extreme case both in terms of the infrequent purchase of its services by most consumers, and the high cost of restarting production once its inputs have been redirected. Less extreme, but more numerous, examples would be hospitals. A hospital is utilized infrequently by most persons and not at all, by some; yet, like the national park, it provides a valuable stand-by service, so that its value cannot be measured by the number of its users or the fees collectable from them alone. This stand-by or option value may be sizable enough to justify the existence of the hospital on efficiency grounds, but the private entrepreneur without the power of taxation may have great difficulty in charging nonusers, and so may find the hospital to be continuously unprofitable. Again, the issue is more than one of the time horizon. The option will have value even for persons who never become patients, as it also will for former patients in the years between their last hospital admission and death. Of course, it must be reiterated that the option value is important for resource-allocation only to the extent that when added to user demand it would affect the level of supply — that is, would make the difference to a firm between remaining open and closing, or between opening in the first place and not doing so, or between providing a given increment of service or not.

A third example may suffice to indicate the frequency with which the option demand concept is relevant. Urban transit firms have come to recognize that persons who normally walk or use private automobiles will occasionally use public transportation — e.g., when weather is bad, or when the auto breaks down. These and other occasional users may patronize the transit system once or twice a year, or even less often. Yet an option demand will exist for the stand-by facilities. A structure of user charges which differentiates between classes of users can perhaps be developed, though cases in which they have been used successfully are difficult to find. In any case, such a structure would still not catch persons who never use the system, but who value its availability.[6]

A system of user charges designed to capture *some* of the option demand would charge the occasional rider more per ride than the regular rider, *ceteris paribus*. Tokens sold in large quantity lots at rates below the cash fare are sometimes used, but differentials are usually minor. If the differential grew, it would be increasingly circumvented by resales from regular to occasional patrons. Thus, the tokens, tickets, etc., would have to be made nontransferable. And so the administrative problems would grow.

It is interesting to note that the argument for levying greater user fees on occasional users (as a means of tapping their option demand) may conflict with the argument for levying greater fees on rush-hour users (as a means of indicating the high marginal cost of the service they consume).[7] Rush-hour users are frequently regular users. Thus, on balance it may be sensible to have lower fees for regular, rush-hour users than for occasional, nonrush-hour users.

Actually, four classes of users may be distinguished: (1) regular nonrush-hour, (2) regular rush-hour, (3) occasional nonrush-hour, (4) occasional rush-hour. Class (1) users would qualify for low charges on both cost and option-demand grounds; at the opposite extreme, class (4) users would be subjected to high charges on both grounds. Between these limits would be the charges to class (3) and class (2) users. Class (2) would be charged *less* than class (3) with respect to the option demand, but *more* with respect to costs. Thus, depending on the relative weights attached to each

---

6. It may be socially profitable to maintain a currently-unprofitable transit system because of the possibility that highway congestion in the future may produce a greater demand for it. However, this is beside the point being made here. Private entrepreneurs may be expected to take this future demand into account insofar as it is translated into sales. But insofar as that demand reflects the (option) demand of persons who, *ex post*, do not purchase the service, it will, presumably, not affect the decisions of private producers regarding the level of services.

7. A strenuous advocate of lower charges for off-peak users of urban transport service in particular is William Vickrey; see, for example, his "Pricing in Urban and Suburban Transport," presented to a session of the American Economic Association, December 28, 1962, mimeographed, p. 4.

factor, a group of rush-hour users might be charged less than a group of nonrush-hour users.

Now to generalize. The fact that the revenue of a private operator is limited, as a practical matter, to user charges prevents his capturing the option demand of nonusers. It follows that the inability of the operator to make a profit does not necessarily imply the economic inefficiency of the firm. If he had the power to tax he could supplement user charges with charges for the option services being generated.

The range of frequency of purchase for various commodities is a wide one, from once-in-a-lifetime attendance at a national park to daily purchase of tap water. "Infrequent purchase" is a matter of degree. Similarly, costs of expanding production to meet the demand of occasional purchasers exist for all commodities, although in varying degrees. It seems, therefore, that in principle the option demand exists for all commodities. The more frequently the commodity is purchased (the smaller the ratio of "occasional" to "regular" purchasers), and the less costly the expansion of output, the smaller will be the significance of the option demand — the easier it will be for sellers to rely on a system of user charges.

Even for those commodities purchased infrequently, the option demand is of no significance so long as production is sufficiently profitable to insure that output can be provided at a level adequate to meet the demand of the infrequent purchaser. The all-night drug store, for example, presumably makes sufficient sales at night, at regular or specially-high prices, to cover its added costs, and so it remains open and provides a stand-by service for many non-customers. Under these conditions the option demand is satisfied as a costless by-product of production for current purchasers. But the option demand becomes important with respect to resource-allocation decisions when user charges (current and discounted future) begin to fall short of costs at the margin of service, so that private entrepreneurs will cease or curtail operations. Recognition of the option demand may dictate continued operation in the social interest, with "losses" made up from charges (taxes) on "occasional" purchasers. This is simply an extension of the well-known proposition that achievement of an optimal level of output in an industry generating external economies (in this case, fulfilling the option demand) requires subsidization. Consequently there appears to be an a priori case for at least consideration of public operation or subsidy when a producer of an infrequently-purchased, nonstorable commodity with sharply-rising short-period marginal costs con-

COLLECTIVE-CONSUMPTION SERVICES 477

templates closing or cutting service because of unprofitable operations. Of course, if the sum of user charges and the value of the option-demand falls short of costs (on a present-value basis), then efficient resource allocation would require that operations be halted or curtailed and resources shifted to alternative uses.

Although it is only at the margin of closing down or, in general, of curtailing supply, that the option demand is relevant, these are precisely the points at which the question is likely to arise: should the private firm be subsidized or possibly operated publicly rather than permit its services to be cut? The argument presented above does not imply an affirmative answer in all cases. It does imply that a negative answer is not necessarily justified, even on the grounds of allocative efficiency.

COUNCIL OF ECONOMIC ADVISERS
WASHINGTON, D.C.

UNIVERSITY OF WISCONSIN

[26]

JOURNAL OF ENVIRONMENTAL ECONOMICS AND MANAGEMENT 1, 132–149 (1974)

Bidding Games for Valuation of Aesthetic Environmental Improvements [1]

ALAN RANDALL

*Department of Agricultural Economics, University of Kentucky,
Lexington, Kentucky 40506*

AND

BERRY IVES AND CLYDE EASTMAN

*Department of Agricultural Economics and Agricultural Business,
New Mexico State University, Las Cruces, New Mexico 88003*

Received March 19, 1974

An empirical case study of the benefits of abatement of aesthetic environmental damage associated with the Four Corners power plant and Navajo mine using the bidding game technique is presented. Bidding games were carefully designed to avoid the potential problems inherent in that technique. The results indicate the existence of substantial benefits from abatement of this aesthetic environmental damage. Aggregate bid curves, marginal bid curves, and estimates of the income elasticity of bid are presented. The effectiveness of the bidding game technique is discussed.

It has proved a difficult and often forbidding task to ascribe economic values to environmental improvements. Yet, rational and informed social decision making requires, among other things, a consideration of the economic costs and benefits of environmental improvements. The difficulties in economic evaluation are compounded in the case of environmental improvements of an aesthetic nature. This article discusses the problems inherent in the valuation of aesthetic environmental improvements and presents a case study in which bidding games were used as the valuation technique.

THE THEORY

Aesthetic damage to an outdoor environment, to the extent that it diminishes the utility of some individuals, is a discommodity and its abatement is a commodity. Abatement of this kind of external diseconomy is both a nonmarket good, since it is nonexclusive, and a public good in the sense of Davis and Whinston [6], since it is inexhaustible at least over a very substantial range. That is, additional consumers of this kind of aesthetic environmental improvement can be added without diminishing the visibility or scenic beauty available to each (at least, until crowding occurs). Additional users can be added at near zero marginal cost, over a substantial range.

Bradford [2] has presented a theoretical framework for the valuation of public goods. Traditional demand curves are inappropriate for the analysis of demand for

[1] Journal Article 506, New Mexico State University, Agricultural Experiment Station, Las Cruces. The authors are grateful for helpful comments from Ralph d'Arge and two anonymous reviewers.

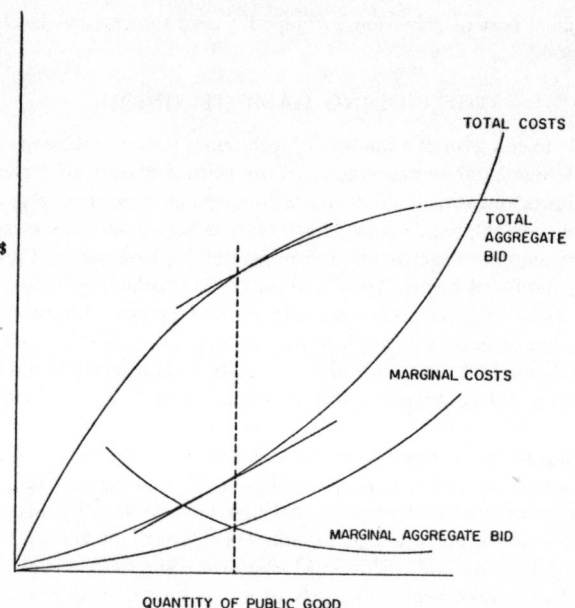

FIG. 1. Collective optimization of the quantity of public good provided.

public goods, since the situation is not one of individuals responding to a parametric
price per unit by choosing an appropriate number of units. Rather, the individual
directly arrives at the total value to himself of various given packages. In the case of
a public good, the individual is unable to exercise any choice over the quantity provided him, except as a member of the collective which makes a collective choice.
Further, the nature of a public good such as aesthetic environmental improvements
is such that increases in the quantity provided are not purely quantitative increases,
but are more in the nature of improvements in quality. Thus, the individual values
alternative packages of a public good, which may differ in quantity and quality.

Bradford proposes the concept of an aggregate bid curve for public goods. Individual bid curves are simply indifference curves passing through a given initial state,
with the numeraire good (which can be dollars) on the vertical axis and the public
good on the horizontal axis.[2] The aggregate bid curve is the algebraic (or vertical, in
diagrammatic analyses) summation of individual bids over the relevant population.

The aggregate bid curve is an aggregate benefit curve, as it measures precisely what
an accurate benefit-cost analysis of provision of a public good would measure as
benefits. Using the approach of methodological collectivism, efficiency in the provision of a public good can be achieved by maximizing the excess of aggregate bid
over total cost, or equating the first derivative of aggregate bid (i.e., marginal bid)

---

[2] If different packages of a public good represented continuous quantitative increases, the individual bid curve would be smooth and would exhibit decreasing marginal utility of increasing quantities
of the public good. However, Bradford's concept of different packages differing in quantity and
quality logically implies that individual bid curves need be neither smooth nor of continually decreasing slope. Bradford insists that, *a priori*, nothing can be said about the slope of the "demand," or
marginal bid curve, for a public good of this nature.

134   RANDALL, IVES AND EASTMAN

with the marginal cost of provision.[3] Figure 1 shows the efficient level of provision of a public good.[4]

THE BIDDING GAME TECHNIQUE

It is possible to conceive of a number of techniques for estimating the aggregate bid curve for environmental improvements. Two general classes of techniques, direct costing techniques and revealed demand techniques, have been suggested in the literature and applied in empirical studies. Each of these has its difficulties, especially when adapted for valuation of aesthetic environmental improvements. These techniques will be briefly discussed below. Then, a third type of technique, bidding games, will be proposed. Bidding game techniques are themselves not without difficulties, but we will argue that there may be applications for which they are the preferable or even the only feasible method for empirical studies. Methods of maximizing the reliability of bidding games will be discussed and an empirical study using bidding games will be presented.

Direct costing methods. Implicit in the concept of a "marginal value of damage avoided by abatement" curve, as proposed by Kneese and Bower [12], is the idea of estimating the benefits of abatement of environmental damage by directly estimating the costs attributable to that damage. Several workers have made progress along these lines. For example, Lave and Seskin [13] have had some success in relating the costs of impairment of human health to levels of air pollution. If all relevant costs of a particular incidence of environmental damage can be identified, evaluated and summed, a curve relating the value of damage avoided to levels of environmental improvements can be fitted. The first derivative of this curve is the "M.V.D.A." curve of Kneese and Bower [12].

These costing techniques are theoretically sound and may often be feasible in practice. However, difficulties may be introduced by the unavailability of information and the pricing and accounting problems inherent in this type of analysis. These techniques will have limited application in valuation of aesthetic environmental improvements, since the costs of aesthetic damages may seldom be directly reflected in the market.

Revealed demand techniques. Revealed demand techniques have been widely used for estimation of the demand for outdoor recreation, often a nonmarket good.[5] A number of applications to valuation of the benefits of air pollution abatement have been made [1, 11, 14, 16, 18]. The principle is as follows. The benefits of provision of a nonmarket good are inferred from the revealed demand for some suitable proxy. In the case of air pollution abatement, the revealed demand for residential land is related by regression analysis to air pollution concentrations. In metropolitan areas, it is possible to obtain information on the concentration of specific air pollutants in different parts of the city. If all other variables relevant to the valuation of urban residential land can be identified[6] and measured, it ought to be possible to determine by

---

[3] In the approach of methodological individualism, Pareto-efficiency is still not achieved since the price to the individual cannot equal the marginal cost to the individual (which is zero) and allow collection of sufficient funds to cover the total cost of provision.

[4] In Fig. 1, the aggregate and marginal bid curves are drawn as smooth curves consistent with diminishing marginal utility. As pointed out in footnote 2, this need not be even the typical case.

[5] See [4].

[6] Some appropriate variables are size and value of structures on the land, distance from places where services and employment opportunities are concentrated, proportion of park land and open space in the neighborhood, density of population, proportion of various racial and ethnic minorities in the immediate vicinity, and the incidence of violent crimes.

regression analysis the extent to which air pollution concentrations affect observed land values. In this way, a proxy measure of the benefits of air pollution abatement is obtained.

There are a number of difficulties with this type of analysis. Since the value ascribed to air pollution control is derived directly from the regression coefficient of the pollution concentration variable, accurate results require perfect and complete specification of the regression equation. In an interesting recent study, Wieand [17] claims that when such regression models are completely specified, the regression coefficient of the pollution concentration variable may not be significantly different from zero. Another difficulty, researchers in the field agree, lies in interpretation of the results. Are all of the benefits of air pollution abatement captured in residential land values? Most think not. For our purposes, the other side of that coin is of interest: Surely some benefits in addition to the aesthetic benefits are captured. Which additional benefits?

In the case study reported below, the geographical area affected by environmental damage includes urban areas, but also rural and agricultural areas, and substantial areas of Indian reservation and National Park, Monument, and Forest lands (which are typically not exchanged in the market). Thus, those revealed demand techniques currently available would seem to be inapplicable to the situation faced in our study.

Bidding games. In analysis of the demand for outdoor recreation, Davis [7] pioneered in the use of bidding games. During personal interviews, the enumerator follows on iterative questioning procedure to elicit responses which enable the fitting of a demand curve for the services offered by a recreation area. Respondents are asked to answer "yes" or "no" to the question: Would you continue to use this recreation area if the cost to you was to increase by X dollars? The amount is varied up or down in repetitive questions, and the highest positive response is recorded. Individual responses may then be aggregated to generate a demand curve for the recreation services provided by the area.

It seems reasonable that bidding games may be adapted to the estimation of the benefits from provision of an inexhaustible nonmarket good such as abatement of aesthetic environmental damage. Bidding games would seem to be the most direct method of estimating Bradford's aggregate benefit curve, which is derived from vertical summation of individual bid curves. The difficulties of interpretation which are inherent in the revealed demand techniques developed thus far do not occur when the bidding game technique is used. The data obtained with bidding games are not cost observations but individuals' perceptions of value. Thus, bidding games can be used in situations where direct costing techniques are ineffective for lack of data. These advantages of bidding games over revealed demand and direct costing techniques seem sufficient to justify attempts to adapt the bidding game technique for use in valuation of aesthetic environmental improvements.

Some General Considerations in the Design of Bidding Games

Bidding games are designed to elicit information on the hypothetical behavior of respondents when faced with hypothetical situations. In the case study presented below, the purpose of bidding games is to provide a measure of the benefits of aesthetic environmental improvements by measuring the willingness of a sample of respondents to pay for such improvements. The efficacy of bidding games used for this purpose depends on the reliability with which stated hypothetical behavior is converted to action, should the hypothetical situation posited in the game arise in actuality.

Willingness to pay is the behavioral dimension of an underlying attitude: concern for environmental quality.[7] Sociologists and public opinion researchers have built up a substantial body of literature which considers ways in which survey techniques of measuring attitudes and their behavioral component can be made as reliable as possible. Some desirable characteristics of such surveys have been identified [5, 9]. The hypothetical situation presented should be realistic and credible to respondents. Realism and credibility can be achieved by satisfying the following criteria for survey instrument design: Test items must have properties similar to those in the actual situation; situations posited must be concrete rather than symbolic; and test items should involve institutionalized or routinized behavior, where role expectations of respondents are well defined. Where the behavioral predisposition under study are affected by attitudes about a number of different things, the test instrument must be designed to focus upon those attitudes which are relevant. An example may be helpful. In the case study reported here, willingness to pay additional taxes to achieve aesthetic environmental improvement is affected by attitudes toward environmental quality, but also by attitudes toward the current tax burden and attitudes toward the idea of receptors of pollutants paying to obtain abatement of emissions. If the survey is carried out for the purpose of measuring the benefits of abatement, the test instrument must be designed to take cognizance of the various diverse attitudes which affect willingness to pay and to allow isolation of the relevant attitudinal dimensions.

Since abatement of aesthetic environmental damage is an inexhaustible, public good, bidding games intended to provide data for valuation of that good must be designed to avoid the effects of the freeloader problem, which encourages nonrevelation of preferences. One method would be to design games in which each respondent is told that all consumers of the good would pay for it on a similar basis, thus eliminating the possibility of freeloading.

With careful design of bidding games to ensure that the responses recorded are predictive of behavior, it should be possible to use the bidding technique to estimate the benefits of environmental improvements with reasonable accuracy.

AN EMPIRICAL APPLICATION:

ESTIMATION OF THE BENEFITS OF ABATEMENT OF AESTHETIC ENVIRONMENTAL DAMAGES ASSOCIATED WITH THE FOUR CORNERS STEAM ELECTRIC GENERATING PLANT

At New Mexico State University, research is under way to examine the socioeconomic impacts of development of the rapidly expanding coal strip-mining and steam electric generation industry in the Four Corners Region (southwestern United States), and to predict the impacts of alternative policies with respect to environmental management and economic development, as such policies would affect the industry. One facet of this research required estimation of the benefits of abatement of aesthetic environmental damage associated with the Four Corners power plant at Fruitland, NM, and the Navajo mine which provides its raw energy source—low energy, low sulfur, high ash, sub-bituminous coal.[8]

_____

[7] Three dimensions of attitudes are recognized [8]: (1) a cognitive dimension, (2) an affectual dimension, and (3) a behavioral dimension.

[8] The following facts may provide some idea of the magnitude of this operation and its attendant environmental problems. In 1970, the power plant had a capacity of 2,080 MW. The mine provides

The mine–power plant complex causes several kinds of aesthetic environmental damage. Particulates, sulfur oxides and nitrous oxides are emitted into the air. The adverse effects of particulate pollutants on visibility is considered the most important aesthetic impact of the complex. The strip-mining process will create some aesthetic damage. Although the soil banks will be leveled, reclamation in the sense of re-establishing a viable plant and animal eco-system is uncertain. Transmission lines radiate from the plant in several directions, passing through the Navajo Reservation and bringing the paraphernalia of development to a landscape which is in some places very beautiful and otherwise untouched.[9]

It was decided to use bidding games to measure the benefits of abatement of the aesthetic environmental damage associated with the Four Corners power plant and the Navajo mine.[10] Considerable attention was devoted to the design and development of bidding games which provide a reliable estimator of these benefits.

Questionnaire Design

The bidding games were part of prepared schedules designed for use in a personal interview survey of samples of users of the Four Corners Interstate Air Quality Control Region environment (i.e., residents and recreational visitors to the region). In preparation for the bidding games, respondents were asked a series of questions about environmental matters, to focus their attention on that topic. Then, the subject of the coal–electricity complex in the Four Corners area was explicitly raised. The respondents were shown three sets of photographs depicting three levels of environmental damage around the Four Corners Power Plant, near Fruitland, NM.

Set A showed the plant circa 1969, prior to installation of some additional emissions control equipment, producing its historical maximum emissions of air pollutants. Another photograph depicted the spoil banks as they appear following strip-mining, but prior to leveling. A third photograph showed electricity transmission lines marring the landscape. Set A depicted the highest level of environmental damage, and accurately represented the actual situation in the early years of operation of the plant.

Set B showed an intermediate level of damage. One photograph showed the plant circa 1972, after additional controls had reduced particulate emissions (i.e., the type of emissions most destructive of visibility). Another showed the spoil banks leveled but not revegetated; a third showed the transmission lines placed less obtrusively (i.e., at some distance from major roads).

Set C was intended to depict a situation where the industries continued to operate,

---

coal at a rate of 8.5 millions tons annually. Over the 40 year projected life span of the mine, 31,000 acres will be stripped. In 1970, approximately 550 people were employed in the mine and power plant, total value of sales of electricity was $146 million, and 96,000 tons of particulates, 73,000 tons of sulfur oxides and 66,000 tons of nitrous oxides were emitted annually.

[9] To place this aesthetic environmental damage in perspective, it may be useful to point out that the Four Corners Interstate Air Quality Control Region includes the greatest concentration of National Parks and Monuments in the United States and a number of Indian reservations, the largest of which are the Navajo and Hopi reservations. The value of the region for tourism and recreation depends largely on its bizarre and unusual landscapes, the enjoyment of which requires excellent long distance visibility and depth and color perception. There exists a substantial minority of "traditional" Native Americans who have strong religious and cultural attachments to nature, and who resent the air pollution, strip-mining, and transmission lines; witness the prolonged litigation about location of the Tucson Gas and Electric Company transmission line from the San Juan power plant, which is under construction about 9 miles from the Four Corners plant.

[10] In that part of the overall study which deals with nonaesthetic environmental damage, direct costing techniques are used.

446 *The Economics of the Environment*

138   RANDALL, IVES AND EASTMAN

but with minimal environmental damage. One photograph showed the plant with visible emissions reduced to zero.[11] A second photograph showed a section of arid land in its natural state; it was intended to depict a situation where the transmission lines were placed underground and the strip-mined land completely reclaimed.

The interviewers pointed out the salient features of each set of photographs to each respondent. For most of the respondents (with the exception of many recreationists), the situations were rooted in real experience: the residents of the region were familiar with the plant and mine, and their operation for the previous eight years. Most remembered situation A well, for that was exactly how it was only a few years earlier. Situation B was a fairly good approximation of the real situation at the time of the interviews. With the help of the photographs, situation C would be readily visualized.

Since the fitting of bid or benefit curves requires an expression of willingness to pay for abatement of aesthetic damages, it was necessary to design games based upon appropriate vehicles of payment. The vehicles for payment were chosen so as to maximize the realism and credibility of the hypothetical situation posited to respondents. As will be discussed below, it was necessary to design and use a series of bidding games, because no one vehicle of payment was appropriate for use with all of the subpopulations sampled. First, the general format applicable to all games is discussed. Then, the particular games used for particular subpopulations are discussed.

For each bidding game played, respondents were asked to consider situation A, the highest level of environmental damage, as the starting point. The bidding games were designed to elicit the highest amount of money which the respondent, an adult speaking for his or her household, was willing to pay in order to improve the aesthetic environment to situation C, and to situation B. Answers were elicited in terms of "yes" or "no" to questions expressed in the form "would you pay amount X . . . ?" A "yes" answer would lead the enumerator to raise the amount and repeat the question, maybe several times, until a "no" answer was obtained. A "no" answer would lead the enumerator to reduce the amount until a "yes" answer was obtained. The amount which elicited the highest "yes" answer was recorded as the amount the respondent was willing to pay.

It was emphasized that the respondent was to assume that the vehicle for payment used in a particular game was the only possible way in which environmental improvements could be obtained. This stipulation was designed to minimize the incidence of zero bids as protests against either the zero liability rule implicit in "willingness to pay" games or the particular method of payment used in a particular game. If a respondent indicated that he was willing to pay nothing at all, he was asked a series of questions to find out why. A respondent indicating that he did not consider his household to be harmed in any way by the environmental damage and, therefore, saw no reason to pay for environmental improvements was recorded as bidding zero. If a respondent indicated that his zero bid was in protest against the game, his answer was analyzed as a nonresponse to the bidding game, since he had refused to play the game by the stated rules.[12]

---

[11] This feat was accomplished by photographing the plant on a day when all units were shut down.

[12] For the purpose of estimating the benefits of abatement, the treatment of "protest bids" as non-responses is legitimate. By definition, a "protest bid" recognizes that positive benefits from abatement exist, but registers a protest against a particular method of financing abatement. We recognize that the elimination of "protest bids" from analyses aimed at estimating the benefits of abatement fails to remove all downward bias from the responses to particular games: some respondents may bid low (i.e., underestimate the benefits to themselves of abatement) in conscious or subconscious protest against the method of financing assumed in a game.

The selection of appropriate vehicles for payment provided a challenge. People are not accustomed to paying for abatement of air pollution and strip-mining damage. However, they are accustomed to paying for many other types of useful goods and services, many of which, such as parks and highway beautification, have aesthetic or "quality of life" components. So selection of realistic vehicles for payment was not impossible. However, the heterogeneous nature of the affected population meant that no single vehicle was suitable for data collection among all groups. In the Four Corners Region, the affected population can be divided into three broad groups: (1) the residents of Indian reservations, primarily Navajos, but also including members of several other tribes; (2) the residents of the nonreservation sections of the region, primarily Anglo-Americans, but with a sprinkling of Spanish-Americans, Native Americans living off the reservations, and other minorities; and (3) the tourists and recreationists who visit the area to enjoy its unique natural, historical and cultural attractions. Different versions of the questionnaire, using bidding games based on different vehicles for payment, were constructed for use with the three different subpopulations of the affected population.

The particular bidding games used are described below.

The sales tax game. Members of all three subpopulations are familiar with the practice of paying sales taxes. For most, this is a frequent occurrence. It is also understood by most that income collected in sales taxes is used to provide useful public services. It does not require much imagination to conceive of a public agency collecting a sales tax from residents of the affected region and using the income to finance environmental improvements.

The sales tax bidding game was used for both the resident samples. It was not used with the recreationist sample, since that group often purchased only a few items in the region, bringing most of their equipment and supplies with them. This would make a regional sales tax largely irrelevant for that group.

Respondents were asked to assume that a regional sales tax was collected on all purchases in the Four Corners Interstate Air Quality Control Region for the purpose of financing environmental improvements.[13] All revenue from the additional tax would be used for abatement of aesthetic environmental damage associated with the power plant and mine, and all citizens would be required to pay the tax. Recreational visitors to the region would contribute to environmental improvement through payment of additional users fees for facilities.

The electricity bill game. The monthly electricity bill seemed to be a suitable vehicle for measurement of willingness to pay. It is the production of electricity which causes the environmental damage, and most people can readily comprehend that reduction of the damage may raise the cost of operating the industry and that passing these additional costs on to consumers of electricity is a not unlikely outcome. For the residents of those sections of the region outside the Indian reservations, payment of a monthly electricity bill is a routinized behavior. Therefore, a bidding game based upon the monthly electricity bill was played with the nonreservation resident sample.

This game was unsuitable for use with the other two samples. Many residents of

---

"Protest bids" were recorded and used in some other types of analyses. For example, the incidence of "protest bids" is an indicator of the relative political acceptability of various methods of financing abatement.

[13] The regional sales tax would be additional to current state and local sales taxes and would be charged on all commodities subject to existing state and local sales taxes.

Indian reservations do not have electricity available in their homes. Recreationists do not pay monthly electricity bills while vacationing away from home.

The respondent was first asked the amount of his monthly household electricity bill. He was then asked to imagine that an additional charge was added to his electricity bill, and the electricity bills of everyone who uses electricity produced in the Four Corners Region, even people as far away as southern California. All of the additional money collected would be used to repair the aesthetic environmental damage caused as a result of electricity production and transmission in the Four Corners region.

The user fees game. Measuring recreationists' willingness to pay for environmental improvements raised problems which prevented use of the electricity bill and sales tax games. For the recreationists, a satisfactory game would need to focus upon (1) the activities associated with vacationing, and (2) the collection of payments while they are in the region and using the regional environment. The payment of user fees for recreation services (i.e., campsite, utilities hook-up, boat launching), seemed to be a promising vehicle for a bidding game for the recreationists. If visitors were concerned about environmental quality in the places where they vacation, the payment of an additional sum along with their usual daily user fees would provide a suitable way to express that concern.

A sample of recreationists in the national parks, monuments and forests and state parks in the region played a bidding game based on user fees. Only recreationists who were not residents of the region were included. They were first asked the total sum of user fees they paid daily. They were then asked to suppose user fees in all the recreation areas in the Four Corners area were increased. All the additional money collected would be spent on environmental improvements. All recreators would pay and the year-round residents would pay, too, through additional regional sales taxes.

The Conduct of the Survey

The bidding games, as described above, were included in prepared schedules which also served as the instrument for collection of data for socioeconomic analysis of citizen environmental concern. Personal interviews were conducted by enumerators who were closely supervised and who had been carefully trained in formal sessions and in two separate field pre-tests of the questionnaire. Interviews were conducted during the summer of 1972.

Usable questionnaires were completed by 526 residents of nonreservation sections of the Four Corners Interstate Air Quality Control Region, 71 residents of Indian reservations and 150 recreators and tourists from outside the region who were using recreation sites within the region. The ratio of reservation residents to nonreservation residents sampled was proportional to their total numbers in the regional population; the size of the recreationist sample was chosen arbitrarily. Respondents from each subpopulation were selected by stratified random sampling. Stratification was based on concentration of air pollutants above the respondent's home or recreation site, as estimated by an atmospheric diffusion model developed as part of the larger research project. The population in higher pollution concentration zones was sampled more heavily.

Analysis and Results

For the *determination of three points on the aggregate bid curve*, corresponding to the situations, A, B, and C, the bidding game results were aggregated by methods appro-

TABLE I

AGGREGATE BIDS FOR ABATEMENT OF AESTHETIC ENVIRONMENTAL DAMAGE
ASSOCIATED WITH THE FOUR CORNERS POWER PLANT, 1972

Item	Situation		
	A	B	C
Emissions (tons of particulates per year)	96,000	26,000	0
Level of abatement (tons of particulates per year)	0	70,000	96,000
Estimated regional aggregate bid ($ millions per year)	0	15.54	24.57
Standard error ($ millions per year)	—	1.24	1.52
95% Confidence limits ($ millions per year)	—	±2.43	±2.97
Estimated consumer aggregate bid ($ millions per year)	0	11.25	19.31
Standard error ($ millions per year)	—	0.68	0.98
95% Confidence limits ($ millions per year)	—	±1.33	±1.92

priate to the stratified random sampling technique used, to provide estimates of the total bid for the relevant population. Two methods of aggregation were used, to generate two different aggregate bid curves.

(1) The results of the sales tax game with area residents (reservation and non-reservation) were added to the results of user fee games played by recreators to estimate a total regional willingness to pay for three levels of environmental improvement.

(2) The results of the electricity bill game were extrapolated over all consumers of power from the Four Corners plant to estimate consumer willingness to pay. This latter procedure involved the ethical premise that, since the production of electricity causes environmental damage, all citizens who consume Four Corners power ought to be willing to pay as much in additional electricity charges for environmental improvements as those who live in the region which suffers the damage. However appealing this ethical premise may be, our survey did not include people outside the region. Thus the consumer bid cannot be interpreted as an estimate of true "willingness to pay." It would be interesting to extend this research to include bidding games for these consumers of Four Corners electricity who do not live or recreate in the affected environment.

While both the regional and consumer aggregate bids are of interest, the authors believe that more faith may be placed in the regional bid since that bid was derived from samples of all segments of its relevant population.

Table I presents the estimated aggregate bids, standard errors, and 95% confidence limits at points A, B, and C. Regional and consumer bids are presented.

Using the estimated aggregate bids (Table I), a *regional aggregate bid curve* and a *consumer aggregate bid curve* were fitted. To fit two-dimensional aggregate bid curves, it was necessary to select a single independent variable to serve as a proxy for the total package of aesthetic environmental improvements under consideration. Situations A, B, and C were defined so that all three forms of aesthetic damage (air pollution, strip-mining, and transmission lines) were successively reduced together from their most obtrusive in situation A to virtual elimination in C. Of the three forms of damage, reduced visibility due to particulate air pollution was considered by respondents to be far and away the most serious. So, abatement of particulate air pollutant emissions (measured as the difference, in tons per year, between the level at A and the levels at

142   RANDALL, IVES AND EASTMAN

TABLE II

Tests of Hypotheses Concerning the Slopes of the Aggregate Bid Curves

	Hypothesis	Confidence of rejecting H_0	
		Regional aggregate bid curve (%)	Consumer aggregate bid curve %
1.	The aggregate bid curve is of linear positive slope[a]	99.9	99.9
2.	The aggregate bid for situation B is one half of that for C[b]	99.9	94.5

[a] Rejection implies that the aggregate bid curve is of increasing positive slope.
[b] Rejection implies that the aggregate bid for B exceeds one half of that for C.

B and C, respectively) was arbitrarily chosen to serve as a single independent variable for graphical analyses.[14]

The form of the curve requires some discussion. It has already been noted [footnote 2] that the usual restraints placed on the slope of demand curves are inappropriate for the first derivatives of aggregate bid curves for public goods, due to the impossibility of separating quantity and quality factors. Here we have a case in point. It seems resonable that "consumers" of abatement of particulate emissions desire the attribute, visibility. Given the reasonable assumption that marginal utility of additional visibility is diminishing, one would expect the first derivative of the aggregate bid curve for visibility to be of negative slope.

Meteorologists have established that an inverse relationship exists between visibility and concentration of particulate pollutants. Visibility increases at an increasing rate as particulate pollution (measured in terms of weight) is abated [3, 10]. Therefore, the slope of the marginal aggregate bid curve for abatement of emissions (in tons per year) is *a priori* unpredictable, since the diminishing marginal utility of visibility and the increasing marginal visibility resulting from additional abatement influence that slope in opposite ways.

In terms of visibility, the aggregate bid curve form which provided the best fit of the three data points was

$$B = c \ln (v),$$

where B = aggregate bid in dollars, c = a constant, and v = visibility.

In terms of abatement of particulate air pollutants (measured in tons per year), the appropriate curve form was

$$B(q) = c \ln \frac{k}{k - q},$$

[14] In the case study at hand, we recognize the inelegance introduced by this procedure. We do not believe it does serious violence to the truth, since most of the aesthetic environmental damage occurring is, in fact, due to particulate air pollutants. We emphasize, however, that this problem should not typically occur in the use of aggregate bid methodology and bidding game techniques. Rather, its occurrence here was a special case and is attributable to our need to value a package of different aesthetic environmental improvements within the following constraints: (1) a limited research budget, which confined us to one personal interview survey, and (2) the need to limit the length of each interview, to avoid exhausting the patience of respondents.

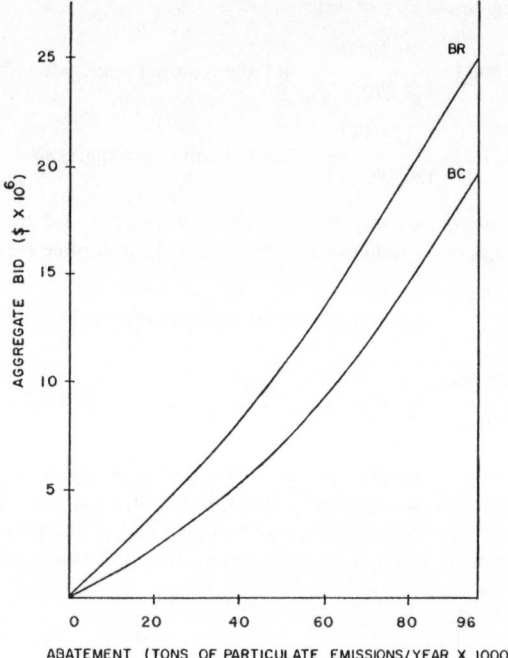

FIG. 2. Estimated aggregate bid curves for abatement of aesthetic environmental damage, Four Corners power plant, 1972. BR, Regional aggregate bid; BC, Consumer aggregate bid.

where k = a parameter relating visibility to emissions, which is determined behaviorally, and q = tons of particulate emissions abated annually.

The aggregate bid curve fitted using this equation form passes through the origin, as logically it must, given that rational citizens would bid zero for zero abatement. The first derivative of the aggregate bid curve is of positive slope.[15] Statistical tests (Table II) resulted in rejection of the hypotheses (1) that the aggregate bid curve was linear, or of decreasing positive slope, and (2) that the aggregate bid at point B was simply one-half of that at C. Regional and consumer aggregate bid curves are presented (Fig. 2).

[15] It must be emphasized that the curve form used provided the best fit, given the three data points available. It would have been desirable to have collected information adequate to generate more data points. The decision to collect data for only three points was made in recognition of limits to the patience of respondents. The multipurpose schedule was already quite lengthy, given the need to collect data relevant to the situation of the respondent, play the bidding games, and collect socio-economic, sociological and attitudinal data.

It is recognized that, if more data points had been available, a different curve form may have been appropriate. The possibility of a sigmoid aggregate bid curve is logically appealing. Such a curve would have a segment of increasing slope, where the increasing marginal visibility from particulate abatement dominates the decreasing marginal utility of additional visibility then, as complete abatement is approached (i.e., somewhere to the right of our point B), the slope may become decreasing as the diminishing marginal utility of visibility becomes dominant. Such a curve form would be consistent with theoretical considerations and with the three data points available.

The fitted aggregate bid curves were:

$$B_r = \$29,175,840 \ln \frac{168,890}{168,890 - q}, \quad \text{for the regional aggregate bid curve, and}$$

$$B_c = \$15,396,700 \ln \frac{134,490}{134,490 - q}, \quad \text{for the consumer aggregate bid curve.}$$

Marginal aggregate bid curves, or *price curves*, were generated by taking the first derivatives of the aggregate bid curves (Fig. 3). The derived price curves were:

$$P_r = \$\frac{29,175,840}{168,890 - q}, \quad \text{derived from the regional aggregate bid curve, and}$$

$$P_c = \$\frac{15,396,700}{134,490 - q}, \quad \text{derived from the consumer aggregate bid curve.}$$

These derived price curves are very useful for public policy analyses with respect to optimal environmental management policies. In Fig. 4, a hypothetical derived price curve is presented, along with a hypothetical marginal cost of abatement curve. In this hypothetical example, the optimal level of abatement is *S*. A standard allowing maxi-

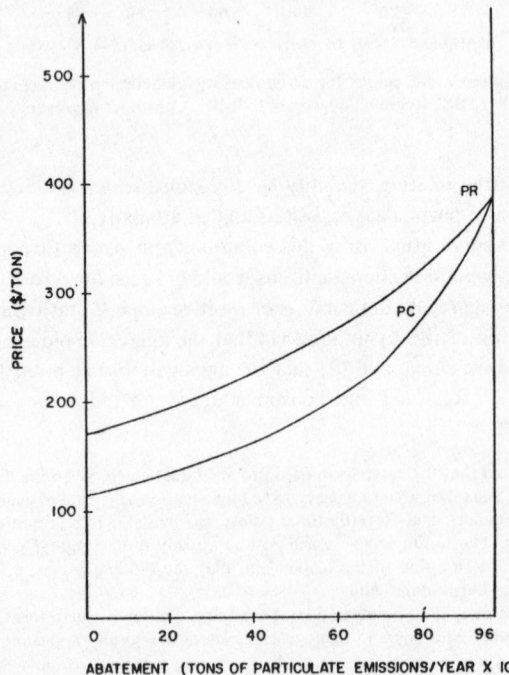

FIG. 3. Derived price curves for abatement of aesthetic environmental damage, Four Corners power plant, 1972. PR, price curve derived from regional aggregate bid; PC, price curve derived from consumer aggregate bid.

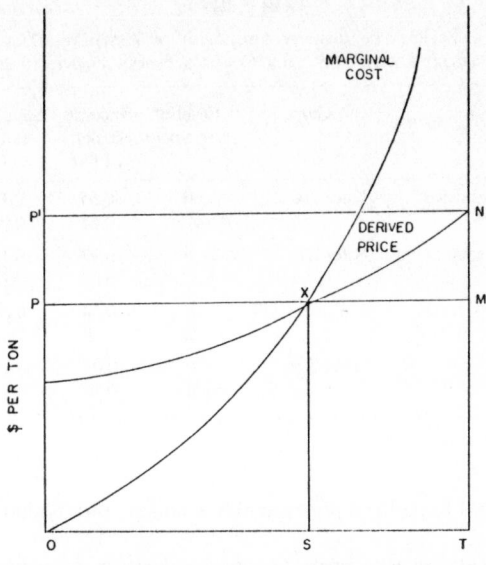

FIG. 4. Optimal standards, penalties and per unit taxes on emissions, given hypothetical marginal cost and price curves.

mum annual emissions of $(T–S)$ tons of particulates would be appropriate, and the penalty for violation of that standard should be set sufficiently high that the polluter's expected penalty per ton of emissions in excess of the standard would be at least P. An alternative institutional framework would call for a fine or tax per ton of particulate emissions. The fine ought to be set at least as high as P per ton. At the level P, the optimal level of abatement would be achieved. A fixed fine per ton of remaining emissions would result in collection of the amount $XMTS$. However, since the derived price curve is of positive slope, the sum of the fines collected would be insufficient to compensate the receptors of the pollutants for their loss in welfare. The necessary amount would be $XNTS$. This amount could be collected, if full compensation were the accepted policy,[16] by using a sliding scale of fines, ranging from P' for the first ton of emissions down to P for all emissions in excess of $T–S$.

If the marginal costs of abatement of aesthetic environmental damage associated with the Four Corners power plant were known,[17] the derived price curves presented

[16] Under a full compensation policy, a derived price curve generated from bidding games based on the concept of willingness to pay (which implicitly places the liability with the receptor of damages) would underestimate both the optimal level of abatement and the appropriate level of fines or taxes. Randall [15] and others have demonstrated that the demand for abatement of an external diseconomy is greater in the full liability situation than in the zero liability situation implicit in willingness to pay games.

[17] We are not yet in a position to present a complete benefit/cost analysis of the abatement of the aesthetic environmental damage associated with the Four Corners power plant and Navajo mine. Preliminary and tentative calculations indicate that, *if our attribution of most of the benefits reported here to abatement of particulate air pollutants is reasonable*, 99.7% abatement of particulate emissions (the current New Mexico standard for 1975) is economically justified on the basis of aesthetic considerations alone. Some additional abatement beyond the 1975 standard may be justified. The economic benefits from that abatement which has already taken place appear to far exceed the costs.

146   RANDALL, IVES AND EASTMAN

TABLE III

INCOME ELASTICITY OF BID FOR ABATEMENT OF AESTHETIC DAMAGES
ASSOCIATED WITH THE FOUR CORNERS POWER PLANT, 1972

Subpopulation	Game	Level of abatement	Income elasticity of bid	Standard error	Significantly greater than zero[a]?
Nonreservation residents	Sales tax	B	0.65	0.10	Yes
		C	0.65	0.08	Yes
Reservation residents	Sales tax	B	0.23	0.18	No
		C	0.24	0.18	No
Nonreservation residents	Electricity bill	B	0.54	0.09	Yes
		C	0.39	0.06	Yes
Recreators	Users fees	B	0.09	0.15	No
		C	0.16	0.11	No

[a] At the 95% level of confidence.

in Fig. 3 could be used to perform policy analyses similar to those in the hypothetical example above.

The *relationship between willingness to pay and household income* is of interest. However, the concept of income elasticity of demand is inappropriate to the public good under study. The calculation of an income elasticity of quantity of abatement demanded would require consideration of the relationship between income and quantity of homogeneous units of abatement demanded at a constant price per unit. However, in this study there were no explicit unit prices for abatement; neither were there individual variations in quantity of abatement demanded, as the quantities were fixed as defined in situations A, B, and C. These conditions result from the inherent nonexclusive nature of abatement of aesthetic environmental damage: Everyone obtains the same quantity and there is no explicit price. This situation is the inverse of the market situation for private goods; dollar bids are the response to a quantity which is given.

Since there existed no market price at which to calculate the income elasticity of demand, an "income elasticity of bid" was estimated. The income elasticity of bid was defined as:

$$e_Y = \frac{dB}{dY}\frac{Y}{B} = b_1\frac{Y}{B},$$

where Y = household income, and B = the individual's total annual bid. A linear regression model was used to determine the statistic b_1. The mean value of Y and B were used, and the calculation was made at each level of abatement.

Calculated income elasticities of bid for the various subpopulations and bidding games are presented in Table III. In all cases, income elasticity of bid was greater than zero, indicating that higher income households were willing to pay a greater amount than lower income households to achieve the same level of abatement of aesthetic damages. For the non-reservation residents, calculated income elasticity of bid

This conclusion is extremely tentative and subject to revision. It is presented in this footnote (at the request of an anonymous reviewer) to provide a "ball park" indication of the conclusions which may arise from our research.

ranged from 0.39 to 0.65, depending on the game and the level of abatement. Income elasticity of bid was significantly greater than zero at the 95% level of confidence. For the residents of Indian reservations and the recreational visitors to the region, lower positive income elasticities were recorded. These were not significantly greater than zero, at the 95% level of confidence.[18]

It was also found that willingness to pay an additional charge in the electricity bill for a particular level of abatement increased as the size of the electricity bill increased. Electric bill elasticity of bid, as defined as

$$e_b = \frac{dB}{d\text{Bill}}\frac{\text{Bill}}{B},$$

was calculated (for the nonreservation resident sample) to be 0.30 for situation B and 0.25 for situation C; at both points, it was significantly greater than zero at the 95% level of confidence. These estimates indicate that willingness to pay for a given level of environmental improvements increased as the size of the electricity bill increased, but at a lesser rate.

The Reliability of the Results

In the statistical sense, our estimates of the aggregate benefits from abatement of aesthetic environmental damage would seem to be of a high order of reliability. The 95% confidence limits of the aggregate bids are quite narrow, compared with the size of the estimated aggregate bids. Statistical estimates of the confidence which may be placed in these estimated aggregate bids are based upon the variance of the responses of the samples, and indicate the confidence with which sample results may be extrapolated to the whole population. These statistics, *per se*, are unable to give any indication of the reliability with which predispositions to behave, as measured by the bidding games, would be transmitted to actions should the hypothetical situation arise.

We argue, nevertheless, that our estimates of the benefits of abatement of aesthetic environmental damages associated with the Four Corners power plant are of a reasonable order of magnitude and, if anything, conservative. (1) We believe the design of the bidding games allows confidence in their efficacy. (2) The individual household bid for abatement, on average, is of the same order of magnitude as the estimates of the value of particulate pollution abatement obtained in revealed demand studies [1], when the latter are converted to a comparable basis. Mean individual household willingness to pay for abatement, measured by the sales tax game played with the nonreservation resident sample, was about $50 annually to achieve situation B and $85 annually to achieve situation C. (3) The estimated aggregate bids for abatement are relatively small given the scale of the operation at Four Corners, as indicated by its 1970 emissions rate and its total annual sales of $146 million [footnote 5]. (4) Theoretical analyses indicate that the demand for abatement of an externality will

[18] The estimates of income elasticity obtained with the nonreservation resident sample may be more reliable, for two reasons. First, the nonreservation sample was considerably larger than either of the other two samples. Second, the range of incomes encountered in the nonreservation resident sample more nearly approached that of society as a whole. The reservation resident sample was representative of its underlying population, in which incomes are concentrated at the extreme lower end of the national range. The visiting recreators had a mean household income about fifty per cent greater than the national average; very few recreators had incomes in the lower half of the national range.

148   RANDALL, IVES AND EASTMAN

be lower under a zero liability rule than under intermediate or full liability rules [15]. The bidding games used were based on zero liability rules, and they should be expected to yield conservative estimates of the benefits of abatement.

It is recognized that three data points provide an inadequate basis on which to draw conclusions with respect to the shapes and slopes of the aggregate bid curves and their first derivatives. However, it is consistent with theoretical considerations and with the limited data available that the aggregate bid curves may have at least a segment with increasing slope.

It would seem that the income elasticity of bid and the electric bill elasticity of bid fall in the range from zero to − 1. This result was consistent with our prior expectations.

CONCLUDING COMMENTS

In the case study reported, bidding games were used to estimate the benefits which would accrue from abatement of the aesthetic environmental damages associated with the Four Corners power plant and the Navajo mine. The problem situation was not amenable to the use of direct costing nor revealed demand techniques.

This study has revealed that substantial benefits may be gained from abatement of aesthetic environmental damage associated with the Four Corners power plant and Navajo mine. These potential benefits have not been revealed or realized in the market place. However, the process of political and institutional change has led to the imposition of increasingly rigorous control standards for particulate emissions from the plant, indicating a recognition, in some broad sense, that benefits may be gained from emissions controls. Our contribution has been to attempt a quantification of these benefits.

We believe that the use of bidding game techniques was successful in meeting the objective, valuation of these benefits. Bidding game techniques seem amenable to use as a research tool for valuation of a wide variety of nonmarket goods. It must be understood, however, that bidding games measure the hypothetical responses of individuals faced with hypothetical situations. Thus, considerable care must be exercised in the design of bidding games and the conduct of surveys for data collection, to ensure that the results obtained are as reliable as possible.

REFERENCES

1. R. J. Anderson, Jr. and T. D. Crocker, Air pollution and housing: Some findings, Paper No. 264, Institute for Research in the Behavioral, Economic and Management Sciences (January 1970).
2. D. F. Bradford, Benefit-cost analysis and demand curves for public goods, *Kyklos* 23, 775–91 (1970).
3. R. J. Charlson, N. C. Ahlquist, and H. Horvath, On the generality of correlation of atmospheric aerosol mass concentration and light scatter, *Atmos. Environ.* 2, 455–464 (1968).
4. M. Clawson and J. L. Knetsch, "Economics of Outdoor Recreation," Johns Hopkins Press, Baltimore (1966).
5. I. Crespi, What kinds of attitude measures are predictive of behavior? *Pub. Opin. Quart.* 35, 327–34 (1971).
6. O. A. Davis and A. B. Whinston, On the Distinction Between Public and Private Goods. *Amer. Econ. Rev.* 57, 360–373 (1967).
7. R. K. Davis, Recreation planning as a economic problem, *Natural Res. J.* 3, 239–249 (1963).
8. J. F. Engel, D. T. Kollat, and R. D. Blackwell, Attitude formation and structure, *in* "Consumer Behavior," Holt, Rinehart, and Winston, New York (1968).
9. H. Erskine, The polls: Pollution and its costs, *Pub. Opin. Quart.* 36, 120–135 (1972).
10. H. Ettinger and G. W. Roger, Particle size, visibility and mass concentration in a nonurban environment, Los Alamos Scientific Laboratory, LA-DC-12197 (1971).

BIDDING GAMES 149

11. J. A. Jaksch and H. H. Stoevener, Effects of air pollution on residential property values in Toledo, Oregon, Agricultural Experiment Station Special Report 304, Oregon State University, Corvallis (1970).
12. A. V. Kneese and B. Bower, "Managing Water Quality: Economics, Technology and Institutions," Johns Hopkins Press, Baltimore (1972).
13. L. Lave and E. Seskin, Air Pollution and Human Health, *Science* 169, 723–732 (1970).
14. H. O. Nourse, The effect of air pollution on house values, *Land Econ.* 43, 181–189 (1967).
15. A. Randall, On the theory of market solutions to externality problems, Agricultural Experiment Station Special Report 351, Oregon State University, Corvallis (1972).
16. R. G. Ridker and J. A. Henning, The determination of residential property values with special reference to air pollution (St. Louis, Missouri), *Rev. Econ. Stat.* 49, 246–257 (1967).
17. K. F. Weiand, Air pollution and property values: A study of the St. Louis area, *J. Reg. Sci.* 13 91–95 (1973).
18. R. O. Zerbe, Jr., The economics of air pollution: A cost-benefit approach, Ontario Dept. of Public Health, Toronto (1969).

[27]

Valuing Public Goods: A Comparison of Survey and Hedonic Approaches

By DAVID S. BROOKSHIRE, MARK A. THAYER,
WILLIAM D. SCHULZE, AND RALPH C. D'ARGE*

Although the theory of public goods has progressed rapidly since Paul Samuelson's seminal article, the empirical measurement of the value of (demand for) public goods only recently has received increased attention. Perhaps the best known and most widely accepted empirical approach has been the use of hedonic prices wherein, for example, it is assumed that either wages or housing values reflect spatial variation in public good characteristics of different communities. This indirect approach, based on theoretical work of Charles Tiebout, Kelvin Lancaster, Sherwin Rosen, and others, has proven quite successful. Among public goods or bads which have been valued using the hedonic approach are climate (I. Hoch), air pollution (Robert Anderson and Thomas Crocker; D. Harrison and D. Rubinfeld), social infrastructure (R. Cummings et al.) and other community characteristics such as noise level (J. Nelson), and ethnic composition (Ann Schnare).

An alternative approach is to directly ask households or individuals to state their willingness to pay for public goods using survey techniques. Despite arguments that strategic bias will invalidate survey results, there exists the need for an alternative to the hedonic approach. As an example, consider the case of a remote and unique scenic vista, valuable

*Assistant professor, University of Wyoming, assistant professor, University of Missouri-Rolla, associate professor, University of Wyoming, and professor, University of Wyoming, respectively. The research reported here was funded under a grant, Methods Development for Assessing Air Pollution Control Benefits, from the U.S. Environmental Protection Agency. We would like to give special thanks to Alan Carlin and Shelby Gerking for their helpful suggestions and contributions. Additional helpful comments were received from A. Myrick Freeman III, John Tschirhart, and James Murdoch. All conclusions are of course our sole responsibility.

to recreators, which is threatened by air pollution from a proposed coal fired plant—a typical situation in the western United States. Although it is possible, in principle, to impute the value of clean air and visibility from the relative decline in local visitation which might follow construction of a power plant, information on the value of visibility at the site is needed prior to construction for socially optimal decision making on plant location and pollution control equipment. The hedonic approach is unavailable both because the scarcity of local population—as opposed to recreators—makes use of wage or property value data impossible and because scenic vistas may themselves be unique. For these reasons, A. Randall et al. first applied survey methods for valuing visibility and other environmental effects of large coal fired power plants in the Four Corners region of New Mexico. Since this initial application, the survey approach has been widely used to value environmental commodities where market data for hedonic analysis is difficult to acquire (see, for example, Brookshire, Ives, and Schulze; Rowe et al.; Brookshire et al.). Other early attempts to value public goods using the survey approach include R. Davis, Peter Bohm, and J. Hammack and G. Brown.

Although results of using the survey approach for estimating the value of public goods appear to be internally consistent, replicable and consistent with demand theory (see Schulze et al.), little work on external validation has been reported. Thus, the purpose of this paper is to report on an experiment designed to validate the survey approach by direct comparison to a hedonic property value study.

The Los Angeles metropolitan area was chosen for the experiment because of the well-defined air pollution problem and because of the existence of detailed property value data. Twelve census tracts were chosen for sampling wherein 290 household interviews were conducted during March 1978. Respondents were asked to provide their willingness to pay for an improvement in air quality at their current location. Air quality was defined as poor, fair, or good based both on maps of the region (the pollution gradient across the Los Angeles metropolitan area is both well defined and well understood by local residents) and on photographs of a distant vista representative of the differing air quality levels. Households in poor air quality areas were asked to value an improvement to fair air quality while those in fair areas were asked to value an improvement to good air quality. Households in good air quality areas were asked their willingness to pay for a region-wide improvement in air quality. The region-wide responses are reported elsewhere (Brookshire et al.).

For comparison to the survey responses, data was obtained on 634 single family home sales which occurred between January 1977 and March 1978 exclusively in the twelve communities used for the survey analysis. As we show in the next section, households, in theory, will choose to locate along a pollution-rent gradient, paying more for homes in clean air areas based on income and tastes. However, *ceteris paribus*, we show that the annualized cost difference between homes in two different air quality areas (the rent differential for pollution) will in theory exceed the annual willingness to pay for an equivalent improvement in air quality for a household in the lower air quality area. Thus, the rent differential associated with air quality improvement from hedonic analysis of the property value data must exceed estimates of household willingness to pay for the survey responses, if the survey responses are a valid measure of the value of air quality improvements. Section II describes the data analysis and experimental design in more detail.

We also conjecture that the willingness to pay for air quality improvements is greater than zero for residents in our sample communities based on statewide political support for air quality regulation. The state of California, principally in response to the air pol-

lution problem in the Los Angeles metropolitan area, has led the nation in imposing automobile emissions standards. The automobile industry, under pressure from the California Legislature, installed the first pollution control devices on California cars in 1961. This initial step was followed nationally in 1963. Again, California imposed the first exhaust emission control regulations in 1966, leading the nation by two years. Over the decade of the 1970's, California has had more stringent automotive emission standards than federal levels, resulting in higher initial costs and sacrifices in both performance and fuel economy. In spite of these difficulties, political support, as reflected both in the State Legislature and in several administrations, has remained strong for auto emission controls.

In Section III the results of the hypotheses tests are presented. As Table 2 illustrates, results of the experiment can be summarized as follows: In the nine census tracts where air quality improvements are possible (poor and fair communities), we cannot reject our dual hypotheses that, in each census tract, household willingness to pay for air quality improvements, as estimated by surveying households, falls below equivalent property value rent differentials and lies above zero. We view these results as a qualified verification of the survey approach for estimating the value of public goods. Further interpretation of the results is contained in the concluding remarks offered in Section IV.

I. A Theoretical Basis

The property value and the survey approaches for valuing public goods have received considerable theoretical scrutiny. Property value studies are conceptually based on hedonic price theory as developed by Rosen and recently summarized by A. Myrick Freeman. The survey approach has been modeled using standard concepts of consumers' surplus by Randall et al., Bohm, and Brookshire, Ives, and Schulze, where the latter two analyses also focus on the possibility of strategic behavior. The considerable empirical evidence now available suggests that strategic bias may be of little consequence both in survey work (see R. C. Bishop and T. A. Heberlein; Brookshire et al.; Rowe et al.; and Schulze et al.) and in experimental economics (see David Grether and Charles Plott; B. Scherr and E. Babb; and Vernon Smith). The hypothetical nature of the questions used in survey analysis may substantially reduce incentives for strategic behavior. However, respondents also may have little incentive to provide accurate answers concerning willingness to pay for public goods. Thus, it has even been suggested that the survey approach produces "noise" since responses are purely hypothetical and have no necessary connection to actual budgetary decisions.

In this section, a theoretical model is developed for comparison of survey responses to a property value study for valuing air quality improvements in the Los Angeles region in order to determine if valid public good measures can be obtained from survey data.

We use the following notation: Let $P =$ the level of air pollution; $X =$ consumption of a composite commodity excluding housing; C = unit cost or price of the composite commodity X; $R =$ rent or periodic cost of housing; $Y =$ household income; and $U(P, X) =$ household utility, a decreasing function of pollution $U_P < 0$ an increasing function of consumption $U_X < 0$.[1]

Each household maximizes utility, $U(P, X)$, subject to the budget constraint

$$Y - CX - R(P) = 0,$$

where we assume the existence of a continuous differentiable rent gradient $R(P)$. (See Rosen for a complete discussion of the generation and existence of rent gradients. Our model is a simple adaptation of Rosen's, so we will not elaborate here.) Two distinct choices are modeled: consumption of the composite commodity, X, and that of housing location by pollution level, P. Presumably, lower rents will be paid for homes in

more polluted areas, so $R'(P) < 0$.[2] The first-order conditions for choice of P and X imply that

$$C(U_P / U_X) = R'(P),$$

or that the marginal rate of substitution between pollution P, and the composite commodity X, valued at the cost of the composite commodity C, equals the slope of the rent gradient $R'(P)$ at equilibrium location and consumption levels.

Figure 1 illustrates the solution graphically and allows us to structure hypotheses for testing the validity of survey results in comparison to the property value approach. The vertical axis measures the quantity of the composite commodity, X, where we assume that the cost C of the composite commodity is unity; that is, the vertical axis measures dollars as well. Pollution is on the horizontal axis. Given household income Y^0, the budget constraint, shown as $Y^0 - R(P)$ in Figure 1, is obtained by vertically subtracting the rent gradient $R(P)$. Thus, household A with preferences shown by indifference curve I_A^0 would maximize utility at point a, choosing to locate at pollution level P^0, consume X^0, and pay rent R^0. If household A's income were to increase to Y^1, the budget constraint would shift vertically to $Y^1 - R(P)$ and the same household would relocate, choosing point b, at a lower pollution level P^1 with higher consumption X^1, given tastes as represented by indifference curve I_A^1. Alternatively, another household, B, with income Y^0 but tastes as shown by I_B^3, would choose point d, locating at P^1 as well but choosing lower consumption X^1. Thus, both tastes and income enter location decisions over pollution levels.

The survey approach used in the Los Angeles metropolitan area to obtain an estimate of the value of air quality asked households how much, at most, they would be willing to pay for an improvement in air quality at the site where they presently live. Thus, the household in equilibrium at point a in Figure 1 asked how much X it would

---

[1] Alternatively we could define the utility function $U(-P, X)$ which would be an increasing quasi-concave function of both arguments.

[2] Primes or subscripts denote derivatives or partial derivatives, respectively, throughout the paper.

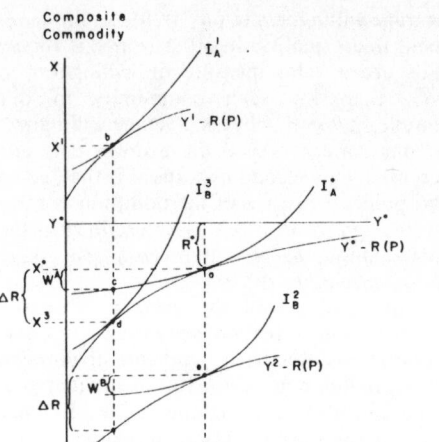

FIGURE 1

Note: With identical housing attributes, the identical rent differential ΔR exceeds individual willingness to pay, W^A and W^B.

forego to experience P^1 rather than P^0 while maintaining the same utility level. Presumably, household A would be indifferent between points a and c and be willing to pay W^A dollars (or units of X) to achieve a reduction in air pollution of ΔP. Unfortunately, as is illustrated in Figure 1, the budget constraint $Y^0 - R(P)$, obtainable by estimating the rent gradient function $R(P)$, does not provide information on the bid for improved air quality W^A. Rather, the change in rent between locations with air quality levels P^0 and P^1, ΔR in Figure 1, must, for any household located at a, equal or exceed the bid W^A, if the second-order conditions for the household optimization problem are generally satisfied. Note, that the rent gradient $R(P)$ need not be strictly concave or convex, but must lie "below" the relevant indifference curves. In fact, no a priori theoretical arguments on the shape of the rent gradient can be made. However, we can establish an upper bound on the willingness to pay for air quality improvement by examining the rent gradient. For example, if household B had a lower income, Y^2, it would locate at point e. Even though house-

hold B is now located at pollution level P^0 like household A, its bid for an air quality improvement ΔP would be W^B, smaller than W^A yet still less than ΔR. Thus, if survey bids are a valid measure of willingness to pay for air quality improvements, then $\Delta R \geqslant W$.

This hypothesis holds for each household even if we consider the case of multiple housing attributes. Including other attributes such as square footage of the home, bathrooms, fireplaces, neighborhood characteristics, etc., denoted by the vector $\vec{Z}$, the model is revised as follows:

$$max \, U(\vec{Z}, P, X);$$

subject to $\quad Y - CX - R(\vec{Z}, P) = 0,$

with first-order conditions[3]

$$C\frac{U_P}{U_X} = R_P(\vec{Z}, P); \quad C\frac{U_{\vec{Z}}}{U_X} = R_{\vec{Z}}(\vec{Z}, P).$$

These first-order conditions constitute, along with frequency distributions for housing characteristics and household preferences, a system of partial differential equations which solve for $R(\vec{Z}, P)$.[4] Thus, a hedonic rent gradient is defined for pollution P, and other household characteristics $\vec{Z}$, as well.

As illustrated in Figure 1, in which housing characteristics other than pollution are not incorporated, budget constraints for different households are obtained by vertically shifting the same rent gradient. Thus, all households face the same rent differential ΔR for a change in pollution level ΔP even though willingness to pay for that change may differ, that is, $W^A \neq W^B$. However, turning to Figure 2, household A, located at P^0, may occupy a house with attributes $\vec{Z}^A$ while household B also located at P^0 may occupy a house with a different set of attributes $\vec{Z}^B$. Household A, with income Y^A, would then face a rent gradient like that

[3] The second expression is, of course, a vector of conditions, one for each attribute.

[4] For a continuous model, one could specify a taste parameter in the utility function and specify a distribution of households over that parameter. To complete a closed model, one also needs the distribution of housing units over characteristics.

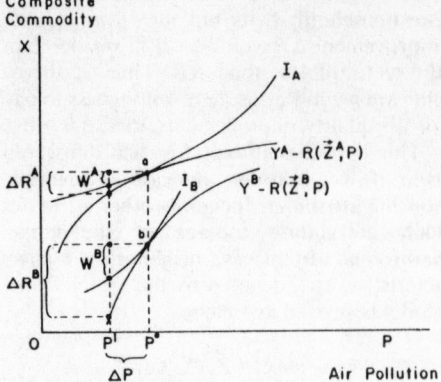

FIGURE 2

Note: With differing housing attributes across house-holds, each rent differential exceeds that household's willingness to pay.

shown in Figure 2 defined by $R(\vec{Z}^A, P)$ and choose point a, but household B with income Y^B, would now face a different rent gradient of $R(\vec{Z}^B, P)$ and choose to locate at point b. Therefore, households with different housing characteristics may face different rent gradients over pollution when projected in the (X, P) plane. In general, ΔR, unlike the case shown in Figure 1, will no longer be constant across households at the same location. However, for each household $i(i = A, B$ in Figure 2), it is still true that the rent differential ΔR^i, for a change in pollution ΔP, calculated for the fixed vector of housing characteristics $\vec{Z}^i$, will exceed that household's willingness to pay, W^i, for the same change in pollution level at the same location. Note that households were asked their willingness to pay with the specific assumption that they remained in the same house and location. Thus, $\vec{Z}^i$ for a particular household was truly fixed—allowing the simple analysis in the (X, P) plane as shown in Figure 2.

The first hypothesis for testing the validity of the survey approach can be constructed as follows: *for each household i in a community*, $\Delta R^i \geq W^i$. It then follows that in each community the average rent differential across households, $\overline{\Delta R}$, must equal or exceed the

average willingness to pay $\overline{W}$ for an improvement in air quality. In other words, if survey bids are a valid measure of willingness to pay, then for each community in our sample, $\overline{\Delta R} \geq \overline{W}$, that is, average willingness to pay cannot exceed the average rent differential. Our second hypothesis is that, given the political history of air pollution control in the state of California as described in the introduction, *mean bids in each community are nonnegative*, $\overline{W} > 0$.

Our dual test of the validity of survey measures must remain somewhat imprecise because hedonic rent gradients themselves only provide point estimates of the marginal rates of substitution (slopes of indifference curves) between pollution and other goods (money) for individuals with possible differing tastes and income. One does not have information necessary to estimate, for example, the shape of I_A^0 in Figure 1 solely on the basis of the slope of the budget constraint, $R'(P^0)$, at point a. Attempts to estimate individual willingness to pay (W^A in Figure 1) from hedonic rent gradients must thus introduce strong assumptions about the nature of preferences. (See Harrison and Rubinfeld for an example of an hedonic approach which derives willingness to pay by implicitly making such assumptions.)

Finally, it should be noted that households were asked to hypothetically give up money for better air quality in this study, and not asked about hypothetical compensation to accept worse air quality. The latter type of question has consistently evoked biased responses (see, for example, Rowe et al.; Bishop and Heberlein).

II. Sampling and Data Analysis

The previous section presented a theoretical framework for a comparison between the survey technique and the property value approach for valuing public goods. In order to empirically implement the comparison, the two approaches require a consistent sampling procedure. This section describes the sampling procedure and results of the separate studies.

Sampling was restricted to households within the Los Angeles metropolitan area.

The first concern was air pollution data. Air monitoring stations are located throughout the Los Angeles area providing readings on nitrogen dioxide (NO_2), total suspended particulate matter (TSP), and other pollutants. The objective was to relate as closely as possible the readings of two constituents of air pollution (NO_2 and TSP) to census tracts used both for the property value and survey studies. The air shed was divided into the following air quality regions: "good" ($NO_2 <$ 9 $pphm$) ($TSP < 90$ $\mu g/m^3$); "fair" (NO_2 9-11 $pphm$) (TSP 90-110 $\mu g/m^3$); and "poor" ($NO_2 > 11$ $pphm$) ($TSP > 110$ $\mu g/m^3$). Improvements from poor to fair and fair to good across the region are each associated with about a 30 percent reduction in ambient pollution levels. Consideration was given to wind patterns and topography of the area in making these distinctions.

Many variables may affect the value households place on air quality. To control for as many of these as possible in advance of the actual experiment, the sample plan identified six community pairs where each pair was relatively homogeneous with respect to socioeconomic, housing, and community characteristics, yet allowed for a significant variation in air quality.[5]

The property value analysis attempts to provide external validation for the survey approach. The absence of such validation explains, in our view, the lack of general acceptance of survey techniques. The objective, then, is to estimate the hedonic rent gradient $R(\vec{Z}, P)$ and calculate rent differentials associated with the poor-fair and fair-good air quality improvements for sample

census tracts. These results are then utilized for comparison to the survey results.

An hedonic rent gradient was estimated in accordance with literature as recently summarized by Freeman.[6] Housing sale price is assumed to be a function of housing structure variables (living area, bathrooms, fireplaces, etc.), neighborhood variables (crime rate, school quality, population density, etc.), accessibility variables (distance employment to centers and beach), and air quality as measured by total suspended particulates (TSP) or nitrogen dioxide (NO_2).[7] The primary assumption of the analysis is that variations in air pollution levels as well as other household, neighborhood, and accessibility attributes are capitalized into home sale price. Implicit or hedonic prices for each attribute are then determined by examining housing prices and attribute levels.

The property value analysis was conducted at the household level in order to provide an appropriate comparison to the survey instrument. Thus, the household data used were at the micro level of aggregation and include a large number of characteristics.[8] Data were obtained for 634 sales of single family homes which occurred between January 1977 and

---

[5] The paired areas with associated census tract marker and air quality level are, respectively: 1) Canoga Park, #1345, fair/El Monte, #4334, poor; 2) Culver City, #2026, fair/Montebello, #4301.02, and part of #5300.02, poor; 3) Newport Beach, central #630.00, fair/Pacific, northeast portion of #2627.02 and southwest intersection, good; 4) Irvine, part of #525, fair/Palos Verdes, portion of good; 5) Encino, portion of #1326, fair/La Canada, south-central portion of #4607, poor; 6) Huntington Beach, central portion of #993.03 poor/Redondo Beach, eastern portion of #6205.01 and #6205.02, good. For a map showing the monitoring station locations in relation to the paired sample areas and the air quality isopleths, see Brookshire et al.

[6] The estimation of a hedonic rent gradient requires that rather restrictive assumptions are satisfied. For example, K. Mäler has raised a number of objections to the hedonic property value approach for valuing environmental goods. These include the possibility that transaction costs (moving expenses and real estate commissions) might restrict transactions leaving real estate markets in near constant disequilibrium; and that markets other than those for property alone might capture part of the value of an environmental commodity. The first of these criticisms is mitigated by the extremely fluid and mobile real estate market of the late 1970's in Los Angeles, where rapidly escalating real property values increased homeowner equity so quickly that "housejumping" became financially feasible. The second of Mäler's concerns, that other prices, for example, golf club fees and wages, capture part of the willingness to pay can be addressed empirically. For example, attempts to test if wages from our survey data across the Los Angeles area reflected differences in pollution level produced negative results.

[7] Note that we use sale price or the discounted present value of the flow of rents rather than actual rent as the dependent variable. Given the appropriate discount rate, the two are interchangeable.

[8] Housing characteristic data were obtained from the Market Data Center, a computerized appraisal service with central headquarters in Los Angeles.

March 1978 in the communities used for the survey analysis. In addition to the immediate attributes of the household, variables which reflected the neighborhood and community were included to isolate the independent influence of air quality differentials on home sale price.

As indicated by Mäler, even under the presumption of correct model specification, estimation of a single equation hedonic rent gradient may be hindered by severe empirical difficulties, primarily multicollinearity. With respect to this problem, in each of three data categories—household, neighborhood, and air quality—multicollinearity forced the exclusion of variables and the usage of proxy variables. For instance, collinearity between number of rooms, number of bedrooms, and living area as quantitative measures of house size allowed the use of only one—living area which serves as a proxy for all. Further, since housing density and population density measure essentially the same phenomenon, only the former is used in the estimated equations. The estimation procedure was not able to separate out the independent influence of each air pollutant. Thus, only one pollution measure, either NO_2 or TSP, was utilized to describe the level of air quality. In order to provide information concerning the sensitivity of our analysis, results are presented for each of these pollutants. Finally, contrary to expectation, a collinearity problem did not exist between distance from beach and air pollution. This can be attributed, in part, to the success of the sample plan in isolating the effects of air quality.

Two alternative nonlinear hedonic equations are presented in Table 1, alternatively using NO_2 or TSP to represent pollution level. A number of aspects of the equations are worth noting. First, approximately 90 percent of the variation in home sale price is explained by the variation in the independent variable set. Second, with only a minor exception, all coefficients possess the expected relationship to the dependent variable and are statistically significant at the one percent level. The exception is the crime rate in both the NO_2 and TSP equations. Third, in their respective equations, the pollution variables have the expected negative influence on sale price and are highly significant. The estimated relationship between house sale price and pollution is also consistent with the graphical analysis of Section I; that is, the rent gradient is convex from below in the pollution/dollars plane. Finally, the stability or relative insensitivity of the regression coefficients to the particular pollution variable indicates that individuals have an aversion to pollution in general rather than to any one pollutant.

Estimation of the rent gradient was also completed using other functional forms with respect to the pollution variable.[9] The functional forms which gave the best fit are presented in Table 1. Rent differentials were calculated both from these and from the other estimated forms with results nearly identical to those presented here.

The next step was to estimate the rent differential ΔR_i for each individual household for each census tract. The rent differen-

[9] Since the calculated individual values of the rent differentials, ΔR_i, could be sensitive to the estimated functional form of the rent gradient with respect to the pollution variable, four alternative functional forms were tried. Where R indicates sale price, P the pollution variable, and $\sum_j \hat{b}_j X_j$ stands for the estimated coefficients $(\hat{b}_j)$ and the other independent variables (X_j) exactly as specified in Table 1, the estimated equations for four alternative functional forms, where NO_2 is used as the pollution variable, are as follows (t-statistics are presented in parenthesis under the estimated coefficients):

(a) $\log R = \sum_j \hat{b}_j Z_j$ $-.224 \log P$ $R^2 = .8884$
                                        (-4.03) $SSR = 18.92$;

(b) $\log R = \sum_j \hat{b}_j Z_j$ $-.0197 P$ $R^2 = .8874$
                                        (-3.29) $SSR = 19.08$;

(c) $\log R = \sum_j \hat{b}_j Z_j$ $-.00297 P^2$ $R^2 = .8866$
                                        (-2.56) $SSR = 19.21$;

(d) $\log R = \sum_j \hat{b}_j Z_j$ $-.0000391 P^3$ $R^2 = .8861$
                                        (-1.88) $SSR = 19.31$.

Clearly, form (a), which is the same as that presented in Table 1, gives the best fit. The *log*-linear (a) and semi-*log* (b) forms imply a curvature for the hedonic rent function similar to that shown in Figures 1 and 2, while the semi-*log* exponential forms, (c) and (d), allow for either a concave or convex rent function in the rent-pollution plane depending on the estimated coefficient. If *TSP* is used as the pollution variable, precisely the same pattern emerges, with functional form (a) giving the best fit. However, rent differentials calculated from any of the functional forms, using either of the pollutants, give results almost identical to those presented in Table 2 which used the *log*-linear NO_2 equation.

TABLE 1—ESTIMATED HEDONIC RENT GRADIENT EQUATIONS[a]
DEPENDENT VARIABLE= *log* (HOME SALE PRICE IN \$1,000)

Independent Variable	NO_2 Equation	*TSP* Equation
Housing Structure Variables		
Sale Date	.018591	.018654
	(9.7577)	(9.7727)
Age	−.018171	−.021411
	(−2.3385)	(−2.8147)
Living Area	.00017568	.00017507
	(12.126)	(12.069)
Bathrooms	.15602	.15703
	(9.609)	(9.6636)
Pool	.058063	.058397
	(4.6301)	(4.6518)
Fireplaces	.099577	.099927
	(7.1705)	(7.1866)
Neighborhood Variables		
Log (Crime)	−.08381	−.10401
	(−1.5766)	(−1.9974)
School Quality	.0019826	.001771
	(3.9450)	(3.5769)
Ethnic Composition	.027031	.043472
(Percent White)	(4.3915)	(6.2583)
Housing Density	−.000066926	−.000067613
	(−9.1277)	(−9.2359)
Public Safety Expenditures	.00026192	.00026143
	(4.7602)	(4.7418)
Accessibility Variables		
Distance to Beach	−.011586	−.011612
	(−7.8321)	(−7.7822)
Distance to Employment	−.28514	−.26232
	(−14.786)	(−14.158)
Air Pollution Variables		
log (*TSP*)		−.22183
		(−3.8324)
log (NO_2)	−.22407	
	(−4.0324)	
Constant	2.2325	1.0527
	(2.9296)	(1.4537)
R^2	.89	.89
Sum of Squared Residuals	18.92	18.97
Degrees of Freedom	619	619

[a] *t*-statistics in parentheses.

tial specifies the premium an individual household would have to pay to obtain an identical home in the next cleaner air region (poor to fair for six communities, fair to good for three communities). Due to the estimated functional form of the rent gradient, the calculated rent differential is dependent upon the value of all other variables.[10]

The average home sale price change based on individual data in each census tract associated with an improvement in air quality, *ceteris paribus*, is shown in column (2) of Table 2. Column (1) of Table 2 lists communities by air quality level. The table only shows results for the *log*-linear NO_2 equation since, as noted above, other specifications

[10] It should be noted that nonlinear estimated equations will give biased but consistent forecasts of rent differentials. However, if a linear estimated equation is

used for either NO_2 or *TSP*, forecast rent differentials are larger than the results from the nonlinear estimated equations presented here.

give nearly identical results. The numbers shown are derived by evaluating the hedonic housing expression, given the household's characteristics, for a pollution change from poor to fair or fair to good as the case may be. The resulting sale price differential is then converted to an equivalent monthly payment through the standard annualization procedure and division by twelve.[11] Since our hypothesis test is posed in terms of the average rent differential in the relevant communities, a community mean and standard deviation are then calculated. Column (3) of Table 2 shows the number of homes for which data was available to calculate average rent differentials and standard deviations for each community. Monthly rent differentials ranged from $15.44 to $45.92 for an improvement from poor to fair air quality and $33.17 to $128.46 for an improvement from fair to good air quality. The higher figures in each case are associated with higher income communities. Again, these average differentials should provide an upper bound for the survey results.

The survey approach followed the work of Davis and Bohm in gathering the information necessary for estimating a David Bradford bid curve. The approach involves the establishment of a hypothetical market via a survey instrument. Through the work of Randall et al. and Brookshire, Ives, and Schulze, the necessary structure for constructing a hypothetical market for the direct determination of economic values within the Hicksian consumers' surplus framework has been developed. The survey reported on here is consistent with this previous literature.

The hypothetical market was defined and described both in technical and institutional detail. The public good (air quality) was described by the survey instrument to the respondent in terms of easily perceived levels of provision such as visual range through photographs[12] and maps depicting good, fair,

[11] A capital recovery factor equal to .0995 which corresponds to the prevailing .0925 mortgage rate in the January 1979–March 1978 period is used.

[12] In developing photographs, two observational paths from Griffith Observatory in Los Angeles were chosen: toward downtown Los Angeles; and looking down Western Avenue. The approximate visibility (discerna-

and poor air quality levels over the region. Respondents had little difficulty understanding the levels of air quality represented to them because of the sharp pollution gradient across the region.

Payment mechanisms[13] were specified within the survey instrument and the respondent was asked to react to alternative price levels posited for different air quality levels. In every case the basis for the bid for better air quality was the existing pollution situation as determined by location of their home shown on a map of the Los Angeles metropolitan area which depicted regional air quality levels. Various starting points for the bidding prices and differing information structures were included in the survey format. Biases from alternative starting points and information structures were not present in the results (see Brookshire et al.).[14]

The survey was conducted over the period of March 1978. A total of 290 completed surveys were obtained for the above mentioned areas. Sampling was random within each paired area.[15]

Table 2 presents the mean bids and standard deviations and number of observations in columns (4) and (5), respectively, for each community for an improvement in air quality. Two types of bids are presented: proposed improvements from poor to fair air quality and from fair to good air quality. In

ble objects in the distance, not visual range) for poor visibility was 2 miles, for fair visibility 12 miles, and for good visibility 28 miles.

[13] Payment mechanisms are either of the lump sum variety, or well-specified schemes such as tax increments or utility bill additions. The choice in the experimental setting varies according to the structure of the contingent market.

[14] Questions have been raised as to problems of biases in the survey approach. Strategic bias (i.e., free-rider problems), hypothetical bias, instrument bias; all have been explored. Generally speaking, problems of bias within the survey approach have not been prevalent. For a general review of the definition of various biases and results of different experiments see Schulze et al., and for investigations of strategic bias utilizing other demand revealing techniques, see Scherr and Babb, and Smith.

[15] Interviewer bias was not present. No records were kept that would enable the testing for nonrespondent bias.

poor communities—El Monte, Montebello, and La Canada—the mean bids ranged from $11.00 to $22.06 per month. For the fair communities — Canoga Park, Huntington Beach, Irvine, Culver City, Encino, and Newport Beach—the mean monthly amounts range from $5.55 to $28.18 to obtain good air quality.

III. Test of Hypotheses

The previous sections have described a theoretical structure and two different empirical estimation techniques for determining the value of urban air quality improvements in the Los Angeles metropolitan area. The theoretical relationship between the valuation procedures ($\overline{\Delta R} \geqslant \overline{W}$) and the hypothesis that survey bids are nonzero ($\overline{W} > 0$) are tested in this section.

Table 2 presents the community average survey bids (col. (4)) and corresponding rent differentials (col. (2)). As is indicated, in each community the sample survey bids are nonzero and less than the calculated rent differentials in absolute magnitude. This establishes that the survey bid bounds are consistent with our theoretical arguments but does not indicate statistical significance, which is provided below.

With respect to the test of equality of mean survey bids to zero, Table 2 (col. (6)) presents the experimental results. The calculated t-statistics indicate rejection of the null hypothesis (that the population mean $\mu_{\overline{W}}$ equals zero) at the 1 percent level in every community sampled. These results are in accordance with the political history of the region and indicate that individual households are willing to pay amounts significantly greater than zero for an approximate 30 percent improvement in air quality.

The comparison of the survey bids to the estimated rent differentials is presented in Table 2 (col. (7)). In this instance the compound hypothesis that population average rent differential ($\mu_{\overline{\Delta R}}$) equals or exceeds the population average survey bid ($\mu_{\overline{W}}$) is again tested using the t-statistic. Rejection of the null hypothesis requires that the calculated t-statistics be negative and of sufficient mag-

nitude.[16] The standard t-test calculations (col. (7)) imply that the hypothesis $\mu_{\overline{\Delta R}} \geqslant \mu_W$ cannot be rejected for the population means $\mu_{\overline{R}}$ and $\mu_{\overline{W}}$ even at the 10 percent critical level. Although we present only the results for the hedonic housing equation in which log (NO$_2$) is the pollution measure, these results remain essentially unchanged for all communities, for all estimated hedonic rent gradients, regardless of the variable (NO$_2$ or TSP) utilized as a proxy for the general state of air quality. The results then are quite insensitive to the particular hedonic model specification, providing a degree of generality to the results.

The hypotheses tests indicate that the empirical analysis is entirely consistent with the theoretical structure outlined above. This conclusion, when combined with the absence of any identified biases (see Brookshire et al.) suggests that survey responses yield estimates of willingness to pay for environmental improvements in an urban context consistent with a hedonic-market analysis. A further implication is that individual households demonstrated a nonzero willingness to pay for air quality improvements rather than free riding. This conforms to the previous survey results of Brookshire, Ives, and Schulze, and Rowe et al., as well as the experimental work of Scherr and Babb, Smith, and Grether and Plott, concerning the role of strategic behavior. This seems to indicate that the substantive effort to devise a payment mechanism free of strategic incentives for consumers (see Theodore Groves and John Ledyard) has been directed towards solving a problem not yet empirically observed.

Another important question is the accuracy of willingness to pay estimates based on surveys. Bishop and Heberlein conclude—based on a survey approach quite different from that cited throughout this study—that survey estimates of willingness to pay might be biased downward by 55 percent for goose

---

[16]For instance, rejection of the null hypothesis ($\mu_{\overline{\Delta R}} \geqslant \mu_{\overline{W}}$) at the 1 percent level would require a calculated t-statistic less than -2.326, given a large number of observations. Since none of the calculated t-statistics are negative, the null hypothesis cannot be rejected (see W. Guenther).

The Economics of the Environment

BROOKSHIRE ET AL.: PUBLIC GOODS

TABLE 2—TESTS OF HYPOTHESES

Community (1)	Property Value Results[a]		Survey Results		Tests of Hypotheses	
	ΔR (Standard Deviation) (2)	Number of Observations (3)	$\overline{W}$ (Standard Deviation) (4)	Number of Observations (5)	t-Statistics $\mu_{\overline{W}} > 0$[b] (6)	t-Statistics $\mu_{\Delta R} \gtrless \mu_{\overline{W}}$[c] (7)
POOR–FAIR						
El Monte	15.44 (2.88)	22	11.10 (13.13)	20	3.78	1.51
Montebello	30.62 (7.26)	49	11.42 (15.15)	19	3.28	7.07
La Canada	73.78 (48.25)	51	22.06 (33.24)	17	2.74	4.10
Sample Population	45.92 (36.69)	122	14.54 (21.93)	56	4.96	5.54
FAIR–GOOD						
Canoga Park	33.17 (3.88)	22	16.08 (15.46)	34	6.07	5.07
Huntington Beach	47.26 (10.66)	44	24.34 (25.46)	38	5.92	5.47
Irvine	48.22 (8.90)	196	22.37 (19.13)	27	6.08	5.08
Culver City	54.44 (16.09)	64	28.18 (34.17)	30	5.42	.11.85
Encino	128.46 (51.95)	45	16.51 (13.38)	37	7.51	12.75
Newport Beach	77.02 (41.25)	22	5.55 (6.83)	20	3.63	7.65
Sample Population	59.09 (34.28)	393	20.31 (23.0)	186	12.02	14.00

[a]Rent differentials for the hedonic housing equation in which $log(NO_2)$ is the relevant pollution variable are presented here.

[b]The hypotheses to be tested were $H_0: \mu_{\overline{W}} = 0$; $H_1: \mu_{\overline{W}} > 0$. All test statistics indicate rejection of the null hypothesis at the 1 percent significance level.

[c]The hypotheses to be tested were $H_0: \mu_{\Delta R} \geq \mu_{\overline{W}}$; $H_1: \mu_{\Delta R} < \mu_{\overline{W}}$. All test statistics indicate that the null hypothesis could not be rejected even at the 10 percent level.

hunting permits. Interestingly, the more traditional travel cost approach gave a downward bias of 67 percent. The basis for calculating both biases was actual repurchase of goose hunting permits. For purposes of comparison, if survey estimates of willingness to pay for air quality improvement are increased by 50 percent over those shown in Table 2, then, for eight out of nine communities, average willingness to pay still lies below estimated average rent gradients. Thus, our results are consistent with the possibility of errors of about 50 percent in estimating willingness to pay, just as in the Bishop and Heberlein study. Although better accuracy would be highly desirable, in many cases

where no other technique is available for valuing public goods, this level of accuracy is certainly preferable to no information for the decision-making process.

The conclusions of this experiment are not without further qualifications. In the next section, possible limitations of survey analysis and conclusions concerning the efficacy of employing surveys to value a wide range of nonmarket commodities are discussed.

IV. Conclusion

There are a number of limitations in generalizing our results to all survey work. First, this experiment was conducted in the South

Coast Air Basin where individuals have both an exceptionally well-defined regional pollution situation and a well-developed housing value market for clean air. The effect of clean air on housing values appears to be exceptionally well understood in the Los Angeles metropolitan area. Thus, the Los Angeles experiment may be a special case in which an informed populace with market experience for a particular public good allowed the successful application of the survey approach. In particular, situations where no well-developed hedonic market exists may not be amenable to survey valuation. Biases due to lack of experience must then be considered a possibility. However, existing studies by Randall et al. and Brookshire, Ives, and Schulze, and Rowe et al. of remote recreation areas certainly suggest that survey approaches provide replicable estimates of consumers' willingness to pay to prevent environmental deterioration, without prior valuation experience.

In summary, this paper set out to both theoretically and empirically examine the survey approach and to provide external validation for survey analysis. The theoretical model described in Section I predicts that survey responses will be bounded below by zero and above by rent differentials derived from the estimated hedonic rent gradient. In order to test the dual hypotheses a survey and a traditional analysis of the housing market were undertaken. Each was based upon a consistent sampling procedure in the Los Angeles metropolitan area. The empirical results do not allow the rejection of either of the two hypotheses, thereby providing evidence towards the validity of survey methods as a means of determining the value of public goods.

REFERENCES

Anderson, Robert and Crocker, Thomas, "Air Pollution and Residential Property Values," Urban Studies, October 1971, 8, 171–80.

Bishop, R. C. and Heberlein, T. A. "Measuring Values of Extra-Market Goods: Are Indirect Measures Biased?," American Jour-

nal of Agricultural Economics, December 1979, 61, 926–30.

Bohm, Peter, "Estimating Demand for Public Goods: An Experiment," European Economic Review, 1972, 3, 11–130.

Brookshire, David et al., "Experiments in Valuing Public Goods," in V. Kerry Smith, ed., Advances in Applied Microeconomics, Greenwich: JAI Press, 1980.

Brookshire, D., Ives, B., and Schulze, W. "The Valuation of Aesthetic Preferences," Journal of Environmental Economics and Management, December 1976, 3, 325–46.

Bradford, David, "Benefit Cost Analysis and Demand Curves for Public Goods," Kyklos, November 1972, 23, 775–82.

Cummings, R., Schulze, W., and Meyer, A. "Optimal Municipal Investment in Boomtowns: An Empirical Analysis," Journal of Environmental Economics and Management, September 1978, 5, 252–67.

Davis, R., "Recreation Planning as an Economic Problem," Natural Resources Journal, October 1963, 3, 239–49.

Freeman III, A. Myrick, "Hedonic Prices, Property Values and Measuring Environmental Benefits: A Survey of the Issues," Scandinavian Journal of Economics, 1979, 81, 154–173.

Grether David and Plott, Charles "Economic Theory and the Preference Reversal Phenomenon," American Economic Review, September 1979, 69, 623–38.

Groves, Theodore and Ledyard, John "Optimal Allocation of Public Goods: A Solution to the 'Free Rider' Problem," Econometrica, May 1977, 45, 783–809.

Guenther, W., Concepts of Statistical Inference, New York: McGraw-Hill, 1973.

Hammack, J. and Brown, G., Waterfowl and Wetlands: Toward Bioeconomic Analysis, Baltimore: Johns Hopkins University Press 1974.

Harrison, D., Jr. and Rubinfeld, D., "Hedonic Housing Prices and the Demand for Clean Air," Journal of Environmental Economics and Management, March 1978, 5, 81–102.

Hoch, I. with Drake, T., "Wages, Climate, and the Quality of Life," Journal of Environmental Economics and Management, December 1974, 1, 268–95.

Lancaster, Kelvin, "A New Approach to Consumer Theory," *Journal of Political Economy*, April 1966, *74*, 132–57.

Mäler, K., "A Note on the Use of Property Values in Estimating Marginal Willingness to Pay for Environmental Quality," *Journal of Environmental Economics and Management*, December 1977, *4*, 355–69.

Nelson, J., "Airport Noise, Location Rent, and the Market for Residential Amenities," *Journal of Environmental Economics and Management*, December 1979, 6, 320–31.

Randall, A., Ives, B., and Eastman, C., "Bidding Games for Valuation of Aesthetic Environmental Improvements," *Journal of Environmental Economics and Management*, August 1974, *1*, 132–49.

Rosen, Sherwin, "Hedonic Prices and Implicit Markets: Product Differentiation in Pure Competition," *Journal of Political Economy*, January/February 1974, *82*, 34–55.

Rowe, R., d'Arge, R., and Brookshire, D. S., "An Experiment in the Value of Visibility,"

Journal of Environmental Economics and Management, March 1980, 7, 1–19.

Samuelson, Paul, "The Pure Theory of Public Expenditures," *Review of Economics and Statistics*, November 1954, *36*, 387–89.

Scherr, B. and Babb, E., "Pricing Public Goods: An Experiment with Two Proposed Pricing Systems," *Public Choice*, Fall 1975, *23*, 35–48.

Schnare, Ann, "Racial and Ethnic Price Differentials in an Urban Housing Market," *Urban Studies*, June 1976, *13*, 107–20.

Schulze, W., d'Arge R., and Brookshire, D. S., "Valuing Environmental Commodities: Some Recent Experiments," *Land Economics*, May 1981, forthcoming.

Smith, Vernon, "The Principal of Unanimity and Voluntary Consent in Social Choice," *Journal of Political Economy*, December 1977, *85*, 1125–40.

Tiebout, Charles "A Pure Theory of Local Expenditures," *Journal of Political Economy*, October 1956, *65*, 416–24.

[28]

Willingness To Pay and Willingness To Accept: How Much Can They Differ?

By W. Michael Hanemann*

In many empirical studies, analysts seek to obtain money measures of welfare changes due not to price changes but to changes in the availability of public goods or amenities, changes in the qualities of commodities, or changes in the fixed quantities of rationed goods. The conventional welfare measures for price changes are the compensating (C) and equivalent (E) variations, which correspond to the maximum amount an individual would be willing to pay (WTP) to secure the change or the minimum amount she would be willing to accept (WTA) to forgo it. Karl-Göran Mäler (1974) was perhaps the first to show that the concepts of C and E can readily be extended from conventional price changes to such quantity changes. For price changes, Robert Willig (1976) demonstrated that C and E are likely to be fairly close in value, with the difference depending directly on the size of the income elasticity of demand for the commodity whose price changes. Subsequently, Alan Randall and John Stoll (1980) examined the duality theory associated with fixed quantities in the utility function and showed that, with appropriate modifications, Willig's formulas for bounds on C and E do, indeed, carry over to this setting.

Within the environmental-economics literature, Randall and Stoll's results have been widely interpreted as implying that WTP and WTA for changes in environmental amenities should not differ greatly unless there are unusual income effects.[1] However,

recent empirical work using various types of interview procedures has produced some evidence of large disparities between WTP and WTA measures.[2] This has led to something of an impasse: how can the empirical evidence of significant differences between WTP and WTA be reconciled with the theoretical analysis suggesting that such differences are unlikely? Can they be explained entirely by unusual income effects or by peculiarities of the interview process?

In this note, I reexamine Randall and Stoll's analysis and show that, while it is indeed accurate, its implications have been misunderstood. For quantity changes, there is no presumption that WTP and WTA must be close in value and, unlike price changes, the difference between WTP and WTA depends not only on an income effect but also on a substitution effect. By the latter, I mean the ease with which other privately marketed commodities can be substituted for the given public good or fixed commodity, while maintaining the individual at a constant level of utility. I show that, holding income effects constant, the smaller the substitution effect (i.e., the fewer substitutes available for the public good) the *greater* the disparity between WTP and WTA. This surely coincides with common intuition. If there are private goods that are readily substitutable for the public good, there ought to be little difference between an individual's WTP and WTA for a change in the public good. However, if the public good has almost no substitutes (e.g., Yosemite National Park, or in a different context, your own life), there is no reason why WTP and WTA could not differ vastly: in the limit, WTP could equal the individual's entire (finite)

*Department of Agricultural and Resource Economics, University of California, Berkeley, CA 94720.
[1]This view is expressed by, for example, Myrick Freeman (1979 p. 3), Mark A. Thayer (1981 p. 30), Jack L. Knetsch and J. A. Sinden (1984 p. 508), Robin Gregory (1986 p. 326), Don L. Coursey et al. (1987 p. 678), and most of the participants in a recent symposium on valuing amenity resources edited by George L. Peterson et al. (1988 pp. 104, 129, 138, 152, 168, 230, 238, 259).

[2]See the summaries in table 3.2 of Ronald G. Cummings et al. (1986) and table 1 of Ann Fisher et al. (1988).

636   THE AMERICAN ECONOMIC REVIEW   JUNE 1991

income, while WTA could be infinite. My argument is developed in the following two sections. Section I deals specifically with the two polar cases of perfect substitution and zero substitution between the public good and available private goods. Section II deals with Randall and Stoll's extension of Willig's formulas and shows that their bounds are, in fact, consistent with substantial divergences between WTP and WTA. Section III presents empirical application of these bounds and relates them to Mäler's concept of weak complementarity.

I. Two Polar Cases

The theoretical setup is as follows. An individual has preferences for various conventional market commodities whose consumption is denoted by the vector x as well as for another commodity whose consumption is denoted by q.[3] This could represent the supply of a public good or amenity; it could be an index of the quality of one of the private goods; or it could be a private commodity whose consumption is fixed by a public agency.[4] The key point is that the individual's consumption of q is fixed exogenously, while she can freely vary her consumption of the x's. These preferences are represented by a utility function, $u(x, q)$, which is continuous and nondeceasing in its arguments (I assume that the x's and q are all "goods") and strictly quasiconcave in x. The individual chooses her consumption by solving

(1) $\max_{x} u(x, q)$ subject to $\sum p_i x_i = y$

taking the level of q as given. This yields a set of ordinary demand functions, $x_i = h^i(p, q, y)$, $i = 1, \ldots, N$, and an indirect utility function, $v(p, q, y) \equiv u[h(p, q, y), q]$,

which has the conventional properties with respect to the price and income arguments and also is nondecreasing in q.[5] Now suppose that q rises from q^0 to $q^1 > q^0$ while prices and income remain constant at (p, y). Accordingly, the individual's utility changes from $u^0 \equiv v(p, q^0, y)$ to $u^1 \equiv v(p, q^1, y) \geq u^0$. Following Mäler, the compensating and equivalent variation measures of this change are defined, respectively, by[6]

(2) $v(p, q^1, y - C) = v(p, q^0, y)$

(3) $v(p, q^1, y) = v(p, q^0, y + E)$.

Dual to the utility maximization in (1) is an expenditure minimization: minimize $\sum p_i x_i$ with respect to x subject to $u = (x, q)$, which yields a set of compensated demand functions, $x_i = g^i(p, q, u)$, $i = 1, \ldots, N$, and an expenditure function, $m(p, q, u) \equiv \sum p_i g^i(p, q, u)$, which has the conventional properties with respect to (p, u) and is nonincreasing in q. In terms of this function, C and E are given by

(2') $C = m(p, q^0, u^0) - m(p, q^1, u^0)$

(3') $E = m(p, q^0, u^1) - m(p, q^1, u^1)$.

It is evident from (2) and (3) that $0 < C < y$ while $E \geq 0$.[7] The questions at issue are: i) is it true that $E/C \approx 1$? and ii) what factors affect this ratio? As a first cut at an answer, I compare two polar cases. In the first case, at least one private good—say, the first—is a perfect substitute for some

---

[3] I am treating q as a scalar here, but it could be a vector without seriously affecting the analysis in this section. In the next section, however, the analysis would become significantly more complex if q were a vector and more than one element of q changed.

[4] These alternative interpretations are offered, respectively, by Mäler (1974), Hanemann (1982), and Randall and Stoll (1980).

[5] These properties are established in my earlier paper (Hanemann, 1982).

[6] I have taken the liberty of defining C and E as the negative of quantities appearing in Willig (1976) and in Randall and Stoll (1980), so that $\text{sign}(C) = \text{sign}(E) = \text{sign}(u^1 - u^0)$.

[7] I assume throughout that $q^1 > q^0$ and $u^1 \geq u^0$. The analysis could be repeated for a case in which quality decreases and $u^1 < u^0$. In that case, C and E are both nonpositive and correspond, respectively, to the compensation that the individual would be willing to accept to consent to the change and the amount that she would be willing to pay to avoid the change. This would reverse the inequalities presented in what follows, but it would not affect the substance of my argument.

transformation of q. Thus, the direct utility function assumes the special form

$$(4) \quad u(x,q) = \bar{u}[x_1 + \psi(q), x_2, \dots, x_N]$$

where $\psi(\cdot)$ is an increasing function and $\bar{u}(\cdot)$ is a continuous, increasing, strictly quasi-concave function of N variables. As W. M. Gorman (1976) has shown, assuming an interior solution, the resulting indirect utility function is

$$(5) \quad v(\mathbf{p}, q, y)$$
$$= \bar{v}\big[p_1, p_2, \dots, p_N, y + p_1 \cdot \psi(q)\big]$$

where $\bar{v}(\cdot)$ is the indirect utility function corresponding to $\bar{u}(\cdot)$. Substitution of (5) into (2) and (3) yields the following:[8]

PROPOSITION 1: *If at least one private market good is a perfect substitute for q, then $C = E$.*

At the opposite extreme, I assume that there is a zero elasticity of substitution not just between q and x_1 but between q and *all* the x's. Thus, the direct utility function becomes

$$(6) \quad u(\mathbf{x}, q)$$
$$= \bar{u}\left[\min\left(q, \frac{x_1}{\alpha_1}\right), \dots, \min\left(q, \frac{x_N}{\alpha_N}\right)\right]$$

where $\alpha_1, \dots, \alpha_N$ are positive constants and $\bar{u}(\cdot)$ is conventional direct utility function. In this case, the indirect utility function $v(\mathbf{p}, q, y)$ has a rather complex structure and changes its form in different segments of $(\mathbf{p}, q, y)$-space. It will be sufficient for my purposes to focus on just one of these segments. Suppose that $q \le y / \Sigma p_i \alpha_i$; then, the maximization of (6), subject to the budget constraint, yields demand functions and an indirect utility function of the form $x_i = h^i(\mathbf{p}, q, y) = \alpha_i q$, and $u =$

$v(\mathbf{p}, q, y) = \bar{u}(q, \dots, q) \equiv w(q)$. In this region of $(\mathbf{p}, q, y)$-space, the individual does not exhaust her budget, and her marginal utility of income is therefore zero. Now suppose that $q^0 \le y / \Sigma p_i \alpha_i$ and $q^1 > q^0$. Since $v(\mathbf{p}, q^1, y) > w(q^0)$, it is evident from (2) that the individual would be willing to pay some positive but limited amount C to secure this change. However, for any positive quantity E, no matter how large, $v(\mathbf{p}, q^0, y + E) = v(\mathbf{p}, q^0, y) = w(q^0)$. This implies the following proposition.

PROPOSITION 2: *If there is zero substitutability between q and each of the private-market goods, it can happen that, while the individual would only be willing to pay a finite amount for an increase in q, there is no finite compensation that she would accept to forgo this increase.*

It should be emphasized that this result obtains only in a portion of $(\mathbf{p}, q, y)$ space; in other regions, even with (6), E would be finite.[9] However, the result in Proposition 2 can also be established for other utility functions that permit some substitutability between q and the x's as long as the indifference curves between q and each of the x's become parallel to the x axis at some point. The implication of these two propositions is that the degree of substitutability between q and private-market goods *does* significantly affect the relation between C and E. In the next section, I show how this observation can be reconciled with the bounds on C and E derived by Randall and Stoll.

II. Randall and Stoll's Bounds

In order to extend Willig's bounds from price to commodity space, Randall and Stoll focus on a set of demand functions different from those considered above. Suppose that the individual could purchase q in a market

---

[8]This result caries over, of course, if *more* than one private good is a perfect substitute for q. In the most general case, $u(\mathbf{x}, q) = \bar{u}[x_1 + \psi_1(q), \dots, x_N + \psi(q)]$ and $C = E = \Sigma p_i[\psi_i(q^1) - \psi_i(q^0)]$.

[9]Indeed, if $\bar{h}^i(\alpha_1 p_1, \dots, \alpha_N p_N, y) \le q^0$, $i = 1, \dots, N$, it can be shown that $v(\mathbf{p}, q^0, y) = v(\mathbf{p}, q^1, y) = \bar{v}(\alpha_1 p_1, \dots, \alpha_N p_N, y)$ and $C = E = 0$, where $\bar{h}^i(\cdot)$ and $\bar{v}(\cdot)$ are the ordinary demand functions and the indirect utility function associated with $\bar{u}(\cdot)$.

at some given price, π. It must be emphasized that this market is entirely hypothetical since q is actually a public good. Instead of (1), she would now solve[10]

$$(7) \qquad \max_{\mathbf{x},q} u(\mathbf{x},q)$$

$$\text{subject to } \sum p_i x_i + \pi q = y.$$

Denote the resulting ordinary demand functions by $x_i = \hat{h}^i(\mathbf{p}, \pi, y)$, $i = 1, \ldots, N$ and $q = \hat{h}^q(\mathbf{p}, \pi, y)$. The corresponding indirect utility function is $\hat{v}(\mathbf{p}, \pi, y) \equiv u[\hat{h}(\mathbf{p}, \pi, y), \hat{h}^q(\mathbf{p}, \pi, y)]$. The dual to (7) is: minimize $\sum p_i x_i + \pi q$ with respect to $\mathbf{x}$ and q subject to $u = u(\mathbf{x}, q)$. This generates a set of compensated demand functions, $x_i = \hat{g}^i(\mathbf{p}, \pi, u)$, $i = 1, \ldots, N$ and $q = \hat{g}^q(\mathbf{p}, \pi, u)$, and an expenditure function, $\hat{m}(\mathbf{p}, \pi, u) \equiv \sum p_i \hat{g}^i(\mathbf{p}, \pi, u) + \pi \hat{g}^q(\mathbf{p}, \pi, u)$. These functions are hypothetical, since q is really exogenous to the individual, but they are of theoretical interest because they shed light on the relation between C and E.

For any given values of q, $\mathbf{p}$, and u, the equation

$$(8) \qquad q = \hat{g}^q(\mathbf{p}, \pi, u)$$

may be solved to obtain $\pi = \hat{\pi}(\mathbf{p}, q, u)$, the inverse compensated demand (i.e., willingness-to-pay) function for q: $\hat{\pi}(\cdot)$ is the price that would induce the individual to purchase q units of the public good in order to attain a utility level of u, given that she could buy private goods at prices $\mathbf{p}$. Let $\pi^0 \equiv \hat{\pi}(\mathbf{p}, q^0, u^0)$ and $\pi^1 \equiv \hat{\pi}(\mathbf{p}, q^1, u^1)$ denote the prices that would have supported q^0 and q^1, respectively. The two expenditure functions dual to (1) and (7) are related by

$$(9) \qquad m(\mathbf{p}, q, u) \equiv \hat{m}[\mathbf{p}, \hat{\pi}(\mathbf{p}, q, u), u]$$
$$- \hat{\pi}(\mathbf{p}, q, u) \cdot q.$$

This implies that[11]

$$(10) \qquad m_q(\mathbf{p}, q, u) = -\hat{\pi}(\mathbf{p}, q, u).$$

Combining (10) with (2') and (3') yields these alternative formulas for C and E, expressed in terms of the willingness-to-pay function:

$$(2'') \qquad C = \int_{q^0}^{q^1} \hat{\pi}(\mathbf{p}, q, u^0) \, dq$$

$$(3'') \qquad E = \int_{q^0}^{q^1} \hat{\pi}(\mathbf{p}, q, u^1) \, dq.$$

It can be shown that sign $(\hat{\pi}_u) = \text{sign}(\hat{h}_y^q)$. Therefore, for given $(\mathbf{p}, q)$, the graph of $\hat{\pi}(\mathbf{p}, q, u^1)$ lies above (below) that of $\hat{\pi}(\mathbf{p}, q, u^0)$, and $E > (<) C$, when q is a normal (inferior) good. Figure 1 shows E and C for the case in which q is normal: E corresponds to the area $q^0 \alpha \gamma q^1$, while C corresponds to the area $q^0 \beta \delta q^1$.

Using techniques pioneered by Willig (1976), Randall and Stoll (1980) establish bounds on the difference between each of C and E and the area under an inverse ordinary demand function for q. From this, they derive bounds on the difference between C and E. However, the requisite inverse ordinary demand function is obtained in a rather special manner. Given any level of q, one can ask what market price π would induce the individual to purchase that amount of public good if it were available in a market, while still allowing her to purchase the quantity of the x's that she actually did buy at market prices $\mathbf{p}$ and with income y. In conducting this thought experiment, one needs to supplement the individual's income so that she can afford q as well as the x's. Thus, for given $(\mathbf{p}, q, y)$, one seeks the price π that satisfies

$$(11) \qquad q = \hat{h}^q(\mathbf{p}, \pi, y + \pi q).$$

---

[10] It is now necessary to assume that $u(\cdot)$ is strictly quasi-concave in both $\mathbf{x}$ and q, rather than $\mathbf{x}$ alone. See footnote 22 for an example in which this is a nontrivial restriction.

[11] Using subscripts to denote derivatives, differentiate (9) and note that $q = \hat{g}^q(\mathbf{p}, \pi, u) = \hat{m}_\pi(\mathbf{p}, \pi, u)$ by Shephard's lemma. Equations similar to (9)–(12) are presented by J. P. Neary and K. W. S. Roberts (1980).

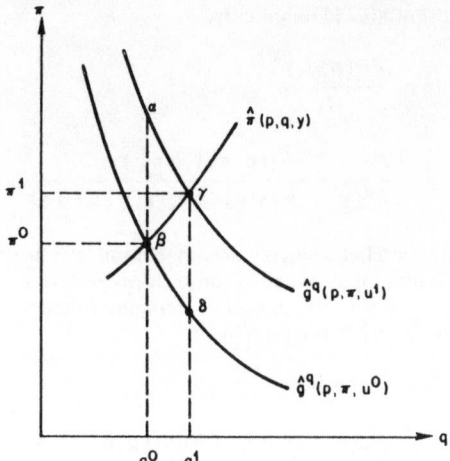

FIGURE 1. WTP AND WTA FOR A CHANGE IN q

The solution will be denoted by $\pi = \hat{\pi}(\mathbf{p}, q, y)$. This inverse function is related to the inverse compensated demand function by the identities[12]

(12a) $\hat{\pi}(\mathbf{p}, q, y)$

$\equiv \hat{\pi}[\mathbf{p}, q, v(\mathbf{p}, q, y)]$

(12b) $\hat{\pi}(\mathbf{p}, q, u)$

$\equiv \hat{\pi}[\mathbf{p}, q, m(\mathbf{p}, q, u)]$.

Both identities play a role in the analysis. From (12a) it follows that $\pi^0 \equiv \hat{\pi}(\mathbf{p}, q^0, u^0) \equiv \hat{\pi}(\mathbf{p}, q^0, y)$ and $\pi^1 \equiv \hat{\pi}(\mathbf{p}, q^1, u^1) = \hat{\pi}(\mathbf{p}, q^1, y)$. Hence, the graph of $\hat{\pi}(\mathbf{p}, q, y)$ as a function of q intersects the graph of $\hat{\pi}(\mathbf{p}, q, u^0)$ at $q = q^0$, and the graph of $\hat{\pi}(\mathbf{p}, q, u^1)$ at $q = q^1$. This is depicted in

Figure 1.[13] From (12b) and (10), one obtains

(13) $m_q(\mathbf{p}, q, u)$

$= -\hat{\pi}[\mathbf{p}, q, m(\mathbf{p}, q, u)]$

which is the fundamental differential equation underlying Randall and Stoll's analysis.[14] Also, by differentiating (12b) and then using (13), it can be shown that the concavity of $\hat{m}(\mathbf{p}, \pi, u)$ in π, which itself follows from the quasi-concavity of $u(\mathbf{x}, q)$ in q, implies the following negativity condition on the Slutsky term associated with $\hat{\pi}(\mathbf{p}, q, y)$: $\hat{\pi}_q - \pi \hat{\pi}_y \le 0$.[15]

Define the quantity

(14) $A \equiv \int_{q^0}^{q^1} \hat{\pi}(\mathbf{p}, q, y)\, dq$

which corresponds to the area $q^0 \beta \gamma \delta q^1$ in Figure 1. This is a sort of Marshallian consumer's surplus, which is to be compared with C and E.[16] Let

$$\xi \equiv \frac{\partial \ln \hat{\pi}(\mathbf{p}, q, y)}{\partial \ln y}$$

be the income elasticity of $\hat{\pi}(\mathbf{p}, q, y)$; Randall and Stoll call this the "price flexibility of income." Assume that, over the range from $(\mathbf{p}, q^0, y)$ to $(\mathbf{p}, q^1, y)$, this elasticity is bounded from below by ξ^L and from above by ξ^U, with neither bound equal to 1. Using

---

[12] Note that $\hat{\pi}(\mathbf{p}, q, y)$ is *not* an inverse ordinary demand function in the sense of Ronald W. Anderson (1980), because it involves an income adjustment as well as a price effect.

[13] It is commonly supposed the $\hat{\pi}_q < 0$, so that $\pi^0 > \pi^1$ when $q^0 < q^1$ (see e.g., Richard E. Just et al., 1982 fig. 7.12), but this is not correct. It can be shown that $\pi^0 \gtreqless \pi^1$ according to whether $\eta \lesseqgtr 1/\alpha$, where η and α are defined in the text below equation (16'). Since $\Sigma \alpha_i \eta_i + \alpha \eta = 1$ by the Engel aggregation condition, where $\alpha_i \equiv p_i \hat{h}^i(\mathbf{p}, \pi, y + \pi q)/(y + \pi q)$ and $\eta_i \equiv (y + \pi q)\hat{h}^i_y(\mathbf{p}, \pi, y + \pi q)/\hat{h}^i(\mathbf{p}, \pi, y + \pi q)$, it follows that $\pi^0 \lesseqgtr \pi^1$ if and only if $\Sigma \alpha_1 \eta_i \lesseqgtr 0$.

[14] This corresponds to Randall and Stoll's equation 7.

[15] Also, because $\hat{m}(\cdot)$ is linearly homogeneous in $(\mathbf{p}, \pi)$, it follows that $\hat{\pi}(\mathbf{p}, q, y)$ is linearly homogeneous in $(\mathbf{p}, y)$.

[16] Its relation to the conventional Marshallian consumer's surplus associated with the demand for the x's is analyzed in Proposition 4.

the mean-value theorem, as in Willig's (1976) equation 18, and integrating (13) yields Randall and Stoll's result, namely, the following.

PROPOSITION 3: *Assume* $\xi^L \le \xi \le \xi^U$ *where* $\xi^L \ne 1$ *and* $\xi^U \ne 1$. *Then*,

(i) $\quad 0 \le \left[1 + (1 - \xi^L) \dfrac{A}{y} \right]^{\frac{1}{1 - \xi^L}} - 1 \le \dfrac{E}{y}$

(ii) $\quad 0 \le 1 - \left[1 - (1 - \xi^U) \dfrac{A}{y} \right]^{\frac{1}{1 - \xi^U}} \le \dfrac{C}{y} \le 1.$

If $\xi^U < 1$, *or if* $\xi^U > 1$ *and* $1 + (1 - \xi^U)\dfrac{A}{y} > 0$,

(iii) $\quad \dfrac{E}{y} \le \left[1 + (1 - \xi^U) \dfrac{A}{y} \right]^{\frac{1}{1 - \xi^U}} - 1.$

If $\xi^L > 1$, *or if* $\xi^L \le 1$ *and* $1 - (1 - \xi^L)\dfrac{A}{y} \ge 0$,

(iv) $\quad \dfrac{C}{y} \le 1 - \left[1 - (1 - \xi^L) \dfrac{A}{y} \right]^{\frac{1}{1 - \xi^L}}.$

Applying a Taylor approximation, as in Willig (1976), and assuming that the conditions in (iii) and (iv) are satisfied, one obtains

(15) $\quad \xi^L \dfrac{A^2}{2y} \le E - C \le \xi^U \dfrac{A^2}{2y}.$

This is commonly interpreted as implying that C and E are likely to be close in value, but whether or not that is correct clearly depends on the magnitudes of A/y and the bounds ξ^L and ξ^U. The magnitude of A/y depends in part on the size of the change from q^0 to q^1; but what can be said about the likely magnitude of the income elasticity, ξ? Could it happen, for example, that $\xi^L = \infty$? To answer that question, dif-

ferentiate (11) implicitly:

(16) $\quad \dfrac{\partial \hat{\pi}(\mathbf{p}, q, y)}{\partial y}$

$$= - \dfrac{\hat{h}_y^q(\mathbf{p}, \pi, y + \pi q)}{\hat{h}_\pi^q(\mathbf{p}, \pi, y + \pi q) + q \hat{h}_y^q(\mathbf{p}, \pi, y + \pi q)}.$$

By the Hicks-Slutsky decomposition, the denominator is equal to the own-price derivative of the compensated demand function for q and is nonpositive:

$$\hat{g}_\pi^q[\mathbf{p}, \pi, v(\mathbf{p}, q, y)]$$

$$= \hat{h}_\pi^q(\mathbf{p}, \pi, y + \pi q) + q \hat{h}_y^q(\mathbf{p}, \pi, y + \pi q)$$

$$\le 0.$$

Converted to elasticity form, (16) becomes

(16') $\quad \xi = - \dfrac{\eta(1 - \alpha)}{\varepsilon}$

where

$$\eta \equiv \dfrac{(y + \pi q) \hat{h}_y^q(\mathbf{p}, \pi, y + \pi q)}{\hat{h}^q(\mathbf{p}, \pi, y + \pi q)}$$

is the income elasticity of the *direct* ordinary demand function for q,

$$\alpha \equiv \dfrac{\pi \hat{h}^q(\mathbf{p}, \pi, y + \pi q)}{y + \pi q}$$

is the budget share of q in relation to "adjusted" income, and

$$\varepsilon \equiv \dfrac{\pi \hat{g}_\pi^q[\mathbf{p}, \pi, v(\mathbf{p}, q, y)]}{\hat{g}^q[\mathbf{p}, \pi, v(\mathbf{p}, q, y)]}$$

is the own-price elasticity of the compensated demand function for q.

The denominator in (16') can be related to the overall elasticity of substitution between q and the private market goods $x_1, \ldots, x_N$. Assume that the prices $p_1, \ldots, p_N$ vary in strict proportion (i.e., $p_i = \theta \bar{p}_i$ for some fixed vector $\bar{p}$ and some positive scalar θ). Let the aggregate Allen-Uzawa elasticity of substitution between q and the Hicksian composite commodity $x_0 \equiv \Sigma \bar{p}_i x_i$ be denoted by σ_0. By adapting W. E. Diewert's (1974) analysis, the following formula can be established relating σ_0 to the compensated own-price elasticity for q: $\varepsilon = -\sigma_0(1 - \alpha)$.[17] Hence, (16') may be written

$$(17) \qquad \xi = \frac{\eta}{\sigma_0}.$$

This equation is my fundamental result. It explains the findings in the preceding section about the importance of substitution elasticities. It demonstrates that for changes in q, unlike for changes in p, the extent of the difference between C and E depends not only on income effects (i.e., η) but also on substitution effects (i.e., σ_0). If, over the relevant range, either $\eta = 0$ (no income effects) or $\sigma_0 = \infty$ (perfect substitution between q and one or more of the x's), then $\xi^L = \xi^U = 0$ and, from Proposition 3, $C = A = E$. On the other hand, if either the demand function for q is highly income elastic or there are very few substitutes for q among the x's so that σ_0 is close to zero, this could generate very large values of ξ and a substantial divergence between C and E.

III. Applications

In the first application of (17), the price flexibility of income, ξ, is assumed to be a constant. In that case, as Randall and Stoll note, the bounds in Proposition 3 hold as equalities, and (for simplicity I focus on the case where $\xi \neq 1$):

$$(18a) \qquad \frac{C}{y} = 1 - \left[1 - (1 - \xi)\frac{A}{y}\right]^{\frac{1}{1-\xi}}$$

$$(18b) \qquad \frac{E}{y} = \left[1 + (1 - \xi)\frac{A}{y}\right]^{\frac{1}{1-\xi}} - 1.$$

However, before these formulas can be used to calculate C and E, one must detemine how A varies with ξ.

If the price flexibility of income is to be constant, the inverse ordinary demand function must take the form

$$(18c) \qquad \hat{\pi}(\mathbf{p}, q, y) = \psi(\mathbf{p}, q) y^\xi$$

where $\psi \geq 0$. Define $G(\mathbf{p}, q) \equiv \int \psi(\mathbf{p}, q) \, dq$; from (14):[18]

$$(18d) \qquad A = y^\xi \left[G(\mathbf{p}, q^1) - G(\mathbf{p}, q^0)\right].$$

Substituting (18c) into (13) and integrating yields the indirect utility function that generates (18c):

$$(18e) \quad v(\mathbf{p}, q, y)$$
$$= T\left(\left[y^{1-\xi} + (1 - \xi)G(\mathbf{p}, q)\right]^{\frac{1}{1-\xi}}, \mathbf{p}\right)$$

where $T(\cdot)$ is some function that is homogeneous of degree zero, increasing in its first argument, and nonincreasing in its other arguments.

---

[17] In deriving this result, one evaluates $\hat{m}(\mathbf{p}, \pi, u)$, $\hat{g}^q(\mathbf{p}, \pi, u)$, and $\hat{g}(\mathbf{p}, \pi, u)$ at $u = v(\mathbf{p}, q, y)$. Hence, the budget shares introduced above satisfy $\alpha \equiv \pi \hat{h}^q(\mathbf{p}, \pi, y + \pi q)/(y + \pi q) = \pi \hat{g}^q(\mathbf{p}, \pi, u)/\hat{m}(\mathbf{p}, \pi, u)$, and $\alpha_j \equiv p_j \hat{h}^j(\mathbf{p}, \pi, y + \pi q)/(y + \pi q) = p_j \hat{g}^j(\mathbf{p}, \pi, u)/\hat{m}(\mathbf{p}, \pi, u)$. In addition to the compensated own-price demand elasticity, ε, I introduce the compensated cross-price demand elasticities $\varepsilon_j = \partial \ln \hat{g}^q(\mathbf{p}, \pi, u)/\partial p_j$. The homogeneity of $\hat{g}^q(\cdot)$ in $(\mathbf{p}, \pi)$ implies that $\varepsilon + \Sigma \varepsilon_j = 0$. Under the assumption that $p_j = \theta \bar{p}_j$, $j = 1, \ldots, N$, the Allen-Uzawa elasticity of substitution between q and the composite good x_0 is given by $\sigma_0 \equiv [(\partial \hat{g}^q/\partial \theta) \cdot \theta/q]/\alpha_0$ where $\alpha_0 \equiv \Sigma \alpha_j = 1 - \alpha$ is the expenditure share of x_0 and θ is treated as its price. Observe that $\partial \hat{g}^q/\partial \theta = \Sigma(\partial \hat{g}^q/\partial p_j) \cdot \bar{p}_j = \Sigma(\partial \hat{g}^q/\partial p_j) \cdot (p_j/\theta) = (q/\theta)\Sigma \varepsilon_j = -(q/\theta)\varepsilon$. Hence, $\sigma_0(1 - \alpha) = (\theta/q)(\partial \hat{g}^q/\partial \theta) = -\varepsilon$.

[18] In order to satisfy the negativity and homogeneity conditions, $\psi(\cdot)$ should be increasing in q and homogeneous of degree $1 - \xi$ in $\mathbf{p}$. It follows that $G(\cdot)$, too, is homogeneous of degree $1 - \xi$ in $\mathbf{p}$.

The corresponding demand function for q, $\hat{h}^q(\mathbf{p}, \pi, y)$ can be derived from (18c) by solving $\max_q [v(\mathbf{p}, q, y - \pi q)]$. In general, a closed-form solution cannot be obtained. However, implicit differentiation of the first-order condition for this maximization yields the following expression for the income elasticity of demand:

$$\eta = \frac{\xi\psi + \xi\psi^2 qy^{\xi-1}}{-q\psi_q + \xi\psi^2 qy^{\xi-1}}.$$

It follows that having a constant ξ is generally *not* consistent with having a constant η or a constant σ_0. An exception occurs when

(19a) $\qquad \xi\psi \equiv -q\psi_q$

in which case $\eta \equiv 1$ and, from (17), $\sigma_0 \equiv 1/\xi$ (i.e., the price flexibility of income is merely the reciprocal of the elasticity of substitution between q and the x's). Integrating (19a) yields $\psi(\mathbf{p}, q) = K(\mathbf{p})q^{-\xi}$ for some function $K(\mathbf{p}) \geq 0$ which is homogeneous of degree $1 - \xi$, and $G(\mathbf{p}, q) = K(\mathbf{p})q^{1-\xi}/(1 - \xi)$. Hence,

(19b) $\quad A/y$

$$= K(\mathbf{p})y^{\xi-1}\left[(q^1)^{1-\xi} - (q^0)^{1-\xi}\right]\Big/(1 - \xi)$$

and the formulas for C and E become

(19c) $\quad C/y$

$$= 1 - \left\{1 - K(\mathbf{p})y^{\xi-1}\left[(q^1)^{1-\xi} - (q^0)^{1-\xi}\right]\right\}^{\frac{1}{1-\xi}}$$

(19d) $\quad E/y$

$$= \left\{1 + K(\mathbf{p})y^{\xi-1}\left[(q^1)^{1-\xi} - (q^0)^{1-\xi}\right]\right\}^{\frac{1}{1-\xi}} - 1.$$

This model with a unitary income elasticity, η, is the only case in which ξ, η, and σ_0 can all be constant simultaneously. It can be shown to be a generalization of the CES utility model $u(\mathbf{x}, q) =$

$[\phi(\mathbf{x})^{1-\xi} + aq^{1-\xi}]^{1/1-\xi}$ with homogeneous aggregator function, $\phi(\cdot)$.[19]

Equation (19b) makes explicit the dependence of A on ξ. From (19c) and (19d), it follows that the ratio E/C is increasing in both $K(\mathbf{p})$ and ξ. Table 1 tabulates this ratio for several values of K and ξ, for cases where $q^0 = 1$ and $q^1 = 3$. Observe that a low elasticity of substitution ($\sigma_0 \approx 0.07$) can generate a fivefold difference between C and E, even when A/y is very small.[20] A similar divergence between C and E can be obtained with a relatively moderate elasticity of substitution ($\sigma_0 = 0.99$), provided that the change matters a lot, in the sense that C/y is large ($C/y \approx 0.8$). However, C is almost identical to E when moderate or large elasticities of substitution are combined with low values of C/y.

The second application is the case in which the inverse demand function takes the form

(20a) $\quad \hat{\pi}(\mathbf{p}, q, y) = \psi(\mathbf{p}, q)e^{\gamma(\mathbf{p})y}$

and the price flexibility of income is $\xi = \gamma(\mathbf{p}) \cdot y$, for some $\gamma(\cdot) \geq 0$ which is homogeneous of degree -1 in $\mathbf{p}$, and some $\psi(\cdot) \geq 0$ which is homogeneous of degree 1 in $\mathbf{p}$. Substituting (20a) into (13) and integrating yields the indirect utility function that generates (20a):

(20b) $\quad v(\mathbf{p}, q, y)$

$$= T\left(-\frac{e^{-\gamma(\mathbf{p})y}}{\gamma(\mathbf{p})} + G(\mathbf{p}, q), \mathbf{p}\right)$$

---

[19] The difference is that the CES model generates an indirect utility function of the form

$$\bar{v}(\mathbf{p}, q, y) \equiv [y^{1-\xi} + K(\mathbf{p})q^{1-\xi}]^{1/1-\xi}$$

whereas the indirect utility function associated with (19a)–(19c) is

$$v(\mathbf{p}, q, y) = T[\bar{v}(\mathbf{p}, q, y), \mathbf{p}].$$

[20] This is the order of magnitude by which WTA exceeds WTP in some of the empirical studies summarized in table 3.2 of Cummings et al. (1986).

TABLE 1—SIMULATIONS OF WTP AND WTA FOR A GENERALIZED
CES UTILITY MODEL

ξ	y	$K(\mathbf{p})$	σ_0	A/y	C/y	E/y	E/C
14	1	0.95	0.0714	0.073	0.05	0.259	5.175
1.01	100	1.4	0.99	1.602	0.796	4.026	5.059
0.677	100	8.1	1.481	2.414	0.991	4.975	5.003
0.677	100	0.1	1.481	0.03	0.029	0.03	1.02

where $G \equiv \int \psi(\mathbf{p}, q) \, dq$, and T is some function that is homogeneous of degree zero, increasing in its first argument, and nonincreasing in the other arguments. The corresponding formula for the elasticity of substitution between q and the x's, expressed as a function of $(\mathbf{p}, q, y)$, can be shown to be

$$(20c) \quad \sigma_0 = \frac{\psi y + q\psi^2 e^{\gamma y}}{-qy\psi_q + \gamma yq\psi^2 e^{\gamma y}}.$$

From (20a) and (20b) it follows that

$$(20d) \quad A = e^{\gamma(\mathbf{p})y}\big[G(\mathbf{p}, q^1) - G(\mathbf{p}, q^0)\big]$$

$$(20e) \quad C = \gamma(\mathbf{p})^{-1} \cdot \ln[1 + \gamma(\mathbf{p})A]$$

$$(20f) \quad E = -\gamma(\mathbf{p})^{-1} \cdot \ln[1 - \gamma(\mathbf{p})A].$$

(note that, when $\gamma A > 1$, $E = \infty$). The ratio E/C is clearly increasing in $\gamma(\mathbf{p})$ and A.

In order to proceed further, it is necessary to take a closer look at A. For this purpose, I focus on the special case of (20) in which $\gamma(\mathbf{p}) = \gamma/p_N$, $\psi(\mathbf{p}, q) = \delta e^{\alpha + \delta q} p_1^{1-\beta} p_N^\beta/(\beta - 1)$, and

$$(21a) \quad v(\mathbf{p}, q, y) =$$

$$T\left(-\frac{p_N}{\gamma}e^{-\gamma y/p_N} + \frac{e^{\alpha + \delta q}}{\beta - 1}p_1^{1-\beta}p_N^\beta, p_2, p_3, \ldots, p_N\right)$$

with γ and δ as positive constants and with $\beta > 1$. This implies the following log-log demand function for good 1:[21]

$$(21b) \quad \ln x_1 = \ln h^1(\mathbf{p}, q, y)$$
$$= \alpha - \beta \ln(p_1/p_N)$$
$$+ (\gamma y/p_N) + \delta q.$$

Since $\lim_{p_1 \to \infty} \partial v(\mathbf{p}, q, y)/\partial q = 0$, good 1 is weakly complementary with q in the sense of Mäler, and C and E can be expressed in terms of the area between the compensated demand curves $g^1(\mathbf{p}, q^0, u)$ and $g^1(\mathbf{p}, q^1, u)$. Furthermore, in this model the quantity A corresponds to the change in the Marshallian consumer's surplus associated with good 1.

$$(21c) \quad A \equiv \int_{q^0}^{q^1} \hat{\pi}(\mathbf{p}, q, y) \, dq$$

$$= \left(\frac{p_1}{\beta - 1}\right)\big[h^1(\mathbf{p}, q^1, y) - h^1(\mathbf{p}, q^0, y)\big]$$

$$= \int_{p_1}^{\infty} \big[h^1(\mathbf{p}, q^1, y) - h^1(\mathbf{p}, q^0, y)\big] dp_1.$$

Hence, the formulas for C and E become

$$(21d) \quad \frac{C}{p_N} = \frac{1}{\gamma}\ln\left\{1 + \left(\frac{\gamma}{\beta - 1}\right)\left(\frac{p_1}{p_N}\right)\right.$$
$$\left. \times \big[h^1(\mathbf{p}, q^1, y) - h^1(\mathbf{p}, q^0, y)\big]\right\}$$

$$(21e) \quad \frac{E}{p_N} = \frac{1}{\gamma}\ln\left\{1 - \left(\frac{\gamma}{\beta - 1}\right)\left(\frac{p_1}{p_N}\right)\right.$$
$$\left. \times \big[h^1(\mathbf{p}, q^1, y) - h^1(\mathbf{p}, q^0, y)\big]\right\}.$$

[21] It follows that, in this model, the income elasticity of demand for good 1 is equal to γy, the price flexibility of income.

TABLE 2—SIMULATIONS OF WTP AND WTA FOR A LOG-LOG UTILITY MODEL

ξ	α	δ	γ	A/y	C/y	E/y	E/C
14	−13.58	0.2	0.14	0.0695	0.0486	0.259	5.334
1.01	1.42	0.3	0.0101	0.959	0.6704	3.414	5.092
0.677	2.151	0.3	0.00677	1.427	0.9987	5.004	5.011
0.677	2.28	0.13	0.00677	0.039	0.0385	0.0396	1.027

These are tabulated in Table 2 for several values of α, γ, and δ for the case in which $p_N = 1$, $p_1 = 1.5$, $\beta = 1.125$, $y = 100$, $q^0 = 1$, and $q^1 = 3$.[22] The simulations confirm that $\xi = \gamma y$ and A are the key determinants of the ratio E/C. When either ξ or A is large, then $E \gg C$; when ξ and A are both small, then $E \approx C$.

This example is a striking illustration of the power of Proposition 3. From mere inspection of the ordinary demand function for x_1 in (21b) it is hardly obvious that the term $\xi = \gamma y$ should be a key determinant of the relationship between WTP and WTA for a change in q.[23] The example also raises another issue: the possibility that the quantity A, which forms the basis for Proposition 3, may be related to the conventional Marshallian consumer's surplus associated with a private market commodity, x_1. Under what circumstances does this carry over to other utility models? Could it, in fact, apply to the

first example based on a generalization of the CES utility model?

By way of answer to the first question, the following lemma establishes that weak complementarity is but one of two conditions that must be satisfied if A is to be equated with a change in the Marshallian consumer's surplus:

LEMMA 1: *Suppose there is a private market good, say x_1, with the properties that* (a) *it is nonessential and weakly complementary with q, and* (b)

$$\frac{\partial \hat{\pi}(\mathbf{p}, q, y)}{\partial p_1} = -\frac{\partial h^1(\mathbf{p}, q, y)}{\partial q}.$$

Then,

$$(22) \quad A = \int_{p_1}^{\infty} [h^1(\mathbf{p}, q^1, y) - h^1(\mathbf{p}, q^0, y)]\, dp_1.$$

PROOF:

Weak complementarity implies $\lim_{p_1 \to \infty} m_q(\mathbf{p}, q, u) = 0$. Nonessentialness implies $\lim_{p_1 \to \infty} m(\mathbf{p}, q, u) < \infty$. Hence, by (13), condition (a) implies $\lim_{p_1 \to \infty} \hat{\pi}(\mathbf{p}, q, y) = 0$. Accordingly, one can express $\hat{\pi}(\cdot)$ as

$$\hat{\pi}(\mathbf{p}, q, y) = -\int_{p_1}^{\infty} \frac{\partial \pi(\mathbf{p}, q, y)}{\partial p_1}\, dp_1$$

$$= \int_{p_1}^{\infty} \frac{\partial h^1(\mathbf{p}, q, y)}{\partial q}\, dp_1$$

where the second equality follows from condition (b). Invoking the definition of A in (14) and changing the order of integration yields (22).

[22]The parameter values in these simulations are chosen to satisfy the inequalities $(\beta - 1)p_N \le \gamma p_1 h^1(\mathbf{p}, q, y) \le \beta p_N$, which ensure that the direct utility function implied by (21) is quasi-concave in x and q. If $u(\mathbf{x}, q)$ were not quasi-concave in q, the formulas in (21d) and (21e), would still be valid, but the Randall-Stoll bounds in Proposition 3 would not apply. That happens with another special case of (20) in which $\gamma(\mathbf{p}) = \gamma / p_N$ but $\psi(\mathbf{p}, q) = \delta p_N e^{\alpha - \beta(p_1/p_N) + \delta q}/\beta$. This generates an ordinary demand function for good 1 that is identical to (21b), except that $\ln(p_1/p_N)$ is replaced by (p_1/p_N). Also, (21c)–(21e) hold for this model, except that $\beta - 1$ is replaced by β. However, the implicit utility function $u(\mathbf{x}, q)$ can be shown to be quasi-convex *in q*.

[23]Also, it is hardly obvious that from the demand function in (21b) one can recover σ_0, the elasticity of substitution between q and the x's (*all* the x's, not just x_1). This is obtained by substituting $\gamma(\mathbf{p}) \equiv \gamma / p_N$ and $\psi(\mathbf{p}, q) \equiv \delta e^{\alpha + \delta q} p_1^{1-\beta} p_N^{\beta}/(\beta - 1)$ into (20c). The corresponding formula for η can be obtained from $\eta = \sigma_0 \xi = \sigma_0 \gamma y / p_N$.

Application of Lemma 1 yields the answer to the second question:

PROPOSITION 4: *Partition the price vector as* $\mathbf{p} = (p_1, \mathbf{p}_{(1)})$. *Equation (22) holds if and only if* $v(\mathbf{p}, q, y)$ *can be expressed in the form*

$$(23) \quad v(\mathbf{p}, q, y) = T\left[G(\mathbf{p}, q), \mathbf{p}_{(1)}y\right]$$

where $\lim_{p \to \infty} G_q(\mathbf{p}, q) = \lim_{p_1 \to \infty} G_{p_1}(\mathbf{p}, q) = 0$.

PROOF:

Observe that the conditions on the derivatives of $G(\cdot)$ ensure that x_1 is nonessential and weakly complementary with q. The main task is to show that the functional structure in (23) is necessary and sufficient to satisfy condition (b) of Lemma 1. First use (10) and (12a), and then twice differentiate the implicit function $v(\mathbf{p}, q, y) - u = 0$ to obtain

$$\frac{\partial \hat{\pi}(\mathbf{p}, q, y)}{\partial p_1}$$

$$= -m_{qp_1}[\mathbf{p}, q, v(\mathbf{p}, q, y)]$$

$$\quad -m_{qu}[\mathbf{p}, q, v(\mathbf{p}, q, y)] \cdot v_{p_1}(\mathbf{p}, q, y)$$

$$= -(v_q v_{yp_1} - v_y v_{qp_1}) / v_y^2.$$

Comparing this with $\partial h^1(\mathbf{p}, q, y)/\partial q = (v_{p_1} v_{qy} - v_y v_{qp_1})^2 / v_y^2$, it can be seen that condition (b) will be satisfied if and only if $v_q v_{yp_1} = v_{p_1} v_{qy}$. However, this is equivalent to requiring that (v_q / v_{p_1}) be independent of y, which in turn is equivalent to (23).

The log-log utility model in (21a) clearly satisfies the conditions of Proposition 4. The generalized CES utility model in (18) could also meet the conditions of the proposition, provided that p_1 appears only in the first argument of $T(\cdot)$.

Equation (23) expresses a restriction on the marginal rate of substitution between q and the price of a weakly complementary private-market good, p_1 (i.e., that it be independent of income). This condition was first introduced by Willig (1978) in his paper

on hedonic price adjustments for valuing marginal changes in q: his theorem 1 characterized the circumstances under which the marginal value of q equals the derivative with respect to q of the Marshallian consumer's surplus for x_1, averaged over the number of units of the good consumed. Proposition 4 expresses a similar result using a different and more compact proof. Combining Propositions 3 and 4 provides a way to value *nonmarginal* changes in q by employing the change in Marshallian consumer's surplus to compute A and then using A to bound WTP or WTA. These two propositions, in effect, establish a new link between Willig's two seminal papers.[24]

IV. Conclusion

A recent assessment of the state of the art of public-good valuation concludes "Received theory establishes that ... WTP ... should approximately equal ... WTA.... In contrast with theoretical axioms which predict small differences between WTP and WTA, results from contingent valuation method applications wherein such measures are derived almost always demonstrate large differences between average WTP and WTA. To date, researchers have been unable to explain in any definitive way the persistently observed differences between WTP and WTA measures" (Cummings et al., 1986 p. 41.)[25] This paper

---

[24] I am very grateful to a referee for pointing out the connection with Willig's theorem 1. In my notation, Willig's theorem states that (23) is equivalent to the equality $v_q(\mathbf{p}, q, y)/v_{p_1}(\mathbf{p}, q, y) = \hat{\pi}(\mathbf{p}, q, y)/h^1(\mathbf{p}, q, y)$.

[25] Some of the debates on divergences between WTP and WTA have focused on the concept of loss-aversion, introduced in the economics literature by Daniel Kahneman and Amos Tversky (1979). This is a different phenomenon from that involved in the Randall-Stoll bounds: it concerns the disparity between the WTP to obtain a change from q^0 to $q^0 + \Delta$ (for some $\Delta > 0$) and the WTP to avoid a change from q^0 to $q^0 - \Delta$, which is not the same as the disparity between WTP and WTA for the same change from q^0 to $q^1 = q^0 + \Delta$. However, the loss/gain disparity can be analyzed using the tools developed in this paper. In a separate paper, I have identified the conditions under which it will *exceed* the disparity between WTP and WTA studied here.

offers an explanation by showing that the theoretical presumption of approximate equality between WTP and WTA is misconceived. This is because, for public goods, the relation between the two welfare measures depends on a substitution effect as well as an income effect. Given that the substitution elasticity appears in the denominator of (17) and that the Engel aggregation condition places some limit on the plausible magnitude of the income elasticity in the numerator, this suggests that the substitution effects could exert a far greater leverage on the relation between WTP and WTA than the income effects. Thus, large empirical divergences between WTP and WTA may be indicative not of some failure in the survey methodology but of a general perception on the part of the individuals surveyed that the private-market goods available in their choice set are, collectively, a rather imperfect substitute for the public good under consideration.

REFERENCES

Anderson, Ronald W., "Some Theory of Inverse Demand for Applied Demand Analysis," *European Economic Review*, November 1980, *14*, 281–90.

Coursey, Don L., Hovis, John J. and Schulze, William D., "The Disparity Between Willingness to Accept and Willingness to Pay Measures of Value," *Quarterly Journal of Economics*, August 1987, *102*, 679–90.

Cummings, Ronald G., Brookshire, David S. and Schulze, William D., *Valuing Public Goods: An Assessment of the Contingent Valuation Method*, Totowa, NJ: Rowman and Allanheld, 1986.

Diewert, W. E., "A Note on Aggregation and Elasticities of Substitution," *Canadian Journal of Economics*, February 1974, *7*, 12–20.

Fisher, Ann, McClelland, Gary H. and Schulze, William D., "Measures of Willingness to Pay versus Willingness to Accept: Evidence, Explanations and Potential Reconciliation," in George L. Peterson, B. L. Driver, and Robin Gregory, eds., *Amenity*

Resource Valuation: Integrating Economics with Other Disciplines, State College, PA: Venture, 1988, pp. 127–34.

Freeman, A. Myrick, *The Benefits of Environmental Improvement: Theory and Practice*, Baltimore: Johns Hopkins University Press, 1979.

Gorman, W. M., "Tricks With Utility Functions," in M. Artis and R. Nobay, eds., *Essays in Economic Analysis*, New York: Cambridge University Press, 1976, pp. 211–43.

Gregory, Robin, "Interpreting Measures of Economic Loss: Evidence from Contingent Valuation and Experimental Studies," *Journal of Environmental Economics and Management*, December 1986, *13*, 325–37.

Hanemann, W. Michael, "Quality and Demand Analysis," in Gordon C. Rausser, ed., *New Directions in Econometric Modeling and Forecasting in U. S. Agriculture*, Amsterdam: North Holland, 1982, pp. 55–98.

Just, Richard E., Hueth, Darrell L. and Schmitz, Andrew, *Applied Welfare Economics and Public Policy*, Englewood Cliffs, NJ: Prentice-Hall, 1982.

Kahneman, Daniel and Tversky, Amos, "Prospect Theory: An Analysis of Decisions Under Risk," *Econometrica*, March 1979, *47*, 263–91.

Knetsch, Jack L. and Sinden, J. A., "Willingness to Pay and Compensation Demanded: Experimental Disparity in Measures of Value," *Quarterly Journal of Economics*, August 1984, *99*, 507–21.

Mäler, Karl-Göran, *Environmental Economics: A Theoretical Inquiry*, Baltimore: Johns Hopkins University Press, 1974.

Neary, J. P. and Roberts, K. W. S., "Theory of Household Behavior Under Rationing," *European Economic Review*, January 1980, *13*, 25–42.

Peterson, George L., Driver, B. L. and Gregory, Robin, eds., *Amenity Resource Valuation: Integrating Economics with Other Disciplines*, State College, PA: Venture, 1988.

Randall, Alan and Stoll, John R., "Consumer's Surplus in Commodity Space," *American Economic Review*, June 1980, *71*, 449–57.

Thayer, Mark A., "Contingent Valuation Techniques for Assessing Environmental Impacts: Further Evidence," *Journal of Environmental Economics and Management*, March 1981, *8*, 27–44.

Willig, Robert, "Consumer's Surplus Without Apology," *American Economic Review*, September 1976, *66*, 589–97.

_____, "Incremental Consumer's Surplus and Hedonic Price Adjustment," *Journal of Economic Theory*, April 1978, *17*, 227–53.

[29]

Social Cost of Environmental Quality Regulations: A General Equilibrium Analysis

Michael Hazilla

American University

Raymond J. Kopp

Resources for the Future

The use of cost-benefit analysis by federal regulatory agencies has expanded greatly in scope and sophistication. Unfortunately, agencies continue to employ private cost rather than social cost to evaluate environmental quality regulations. Furthermore, general equilibrium impacts and intertemporal effects of regulations are typically not included in the evaluation. In this paper we estimate the social cost of environmental quality regulations mandated by the Clean Air and Clean Water acts. We construct an econometric general equilibrium model of the United States to demonstrate that social cost estimates diverge sharply from private cost estimates. We also demonstrate that general equilibrium impacts are significant and pervasive and that intertemporal effects of the regulations, heretofore ignored, are significant.

I. Introduction

By presidential executive order, federal agencies are required to analyze new regulations, or changes in existing regulations, using benefit-

This research was supported in part by the U.S. Environmental Protection Agency, Office of Air Quality Planning and Standards, under contract no. 68-02-35-82. Although the research described in this article has been funded in part by the U.S. Environmental Protection Agency and the Senate Research Committee of the American University, no official endorsement should be inferred. We acknowledge helpful comments provided by Maureen Cropper, Robert Haveman, Dale Jorgenson, Al McGartland, John Mullahy, Wallace Oates, Sam Peltzman, Paul Portney, and V. Kerry Smith.

[*Journal of Political Economy*, 1990, vol. 98, no. 4]

cost analysis.[1] Even though it improves on the economic analysis of public policies, the executive order includes neither explicit guidelines for conducting analyses nor precise definitions of benefits and costs. In the absence of formal guidelines, one might conclude that the executive order mandates an interpretation of benefits and costs consistent with applied welfare economics. More specifically, one might infer that benefits and costs are measured on the basis of the compensation principle.[2] Unfortunately, a theoretically precise social cost measure is not used in practice, and current procedures, based on private costs, are subject to errors of unknown magnitude and without basis in modern applied welfare economics.[3] The objective of this paper is to improve on these procedures by using compensating variation welfare measures to evaluate the social cost of environmental quality regulations promulgated under the Clean Air and Clean Water acts.

While federal agencies conducting benefit-cost analyses have, for the most part, employed benefit measures consistent with economic theory, they have inappropriately used private expenditures as a measure of social cost. From a social welfare perspective, the correct theoretical cost measure is the monetized change in social welfare due to reallocation of resources from production of goods and services to pollution abatement activities. If one assumes that social welfare can be measured using a function additive in individual utilities, then social cost is equal to the sum of individual compensating variations. Moreover, under the additivity assumption, a theoretically consistent social cost estimate can be constructed from observable market information.

It is well known that the cost of regulations, as calculated by agencies such as the U.S. Environmental Protection Agency (EPA), is not based on the theoretical concept of social cost. Rather, agencies equate social cost with annualized engineering costs of installed capital and related operating and maintenance expenses. Setting aside

---

[1] For instance, Executive Order 12291, issued by President Ronald Reagan, states that "in promulgating new regulations, reviewing existing regulations, and developing legislative proposals concerning regulation, all agencies, to the extent permitted by law shall adhere to the following requirements: . . . b) Regulatory action shall not be undertaken unless the potential benefits to society for the regulation outweigh the potential costs to society" (*Fed. Register* 46 [February 19, 1981]: 13193–98).

[2] More precisely, benefits are measured using the maximum amount of money individuals would be willing to pay to live in a world with the policy in force rather than not. Conversely, one could assess the cost of the policy as the minimum amount of money necessary to compensate individuals to endure the policy's adverse effects.

[3] Benefits and costs are measured using a money metric of the gains or losses in utility associated with changes in the individual's economic circumstances. It is important to recognize that there is some controversy regarding use of money metric utility (see, e.g., Blackorby and Donaldson 1986).

these theoretical issues, one still finds problems with the use of engineering costs. For example, engineering costs generally do not account for partial equilibrium adjustments, let alone general equilibrium effects. Furthermore, engineering notions of cost are static and do not consider intertemporal regulatory impacts on household and firm decision making.

Some regulatory agencies acknowledge that their cost estimate is inconsistent with benefit measures and that it does not account for dynamic and general equilibrium impacts of regulation. Agencies and many economists believe, however, that engineering cost estimates are suitable proxies for social cost and maintain that dynamic, general equilibrium impacts are insignificant. If this conjecture is valid, then static engineering cost estimates are appropriate for social cost measurement. If, on the other hand, one can demonstrate empirically that engineering estimates are poor proxies for social cost and that dynamic, general equilibrium effects are important, then one can argue that social cost estimates must be based on the precepts of welfare economics and encompass general equilibrium and intertemporal effects.

This paper contrasts static engineering cost estimates, based on private expenditures, with social cost estimates derived from modern applied welfare economics. To estimate the dynamic social cost of environmental quality regulations, we construct an econometric general equilibrium model of the U.S. economy. The model encompasses both static and intertemporal behavioral adjustments. Most important, the general equilibrium model includes an explicit characterization of household utility that is used to assess welfare changes.

The model maintains certain assumptions that the reader should keep in mind when interpreting the results.[4] Like the majority of computable general equilibrium models, the model employed maintains the assumption of perfect competition in all markets. Production is modeled using a single form of malleable capital, and all inputs are assumed mobile. The capital stock is fixed in any given period and augmented at the end of the period by current-period net investment. The household is modeled using myopic expectations and assigned an initial wealth endowment. Transactions costs are assumed to be zero. Prices within the model are measured relative to a wage numeraire. Labor supply is endogenous while population growth is specified exogenously. Finally, as the major intertemporal link, household labor supply determines household income and savings. Household savings determine investment and the capital stock available in the

---

[4] One may, of course, find a model with different assumptions, but those in our model are standard.

next period. Through this intertemporal link, perturbations in the current-period labor market are transmitted to the capital market in the next period.

An outline of the paper follows. A broad review of the legislative basis for the environmental quality regulations is developed in Section II. The EPA estimates of the private cost of compliance with the Clean Air and Clean Water acts are also presented. Section III outlines the general equilibrium model.[5] Section IV describes modeling technology-based regulations, and Section V presents the social cost estimates of regulatory compliance. Concluding remarks are presented in Section VI.

II. Private Costs of Regulation

The majority of environmental regulations, promulgated during the 1970s and early 1980s, have been associated with the Clean Air and Clean Water acts. The 1970 Clean Air Act requires the EPA to establish national ambient air quality standards (NAAQS) for six pollutants.[6] In response to the legislation, the EPA established two regulatory programs. The first focuses on mobile emission sources, while the second concentrates on stationary sources. Each state is required to develop an environmental strategy that ensures that ambient air quality meets the NAAQS standards. This state-level strategy is termed the state implementation plan.

The EPA's responsibility to regulate waterborne pollutants emanates from the Federal Water Pollution Control Act of 1972 and amendments to the Clean Water Act of 1977. The legislation requires the EPA to establish regulations limiting industrial pollutant discharge. Like the Clean Air Act, the water legislation specifies the engineering character of the control technologies. The law initially requires application of "best practicable control technology" currently available but also mandates future implementation of the "best available technology" economically achievable. Similarly, new sources of emissions are regulated under "new source performance standards."[7]

Finally, in addition to the regulatory powers they confer, the Clean Air and Clean Water acts require the EPA to provide Congress with detailed compliance cost estimates. The most recent report, completed in 1983 and encompassing the regulatory framework existing

---

[5] Unfortunately, space limitations do not permit a full and detailed discussion of the model employed in this analysis. A longer version of the present paper and a detailed technical appendix are available on request from the authors.

[6] The six criteria pollutants are particulate matter, sulfur oxides, nitrogen oxides, carbon monoxide, ozone, and lead.

[7] See Portney (1989) for a complete discussion of air and water quality regulations.

in December 1982, forms the basis for our social cost analysis (see U.S. Environmental Protection Agency 1984).

The EPA cost estimates are composed of annualized capital costs of equipment and installation, and direct operating and maintenance expenditures associated with this equipment. These costs pertain only to regulatory actions resulting from the Clean Air and Clean Water acts and exclude voluntary expenditure, or expenditures required by state or local government and other federal laws. Annual 1981 compliance costs reported by the EPA to Congress are displayed by major industries in column 1 of table 1. Total annual cost over the period 1981–90 is reported in column 2 of table 1. The EPA report states that the average annual cost of the regulations in 1981 dollars between 1970 and 1978 was $19 billion, was $40 billion between 1979 and 1981, and will be $58 billion between 1981 and 1990.

In fairness, we note that the EPA does not claim that the estimates reported in table 1 represent social costs, but rather that the estimates are initial private costs of complying with the acts. However, these private cost estimates do not account for general equilibrium cost effects that can be transmitted from a regulated industry to those not directly affected by regulation. The neglect of such secondary effects can understate the private costs.

III. The General Equilibrium Model

Overview

Measuring the social cost of significant and complex regulatory programs, such as the Clean Air and Clean Water acts, requires a modeling structure with particular features. The most important feature is the ability to measure social cost using household willingness to pay rather than measures based on compliance expenditure. This requirement can be satisfied by constructing appropriate demand and supply curves for goods whose prices may be affected and measuring the net change in consumer and producer surplus. Alternatively, one can characterize household preferences with an indirect utility or expenditure function and proceed to monetize the changes in utility due to price and income changes brought about by the regulatory program. If one expects the regulatory program to change several prices and incomes, then measuring the social cost using compensating or equivalent variation measures (derived from expenditure functions) is preferable to using net changes in consumer and producer surplus. The modeling framework adopted follows the work of Jorgenson and Slesnick (1985a) and models household preference using a hierarchy of indirect utility functions. Measures of compensating variation may be readily obtained from these functions.

TABLE 1

Estimated Annual Capital and Operating Expenses Associated with Clean Air and Clean Water Acts Regulations (Millions of 1981 Dollars)

Sector	Annual Cost, 1981 (1)	Cumulative Annual Cost, 1981–90 (2)
Energy:		
Coal mining	103	1,189
Oil and gas extraction	576	6,318
Petroleum refining	1,153	12,346
Electric utilities	7,760	99,132
Coal gasification		302
Food processing:		
Feedlots and meat processing	182	2,725
Other food processing	1,389	14,324
Chemicals:		
Basic inorganic chemicals	403	4,008
Organic chemicals	1,019	15,837
Agricultural chemicals	246	3,358
Formulated chemicals	286	2,944
Construction materials	397	4,742
Metals:		
Ore mining and dressing	166·	1,657
Iron and steel	1,596	22,223
Aluminum	199	2,348
Copper	416	3,644
Nonferrous metals	243	2,876
Soft goods:		
Pulp and paper	1,173	11,987
Textiles	27	355
Leather and rubber	66	1,022
Manufacturing:		
Electroplating	0	910
Surface coatings	122	2,375
Furniture manufacture	7	70
Lead acid batteries	6	64
Services:		
Dry cleaning	0	467
Hospitals	102	1,668
Photographic processing	2	21
Municipal waste incineration	26	250
Other industrial costs:		
Boilers	2,547	26,599
Incinerators	157	2,488
Government expenditures	16,125	197,013
Mobile sources	6,047	80,554
Total expenditures	42,541	525,816

Source.—U.S. Environmental Protection Agency (1984).

   Assessing the reasonableness of static partial equilibrium assumptions underlying the use of expenditures as social cost measures also requires a modeling framework that allows for dynamic general equilibrium responses to regulatory programs. The model we develop departs from the static partial equilibrium analyses by drawing on recent developments in econometric general equilibrium models. The model incorporates intertemporal household behavior and is suitable for assessing long-run impacts of regulatory programs on neoclassical economic growth.

   The final important modeling feature concerns production. Imposing command and control technological requirements on industries subject to environmental regulation requires a detailed econometric production model. In our model, pollution control regulations can be imposed directly on the technologies. The model we develop contains 36 production sectors. Pollution control impacts are modeled through modification of the derived input demand equations in each sector.[8]

General Framework

To our knowledge, a model possessing the full set of attributes discussed above, which might be used to examine the usefulness of compliance expenditures as proxies for social cost, does not exist. Many computable general equilibrium models exist—some relying on calibration techniques and others based on a full set of econometrically estimated parameters—but in some aspect we have found them deficient.[9] The most popular and sophisticated calibration model is described in Ballard et al. (1985). Calibration models employ input-output matrices to describe derived input demand and constrain, a priori, substitution possibilities. The premier econometric general equilibrium model developed by Hudson and Jorgenson (1974), and extended by Hudson (1981) and Goettle and Hudson (1984), allows

   [8] Experience with the 36-sector model suggests that a more aggregate sectoral model may have produced similar results. The nine-sector model in Hudson and Jorgenson (1974) comes to mind; however, we have not undertaken a model aggregation to confirm this conjecture. Most of the initial compliance expenditures are borne by the motor vehicle and energy sectors, a small set of industrial boilers, the iron and steel industry, and organic chemicals. Neglecting the other sectors may have little effect on the results. It is important, however, to recognize that large disaggregate models may now be routinely constructed, and thus there is little reason (other than computer time) to employ more aggregate versions.
   [9] Many parameters in models of the Shoven and Whalley (1972) type are determined by a method known as "calibration." Such a method employs a single observational vector of endogenous variables to solve for the parameters of the model's behavioral equations consistent with observed values. The econometric approach to general equilibrium model building is discussed in Jorgenson (1984).

for substitution possibilities, intertemporal household behavior, and neoclassical growth, but it models production at a high level of aggregation.[10]

We have selected an econometric general equilibrium approach over one based on calibration methods because substitution and intertemporal dynamics are fundamental components in the evaluation of environmental quality regulations. Nevertheless, while we have utilized the Hudson-Jorgenson framework, we have also econometrically estimated disaggregate production sectors in a manner internally consistent with the remainder of the model.[11] The result is a new model, directly descendant from Hudson and Jorgenson, in which production is characterized econometrically, using "Diewert" flexible functional forms.[12] The sectoral econometric models correspond to two-digit industry groups in the Standard Industrial Classification.

The Structure of Production

Production in the model is disaggregated into 36 producing sectors. With the exception of government services, each sector is algebraically formulated as a hierarchical system of translog cost functions exhibiting constant returns to scale. This system gives rise to competitive derived demand equations for capital and labor, four forms of energy, and 30 intermediate inputs.

The translog system is estimated subject to symmetry, linear homogeneity, monotonicity, and concavity constraints. The symmetry and linear homogeneity parametric restrictions are well known, but imposing monotonicity and concavity constraints is a recent development (see Hazilla and Kopp 1986c). The econometric model is estimated using data from 1958–74 predating the Clean Air and Clean Water acts.[13] While it is possible to estimate the model using post-1974 data, the objective is to characterize the base case economy using the preregulation technologies.

---

[10] The Hudson-Jorgenson (1974) model divides the production side of the economy into nine sectors, but manufacturing activity is represented as one sector.

[11] The Hudson-Jorgenson model is probably the most well known of the numerical general equilibrium models and is described in various publications. Hudson and Jorgenson (1974, 1976) provide the most complete discussions readily available to the interested reader. Complete discussions of the model's inner workings are found in Berndt et al. (1981) and Hudson (1981). Other published sources include Hudson and Jorgenson (1978a, 1978b).

[12] A function $f(x)$ is Diewert flexible if at a point x^* it has enough free parameters so that $f(x^*)$, $\nabla f(x^*)$ (the N-dimensional gradient vector of f evaluated at x^*), and $\nabla^2 f(x^*)$ (the $N \times N$ Hessian matrix of second-order partial derivatives of f) can attain arbitrary values. See Diewert and Wales (1986).

[13] The data are extensively discussed in Hazilla and Kopp (1986b).

ENVIRONMENTAL QUALITY   861

The Structure of Consumption

The consumption side of the model is drawn from Berndt et al.
(1981). The model relies on the notion of a representative household
and implies that households share common preferences.[14] These
common preferences, described by a set of hierarchical indirect translog utility functions, serve to model both intertemporal and intratemporal household decisions.

The initial intertemporal decision faced by households concerns
the choice between present and future consumption. That is, a household must allocate a lifetime wealth endowment between present and
future consumption of goods and leisure. Following this choice, the
household focuses on two sequential intratemporal decisions. The
first is to select the proportions of current-period consumption to take
in the form of goods and leisure. This choice determines household
labor supply and leisure. The second sequential decision is household
allocation of current-period goods consumption among the following
commodity groups: energy, durable goods, imported goods, agriculture and construction, manufacturing, commercial and transportation, and other services.[15]

Social Welfare Measures

Social costs of environmental regulations may be measured at any
level in the household preference hierarchy from the uppermost intertemporal wealth-consumption decision to the intratemporal decisions regarding commodity consumption. Because household behavioral response is limited, the lówer in the hierarchy one performs the
measurement, the larger will be the estimates of social cost. Since the

---

[14] The assumption of a representative household may be relaxed by relying on the
exact aggregation theorems due to Lau (1977a, 1977b); see also Jorgenson and Slesnick
(1985b) and Hazilla and Kopp (1986a). This amendment to the model adds to the
computational burden and for that reason is not utilized in the current study. Hazilla
and Kopp (1986a), examining a specific environmental regulation but over a shorter
time period, utilized the detailed consumer model provided by Jorgenson, Lau, and
Stoker (1982) in place of the representative household model. While the latter model
permits one to distribute the costs of regulation over demographic groups, it does not
produce aggregate social welfare losses significantly different from the representative
household model.

[15] The hierarchical indirect utility functions were estimated by Berndt et al. (1981)
subject to adding-up, monotonicity, symmetry, and convexity restrictions using techniques attributed to Lau (1974). Although not of direct interest to our discussion, we
should point out that the model incorporates a government and foreign-trade sector.
The government sector collects taxes on capital and labor income, purchases goods and
services (government expenditures), and provides transfer payments to consumers and
subsidies to producers. A foreign-trade sector, which serves as an alternative to domestic supply, closes the model.

purpose of this study is to draw sharp contrast between private expenditures and social costs, we measure the welfare cost of environmental regulations using the indirect utility function describing preferences for goods and leisure.[16]

Social welfare is measured using the expenditure function and the Hicksian notion of compensating variation (Hicks 1946). The expenditure function is derived from an econometrically estimated indirect utility function. If we let $e(v, p)$ denote the expenditure function, compensating variation is defined as

$$CV = e(v^0, p^0) - e(v^0, p^1), \tag{1}$$

where CV represents the difference between the minimum expenditure necessary to achieve a utility level v^0, given commodity prices p^1, and the expenditure necessary to maintain v^0 at reference prices p^0. With this definition, a positive value for the compensating variation suggests a welfare gain whereas a negative value implies a welfare loss.[17]

IV. Technology-based Regulations

The Clean Air and Clean Water acts' compliance expenditures may be divided into three categories. The first and largest is private firm expenditures on air and water pollutant abatement equipment. The second category also includes pollution abatement expenditures but pertains to those made by federal, state, and local governments. The last group involves direct consumer expenditures such as increased cost of unleaded gasoline purchases and vehicle inspection fees.

The major portion of compliance cost is borne by stationary sources of air and water pollution, which, in our model, are represented by

---

[16] The goods-leisure indirect utility function lies just below the uppermost portion of the hierarchy describing the decision to consume out of total lifetime endowment. Berndt et al. (1981) estimate the preferences for endowment consumption such that the present period's consumption of endowments depends on time and the price of consumption, while the share out of total endowments depends only on time. Given this simplified view of the intertemporal consumption decision, we have chosen to measure welfare using the more econometrically interesting goods-leisure function. We do recognize that this choice somewhat overstates the welfare loss.

[17] When one is considering the welfare costs of significant government policies such as the Clean Air and Clean Water acts, however, income effects can be significant. Accordingly, to account for an income effect, CV may be calculated using

$$CV^* = e(v^0, p^0) - e(v^0, p^1) + y^1 - y^0$$
$$= y^1 - e(v^0, p^1),$$

where y^0 is the reference period income and y^1 is the postregulation income. The measure of social cost employed in this paper is based on CV^*.

the production sectors. In contrast to other forms of regulation, environmental regulations often require producers to employ resources that include the services of specialized capital, operating and maintenance labor, and the purchase of related intermediate inputs. Since input choice is endogenous in a general equilibrium model, representing technology-based regulations is markedly different from the characterization of policies that affect a general equilibrium solely through exogenous economic variables.

Technology-based regulations, the focus of our study, are modeled by specifying four aggregate input qualities—capital (K), labor (L), energy (E), and intermediate materials (M)—needed to comply with the regulations. Under a technology-based regulation, the structure of each production sector is modified to account for increased input usage. To illustrate the technique, consider a production sector whose technology is characterized by constant returns to scale and nonneutral technological change. The technology is represented by the translog cost function

$$\ln c = \alpha_0 + \sum_i \alpha_i \ln p_i + \frac{1}{2} \sum_i \sum_j \gamma_{ij} \ln p_i \ln p_j + \ln q$$
$$+ \alpha_t t + \frac{1}{2}\gamma_{tt} t^2 + \sum_i \gamma_{ti} t \ln p_i, \quad i, j = K, L, E, M, \tag{2}$$

where ln denotes the natural logarithm of cost (c), input prices (p_i), and output (q); t represents technological change; and α and γ are parameter vectors. In the absence of the environmental regulation, the optimal (sectoral) input demand equations are

$$x_i^* = \frac{\partial c}{\partial p_i} = \frac{c}{p_i}\left(\alpha_i + \sum_j \gamma_{ij} \ln p_j + \gamma_{ti} t\right), \tag{3}$$

where $c = \exp(\ln c)$. If Δ_i represents the increased quantity of the ith input required by the regulation, the demand equations would be modified as

$$\bar{x}_i = x_i^* + \Delta_i, \tag{4}$$

where $\bar{x}_i$ is the postregulation quantity of the ith input demanded.

Using (4), one can integrate back to the cost function

$$c = c(p, q) + \sum_i p_i \Delta_i q, \tag{5}$$

where Δ_i now represents input requirements per unit of output.

A second and somewhat more complicated approach, but one that reduces computational burden, is to embed pollution control expenditures directly into the technology. To illustrate this approach, consider the input demand equations

$$x_i^* = \frac{c}{p_i}\left(\alpha_i + \sum_j \gamma_{ij} \ln p_j + \gamma_{ti}l_i\right) \tag{6}$$

and cost function

$$c = \exp\left(\alpha_0 + \sum_i \alpha_i \ln p_i + \tfrac{1}{2}\sum_i \sum_j \gamma_{ij} \ln p_i \ln p_j + \alpha_t l_c + \tfrac{1}{2}\gamma_{tt}l_c^2\right.$$
$$\left. + \sum_i \gamma_{ti}l_i + \ln q\right) \quad \text{for } i, j = K, L, E, M,$$

where the technology variable (t) is replaced with t_c and t_i ($i = K, L, E,$ and M). Without the regulations, $t = t_c = t_i$ for all i. Under the regulations, t_c and t_i may be used to solve the system

$$x_i^* + \Delta_i q = \frac{\partial c}{\partial p_i},$$

$$\tag{7}$$

$$c + \sum_i p_i \Delta_i q = \exp c(\mathbf{p}, q, \mathbf{t}),$$

where $\mathbf{p} = [p_K, p_L, p_E, p_M]$ denotes the input price vector and the technology vector is $[t_c, t_K, t_L, t_E, t_M]$.

The second approach is employed in this study since it yields tractable demand equations. One should note that even though the technology terms are altered in this approach, biases and rate of technological progress are unchanged. Most important, however, imposing regulation does not affect theoretical properties of the cost functions.

There are two additional features of modeling technology-based regulation that are important for interpreting the social cost estimates. First, within a general equilibrium framework, the social cost of increased government expenditures to finance, for example, expenditures on municipal sewage treatment plants, can be significant. An exogenously imposed fixed deficit rule is used to account for increased taxes necessary to finance the expenditures. Arguably, it may be more realistic to finance these expenditures with an increased deficit, but, for expediency, we have forgone this added complexity.

Second, we have modeled the impact of regulations on consumer expenditures by taking into account that the majority of consumer expenditures associated with the acts result from regulations affecting mobile sources (private vehicles). These expenditures take the form of increased vehicle operating and maintenance expenses. Although one could incorporate operating and maintenance expenses within the appropriate consumer commodity group in the model, the source

TABLE 2

ANNUAL SOCIAL COST AND EPA COMPLIANCE COST ESTIMATES OF THE CLEAN AIR
AND CLEAN WATER ACTS (Billions of Current Dollars)

Year	Social Cost	EPA Compliance Cost
1975	6.8	14.1
1981	28.3	42.5
1985	70.6	56.0
1990	203.0	78.6
1981–90	977.0	648.0

of expenditure information does not distinguish these expenses from
the costs of control technologies (see U.S. Environmental Protection
Agency 1984). Accordingly, incremental vehicle expenditures, required by control technologies, have been aggregated into the vehicle
purchase price.

V. Estimates of Social Cost

Estimates of the social cost of environmental regulations are based on
general equilibrium price and income vectors derived from two simulations. The first, termed the base case simulation, pertains to the
period 1970–90. The base case simulation uses both historical values
(1970–85) and Data Resources Incorporated forecasts (1986–90) for
the exogenous variables. The second simulation, termed the regulatory scenario, uses the same exogenous variables but introduces regulation on the production technologies using the second method described in Section IV.

The estimates of social cost based on measures of compensating
variation are displayed in table 2. The general equilibrium model
estimate of the social cost of federal air and water pollution control
regulations in 1981 was approximately \$28 billion. This may be di-
rectly compared to the EPA's \$42.5 billion engineering cost estimate.
These results imply that a 1981 benefit-cost analysis of the regulations
based on the EPA estimates would understate the net benefits of the
Clean Air and Clean Water acts by \$14.5 billion.

The advantage of a general equilibrium analysis is its ability to
capture the complexity of economic adjustments that are intractable
within an analytical framework. Unfortunately, this feature adds to
the difficulty of interpreting the results since one cannot explicitly
formulate the adjustment path. In the current context, the divergence between cost estimates is due in large part to a demand-driven
decrease in control costs and the substitution effect.

The significance of the demand effect is best demonstrated by considering the electric generating sector. This sector incurs the largest private-sector control costs, the largest increase in customer prices, and the largest decline in demand (produced output declines by 13 percent). In equilibrium, the 13 percent decline in demand implies a decreased need for generating capacity and a complementary decline in regulatory compliance expenditures. Though not as pronounced, the same demand phenomenon is observed in the petroleum refining, food processing, chemicals, iron and steel, and pulp and paper sectors. Since the EPA methodology does not take into account the effect of changes in demand on compliance expenditures, it overstates these expenditures.

The significant decline in electricity demand is also indicative of both producer and consumer substitution. The ability of the economy to substitute "clean" goods (lower polluting) for "dirty" goods (higher polluting) gives rise to a significant difference between private expenditures and social costs. This substitution may be readily seen by examining the labor-leisure portion of the consumer model in which welfare costs are estimated.

The 1981 equilibria show that while household expenditure on goods and services is $43.6 billion less under the regulation scenario, household leisure consumption also increases by $14.6 billion (measured in postregulation prices). Admittedly, this is only an approximate measure of compensating variation, but the difference between the decline in consumption and increased leisure ($28 billion) provides a reasonable estimate and serves to highlight the labor-leisure consumer response.

While the 1981 social cost estimate is significantly lower than the EPA estimate, one cannot conclude that social costs are always less than comparable estimates based on private expenditures. Economists have long recognized that governmental regulations have significant dynamic impacts.[18] For example, the EPA estimates that federal air and water pollution control costs are $525.8 billion (1981 dollars) between 1981 and 1990. If we uniformly distribute these expenditures over the 10-year interval and then convert to nominal dollars (using the personal consumption expenditure price index in the model), the total nominal pollution control cost is approximately $648 billion. By contrast, the general equilibrium social cost estimate is $977 billion. Very few policymakers have recognized that social costs

---

[18] In addition to the effect on investment, capital accumulation, and labor supply, regulation may also induce subtle changes that affect sectoral productivity and technological change. Productivity effects due to input prices are captured by the nonneutral treatment of technological change in the translog cost function.

TABLE 3

PERCENTAGE CHANGE IN SELECTED MACRO VARIABLES BETWEEN BASE AND SCENARIO

Macro Variable	1981	1990
Real consumption	−2.68	−6.53
Real growth private domestic investment	−4.15	−8.35
Real gross national product	−2.43	−5.85
Real private domestic capital stock	−2.02	−5.96
Real household labor supply	−.84	−1.18
Current value of gross national product	−.25	−.14
Price index for consumer goods	2.05	6.29
Government revenue from taxes on capital	5.02	12.50
Government revenue from taxes on labor	5.57	12.80

can exceed private expenditures, but it is a direct result of household behavior in which leisure is substituted for consumption.

It is useful to examine some indicators of macroeconomic activity in the base case and regulatory scenarios before discussing the intuition behind leisure-consumption substitution. For comparative purposes, we recount the EPA cost estimate and the macroeconomic discussion. The U.S. EPA 1984 executive summary states that "the 1981 annualized cost of pollution control due to federal regulations was estimated to be $42.3 billion or about one percent of GNP in 1981. The cumulative cost from 1970 to 1978 was $171 billion and the projected cost over the period 1981 to 1990 is estimated at $525.8 billion" (p. 3). The report concludes that consumer prices in 1981 were 3.3 percent higher than they would have been without federal pollution control regulations and that GNP was marginally lower (less than 1 percent).

Table 3 displays percentage changes in selected macro variables between the base case and regulatory scenario for 1981 and 1990. On the basis of the general equilibrium model regulation scenario simulations, consumer prices are found to be only 2 percent higher in 1981 but 6 percent higher in 1990. While the effect on current-dollar GNP is negligible, real GNP is about 2 percent lower in 1981 and 6 percent lower in 1990. The magnitude of the price increase in 1981 is approximately the same in both simulations. In contrast, significantly larger price increases in 1990 under the regulatory scenario suggest that the dynamic consequences of regulation, not addressed in the EPA report, are important.

Consider changes in levels of investment, capital stock, and labor supply brought about by the regulations, reported in table 3. The factor underlying the decrease is the household labor supply decision. In this case, since the relative price of consumption to leisure has increased, labor supply declines under the postregulation scenario.

TABLE 4

CHANGES IN SECTORAL VARIABLES BETWEEN BASE AND IMPACT SCENARIOS (Evaluated in 1990)

Sector	Percentage Change in Output Price	Percentage Change in Output Quantity	Percentage Change in Employment
Agriculture, forestry, and fisheries	6.11	-5.67	-3.78
Metal mining	5.02	-4.72	-.48
Coal mining	5.95	-3.38	1.54
Crude petroleum and natural gas	22.65	-15.28	.00
Nonmetallic mining and quarrying	5.88	-5.86	-3.92
Construction	2.98	-4.48	-1.58
Food and kindred products	7.38	-6.66	-4.79
Tobacco manufactures	5.33	-4.86	-.53
Textile mill products	5.49	-4.74	-4.22
Apparel and other fabricated textile products	3.36	-3.92	-1.67
Lumber and wood products except furniture	5.02	-5.59	-3.91
Furniture and fixtures	3.21	-4.32	-3.22
Paper and allied products	9.64	-7.12	-.94

Continued overleaf

TABLE 4 (continued)

Printing, publishing, and allied products	3.80	−3.91	−.97
Chemicals and allied products	11.33	−8.88	−2.95
Petroleum refining and allied industries	8.64	−5.12	.23
Rubber and miscellaneous plastic products	6.88	−5.60	−1.47
Leather and leather products	3.75	−4.29	−2.31
Stone, clay, and glass products	5.53	−5.07	−.89
Primary metal products	15.51	−10.51	−1.71
Fabricated metal products	7.31	−6.41	−1.42
Machinery excluding electrical	3.98	−4.04	−.52
Electrical machinery	5.52	−5.01	−3.89
Motor vehicles and equipment	36.63	−19.73	7.68
Transportation equipment and ordnance	3.42	−4.16	−3.29
Instruments	4.32	−3.69	−1.91
Miscellaneous manufacturing	5.42	−5.19	−2.97
Transportation and warehousing	3.08	−2.41	−.49
Communications	2.73	−3.53	−.60
Electrical utilities	44.41	−28.95	1.99
Gas utilities	8.85	−5.73	1.60
Wholesale and retail trade	3.39	−3.49	1.10
Finance, insurance, and real estate	5.12	−4.97	−2.64
Other services	3.27	−3.26	−1.57

Reduced labor supply also induces a decline in income and saving. The decline in saving causes investment to fall and, with it, capital stock growth. While supplied labor hours and capital availability increase over time under the regulatory scenario, both increase at a diminished rate. Consequently, household real income declines and aggregate economic growth is retarded.[19]

As noted above, in our model, the macroeconomic impacts of environmental regulations are the result of microeconomic decisions, largely dominated by household behavior. An equally important set of decisions are, however, also made by production sectors in the economy. The impact of producer decisions is displayed in table 4. We summarize the effect of producer decisions by reporting the percentage change in output price and quantity and employment between the base case and the regulatory scenario. The production sectors most severely affected by the regulations are electric utilities, motor vehicles, crude petroleum and natural gas, primary metals, and chemicals and allied products. In these sectors, environmental regulation induced output price increases that exceed 10 percent (44 percent in electric utilities) and an output decline that ranges between 8 and 28 percent in 1990. All industries experienced declines in labor productivity, and some sectors experienced declines in employment. These impacts can also be substantial; for example, employment falls 7.6 percent in the motor vehicle sector.

Sectoral regulatory impacts reported in table 4 highlight a point often made by economists but largely ignored by regulators: regulations affecting production sectors that supply important intermediate products can have significant secondary impacts. Table 4 reveals that while pollution control investments were required in only 13 sectors, the cost of production increased, and output and labor productivity fell, in *all* production sectors. A good example of the magnitude of the secondary effects is found in the finance, insurance, and real estate sector of the economy. The finance sector was not required to invest in pollution abatement equipment and obviously did not incur higher operating costs as a *direct* consequence of the Clean Air and Clean Water acts. Thus, under the EPA cost methodology, the sector would bear no regulatory cost. But on the basis of the general equilibrium analysis, the cost of production in the finance sector is 2 percent higher in 1981 as a result of indirect impacts of the regulation—more

[19] Unfortunately, there is no macro policy fix to this problem. The economy is already fully employed in the postregulation world, and the prices are "correct" in the sense that there exist no noncompetitive distortions. The problem arises from the fact that real wages have fallen and households have adjusted accordingly.

specifically, higher factor prices. Higher production costs represent another private cost to the sector and are another source of error in the EPA cost estimate.

VI. Conclusions

Applied welfare economics can play a central role in policy evaluation. Empirical work in applied policy analysis must be guided by theoretically precise measures of social cost and dynamic general equilibrium considerations. The issuance of several presidential executive orders over the past decade appears to give applied welfare economics a formal position in the analysis of government regulatory policy. Unfortunately, the lack of specificity in the orders, regarding the definition of costs, has allowed federal agencies to continue equating the cost of regulation with private expenditures in an assessment of regulatory impacts. Many economists believe that private expenditures are suitable proxies for the social cost. Our findings demonstrate that private expenditures are poor measures of social cost.

In addition to highlighting the divergence between private compliance expenditures and social costs, the analysis serves to reinforce a frequent conjecture about the effects of regulation on the economy. Specifically, regulations affect intertemporal microeconomic decisions and cause social cost to increase over time. Failure to quantify and account for these intertemporal phenomena in a benefit-cost analysis will likely lead to errors of unknown magnitude. On the basis of our findings of significant intertemporal impacts, currently practiced methods are unacceptable.

It is difficult to overemphasize the importance of approaching policy analysis from a general equilibrium perspective. This emphasis is reinforced by our finding that while only a subset of the industries are directly affected under the regulation scenarios, all production sectors in the model ultimately bear the burden of regulations. This finding suggests that even expenditure-based estimates of costs would be inaccurately estimated.

Although perhaps obvious, one final point deserves mention. Our attention has focused on costs associated with environmental quality regulations. Any normative judgment about the desirability of the regulations depends on comparing appropriately measured costs with corresponding benefits. While benefits have generally been measured using an appropriate willingness-to-pay criterion, an intertemporal general equilibrium approach to benefit estimation might show similar divergences from reported results based on static partial equilibrium analysis.

References

Ballard, Charles L.; Fullerton, Don; Shoven, John B.; and Whalley, John. *A General Equilibrium Model for Tax Policy Evaluation.* Chicago: Univ. Chicago Press (for NBER), 1985.

Berndt, Ernst R.; Fraumeni, Barbara M.; Hudson, Edward A.; Jorgenson, Dale W.; and Stoker, Thomas M. "Econometrics and Data of the 9 Sector Dynamic General Equilibrium Model." Final report to the Macroeconomic Analysis Division, Energy Information Administration. Vol. 3. Washington: Dept. Energy, 1981.

Blackorby, Charles, and Donaldson, D. "Money Metric Utility: A Harmless Normalization?" Discussion Paper no. 86-09. Vancouver: Univ. British Columbia, Dept. Econ., 1986.

Diewert, W. E., and Wales, Terence J. "Semiflexible Functional Forms." Discussion paper. Vancouver: Univ. British Columbia, Dept. Econ., 1986.

Goettle, Richard J., IV, and Hudson, Edward A. "Final Report on the Dynamic General Equilibrium Model." Report. Washington: Emergency Management Agency, February 1984.

Hazilla, Michael, and Kopp, Raymond J. "The Social Cost of Alternative Ambient Air Quality Standards for Total Suspended Particulates: A General Equilibrium Analysis." Final report. Research Triangle Park, N.C.: Office of Air Quality Planning and Standards, U.S. Environmental Protection Agency, 1986. (*a*)

——. "Systematic Effects of Capital Service Price Definition on Perceptions of Input Substitution." *J. Bus. and Econ. Statis.* 4 (April 1986): 209–24. (*b*)

——. "Testing for Separable Functional Structure Using Temporary Equilibrium Models." *J. Econometrics* 33 (October/November 1986): 119–41. (*c*)

Hicks, John R. *Value and Capital: An Inquiry into Some Fundamental Principles of Economic Theory.* 2d ed. Oxford: Clarendon, 1946.

Hudson, Edward A. "The 9 Sector Dynamic General Equilibrium Model: Specification and Structure." Final report to the Macroeconomic Analysis Division, Energy Information Administration. Vol. 2. Washington: Dept. Energy, 1981.

Hudson, Edward A., and Jorgenson, Dale W. "U.S. Energy Policy and Economic Growth, 1975–2000." *Bell J. Econ. and Management Sci.* 5 (Autumn 1974): 461–514.

——. "Tax Policy and Energy Conservation." In *Econometric Studies of U.S. Energy Policy,* edited by Dale W. Jorgenson. Amsterdam: North-Holland, 1976.

——. "The Economic Impact of Policies to Reduce U.S. Energy Growth." *Resources and Energy* 1 (November 1978): 205–29. (*a*)

——. "Energy Prices and the U.S. Economy, 1972–1976." *Natural Resources J.* 18 (October 1978): 877–97. (*b*)

Jorgenson, Dale W. "Econometric Methods for Applied General Equilibrium Analysis." In *Applied General Equilibrium Analysis,* edited by Herbert E. Scarf and John B. Shoven. Cambridge: Cambridge Univ. Press, 1984.

Jorgenson, Dale W.; Lau, Lawrence J.; and Stoker, Thomas M. "The Transcendental Logarithmic Model of Aggregate Consumer Behavior." In *Advances in Econometrics,* vol. 1, edited by R. L. Basmann and George F. Rhodes, Jr. Greenwich, Conn.: JAI, 1982.

Jorgenson, Dale W., and Slesnick, Daniel T. "Efficiency versus Equity in Natural Gas Price Regulation." *J. Econometrics* 30 (October/November 1985): 301–16. (*a*)

ENVIRONMENTAL QUALITY   873

————. "General Equilibrium Analysis of Economic Policy." Paper presented at the Econometric Society Fifth World Congress, Cambridge, Mass., August 1985.

Lau, Lawrence J. "Econometrics of Monotonicity, Convexity and Quasi-Convexity." Technical Report no. 123. Stanford, Calif.: Stanford Univ., Inst. Math. Studies Soc. Sci., 1974.

————. "Complete Systems of Consumer Demand Functions through Duality." In *Frontiers of Quantitative Economics,* vol. 3A, edited by Michael D. Intriligator. Amsterdam: North-Holland, 1977.

————. "Existence Conditions for Aggregate Demand Functions." Technical Report no. 248. Stanford, Calif.: Stanford Univ., Inst. Math. Studies Soc. Sci., 1977 (rev. February 1980).

Portney, Paul R. *Environmental Regulation in the U.S.: Public Policies and Their Consequences.* Washington: Resources for the Future, 1989.

Shoven, John B., and Whalley, John. "A General Equilibrium Calculation of the Effects of Differential Taxation of Income from Capital in the U.S." *J. Public Econ.* 1 (November 1972): 281.

U.S. Environmental Protection Agency. "Final Report: The Cost of Clean Air and Water: Report to Congress 1984." Washington: U.S. Environmental Protection Agency, May 1984.

Part V
The Enforcement of Environmental Policies

[30]

JOURNAL OF ENVIRONMENTAL ECONOMICS AND MANAGEMENT 1, 219–236 (1974)

The Economics of Enforcing Air Pollution Controls[1]

PAUL B. DOWNING

Virginia Polytechnic Institute and State University, Blacksburg, Virginia 24060

AND

WILLIAM D. WATSON, JR.

Resources for the Future, Inc., Washington, DC 20036

Received February 7, 1974

The goal of this paper is to determine the likely effect on a firm's control actions of alternative implementation and enforcement policies available to the control agency. Three alternatives are studied, legal enforcement through the new source performance standards set forth by EPA, and two effluent fee enforcement alternatives. First, a generalized model of the effects of implementation and enforcement policies on the firm's control actions is developed. This model assumes that the firm is an expected cost minimizer. The model is then applied to the case of particulate matter discharges from coal-fired power plants in order to estimate empirically the effect of policy alternatives on the firm's control efforts. Finally, the results of the model and its empirical application are used to develop policy functions which relate control to the values of various policy parameters. These results lead us to several policy recommendations.

INTRODUCTION

The use of the environment by a firm can impose uncompensated costs on other firms or on individuals. There are two general methods which may be employed to internalize these costs to the polluting firm: namely, emission standards and emission charges.[2] In assessing the cost of pollution control typical studies look only at the cost of the control device or process change without concern for the institutional constraints placed on the firm by the control agency and the legislature. Yet it is clear that the firm incurs differential expenses in addition to (or instead of) the actual installation and operation costs of the control device or process change itself. These additional expenses can include compliance testing or other certification expenses, legal expenses, fines, and other enforcement costs. These expenses are a function of the implementa-

---

[1] The authors are respectively Associate Professor of Economics, Virginia Polytechnic Institute and State University and Research Associate, Resources for the Future. This research was completed while the authors were on the staff of the Washington Environmental Research Center, U.S. Environmental Protection Agency. However, the views expressed here are those of the authors and do not necessarily reflect those of EPA. The authors would like to express their appreciation to their colleagues at EPA, Resources for the Future, and the Brookings Institution for helpful comments at various stages of this research.

[2] Other possible control instruments such as subsidies and marketable permits have been neglected in this study.

219

220   DOWNING AND WATSON

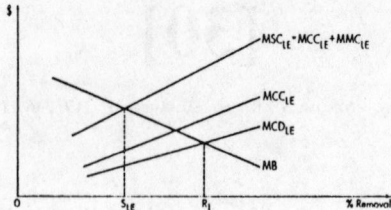

FIG. 1. Standards enforcement.

tion and enforcement rules employed by the control agency. Hence they are likely to vary with the method of internalization (policy instrument) chosen.

Optimal Emission Standards

Before we proceed with the development of our model, a general framework is provided by investigating how the cost to the firm of complying with control requirements and the cost to society of insuring that the firm complies affect the optimal level of pollution control.[3] It is likely that both these costs will differ between the two implementation and enforcement alternatives. Let us first investigate legal enforcement (LE) and then turn our attention to effluent fee (EF) enforcement. In Fig. 1 we plot increasing percent removal of a pollutant (R) on the horizontal axis and dollar costs on the vertical axis. The marginal cost of a control device (MCD_{LE}) increases as removal increases. This is the cost function measured in the usual control cost study. However, the cost of the device is not the full cost born by the firm. Depending upon the form of legal enforcement the firm may have to conduct compliance tests, incur monitoring costs, keep records and meet other requirements imposed by the control agency. Interpreting these curves as planning horizon cost curves it is clear that at least some of these compliance costs vary with R. Thus, the marginal cost of control for legal enforcement (MCC_{LE}) which the firm actually faces includes both MCD_{LE} and these other costs and lies above MCD_{LE}.

The marginal social cost of control using legal enforcement (MCS_{LE}) includes the cost to the firm (MCC_{LE}) and the cost to the control agency of carrying out enforcement activities in an attempt to insure that its rules and regulations are carried out (MMC_{LE}). The control agency must inspect the site to determine that the firm has the required controls installed and operating and that it does not cheat by turning the devices off when the control agency personnel are not around. It is reasonable to assume that at least some of these costs vary with the level of removal. This is because it is likely that the payoff to cheating will increase as the required level of control increases. Control agency enforcement efforts should increase in an attempt to counteract this incentive.

Assuming the usual declining marginal benefit function (MB), the optimal level of control for this set of control instruments would be where $MCS_{LE} = MB$ or S_{LE} in Fig. 1. Note that when it is recognized that social control costs are greater than the cost of the device itself, the optimal level of control of pollution is less than the level usually determined in empirical studies (R_1). The neglect of these costs would lead to the setting of a standard which is inefficiently stringent.

[3] Anderson and Crocker (1971) suggest that these issues are of vital importance in control instrument decisions but do not cite any literature which explores their effects on control.

The same conceptual set of control cost functions hold for the effluent fee enforcement case. However, each of these functions may differ from their legal enforcement equivalents in their actual location on the graph. There are compliance costs for the effluent fee enforcement system as well. The firm must record emissions, pay the fee, deal with periodic checks by control agency personnel, etc. It is reasonable to assume that these compliance costs would increase with the level of removal. Likewise, the marginal management costs to the control agency are likely to increase with the level of removal. This is because higher removal and consequently greater effluent fees makes cheating more profitable to the firm. This in turn necessitates greater checking by the control agency.

If society's goal is to control pollution at least cost (and if it wished to neglect distributional issues), it should pick that institutional form which is least costly. Economists have often argued that the best institutional form for pollution control is the effluent fee. For this to be true it is necessary that the net social benefit of control for the effluent fee enforcement system be greater than the net social benefit of control for the legal enforcement system where each is at its optimal level (i.e., $MSC = MB$).

In order to determine if the economists' argument is correct it is necessary to know both MCC and MMC under legal enforcement and effluent fee enforcement. While logical arguments can be made to support the economist's argument, the other side also has merit. The determination will probably rest on empirical evidence yet to our knowledge no such estimates exist. This paper attempts to fill part of this gap by determining the firm's cost functions under alternative enforcement policies. The determination of the control agency's cost functions are left for future research.

AN ENFORCEMENT MODEL OF THE FIRM'S CONTROL BEHAVIOR

In this section we derive a model of the firm's reactions to enforcement strategies. We then explore various cases to determine the likely reaction of the firm to alternative values of the policy variables under differing technological and time frame assumptions. In the following section this model is applied to the case of new source performance standards for fly ash discharge from coal-fired power plants.

Becker (1968) developed a model of the economics of crime and punishment which consists of a damages function, an enforcement cost function, a supply of offenses function, and a punishment function. Becker's supply of offenses function can be interpreted in terms of air pollution control. The polluter's supply of offenses (the number of times he exceeds the standard) are assumed to be a function of the probability of his being convicted, the fine he pays per conviction, and what Becker calls "a portmanteau variable" representing the sum of all other influences It is this supply of offenses (emissions) function that we explore for the air pollution case in this paper. Specifically stated, our goal is to intestigate the reactions of an individual firm to alternative standards, conviction probabilities, and fines (the policy variables) under different implementation schemes.

Cost of Pollution Control to the Firm

It is assumed for the purposes of this paper that the firm seeks to minimize the expected cost of control of pollutants [E(CC)].[4] These expected costs are the sum of

[4] While our model does not specifically consider the tradeoffs involved in the interrelationships between control costs and total product output of the firm, the conclusions reached here do hold in the general case. For a model which relates pollution control costs to the optimal output of the firm see Fan and Froehlich (1972).

the expected cost of control devices [E(CD)] and the expected cost of compliance and enforcement actions imposed on the firm for compliance or noncompliance with required controls or standards [E(EC)]. The firm's objective function[5] is then

$$\min E(CC) = E(CD) + E(EC), \tag{1}$$

given a fixed set of control regulations (the policy variables). Both CD and EC are stochastic in this formulation. Device costs include both capital and installation costs (KC) and operation and maintenance costs (OM). For many devices OM will have some distribution about an expected value because the device might partially or fully fail during the period (as when a catalytic reactor gets poisoned). Enforcement costs are stochastic because the control efficiency of the device is stochastic causing the incidence of violation to be uncertain. A complete analysis of E(CD) is not necessary for our purposes. It is assumed here (and has been shown for the electrostatic precipitator case we explore empirically) that:

$$\partial E(CD)/\partial R > 0$$

and

$$\partial^2 E(CD)/\partial R^2 > 0$$

The arguments in the E(EC) function are somewhat different depending upon the implementation and enforcement method used. For the legal enforcement method now employed for new sources by EPA the expected enforcement and compliance costs are a function of the expected number of days the firm is detected to be in noncompliance during the year [E(N)] times the expected penalty imposed on the firm for each violation [E(P)].

$$E(EC) = f[E(N) \cdot E(P)]. \tag{2}$$

E(N) is a function of the expected control efficiency of the device installed by the firm [E(R)] given the various rules and regulations imposed upon the firm by the control agency and/or the legislature.

$$E(N) = g[E(R)|I, S, C], \tag{3}$$

where

      I = the frequency, accuracy, and form of the inspection and monitoring actions of the control agency,
      S = the emission standard set by the control agency,
      C = the requirements set by the control agency for certification of the effectiveness of the firm's control device (usually through some sort of compliance testing procedure).

That is, for any given set of control agency policies, the higher E(R) the lower E(N). If the control agency were to increase its enforcement efforts by increasing the frequency of inspections, improving the accuracy of monitoring, or making compliance tests more strict, any given E(R) would imply a larger E(N). Likewise, a more stringent emission standard would increase E(N).

---

[5] This objective function can easily be translated into Becker's supply of offenses function. However, it is stated in stochastic form rather than deterministic form since many of the terms are stochastic in nature. The first derivative of this function represents the value to the firm of a violation and hence under perfectly competitive conditions the opportunity cost to society of pollution control.

ENFORCING AIR POLLUTION CONTROLS 223

The expected penalty is a function of the probability of being convicted of being in violation (PC), the money fine imposed on the firm by the courts if convicted of being a polluter (F), the damages to the firm's image if convicted (DI) and the possible shutdown time (ST) for required repairs or construction if found in violation by either the control agency or the courts.

$$E(P) = h(PC, F, DI, ST). \qquad (4)$$

PC is a function of the legal costs incurred by the firm to defend itself against the control agency (LC). The effectiveness of a dollar spent on defense demands upon the control agency's prosecution efforts (CAP).

$$PC = k(LC|CAP). \qquad (5)$$

The firm will minimize its cost where

$$\partial E(CC)/\partial R = \partial E(CD)/\partial R + \partial E(EC)/\partial R = 0. \qquad (6)$$

Since enforcement costs decline as removal increases, this condition can be satisfied. For a set of policy parameter values Eq. 6 defines the values of MCC_{LE} and MCD_{LE} as equal to the values of $\partial E(CC)/\partial R$ and $\partial E(CD)/\partial R$, respectively.

In the case of pure effluent fee enforcement the E(EC) function is less complex. Expected enforcement costs are simply a function of R and the level of the effluent fee (EF) per unit of emissions given some monitoring and inspection system and possibly some certification of the control device as well.

$$E(EC) = m(R, EF|I, C), \qquad (7)$$

where under usual circumstances

$$\partial E(EC)/\partial R < 0,$$

and

$$\partial^2 E(EC)/\partial EF^2 > 0.$$

Alternative Enforcement Strategies

Having discussed the factors which affect the firm's expected cost of environmental control, we turn our attention to the effects of alternative enforcement strageties on their expected cost and the firm's reaction in terms of pollution control.

Let us assume that the control agency has an air quality goal which it is attempting to reach using the legal enforcement method. It has several policy tools available by which it can effect the control efforts of the firm. It can set higher or lower emission standards, change penalties for noncompliance, make court actions more prompt, and impose external pressures on the firm through public statements.

Standard. The firm will react to higher standards by installing more effective devices, but only if the expected penalties and court costs are higher than the cost of control. It will delay as long as the court cost of delaying actions is less than the interest on the cost of control devices and savings in operation and maintenance expenses. For a given envorcement effort against the firm, a higher standard will cause the firm to attempt more delaying actions.

Monitoring. The lack of any monitoring of the control actions of the firm will make any standard set by the control agency ineffective. The frequency and type of monitoring will also affect the firm's compliance.[6]

---

[6] For an investigation of monitoring alternatives applied to automotive emissions see Downing (1974).

224   DOWNING AND WATSON

There are two stages of our legal enforcement model. One for the situation before the firm takes any control action and another for the situation after the installation of control equipment. This is because control and enforcement costs differ in the two cases. To make this distinction clear, Eq. (1) is rewritten as follows.

$$\min E(CC) = [KC + E(EC_B)] + [E(OM) + E(EC_A)], \qquad (8)$$

where

$E(EC_B)$ = expected enforcement cost before installation of a control device,

$E(EC_A)$ = expected enforcement cost after installation of a control device (i.e., during operation).

In the before installation case all of Eq. (8) holds although it is possible that the firm will perceive $E(EC_A)$ as zero in which case the last two terms drop out.

After installation of the required devices the first two terms on the right hand side of Eq. (8) are inoperative. The firm is faced with the choice of operating the device or not and its decision clearly depends upon $E(EC_A)$. This in turn depends upon I_A. Assuming that each violation detected by an inspection is a separate offense (the usual case in control legislation), an increase in monitoring frequency will *ceteris paribus* yield more control. The device will be operated more effectively and more often. But the form as well as the frequency of inspection will affect this result. Unannounced inspections will be more effective in stimulating proper operation and maintenance of devices. Indeed it has been observed that when control authority personnel go home at night firms take the opportunity to plow the accumulated fly ash out of the stack. This can be safely done because, in effect the control agency has announced noninspection.

Penalty. It is perhaps obvious that increasing the level of penalty imposed (rather than threatened) will increase compliance by the firm. The timing of the imposition of a penalty can also have a substantial effect on the firm's control effort. If the expected value of the penalty is constant, it will induce firms to employ legal delaying actions if the legal costs are less than the interest on the expected value of the penalty. If the penalty were made a fee and hence payable upon release of the pollution, its present value would be increased. Thus, an effluent tax is more effective than an equivalent penalty per pound because it is payable on release rather than after court action. As a corollary to this result, the control agency can make the effective penalty larger by increasing the speed of bringing accused violators into court. There is another reason to believe that an effluent fee will be more effective than a penalty. The direct payoff for cheating 10% on reporting emissions in the effluent fee case saves the firm 10% of the fee. In the penalty case, because of the zero/one nature of the violation definition, this level of cheating may save 100% of the penalty. It pays more to cheat in the legal enforcement system than in the effluent fee system.

In addition to the above policy alternatives, the control agency has two more options. First, it can try to obtain more tightly written laws which would increase the probability of obtaining a conviction (make the penalty more certain) and/or improve their preparation to the same end.[7] Second, the control agency can increase the damage to the firm's image by publicly announcing violations.[8]

---

[7] Tittle (1969) as shown that greater certainty of punishment for a crime is associated statistically with lower offense rates.

[8] It has another opion—to shift to an alternative enforcement scheme. This may be preferable since in the current legal enforcement scheme noncompliance is ". . . enforced by criminal process, probably the most cumbersome coercive tool we have. The violator is protected by all the constitutional protections which apply to any criminal trial. He can demand a trial by jury and unanimous verdict (and this against the heavy burden of proof faced by the prosecution)." (Krier, 1970, pp. 5–29.)

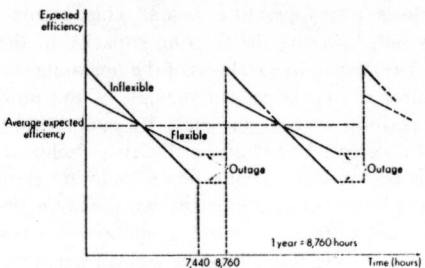

FIG. 2. Precipitator operating curves.

A SIMULATION OF ENFORCEMENT ALTERNATIVES

We have presented a general theory of a firm's reactions to environmental control implementation and enforcement alternatives. In order to demonstrate some of these propositions and determine their empirical significance a simulation study was conducted for enforcing the federal new source performance standards for particulate matter discharges from coal-fired power plants. The simulation model employed allows us to determine the likely control actions of the firm (and related costs) resulting from alternative levels of enforcement policy parameters and implementation schemes. In effect, via this analysis we will be examining a variety of enforcement "experiments."[9]

Ideally it is desirable to find the set of enforcement policy parameters which minimize the sum of costs for both firms and enforcement agencies. This analysis, however, covers only costs to firms since data and information on enforcement agency costs are almost nonexistent. Nonetheless it will be seen that the partial results reported here are rich in policy implications.[10]

The Simulation Model

We have simulated six policy scenarios:

	Inflexible technology	Flexible technology
Compliance test with fine for violating an opacity standard	S1	S2
Compliance test with tax on emitted fly ash	S3	S4
Emission tax only	S5	S6

Our model describes the firm's least-cost effort to control fly ash discharges given each of the three enforcement policy sets listed above and two variants of electrostatic precipitator technology: inflexible and flexible.

Figure 2 demonstrates the difference between flexible and inflexible precipitator technology. Expected collection efficiency is measured on the vertical axis; operating hours are measured on the horizontal axis. A typical base loaded power plant will operate about 7440 hours per year, the remaining hours in that year will be outage hours when normal maintenance is performed on generating equipment and pollution control devices. The two curves labelled "inflexible" and "flexible" show that precipi-

---

[9] A detailed explanation of the simulation model can be found in Downing and Watson (1973).

[10] It is assumed throughout that managers of coal-fired power plants attempt to minimize expected costs over their planning horizons and that available cost effective fly ash control technology is electrostatic precipitation (see Watson (1974)).

tator efficiency declines over operating hours. This occurs because precipitator discharge electrodes fail, lowering the filtering capacity of the precipitator (Greco and Wynot (1971)). The dashed-line sections of the operating curves represent precipitator maintenance time during scheduled outages of the power plant. On restart, precipitators again perform at top efficiency. By comparing the two performance curves it is seen that a flexible precipitator's efficiency declines less rapidly during an operating cycle. This results from having power shunting electonic instrumentation which optimizes precipitator filtering capacity as discharge electrodes fail. In comparison with a larger inflexible precipitator, a smaller sized flexible precipitator can produce the same average collection efficiency over an operating cycle.

The Legal Enforcement Model

Equation 8 is used as the starting point for our simulations of the firm's reaction to alternative values of the control agency's policy parameters. The firm is assumed to be minimizing its expected costs of control subject to the constraints placed on it by control agency policy. A wide range of policy options are explored. For each set of policy parameters the legal enforcement simulation model considers a number of precipitators of different sizes and consequently different expected collection efficiencies. For each precipitator the model computes the probability of passing a start-up compliance test at some specified compliance test standard. It also computes the expected number of days per year when each precipitator would violate a specified opacity standard. Using these two pieces of information it then computes and sums costs in order to determine total expected costs.

The model begins by computing and summing precipitator installation costs and compliance test costs. Using the probability of passing the compliance test as a weighting factor it then adds in operating, maintenance and stack monitoring costs plus fines for violating the opacity standard, all of these costs, of course, having been computed for a precipitator of the originally specified size. A given precipitator, however, may fail the compliance test. If it fails the model assumes that the precipitator is enlarged to a size which has virtually no probability of failing a subsequent compliance test. In such cases, a power plant would then incur the installation and penalty costs[11] for an enlarged precipitator and its operating, maintenance and stack monitoring costs plus fines for violating a specified opacity standard during operation of the enlarged precipitator. The model sums these costs and uses the probability of failing the compliance test (1-probability of passing) as a weighting factor. The sum of the expected costs yields total expected out-of-pocket costs for a precipitator of some specified size, for a specified compliance test standard and opacity standard, and for a single compliance test.[12] The model then allows successive runs of the compliance test. This changes the probability of passing and failing the compliance test and changes the weighting factors in computing total expected costs. At this stage, the model finds the number of compliance tests at which total expected out-of-pocket costs are a minimum. It then goes on to successively larger sized precipitators, computing costs in exactly the same

---

[11] Penalty costs in this case are the increased costs of producing the power from alternative sources and the interest on investment in the plant during the six months that would be required to complete the expansion.

[12] Two very computationally complicated variants of this model were investigated. One was least cost selection of load shedding or fines when the opacity standard was violated. Another was least cost selection of serial enlargement or a single state enlargement. In a sensitivity analysis, both variants in combination produced results approximately equal to those of the simpler basic model.

fashion for the given set of compliance test and opacity standards. It also holds constant throughout, the flue gas flow rate, the number of averaged stack samples taken during a compliance test and the expected fine for violating the opacity standard. As a final step it finds the precipitator size or efficiency which minimizes total expected out-of-pocket costs to the firm for the given set of enforcement policy parameters. The set of exogenous enforcement policy parameters is then changed and the model rerun.

The only difference between policy scenarios S1 and S2 (similarly S3 and S4) is the selection of precipitator technology. In going from S1 to S2 (and S3 to S4) everything else is held constant in running the model including the exogenous enforcement policy parameters.

Federally promulgated regulations require that the average of at least three separate stack samples must provide a reading which satisfies the compliance test standard before a power plant is allowed to begin full time operation. The model simulates this by repeated sampling from the appropriate density functions, averaging of the sample efficiencies, and computation of pass and fail probabilities. As the number of averaged stack samples is increased, cost minimizing power plants will tend to pick more efficient precipitators.

The probability density functions associated with the compliance tests are also affected by boiler load conditions during compliance tests. When boilers are loaded at peaking levels, the flue gas flow rate through a precipitator can be about 15% above the normal level. Clearly the probability of failing is less under normal load conditions. On the other hand, compliance tests under high load conditions make the compliance test more effective in enforcing a given fly ash emission standard. The model allows for flue gas flow rate variations in simulating compliance tests and hence in computing probabilities of pass and fail.

The Emission Tax Model

For a precipitator of given size and for a given emission tax per ton of fly ash discharged, the emission tax cost model computes total emission taxes. To these it adds installation costs, operating, maintenance and stack monitoring costs to obtain total expected out-ot-pocket costs. Precipitator size is then incremented and total costs recomputed. Computation is truncated when the model finds the precipitator size or efficiency which minimizes the sum of precipitator costs and total taxes for the given emission tax. The emission tax, which is a constant value per ton, is then incremented and the model rerun. Unit emission taxes which vary over time with meterorological conditions for example, and unit taxes which increase as total emission increase, are not specifically considered. However, such emission taxes would not change our basic results.

Simulation Results

The objective of the simulation model is to provide cost and performance functions for each of the policy scenarios. The following functions are of interest: expected out-of-pocket costs to the firm as a function of enforcement policy parameters; expected precipitator efficiency as a function of enforcement policy parameters; and expected out-of-pocket costs to the firm as a function of removal efficiency.

The following ranges of enforcement policy parameters are covered in the simulated scenarios:

Before installation parameters	Range
Compliance test standard (S_{LEB})	0.04–0.14 lb/million
Compliance test conditions (C)	(Btu discharge rate)
No. of averaged stack samples (N)	3–50 stack samples
No. of successive compliance tests (M)	3–15 tests
Flue gas flow rate (FR)	1 V–1.15 V (V is the normal load flue gas flow rate)
After installation parameters	
Opacity standard (S_{LEA})	5–40%
Fine/day of violation (F_A)	$500–$50,000/day
Probability of conviction (PC_A)	0–1
Emission tax parameter	
Tax/ton of fly ash (T)	$5–$180/ton

Scenarios S1 through S4 use of combination of structured and randomly chosen enforcement policy parameters. Our objective was to uniformly cover a relatively wide range of enforcement policy combinations. In all, 50 different policy combinations were selected for these simulations. These policy combinations allow for variations in the above policy parameters only. Several options available to the firm and/or the control agency were not included because of inability to observe and quantify relevant parameter values. Thus, we assume that the firm will attempt to comply with the control agency's requirements rather than carry on a prolonged legal battle although the latter is possible or perhaps likely. Delay of the payment of a penalty through legal action is also assumed to be zero as is damage to the corporate image (DI). While we do allow for variations in the probability of conviction, we do not explicitly investigate the trade-offs implicit in Eq. 5. These regretable but necessary omissions in the assessment of the firm's reaction to policy alternatives result in a bias toward overly optimistic estimates of control. Firms may, and often have in the past, take the legal delay alternative we exclude from our analysis. In the case of the emission-tax-only scenarios, the model was run for only a maximum of 10 different tax rates since each emission tax produces a unique least-cost response. For each set of enforcement policy parameters the model computes expected precipitator efficiency, expected least-costs of fly ash control and expected fines or emission taxes paid. Furthermore, in order to provide for differential response due mainly to economies of scale, the model considers four different plant sizes, 1300 MW, 800 MW, 200 MW, and 25 MW. That is, for each power plant size per scenario, the simulation experiments provide 50 observations (scenarios S1 through S4) or a maximum of 10 observations (scenarios S5 and S6) on firm least-cost behavior as a function of enforcement policy parameters.

Since the model is too complex to solve analytically regression analysis has been used to summarize these "experimental" data. In effect, this "solves" the model. The following functions have been fitted.

Scenarios S1 through S4:

$$C = A(S_{LEB})^{n_1}(N)^{n_2}e^{MD \cdot n_3}(FR)^{n_4}(S_{LEA})^{n_5}(FT)^{n_6}; \qquad (9)$$

$$E = 100 - 100 \cdot EXP[-B(S_{LEB})^{b_1}(N)^{b_2}e^{MD \cdot b_3}(FR)^{b_4}(S_{LEA})^{b_5}(FT)^{b_6}]. \qquad (10)$$

Scenarios S5 and S6:

$$C = A(T)^{n_6}; \qquad (11)$$

ENFORCING AIR POLLUTION CONTROLS   229

TABLE I
CURRENT ENFORCEMENT PRACTICE

Plant Size (MW)	Expected average efficiency[a] (%, inflexible technology)	Expected cost (1000's of 1967 dollars, discounted)	Expected time in violation[a] (%)
25	99.1%	$ 720	0%
200	98.0	1,900	61
800	97.7	5,200	70
1300	97.7	7,800	70

[a] During base load year at normal flue gas flow rates. Time in violation would be higher and average efficiency lower to the extent that plants are operated above normal loads, for example, under peak load demand conditions.

$$E = 100 - 100 \cdot EXP[-B(T)^{b_6}]. \tag{12}$$

All scenarios:

$$C = D(ln(100/(100 - E)))^{d_1}(N)^{d_2}; \tag{13}$$

$$C - FT = G(ln(100/(100 - E)))^{g_1}(N)^{g_2}. \tag{14}$$

C is total expected discounted cost. It includes out-of-pocket firm pollution control costs, associated firm management costs, and total fines or emission taxes. E is average expected precipitator collection efficiency (%) during base-load years. FT is total expected discounted fine or emission tax. MD is a dummy variable which is 1 when the maximum number of allowable successive compliance tests is 3, and 0 when greater than 3.

Individual enforcement policy coefficients within the indicated functional forms are not constrained in the simulation model. They may or may not be significant depending upon least cost tradeoffs. Therefore in "solving" the model the regressions can help to determine which enforcement policy coefficients are significant and therefore exert an influence on the firm's control efforts. The results of the regressions were consistent with prior expectations.[13] The regression coefficients for the compliance test standard (S_{LEB}) and the opacity standard (S_{LEA}) were negative and the remaining coefficients were positive.

The role of effective fine in scenarios S1 and S2 needs further elaboration. The fine appears to be an insignificant determinant of behavior in scenarios S1 and S2. This is misleading. In the model itself, costs (excluding effective fines) are nearly constant over a wide range of precipitator sizes. Consequently, the impact of any positive effective fine is to usually induce a cost minimizing firm to pick a fine-avoiding precipitator. Furthermore, increasing the dollar fine per conviction usually makes the cost curve more steep around the least cost precipitator size, but does not shift the least cost point. Hence, the impact of effective fine on firm behavior is a zero–one effect. If the effective fine is any positive value (fine positive, probability of conviction positive) then the promulgated opacity standard is operative (i.e., the opacity standard impacts firm behavior in relationship to its specified value). A positive effective fine, of course, also promotes maintenance of pollution control devices since even very lax opacity standards would be violated if firms did not maintain their control devices.

One final result of our simulation analysis is of interest. Our best assessment of EPA's

[13] For greater detail on the regression models and results see Downing and Watson (1973).

230   DOWNING AND WATSON

current choice of policy parameters for the enforcement of the new source performance standards for coal-fired power plants is[14]

Compliance test standard	0.1 lb/million Btu
No. of successive compliance tests	15 or less
No. of averaged stack samples	3
Flue gas flow rate	1.1 V
Opacity standard	30%
Fine/day of violation	$500–$50,000/day

Using these values in the model, we find that most plants will control to less than the standard and almost never be cited for a violation. In fact, plants larger than 100 MW will be in violation from 50 to 70% of the time depending upon plant size (see Table 1). The reason why plants are not cited for a violation is that the enforced opacity standard allows about three times the emission of the compliance test standard. We also find that small plants control to a higher percent removal than large plants even though it is relatively more expensive for them to do so. This is because large plants enjoy economies of scale which allow them (relative to small plants) to make more favorable cost-reducing tradeoffs against enforcement policy parameters. Furthermore, all firms choose inflexible technology since its out-of-pocket cost to the firm is less than flexible technology. This is an inefficient choice for society, however, since the real resource cost of the same level of average control using flexible technology is less (see below). In fact, savings in the resource costs of control are probably an underestimate of the societal savings since flexible technology has a higher last day efficiency than inflexible technology. Thus, if marginal damages decline with control as is usually the case, then the increased damages due to a lower first day efficiency for the flexible

---

[14] The final new source performance standard rules and regulations particulate matter discharges from fossil-fueled steam generators were issued by the U.S. Environmental Protection Agency on December 23, 1971 (*Fed. Reg*, December 23, 1971, pp. 24876–24895). Particulate matter discharges (which are mainly fly ash and unburned carbon particles) are not to exceed 0.1 lb/million Btu heat input maximum 2-hr average. This standard is applicable to any power plant unit of more than 250 million Btu/hr input or approximately 25 MW in capacity whose construction is commenced after August 17, 1971. Eventually, with the retirement of prestandard plants, every plant will be subject to the standard.

Under these regulations, firms are required to pass compliance tests on fly ash control devices before new plants go into operation. A plant is certified for operation when, on the basis of prescribed stack testing procedures, discharges during the test period are no greater than the standard. During operation, opacity of stack discharges is to be continuously monitored by the firm at its expense and reported to EPA. If the firm violates the opacity standard (20% opacity) it can be charged in a civil action under the provisions of the Clean Air Act and if convicted, fined as much as $50,000/day of violation.

These regulations have several peculiar features. For one thing, the start-up compliance test can be run an unlimited number of times. Secondly, the conditions under which compliance tests are to be conducted are not clearly defined. Beyond some general stipulations, the rules and regulations do not specify test conditions. Presumably EPA technical personnel will be on hand to check test conditions. The tests, themselves, will be conducted by utility company personnel. A strong fraternity of engineering interests is likely to pervade compliance testing activities with liberal interpretations of test conditions "being understood" by the participants. A third feature is that the average of as few as three compliance test stack samples is the measurement for comparison with the promulgated standard. As demonstrated, the number of successive compliance tests, the stringency of test conditions, and the number of averaged compliance test stack samples markedly influence firm behavior.

A peculiar feature of the federally promulgated opacity standard the basis or detecting a violation during operation, is that it allows roughly twice the quantity of discharges as are allowed by the particulate matter discharge standard. This too influences firm pollution control effort.

device are more than off-set by the higher damage savings due to its greater last day efficiency.

POLICY ANALYSIS

Cost Comparisons

We can now use our simulation results, summarized by our regression equations, to investigate tradeoffs among the alternative enforcement schemes.

Four straightforward results evolve from a comparison of out-of-pocket cost to the firm over the different enforcement schemes and from a comparison of resource costs (cost minus total fine or total tax) over the different enforcement schemes.

First, at high collection efficiencies the expected resource costs of flexible technology are generally less than those of inflexible technology at all plant sizes and for each of the three enforcement schemes. Figures 3a–3c show some representative curves for a 1300 MW plant. Under enforcement schemes using compliance tests, firms will incur enlargement costs weighted by the probability of failing the compliance test. These enlargement costs tend to be quite large while their weighting factors—the probabilities of compliance test failure—tend to decline at high efficiencies. This produces relatively small expected enlargement costs at high collection efficiencies. Hence at high efficiencies flexible devices have smaller expected resource costs than inflexible devices (for the same average efficiency) because the saving from their smaller original-size costs exceed the sum of their extra instrumentation costs, their higher power input costs, and their larger (but relatively small) enlargement costs. This is demonstrated by Fig. 3a and b: flexible costs are less than inflexible when collection efficiency is approximately 95% or greater. Under emission-tax-only enforcement and at high collection efficiencies a flexible precipitator also has smaller expected resource costs than an inflexible precipitator (see Fig. 3c). The reason is that the smaller original-size costs for flexible

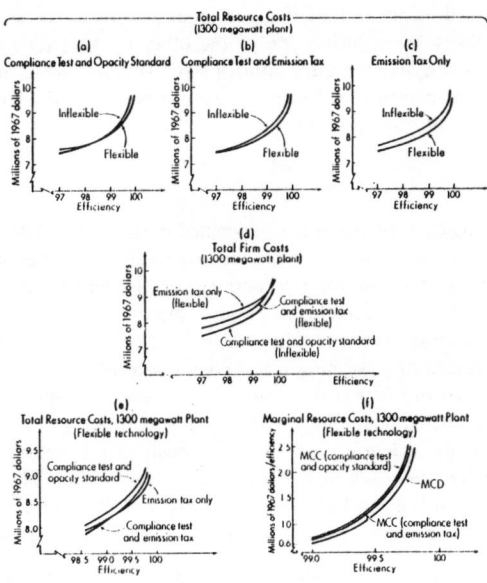

FIG. 3. Cost comparisons.

precipitators provide savings which exceed their extra instrumentation and power costs. In this case there is no question of a plant failing a compliance test and incurring enlargement costs. Therefore, since enlargement costs need not be overcome by flexible cost savings, flexible precipitators enjoy an even greater cost advantage over inflexible under emission-tax-only enforcement then they do under compliance test (with an opacity standard or emission tax) enforcement. This is demonstrated by the relatively larger cost advantage for flexible technology in Fig. 3c; in Fig. 3a and b flexible technology enjoys a relatively smaller cost advantage.

Second, the lowest out-of-pocket cost to the firm occurs with enforcement via a compliance test and opacity standard (with inflexible technology), the next from the lowest is a compliance test with emission tax (with flexible technology), and the third from the lowest is the emission tax only (with flexible technology). Out-of-pocket costs, of course, include fines and emission taxes paid under each of the enforcement schemes. Figure 3d presents each of these costs for a 1300-MW plant. On the other hand, a comparison of resource costs (all for flexible technology) gives the exact opposite ordering (see Fig. 3e). Hence the enforcement schemes which use emission taxes and resource-saving flexible technology and which consequently are attractive to a cost-minimizing resource manager are unattractive to the firms being regulated and vice versa. An implication is that there will be some resistance by firms to a shift toward enforcement schemes which use emission taxes even though this is desirable from the viewpoint of resource cost minimization.

In our earlier discussion of efficient enforcement a distinction was made between resource costs of control only (MCD) and marginal resource costs of control including marginal firm management costs (MCC). We now have quantitative measures of these costs (see Fig. 3f). On the average (at high efficiency levels) there is about 6% difference between MCC and MCD under compliance-test-with-emission-tax enforcement and about a 6.6% difference under compliance-test-with-opacity-standard enforcement.[16] It would appear that if a marginal benefit curve crosses these cost curves at high efficiency levels, using one or the other to determine efficient control levels results in approximately the same control level. It is well to recall however, that the proper inclusion of marginal enforcement agency costs could significantly impact determination of efficient control levels.

Policy Frontiers

Particular technologies were deliberately specified in the above ordering of preferred costs by the firm. This is necessary because the firm in reacting to enforcement policy parameters chooses the precipitator size and *technology* which minimizes its costs. Indeed, different mixes of enforcement policy parameters will induce it to pick flexible technology in some cases and inflexible technology in others. We proceed now to investigate the conditions governing technology selection.

The curve labeled AA in Fig. 4 is the locus of compliance test standards and opacity standards for which flexible technology and inflexible technology are equal in our-of-pocket costs. This locus is determined by setting costs as a function of enforcement policy parameters from scenarios S1 and S2, equal to each other. The dashed perpendiculars and the area to the northeast of these perpendiculars indicate approximate feasible choices for the compliance test and opacity standards. The crossed area to

---

[16] Cost differences of about the same relative magnitude occur at other plant sizes. Note that we have assumed that record keeping and fee playing costs do not vary with the removal rate.

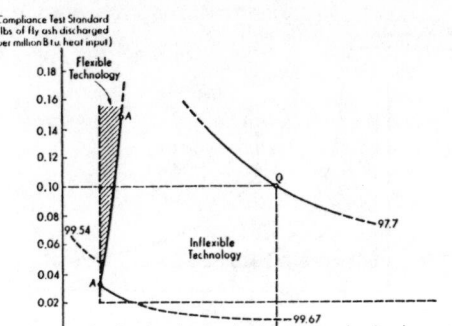

Fig. 4. Enforcement by compliance test and opacity standard, 1300-MW plant. An average of three stack samples ($N = 3$), no limits on the number of successive compliance tests (MD $=$ 0), and an intermediate level for the flue gas flow rate (1.1V) are representative of current enforcement practice. (similar tradeoffs occur at other plant sizes.)

the left of AA is the policy area within which flexible technology is cheaper in out-of-pocket costs. To the right, inflexible technology is cheaper. The curve labeled 99.54 is the locus of compliance test and opacity standards (given flexible technology) which would induce a cost minimizing firm to select a 99.54% efficient precipitator (in effect an isoquant). The curve labeled 99.67 is a similar locus given inflexible technology. Note that the iso-efficiency curves are only relevant for the policy areas where their technologies are less costly. A 99.54% efficient flexible precipitator and a 99.67% efficient inflexible precipitator are devices which would meet the new source fly ash discharge standard even on the last day of their operating cycles at peak load fly ash flow rates (1.15 V).Current legal enforcement practice is somewhere in the vicinity of the point labeled Q.[16] As indicated by the iso-efficiency curve passing through Q, a cost minimizing 1300-MW plant would install a precipitator having a base-load efficiency of about 97.7%. This is substantially below 99.67%, the base-load efficiency needed to meet the federally promulgated new source fly ash standard.

Furthermore, as is clearly indicated, current legal enforcement practice induces the firm to pick inflexible technology even though resource costs are greater than flexible technology. This can be explained as follows. For a relatively tight compliance test standard a cost minimizing firm will pick roughly the same sizes of flexible and inflexible precipitators to avoid high enlargement costs. Therefore the "first day" efficiencies of the two devices will be approximately the same while the installation costs of the equivalent size flexible precipitator will be higher because of extra flexible instrumentation costs. Moreover, the flexible precipitator will have a higher average operating efficiency and consequently higher operating costs. Thus, for a given set of S1 and S2 enforcement parameters (and specifically a relatively tight compliance test standard) a cost minimizing firm would pick an inflexible precipitator of lower average operating efficiency but the same first day efficiency.

Similar analysis has been carried out for scenarios S3, S4, S5, and S6. The results are summarized in Fig. 5. FF is the locus of compliance standards and emission taxes

[16] The enforced opacity standard is likely to be 30% or higher, rather than the promulgated 20%. In the past courts have levied fines only when violations were considerably greater than the relevant standards and when firms were uncooperative and recalcitrant.

234   DOWNING AND WATSON

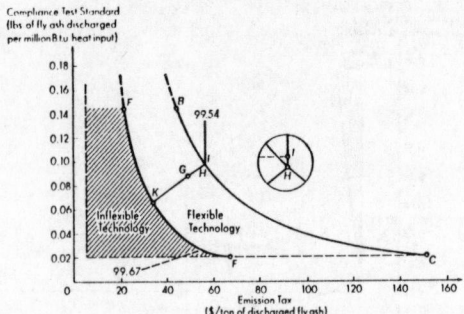

Fig. 5. Enforcement by compliance test and emission tax, 1300-MW plant. An average of three
stack samples (N = 3), no limits on the number of successive compliance tests (MD = 0), and an
intermediate level for the flue gas flow rate (1.1V) are representative of current enforcement practice.
(Similar tradeoffs occur at other plant sizes.)

for which total flexible and inflexible precipitator out-of-pocket costs for a 1300-MW
plant are equal. This locus or policy frontier is determined by setting 1300-MW costs
as a function of enforcement policy parameters from scenarios S3 and S4, equal to
each other. In the crossed area to the left of FF, inflexible technology is cheaper. To
the right, flexible is less costly. BC is the locus of compliance test standards and emission taxes using compliance-test-with-emission-tax enforcement and emission-tax-only
enforcement for which precipitator efficiency is equal in a comparison of these two
alternative enforcement schemes. The curves labeled 99.54 and 99.67 are iso-efficiency
curves for a flexible precipitator under emission tax enforcement and an inflexible
precipitator under compliance-test-tax enforcement. The point labeled G is the compliance test standard and emission tax combination where total expected costs to the
firm for a 99.54% efficient precipitator are equal to tax-only enforcement at H. To the
left of G on the 99.54% iso-efficiency curve, the test-tax policy combinations result in
smaller costs to the firm while to the right of G they are more expensive than tax only
enforcement (indicated by point H). At point I, a compliance standard of 0.1 (the
current EPA standard) combined with an emission tax of $56/ton would induce a cost
minimizing firm to pick a law-abiding 99.54% efficient precipitator. However, note
that an emission tax alone of the same amount would produce the same level of control
at less expected cost to the firm. Point K is the least cost point for the firm under
compliance-test-tax enforcement.

Figure 5 also indicates that flexible technology enjoys a relative policy advantage
under emission tax enforcement. This occurs because increased flexibility allows the
firm, for a given precipitator size, to reduce total emission taxes. Loosely speaking,
flexible technology will cost less than inflexible as long as this emission tax savings
(offset by some additional fly ash disposal costs) exceeds the additional flexible
instrumentation costs. This may, of course, not occur if the emission tax rate is relatively small or if the compliance test standard is relatively tight. In these cases enlargement costs dominate technology selection and inflexible technology clearly has a cost
advantage over flexible technology.

Enforcement Policy and Technology Development

The model contains two "types" (really degrees) of precipitator technology, labeled, for convenience flexible and inflexible. These particular variants were modeled because they are feasible choices in today's technology choice set. Over time though, one would expect that precipitators even more efficiency-flexible than these could be developed. This raises an important issue, namely, do different enforcement schemes either encourage or discourage the development and adoption of efficiency-enhancing technology?

The answer is that emission tax enforcement schemes encourage such developments while enforcement by compliance test and opacity standard discourages them.

The crux of the matter is that enforcement by compliance test and opacity standards tends, for the most part, to encourage good first day performance by firms. Hence, flexible technology development which improves over-the-operating-cycle efficiency is not cost effective for the firm under these enforcement circumstances. Moreover, improving flexibility generally shrinks the relevant policy area within which flexible technology would be adopted under such an enforcement scheme. In comparison, emission tax enforcement rewards over-the-operating-cycle performance. Hence, costs to the firm tend to fall as flexibility increases, given emission tax enforcement of environmental standards. This is true over a wide policy range even when emission taxes are combined with compliance tests. Or in terms of Fig. 5, gains in precipitator flexibility would cause the technology policy frontier, FF, to shift toward the origin.

The important conclusion is that the resource costs of pollution control as well as potential damages for a given average removal efficiency fall as technology is made more flexible and so it is important to devise enforcement schemes which encourage firms in this direction. We have seen that compliance-test-opacity-standard enforcement will usually fail in this regard while emission tax enforcement schemes will generally suceed.

SUMMARY AND CONCLUSIONS

The optimal level of control and emissions has been shown to depend upon the cost of the control devices and process changes, the management costs imposed on the firm by the control agency, and the management cost of the control agency itself (and, of course, the benefits of control). These costs differ among alternative implementation and enforcement schemes. In order to determine the optimal implementation and enforcement scheme it is necessary to determine the optimal control level, and hence values of policy parameters, for each alternative. The net benefit of control for each alternative could then be compared and the scheme with the largest net benefit chosen. While we cannot prove it without further research, the evidence we present indicates that an effluent fee enforcement scheme would be optimal in controlling fly ash emissions from coal-fired power plants. However, we do not expect this result to apply universally. Some form of legal enforcement may be preferred in many cases. This is especially true in cases where continuous monitoring of emissions is technically difficult and expensive.

Assuming that firms are expected cost minimizers we find that different implementation and enforcement techniques imply different reactions to control agency policy. Under a legal enforcement system the relevant policy parameters are inspection and monitoring techniques, emission standards, device certification procedures, probability of conviction if accused of a violation, fines and shutdown penalties, and damage to the corporate image. For example, in our simulation of fly ash control we find that stricter compliance tests and less stringent opacity standards can yield the same level

236   DOWNING AND WATSON

of control. The model indicates that a higher marginal fine or penalty would yield greater control. In our empirical case, however, we find that any positive effective fine will have the same effect on the firm's control decision. This probably is not a general result.

In effluent fee enforcement the relevant policy parameters are the marginal fee, the device certification process if any, and the inspection and monitoring system employed. As expected, higher effluent fees yield greater control. When a certification procedure is added to the effluent fee we find that a tradeoff between the certification standard and the effluent fee exists. This is born out in our empirical test. However, there is a range of effluent fees for which any feasible compliance test will have no effect on the firm's control efforts.

Under current enforcement practice, most coal-fired power plants will not meet the federal new source fly ash standard being in violation as much as 70% of the year. We suspect that this noncompliance result holds for most enforcement schemes currently employed by various control agencies. Our analysis indicates that owners of power plants, especially large ones, have a strong incentive to seek relaxations in compliance test conditions. We also find that smaller plants are relatively more costly to control and, therefore, should be subject to relatively less tsringent penalties or standards.[17] It should be noted that our simulations assume that firms comply with the letter (if not the spirit) of the law rather than fight its implementation. If firms were to take advantage of all the legal delaying tactics available to them, emission reductions such as we determine in this study will be optimistic both as to amount and timing.

[17] Becker (1968, pp. 189 and 196) derived a similar result on theoretical grounds. He argues that penalties (or standards) should be less for smaller violators (plants) and that high income firms should be prosecuted more thoroughly rather than less thoroughly as we have found in our analysis.

REFERENCES

1. R. J. Anderson, Jr. and T. D. Crocker, The economics of air pollution: A literature assessment, in "Air Pollution and The Social Sciences" (Downing, Ed.), Praeger, New York (1971).
2. G. A. Becker, Crime and punishment: An economic approach, *J. Pol. Econ.* 76, 169–217 (1968).
3. P. F. Dienemann, "Estimating Cost Uncertainty Using Monte Carlo Techniques," Rand Corp., Santa Monica, California (1966).
4. P. B. Downing, An economic analysis of periodic vehicle inspection programs, *Atmospheric Environ.* 7, 1237–1246 (1973).
5. P. B. Downing and W. D. Watson, Jr., "Enforcement Economics In Air Pollution Control," Socioeconomic Environmental Studies Series No. EPA-600/5-73-014, U. S. Environmental Protection Agency Government Printing Office, Washington, D.C. (1973).
6. L.-S. Fan and B. R. Frochlich, Pollution control and the behavior of the firm, *Engrg. Econ.* 17, 261–267 (1972).
7. *Fed. Reg.*, Thursday December 23, 1971, Vol. 36, No. 247, Part II.
8. J. Greco and W. A. Wynot., Operating and maintenance problems encountered with electrostatic precipitators, *Proc. Amer. Power Conf.* 33, 345–353 (1971).
9. J. Krier, Air pollution and legation institutions, in "The Contribution of the Social Sciences to the Solution of the Air Pollution Problem," (Downing, Ed.) Taskforce Assessments, Project Clean Air, Statewide Air Pollution Research Center, University of California, Riverside (1970).
10. C. R. Tittle, Crime rates and legal sanctions, *Social Problems* 16, 409–422 (1969).
11. W. D. Watson, Jr., "Costs of Air pollution Control in the Coal-Fired Electric Power Industry," Ph.D. dissertation, University of Minnesota, University Microfilms, Ann Arbor (1970).
12. W. D. Watson, Jr., Stochastic operating characteristics and cost functions of electrostatic precipitators, *Engrg. Econ.* 18, 79–98 (1973).
13. W. D. Watson, Jr., Costs and benefits of fly ash control, *J. Econ. Bus.*, May 1974.
14. H. J. White, "Industrial Electrostatic Precipitation," Reading, Massachusetts Addison-Wesley, (1968).

JOURNAL OF ENVIRONMENTAL ECONOMICS AND MANAGEMENT 5, 26–43 (1978)

Firm Behavior Under Imperfectly Enforceable Pollution Standards and Taxes

Jon D. Harford [1]

Department of Economics, State University of New York at Albany, New York 12222

Received November 2, 1976

Assuming expected profit maximization, the behavior of the firm under imperfectly enforceable pollution standards is examined. Among other results, it is found that cost subsidies can reduce the size of violation and amount of wastes, and that the shape of the expected penalty function determines the direction of the firm response to tighter standards. Under imperfectly enforceable pollution taxes, it is found, among other results, that the firm's actual level of wastes is independent of proportional changes in the expected penalty for pollution tax evasion, and that the marginal cost of actual waste reduction equals the unit tax on reported wastes. Some normative aspects of the results are discussed.

I. INTRODUCTION

In this paper we present simple theoretical models of firm behavior under imperfectly enforceable pollution standards and pollution taxes, respectively. Such models are motivated by the nature of the current and past pollution control efforts in this country and encouraged intellectually by coexisting literatures on approaches to externalities and the economics of crime. Although the model presented here has some strong simplifying assumptions, it presents a point of view distinctly different from most treatments of externalities and allows derivation of some interesting results.

The approach to pollution control adopted by the federal government has by and large been based upon the use of standards, both ambient and emission (or effluent). In the case of air pollution, the Clean Air Act of 1970 gives the Environmental Protection Agency the power to set emission standards on a wide variety of sources with the goal of meeting ambient air quality standards. In the case of water pollution, The Federal Water Pollution Control Act Amendments of 1972 give broad power to the EPA to set effluent standards on practically all industrial and municipal sources with the goal of meeting ambient water quality standards, which, according to legislative intent, are to become increasingly stringent.

In the case of both air and water pollution standards it has been the case that these standards have not always been complied with. For support of this understatement with respect to water pollution controls one should consult Kneese's

---

[1] The author gratefully acknowledges support from the Research Foundation of the State of New York for the researching and writing of this paper.

paper in Bain [2] and Zwick's [15] even less charitable view. In fact, major aspects of the recent water pollution legislation have been aimed at reducing the costs of enforcing pollution standards by making the EPA's power greater and more sharply defined. Both pieces of legislation mentioned have clauses setting penalties for violations of standards.

It may be that once full monitoring of pollution sources is effective, the probability of successfully violating standards without being caught and punished will be close to zero. However, past experience does not support the view that perfect enforcement of pollution standards would be of trivial costs in comparison with the benefits.

Because of the above considerations it is of interest to examine the behavior of a profit maximizing firm under imperfectly enforced pollution standards. However, it is also of interest to examine the behavior of the firm under imperfectly enforceable pollution taxes. One reason would be the substantial literature that has been devoted to proving that under perfect competition the tax per unit of pollution equal to marginal damages with no compensation of victims is the Pareto optimal policy (and that in general virtually all other solutions cannot attain Pareto optimality). Baumol and Oates [4] present a general proof of this proposition and discuss some of the substantial literature that led up to this conclusion. A second reason for studying the effect on the firm of an imperfectly enforceable pollution tax is that it provides us with a comparison set of results for the standards case. We find, in fact, that the pollution tax case does have interesting properties, the main one being a type of separability between the amount of pollution released and the amount of unreported pollution, or tax evasion, that occurs.

If there is a second major federal approach to pollution control it would be that of providing cost subsidies. For firms this is done mostly through the special form of accelerated depreciation allowed on pollution control capital as provided for in the Tax Reform Act of 1969. Such subsidies, by themselves, would seem to provide no positive incentive for pollution control. They merely reduce the cost of doing something which adds nothing to revenues. However, in a world of imperfectly enforceable controls, we can show that such subsidies reduce the tendency to violate standards.

Lastly, we will point out some implications of the analysis for the characterization of optimal levels of pollution control. Since firms that violate standards and evade taxes change the trade-offs in the economy one would expect a change in the set of efficient resource allocations in comparison with a world of perfectly costless enforcement or perfectly compliant firms.

In Section II we will examine the expected profit maximizing firm's response to imperfectly enforceable pollution standards. In Section III we examine the firm's behavior under evadeable pollution taxes. In Section IV we discuss some of the normative implications of the analysis, and Section V presents some conclusions.

II. THE FIRM RESPONSE TO STANDARDS

Let us consider a firm which produces a good x from which it receives revenue $R(x)$. The firm may be either a perfect competitor of some form of imperfect competitor. The costs C of producing the good x depend, not only on the quantity of x, but also on the amount of emitted wastes w. So by definition $C \equiv$

28   JON D. HARFORD

$C(x, w)$. This cost function is taken to reflect all of the process changes which would reduce created wastes and any efforts which would "neutralize" wastes already created. Emitted wastes are those which are created and not neutralized, and all references to firm wastes (or actual wastes) will mean emitted wastes as here defined.

We will indicate partial derivatives by subscripts. Thus, marginal output costs and marginal revenue are C_x and R_x, respectively. Under usual circumstances we would expect $|R_{xx} - C_{xx}| < 0$, where the subscripts indicate second partial derivatives, which we will assume exist for all of the relevant functions unless noted otherwise. In order for the firm to find it profitable to emit pollution in the absence of any external constraints it must be true that C_w is negative over a range from zero pollution up to some level w_o. "w_o" is the point where $C_w = 0$, and would be the amount of pollution released in the absence of any controls. We may assume that C_w becomes positive after this point; that is, it would increase costs to release any more pollution. Of course, the firm would never operate on this portion of its cost curve. Consistent with this description, we will assume that $C_{ww} > 0$. If costs were separable in pollution and output we would have $C_{xw} = 0$, but it is more reasonable to assume that $C_{xw} = C_{wx} < 0$, over the relevant range of the cost function.

Now assume that a particular pollution control board (PCB) or the EPA imposes a particular allowable level of released wastes, labeled w_s, which is less than what the firm would have otherwise chosen. The PCB wishes to see this standard complied with. Therefore it sets penalties in the form of fines (and perhaps prison terms) and expends resources on activities which create a probability of discovering and convicting standards violators greater than zero but less than one. For present purposes, the discovery of a violation, any adjudication process, and the receipt of a penalty for the violation will be treated as one event. For any size of violation, $v = (w - w_s)$, the firm sees the probability of discovery and punishment and the level of fine as parameters.

Generally we would expect that any fine f will be a positive function of the size of violation. It is also plausible that the probability p of detecting a violation will be a positive function of the size of violation. Thus we would suppose that f_v and p_v are ordinarily greater than zero. We will be assuming risk neutrality for the firm, so that the expected fine, $g = pf$, is all that matters to the firm. To facilitate the analysis and reduce the number of terms let us write $g = F_s PG(v)$, where F_s and P are shift parameters for the general size of fines under standards and the general level of the probability of detection and punishment of violators, respectively. Because of their nature, the terms F_s and P can be taken to be equal to one without loss of generality. Thus, $G(v) = f(v)p(v)$, and it is assumed to be continuous and twice differentiable; and

$$G' = f'p + p'f \tag{1a}$$

$$G'' = f''p + 2p'f' + p''f, \tag{1b}$$

where the primes indicate the order of differentiation.

It is conceivable that there could be a discontinuity at $v = 0$. This would require that there be a sudden jump from zero to some positive value in the probability of punishment as one goes from no violation to one of arbitrarily small size *and* that there be some minimum level of fine. We mention this as a possibility since such a discontinuity would tend to produce extreme solutions.

As a practical matter, however, laws are seldom enforced in such a way as to produce a significant discontinuity of this sort. Before going on it should be noted that both f'' and p'' may be negative and still have G'' positive.

The structure of the fines is something to be determined by the PCB and presents an optimization problem. It may be suggested that characterizing the optimal structure of fines is an interesting problem and quite possibly a very difficult one in general. The probability of detection as a function of the size of violation might be either something given in the nature of the production function of detection, or a result of conscious allocation of resources. For a situation involving different types of crimes, the latter interpretation is more plausible (and the concept of crime size less clear) while for crimes of the same type this writer would lean toward the former interpretation. In either case, we assume the firm views these functions as given, and, given risk neutrality, is concerned only with the product of these functions and its derivatives.

In order to complete our picture, let us assume that the firm receives a subsidy at a rate b, where b is between zero and one, for the costs of eliminating wastes. In reality subsidies usually apply only to explicit capital expenditures on pollution control and seldom or never to the costs of all potential ways of reducing pollution, which would include process changes and non-capital inputs into waste neutralization. Indeed, it would be difficult to divide costs between output and pollution control if costs are not additively separable in the technical sense. We will ignore this practical difficulty and assume the total subsidy is $b(C(x, w) - C(x, w_o))$ where w_o is taken to be the level of wastes that the firm would produce in the absence of pollution controls and cost subsidies. Since w_o is a constant, we may define $C(x, w_o) = C^o(x)$.

Given the previous definitions, expected profits, Π_s, is of the following form:

$$\Pi_s = R(x) - C(x, w) + b[C(x, w) - C^o(x)] - PF_sG(v). \qquad (2)$$

The firm is assumed to choose output x and the level of waste w so as to maximize expected profits. The assumption of risk neutrality is not perfectly general, of course, but even for nonrisk neutral firms risk neutrality is a good approximation for relatively small risks, which is probably a fair description of most risks associated with violating pollution standards.[2]

The first order necessary conditions for an interior maximum are:

$$R_x - C_x + b(C_x - C_x^o) = 0 \qquad (3a)$$

$$-(1 - b)C_w - PF_sG' = 0. \qquad (3b)$$

Condition (3a) says that marginal revenue should equal marginal costs less the subsidized fraction of the difference between the marginal costs of output at the base level of waste and the marginal costs of output at the chosen level of

---

[2] Given the basic tenet of portfolio theory that one can evaluate the risk of any asset only in the context of its relationship to the array of all assets, it is difficult to see how one would make rigorous sense out of the idea of either risk averseness or risk preference for a firm that may be owned by thousands of stockholders with differing portfolios and preferences for risk. The present assumption can at least be defended on the grounds that in the long run (assuming survival of the firm and some version of the law of large numbers) the risk neutral firm will have had greater average profits than either the risk averse or risk preferring firm. To put it another way, if all profits were reinvested for all firms at some constant rate of return, then the risk neutral firms would eventually be the largest.

wastes. If the cost function is separable in x and w, the last term is zero and we get the conventional answer that marginal revenue should equal marginal cost. If $C_{xw} < 0$, we would expect $(C_x - C_x^o) > 0$, and therefore, that marginal revenue would be less than marginal costs. With such a cost function and subsidy one ends up subsidizing output as well as pollution control. This is no doubt part of the reason why most actual cost subsidies are for types of pollution control equipment that have no obvious connection to the production of output. This, of course, means that pollution control is not achieved in a least cost manner from society's viewpoint.

Condition (3b) tells us that the unsubsidized fraction of marginal costs of reducing wastes should equal the increase in the expected monetary value of the fine with a one unit increase in actual waste. Clearly it may often be the case that equality in (3b) does not hold. For example, if both the fine and the probability of receiving a penalty are fixed and independent of the violation size, then $G' = 0$, and $C_w = 0$ will appear to be the maximizing condition, which is what it would be in the absence of standards. However, if the expected fine is high enough one will get the other "corner" solution where $w = w_s$.

The two possibilities for the case just mentioned are illustrated in Fig. 1. We have drawn costs as a function of wastes while holding output constant. For simplicity we have assumed a zero subsidy in this and following figures. Two different fixed sizes of expected fine are indicated by G_1 and G_2. The level of costs under complete compliance is indicated by C_2, and under no effort at compliance the costs are C_1. Since $C_1 + G_1 < C_2$, the firm makes no effort at pollution control under expected fine G_1. Under expected fine G_2, the firm chooses zero violation since $C_1 + G_2 > C_2$.

In general, the possibilities for corner solutions depend upon the relative heights and shapes of the cost and expected fine functions, as well as the levels of w_s and b. Figure 2 shows a case where an interior solution, characterized by $w_o > w^o > w_s$, exists. The full compliance level of costs OM_2 is greater than the costs at the minimum point of the $C + G_3$ curve where wastes are w^o and costs are at height OM_1. It is due to the increasing nature of the expected fine and the decreasing marginal costs of waste prevention that w^o is to the left of w_o.

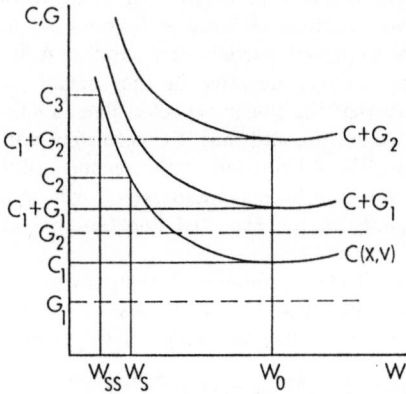

FIG. 1. Choice of violation size with constant expected fine.

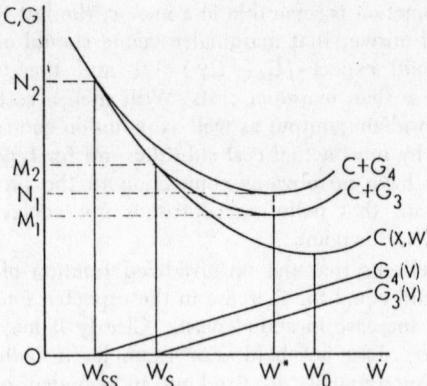

FIG. 2. Choice of violation size with a constant slope expected fine function.

Careful perusal of variations on Fig. 2 indicates that as long as $G'' \geqq 0$, a (further) requirement for a positive violation level is that

$$-C_w|_{w=w_s} > G'|_{v=0},$$

given a zero subsidy and the other assumptions on the cost function. Since the marginal costs of reducing wastes decrease as wastes increase, while the slope of the expected fine function is here assumed to be non-decreasing, we must have marginal costs of waste reduction at the allowed level of wastes greater than the rate of increase in the expected penalty with respect to the first unit of illegal wastes in order to have a positive violation.

To gain further insight into the possibilities of corner solutions we shall now consider the second order conditions for a maximum. These conditions are that the determinant of the Hessian matrix,

$$H_s = \begin{vmatrix} (R_{xx} - (1-b)C_{xx} - bC_{xx}^o) & -(1-b)C_{xw} \\ -(1-b)C_{xw} & -(1-b)C_{ww} - PF_sG'' \end{vmatrix} > 0, \quad (4)$$

and that the terms on the diagonal be negative. This expression has the common implication that the cross partials of the cost function should not be too large in comparison with the repeated partials in w and x. A further implication is that G'' cannot be too strongly negative or the second order conditions will not hold. One may note that the linear expected fine function in Fig. 2 implies that its second derivative is zero, and thus it is consistent with satisfaction of the second order conditions. The satisfaction of the second order conditions ensures us that there is at most one interior maximum, which will be the global maximum if there is no discontinuity in the expected fine function at the zero violation level.

We may now list and discuss a number of comparative static results showing rates of change of controlled variables with respect to parameter changes. In the following results we have taken advantage of the normalization $P = F_s = 1$.

$$\frac{\partial w}{\partial P} = \frac{\partial w}{\partial F_s} = \frac{[R_{xx} - (1-b)C_{xx} - bC_{xx}^o]G''}{H_s} < 0 \quad (5a)$$

32 JON D. HARFORD

$$\frac{\partial w}{\partial w_s} = \frac{-[R_{xx} - (1-b)C_{xx} - bC_{xx}{}^o]G''}{H_s} \geqq 0, \qquad \text{as} \qquad G'' \gtreqless 0. \tag{5b}$$

$$\frac{\partial w}{\partial b} = \frac{-[R_{xx} - (1-b)C_{xx} - bC_{xx}{}^o]C_w + (1-b)C_{xw}(C_x - C_x{}^o)}{H_s} < 0 \tag{5c}$$

$$\frac{\partial x}{\partial P} = \frac{\partial x}{\partial F_s} = \frac{(1-b)C_{xw}G'}{H_s} < 0 \tag{5d}$$

$$\frac{\partial x}{\partial w_s} = \frac{-(1-b)C_{xw}G''}{H_s} \gtreqless 0 \tag{5e}$$

as $G'' \gtreqless 0$, assuming $C_{xw} < 0$.

$$\frac{\partial x}{\partial b} = \frac{(C_x - C_x{}^o)[(1-b)C_{ww} + G''] - (1-b)C_wC_{xw}}{H_s} \gtreqless 0. \tag{5f}$$

These results are based on the assumption that both the first and second order conditions for a maximum are satisfied. On this basis the relationships in (5a) tell us that wastes created and released will decrease with increases in the level of fines or increases in the probability of detection at all sizes of violation. In other words, a general increase in expected fines decreases the actual level of wastes and the size of violation which the firm chooses. We also find from (5b) that an increase in the cost subsidy will reduce the size of any standards violation, a result due basically to the fact that the relative cost of complying with the standard has been reduced. This provides a rationale for the commonly used cost subsidies, which economists have tended to ignore or presume to be useless in situations where none of the benefits of reducing pollution are internal to the firm.

On the output side we find that increased fines and probability of detection tend to reduce the expected profit maximizing level of output to the extent that marginal costs of output are increased by reductions in the emitted wastes. Thus, without separability we would tend to find that limitations on the amount of wastes would tend to reduce the profit maximizing level of output for the firm.

Interestingly enough, the direction of change in waste and output levels with respect to a change in the allowable wastes under the standard is dependent upon G'', the second derivative of the expected fine function with respect to the size of the violation. If the slope of G is increasing, then waste and output will move in the same direction as allowable wastes under the standard. This is the more intuitive result. One may conjecture that it is likely though not certain that this would be the most relevant case. If $G'' > 0$, it can be plausibly argued from the relevant expressions that the increase in wastes will be less than the allowable wastes under the standard, i.e., that the size of violation will decrease with a loosening of the standard.

However, there is nothing in the second order conditions which definitely rules out the case where the slope of the expected fine function is decreasing. In this case we find that making the standard marginally stricter will increase the actual amount of waste released by the firm. To give the reader a better feel for the situation we refer to Fig. 2, which illustrates what occurs in the border line case where the slope of the expected penalty function is constant. The shift in the wastes standard from w_s to w_{ss} has the effect of shifting upward the curve representing the sum of costs plus the expected penalty to $C + G_4$. Thus costs at w° increase from a height of OM_1 to ON_1. However, due to the parallel nature of the shift, ON_1 now represents the new minimum of the sum of costs plus expected penalty. In other words, there is no change in actual wastes emitted. The size of the violation increases in the same magnitude as the reduction in the allowed level of wastes.

Finally, we note that the change in output with respect to a change in the cost subsidy rate is in general ambiguous in sign. This is due to the existence of two counteracting effects. The subsidy reduces the cost of pollution control which allows more output for the same pollution control efforts and total costs. However, because the subsidy encourages less pollution it indirectly increases the marginal costs of output. Which effect dominates depends upon the size of practically all of our parameters and the first and second partial derivatives of the cost function. In the special case of separability between output and wastes in the cost function, we can assert that the change in output with respect to a change in the subsidy rate will be zero.

All of these comparative static results are under the assumption that the first order conditions are satisfied with equality and the second order conditions hold. If, on the other hand, we do not have an interior solution, we would still expect that small changes in the parameter values would have either no effect, or effect waste and output levels in the direction indicated by the comparative statics results.

This expectation tends to hold up even with respect to variations in w_s in the case where complying with the standards maximizes expected profits. One might be tempted to expect that permitted and actual wastes would move in the same direction regardless of the shape of the expected fine function. That this may not be the case is illustrated within Fig. 1. When the allowable level of wastes is decreased from w_s to w_{ss} under the assumption that the expected fine is a constant G_2 we find that overall expected costs are now lowest at the level of w_o wastes, i.e., costs at full compliance with the stricter standard C_3 are greater than $(C_1 + G_2)$. Thus, in this case, increasing the strictness of the standard increases the actual level of wastes from w_s to w_o. To put it another way, the firm may go from full compliance to totally ignoring the standard as it increases in strictness if the expected fine does not increase rapidly enough with the size of violation. For the special case illustrated by Fig. 1, Anderson [1] preceded us in discovering this result.

All of the previous results are about individual firms and, therefore, one needs to know something about industry structure in order to discuss effects of pollution standards on aggregate of firms. For firms operating in an environment where expected long run economic profits should be zero, average costs become important for determining the amount of wastes which the industry will generate since average costs determine the size of the industry in terms of output. Thus, even in the seemingly perverse case where tightening standards increases the firm's waste creation, we would expect (and Figs. 1 and 2 confirm) that the firm's average costs would increase. This would tend to reduce the size of a competitive industry and work in the opposite direction from the "counterproductive" effect on the individual firm.

34   JON D. HARFORD

In the same vein, an increase in the cost subsidy rate for pollution control would be expected to reduce the average costs of output for the firm even though the marginal effect is uncertain. Thus the size of the industry would be larger with the subsidy, ceterus paribus, even though each individual firm may produce less pollution. It is possible that the larger industry size would increase pollution relatively more than any reduction in the pollution per unit of output that the cost subsidy might induce. The overall effect will depend upon a number of factors including the elasticity of the market demand for the output.

III. EVADEABLE POLLUTION TAXES

It is of interest to compare the kind of results we obtain with pollution standards with those we would get in the case where a tax per unit of waste emitted is imposed. To make the comparison reasonable, it is assumed that the pollution tax is evadeable. This may be interpreted as meaning that actual wastes released, w, are greater than the reported wastes, w_r, where the tax is directly on reported wastes only. The firm's costs C are a function of ouput x and the actual wastes released w in the same manner assumed in the case of standards. (We no longer assume any cost subsidy.) All of the remarks about the signs of the derivatives of the cost function still apply.

The unit tax t is applied to w_r so that total pollution tax paid equals t times w_r. In order to prevent the firm from evading all taxes by reporting zero released wastes, the pollution taxing agency imposes penalties for evasion of pollution taxes. The size of the evasion will be measured by $v = (w - w_r)$, where we re-use the letter v to reflect the size of violation in this different case. There is some justification for this procedure. In the cases of standards, the reported wastes would always be w_s since there is no incentive to have actual or reported wastes less than w_s, and reported wastes above w_s would be asking for a penalty. So even in the standards case the violation size v could be interpreted as the difference between actual and reported wastes.

Again we will use the function $G(v) = pf$ to reflect the shape of the expected fine as a function of the violation size where p and f have the same meaning as before. The shift parameter of the probability of detection and punishment will again be labeled P, which will be taken to be equal to one. We shall distinguish between two components of what we shall call the expected penalty function. The first component consists of a fine shift parameter F, also taken to be equal to one, multiplied by $PG(v)$ to reflect the expected fine size. The second component will be the tax that will be collected on unreported but discovered wastes. Thus, in addition to any expected fine and the tax on reported wastes, there is an expected tax on unreported wastes of $Ppvt$. To reduce the number of terms in later expressions we will define $B = pv$. We note that

$$B' = p + p'v \tag{6a}$$

$$B'' = 2p' + p''v. \tag{6b}$$

If we again use $R(x)$ to denote total revenue as a function of output, we may write expected profits as

$$\Pi_t = R(x) - C(x, w) - tw_r - FPG(v) - PB(v)t. \tag{7}$$

The firm now has three control variables, x, w, and w_r, with which it attempts to maximize expected profits. Accordingly, we will have three first order necessary conditions for a maximum, which are:

$$R_z - C_z = 0, \tag{8a}$$

$$-C_w - FPG' - PB't = -C_w - G' - B't = 0, \tag{8b}$$

$$-t + FPG' + PB't = -t + G' + B't = 0. \tag{8c}$$

Condition (8a) informs us that marginal revenue should equal marginal cost, the same type of result one would get if there were no pollution tax (although the level of marginal costs will be affected by the actual level of pollution control). Condition (8b) indicates that the marginal cost of reducing actual waste should be equal to the marginal increase in the expected penalty (expected fine plus additional tax) with a unit increase in violation size. Condition (8c) tells us that the increase in expected penalty from a unit decrease in reported wastes should equal the unit tax on reported wastes.

If these conditions hold, it is obvious but interesting the $-C_w = t$. In other words, the marginal cost of actual pollution reduction by the firm will equal the unit tax on *reported* pollution. This implies that the actual waste level of the firm does not directly depend upon the size of our shift parameters for the fine or the probability of discovery of the violation. Furthermore, if the expected punishment levels are generally so high that the firm maximizes expected profits by having actual and reported wastes the same [$(G' + B't) > t$ at all positive v would cause this situation], then it would still clearly be true that the marginal costs of waste reduction would equal the unit tax on reported wastes, since reported and actual wastes are the same.

At the other extreme of corner solutions, however, this result would not hold. If expected punishment costs are sufficiently low and increase so slowly that the unit tax on reported wastes is everywhere greater than the increase in expected penalty with respect to violation size, one would get a case where reported wastes are equal to zero, and the marginal costs of actual waste reduction would be equal to the smaller magnitude of the increase in expected penalty costs.

Practically speaking, corner solutions where reported wastes are zero are unlikely. It would be irrational to set penalties so low that no pollution tax at all was collected. Moreover, if it is obvious that every firm generates some wastes, reporting zero wastes would be a clear signal of a violation.

Deriving the Hessian matrix of second order derivatives we can characterize the second order conditions for a maximum in terms of restrictions on the signs of its determinant and principal minors. We have the restrictions that the determinant

$$H_t = \begin{vmatrix} (R_{zz} - C_{zz}) & -C_{zw} & 0 \\ -C_{zw} & (-C_{ww} - A) & A \\ 0 & A & -A \end{vmatrix} < 0, \tag{9}$$

where $A = G'' + B''t$, and that all the diagonal elements must be negative, while all second order minors should be positive. These restrictions imply that the expression represented by A must be positive for an interior maximum to be unique, and a global maximum if there is no discontinuity in the expected penalty function at the zero violation level. Thus, the expected penalty function must have an increasing slope to satisfy the second order conditions and provide the possibility of an interior solution in the pollution tax case, whereas the expected fine function did not have to have a positive curvature in order for an interior solution to exist. It is still true, however, that the expected fine function, by itself, does not have to have a positive curvature if the function B has a sufficiently strong positive curvature.

Although we have a larger matrix, the comparative statics analysis turns out to be simpler in some ways than in the standards case. Equating the shift parameters to one we have the following results:

$$\frac{\partial w}{\partial P} = \frac{\partial w}{\partial F} = 0 \tag{10a}$$

$$\frac{\partial x}{\partial P} = \frac{\partial x}{\partial F} = 0 \tag{10b}$$

$$\frac{\partial w}{\partial t} = \frac{-(R_{xx} - C_{xx})A}{H_t} < 0 \tag{10c}$$

$$\frac{\partial x}{\partial t} = \frac{-C_{xw}A}{H_t} < 0 \tag{10d}$$

$$\frac{\partial w_r}{\partial F} = \frac{G'[(R_{xx} - C_{xx})C_{ww} + C_{xw}^2]}{H_t} > 0 \tag{10e}$$

$$\frac{\partial w_r}{\partial P} = \frac{((G' + B't)}{G'} \left(\frac{\partial w_r}{\partial F} \right) > 0 \tag{10f}$$

$$\frac{\partial w_r}{\partial t} = \frac{-[(R_{xx} - C_{xx})C_{ww} + C_{xw}^2](1 - B')}{H_t} + \frac{\partial w}{\partial t} < 0 \tag{10g}$$

$$\frac{\partial v}{\partial t} = \frac{\partial w}{\partial t} - \frac{\partial w_r}{\partial t} > 0 \tag{10h}$$

First of all, quite consistently with previous statements, we find that the actual level of wastes released is independent of the level of fines or probability of detection and punishment. Small changes in P and F have no effect on w. Furthermore, small changes in P and F have no effect on the firm's level of output. This follows quite intuitively; if the optimal level of actual waste does not change, then costs as a function of output would not change, and, therefore, marginal revenue would equal marginal costs at the same output level both before and after any shift in fines or the probability of punishment.

We find that actual wastes decline as the tax on reported wastes is increased. This occurs because of the connection of both actual and reported wastes to the rate of change in the expected penalty with respect to violation size. If costs are not separable in output and wastes, we find that output is a negative function of the tax on wastes. If costs are separable, then the firm's output will not be directly affected by the tax on reported wastes.

Result (10f) indicates that increases in the probability of capture at all sizes of violation will increase reported wastes. Since actual wastes are not affected by such a parameter shift, this implies a reduction in violation size at the same absolute rate. Using this result and explicitly writing out and simplifying (10f), one can derive the following relationship between the elasticity of violation size with respect to the general probability of detection, and the elasticity of the slope of the expected penalty function.

$$\left(\frac{\partial v}{\partial P} \right) \frac{P}{v} \equiv e_{P_\rho} = \frac{-1}{e_{vz}} \equiv -\left(\frac{Z}{Z'} \right) \frac{P}{v} \tag{11}$$

where $Z = G' + B't$, and use is made of the normalization $P = 1$.

This relationship says that the elasticity of violation size (in absolute value) with respect to a proportional shift in the probability of punishment is inversely related to the relative positive curvature of expected punishment as a function of violation size. To say it another way, if the rate of increase in the increase in expected punishment with violation size is relatively small, then a proportional increase in the probability of being fined at all levels of punishment will elicit a relatively large decrease in violation size.

The rate of change in reported wastes with respect to a change in the tax on reported wastes may be broken up into two parts: A term exactly equal to the effect on actual wastes, and a term which reflects the direct tax and penalty effects of a tax shift. It has already been determined that an increase in the pollution tax reduces actual wastes, and accordingly this component reduces the reported wastes to the same extent. The other term in (10g) will be negative if $(1-B')$ is positive. An examination of the first order condition (8c) indicates that this must be true if the slope of the expected fine function is positive, which we assume to be the case. Since both terms are negative, reported wastes will decline to a greater extent than actual wastes when the pollution tax is increased. This, as (10h) indicates, means that an increase in the pollution tax increases the size of the violation that the firm chooses. As one might expect, raising the tax rate causes more evasion and presumably a more difficult enforcement problem.

Given the insensitivity of actual wastes to the general level of fines and the probability of punishment, one might be tempted to conclude that their exact magnitude is of little or no consequence over a considerable range. This idea has a rough validity for all firms in the short run, and firms in noncompetitive industries in the long run. It is definitely not true in the long run for those firms in industries where expected long run economic profits tend toward zero. In these industries it is the long run average costs which determine the industry size in terms of output. A lower level of enforcement of payment of pollution taxes may not change the actual level of wastes emitted by any firm, but the implied lower level of some combination of pollution taxes, and penalty payments will imply lower average costs and more firms in the industry. In this regard it should be noted that, ceteris paribus, firms with the same expected fine function will have lower average costs under the imposition of standards than under the imposition of pollution taxes. It is roughly on this point, as Buchanan and Tullock [7] explain, that standards fail to produce a Pareto optimal (or pollution tax equivalent) resolution to a pollution externality under perfect competition.

This model may not be irrelevant to the current situation in the area of water pollution control. The recent federal legislation states that municipalities must charge fees to firms for accepting their wastes, fees which must be designed to cover the costs of treating those wastes. If the firm were not legally allowed to channel any wastes directly into public waters, then, with proper interpretation, this model might almost directly apply. The fee for municipal acceptance of firms' effluent would correspond to the tax on reported, in this case delivered, wastes. Violations might take the form of illegal dumping of wastes in the river, or channeling more wastes to the municipal treatment plant than the firm pays for in effluent fees. (More complicated and subtle versions of the same problem might involve the firm reneging on pretreatment requirements or negotiating reductions in other types of taxes (such as the local property tax) to compensate for the newly instituted effluent fees.) Even if the firm is allowed to release a fixed level of wastes, w_s, directly into public waters, we may simply define the size of violation as $v_o = [w - (w_s + w_r)]$, and the previous results are not qualitatively altered, although chosen values of the control variables would differ.

If one modifies the definition of the violation size as just suggested, one gets the additional results that $\partial w_r/\partial w_s = -1$, and $\partial w/\partial w_s = 0$. The former result says that there would be a one to one reduction in reported waste (subject to effluent fees by the municipality) with any increase in the allowable standard of wastes disposable directly into public waters. Put another way this result is quite striking. It tells us that making the standard stricter would not increase the violation size, but simply cause an increase in the amount of wastes going to the treatment plant and *paying* the effluent fee. The latter result indicates that changing the standard would have no effect on the actual amount of wastes created, which is in contrast to the pure standards case, but quite in spirit with our results in the pollution tax case.

Inevitably one runs into difficulty in trying to fit reality to a model. Relevant here is the fact that legislatively described fines are often in terms of days of violation rather than being geared to the quantity of pollutant. Even so, or perhaps because of this, the actual level of fines is left to the discretion of the courts within the constraint of maximum and minimum fines.[3] This methodology could produce its own peculiarities. Another complicating factor is the actual variety and interactability of real world wastes. And, with at least two, and perhaps three, levels of government (with varying views of benefits and costs) participating in pollution control with regard to the same set of potentially geographically mobile firms, the actual situation becomes extremely complicated.

IV. NORMATIVE IMPLICATIONS

The analysis heretofore has been predictive in the sense of simply drawing out the implications for a firm's behavior under expected profit maximization. We will now attempt a discussion of the normative implications of an analysis that includes the possibility of evading the pollution taxes, which are imposed pre-

[3] For example, within Title III, Section 309 of the Federal Water Pollution Control Act Amendments of 1972 it is stated that any firm or municipality (or the persons responsible) violating an applicable pollution standard ". . . shall be punished by a fine of not less than $2250 nor more than $25,000 per day of violation, or by imprisonment for not more than one year, or by both." Except for the expectation that the courts will use their discretion wisely in gearing fines to the actual damages caused by the pollution, this would appear to be an unsatisfactory way to relate fines to the severity of the violation.

sumably to reduce an externality to an efficient level. The discussion will speak in terms of a pollution tax rather than a standard, since it is the former which has been most favored by economists for its potential to improve efficiency. We will use the intuitive, but not completely rigorous, concepts of damages and costs measured in dollar values. Hopefully this problem may be treated within a rigorous general equilibrium framework at some future point. At this point, however, the technical problems with more precise approach appear too complex to explore.

The results derived indicate that the larger the pollution tax, the greater the evasion of that tax. This points to increasing enforcement costs as attempts are made to reduce actual pollution. We therefore have increasing marginal costs of reducing pollution which include additional costs of enforcing pollution taxes (or standards). This would argue for a reinterpretation of the rule that pollution should be eliminated to the point where marginal damages are equal to the marginal costs of treatment or prevention. Under present assumptions we should have marginal damages equal to the marginal costs of treatment or prevention plus the marginal costs of enforcing the treatment or prevention.

This point can be argued somewhat more rigorously by a modification of Becker's [5] approach to the optimal level of crime and law enforcement, which is to minimize the sum of the damage caused by crime plus the costs of capturing and punishing criminals. In this context we wish to minimize the sum of the damages caused by pollution plus the costs of treating or preventing pollution plus the costs of enforcing the taxes or other instruments by which pollution control is encouraged.

Let us define the value of the damage done to society by an aggregate level of waste W as $D(W)$. On the basis of previous analysis we would expect aggregate wastes to be a decreasing function of the unit pollution tax t. It is also consistent with previous results to assert that the aggregate level of waste should be a decreasing function of the general level of fines F and the general probability of detection and punishment for an evasion of pollution taxes, P. (P and F are now viewed as control variables of the government rather than as parameters.) Previous results indicate that the later two factors may ordinarily have no effect on the actual level of the firm, but, as we have argued before, expected punishment levels will effect the number of firms (and thus aggregate wastes) in a competitive industry via the effects on expected average costs. The costs of removing or preventing wastes are an increasing function of how much lower wastes are than than they would be if no efforts were made to incur or prevent wastes. This base level of wastes will be labeled W_o, while the aggregate costs of neutralizing wastes will be $S = S(Y)$, where $Y = (W_o - W)$.

Costs of enforcement of the pollution tax, E, will be an increasing function of the probability of capturing violators, P, and an index of the number of violators, V. No analysis of the shape of the function relating the probability of detection and the size of the violation will be attempted. However, the variable V is taken to reflect some index of the number and size of violations, which would in general depend upon the ease of detecting violations of different sizes. The level of the index of violations will itself be a negative function of the probability of detection and punishment, and the general level of fines F, but it should be a positive function of the height of the unit tax t on reported wastes. Thus, we have $E = E[P, V(P, F, t)]$.

Lastly, consistent with Becker, it will be assumed that there are social costs of punishment. These social costs are assumed to be a linear function of the general probability of punishment times the general magnitude of punishment. Specifically, total punishment costs are hPF, where h is a parameter which reflects general population size and other factors. Again, for simplicity, we avoid consideration of the structure of fines over the violation size. Given the fact that punishment in this context is likely to be a fine, the assumption that there are non-negligible social costs to punishment may not be very appealing to some. Harris [9] suggests another rationale for social costs of punishment: that of wrongful punishment. Occasionally, the innocent may be fined and this can be looked upon as causing social costs. On a more general note Stigler [12] points to the idea of marginal deterrence rather than social costs of punishment as the critical factor in the determination the appropriate level of punishment for any crime. This may be interpreted as saying that the higher the punishment for a given type of crime the greater the occurrence of other types of crimes with their attendant social costs. Further discussion of how, and how well, these rationales serve in arguing for social costs of punishment is not warranted here, except to say that Stigler's line of thought quickly leads us back to the tricky problem of determining an optimal structure of punishment.[4] For the moment we will simply work with our simple assumption.

We may now write the sum of pollution damage costs plus the costs of treatment/prevention plus the costs of enforcement of pollution taxes as

$$L = D(W) + S(Y) + E(P, V) + hPF. \tag{12}$$

The social goal is to minimize total social costs through the choice of F, P, and t. The three first order necessary conditions for minimum social costs are: where the subscripts indicate partial derivatives.

$$(D_W - S_Y)W_t + E_V V_t = 0 \tag{13a}$$

$$(D_W - S_Y)W_P + E_P + E_V V_P + hF = 0 \tag{13b}$$

$$(D_W - S_Y)W_F + E_V V_F + hP = 0, \tag{13c}$$

For present purposes it is condition (13a) that is of main interest, and so we will forego any comment on conditions (13b) and (13c), except to say that they indicate the usual balancing of marginal damages and marginal costs as they relate to the variables P and F, respectively. Condition (13a) can be rearranged to read

$$D_W = S_Y - (E_V V_t)/W_t. \tag{14}$$

---

[4] If one examines the concept of marginal deterrence closely it becomes evident that, unless there is some maximum feasible costless punishment, the need for marginal deterrence alone will not always lead one to a finite punishment for any crime. The basic reason for this is that one can mathematically conceive of infinite *rates* of punishment. In the context of this paper, one might have an infinite amount of fine per unit of violation and thus preserve marginal deterrence without having finite punishments. Clearly, in any practical sense, there is a maximum feasible costless punishment. Assuming for the moment that fines have zero social costs, it is clear that any fine cannot exceed the economic worth of the firm or individual fined. Given that there is a maximum feasible costless punishment, the concept of marginal deterrence should enable one to reasonably consider what an optimal structure of punishments should be.

Given our assumptions about the various functional relationships involved, the expression to the right of the minus sign is itself negative. This implies that the damages caused by one more unit of waste should be greater than the costs of physically eliminating the unit by the amount of the extra expenditure on enforcement induced by the increase in tax evasion caused by the additional pollution tax required to reduce pollution by the last unit.

Of course, a full assessment of the normative implications of pollution controls must recognize that the imperfections may be just as great in enforcing non-pollution types of taxes and controls. Imperfections in controls are simply another set of factors to consider in forming policy toward the existence of pollution types of externalities, along with market structure, various uncertainties, and dynamic considerations.

V. CONCLUSION

This paper has presented models of an expected profit maximizing firm under imperfectly 'enforceable pollution standards and under imperfectly enforceable pollution taxes. We have found that under standards increasing the expected level of the penalty will reduce the level of wastes released by the firm, but that increasing the strictness of the standard will only reduce the firm's wastes if the slope of the expected fine function with respect to the size of the standards violation is increasing. We have also found that the use of cost subsidies for pollution control expenses can serve the useful function of reducing the level of the firm's violation of the standard and thus its actual level of wastes.

Under imperfectly enforceable pollution taxes the analysis has established the neat result that the marginal costs of pollution reduction by the firm will be equated to the constant rate of the pollution tax as long as the slope of the expected penalty function is increasing. This implies that on the firm level the amount of pollution tax evasion is independent of the actual wastes, which are determined by the pollution tax rate. The level of tax evasion is determined by equating the increase in expected penalty with respect to a unit reduction in reported wastes to the decrease in tax paid. Therefore, the general level of fines and the probability of punishment affect reported wastes but not actual wastes. Further results indicate that increasing the tax rate on reported wastes will reduce actual wastes released by the firm, but it will reduce reported wastes even more, implying an increase in pollution tax evasion.

We have also suggested that, with proper reinterpretation of the violation size as the difference between actual wastes and an allowable standard of wastes plus an amount of (reported) wastes going to a fee charging treatment plant, one can apply the pollution tax model to current situation in the area of water pollution. Under this reinterpretation, changes in the allowable standard of wastes has no effect on wastes leaving the firm, or violation size, but are offset exactly by the amount of wastes going to the treatment plant.

In considering the implications of these results for policy it has been mentioned that effects of various policies on the expected average costs of firms are important and may not always work in the same direction as the effect on the individual firm's marginal decision. Furthermore, in Section IV, we suggested a reinterpretation of the intuitive rule of efficiency in pollution control that the marginal damages of pollution should equal the marginal costs of eliminating

42   JON D. HARFORD

pollution. The version which this paper suggests is that the marginal damages should be equal to the marginal costs of physically eliminating the pollution plus the additional costs of enforcing any pollution control instrument to the extra degree required to induce the unit reduction in pollution.

Throughout this paper we have assumed that the pollution control agency faces firms which believe that they cannot effect the penalty structure or subsidy rate of the agency. If the number of different polluters is small, this assumption may not be valid. Firms may adopt various kinds of strategic behavior and threats in order to affect the penalty structure. They may threaten to go out of business, or to move to a region where the agency does not have authority. Firms might collude to violate pollution control laws simultaneously, thereby overloading the agency's ability to enforce its laws with any effectiveness. The agency may be able to adopt various counterstrategies in this regulatory duopoly game. The outcome of such a situation is not easily determined, but there are counterparts to it in many types of regulation. Assuming that it is desirable to minimize the possibilities of such strategic behavior on the part of firms, it appears preferable to formulate and administer pollution controls at the most inclusive level of government possible.

This paper raises a number of (other) unsolved problems. One of the more interesting ones is the development of the concept of an optimal structure of penalties. This will likely involve an examination of both the structure of fines and penalties per se, and the technical and resource allocational nature of the probability of detecting and punishing violations of different sizes. Another problem would be to develop a more explicit and rigorous model to analyze the optimal level of pollution, pollution taxes, and enforcement of pollution taxes than that developed in Section IV of this paper. That analysis might be interpreted as suggesting that one should have a lower pollution tax rate in a case where there are enforcement problems than when there are not, but such a conclusion is not explicit, and we suspect that it may not always be true. A more explicit analysis would clarify this and other significant ambiguities.

REFERENCES

1. Robert J. Anderson, Jr., Environmental management economics, *in* "Regional Environmental Management: Selected Proceedings of the National Conference," (Coate and Bonner, Eds.), pp. 201–208, John Wiley and Sons, New York (1975).
2. J. S. Bain (Ed.), "Environmental Decay," Little Brown and Company, New York, (1973).
3. W. J. Baumol, On taxation and the control of externalities, *Amer. Econ. Rev.* 62, 307–322 (1972).
4. W. J. Baumol and W. E. Oates, "The Theory of Environmental Policy," Prentice-Hall, Englewood Cliffs (1975).
5. G. Becker, Crime and punishment: An economic approach, *J. Polit. Econ.* 6, 169–217 (1968).
6. J. M. Buchanan, External diseconomies, corrective taxes, and market structure, *Amer. Econ. Rev.* 59, 174–177 (1969).
7. J. H. Buchanan and G. Tullock, Polluters profits and political response: Direct controls versus taxes, *Amer. Econ. Rev.* 65, 139–147 (1975).
8. M. E. Darby and E. Karni, Free competition and the optimal amount of fraud, *J. Law Econ.* 67–88 (1973).
9. J. R. Harris, On the economics of law and order, *J. Polit. Econ.* 78, 165–174 (1970).

IMPERFECTLY ENFORCEABLE STANDARDS	43

10. S. Rose-Ackerman, The economics of corruption, *J. Pub. Econ.* 4, 187–203 (1975).
11. W. Schulze and R. C. d'Arge, The Coase proposition, information constraints, and long-run equilibrium, *Amer. Econ. Rev.* 64, 763–772 (1974).
12. G. J. Stigler, The optimum enforcement of the laws, *J. Polit. Econ.* 78, 526–536 (1970).
13. U. S. Congress, "Clean Air Amendments of 1970," (PL91-604) USGPO, Washington, D. C. 1970.
14. U. S. Congress, "The Federal Water Pollution Control Act Amendments of 1972," (PL92-500) USGPO, Washington, D. C. (1972).
15. D. Zwick, "Water Wasteland," Bantam, New York (1972).

[32]

Journal of Public Economics 37 (1988) 29–53. North-Holland

ENFORCEMENT LEVERAGE WHEN PENALTIES ARE RESTRICTED

Winston HARRINGTON*

Resources for the Future, Inc., 1616 P Street, N.W., Washington, DC 20036, USA

Received January 1987, revised version received April 1988

1. Introduction

In the United States, empirical studies of the enforcement of continuous compliance with environmental regulations, especially air and water pollution regulations, have repeatedly demonstrated the following:

(i) For most sources the frequency of surveillance is quite low.

(ii) Even when violations are discovered, fines or other penalties are rarely assessed in most states.

(iii) Sources are, nonetheless, thought to be in compliance a large part of the time.[1]

The evidence for the apparently low level of enforcement activity is found in a number of case studies of state and local enforcement of air and water quality regulations conducted jointly by the Environmental Protection Agency (EPA) and Council on Environmental Quality (CEG), together with periodic surveys of implementation of air and water quality legislation conducted by the General Accounting Office (GAO).[2] These surveys show

*This research was partially supported by the National Science Foundation, Grant No. PRA 8413311. I would also like to thank, without implicating, Carol A. Jones, Arun Malik, Wallace E. Oates, Paul Portney, Clifford S. Russell, Robert Schwab and Michael Toman for discussion and comments on earlier drafts.

[1]Because several different environmental regulations or requirements are enforced, 'compliance' is a somewhat ambiguous term, and depending on context may mean (1) initial compliance, in which the objective is to force the regulated source to install the abatement equipment that enables the regulation to be met, (2) compliance with reporting requirements, which aim to force the firm to meet regulatory requirements on the reporting of data to the authorities, or (3) continuous compliance, which attempts to force the source to keep emission discharges within regulatory limits. There have been well-publicized examples of heavy penalties for violation of environmental regulations, but these are largely confined to the first two categories. Continuous compliance with discharge limitations, which is of course what determines environmental quality, is hardly enforced via penalties at all.

[2]The results of these case studies are summarized in U.S. EPA (1981a, 1981b) and in Russell, Harrington and Vaughan (1986) and U.S. GAO (1982). Also see U.S. GAO (1979), Downing and Kimball (1982), Willick and Windle (1973), Environmental Law Institute (1975), Harrington (1981) and Russell (1982), and Abbey and Harrington (1981) for reports on some other enforcement surveys.

Table 1

State enforcement activity (annual averages, 1978–1983).

			Penalties		
State	NOVs issued	Civil actions brought	Number of penalties assessed	Average of penalties assessed	Average penalty per NOV
Colorado	124	3.6	0.5	$120	$0.48
Connecticut	800	2.3	21.5	363[a]	9.75
Indiana	59[b]	NA	21	4,050[c]	1,442.37
Kentucky	194	5.2	5.2	2,520[d]	67.52
Massachusetts	NA	0	0	0	0
Minnesota	41	NA	10	10,900	2,658.53
Nebraska	59[e]	NA	0.2	200	0.67
Nevada	31.5	0.3	2.3	45	3.33
New Jersey	1,167	NA	350	1,430	428.45
Oregon	197	NA	30.7	705	110.00
Pennsylvania	NA	NA	176[f]	1,480	–
Rhode Island	5	7.2	0	0	0
South Carolina	68[g]	5.5	2.2	24,250[h]	NA
South Dakota	17	1.2	0.3	1,000	20.00
Tennessee	193[i]	8.4	0	0	0
Virginia	161	7.8	3	200	3.79
Wisconsin	80.5[j]	13.5	7.7	7,951	760.00

Note: NA = not available.

[a]Refers to amounts assessed; over the same period actual collections were 62 percent of assessments.

[b]Includes both NOVs and compliance orders.

[c]Excludes one penalty of $415,000, which was cancelled when company bought equivalent amount of air pollution equipment.

[d]Excludes performance bonds (two required for total of $45,000 in last five years).

[e]Excludes Lincoln and Omaha.

[f]Only data from the last quarter of 1983 was readily available. This figure is an extrapolation to an annual average.

[g]No NOVs were issued before 18 April 1983. From 1 July 1983 to 31 March 1984, 51 NOVs were issued.

[h]Excludes one fine of $1,700 per month until compliance was restored and one fine of $250,000 dropped in lieu of a donation of a like sum to a technical college.

[i]Does not include NOVs from Continuous Monitoring Data, which were extremely numerous.

[j]1980–1983 only.

that the typical source can expect to be inspected on the order of once or twice each year. When a violation is discovered, by far the most common response is for the agency to send the firm a Notice of Violation (NOV), ordering it to return to compliance but taking no further action. The reticence to use penalties is exhibited in table 1, which reports the results of an RFF survey of state-level enforcement activity conducted in 1984. As shown, most states levied penalties for less than 5 percent of the notices of violation (NOVs) issued each year, although some states, such as Pennsylvania and

New Jersey, made frequent use of penalties. Also, the size of the penalties is generally very small.

Many of these same case studies also provide evidence for the third assertion. States are required to report annually on the compliance status of major stationary sources of air pollution, and these reports routinely indicate that well over 90 percent of all sources are in compliance. Spot-checks by the EPA (which used to have a program to reinspect a random 10 percent of sources reported by the states to be in compliance) have shown that most of such sources actually were in compliance. During 1977, for example, 22 percent of such sources were found to be in violation by the EPA [U.S. GAO (1982)]. In water quality enforcement, surveys by GAO in 1978 and 1980 revealed that 55 percent of industrial waste dischargers and 34 percent of municipal waste dischargers had committed 'serious' violations of permit requirements at some time during the past year [U.S. GAO (1982)]. Note, however, that while violations are frequent, they are far from universal.

Other surveys have disclosed similar results. The EPA–CEQ studies mentioned above collectively estimated that the sources examined were in violation of the standards about 9 percent of the time [U.S. EPA (1981b)]. However, the authors of these studies made the assumption that those sources were in compliance except when available plant data indicated otherwise, so that they probably underestimated the time in violation. In New Mexico, about 30–40 percent of all surveillance visits by agency personnel uncovered emission violations [Harrington (1981)].

But even though empirical support for all three statements can be found, together they seem mutually contradictory. Indeed, the truth of the three statements seems to violate both common sense and most existing models of environmental enforcement. For if enforcement activity is carried on at such a low level, and if violations are rarely punished even if discovered, why would any firm bother to comply? Reconciliation is indeed difficult in static economic models of environmental enforcement, in which the penalty facing the firm depends on the firm's rate of emissions, not on its previous compliance record.

All three observations, however, can be made consistent with a dynamic repeated-game model in which the regulated firm and the enforcement agency can react to previous actions by the other.

In this paper such a model will be described and its properties examined. The enforcement agency sets the parameters of the game, which in turn determine the average rate of compliance, the firm's expected compliance cost and the agency's expected enforcement cost. A key feature of this game is the assumption that the size of the penalty that the agency can impose in any period is restricted.

The interest in such a model is justified in part by the very low level of fines currently imposed for violations of continuous compliance. The rarity of penalties might be attributable to a number of causes. In most states there is a restriction on size of penalties that can be levied each day (usually $1000 or $5000). In addition, agencies can often cite violations occurring only on the day of surveillance events, even though the inspector may believe the violation has been occurring for some time.[3] Even when a maximum fine is not imposed by statute, there may be a practical or political limit to the size of penalties. Severe but rarely-imposed penalties might seem capricious and unfair. Also, there is an upper limit to the fine that can be imposed on any given firm such that the firm is not driven into bankruptcy [Braithwaite (1982)]. In any event, levying penalties can be a costly activity for the agency, just as surveillance is.

In section 2 the enforcement game is described and analyzed from the firm's point of view. The firm's optimum strategy is a two-state Markov decision problem, one for which parameters selected beforehand by the agency determine transition probabilities and payoffs, and hence the firm's compliance rate. The main result of this section is that the firm may have an incentive to comply with regulation even though its cost of compliance each period exceeds the expected penalty for violation, or even the maximum penalty that can be levied in any period. The property will be called 'leverage'. Section 3 discusses the optimum choice of parameters for the agency. It will be shown that when these optimum parameters are selected, no penalties are ever collected for violations. In addition, compared to state-independent enforcement schemes this model allows a target compliance level for less enforcement effort, although the advantage is not very great if the target compliance rate is high. In section 4 it is shown that introducing a third state into the model increases the cost-effectiveness off enforcement by the agency by turning the game into a 'threat game'. Finally, in section 5 these results will be discussed in light of the empirical findings that motivated the paper in the first place.

2. A dynamic model of firm behavior

The economic approach to enforcement began with the seminal article by Becker (1968). In contrast to the then-prevailing views in criminology, Becker assumed rational economizing behavior among criminals, whose expectations of gains from illicit activity had to be countered by an expectation that some violators would be caught and punished. The structure of penalties is thus an important determinant of the crime rate.

Unlike criminal activity, violation of environmental regulations is usually inadvertent rather than willful, especially after initial compliance has been

---

[3]In contrast, large fines have been assessed for violations of initial compliance or reporting violations, which are relatively easy to detect and also easy to infer more than one day's violation.

achieved. Nonetheless, plant operators have choices in maintenance and operation of abatement equipment, choices that can strongly affect the frequency, duration and magnitude of violations. Environmental regulations must therefore be continuously enforced, and the application of Becker's insights to this problem is straightforward.

Most of the early enforcement literature is static [e.g. Downing and Watson (1974), Harford (1978), Storey and McCabe (1980), Viscusi and Zeckhauser (1979), and Linder and McBride (1984)]. In a static analysis there is no way for the agency and the firm to react to each other's actions; with the expected penalty a function of the rate of violation, the firm makes a single choice of the rate of violation. Penalties for violating emission regulations are treated like any other cost, whereupon the optimal rate of violation of environmental regulations by a firm occurs when the marginal gain from violation equals to marginal expected penalty.

It is certainly consistent with this approach to consider enforcement a simple two-person game, as, for example, Brams and Davis (1983) have done in the context of arms control. The players of the game are the enforcement agency and a single regulated, risk-neutral firm. In a given play of the game, the agency chooses between two actions: to inspect or not to inspect. The firm also chooses between two actions: to comply or to violate the regulation. Compliance has the same cost for the firm regardless of what the agency does. This compliance cost can be avoided by violating the regulation, but if the agency inspects, thus discovering the violation, the firm must pay the cost to return to compliance plus a penalty. The agency, in contrast, is rewarded for every period that the source is in compliance (or penalized whenever the source is in violation). Thus, the agency's objective is to minimize the frequency of violation, subject to a fixed enforcement budget.

In a single play of this game the agency inspects the firm with a certain probability. If the agency announces beforehand what the inspection probability will be, the best strategy for the firm is nonrandom: the firm is better off complying with probability one if $pF > c$, where p is the inspection frequency, F the fine for violation, and c the cost of compliance. Otherwise it violates. Unfortunately, the expected penalty required to achieve this result seems to be very high, implying much higher inspection frequencies and penalties than actually experienced in environmental regulation.

But if the enforcement game is played repeatedly, the agency can alter the expected penalty and the inspection frequency based on the firm's past performance. Landsberger and Meilijson (1982) have shown, in a model of income tax compliance, that an enforcement regime in which the probability of an audit depends on the outcome of the most recent audit is more cost-effective than a system in which the audit frequency is independent of past audit outcomes. That is, greater tax revenues can be collected for the same level of enforcement resources. In Landsberger and Meilijson's model all taxpayers are placed in one of two states, with movement from one state to the other depending on the occurrence and outcome of an audit. Greenberg (1984) added to this model a third state, from which no escape is allowed, so that once in this state one faces a sure audit each period. He demonstrated a result that seems, as the author himself admitted, almost too good to be true: regardless of the agency's budget, the rate of violations can be made arbitrarily small (though greater than zero).

The free-lunch aspect of this model was attributed primarily to a hidden assumption, namely that the agency could determine with perfect accuracy whether the taxpayer was cheating. If false positives are possible, every taxpayer is eventually in the third state, forcing the agency to audit everyone every period. As Greenberg observed, to prevent this outcome some escape from the third state would have to be allowed, and this would impose some limits on the performance of the model. This false positive problem in Greenberg's model is examined in the context of environmental regulation in Russell (1984) and Russell, Harrington and Vaughan (1986).

There is another 'hidden' assumption that is also important in the performance of this model: Greenberg assumes that there is no maximum panalty, or at least that the penalty that the agency can impose exceeds the firm's per-period compliance cost. That is to say, if the firm is certain that an inspection will occur, the penalty for a violation is assumed large enough so that it will choose to comply.

In other words, it is assumed that the penalty can be made as large as is necessary. This recalls the treatment of the static (i.e. state-independent) model examined by earlier authors. In the static model, the penalty can always be made large enough so that the firm will always comply. (In the notation used earlier, the firm will always comply if $F > c/p$.) To be sure, the penalty must meet a much less stringent requirement, for Greenberg's model only requires $F > c$.

Here that assumption will be relaxed. The interest will be in the relationship between the firm's compliance cost and the average level of compliance that can be achieved when both enforcement budgets and the maximum feasible penalty are limited. It will also be evident just what the addition of a third state adds to the cost-effectiveness of enforcement.

Suppose, then, that the agency classifies firms into two groups, one of which faces more severe enforcement than the other. Each firm can then move from one group to the other based on its performance. More precisely, let G_1 and G_2 denote the two groups of firms, and suppose the inspection probability in G_i is p_i and the penalty for violation is F_i, with $p_1 < p_2$ and $F_1 < F_2$. Violations discovered in G_1 are punished by exile into G_2 and compliance discovered in G_2 is rewarded with the chance of a return to G_1. Let u denote the probability that a firm found in compliance in G_2 is returned to G_1. Thus, the agency and firm are players in a pair of linked

Table 2

Payoff matrices for the enforcement games.

	Group 1		Group 2	
	Comply	Violate	Comply	Violate
No inspection	c	0	c	0
Inspection	c	F_1, $\rightarrow G_2$	c $P(\rightarrow G_1) = u$	F_2

games with payoff matrices as shown in table 2 (only payoffs to the firm are shown).

Before examining the properties of this model several simplifying assumptions are to be noted. First, in many real-world applications the rate of emissions is continuous, and hence the degree of noncompliance is important. In these models, however, the firm has only two discrete choices: compliance or noncompliance. Second, the probability of an inspection is assumed not to be affected by the incidence of a violation. But often the occurrence of a violation can be detected, or at least suspected, offsite, raising the probability of an inspection. Third, it is assumed that an inspection will determine without error whether a violation has occurred. This assumption is discussed above.

From the firm's standpoint this monitoring and enforcement scheme poses a Markov decision problem, as discussed in Kohlas (1982). The firm moves from group to group according to transition probabilities that depend not only on the current state of the system but on the action taken during that period by the firm (i.e. to comply or not). In addition, each period the firm receives a payoff (or incurs a cost) that likewise depends on the state of the system and the action taken. A *decision* at any time is a map from states to actions, and a *policy* is a sequence of decisions over time.

Let r_{ti}^a denote the payoff if action a is chosen when in state i at time t. If these payoffs are constant over time, i.e.

$$r_{ti}^a = r_i^a, \quad t = 0, 1, 2, \ldots,$$

and if future payoffs are discounted by a discount factor β, $0 \leq \beta < 1$, the following ergodic theorem can be proved [see Kohlas (1982)]: (a) the expected gains of any policy over an infinite time horizon are finite, (b) the optimum policy is a *stationary* policy [i.e. if $\{f_0, f_1, \ldots\}$ is optimum then $f_n(i) = g(i)$ for some decision rule g], and (c) the optimum policy g is independent of the initial state of the system (although the expected gains of that policy are not).

Applied to the monitoring problem, the states are the two groups G_1 and

G_2. A policy for the firm is a map $f:\{1,2\}\to\{0,1\}$ of states into decisions to comply with or violate the regulations, and the firm's problem is to choose the policy that minimizes the expected cost over future periods. The stationary property means that there are four policies possible.

The transition probabilities p_{ij}^a are given as follows:

	$a=0$ (comply)			$a=1$ (cheat)	
	G_1	G_2		G_1	G_2
G_1	1	0	G_1	$1-p_1$	p_1
G_2	p_2u	$1-p_2u$	G_2	0	1

Denote the four available policies by f_{00}, f_{01}, f_{10}, f_{11}, where, for example, f_{00} is the policy of complying when in both states and f_{01} is the policy of complying if in G_1 and cheating if in G_2. Let $E^{ij}(m)$ denote the expected cost, in present value, of policy f_{ij} when initially in state m. By the stationary property, the expected present value must be the cost this period plus the expected present value discounted one period. For example, consider the present value of f_{00}, the policy of compliance in both groups. Thus,

$$E^{00}(1)=c+\beta E^{00}(1),$$

$$E^{00}(2)=c+\beta p_2 u E^{00}(1)+\beta(1-p_2u)E^{00}(2).$$

Solution of these simultaneous equations gives the present value of the policy f_{00}. The four sets of simultaneous equations giving the present values of the four policies can be conveniently displayed as follows:

Group 1	*Group 2*
Comply(0): $E_1=c+\beta E_1$	$E_2=c+\beta p_2 u E_1+\beta(1-p_2)E_2$
Violate(1): $E_1=(1-p_1)\beta E_1+p_1(F_1+\beta E_2)$	$E_2=p_2F_2+\beta E_2$

To evaluate policy f_{ij}, solve the system of equations formed by taking the ith equation column 1 and the jth equation of column 2.

The optimum policy g takes on values $g(k)=v_k$, $k=1,2$, that satisfy:

$$v_k=\min_{i,j} E^{ij}(k).$$

The ergodic theorem assures that such a policy exists.

To find v_1 and v_2, first find the solution of the four simultaneous equation systems for the $E^{ij}(m)$, which are given in table 3. Examination of these solutions reveals several characteristics this game, as follows.

Table 3
Expected cost of alternative policies.

Policy	$E^{ij}(1)$	$E^{ij}(2)$
f_{00}	$\dfrac{c}{1-\beta}$	$\dfrac{c}{1-\beta}$
f_{10}	$\dfrac{cp_1\beta+p_1F_1(1-\beta+p_2u\beta)}{(1-\beta)(1-\beta+p_1\beta+p_2u\beta)}$	$\dfrac{c(1-(1-p_1)\beta)+\beta p_2up_1F_1}{(1-\beta)(1-\beta+p_1\beta+p_2u\beta)}$
f_{11}	$\dfrac{p_1F_1(1-\beta)+\beta p_1p_2F_2}{(1-\beta)(1-(1-p_1)\beta)}$	$\dfrac{p_2F_2}{1-\beta}$

Lemma 1. f_{01} *is never optimal.*

This follows because f_{01} is dominated by f_{00} when $c<p_2F_2$ and by f_{11} when $c\geq p_2F_2$.

Lemma 2. For each initial state k, the remaining $E^{ij}(k)$, considered as functions of the compliance cost c, are of the form $A+Bc$, where

for E^{00}; $A=0$, $B>0$,

for E^{10}; $A>0$, $B>0$,

for E^{11}; $A>0$, $B=0$,

Lemma 3. When $c=L_0=p_1F_1$, $E^{00}=E^{10}<E^{11}$, and the firm is indifferent between f_{00} and f_{10}.

L_0 is found by setting $E^{00}(2)$ equal to $E^{10}(2)$ and solving for c (the expected values for group 1 could also be used).

Lemma 4. Similarly, $E^{10}=E^{11}<E^{00}$ when $c=L_1$, where

$$L_1=p_2F_2+\frac{p_2\beta u(p_2F_2-p_1F_1)}{[1-(1-p_1)\beta]}. \tag{1}$$

These results can be summarized in the following proposition.

Proposition 1. If g denotes the optimal policy, then

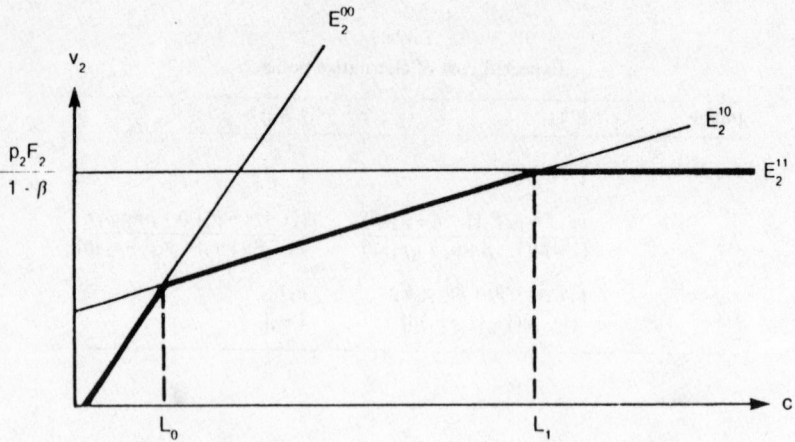

Fig. 1. Expected cost of the firm's optimum policy as a function of compliance cost.

$$g = \begin{cases} f_{00}, & \text{if } c \leq L_0, \\ f_{10}, & \text{if } L_0 \leq c \leq L_1, \\ f_{11}, & \text{if } L_1 \leq c. \end{cases}$$

Inasmuch as each f_{ij} is a linear function of c, the expected costs of the optimum policy, $v_1(c)$ and $v_2(c)$, are piecewise linear functions of c, as shown in fig. 1 for $k=2$ (for $k=1$ the threshold values L_0 and L_1 are the same but the expected cost is lower).

Since $p_2 F_2 \geq p_1 F_1$, the threshold L_1 must be at least as great as $p_2 F_2$, the expected penalty in Group 2, and will equal $p_2 F_2$ only in degenerate cases:

(i)   no monitoring in Group 2 ($p_2 = 0$);
(ii) perfect myopia ($\beta = 0$);
(iii) no escape from Group 2 ($u = 0$);
(iv) no difference in expected penalty between the groups.

In all other cases we must have $L_1 > p_2 F_2$.

Proposition 1 classifies firms as f_{00}, f_{10} or f_{11} firms depending on its optimum strategy, which in turn depends on its compliance costs and the enforcement parameters chosen by the enforcement agency.

Let C_{ij} be the probability that an f_{ij} firm is in compliance. Then $C_{00} = 1$ and $C_{11} = 0$. An f_{10} firm is more interesting, because it complies only part of the time. When f_{10} is optimum, the system has the following transition matrix:

	G_1	G_2
G_1	$1 - p_1$	p_1
G_2	$p_2 u$	$1 - p_2 u$

In this case, the firm cheats when it is in G_1 and complies in G_2. The irony of this model is that the firms with the status of 'good guys' are the ones that can afford to cheat, while those with a 'bad guy' reputation comply until moved back into the G_1.

For an f_{10} firm the frequency of compliance in steady state is the stationary probability of being in G_2, or

$$C_{10} = \frac{p_1}{p_1 + p_2 u}. \tag{2}$$

Likewise, let I_{ij} be the probability that an f_{ij} firm is inspected. Clearly, $I_{00} = p_1$, and $I_{11} = p_2$, because f_{00} firms are eventually in Group 1 with probability one, and f_{11} firms are eventually in Group 2. Also,

$$I_{10} = \frac{p_1 p_2 (1 + u)}{p_1 + p_2 u}. \tag{3}$$

Note that $C_{00} > C_{10} > C_{11}$, but, since $p_1 < p_2$, $I_{00} < I_{10} < I_{11}$. Thus, firms with better compliance records are those with less frequent surveillance.

The expected fine per period paid by an f_{10} firm is $p_1 F_1 (1 - C_{10})$. If $F_1 = 0$, no fines will be collected, yet the firm will be in compliance part of the time. In a static model, by way of contrast, absence of fines requires either perfect compliance or perfect noncompliance. Furthermore, the firm's compliance cost c can easily exceed the expected fine in G_2 (which is $p_2 F_2$), because $L_1 > p_2 F_2$. Thus, in this dynamic model compliance can be achieved even though the expected penalty would not be large enough to ensure compliance in a static model. The reason, of course, is that compliance in G_2 allows the firm eventually to return to G_1, where the cost of cheating is much lower.

3. Formulating agency enforcement policy

In this section I describe the policy selection of an enforcement agency playing the two-group game described above, and consider the consequences of adding a third group as described by Greenberg and Russell. The enforcement agency wishes to minimize the resources devoted to monitoring and enforcement, consistent with achieving a target compliance rate by the regulated firm, assumed to have a known compliance cost c^*. To carry out this task it can modify five variables: the two monitoring frequencies, p_1 and p_2, the two penalties, F_1 and F_2, and the probability u of being allowed back into Group 1 after being found in compliance. $T = 1/p_2 u$ is the expected duration in Group 2, assuming compliance. Suppose the target long-run (i.e.

steady state) compliance rate is Z, and suppose that the maximum fine the agency is allowed to impose is F^*.

The agency has at least three objectives in setting up its enforcement policy. (Of course, it will in general be impossible to optimize on all three objectives simultaneously, and the agency's problem is one of constrained optimization, optimizing on one objective while meeting target levels on the other two.) It wishes to minimize the average inspection rate I^*, it wishes to make the average rate of compliance as high as possible, and it wishes to give firms with the highest compliance cost possible the incentive to comply. In the terminology of the two-group model discussed in the previous section, this last objective boils down to making L_2 as large as possible. This property will be called leverage, and is defined as follows. Suppose a target compliance rate Z is given, and let W be the set of all compliance costs such that any firm with a compliance cost $c \in W$ complies with probability exceeding Z. Now put $\Delta = \mathrm{lub}(W) - F$ and call Δ the leverage of the enforcement policy for the compliance rate Z.

If the agency's target is perfect compliance ($Z = 1$), then the inspection resources must be large enough so that $I^* F^* > c^*$, just as in the static model. Also necessary for perfect compliance is for the maximum allowable fine to exceed c^*. At the other extreme, the agency cannot elicit any compliance at all if c^* exceeds $F^*/(1 - \beta)$, because the cost of complying even once exceeds the present value of all future fines. If $c^* < F^*/(1 - \beta)$, then some degree of compliance can be achieved.[4]

Suppose $c^* < F^*/(1 - \beta)$, so that some level of compliance is feasible and suppose the target $Z < 1$ is given. The agency's problem is to find parameters (p_1, p_2, F_1, F_2, u) to minimize:

$$I_{10} = \frac{p_1 p_2 (1 + u)}{p_1 + p_2 u} \tag{4}$$

subject to the following constraints:

$$L_1 = p_2 F_2 + \frac{p_2 \beta u (p_2 F_2 - p_1 F_1)}{[1 - (1 - p_1)\beta]} \geqq c^*, \tag{5}$$

$$C_{10} = \frac{p_1}{p_1 + p_2 u} \geqq Z, \tag{6}$$

$$0 \leqq F_1 \leqq F^*; \quad 0 \leqq F_2 \leqq F^*.$$

---

[4] Let $F_1 = 0$, $F_2 = F^*$, $p_2 = u = 1$, and $p_1 = \varepsilon$. By choosing ε small enough, L_1 can be made as close as desired to $F^*/(1 - \beta)$ and we can assure that $I_{10} < I^*$. Of course, that makes C_{10} pretty close to zero, though still positive.

Although a full solution to this optimization problem is complicated and would probably not provide much insight, several interesting observations can be made.

Observation 1. The optimum penalties F_1 and F_2 must be 0 and F^*, respectively. This follows because the penalties do not affect the values of I_{10} or C_{10}, and the choice of fines maximizes L_1 for a given choice of the other parameters.

Observation 2. At the optimum no fines are ever collected, because the firm violates only in Group 1, where $F_1 = 0$.

Observation 3. It also follows that an increase in the penalties does not affect the rate of compliance, unless it changes the compliance class to which the firm belongs (e.g. a f_{10} firm becomes a f_{00} firm).

Observation 4. If the compliance cost exceeds the maximum allowable fine $(c^* > F^*)$, then the maximum feasible target compliance rate Z is F^*/c^*. To see this, consider the unexpected role of p_2, the inspection frequency in Group 2. Increasing p_2 might seem to decrease the average rate of compliance, ceteris paribus, because a firm in G_2 is already in compliance, and an increase in the inspection rate in that group is just an enhanced opportunity to be returned to G_1 to do some cheating. Although this may suggest making p_2 as small as possible, there is a minimum value for p_2 consistent with Z. This minimum value may be found by considering the numerator and denominator in the expression (1) defining L_1:

Numerator: $p_2\beta u(p_2 F_2 - p_1 F_1) \leq p_2 u(p_2 F^*)$, since $\beta \leq 1$, $F_1 = 0$ and $F_2 = F^*$.
Denominator: $1 - (1 - p_1)\beta = 1 - \beta + p_1\beta \geq (1-\beta)p_1 + p_1\beta = p_1$. Thus,

$$c^* \leq L_1 \leq p_2 F^* \left[1 + \frac{p_2 u}{p_1} \right] = \frac{p_2 F^*}{C_{10}} \leq \frac{p_2 F^*}{Z}.$$

This means that p_2 must be at least Zc^*/F^*. In particular, if $c^* > F^*$, the maximum feasible target compliance rate Z is F^*/c^*, in which case $p_2 = 1$.

Observation 5. Let t be the compliance rate that can be achieved in a state-independent enforcement strategy with the same resources I^* that achieve a compliance rate Z in the two group model. Then $Z \geq t \geq Z^2/(1 + u)$.

This observation concerns the comparison of this state-dependent enforcement strategy with one that is independent of prior behavior by the firm. As noted above, this repeated game can achieve some degree of compliance for firms that would have incentives to be always in violation in the standard state-independent model. Even for those firms for which the standard model achieves some compliance, the optimum choice of parameters for the repeated game achieves a greater compliance rate for a given inspection budget. However, the greater the target compliance rate Z, the less the advantage of the repeated game over a state-independent model, because Z and Z^2 become increasingly close.

Consider first a *random* enforcement strategy, in which the agency inspects in each period with probability I^*, regardless of past outcomes. If the firm's compliance cost c^* is less than the expected penalty I^*F^*, then the firm complies at all times; if $c^* > I^*F^*$, then the firm never complies. With a nonrandom strategy the agency can achieve partial compliance with a state-independent model even when $I^*F^* < c^* < F^*$, in the following way. The agency announces that for some fraction t of the year, inspections will occur with a frequency of c^*/F^*, and the rest of the year no inspections will take place. Assuming the firm knows which is which, its incentive will be to comply during the first interval and violate during the second. If the average inspection rate for the year is I^*, the average compliance rate is:

$$t = I^*F^*/c^*.$$

To compare this level of compliance to that achieved with equal inspection resources in the two-group model, note that from (4) and (6):

$$I^* = Zp_2(1 + u),$$

and from Observation 4 above:

$$c^* \leqq p_2 F^*/Z.$$

Substitution into the expression for t yields:

$$t \geqq Z^2(1 + u). \tag{7}$$

This expression says that the closer Z gets to 1, the less difference there is between Z and t. The bound (7) is fairly tight when β is close to unity (i.e. a low discount rate) and optimal values for the parameters p_1, p_2 and u are chosen. For example, suppose target enforcement rate $Z = 0.8$, compliance cost $c^* = 50$ per month, the maximum penalty $F^* = 100$, and the discount rate is 10 percent per year (which makes $\beta = 0.992$ per month). Then the optimum values of p_1, p_2 and u (per month) are approximately:

$$p_1 = 0.05, \quad p_2 = 0.41, \quad u = 0.03,$$

and the minimum inspection frequency is $I^* = 0.341$. Applying these resources in a state-independent model we would have $t = 0.68$ and $Z^2(1 + u) = 0.66$.

To summarize the distinction between the state-independent and state-dependent models discussed above, it has been shown that the state-independent model can offer an incentive for partial compliance as long as compliance cost c^* does not exceed the maximum per-period penalty F^*. The compliance rate that can be achieved by the agency depends on the rate of inspection, but it can be as high as 1 if inspections are sufficiently frequent. The state-dependent model can achieve partial compliance even if $c^* > F^*$; in fact, c^* may be as large as $F^*/(1 - \beta)$ before the firm can be given no incentive to comply at all. When $c^* > F^*$, however, Z must be less than F^*/c^*.

Besides having greater leverage, the state-dependent model is more cost-effective than the state-independent model when $c^* < F^*$. Unfortunately, as the desired compliance rate approaches unity, this advantage begins to disappear. This raises the question of what the addition of a third group might accomplish in this same context of restricted penalties.

4. The advantages of a three-group model

As noted above, Greenberg proposed a third, absorbing state for his tax compliance model. The strength of this model was that it allows the agency to threaten a noncomplying firm with a dire result (eternal compliance) without having to commit the vast resources (constant surveillance) that would ordinarily be necessary to achieve that result. By making such a threat, arbitrarily good compliance could be achieved with arbitrarily small budgets. However, that outcome depends on the assumption that penalties are large enough to induce compliance when an inspection is certain (i.e. $F^* > c$). In this section the cost-effectiveness and leverage of this model are examined when that assumption no longer holds.

It will be assumed that, as in Greenberg's model, the third state is an absorbing state, from which no escape is possible and which faces inspections with certainty. The fine in the third group F_3 cannot exceed the maximum allowable fine F^*; in fact, it will be assumed that the penalty in Groups 2

44   *W. Harrington, Enforcement leverage*

Table 4
Expected cost of alternative policies: Three-group model.

Policy	$E^{ijk}(1)$	$E^{ijk}(2)$	$E^{ijk}(3)$
f_{000}	$\dfrac{c}{1-\beta}$	$\dfrac{c}{1-\beta}$	$\dfrac{c}{1-\beta}$
f_{100}	$\dfrac{cp_1\beta+p_1F_1(1-\beta+p_2u\beta)}{(1-\beta)(1-\beta+p_1\beta+p_2u\beta)}$	$\dfrac{c(1-(1-p_1)\beta)+\beta p_2up_1F_1}{(1-\beta)(1-\beta+p_1\beta+p_2u\beta)}\quad\dfrac{c}{1-\beta}$	
f_{110}	$\dfrac{(1-(1-p_2)\beta)(1-\beta)p_1F_1+(1-\beta)p_1p_2\beta F_2+p_1p_2\beta^2c}{(1-(1-p_1)\beta)(1-(1-p_2)\beta)(1-\beta)}$	$\dfrac{p_2F_2(1-\beta)+p_2\beta c}{(1-(1-p_2)\beta)(1-\beta)}$	$\dfrac{c}{1-\beta}$
f_{111}	$\dfrac{(1-(1-p_2)\beta)(1-\beta)p_1F_1+(1-\beta)p_1p_2\beta F_2+p_1p_2\beta^2F_2}{(1-(1-p_1)\beta)(1-(1-p_2)\beta)(1-\beta)}$	$\dfrac{p_2F_2(1-\beta)+p_2\beta F_2}{(1-(1-p_2)\beta)(1-\beta)}$	$\dfrac{c}{1-\beta}$

and 3 will both be the same, or $F_2=F_3$. Analogous to the two-group case, let $f_{ijk}(i,j,k=0,1)$ denote the eight possible policies for the firm, and $E^{ijk}(m)$ the expected cost of f_{ijk} when m is the initial state $(m=1,2,3)$. As before, the $E^{ijk}(m)$ are found by solving the system of simultaneous equations formed by taking the appropriate equation from the table below (the ith equation of the first column, the jth equation of the second, and the kth of the third):

	Group 1	Group 2	Group 3
Comply:	$E_1=c+\beta E_1$	$E_2=c+\beta p_2uE_1+\beta(1-p_2u)E_2$	$E_3=c+\beta E_3$
Violate:	$E_1=(1-p_1)\beta E_1$		
	$+p_1(F_1+\beta E_2)$	$E_2=p_2(F_2+\beta E_3)+(1-p_2)E_2$	$E_3=F_2+\beta E_3$

Four of these policies are clearly nonoptimal regardless of the enforcement parameters or the firm's compliance cost: f_{001}, f_{010}, f_{101} and f_{011}. For f_{001} and f_{101}, in fact, the absorbing group is never entered because the firm complies in Group 2. The policies f_{010} and f_{011} are extensions of the dominated policy in the two-group model and are also dominated in this model. For the remaining four policies, the expected costs in each initial state are given as functions of c and the agency enforcement parameters in table 4.

Unlike the two-group case, the steady-state compliance and inspection frequencies for the other four policies depend on the initial state. If a firm starts in Group 3, it can never get out regardless of the policy adopted. In addition, a firm using policy f_{110} or f_{111} is eventually in Group 3 with certainty; the inspection rate is 1 and the compliance rate is either 1 (f_{110}) or 0 (f_{111}). The stationary probabilities for the other two policies are similar in form to those encountered in the two-group model. For f_{000} the inspection rate is p_1 and the compliance rate is 1, while for f_{100} the inspection rate is $I_{10}=p_1p_2(1+u)/(p_1+p_2u)$ and the compliance rate is $C_{10}=p_1/(p_1+p_2u)$.

To find the firm's best policy as a function of its compliance cost c, proceed as in the two group case, finding the point of indifference for each pair of policies. The results can again be summarized in a series of lemmas.

Lemma 5.   *The $E^{ijk}(m)$ are of the form $A + Bc$, where*

   for f_{000}: $A = 0, B > 0$,

   for f_{100}: $A > 0, B > 0$,

   for f_{110}: $A > 0, B > 0$,

   for f_{111}: $A > 0, B = 0$,

Lemma 6.   *When the E^{ijk} are evaluated for particular values of c, we have the following:*

   for $c = p_1 F_1$: $E^{000} = E^{100} < E^{110}$,

   for $c = F_2$: $E^{110} = E^{111}$,

   for $c = L_2$: $E^{100} = E^{111}$,

where

$$L_2 = \frac{p_2 F_2}{1 - (1 - p_2)\beta} + \frac{\beta p_2 u(p_2 F_2 - p_1 F_1)}{(1 - (1 - p_1)\beta)(1 - (1 - p_2)\beta)} = \frac{L_1}{1 - (1 - p_2)\beta}. \tag{10}$$

Again, the expected cost is a piecewise linear function. If $L_2 \geq F_2$ the expected cost functions for the optimal policy, v_1 and v_2,[5] consist of three linear segments, as shown in fig. 2(a). The policy f_{110} is dominated and is never optimal. On the other hand, if $L_2 < F_2$, as shown in fig. 2(b), the optimal policy consists of four segments. f_{110} is no longer dominated. To summarize:

Proposition 2.   *(a) If $L_2 \geq F_2$, then the optimum policy g is:*

$$g = \begin{cases} f_{000}, & \text{if } c \leq L_0, \\ f_{100}, & \text{if } L_0 \leq c \leq L_2, \\ f_{111}, & \text{if } L_2 \leq c. \end{cases}$$

[5]The expected cost function v_3 for when Group 3 is the initial state is ignored; it is not very interesting since escape from Group 3 is impossible.

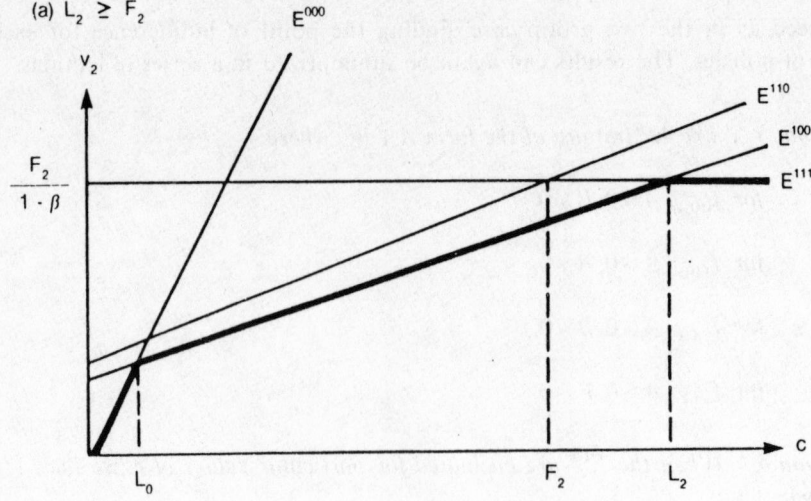

(a) $L_2 \geq F_2$

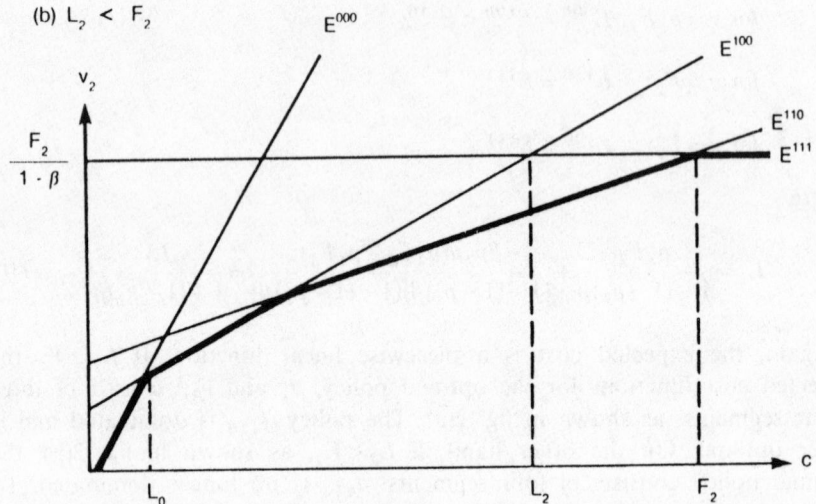

(b) $L_2 < F_2$

Fig. 2. Expected cost of the firm's optimum policy as a function of compliance cost: three-group model.

(*b*) *If* $L_2 < F_2$, *then the optimum policy is:*

$$g = \begin{cases} f_{000}, & \text{if } c \leqq L_0, \\ f_{100}, & \text{if } L_0 \leqq c < w, \\ f_{110}, & \text{if } w \leqq c < L_2, \\ f_{111}, & \text{if } L_2 \leqq c, \end{cases}$$

Table 5

Inspection resources required to achieve target compliance
rates: Two-group vs. three-group models.

I.	Maximum fine, F^*	100
	Compliance cost, c^*	150
	Target compliance rate, Z	0.6
	Discount factor, β	0.992

Two groups	Three groups
$p_1 = 0.062$	$p_1 = 0.078$
$p_2 = 0.943$	$p_2 = 0.103$
$u = 0.044$	$u = 0.503$
$I = 0.591$	$I = 0.093$

II.	Maximum fine, F^*	100
	Compliance cost, c^*	100
	Target compliance rate, Z	0.9
	Discount factor, β	0.992

Two groups	Three groups
$p_1 = 0.082$	$p_1 = 0.069$
$p_2 = 0.908$	$p_2 = 0.074$
$u = 0.010$	$u = 0.103$
$I = 0.826$	$I = 0.074$

where w is the value of c where $E^{100}(1) = E^{110}(1)$ and $E^{100}(2) = E^{110}(2)$.

Given a firm with compliance cost c^*, the agency's problem, as in the two-group case, is to find the optimum parameters so that the inspection budget I is minimized subject to meeting the steady-state target compliance frequency Z. Naturally, the agency wishes to avoid setting parameters that might give the firm an incentive to adopt the policy f_{111}. This is the worst of all worlds for the agency, because it must inspect every period and yet the firm continues to violate. The policy f_{110} is almost as bad, for constant inspections are again required. The implication is that the agency must choose parameters to ensure that L_2 exceeds both F_2 and the compliance cost c^*.

The addition of a third group can result in a spectacular reduction in the minimum resources required to achieve a given level of compliance. This advantage in cost-effectiveness is illustrated by two numerical examples, shown in table 5. In the first, $F^* = 100$, $c^* = 150$, $\beta = 0.992$ and the target compliance rate Z is 0.6. The group fines are set so that, for the two-group model, $F_1 = 0$ and $F_2 = F^* = 100$, and for the three-group model, $F_1 = 0$ and $F_2 = F_3 = F^* = 100$. As shown, the steady-state inspection rate I falls from 0.591 to 0.093 when the third group is added, primarily due to the sharp decline in p_2, the inspection rate in the second group. This represents a reduction of nearly 85 percent. This advantage remains even when the target compliance rate is high. In the second example, $Z = 0.9$, $c^* = 100$ and the inspection rate required with three groups is 91 percent less than that required with two groups.

Yet even though the three-group model is much more cost-effective than the two-group model, the leverage is the same. Just as in the two-group model, the maximum feasible compliance frequency Z that can be achieved when the firm's compliance cost is c^* and the maximum penalty is F^* is F^*/c^*. To see this, consider expression (10) defining L_2. Since $1 - (1 - p_2)\beta > p_2$,

$$\frac{p_2 F_2}{1 - (1 - p_2)\beta} < F_2,$$

and

$$\frac{\beta p_2 u (p_2 F_2 - p_1 F_1)}{(1 - (1 - p_1)\beta)(1 - (1 - p_2)\beta)} < \frac{\beta u p_2 F_2}{1 - (1 - p_1)\beta}.$$

In addition, $1 - (1 - p_1)\beta > p_1$ and $p_2 u / p_1 = (1 - Z)/Z$ therefore,

$$\frac{\beta u p_2 F_2}{1 - (1 - p_1)\beta} < \left[\frac{1 - Z}{Z} \right] F_2.$$

Hence, $L_2 < F_2 + F_2 (1 - Z)/Z = F_2/Z$.

This is why, in example II of table 5, the compliance cost was assumed to be 100 and not 150 as in example I. With $F^* = 100$ and $c^* = 150$, a compliance rate of 0.9 is not feasible in either the two-group or the three-group model.

5. Conclusion

In this paper the behavior of enforcement agencies and regulated firms has been analyzed in a repeated game setting in which each can react to the previous actions of the other. It has been argued that the two-group state-dependent model described in sections 2 and 3 offers an explanation for a number of characteristics of the current enforcement of air and water quality regulations, some of which are rather difficult to explain using the standard, static model. In addition, these adaptive models, especially the three-state model described in section 4, are more cost effective than the nonadaptive or state-independent models that comprise the bulk of the economic literature on enforcement of environmental regulations. In effect, these models work by offering a bribe and threatening a penalty at the same time.

The salient behavioral characteristics of the state-dependent enforcement model are, first, that firms are divided into classes depending on compliance cost. Low-cost firms (f_{00}) are always in compliance, and high-cost firms (f_{11}) are always in violation. In the middle is the class f_{10}, consisting of firms that move in and out of compliance, depending on the results of the most recent inspection. In fact, studies of compliance do show that many firms are apparently always in compliance, and there are a few firms that are found to be in violation at nearly every inspection and that are subject to incessant complaints of nearby residents. However, it is not clear that compliance cost is the most important determinant of a firm's behavior.[6] Among other determinants is the firm's financial health: firms on the brink of bankruptcy, or plants about to be closed by parent firms, appear much more likely to commit violations.

Second, in these models at least partial compliance is achieved without ever having penalties imposed on violators. As shown above, this requires the penalty in G_1 (i.e. F_1) to be set to zero. As noted in the Introduction, compliance without penalties seems to be a common characteristic of air and water quality enforcement by state governments in the United States. Note, however, that if $F_1 = 0$, then the group of perfectly-complying firms consists only of those with zero compliance costs. It would not be unheard of for the relevant compliance costs to be zero, since to achieve compliance the firm may have installed abatement equipment with very low operating cost or modified the production process to eliminate residuals generation.

It should be noted also that there are other explanations of compliance without penalties, some of which would apply to particular firms, but hardly to all firms. An elaborate model is not required to explain the compliance of firms with zero compliance cost or firms that for whatever reason may be inherently law-abiding, for example. A competing explanation with a wider application is the existence of other penalties for noncompliance besides money fines. As suggested in Downing (1984) and Harrington (1985), a noncomplying firm may face bad publicity; it may be ordered to conduct costly stack tests; it may be forced to attend time-consuming meetings or conduct maintenance operations at inconvenient times. Such informal incentives may often be important, but are difficult to identify. No one has demonstrated empirically that an unofficial sanction such as fear of adverse publicity actually has improved continuous compliance with environmental regulations.

Third, these models 'work' better if the desired rate of compliance is not too close to unity. The two-group model has an advantage in cost-effectiveness over a state-independent model that vanishes as the compliance rate approaches unity. In both the state-dependent models examined, the leverage depended on the target compliance rate: the lower the compliance

---

[6]The relevant cost, of course, is the variable operating cost. Fixed costs are excluded because they are unaffected by compliance.

frequency, the higher the compliance cost that could be accommodated. If, as this suggests, the marginal cost of enforcing compliance is increasing, then agencies might be willing to tolerate a high rate of noncompliance to minimize costs. And in fact, results of case studies of enforcement do find low compliance rates, although again there may be a number of alternative explanations for this observation.

On the other hand, there are some apparent truths from these case studies that do not match up well with comparable aspects of the state-dependent model, although often only modest extensions of the model are required. For example, in the model fines are assessed upon the second consecutive violation of the regulation, whereas in reality, sources are often caught violating standards over and over again before a penalty is exacted. This phenomenon can be imitated by introducing a parameter u', analogous to u, governing the transition from Group 1 to Group 2. Alternatively, one could visualize a model with firms divided into n groups, with no penalties being assessed for violations if in the first $m < n$ groups. But this alteration would probably introduce computational unwieldiness without a corresponding gain in insight.

In short, these models are consistent with several broad observations about enforcement and compliance of air and water quality regulations, or can be made so with minor alterations. But although such consistencies are suggestive, they do not constitute a proper test for a theory. Instead, one should ask: Do these models generate any testable hypotheses that distinguish them from other theories? Are the behavioral assumptions that underlie the model reasonable?

It turns out that testable hypotheses are hard to come by, though hardly nonexistent. Let me propose the following two. First, according to (6) the rate of compliance for any f_{10} firm depends not on the cost of compliance, but on the transition probabilities in the two groups, p_1 and p_2, plus the parameter u. Assuming that the parameters for all firms are the same, the rate of compliance for such firms will be the same also.

Second, and of more interest, is the effect of finding a violation on subsequent behavior by the firm. If the firm is inspected and found to be in violation, then the probability of a violation at the next inspection is reduced. If found in compliance, on the other hand, the probability of a violation is *increased*. That is, suppose we have a record of inspections of a firm over time, $(I_1 I_2 I_3 \ldots)$, where $I_n = 1$ if the plant was found in violation of the nth inspection and 0 otherwise. Then

$$P\{I_n = 0 \mid I_{n-1} = 0\} < P\{I_{n-1} = 0\} < P\{I_n = 0 \mid I_{n-1} = 1\}.$$

In static models, by way of contrast, the outcome of the current inspection is not affected by the outcome of the previous inspection. This effect, if it exists, may be difficult to find in practice, because the inspection may cause the firm to revise upward its estimate of the probability of an inspection. An inspection could in this case lead to improved compliance even if the firm was found in compliance, just as borderline speeders often slow down upon seeing a highway patrol car.

As for the reasonableness of the assumptions of the model, enforcement authorities admittedly do not formally and consciously pursue a game-theoretic policy of any sort. But they do tend to adjust the inspection frequency and penalties to the past performance of sources. In addition, enforcement officials typically have a very good idea who the 'bad actors' are. These sources are burdened with more frequent surveillance and greater likelihood of being fined for violations. Also, in the assessment of penalties the recalcitrance of the source is probably more decisive than the likely environmental consequences of a violation. The two-group model may capture the essence of agency behavior, even if it is not the formal procedure used.

It may also be questioned whether firms are so cynical as to commit wilful violations just when they think they can get away with it. This objection is another way of saying that firms are not pure cost minimizers. Perhaps not, but cost minimization remains a useful simplifying assumption. As noted earlier, violations result from a conjunction of numerous stochastic events, such as variation in input quality, process upsets, and breakdowns in abatement equipment, rather than deliberate acts. A firm has considerable discretion in the care with which abatement equipment is operated and maintained. It stands to reason that its diligence would be the greater during those times when violations were likely to be costly.

The assumption that there is a maximum penalty also deserves comment. On paper, most environmental agencies probably do possess sufficient power to force firms to comply with regulations. Even when fines are limited, agencies may seek an injunction shutting the plant down. To take such an extreme action, however, is costly for the agency and the outcome is uncertain. Melnick (1982) has shown how reluctant U.S. courts have been to impose draconian measures on recalcitrant firms when such measures would result in unemployment. Thus, enforcement agencies often have the authority to take drastic action, but it is not a step that would be taken lightly. Given such limitations it makes sense to consider what can be achieved with limited penalties.

I think there is yet another assumption being made in these models that is perhaps less obvious but probably more questionable: both the firm and the agency are assumed to know a lot about the other. The firm is assumed to know what enforcement parameters the agency is using, and to know, at any instant in time, to which group it is assigned. For its part, the agency is assumed to know the firm's cost of compliance. In the real world these assumption may not hold. This means that both the agency and the firm can make mistakes, the agency in the original choice of the parameters of the game and the firm in its choice of strategy, as well as in its choice of action in any given period. Furthermore, both will know this and will tend to act cautiously. For example, suppose a firm had been in compliance for some time after a violation. How is it to tell when it is 'safe' to relax and begin to commit violations again? Presumably inferences could be formed from the pattern of inspections, but necessarily there will be a delay, for some time will elapse between the time the firm's status is changed and the firm can infer the fact. During this period of delay the firm would be in compliance, thus raising the firm's overall compliance rate, but the arractiveness of returning to Group 1 would be reduced.

Incorporation of this reality into the model would allow the investigation of an interesting theoretical question: Who would benefit if both parties were to conceal from the other the requisite information? One can visualize a second game, to be played before continuous enforcement begins, in which the agency announces the enforcement parameters to be used, the firm announces its compliance cost, and each must decide whether to believe the other.

In contrast to the two-group model, the three-group model discussed in section 4 is not represented as a description of current enforcement practice. There probably are not any enforcement authorities that threaten repeat violators with perpetual surveillance. Nonetheless, this model has much to recommend it, for it promises to enforce high compliance rates with relatively small enforcement budgets. When penalties are limited the performance of the model is not arbitrarily high, as in Greenberg's original model. The limitation on penalty size appears to affect the maximum compliance rate that can be achieved, but the inspection resources required remain quite small, though not arbitrarily so. Practical implementation of this model would require some way of allowing firms to escape from the third group, for otherwise most firms would eventually end up there. Leakage into the absorbing state would occur either because of inevitable mistakes by the agency in determining violations, as Greenberg and Russell have pointed out, or inadvertent violations by the firm. Allowing an escape from Group 3 would, no doubt, compromise to some degree the cost-effectiveness of the model. Determination of just how much is a subject of future research.

References

Abbey, David and W. Harrington, 1981, Air quality regulation and management in the four corners states, Southwestern Journal of Economics and Business 1, no. 2.
Becker, Gary S., 1968, Crime and punishment: An economic analysis, Journal of Political Economy 76, no. 2.

Braithwaite, John, 1982, The limits of economism in controlling harmful corporate conduct, Law and Society Review 16, no. 3.

Brams, Stephen J. and M.D. Davis, 1983, The verification problem in arms control: A theoretical analysis, Economic Research Report 83-12 (New York University Department of Economics, New York, NY).

Downing, Paul, 1984, Environmental economics and policy (Little Brown & Co., Boston, MA).

Downing, Paul and James Kimball, 1982, Enforcing pollution control laws in the United States, Policy Studies Journal 11, no. 1, Sept.

Downing, Paul and W.D. Watson, 1974, The economics of enforcing air pollution controls, Journal of Environmental Economics and Management 1, 219–236.

Environmental Law Institute, 1975, Enforcement of federal and state water pollution controls (Report prepared for the National Commission on Water Quality, Washington, DC).

Greenberg, Joseph, 1984, Avoiding tax avoidance: A (repeated) game-theoretic approach, Journal of Economic Theory 32, no. 1, 1–13.

Harford, John, 1978, Firm behavior under imperfectly enforceable standards and taxes, Journal of Environmental Economics and Management 5, no. 1.

Harrington, Winston, 1981, The regulatory approach to air quality management: A case study of New Mexico (Resources for the Future, Washington, DC).

Harrington, Winston, 1985, Enforcement of continuous compliance with air quality regulations (unpublished Ph.D. dissertation, University of North Carolina, Chapel Hill, NC).

Kohlas, J., 1982, Stochastic methods of operations research (Cambridge University Press, New York).

Landsberger, Michael and Isaac Meilijson, 1982, Incentive generating state dependent penalty system, Journal of Public Economics 19, 333–352.

Linder, Stephen H. and Mark E. McBride, 1984, Enforcement costs and regulatory reform: The agency and firm response, Journal of Environmental Economics and Management 11, no. 4, 327–346.

Melnick, Shep, 1982, Regulation and the Courts: The case of the Clean Air Act (The Brookings Institution, Washington, DC).

Russell, Clifford S., 1982, Pollution monitoring survey summary report (Resources for the Future, Washington, DC).

Russell, Clifford S., 1984, Imperfect monitoring of sources of externalities: Lessons from single and multiple play games, Discussion paper QE84-01 (Resources for the Future, Washington, DC).

Russell, Clifford S., W. Harrington and W.J. Vaughan, 1986, Enforcing pollution control laws (Johns Hopkins University Press, Baltimore, MD).

Storey, D.J. and P.J. McCabe, 1980, The criminal waste discharger, Scottish Journal of Political Economy 27, no. 1.

U.S. Environmental Protection Agency, 1981a, Profile of nine state and local air pollution agencies (Office of Planning and Evaluation, The Agency, Washington, DC).

U.S. Environmental Protection Agency, 1981b, Characterization of air pollution control equipment operation and maintenance problems (Office of Planning and Evaluation, The Agency, DC).

U.S. General Accounting Office, 1979, Improvements needed in controlling major air pollution sources, Discussion paper CED-78-165 (The Agency, Washington, DC).

U.S. General Accounting Office, 1982, Cleaning up the environment: Progress achieved but major unresolved issues remain, Discussion paper CED-82-72 (The Agency, Washington, DC).

Viscusi, W. Kip and R.J. Zeckhauser, 1979, Optimal standards with incomplete enforcement, Public Policy 27, no. 4.

Willick, W. and T. Windle, 1973, Rule enforcement by the Los Angeles air pollution control district, Ecology Law Quarterly 3, 507–534.

Part VI
The Economics of Conservation

[33]

CONSERVATION RECONSIDERED

By JOHN V. KRUTILLA*

"It is the clear duty of Government, which is the trustee for unborn generations as well as for its present citizens, to watch over, and if need be, by legislative enactment, to defend, the exhaustible natural resources of the country from rash and reckless spoliation. How far it should itself, either out of taxes, or out of State loans, or by the device of guaranteed interest, press resources into undertakings from which the business community, if left to itself, would hold aloof, is a more difficult problem. Plainly, if we assume adequate competence on the part of governments, there is a valid case for *some* artificial encouragement to investment, particularly to investments the return from which will only begin to appear after the lapse of many years."

A. C. PIGOU

Conservation of natural resources has meant different things to different people. But to the economist from the time of Pigou, who first took notice of the economics of conservation [10, p. 27ff], until quite recently, the central concerns have been associated with the question of the optimal intertemporal utilization of the fixed natural resource stocks. The gnawing anxiety provoked by the Malthusian thesis of natural resource scarcity was in no way allayed by the rates of consumption of natural resource stocks during two world wars occurring between the first and fourth editions of Pigou's famous work. In the United States, a presidential commission, reviewing the materials situation following World War II, concluded that an end had come to the historic decline in the cost of natural resource commodities [12, pp. 13-14]. This conclusion reinforced the concern of many that the resource base ultimately would be depleted.

More recently, on the other hand, a systematic analysis of the trends in prices of natural resource commodities did not reveal any permanent interruption in the decline relative to commodities and services in general [11]. Moreover, a rather ambitious attempt to test rigorously the thesis of natural resource scarcity suggested instead that technological progress had compensated quite adequately for the depletion of the higher quality natural resource stocks [1]. Further, given the present state of the arts, future advances need not be fortuitous occurrences;

* The author is indebted to all of his colleagues at Resources for the Future and to Harold Barnett, Paul Davidson, Otto Davis, Chandler Morse, Peter Pearse, and Ralph Turvey for many helpful suggestions on an earlier draft of this paper.

rather the rate of advance can be influenced by investment in research and development. Indeed, those who take an optimistic view would hold that the modern industrial economy is winning its independence from the traditional natural resources sector to a remarkable degree. Ultimately, the raw material inputs to industrial production may be only mass and energy [1, p. 238].[1]

While such optimistic conclusions were being reached, they were nevertheless accompanied by a caveat that, while we may expect production of goods and services to increase without interruption, the level of living may not necessarily be improved. More specifically, Barnett and Morse concluded that the quality of the physical environment—the landscape, water, and atmospheric quality—was deteriorating.

These conclusions suggest that on the one hand the traditional concerns of conservation economics—the husbanding of natural resource stocks for the use of future generations—may now be outmoded by advances in technology. On the other hand, the central issue seems to be the problem of providing for the present and future the amenities associated with unspoiled natural environments, for which the market fails to make adequate provision. While this appears to be the implication of recent research,[2] and is certainly consistent with recent public policy in regard to preserving natural environments, the traditional economic rationale for conservation does not address itself to this issue directly.[3] The use of Pigou's social time preference may serve only to hasten the conversion of natural environments into low-yield capital investments.[4] On what basis, then, can we make decisions when we confront a choice entailing action which will have an irreversible adverse consequence for rare phenomena of nature? I investigate this question below.

Let us consider an area with some unique attribute of nature—a geomorphologic feature such as the Grand Canyon, a threatened species, or an entire ecosystem or biotic community essential to the survival of the threatened species.[5] Let us assume further that the area can be used

---

[1] The conclusions were based on data relevant to the U.S. economy. While they may be pertinent to Western Europe also, all of my subsequent observations are restricted to the United States.

[2] For example, see [7].

[3] It must be acknowledged that with sufficient patience and perception nearly all of the argument for preserving unique phenomena of nature can be found in the classic on conservation economics by Ciriacy-Wantrup [3].

[4] An example of this was the recent threat to the Grand Canyon by the proposed Bridge and Marble Canyon dams. Scott makes a similar point with reference to natural resource commodities [13].

[5] Uniqueness need not be absolute for the following arguments to hold. It may be, like Dupuit's bridge, a good with no adequate substitutes in the "natural" market area of its

for certain recreation and/or scientific research activities which would be compatible with the preservation of the natural environment, or for extractive activities such as logging or hydraulic mining, which would have adverse consequences for scenic landscapes and wildlife habitat.

A private resource owner would consider the discounted net income stream from the alternative uses and select the use which would hold prospects for the highest present net value. If the use which promises the highest present net value is incompatible with preserving the environment in its natural state, does it necessarily follow that the market will allocate the resources efficiently? There are several reasons why private and social returns in this case are likely to diverge significantly.

Consider the problem first in its static aspects. By assumption, the resources used in a manner compatible with preserving the natural environment have no close substitutes; on the other hand, alternative sources of supply of natural resource commodities are available.[6] Under the circumstances and given the practical obstacles to perfectly discriminating pricing, the private resource owner would not be able to appropriate in gate receipts the entire social value of the resources when used in a manner compatible with preserving the natural state. Thus the present values of his expected net revenues are not comparable as between the competing uses in evaluating the effciency of the resource allocation.

Aside from the practical problem of implementing a perfectly discriminating pricing policy, it is not clear even on theoretic grounds that a comparison of the total area under the demand curve on the one hand and market receipts on the other will yield an unambiguous answer to the allocative question. When the existence of a grand scenic wonder or a unique and fragile ecosystem is involved, its preservation and continued availability are a significant part of the real income of many individuals.[7] Under the conditions postulated, the area under the demand curve, which represents a maximum willingness to pay, may be significantly less than the minimum which would be required to compensate such individuals were they to be deprived in perpetuity of the opportunity

---

principal clientele, while possibly being replicated in other market areas to which the clientele in question has no access for all practical purposes.

[6] The asymmetry in the relation posited is realistic. The historic decline in cost of natural resource commodities relative to commodities in general suggests that the production and exchange of the former occur under fairly competitive conditions. On the other hand, increasing congestion at parks, such as Yellowstone, Yosemite, and Grand Canyon, suggests there are no adequate substitutes for these rare natural environments.

[7] These would be the spiritual descendants of John Muir, the present members of the Sierra Club, the Wilderness Society, National Wildlife Federation, Audubon Society and others to whom the loss of a species or the disfigurement of a scenic area causes acute distress and a sense of genuine relative impoverishment.

to continue enjoying the natural phenomenon in question. Accordingly, it is conceivable that the potential losers cannot influence the decision in their favor by their aggregate willingness to pay, yet the resource owner may not be able to compensate the losers out of the receipts from the alternative use of the resource. In such cases—and they are more likely encountered in this area—it is impossible to determine whether the market allocation is efficient or inefficient.

Another reason for questioning the allocative efficiency of the market for the case in hand has been recognized only more recently. This involves the notion of *option demand* [14]. This demand is characterized as a willingness to pay for retaining an option to use an area or facility that would be difficult or impossible to replace and for which no close substitute is available. Moreover, such a demand may exist even though there is no current intention to use the area or facility in question and the option may never be exercised. If an option value exists for rare or unique occurrences of nature, but there is no means by which a private resource owner can appropriate this value, the resulting resource allocation may be questioned.

Because options are traded on the market in connection with other economic values, one may ask why no market has developed where option value exists for the preservation of natural environments.[8] We need to consider briefly the nature of the value in question and the marketability of the option.

From a purely scientific viewpoint, much is yet to be learned in the earth and life sciences; preservation of the objects of study may be defended on these grounds, given the serendipity value of basic research. We know also that the natural biota represents our reservoir of germ plasm, which has economic value. For example, modern agriculture in advanced countries represents cultivation figuratively in a hot-house environment in which crops are protected against disease, pests, and drought by a variety of agricultural practices. The energy released from some of the genetic characteristics no longer required for survival under cultivated conditions is redirected toward greater productivity. Yet because of the instability introduced with progressive reduction of biological diversity, a need occasionally arises for the reintroduction of some genetic characteristics lost in the past from domestic strains. It is from the natural biota that these can be obtained.

The value of botanical specimens for medicinal purposes also has been long, if not widely, recognized. Approximately half of the new drugs currently being developed are obtained from botanical specimens.[9] There is a traffic in medicinal plants which approximates a third

---

[8] For a somewhat differently developed argument, see [6].

[9] For an interesting account of the use of plants for medicinal purposes, see [8].

KRUTILLA: CONSERVATION 781

of a billion dollars annually. Cortisone, digitalis, and heparin are among the better known of the myriad drugs which are derived from natural vegetation or zoological sources. Since only a relatively small part of the potential medicinal value of biological specimens has yet been realized, preserving the opportunity to examine all species among the natural biota for this purpose is a matter of considerable importance.

The option value may have only a sentimental basis in some instances. Consider the rallying to preserve the historical relic, "Old Ironsides."[10] There are many persons who obtain satisfaction from mere knowledge that part of wilderness North America remains even though they would be appalled by the prospect of being exposed to it. Subscriptions to World Wildlife Fund are of the same character. The funds are employed predominantly in an effort to save exotic species in remote areas of the world which few subscribers to the Fund ever hope to see. An option demand may exist therefore not only among persons currently and prospectively active in the market for the object of the demand, but among others who place a value on the mere existence of biological and/or geomorphological variety and its widespread distribution.[11]

If a genuine value for retaining an option in these respects exists, why has not a market developed? To some extent, and for certain purposes, it has. Where a small natural area in some locality in the United States is threatened, the property is often purchased by Nature Conservancy,[12] a private organization which raises funds through voluntary subscriptions.[13] But this market is grossly imperfect. First, the risk for private investors associated with absence of knowledge as to whether a particular ecosystem has special characteristics not widely shared by others is enormous.[14] Moreover, to the extent that the natural environment will support basic scientific research which often has unanticipated practical results, the serendipity value may not be appropriable by those paying to preserve the options. But perhaps of greatest significance is that the preservation of the grand scenic wonders, threatened species, and the like involves comparatively large land tracts which are not of merely

[10] The presumption in favor of option value is applicable also to historic and cultural features; rare works of art, perhaps, being the most prominent of this class.

[11] The phenomenon discussed may have an exclusive sentimental basis, but if we consider the "bequest motivation" in economic behavior, discussed below, it may be explained by an interest in preserving an option for one's heirs to view or use the object in question.

[12] Not to be confused with a public agency of the same name in the United Kingdom.

[13] Subscriptions to World Wildlife Fund, the Wilderness Society, National Parks Association, etc. may be similar, but, of course, much of the effect these organizations have on the preservation of natural areas stems not from purchasing options, but from influencing public programs.

[14] The problem here is in part like a national lottery in which there exists a very small chance for a very large gain. Unlike a lottery, rather large sums at very large risk typically would be required.

local interest. Thus, all of the problems of organizing a market for public goods arise. Potential purchasers of options may be expected to bide time in the expectation that others will meet the necessary cost, thus eliminating cost to themselves. Since the mere existence or preservation of the natural environment in question satisfies the demand, those who do not subscribe cannot be excluded except by the failure to enroll sufficient subscribers for its preservation.

Perhaps of equal significance to the presumption of market failure are some dynamic characteristics of the problem suggested by recent research. First, consider the consumption aspects of the problem. Davidson, Adams, and Seneca have recently advanced some interesting notions regarding the formation of demand that may be particularly relevant to our problem [5, p. 186].

> When facilities are not readily available, skills will not be developed and, consequently, there may be little desire to participate in these activities. If facilities are made available, opportunities to acquire skill increase, and user demand tends to rise rapidly over time as individuals learn to enjoy these activities. Thus, participation in and enjoyment of water recreational activities by the present generation will stimulate future demand without diminishing the supply presently available. Learning-by-doing, to the extent it increases future demand, suggests an interaction between present and future demand functions, which will result in a public good externality, as present demand enters into the utility function of future users.

While this quotation refers to water-based recreation, it is likely to be more persuasive in connection with some other resource-based recreation activity. Its relevance for wilderness preservation is obvious. When we consider the remote backcountry landscape, or the wilderness scene as the object of experience and enjoyment, we recognize that utility from the experience depends predominantly upon the prior acquisition of technical skill and specialized knowledge. This, of course, must come from experience initially with less arduous or demanding activities. The more the present population is initiated into activities requiring similar but less advanced skills (e.g., car camping), the better prepared the future population will be to participate in the more exacting activities. Given the phenomenal rise of car camping, if this activity will spawn a disproportionate number of future back-packers, canoe cruisers, cross-country skiers, etc., the greater will be the induced demand for wild, primitive, and wilderness-related opportunities for indulging such interest. Admittedly, we know little about the demand for outdoor experiences which depend on unique phenomena of nature—its formation, stability, and probable course of development. These are important questions for research, results of which will have significant policy implications.

In regard to the production aspects of the "new conservation," we need to examine the implications of technological progress a little further. Earlier I suggested that the advances of technology have compensated for the depletion of the richer mineral deposits and, in a sense, for the superior stands of timber and tracts of arable land. On the other hand, there is likely to be an asymmetry in the implications of technological progress for the production of goods and services from the natural resource base, and the production of natural phenomena which give rise to utility without undergoing fabrication or other processing.[15] In fact, it is improbable that technology will advance to the point at which the grand geomorphologic wonders could be replicated, or extinct species resurrected. Nor is it obvious that fabricated replicas, were they even possible, would have a value equivalent to that of the originals. To a lesser extent, the landscape can be manufactured in a pleasing way with artistry and the larger earth-moving equipment of today's construction technology. Open pit mines may be refilled and the surroundings rehabilitated in a way to approximate the original conditions. But even here the undertaking cannot be acccomplished without the cooperation of nature over a substantial period of time depending on the growth rate of the vegetal cover and the requirements of the native habitat.[16] Accordingly, while the supply of fabricated goods and commercial services may be capable of continuous expansion from a given resource base by reason of scientific discovery and mastery of technique, the supply of natural phenomena is virtually inelastic. That is, we may preserve the natural environment which remains to provide amenities of this sort for the future, but there are significant limitations on reproducing it in the future should we fail to preserve it.

If we consider the asymmetric implications of technology, we can conceive of a transformation function having along its vertical axis amenities derived directly from association with the natural environment and fabricated goods along the horizontal axis. Advances in technology would stretch the transformation function's terminus along the horizontal axis but not appreciably along the vertical. Accordingly, if we simply take the effect of technological progress over time, considering tastes as constant, the marginal trade-off between manufactured and natural amenities will progressively favor the latter. Natural environments will represent irreplaceable assets of appreciating value with the passage of time.

If we consider technology as constant, but consider a change in tastes progressively favoring amenities of the natural environment due to the learn-by-doing phenomenon, natural environments will similarly for this

---

[15] I owe this point to a related observation, to my knowledge first made by Ciriacy-Wantrup [3, p. 47].

[16] That is, giving rise to option value for members of the present population.

reason represent assets of appreciating value. If both influences are operative (changes in technology with asymmetric implications, and tastes), the appreciating value of natural environments will be compounded.

This leads to a final point which, while a static consideration, tends to have its real significance in conjunction with the effects of parametric shifts in tastes and technology. We are coming to realize that consumption-saving behavior is motivated by a desire to leave one's heirs an estate as well as by the utility to be obtained from consumption.[17] A bequest of maximum value would require an appropriate mix of public and private assets, and, equally, the appropriate mix of opportunities to enjoy amenities experienced directly from association with the natural environment along with readily producible goods. But the option to enjoy the grand scenic wonders for the bulk of the population depends upon their provision as public goods.

Several observations have been made which may now be summarized. The first is that, unlike resource allocation questions dealt with in conventional economic problems, there is a family of problems associated with the natural environment which involves the irreproducibility of unique phenomena of nature—or the irreversibility of some consequence inimical to human welfare. Second, it appears that the utility to individuals of direct association with natural environments may be increasing while the supply is not readily subject to enlargement by man. Third, the real cost of refraining from converting our remaining rare natural environments may not be very great. Moreover, with the continued advance in technology, more substitutes for conventional natural resources will be found for the industrial and agricultural sectors, liberating production from dependence on conventional sources of raw materials. Finally, if consumption-saving behavior is motivated also by the desire to leave an estate, some portion of the estate would need to be in assets which yield collective consumption goods of appreciating future value. For all of these reasons we are confronted with a problem not conventionally met in resource economics. The problem is of the following nature.

At any point in time characterized by a level of technology which is less advanced than at some future date, the conversion of the natural environment into industrially produced private goods has proceeded further than it would have with the more advanced future technology. Moreover, with the apparent increasing appreciation of direct contact with natural environments, the conversion will have proceeded further, for this reason as well, than it would have were the future composition of tastes to have prevailed. Given the irreversibility of converted natural

[17] See [2]; also [9].

environments, however, it will not be possible to achieve a level of well-being in the future that would have been possible had the conversion of natural environments been retarded. That this should be of concern to members of the present generation may be attributable to the bequest motivation in private economic behavior as much as to a sense of public responsibility.[18]

Accordingly, our problem is akin to the dynamic programming problem which requires a present action (which may violate conventional benefit-cost criteria) to be compatible with the attainment of future states of affairs. But we know little about the value that the instrumental variables may take. We have virtually no knowledge about the possible magnitude of the option demand. And we still have much to learn about the determinants of the growth in demand for outdoor recreation and about the quantitative significance of the asymmetry in the implications of technological advances for producing industrial goods on the one hand and natural environments on the other. Obviously, a great deal of research in these areas is necessary before we can hope to apply formal decision criteria comparable to current benefit-cost criteria. Fully useful results may be very long in coming; what then is a sensible way to proceed in the interim?

First, we need to consider what we need as a minimum reserve to avoid potentially grossly adverse consequences for human welfare. We may regard this as our scientific preserve of research materials required for advances in the life and earth sciences. While no careful evaluation of the size of this reserve has been undertaken by scientists, an educated guess has put the need in connection with terrestrial communities at about ten million acres for North America [4, p. 128]. Reservation of this amount of land—but a small fraction of one per cent of the total relevant area—is not likely to affect appreciably the supply or costs of material inputs to the manufacturing or agricultural sectors.

The size of the scientific preserve required for aquatic environments is still unknown. Only after there is developed an adequate system of classification of aquatic communities will it be possible to identify distinct environments, recognize the needed reservations, and, then, estimate the opportunity costs. Classification and identification of aquatic environments demand early research attention by natural scientists.

Finally, one might hope that the reservations for scientific purposes would also support the bulk of the outdoor recreation demands, or that substantial additional reservations for recreational purposes could be

[18] The rationale above differs from that of Stephen Marglin which is perhaps the most rigorous one relying on a sense of public responsibility and externalities to justify explicit provision for future generations. In this case also, my concern is with providing *collective consumption goods for the present and future*, whereas the traditional concern in conservation economics has been with provision of *private intermediate goods for the future*.

786   THE AMERICAN ECONOMIC REVIEW

justified by the demand and implicit opportunity costs. Reservations for recreation, as well as for biotic communities, should include special or rare environments which can support esoteric tastes as well as the more common ones. This is a matter of some importance because outdoor recreation opportunities will be provided in large part by public bodies, and within the public sector there is a tendency to provide a homogenized recreation commodity oriented toward a common denominator. There is need to recognize, and make provision for, the widest range of outdoor recreation tastes, just as a well-functioning market would do. We need a policy and a mechanism to ensure that all natural areas peculiarly suited for specialized recreation uses receive consideration for such uses. A policy of this kind would be consistent both with maintaining the greatest biological diversity for scientific research and educational purposes and with providing the widest choice for consumers of outdoor recreation.

REFERENCES

1. H. J. BARNETT AND C. MORSE, *Scarcity and Growth: The Economics of Natural Resource Availability.* Baltimore 1963.
2. S. B. CHASE, JR., *Asset Prices in Economic Analysis.* Berkeley 1963.
3. S. V. CIRIACY-WANTRUP, *Resources Conservation.* Berkeley 1952.
4. F. DARLING AND J. P. MILTON, ed., *Future Environments of North America, Transformation of a Continent.* Garden City, N.Y. 1966.
5. P. DAVIDSON, F. G. ADAMS, AND J. SENECA, "The Social Value of Water Recreation Facilities Resulting from an Improvement in Water Quality: The Delaware Estuary," in A. V. Kneese and S. C. Smith, ed., *Water Research,* Baltimore 1966.
6. A. E. KAHN, "The Tyranny of Small Decisions: Market Failures, Imperfections, and the Limits of Economics," *Kyklos,* 1966, 19 (1), 23-47.
7. A. V. KNEESE, *The Economics of Regional Water Quality Management.* Baltimore 1964.
8. M. B. KREIG, *Green Medicine: The Search for Plants that Heal.* New York 1964.
9. F. MODIGLIANI AND R. BRUMBERG, "Utility Analysis and the Consumption Function: An Interpretation of Cross-Section Data," in K. K. Kurihara, ed., *Post-Keynesian Economics,* New Brunswick 1954.
10. A. C. PIGOU, *The Economics of Welfare.* 4th ed., London 1952.
11. N. POTTER AND F. T. CHRISTY, JR., *Trends in Natural Resources Commodities: Statistics of Prices, Output, Consumption, Foreign Trade, and Employment in the United States, 1870-1957.* Baltimore 1962.
12. The President's Materials Policy Commission, *Resources for Freedom, Foundation for Growth and Security,* Vol. I. Washington 1952.
13. A. D. SCOTT, *Natural Resources: The Economics of Conservation.* Toronto 1955.
14. B. A. WEISBROD, "Collective Consumption Services of Individual Consumption Goods," *Quart. Jour. Econ.,* Aug. 1964, 77, 71-77.

[34]

The Economics of Environmental Preservation: A Theoretical and Empirical Analysis

By Anthony C. Fisher, John V. Krutilla, and Charles J. Cicchetti*

Concern over the adequacy of nature's endowments has been reflected in economic literature at least from the time of Malthus. For Malthus, the natural environment was essentially a source of increasingly scarce resources to sustain economic activity. Recent theoretical contributions in this framework have sought to develop programs for the optimal intertemporal consumption of fixed and renewable natural resource stocks.[1] Some evidence, on the other hand, suggests that technological progress has so broadened the resource base that the scarcity foreseen by Malthus and assumed, for example, in the stationary utility function postulated by Plourde, has not in fact been realized.[2] Yet, though the statistical evidence is that the direct costs of production from natural resources have fallen (relatively) over time, it seems likely that some of the environmental costs have risen.

It is desirable to distinguish two kinds of environmental costs. One is pollution, concerning which there is a relatively large and growing literature,[3] which we do not address in this paper. The other is the transformation and loss of whole environments as would result, for example, from clear cutting a redwood forest, or developing a hydroelectric project in the Grand Canyon. Surely there are important economic issues here, yet although there is a vast literature dating back to the 1930's on benefit-cost criteria for water resource projects, economists have said. virtually nothing about the environmental opportunity costs of these projects. Where reference is made to the despoliation of natural environments, note is made only in passing to "extra-economic" considerations.[4] Similarly in the texts on land economics no mention is made of the economic issues involved in the allocation of wildlands and scenic resources, nor do the costs of land development include the opportunity returns foregone as a result of destroying natural areas.

More recently Krutilla has argued that private market allocations are likely to preserve less than the socially optimal

* Fisher's work was done at Brown University and Resources for the Future, Inc. Krutilla and Cicchetti are at Resources for the Future, Inc. This paper represents work done in the Natural Environments Program, Resources for the Future, Inc. Fisher's work was additionally supported partially by NSF Grant GS2530 to the Institute for Mathematical Studies in the Social Sciences, Stanford University. We are indebted to George Borts, John Brown, and Harl Ryder for many perceptive comments and suggestions. We are also grateful to our colleagues at Resources for the Future; to faculty and students of the Natural Resources Institute, Oregon State University 1969, and to Darwin Nelson, Arnold Quint, and Donald Sander of the Federal Power Commission for many constructive suggestions. We wish to acknowledge as well comments on an earlier draft of this paper from Gardner Brown, Ronald Cummings, A. Myrick Freeman III, Richard Judy, Clifford Russell, V. Kerry Smith, and an anonymous reviewer.

[1] See for example, studies by Vernon Smith, Charles Plourde, Oscar Burt and Ronald Cummings.

[2] See the studies by Neal Potter and Francis Christy, and Harold Barnett and Chandler Morse.

[3] For a summary of this literature, see E. J. Mishan.

[4] See for example, *Proposed Practices for Economic Analysis of River Basin Projects*, p. 44, Krutilla and Otto Eckstein, p. 265, Roland McKean, p. 61, and Maynard Hufschmidt, Krutilla, and Julius Margolis, pp. 52–53.

The Economics of the Environment

amount of natural environments. More-over, he concludes that the optimal amount is likely to be increasing over time—a particularly serious problem in view of the irreversibility of many environmental transformations.

In this paper we extend Krutilla's discussion in two ways. First, in Sections I and II we develop a model for the allocation of natural environments between preservation and development. Then, in Section III, we apply the model to a currently debated issue: Should the Hells Canyon of the Snake River, the deepest gorge on the North American continent, be preserved in its current state for wilderness recreation and other activities,[5] or further developed as a hydroelectric facility?

I

Before proceeding with the discussion of allocation between preservation and development, we observe that a natural area may have not just one, but several uses in each state. For the development alternative, we abstract from this problem by assuming allocation to the highest valued use or combination of uses via the market, or some appropriate mix of market, government intervention and bargaining.[6] Similarly for an area reserved from development, we make the same assumption; i.e., the area is used optimally for recreation.[7] Our objective at this stage, then, is

to formulate a model for guiding choice between the two broad alternatives of preservation and development.

We begin in this section with a rather general model for the optimum use of natural environments. In succeeding sections a more specific methodology will be developed and used to evaluate the Hells Canyon alternatives.

As a defensible definition of optimum use we propose that use which maximizes the present value of net social returns, or benefits, from an area. In symbols, we wish to maximize

$$(1) \quad \int_0^\infty e^{-\rho t}[B^P(P(t), t) + B^D(D(t), t) \\ - I(t)]dt$$

where B^P and B^D are expected net social benefits (benefits minus costs) at time t, from P units of preserved area, and D units of developed; I is the "social overhead" capital investment cost at time t of transforming from preserved into developed; and ρ is the social discount rate. Note that the opportunity costs of development, the benefits B^P from preservation, generally ignored in benefit-cost calculations, here enter explicitly into the expression to be maximized.

There are several constraints, imposed by nature and past development, on the maximization of (1). We recognize, first, that the amount of any given area developed, residually determines the amount preserved. In symbols,

$$(2) \quad\quad\quad P + D = L$$

where L is the fixed amount of land in the area.[8] Second, current and future choice is

[5] For a discussion of some of the uses of a preserved natural environment, including some suggestions as to how benefits might be evaluated, see Krutilla.

[6] At least two types of externality, pollution and crowding, are likely to be significant in the commercial exploitation of a natural area, making an efficient allocation in general unattainable in the absence of some form of government intervention or private bargaining to internalize. For a summary discussion of the general externality problem, see Mishan. For an interesting treatment of the crowding problem in particular, see Smith.

[7] The problem is that beyond some point, expanding recreation activity can result in congestion disutility to

recreationists, or ecological damage, or both. For a detailed discussion, see Fisher and Krutilla.

[8] For sufficient flexibility in application, we think of D as the number of units affected by the development activity, adjusted perhaps for the character of the activity.

constrained by the results of past choices. In symbols,

(3) $P(0) = P_0$ and, $D(0) = D_0$,

i.e., initial values for preserved and developed portions of the area are given. The dynamic and irreversibility constraints are:

(4) $D = \sigma I$,

where σ is a positive constant of transformation with dimensions area/money,[9] and

(5) $I \geq 0$

Clearly, were the converse true, i.e., were the transformation reversible, much of the conflict between preservation and development would vanish. It seems to us that it is precisely because the losses of certain natural environments would be losses virtually in perpetuity that they are significant.

Finally, we assume concave benefit functions B^P and B^D, so that returns to increasing preservation or development are positive but diminishing; in symbols,

(6) $B_P^P, B_D^D > 0$ and, $B_{PP}^P, B_{DD}^D < 0$

It is conceivable that initial stages of water resource development may be characterized by increasing returns. This will not in general be true of river systems in advanced stages of development, such as the Columbia River system, of which the Hells Canyon reach of the Snake River is a part. Accordingly, while the larger High Mountain Sheep project is more profitable than the smaller Pleasant Valley-Low Mountain Sheep, any increase in scale beyond High Mountain Sheep runs into

severely diminishing returns, as the higher pool reduces the existing developed head upstream. Moreover, though this anticipates the analysis just a bit, what really matters is the behavior of development benefits *net* of opportunity costs. And the marginal opportunity costs of development, the benefits from preservation, are *increasing* as *development* increases.[10]

We now proceed with a control-theoretic solution of this problem in the general case, in which no restrictions are placed on the time paths of the benefit functions.[11] The Hamiltonian is

(7) $H = e^{-\rho t}[B^P(P, t) + B^D(D, t)$
$\qquad\qquad - I(t)] + p(t)\sigma I(t)$

where the first term on the right-hand side, $e^{-\rho t}[B^P(P, t) + B^D(D, t) - I(t)]$, is the (discounted) flow of net benefits at time t, and $p(t)$ is the (discounted) shadow price (value of future benefits) of development. Setting $q(t) = p(t)\sigma - e^{-\rho t}$, H can be simplified to

(8) $H = e^{-\rho t}[B^P(P, t) + B^D(D, t)]$
$\qquad\qquad + q(t)I(t)$

Note the relationship of q to p. If technology or demand relationships are changing, then p and hence q will be affected.

Applying the maximum principle of Pontryagin, et al., I is chosen to maximize H subject to the irreversibility restriction (5):

(9) H is maximized by $\quad I = 0 \quad q < 0$
$\qquad\qquad\qquad\qquad\quad I \geq 0 \quad q = 0$

For $q > 0$, investment would have to be infinite over an interval. Quite apart from its impracticality, this possibility can be ruled out because it leads to a contradic-

---

[9] In specifying the constraint in this fashion we are assuming "constant returns" to increasing investment. This seems at least as plausible, in the general case, as either increasing or decreasing returns, as would be implied by some more complicated functional form for the relationship between investment and development.

[10] This follows from the other half of equation (6), namely that $B_P^P > 0$ and $BP_{PP}^P < 0$.

[11] Problems similar in form to (1)–(6) have recently been studied by Arrow and Kurz and by Arrow. In the remainder of this section we draw heavily on their work.

tion. Obviously, past development could not have been optimal; more should have been invested earlier.

Since, from (2) P and D are not independent, H can also be written

$$(10) \quad H = e^{-\rho t}[B^P(L - D, t) + B^D(D, t)] + q(t)I(t)$$

Again applying the maximum principle,

$$(11) \quad P = -\frac{\partial H_{max}}{\partial D} = -e^{-\rho t}(-B^P_P + B^D_D)$$

Since equation (9) is written in q, not p, let us write

$$(12) \quad \dot{q} = \sigma P + \rho e^{-\rho t} = \sigma e^{-\rho t}(B^P_P - B^D_D) + \rho e^{-\rho t} = e^{-\rho t}[\rho - \sigma(B^D_D - B^P_P)],$$

and,

$$(13) \quad q(t_1) - q(t_0) = \int_{t_0}^{t_1} e^{-\rho t}[\rho - \sigma(B^D_D - B^P_P)]dt$$

From (9), the optimal development path is a sequence of intervals satisfying alternately the conditions $q(t) = 0$ and $q(t) < 0$. Following Kenneth Arrow, define intervals in which $q(t) = 0$ as free intervals, intervals in which $q(t) < 0$ as blocked (no investment) intervals. In a free interval, $\dot{q} = 0$, so

$$(14) \quad \rho = \sigma(B^D_D - B^P_P)$$

Assume, however unrealistically, that investment were costlessly reversible, except for prior interest charges. This would be equivalent to renting the area for this period, at a rate equal to the rate of interest. As in the related capital accumulation problem, optimal investment policy would then have the myopic property

$$(15) \quad \frac{\rho}{\sigma} = B^D_D(D^*, t) - B^P_P(P^*, t),$$

or

$$B^D_D(D^*, t) = \frac{\rho}{\sigma} + B^P_P(P^*, t),$$

which may be interpreted to mean that optimal investment policy equates the marginal benefits from development B^D_D to the sum of direct and marginal opportunity costs $(\rho/\sigma + B^P_P)$ at any point in time.

Combining (14) and (15), we have

$$(16) \quad D(t) = D^*(t) \text{ on a free interval}$$

Again, following Arrow, define a rising segment of $D^*(t)$ as a riser. Then, since $D(t)$ is increasing on a free interval, $D^*(t)$ is increasing, and a free interval lies within a single riser.

On a blocked interval (t_0, t_1), $0 < t_0 < t_1 < \infty$, it follows that $D(t_0) = D^*(t_0)$ and $q(t_0) = 0$, since t_0 is also the end of a free interval. Since $I = 0$, $D(t)$ is constant, so $D(t) = D^*(t_0)$, $t_0 \leq t \leq t_1$. Similarly, since t_1 is the start of a free interval, $D(t) = D^*(t_1)$, $t_0 \leq t \leq t_1$ and $q(t_1) = 0$. Summarizing, on a blocked interval (t_0, t_1), $0 < t_0 < t_1 < \infty$,

$$(17) \quad D^*(t_0) = D^*(t_1),$$

$$(18) \quad \int_{t_0}^{t_1} e^{-\rho t}r[D^*(t_0), t]dt = 0$$

where

$$r(D, t) = \rho - \sigma[B^D_D(D, t) - B^P_P(P, t)],$$

$$(19) \quad \int_{t_0}^{t} e^{-\rho t}r[D^*(t_0), t]dt < 0, t_0 < t < t_1,$$

and

$$(20) \quad \int_{t}^{t_1} e^{-\rho t}r[D^*(t_0), t]dt > 0, t_0 < t < t_1$$

Equations (18)–(20) can be given economic interpretations. Holding $D(t)$ $=D^*(t_0)$, net marginal benefits $(B_D^D - B_P^P)$ first exceed (constant) marginal costs, since we do not invest, or push development, to the point $(D^*(t))$ at which they are equal. As short-run optimal development $(D^*(t))$ begins to fall, however, beyond some point there is too much development, i.e., $D(t)=D^*(t_0)>D^*(t)$. From this point, marginal benefits are less than marginal costs. Equation (18) then says that over the full interval (t_0, t_1) the sum of (discounted) marginal costs just equals the sum of (discounted) marginal benefits. Equation (19) says that, over an interval starting at t_0 and ending at any time t short of t_1, marginal benefits exceed marginal costs. Equation (20) is, of course, not independent of (18) and (19), and says that, over an interval starting at any time t beyond t_0 and ending at t_1, marginal benefits are less than marginal costs.

Myopic (D^*) and "corrected" (D) optimal development paths are shown in Figure 1. Note that at a point such as

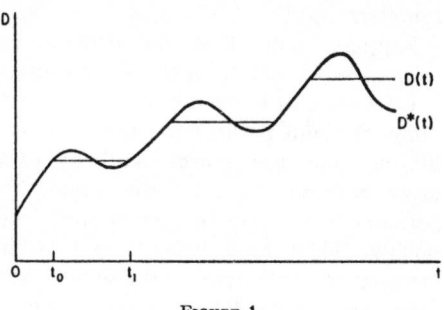

FIGURE 1

t_0 at which D^* is rising, if it will be falling in the relatively near future, then the present value of benefits may be sufficiently low for $q<0$, and investment should cease (equation (9))—until t_1 (equation (17)). We should observe, then, an alternating sequence of rising segments and plateaus in the path of optimal growth over time of the stock of developed land.

The divergence of this corrected path from the myopic is a crucially important result. It says that it will in general be optimal to refrain from development even when indicated by a comparison of current benefits and costs if, in the relatively near future, "undevelopment" or disinvestment, which are impossible, would be indicated.[12]

II

In the foregoing analysis no restrictions were placed on the patterns of time variation of the benefit functions. But when we come to consider the Hells Canyon project, and quite probably other similar proposals, both theoretical and empirical considerations suggest that benefits from development are likely to be decreasing, whereas benefits from preservation are likely to be increasing. The former, at least, may seem implausible. After all, shouldn't the demands of a growing economy increase the benefits from development of a natural area such as a hydroelectric power site? In this section we first explore this question, and the related one concerning the time pattern of benefits from preservation, then go on to show how the suggested restrictions affect optimal policy.

The traditional measure of the benefits of a hydroelectric power project, at any point in time, is simply the difference in costs between the most economic alternative source and the hydro project. This assumes, of course, that the amount of power provided by the project will be provided in any event, so that gross benefits are equal and the net benefit of the project is the saving in costs.[13] However, over the relatively long life of a hydro

---

[12] This result was anticipated by Krutilla, who noted " . . . our problem is akin to the dynamic programming problem which requires a present action (which may violate conventional benefit-cost criteria) to be compatible with the attainment of future states of affairs" (p. 785).

[13] For a fuller discussion of this point, see Peter Steiner.

project, costs of the (best) alternative source of energy will be decreasing as plants embodying new technologies replace the shorter-lived obsolete plants in the alternative system. This means that the benefits from developing the hydro project are correspondingly decreasing over the life of the project. In the traditional benefit-cost analysis this adjustment is not made. Benefits are calculated as of the construction date, implicitly assuming that the technology of alternative sources is fixed over the entire life of the project. For purposes of discussion in this section, a simplified process of technical change and replacement involving some constant rate of decrease of benefits is considered. The implications of a more complicated and realistic process are derived in the Appendix, and applied in our computations in the next section.

Benefits from not developing, on the other hand, appear to be increasing over time. The benefit from a nonpriced service such as wilderness recreation in the Hells Canyon, at any point in time, is the aggregate consumer surplus or area under the aggregate demand curve for the service. Much evidence suggests that demand for wilderness recreation in general, and for the Hells Canyon area in particular, is growing rapidly. This growth is due perhaps to growing population and per capita income, with the extra income used by consumers in part to "purchase" more leisure for themselves. Rising education levels, which seem to be associated with increasing preferences for taking this leisure in a natural environment doubtless also account for the rapidly growing demands.[14] Growth in demand can be broken down into two components: a quantity and a price shift. The effect of

[14] For an illustration of the rapid growth in wilderness recreation, see the figures for National Forest wilderness, wild and primitive area recreation, reported by Irving Hoch.

population growth, for example, given unchanging distributions of preferences and income, would be to increase the quantity demanded by the same percentage at any given "price," or willingness-to-pay.

On the other hand, for any fixed quantity, assuming growth of incomes, a set of conditions which will guarantee an increase in price to occur can be summarized as follows: if (a) present services of the environmental resource have no good substitutes among produced goods, (b) income and initial price elasticities of demand for such services are larger than for produced goods in general, and (c) the fraction of the budget spent on the environmental services in fixed supply is smaller than for produced goods in general, then the relative "price" or value of the environmental services in fixed supply will increase over time relative to the price of the produced goods at those levels of use short of the point at which congestion externalities occur.[15] Additionally, changes in consumer preferences clearly can affect both the quantity and the price shift parameters.

Suppose, now, that the demand for wilderness recreation in the Hells Canyon is expanding at some rate in the quantity dimension, due perhaps to changes in population and preferences, and at some other rate in the price dimension, due perhaps to changes in income and technology. Then total benefits will be increasing at a rate equal to the sum of these rates, assuming a linear imputed demand function.[16]

[15] These conditions can be derived from the Hicks–Allen two-good general equilibrium model. Details can be furnished by the authors on request.

[16] Let P_t = the vertical intercept at time t

Q_t = the horizontal intercept at time t

r_v = rate of growth in willingness to pay (vertical shift)

γ = rate of growth in quantity (horizontal shift)

B_t = benefits at time t

Then

It is easily seen that as benefits from preservation increase relative to benefits from development, the optimal short-run level of development $D^*(t)$ decreases.[17]

We can now show, in the analytical framework of the preceding section, the effect of this trend on optimal policy. If $D^*(t)$ is monotone decreasing, then there is in effect an infinite blocked interval. Development is either frozen at the initial level $D(0)$, or jumps, at $t=0$, to some higher level $\overline{D}$, and is then frozen. If there is some initial investment, obviously $q(0) = 0$. Also, $\lim_{t \to \infty} q(t) = 0$, because

$$(21) \quad -e^{-\rho t} \leq q(t) = \sigma p(t) - e^{-\rho t} \leq 0,$$

(a) $\quad B_t = (1/2)P_t Q_t$

$\qquad = 1/2\,(P_0 e^{r_v t})(Q_0 e^{\gamma t})$

$\qquad = 1/2\,P_0 Q_0 e^{(r_v + \gamma)t}$

The increment over an infinitesimal period is

(b) $\quad \dfrac{dB_t}{dt} = 1/2 P_0 Q_0 e^{(r_v+\gamma)t}(r_v + \gamma),$

and the percent rate of increase is

(c) $\quad \dfrac{\dfrac{dB_t}{dt}}{B_t} = \dfrac{1/2 P_0 Q_0 e^{(r_v+\gamma)t}(r_v + \gamma)}{1/2 P_0 Q_0 e^{(r_v+\gamma)t}}$

$\qquad = r_v + \gamma$

[17] Ignoring investment, total benefits at any time t from an area of size L, where $L = P + D$, and benefits B^P from the preserved area P are increasing relative to benefits B^D from developed area D at a rate of α', are

(a) $\quad B = B^P(P, t)e^{\alpha' t} + B^D(D, t)$

$\qquad = B^P(L - D, t)e^{\alpha' t} + B^D(D, t)$

Optimal D, D^*, is found by differentiating with respect to D and setting equal to zero.

(b) $\quad \dfrac{\partial B}{\partial D} = -B_P^P e^{\alpha' t} + B_D^D = 0$

or

$$B_D^D = B_P^P e^{\alpha' t}$$

As t increases, $e^{\alpha' t}$ increases, so that B_P^P (the marginal benefits of preservation) must be decreasing, implying that P^* is increasing—and D^* decreasing.

and

$$(22) \qquad \lim_{t \to \infty} - e^{-\rho t} = 0$$

On the blocked interval $(0, \infty)$ then, $D(t) = \overline{D}$, with

$$(23) \qquad D(0) \leq \overline{D},$$

$$(24) \qquad \int_0^\infty e^{-\rho t} r(\overline{D}, t)dt \geq 0$$

(but the strict inequality cannot hold in both) and

$$(25) \quad \int_t^\infty e^{-\rho t} r(\overline{D}, t)dt > 0 \quad 0 < t < \infty$$

For the projected development in the Hells Canyon, the interpretation of the analytical results is that it should be undertaken immediately, if at all. In symbols, if

$$(26) \quad \int_0^\infty [B^P(L - \overline{D}, t) + B^D(\overline{D}, t)$$

$$- I(t)]e^{-\rho t}dt > \int_0^\infty [B^P(L - D(0), t)$$

$$- I(t)]e^{-\rho t}dt,$$

where $\overline{D} > D(0)$, then some initial development, to a level of $\overline{D}$, will be optimal. If the inequality is reversed, then no further development beyond $D(0)$ should be undertaken. In the next section, a partial and approximate evaluation of these present value integrals is attempted, with $\overline{D}$ corresponding to the most profitable level of development, the High Mountain Sheep project.

Before proceeding with the evaluation, a few qualifying remarks about the analytical results may be made. First, although a particular program, in this case nondevelopment, may be indicated given current anticipations, it can be revised (in the direction of further development) at any time following the emergence of new and unanticipated relationships in the economy, as for example, a reversal of the historic decline in energy costs. Or, though a particular level of development, corresponding say to High Mountain Sheep in the Hells Canyon, may be optimal for the purposes of power generation, a more intensive level may be indicated by the inclusion of another purpose, for example, flat water recreation. In fact, this is not now true for development in the Hells Canyon, because the separable costs of high density recreation facilities would exceed their benefits.[18]

Second, the somewhat abstract nature of the development measure D might be noted. D can increase, for example, by developing additional sites along the river, the construction of facilities to accommodate larger numbers of flat water recreation seekers, the penetration by roads of virgin sections, etc.

Third, to what extent, if any, has the case for preservation been overstated by the absolute restriction on reversibility, and can the restriction be relaxed? Our view, as stated earlier, is that the irreversibility of development is fundamental to the problem. This does not, however, mean that it must be absolute. Two kinds of reversal are possible, or at least conceivable. One is the restoration of an area by a program of direct investment. This would seem to have little relevance, however, for the sorts of phenomena with which we are mainly concerned: an extinct species or ecological community that cannot be resurrected, a flooded canyon that cannot be replicated, an old-growth redwood forest that cannot be restored, etc.[19]

The other kind of reversal is the natural reversion to the wild, which, though also

---

[18] See testimony of Krutilla, *FPC* hearings, R-5840 and R-6494-6499.

[19] This is not to deny its relevance in some contexts, as shown for example in the clean-up and revegetation of certain former coal mining areas.

seemingly of little relevance to our main concerns, is easily fit into the analytical framework. Suppose some (constant, though this is not necessary) nonzero rate of reversion, δ. Then $D'(t) = D(t)\, e^{-\delta t}$, where $D'(t)$ is development subject to reversion. It is not clear how much additional flexibility this gives to investment policy. Even in situations in which δ is significantly different from zero, it may be much smaller than the desired rate of decrease as determined by changing technology and demand and unconstrained by nature.

III

In this section we present estimates of the costs and benefits associated with the alternatives for Hells Canyon. There are various services which the canyon can provide if preserved in its natural state. The value of some have become measurable through recent advances in economic analysis, for example, outdoor recreation, while the value of others are still intractable to economic measurement, for example, preservation of rare scientific research materials. Since we cannot measure the benefits in toto, we ask, rather, what would the present value of preserving the area need to be to equal or exceed the present value of the developmental alternative. Owing to the inverse relationship between π and α_t (see below) the initial year's preservation benefit may need to be only very modest in comparison with the development benefit. This is illustrated in simplified, discrete form in equation (27) below.

$$(27) \quad b_p^m = \sum_{t=1}^{T} \frac{b_0/(1+\pi)^t}{(1+i)^t} \div \sum_{t=1}^{T'} \frac{\$1(1+\alpha_t)^t}{(1+i)^t}$$

where:

b_p^m = the minimum initial year's benefit

required to make the present value of benefits from preserving the area equal to the present value of the development benefits,

$b_0=$ the initial year's development benefit,

$\pi=$ the simplified representation of technological change for the development alternative and is defined in the Appendix

$T=$ the relevant terminal year for the development alternative,

$T'=$ the relevant terminal year for the preservation alternative,

$i=$ the discount rate,

$\alpha_t=$ the percent rate of growth in annual benefits as described in footnote 16.

This is the required initial year's benefit from preservation which makes the two alternatives equivalent and relation (26) an equality.

The terminal years for each choice, T and T', are determined by the years in which the discounted annual benefit falls to zero. They need not and probably would not be the same. Any change in the relative annual values of the incompatible alternatives would result in different relevant time horizons.[20] For convenience in computation, we select T and T' as the years in which the increment to the present value of net benefits of each alternative falls to $0.01 per $1.00 of initial year's benefits.

Now π in the numerator of equation (27) is derived from our technical change model (see the Appendix). The value of π depends on a) investment per unit of thermal capacity, b) cost per kilowatt hour of thermal energy, and c) the rate of advance in technical efficiency. We have relied on construction cost data provided by Fed-

eral Power Commission (*FPC*) staff witnesses;[21] taken energy costs to be increasing from 0.98 mills per kilowatt hour in the early stage to 1.28 mills per kilowatt hour in the later period of analysis owing to projected increases in cost of processing nuclear materials;[22] and selected rates of technological progress of 3 to 5 percent, believed to bracket the relevant range.[23] Using such data in our technological change model we find that gross hydroelectric benefits will be overstated between 5 and 11 percent when technological change is not introduced into the analysis.[24] While the difference in *gross* benefits may not be very large, if the two alternatives are close cost competitors, such small differences can make a large difference in *net* benefits. In short, using a medium value for all of the parameters tested results in a reduction in the net present value by approximately a half in the Hells Canyon hydroelectric evaluation.[25]

[20] Since control theory has not previously been applied in public sector benefit-cost studies, the time horizons have been selected arbitrarily.

[21] See testimony of *FPC* witness Joseph J. A. Jessell, *FPC* hearings, and Exhibit No. R-54-B.

[22] See testimony of *FPC* witness I. Paul Chavez, "In the Matter of . . . , " and Exhibit No. R-107-B.

[23] The rate of technological change was computed from data presented in the biennial reports of *Electrical World* over a period representing a consistent method of reporting, 1950–68. It must be acknowledged that the model used for computational purposes is applicable to the period of the past, dominated by use of fossil fuels and not specifically relevant to the yet unspecified changes in technology of the future, doubtless to be tied closely to nuclear reactors. The argument, however, is that while the relevant models would differ, the effects of technological change on costs of generation will be of the same or greater order of magnitude and should not be ignored. (See testimony of Krutilla, *FPC* hearings, R-5838.) Although, as noted earlier, at least some of the reduction in costs may be balanced by a rise in environmental pollution from the more efficient fossil fuel plants, estimated costs of dealing with the thermal pollution from a nuclear plant *are* included in our calculations (though not the possible but unknown costs of radioactive waste disposal).

[24] See Table 1, Exhibit R-670, *FPC* hearings, for the complete range of values resulting from the computational model given in the Appendix.

[25] See testimony of John V. Krutilla, *FPC* hearings, R-5842-3 and Exhibit Nos. R-669 and R-671.

In our discussion of benefits from preservation in the last section, especially in footnote 16, we took α_t to be constant. This is plausible, however, only so long as the capacity of the area for recreation activity is not reached. If demand for the wilderness recreation services of the area is growing, congestion externalities eventually will arise. That is, a point will be reached beyond which use of the area by one more individual per unit time will result in a diminution of the utility obtained by others using the area. For purposes of this analysis, this point is taken as the "carrying capacity" of the area. If the benefits of additional use exceeded the congestion costs, total benefits could be increased by relaxing this constraint.[26] But we seek here to define a quantity of constant quality services, the value of which will be a lower bound for preservation benefits. Counting from the base year, let k be the year in which use of the area reaches capacity, m the year in which γ falls to the rate of growth of population, and d the rate of decay of γ.

Beyond some point, then, annual benefits do not grow at a uniform rate over time but depend upon the values taken by γ, r_y, k, d, and m. The particular values taken, i.e., γ of 10 percent and k of 20 years, with alternative assumptions for purposes of sensitivity analyses, were chosen for reasons given elsewhere.[27] A discount rate of 9 percent with alternatives of 8 and 10 percent was the result of independent study.[28] The selection of the value of m for 50 years, with alternative assumptions of 40 and 60, was governed by both the rate of growth of general demand for wilderness or primitive area recreation, and the estimated "saturation

level" for such recreational participation for the population as a whole. Finally, the range of values for r_y was taken from what we know about the conventional income elasticity of demand[29] as related to the special case of a unique resource in fixed supply and growth in per capita income over the past two or three decades.[30]

To contrast the results of our analysis with traditional benefit-cost analysis, consider the computed initial year's preservation benefit (Table 1) corresponding to i of 9 percent, r of 0.04, γ of 10 percent and k of 20 years, m of 50 years and r_y of 0.05; namely, $80,122. This sum compares with the sum of $2.9 million, which represents the "levelized" annual benefit from the hydro-electric development, when neither adjustments for technological progress have been made in hydroelectric power value computations, nor any site value (i.e., present value of opportunity benefits foreclosed by altering the present use of Hells Canyon) is imputed to costs. Typically then, the question would be raised whether or not the preservation value is equal to or greater than the $2.9 million annual benefits from development.

Let us now consider the readily quantifiable opportunity benefits which would be foreclosed by development of the canyon. These are based on studies conducted by the Oregon and Idaho fish and game commissions in cooperation with the U.S. Forest Service and monitored by an observer representing the applicants for the *FPC* license. Presented in summarized form they appear in Table 2.[31]

While systematic demand studies of the several different recreational activities were not conducted in connection with the imputed values, given what is known about prices paid for fishing and hunting rights where such rights are vested in

---

[26] For a detailed discussion of this and other considerations in determining the capacity of a natural area for recreation activity, see Fisher and Krutilla.

[27] See testimony of John V. Krutilla, *FPC* hearings, R-5859-73.

[28] See Eckstein and Arnold Harberger, and also James Seagraves.

[29] See Cicchetti, Joseph Seneca and Paul Davidson.

[30] See footnote 15.

[31] See testimony of John V. Krutilla, *FPC* hearings, R-5877-, Table 3 R-5878-9, R-5880-4.

TABLE 1—INITIAL YEAR'S PRESERVATION BENEFITS, b_p^m, (GROWING AT THE RATE α_t) REQUIRED IN ORDER TO HAVE PRESENT VALUE EQUAL TO DEVELOPMENT

r_y	$\gamma = 7.5$ Percent $k = 25$ years	$\gamma = 10$ Percent $k = 20$ years	$\gamma = 12.5$ Percent $k = 15$ years
$i = 8$ Percent,	$m = 50$ years,	$r = 0.04$,	$PVC_{1...T} = \$18,540,000$
0.04	\$138,276	\$109,149	\$106,613
0.05	87,568	70,363	70,731
0.06	48,143	39,674	41,292
$i = 9$ Percent,	$m = 50$ years,	$r = 0.04$,	$PVC_{1...T} = \$13,809,000$
0.04	\$147,422	\$115,008	\$109,691
0.05	101,447	80,122	78,336
0.06	64,300	51,700	52,210
$i = 10$ Percent,	$m = 50$ years,	$r = 0.04$,	$PVC_{1...T} = \$ 9,861,000$
0.04	\$142,335	\$110,240	\$103,030
0.05	103,626	80,888	77,232
0.06	71,369	56,397	55,194

Sources: Exhibit No. R-671, R-672, *FPC* hearings, and Transcript R-5869-5873.
Where:

i = discount rate
r_y = annual rate of growth in price for a given quantity
γ = annual rate of growth of quantity demanded at given price
k = number of years following initial year upon which carrying capacity constraint becomes effective
m = number of years after initial year upon which γ falls to rate of growth of population
$PVC_{1...T}$ = present value of development (adjusted)
r = annual rate of technological progress in the development case

private parties, we feel our estimates are rather conservative.[32]

[32] See also William Brown, Ajmer Singh and Emery Castle; Stephen Mathews and Gardiner Brown; and Peter Pearse for more systematic evaluation of the Oregon and Washington Steelhead-Salmon Fisheries and other big game resource values, and the estimated willingness to pay. On the basis of all the evidence available to us the imputation of values in the Hells Canyon case appear to be most conservative. It should be noted, however, that two assumptions are made in order that the values appearing in Table 2 represent net benefits, consistent with the benefits estimated for the hydro development. One assumption is that there are no adequate substitutes of like quality, i.e., other primitive scenic areas are either congested or being rationed, conditions which are widely encountered in national parks and over much of the wilderness system. Secondly, it is assumed that the demand unsatisfied by virtue of the transformation of the Hells Canyon would impinge on the margin in other sectors of the economy characterized by free entry and feasibility of augmenting supplies, i.e., incremental costs will equal incremental benefits.

Considering the estimates one might argue, for example, that the preservation benefits shown are roughly only a third (\$.9 to \$2.9 million) as large as would be

TABLE 2—ESTIMATED INITIAL YEAR'S QUANTIFIABLE PRESERVATION BENEFITS

Recreation Activity	Visitor Days Initial Year	Unit Value	Imputed Benefits
Streamside Use Angling	84,000	\$ 5.00	\$420,000
Canyon Area Hunting Big game	7,000	25.00	175,000
Upland bird	1,000	10.00	10,000
Increased value of remaining hunting experience	29,000	10.00	290,000
Total Quantifiable Opportunity Benefits			\$895,000

required in comparisons based on traditional analysis of similar cases. By introducing the differential incidence of technological progress on, and growth in demand for, the mutually exclusive alternative uses of the Hells Canyon, we reach quite a different conclusion. The initial year's preservation benefit, subject to reevaluation on the basis of sensitivity tests, appears to be an order of magnitude ($900,000 to $80,000) larger than it needs to be to have a present value equaling or exceeding the present value of the development alternative. Thus we get results significantly different from traditional analysis.

What about the sensitivity of these conclusions to the particular values the variables used in our two simulation models are given? Sensitivity tests can be performed with the data contained in Table 1, along with additional information available from computer runs performed. Some of these checks are displayed in Table 3.

TABLE 3—SENSIVITIY OF ESTIMATED INITIAL YEAR'S
REQUIRED PRESERVATION BENEFITS TO CHANGES IN
VALUE OF VARIABLES AND PARAMETERS
(at $i = 9$ percent)

Variable	Variation in Variable From	To	Percent Change	Percent Change in Preservation Benefit
r_y	0.04	0.05	25	39–49
r	0.04	0.05	25	25
k^a (years)	20	25	25	30–40
γ (percent)	10	12.5	25	−4 to +7
m (years)	40	50	25	3

* The 25 percent change in years before carrying capacity is reached translates into a 40 percent change in carrying capacity at the growth rate of 10 percent used here.

Given the estimated user days and imputed value per user day, the conclusion regarding the relative economic merit of the two alternatives is not sensitive within a reasonable range, to the particular values chosen for the variables and parameters used in the computation models.

There is need, however, for another set of tests when geometric growth rates are being used. We might regard these as "plausibility analyses." For example, the ratio of the implicit price to the projected per capita income in the terminal year was examined and found to equal 2.5×10^{-3}. At today's per capita income level this is comparable to a user fee of approximately $10.00. Similarly, the ratio of the terminal year's preservation benefit to the GNP in the terminal year is found to be 4.0×10^{-7}. This value compares with a ratio of the total revenue of the applicants in 1968 to GNP of 5.0×10^{-4}. The year at which the growth rate in quantity of wilderness-type outdoor recreation services demanded falls to the rate of growth of the population must also be checked to ensure that the implicit population participation rate is something one would regard as plausible. Such tests were performed in order to avoid problems which otherwise would stem from use of unbounded estimates. We found our assumed initial rate of 10 percent, appropriately damped over time, was a realistic value.

Finally, since the readily observed initial year's benefits appear to be in excess of the minimum which would be required to have their present value exceed the present value of development, the computation is concluded at this point. Note, however, that since the analysis relies implicitly on the price compensating measure of consumer surplus, the resulting estimate of preservation value would be for this reason, as well as the restricted carrying capacity, a lower bound. Moreover, in seeking maximum expected benefits, we have implicitly assumed a neutral attitude toward risk. In fact, some preliminary findings as to the effect of uncertainty on optimal environmental policy suggest that there may be a kind of risk premium, or other adjustment, in the direction of re-

FISHER, KRUTILLA, AND CICCHETTI: ENVIRONMENT 617

ducing benefits from development relative to preservation.[33]

IV

In Section I of this study we propose a model for the allocation of natural environments between preservation and development, and show that it will in general be optimal to refrain from some development indicated by current benefits and costs if, in the relatively near future, "undevelopment," which is impossible, would be indicated. In Section II we show that if, as in the case of the proposed development in the Hells Canyon, benefits from development are decreasing over time relative to benefits from preservation, it will be optimal to proceed with the development immediately, if at all.[34] In Section III we consider this question in detail for the case of the Hells Canyon, and show that it will not, in fact, be optimal to undertake even the most profitable development project there. Rather the area is likely to yield greater benefits if left in its natural state.

APPENDIX

Over the first 30-year period, taken as the useful life of a thermal facility, let PVC_t represent the present value of annual costs per kilowatt of the thermal alternative in year t:

$$PVC_1 = C_1 + E(8760F)$$

$$PVC_2 = \left\{ C_1 + [E8760(F - k)] + \frac{E}{(1 + r)}(8760k) \right\} \left(\frac{1}{(1 + i)} \right)$$

$$\vdots$$

[33] See Cicchetti and A. Myrick Freeman, and Fisher. This is an important question and one which bears on the design of optimal policies for pollution control as well, but further consideration is beyond the scope of this paper.

[34] This is consistent with the obvious differences in views held by members of affluent societies and less

$$PVC_n = \left\{ C_1 + E[8760(F - (n - 1)k)] \right. $$
$$\left. + \frac{E}{(1 + r)^{n-1}} [8760(n - 1)k] \right\}$$
$$\cdot \left(\frac{1}{1 + i} \right)^{n-1} \quad \text{for } 1 < n < 30$$

where

$C_1 =$ Capacity Cost/KW/yr during first 30-year period
$E =$ Energy Cost/KWh
$F =$ The plant factor; (.90)
$k =$ a constant representing the time decay of the plant factor (.03)
$i =$ the discount rate
$r =$ the annual rate of technological progress

Writing out the nth term yields:

$$PVC_n = \frac{C_I}{(1 + i)^{n-1}} + \frac{8760EF}{(1 + i)^{n-1}}$$
$$- \frac{8760Ek(n - 1)}{(1 + i)^{n-1}} + \frac{8760Ek(n - 1)}{[(1 + r)(1 + i)]^{n-1}}$$

These terms can be summed individually using standard formulas for geometric progressions and then factored to form:

$$PVC_{1, \ldots, 30} = \sum_{n=1}^{30} PVC_n = (C_I + 8760EF)$$
$$\cdot \left[\frac{1 - a^{30}}{1 - a} \right] - \frac{8760Ek}{i}$$
$$\cdot \left\{ \frac{1 - a^{29}}{1 - a} - 29a^{29} \right\}$$
$$+ \frac{8760Ek}{(1 + r)(1 + i) - 1} \left\{ \frac{1 - b^{29}}{1 - b} - 29b^{29} \right\}$$

where

$$a = \left(\frac{1}{1 + i} \right)$$

$$b = \frac{1}{(1 + r)(1 + i)}$$

developed countries on these and related environmental issues.

Over years 31, . . . , T the cost expressions are similar except that we are dealing with only $T-30$ additional years and all terms thus get discounted by a factor of $(1/1+i)^{30}$. Hence, using similar formulas for the sum of geometric series the present value of annual costs per kilowatt from this later period is determined to be:

$$PVC_{31,\ldots,T} = \sum_{p=31}^{T} PVC_p = \left(\frac{1}{1+i}\right)^{30}$$

$$\cdot \left\{ C_{II} + 8760E'F\right) \left[\frac{1 - a^{(T-30)}}{1 - a}\right]$$

$$- \frac{8760E'k}{i}\left[\frac{1 - a^{(T-31)}}{1 - a} - 19a^{(T-31)}\right]$$

$$+ \frac{8760E'k}{(1 + r)(1 + i) - 1}$$

$$\left[\frac{1 - b^{(T-31)}}{1 - b} - 19b^{(T-31)}\right]\right\}$$

where

$$C_{II} = \frac{C_I}{(1 + r)^{30}}$$

$$E' = \frac{E}{(1 + r)^{30}}$$

The overall present value is:

$$PVC_{1,\ldots,T} = PVC_1 + \ldots + PVC_{30}$$

$$+ PVC_{31} + \ldots + PVC_T$$

Traditional analyses are based essentially on the model given below.

$$K = \sum_{n=1}^{T} \frac{[C_I + E(8760F)]}{(1 + i)^{n-1}}$$

or, which is equivalent,

$$= [C_I + E(8760F)]\left[\frac{1 - a^T}{1 - a}\right]$$

We can therefore determine a relationship between the traditional measure of development benefit (K) and the measure outlined in this appendix $(PVC_{1,\ldots,T})$ in order to

define the simplified measure of technological change (π) utilized in the text above.

$$\frac{K}{PVC_{1,\ldots,T}} = \sum_{t=1}^{T} \frac{b_0}{(1 + i)^t}$$

$$\div \sum_{t=1}^{T} \frac{b_0/(1 + \pi)^t}{(1 + i)^t}$$

$$= T \Big/ \sum_{t=1}^{T} \frac{1}{(1 + \pi)_t}$$

REFERENCES

K. J. Arrow, "Optimal Capital Policy with Irreversible Investment," in J. N. Wolfe, ed., *Value, Capital and Growth*, Chicago 1968, pp. 1–20.

—— and M. Kurz, "Optimal Growth with Irreversible Investment in a Ramsey Model," *Econometrica*, Mar. 1970, *38*, 331–44.

—— and A. C. Fisher, "Environmental Preservation, Uncertainty, and Irreversibility," *Quart. J. Econ.*, forthcoming.

H. J. Barnett and C. Morse, *Scarcity and Growth*, Baltimore 1963.

W. G. Brown, A. Singh, and E. N. Castle, "Net Economic Value of the Oregon Salmon-Steelhead Sport Fishery," *J. Wildlife Manage.*, Apr. 1965, *29*, 66–79.

O. R. Burt and R. Cummings, "Production and Investment in Natural Resource Industries," *Amer. Econ. Rev.*, Sept. 1970, *60*, 576–90.

C. J. Cicchetti, J. Seneca, and P. Davidson, *The Demand and Supply of Outdoor Recreation*, Washington 1969.

C. J. Cicchetti and A. M. Freeman, III, "Option Demand and Consumer Surplus," *Quart. J. Econ.*, Aug. 1971, *85*, 528–39.

O. Eckstein, *Water Resource Development*, Cambridge 1958.

——, in *Economic Analysis of Public Investment Decisions: Interest Rate Policy and Discounting Analysis*, Hearings, Joint Economic Committee, 90th Congress, 2d Sess., Washington 1968.

A. C. Fisher and J. V. Krutilla, "Determination of Optimal Capacity for Resource-Based Recreation Facilities," *Natur. Resources J.*, forthcoming.

A. Harberger, in *Economic Analysis of Public Investment Decisions: Interest Rate Policy and Discounting Analysis*, Hearings, Joint Economic Committee, 90th Congress, 2d Sess., Washington 1968.

J. R. Hicks and R. G. D. Allen, "A Reconsideration of the Theory of Value," Part I, II, *Economica*, Feb., May 1934, *1*, 52–76; 196–219.

I. Hoch, "Economic Analysis of Wilderness Areas," in *Wilderness and Recreation—a Report on Resources, Values and Problems*, ORRRC Study Report No. 3, Washington 1962, pp. 203–64.

M. M. Hufschmidt, J. V. Krutilla, and J. Margolis, *Standards and Criteria for Formulating and Evaluating Federal Water Resources Development. Report to the Bureau of the Budget*, Washington 1961.

J. V. Krutilla, "Conservation Reconsidered," *Amer. Econ. Rev.*, Sept. 1967, *57*, 777–86.

――― and O. Eckstein, *Multiple Purpose River Development*, Baltimore 1958.

S. B. Mathews and G. S. Brown, *Economic Evaluation of the 1967 Sport Salmon Fisheries of Washington*, Washington Dept. of Fisheries Technical Report 2, Olympia 1970.

R. N. McKean, *Efficiency in Government Through Systems Analysis*, New York 1958.

E. J. Mishan, "The Postwar Literature on Externalities: An Interpretive Essay," *J. Econ. Lit.*, Mar. 1971, *9*, 1–28.

P. H. Pearse, "A New Approach to the Evaluation of Non-Priced Recreation Resources," *Land Econ.*, Feb. 1968, *44*, 87–99.

C. G. Plourde, "A Simple Model of Replenishable Natural Resource Exploitation," *Amer. Econ. Rev.*, June 1970, *60*, 518–22.

N. Potter and F. T. Christy, Jr., *Trends in Natural Resource Commodities*, Baltimore 1962.

J. A. Seagraves, "More on the Social Rate of Discount," *Quart. J. Econ.*, Aug. 1970, *84*, 430–50.

V. L. Smith, "Economics of Production from Natural Resources," *Amer. Econ. Rev.*, June 1968, *58*, 409–31.

P. O. Steiner, "The Role of Alternative Cost in Project Design and Selection," *Quart. J. Econ.*, Aug. 1965, *79*, 417–30.

H. Wold and L. Jureen, *Demand Analysis*, New York 1953.

Federal Power Commission (*FPC*), "In the Matter of: Pacific Northwest Power Company and Washington Public Power Supply System," hearings, Washington 1970.

Policies, Standards, and Procedures in the Formulation, Evaluation, and Review of Plans for Use and Development of Water and Related Land Resources, prepared under the direction of the President's Water Resources Council, Senate Document no. 97, 87th Cong., 2d sess., Washington 1964.

――――, Supp. no. 1, "Evaluation Standards for Primary Outdoor Recreation Benefits," Ad Hoc Resources Council, Washington 1964.

Proposed Practices for Economic Analysis of River Basin Projects, report to the Inter-Agency Committee on Water Resources, prepared by the Subcommittee on Evaluation Standards, Washington 1958.

"Steam Station Cost Survey," *Electrical World*, Nov. 3, 1969.

[35]

ENVIRONMENTAL PRESERVATION, UNCERTAINTY, AND IRREVERSIBILITY *

KENNETH J. ARROW
ANTHONY C. FISHER

I

A number of recent contributions by economists have provided a clear insight into the causes of the varied forms of environmental deterioration, and have also suggested, implicitly or explicitly, policies for more efficient management of environmental as well as other resources.[1] Yet, as Allen Kneese has pointed out in a review of empirical studies of pollution damages, "a general shortcoming of [these studies] has been that they have treated a stochastic or probabilistic phenomenon as being deterministic."[2] The purpose of this paper is to explore the implications of uncertainty surrounding estimates of the environmental costs of some economic activities. It is shown in particular that the existence of uncertainty will, in certain important cases, lead to a reduction in net benefits from an activity with environmental costs. In such cases the implication for an efficient control policy will generally involve some restriction of the activity.

Any discussion of public policy in the face of uncertainty must come to grips with the problem of determining an appropriate attitude toward risk on the part of the policy maker. Thus in the essay quoted above, Kneese asks, "Is the concept of mathematical expectation applicable here or must we give attention to higher moments of the probability distribution. . . ?"[3] Although the question has not, to our knowledge, received consideration in just this form in the environmental literature, received theory does shed some light on the issue it poses.

* Research reported in this paper has been supported by a grant from the Natural Environments Program at RFF and also in part by NSF Grant GS 2530 to the Institute for Mathematical Studies in the Social Sciences, Stanford University. Comments and suggestions by Harl Ryder and a referee are gratefully acknowledged.

1. Also some not so recent, as in the classic work of Pigou. For a review of some more recent contributions, see E. J. Mishan, "The Postwar Literature on Externalities: An Interpretative Essay," *Journal of Economic Literature*, Vol. 9 (March 1971), 1–28.

2. A. V. Kneese, *Economics and the Quality of the Environment — Some Empirical Experiences*, Reprint Number 71 (Washington, D.C.: Resources for the Future, 1968), p. 172.

3. *Ibid.*, p. 172.

PRESERVATION, UNCERTAINTY, AND IRREVERSIBILITY 313

Burton Weisbrod first suggested that where there is uncertainty in demand for a publicly provided good or service, there may be some benefit ("option value") to the individual in addition to the conventional price-compensating consumer surplus.[4] More recently Charles J. Cicchetti and A. Myrick Freeman III have shown that, where there is uncertainty in either demand or supply, Weisbrod's option value will be positive for risk-averse individuals.[5] In the Cicchetti-Freeman analysis this extra benefit from the public good is in fact equivalent to a premium for risk bearing. Examples of such goods in the environmental sector (to which we will return) might be the preservation of certain valuable natural phenomena or the abatement of pollution.

At this point a very interesting corollary question arises. It is this: even assuming a nonneutral attitude toward risk, hence the need for some adjustment of expected benefits and costs *to the individual,* as demonstrated by Cicchetti and Freeman, does it necessarily follow that the social calculus should properly make the same adjustment? It does seem plausible, but a challenge to this point of view has been put forward in an analysis of the evaluation of benefits from more traditional public investments by Arrow and Lind.[6] They show that, as the net returns to an investment of given size are shared by an increasingly large number of individuals, the individual risk premium, and more importantly and perhaps unexpectedly, the aggregate of all such premiums go to zero. Only expected returns, then, should be taken into account in evaluating the investment.

This is the approach taken in the next section, in which the discussion focuses on a decision as to how far, if at all, to proceed with some form of commercial development of an unspoiled natural area that is also capable of yielding benefits in its preserved state. In particular, the question considered is, does the introduction of uncertainty as to the costs or benefits of a proposed development have any effect on an appropriately formulated investment criterion beyond the replacement of known values with their expectations? It turns out that, if the development involves some irreversible transformation of the environment, hence a loss in perpetuity of the benefits from preservation, and if information about the costs and

4. B. A. Weisbrod, "Collective-Consumption Services of Individual-Consumption Goods," this *Journal,* Vol. 78 (Aug. 1964), 471–77.
5. C. J. Cicchetti and A. M. Freeman III, "Option Demand and Consumer Surplus: Further Comment," this *Journal,* Vol. 85 (Aug. 1971), 528–39.
6. K. J. Arrow and R. C. Lind, "Uncertainty and the Evaluation of Public Investment Decisions," *American Economic Review,* Vol. 60 (June 1970), 364–78.

314   *QUARTERLY JOURNAL OF ECONOMICS*

benefits of both alternatives realized in one period results in a change in their expected values for the next, the answer is yes — net benefits from developing the area are reduced and, broadly speaking, less of the area should be developed.

II

In this section we are concerned primarily with the effect of uncertainty on the criteria for choice between two alternative uses of a natural environment — preservation and development. As an example of the type of problem to which the analysis might be applied, consider the choice, at each moment in time, between preserving (part of) a virgin redwood forest for wilderness recreation, on the one hand, or opening (part of) it up to clear-cut logging, on the other. Although this sort of transformation may be technically reversible, the length of time required for regeneration of the forest for purposes of wilderness recreation is so great that, given some positive rate of time preference, it might as well be irreversible.

A problem having just these characteristics has in fact been studied by Fisher, Krutilla, and Cicchetti.[7] Without going into the structure of the problem in more detail, their results, following results obtained by Arrow [8] and by Arrow and Kurz [9] in dynamic optimization theory, can be summarized as follows. First, it will in general be optimal to refrain from some development that is currently profitable if in the near future "undevelopment," which is impossible, would be indicated. Second, if net benefits from development are in fact decreasing over time relative to benefits from preservation, as shown in an empirical application to proposed further development of hydroelectric capacity along the Hells Canyon reach of the Snake River, it will be optimal to develop either immediately or not at all. It is then shown that even the most profitable of current development projects there can be expected at this time to yield a smaller return than the preservation-recreation alternative.

The notion of "irreversibility" underlying these results might be spelled out a bit more. Ordinarily, it would be technical. Thus the construction of a major dam or series of dams in the Hells

7. A. C. Fisher, J. V. Krutilla, and C. J. Cicchetti, "The Economics of Environmental Preservation: A Theoretical and Empirical Analysis," *American Economic Review*, Vol. 62 (Sept. 1972), 605–19.

8. K. J. Arrow, "Optimal Capital Policy and Irreversible Investment," in J. N. Wolfe, ed., *Value, Capital and Growth* (Chicago: Aldine Publishing Company, 1968), pp. 1–20.

9. K. J. Arrow and M. Kurz, "Optimal Growth with Irreversible Investment in a Ramsey Model," *Econometrica*, Vol. 38 (March 1970), 331–44.

PRESERVATION, UNCERTAINTY, AND IRREVERSIBILITY 315

Canyon clearly could not be undone in such a way as to make possible the enjoyment of the recreational and other services currently provided by the free-flowing stream through the deepest canyon on the North American continent.

Conceivably, construction of an alternative power source could preclude development of the hydroelectric potential there. This would, however, be an economic decision, and one that might in any case be reversed — although this would not be indicated by a continuation of present trends in benefits from wilderness preservation versus power development there, as assumed in the Fisher-Krutilla-Cicchetti study.

Of course, a technically irreversible development could be characterized as one that would be infinitely costly to reverse. More generally, the cost of reversal may take intermediate values that would vary with the alternative chosen. For the remainder of this section, however, it may be helpful to rely on the intuitive notion of a technically irreversible development, such as the placing of a dam.

As the Fisher-Krutilla-Cicchetti study adopts the risk-neutral approach in its specification of only expected costs and gains in the investment criterion with no adjustment, for example, for option value in preserving, the bias against development is due solely to the restriction on reversibility. By joining to this restriction the additional and plausible assumption that realizations in one period affect expectations in the next, as spelled out in the following simple model, we discover, consistent with the continuing assumption of risk neutrality, a "quasi-option value" having an effect in the same direction as risk aversion, namely, a reduction in net benefits from development.

Consider, now, the development of an area d over a two-period time horizon consisting of a first period followed by all future intervals compressed into a single second period. Though not particularly elegant, this formulation seems sufficient to capture the essential features of the process described above.

Let $d =$ unity (a normalized unit of land)
  $d_1 =$ the amount of land developed in the first period
  $d_2 =$ the amount of land developed in the second period
  $b_p =$ benefits from preservation of d in first period
  $b_d =$ benefits from development of d in first period
  $\beta_p =$ expected benefits, conditional on b_p and b_d, from preservation of d in second period

$\beta_d =$ expected benefits, conditional on b_p and b_d, from development of d in second period

$c_1 =$ investment costs in first period

$c_2 =$ investment costs in second period.

Several remarks can be made concerning the structure of this model.

1. Though explicitly dynamic, it need not deal with time discounting in any meaningful way. Thus the second-period benefits and costs β_p, β_d, and c_2 can be viewed as present values, and the results are not affected.

2. It is assumed that development entails investment costs but preservation does not. Costs of preservation could easily be introduced (where meaningful) but again, results would not be affected, and extra terms would clutter the model. The real difference between the alternatives is that one is assumed to be reversible, and the other not.

3. Note that second-period expectations are conditional on first-period realizations. Some amount of development is planned at the start of the first period, but the plan can be revised (at least in the direction of additional development) at the start of the second period, based upon information that has accumulated concerning benefits in the first period.

4. Note, finally, that all benefits are specified as coefficients, so that constant returns to any level of development or preservation are assumed. Later on, this assumption is relaxed.

Let us focus now on the decision at the start of the second period. If $\beta_d - \beta_p > c_2$, then $d_2 = 1 - d_1$. If $\beta_d - \beta_p < c_2$, then $d_2 = 0$. Define $z = \beta_d - \beta_p$, $w = b_d - b_p - c_1$, and event A as $z > c_2$. If A occurs, total benefits from the area are

$$(1) \qquad b_p(1-d_1) + b_d d_1 - c_1 d_1 + \beta_d - c_2(1-d_1) = w d_1 + c_2 d_1 + b_p + \beta_d - c_2.$$

If A does not occur, then benefits are

$$(2) \qquad b_p(1-d_1) + b_d d_1 - c_1 d_1 + \beta_p(1-d_1) + \beta_d d_1 = w d_1 + z d_1 + b_p + \beta_p.$$

The expected benefits from developing $d_1 > 0$ in the first period are

$$(3) \qquad E[(w + \min(c_2, z)) d_1 + b_p + \max(\beta_d - c_2, \beta_p)].$$

Now suppose that $d_1 = 0$. If A occurs, total benefits from the area are $b_p + \beta_d - c_2$; if A does not occur, benefits are $b_p + \beta_p$; and expected benefits are $E[b_p + \max(\beta_d - c_2, \beta_p)]$. Then the difference

PRESERVATION, UNCERTAINTY, AND IRREVERSIBILITY 317

(in expected benefits) between developing $d_1 > 0$ and $d_1 = 0$ is

(4) $E[(w + \min(c_2, z))d_1 + b_p + \max(\beta_d - c_2, \beta_p)] - E[b_p + \max (\beta_d - c_2, \beta_p)] = E[(w + \min(c_2, z))d_1]$.

We are interested in the sign of the expression $E[w + \min(c_2, z)]$. If it is positive, it will be optimal to develop in the first period.

Now suppose that the decision maker ignores uncertainty, i.e., he lets z and w be replaced by known numbers $E[z]$ and $E[w]$, so that the criterion is $E[w] + \min(c_2, E[z])$. Either $c_2 < E[z]$, or $c_2 > E[z]$. Consider the case in which $c_2 < E[z]$, so that the criterion is $E[w] + c_2$. Clearly,

(5) $\min(c_2, z) \leqslant c_2$;

with

(6) $P[\min(c_2, z) < c_2] > 0$,

where $P[\ ]$ represents the probability of occurrence of the expression in brackets. Thus

(7) $E[\min(c_2, z)] < c_2$;

and

$$E[w + \min(c_2, z)] < E[w] + c_2.$$

The expected value of benefits under uncertainty is seen to be less than the value of benefits under certainty. There exists a range of values for z and w for which development should not, then, take place under uncertainty but should under certainty. An interpretation of this result might be that, if we are uncertain about the payoff to investment in development, we should err on the side of underinvestment, rather than overinvestment, since development is irreversible. Given an ability to learn from experience, underinvestment can be remedied before the second period, whereas mistaken overinvestment cannot, the consequences persisting in effect for all time.

Similarly, for the case in which $c_2 > E[z]$,

(8) $\min(c_2, z) \leqslant z$;

with

(9) $P[\min(c_2, z) < z] > 0$.

Thus

(10) $E[\min(c_2, z)] < E[z]$.

Note that the assumed rigidity of the benefit (and cost) coefficient requires that, if the criterion is positive, the entire area be developed. Our result then states that the entire area is less likely to be developed under uncertainty. It might be desirable to have a result of this type in more flexible form, in particular that less of a

318   *QUARTERLY JOURNAL OF ECONOMICS*

given area be developed under uncertainty — rather than less chance of the entire area's being developed.

Let (as yet) undeveloped area d be divided into n units, $\mu_1, \mu_2, \ldots, \mu_n$, each with fixed coefficients. Suppose, now, we consider development of d on a unit-by unit basis, proceeding exactly as above, but with the benefit and cost coefficients referring, respectively, to the first unit considered, then the second, etc. Under the plausible assumption of diminishing returns to both development and preservation, it is easily verified that, if it does not pay to develop the first unit considered, then it does not pay to develop any of the others. If, on the other hand, it pays to develop the first unit, then the second must be considered and so on. Corner solutions are possible as before, but so are interior solutions of part preserved and part developed.

In order to avoid confusion over the terms "constant returns" and "diminishing returns," we can define them more precisely. Let each of the n units μ_i, $i = 1, \ldots, n$ be further divided into m subunits μ_{ij}, $i = 1, \ldots, n$, $j = 1, \ldots, m$, each with fixed coefficients. Constant returns to, say, first-period development within any unit μ_i can be represented as

$$b_{di_1} = b_{di_2} = \ldots = b_{di_m},$$

with

$$b_{di_1} + b_{di_2} + \ldots + b_{di_m} = b_{di},$$

where b_{di_1} = benefits from development in the first period of unit μ_{i_1}, etc. Diminishing returns to development across units μ_i can be represented as $\dfrac{db_{di}}{di} < 0$. (Note that $\dfrac{db_{pi}}{di} > 0$, as benefits from preserving the marginal unit increase with the number of units already developed.) In this formulation the size and number of units μ_i are defined by the condition that returns are constant within each.

III

The foregoing analysis indicates that, even where it is not appropriate to postulate risk aversion in evaluating an activity, something of the "feel" of risk aversion is produced by a restriction on reversibility. If one takes the view that some means of spreading the risk associated with the uncertain environmental costs of the activity is likely to be feasible in most cases, then there are clear policy implications to this result, as it sharply distinguishes between reversible and irreversible changes in the environment.

PRESERVATION, UNCERTAINTY, AND IRREVERSIBILITY 319

One such implication, however, is *not* the overthrow of marginal analysis. Just because an action is irreversible does not mean that it should not be undertaken. Rather, the effect of irreversibility is to reduce the benefits, which are then balanced against costs in the usual way.

The analysis can be applied to problems of pollution control as well. Let b_d and β_d represent the benefits from an investment, and c_1 and c_2 the direct costs, as before. Then b_p and β_p can be taken to represent the benefits (reduced losses) from the cleaner or less toxic air, or water, that would be enjoyed were the investment not made.

Of course, the dynamic model is relevant only if the pollution is in some sense irreversible, as is the extinction of a form of life, or the destruction of a unique geomorphological phenomenon. This is an empirical matter. Clearly, much pollution is short-lived, sufficiently diffused or degraded by the assimilative medium to render it negligible in concentration and harmless in effect beyond some point in time. To this type of pollution the model does not apply.

On the other hand, there is evidence that some pollution does accumulate in the environment, perhaps sufficiently to be considered irreversible. Recent research has shed light on the toxicity and the persistence, indeed the increasing concentration, of the "hard" or nondegradable pesticides such as DDT, for example, and of industrial substances such as lead. A decision on a project involving discharge into the ambient environment of any of these or other potentially harmful and persistent substances should then take into account the continuing effect, as in the analysis of the preceding section. The same reasoning would apply to cumulative "macro" environmental effects, such as the increasing concentration of carbon dioxide in the global atmosphere, with its attendant climatic changes, as predicted by some ecologists.

The point about uncertainty, information, and irreversibility might be made still more generally, i.e., without reference to environmental effects. Essentially, the point is that the expected benefits of an irreversible decision should be adjusted to reflect the loss of options it entails.[1]

HARVARD UNIVERSITY
UNIVERSITY OF MARYLAND AND RESOURCES FOR THE FUTURE

1. For an earlier statement see A. G. Hart, "Risk, Uncertainty, and the Unprofitability of Compounding Probabilities," in *Studies in Mathematical Economics and Econometrics*, ed. by O. Lange, F. McIntyre, and T. O. Yntema (Chicago: University of Chicago Press, 1942).

Name Index